Advanced Numerical and Computational Methods for Engineering and Applied Mathematical Problems

Advanced Numerical and Computational Methods for Engineering and Applied Mathematical Problems

Editors

Lihua Wang
Benny Yiu-Chung Hon
Sheng-Wei Chi

Basel • Beijing • Wuhan • Barcelona • Belgrade • Novi Sad • Cluj • Manchester

Editors
Lihua Wang
Tongji University
Shanghai
China

Benny Yiu-Chung Hon
City University of Hong Kong
Hong Kong
China

Sheng-Wei Chi
University of Illinois at Chicago
Chicago, IL
USA

Editorial Office
MDPI AG
Grosspeteranlage 5
4052 Basel, Switzerland

This is a reprint of articles from the Special Issue published online in the open access journal *Mathematics* (ISSN 2227-7390) (available at: https://www.mdpi.com/journal/mathematics/special_issues/Numer_Comput_Methods_Eng_Math).

For citation purposes, cite each article independently as indicated on the article page online and as indicated below:

Lastname, A.A.; Lastname, B.B. Article Title. *Journal Name* **Year**, *Volume Number*, Page Range.

ISBN 978-3-7258-2559-2 (Hbk)
ISBN 978-3-7258-2560-8 (PDF)
doi.org/10.3390/books978-3-7258-2560-8

© 2024 by the authors. Articles in this book are Open Access and distributed under the Creative Commons Attribution (CC BY) license. The book as a whole is distributed by MDPI under the terms and conditions of the Creative Commons Attribution-NonCommercial-NoDerivs (CC BY-NC-ND) license.

Contents

About the Editors vii

Victor V. Kuzenov, Sergei V. Ryzhkov and Aleksey Yu. Varaksin
The Adaptive Composite Block-Structured Grid Calculation of the Gas-Dynamic Characteristics of an Aircraft Moving in a Gas Environment
Reprinted from: *Mathematics* **2022**, *10*, 2130, doi:10.3390/math10122130 1

Yu Chen and Nick Gibbons
Simulations of Hypersonic Boundary-Layer Transition over a Flat Plate with the Spalart-Allmaras One-Equation BCM Transitional Model
Reprinted from: *Mathematics* **2022**, *10*, 3431, doi:10.3390/math10193431 15

Qinghui Luo, Yueting Zhou, Lihua Wang and Shenghu Ding
The Effect of Adhesion on Indentation Behavior of Various Smart Materials
Reprinted from: *Mathematics* **2022**, *10*, 4511, doi:10.3390/math10234511 40

Xing Zhou, Qinfeng Di, Xiaoliang Wang, Dakun Luo, Feng Chen and Wenchang Wang
A Collapse Strength Model for a 7″ Crescent-Worn Casing Connection Considering Sealing Integrity
Reprinted from: *Mathematics* **2023**, *11*, 489, doi:10.3390/math11020489 90

Minghao Hu, Lihua Wang, Fan Yang and Yueting Zhou
Weighted Radial Basis Collocation Method for the Nonlinear Inverse Helmholtz Problems
Reprinted from: *Mathematics* **2023**, *11*, 662, doi:10.3390/math11030662 105

Naif Abdulaziz M. Alkuhayli
Enhancing the Heat Transfer Due to Hybrid Nanofluid Flow Induced by a Porous Rotary Disk with Hall and Heat Generation Effects
Reprinted from: *Mathematics* **2023**, *11*, 909, doi:10.3390/math11040909 134

Amir Abbas, Radhika Khandelwal, Hafeez Ahmad, Asifa Ilyas, Liaqat Ali and Kaouther Ghachem
Magnetohydrodynamic Bioconvective Flow of Williamson Nanofluid over a Moving Inclined Plate Embedded in a Porous Medium
Reprinted from: *Mathematics* **2023**, *11*, 1043, doi:10.3390/math11041043 151

Zhizhong Yan and Ercong Cheng
A Novel Monte Carlo Method to Calculate the Thermal Conductivity in Nanoscale Thermoelectric Phononic Crystals Based on Universal Effective Medium Theory
Reprinted from: *Mathematics* **2023**, *11*, 1208, doi:10.3390/math11051208 179

Xiujie Cao and Jingjun Yu
LLE-NET: A Low-Light Image Enhancement Algorithm Based on Curve Estimation
Reprinted from: *Mathematics* **2024**, *12*, 1228, doi:10.3390/math12081228 194

Robin Herkert, Patrick Buchfink, Tizian Wenzel, Bernard Haasdonk, Pavel Toktaliev and Oleg Iliev
Greedy Kernel Methods for Approximating Breakthrough Curves for Reactive Flow from 3D Porous Geometry Data
Reprinted from: *Mathematics* **2024**, *12*, 2111, doi:10.3390/math12132111 212

Intesar F. El Ramley, Nada M. Bedaiwi, Yas Al-Hadeethi, Abeer Z. Barasheed, Saleha Al-Zhrani and Mingguang Chen
A Novel Underwater Wireless Optical Communication Optical Receiver Decision Unit Strategy Based on a Convolutional Neural Network
Reprinted from: *Mathematics* **2024**, *12*, 2805, doi:10.3390/math12182805 . . . . **229**

About the Editors

Lihua Wang

Lihua Wang, Ph.D., Professor in the School of Aerospace Engineering and Applied Mechanics of Tongji University (Shanghai, China) and Deputy Director of the Department of Mechanics. She is a General Council Member of the International Association for Computational Mechanics (IACM), a General Council Member of the International Chinese Association for Computational Mechanics (ICACM), a Committee Member of the Chinese Association of Computational Mechanics, and a Vice-chairman Committee Member of the South China Liaison Committee of Computational Mechanics. She is the recipient of several awards, including the APACM Award for Young Investigators in Computational Mechanics, the Qian Linxi Computational Mechanics Award (Young Investigators), the ICACM Young Investigator Award, and the Du Qing-Hua Medal & Young Researcher Award of Computational Methods in Engineering. She has authored more than 100 peer-reviewed journal articles in journals including CMAME, IJNME, JCP, etc., and has been invited to deliver more than 10 plenary and invited lectures at international conferences. She has served as associate editor of the *Chinese Quarterly of Mechanics* and as an editorial board member for five international/Chinese journals. Her research interests include the development of meshfree methods and machine learning, fluid–structure interaction, inverse problems, functionally graded materials, rigid–flexible coupling dynamics, etc.

Benny Yiu-Chung Hon

Benny Yiu-Chung Hon, Ph.D., Adjunct Professor in the Department of Mathematics of the City University of Hong Kong (Hong Kong, China). Recently, Professor Benny Y. C. Hon was awarded the Top 2% most highly cited scientists by Prof. John Ioannidis and his team at Stanford University based on the Top Scientists Ranking for 2022–2024. He is now serving as an Associate Editor for the *Journal of Inverse Problems in Science and Engineering* (IPSE) and the *Journal of Applicable Analysis*; a member of the editorial board for six international journals including the journals *Advances in Computational Mathematics and Engineering Analysis with Boundary Elements* with recent emphasis on meshless and mesh reduction methods. He is particularly keen on promoting the meshless radial basis functions method for solving real physical problems such as simulations of tides and waves; multiphasic fluid flows; micro-electro-mechanical systems; inverse heat conduction; image reconstruction; financial options pricing; and non-local nonlinear peridynamic models. His current research focus is on the development of an AI-integration-based meshless computational method, which has been shown to have distinct advantages in being truly meshless, highly accurate, and unconditionally stable for solving multi-dimensional boundary value problems (BVPs) under various kinds of stiffness boundary conditions defined in irregular domains.

Sheng-Wei Chi

Sheng-Wei Chi, Ph.D., Associate Professor in the Department of Civil and Materials Engineering at the University of Illinois at Chicago (Chicago, IL, USA). He received his Ph.D. from the Department of Civil and Environmental Engineering at the University of California, Los Angeles in 2009 and continued his postdoctoral education at UCLA before his appointment at UIC. He won the College of Engineering Advising Award at UIC in 2014, 2017, and 2018 and the College of Engineering Faculty Research Award at UIC in 2017. His research interests include image-based computational methods for biomedical applications, multiscale material modeling, advanced numerical methods, including meshfree methods, collocation methods, and generalized finite element methods, large deformation and contact mechanics, and fragment and impact simulations.

Article

The Adaptive Composite Block-Structured Grid Calculation of the Gas-Dynamic Characteristics of an Aircraft Moving in a Gas Environment

Victor V. Kuzenov [1], Sergei V. Ryzhkov [1,*] and Aleksey Yu. Varaksin [2]

[1] Thermal Physics Department, Bauman Moscow State Technical University, Moscow 105005, Russia; vik.kuzenov@gmail.com

[2] Joint Institute for High Temperatures, Russian Academy of Sciences, Moscow 125412, Russia; varaksin_a@mail.ru

* Correspondence: svryzhkov@bmstu.ru; Tel.: +7-(499)-263-6570

Citation: Kuzenov, V.V.; Ryzhkov, S.V.; Varaksin, A.Y. The Adaptive Composite Block-Structured Grid Calculation of the Gas-Dynamic Characteristics of an Aircraft Moving in a Gas Environment. *Mathematics* **2022**, *10*, 2130. https://doi.org/10.3390/math10122130

Academic Editors: Lihua Wang, Benny Y. C. Hon and Sheng-Wei Chi

Received: 30 May 2022
Accepted: 17 June 2022
Published: 19 June 2022

Publisher's Note: MDPI stays neutral with regard to jurisdictional claims in published maps and institutional affiliations.

Copyright: © 2022 by the authors. Licensee MDPI, Basel, Switzerland. This article is an open access article distributed under the terms and conditions of the Creative Commons Attribution (CC BY) license (https://creativecommons.org/licenses/by/4.0/).

Abstract: This paper considers the problem associated with the numerical simulation of the interaction between the cocurrent stream occurring near a monoblock moving in the gas medium and solid fuel combustion products flowing from a solid fuel rocket engine (SFRE). The peculiarity of the approach used is the description of gas-dynamic processes inside the combustion chamber, in the nozzle block, and the down jet based on a single calculation methodology. In the formulated numerical methodology, the calculation of gas-dynamic parameters is based on the solution of unsteady Navier–Stokes equations and the application of a hybrid computational grid. A hybrid block-structured computational grid makes it possible to calculate gas flow near bodies of complex geometric shapes. The simulation of the main phase of interaction, corresponding to the stationary mode of rocket flight in the Earth's atmosphere, has been carried out. A conjugated simulation of the internal ballistics of SFRE and interaction of combustion products jets is conducted.

Keywords: mathematical model; mesh generation; Navier–Stokes equations; numerical computation

MSC: 65N55; 65M50; 76D05

1. Introduction

A significant number of experimental and theoretical works are devoted to the study of the structure of jets of combustion products of rocket engines in which, as a rule, the influence of such dimensionless similarity criteria as the Mach number at the nozzle exit M_a and in the cocurrent flow M_∞, the adiabatic index γ, the degree of non-design $n = P_a/P_\infty$, Reynolds number $\text{Re} = (\rho_a u_a r_a)/\mu_a$ and the angle of inclination nozzle contour in the outlet section θ_a (where μ_a is the viscosity coefficient at the nozzle exit, u_a is the longitudinal velocity component at the nozzle exit, r_a is the nozzle exit radius and M_∞ and P_∞ are the Mach number and wake pressure at infinity).

Thanks to these studies, it was established that when a supersonic jet flows into a cocurrent supersonic flow, a complex flow structure is formed: hanging barrel-shaped shock waves appear in the external flow and inside the jet, rarefaction waves arise inside the jet, and an expanding mixing layer is formed at the outer boundary of the jet. In this case, the gaseous medium into which the outflow occurs can be at rest relative to the solid propellant rocket engine SFRE (outflow into the flooded space) or move relative to it at a speed W_∞ (interaction with a cocurrent flow). An increase in pressure P_∞ leads to the appearance of an initially oblique hanging shock at the nozzle exit, and at a higher counterpressure, the appearance of a Y-shaped system of shocks, consisting of two oblique and one direct shocks, is observed. At a certain threshold value of pressure, the $P_{\infty,\kappa p}$ Y-shaped system of shocks enters the nozzle, separating the boundary layer from the nozzle wall and significantly changing the gas-dynamic flow inside the nozzle apparatus.

It is important to note here that the described picture of the gas flow inside the nozzle apparatus is observed when the gas jet flows into the flooded space and can change under conditions of interaction with the external gas flow. Due to the difference in flow rates in the outgoing jet and the cocurrent flow, a central zone of reverse currents appears, which has a toroidal shape. The size and location of the reverse flow zones strongly affect the performance of the solid propellant rocket engine combustion chambers, which requires appropriate research.

In addition, this paper also considers the issue of the impact of a shock wave resulting from the impact on the oncoming undisturbed supersonic air flow of the head part of a solid propellant rocket engine on the thermal physical parameters of the cocurrent air jet and combustion products flowing from the nozzle apparatus of a solid-fuel rocket engine.

The paper presents a theoretical model of a solid fuel rocket, which allows calculating the characteristics of gas-dynamic processes in the nozzle block of a solid fuel rocket engine (SFRE) as well as calculating the interaction of the combustion product jet with the surrounding gas medium based on a unified numerical methodology. The computational studies are carried out within the framework of viscous (Navier–Stokes equations) gas flow. Earlier multigrid methods have been created, and the computation for convection–diffusion equations on nonuniform grids and equations with dynamic boundary conditions was performed. Numerical simulations have been developed for different flows and aerodynamic applications [1–3].

The important point in the numerical modeling of Navier–Stokes equations is the construction of a computational grid in complicated two- and three-dimensional domains Ω, which represents the computational domain Ω in the form of separate finite elements (cells). In this paper, the hexagonal irregular grid method, based on the hybrid non-structural multi-block structuring grids, is used for such domains. For this purpose, uniform partitioning of the domain into rectangular cells of size D_s, and the boundary of the computational domain Ω is presented as a piecewise-smooth contour $\partial\Omega$ consisting of curvilinear segments approximated by Bezier curves, is applied as an initial approximation. The numerical technique used in this research makes it possible to construct nonorthogonal structured grids even in those areas where non-structured computational grids are normally used to discretize the computational domain.

2. Method for Constructing Adaptive Grids

It is known from practical calculations that structured computational grids are preferable for solving problems in plasma dynamics and aerodynamics. However, the range of technical objects, the surface geometry of which can be described by structured computational grids, is rather limited. Therefore, there is a compromise option—a hybrid unstructured block-tetrahedral computational grid.

The use of a complex block-structured grid involves shaping the geometry of the computational domain by representing it as a group of hexahedral block-primitives (Figure 1), each of which constructs its structured grid Ω_h consistent with the grid in neighbouring blocks. The implementation of this approach requires that the blocks-primitives are docked on the boundaries with each other, and the computational grid formed in each block is combined into a single unstructured grid with common node numbering (Figure 2).

To approximate the curvilinear surfaces of faces, a Bezier projective surface is used, which is defined by a finite set of ordered points of three-dimensional space called the matrix of poles p_{ij} and the matrix of weights w_{ij} assigned to the same points. By changing the positions of the poles p_{ij} (control points) and the values of weights w_{ij}, we can control the closeness of the shape of the Bezier projective surface $\vec{r}(u,v)$ to the shape of the smooth curvilinear surfaces of the faces. Note here that the larger (relative to other points) the value of the weighting factor w_{ij}, the closer the Bezier surface is to the corresponding point on the face surface of the primitive block (decreasing the weight of the vertex will have the opposite effect).

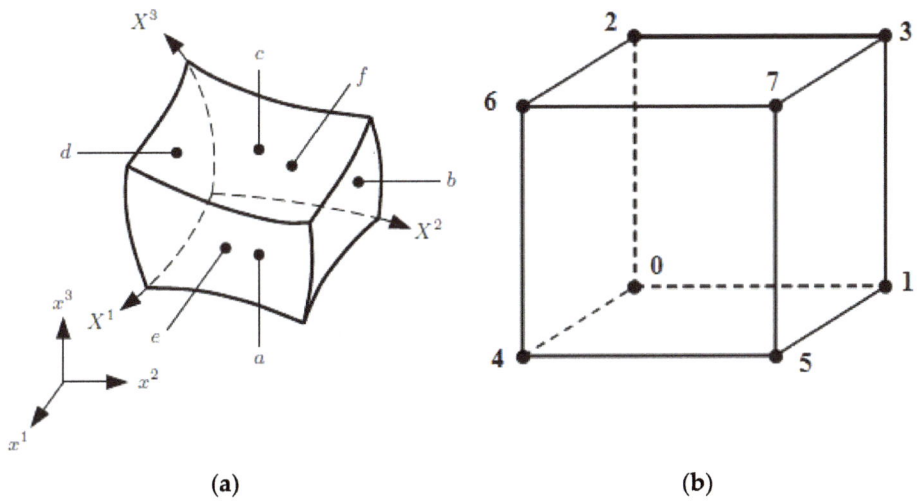

Figure 1. View of the primitive (**a**) curvilinear and (**b**) Cartesian block in the grid domain Ω_h.

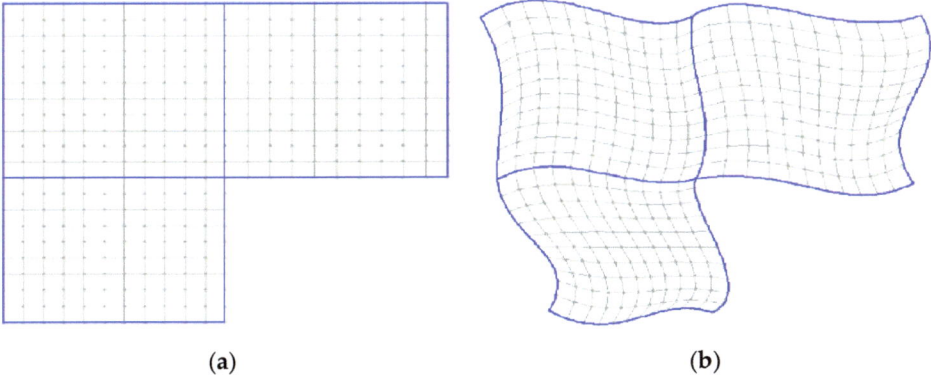

Figure 2. Forming a computational grid of primitive blocks in the computational domain Ω in (**a**) Cartesian and (**b**) curvilinear domains.

Analytically, a Bezier projective surface of order $n \times m$ (its representation is related to Bernstein basis polynomials $B_i^n(v)$, $B_j^m(u)$) is described by a fractional-rational function $\vec{r}(u,v)$ of the following form (the weights w_{ij} of the angular vertices are considered to be equal to 1):

$$\vec{r}(u,v) = \sum_{i=0}^{n} \sum_{j=0}^{m} B_i^n(v) B_j^m(u) \langle w_{ij} \rangle \vec{p}_{ij} =$$

$$= \left(\sum_{j=0}^{m} B_0^n(v) B_j^m(u) \langle w_{0j} \rangle \vec{p}_{0j} + \ldots + \sum_{j=0}^{m} B_n^n(v) B_j^m(u) \langle w_{nj} \rangle \vec{p}_{nj} \right),$$

$$\langle w_{ij} \rangle = \frac{w_{ij}}{\sum_{i=0}^{n} \sum_{j=0}^{m} B_i^n(v) B_j^m(u) w_{ij}}, \ 0 \le u \le 1, 0 \le v \le 1,$$

$$B_i^n(v) = \binom{n}{i} v^i (1-v)^{n-i}, \ B_j^m(u) = \binom{m}{j} u^j (1-u)^{m-j}, \ \sum_{i=0}^{n} \sum_{j=0}^{m} B_i^n(v) B_j^m(u) = 1,$$

where $\binom{n}{i} = C_n^i = \frac{n!}{i!(n-i)!}$, $\binom{m}{j} = C_m^j = \frac{m!}{j!(m-j)!}$ are the binomial coefficients, and $\vec{p}_{ij}$ is the pole matrix consisting of vectors (with x, y, z components) of control points.

When writing this formula, it is assumed that there is a set of control points conventionally arranged as $n + 1$ rows of $m + 1$ points in each row. The indices of point $\vec{p}_{ij}$ mean that the given j-th control point is located in the i-th row (the first index equals the number of the row; the second index equals the number of the point in the row). Note also that the expression for $\vec{r}(u,v)$ is a convex hull of the poles $\vec{p}_{ij}$. That is, the projective Bezier surface will be located inside this convex hull, "stretched" on these poles.

The Bezier surface can (for the convenience of further calculations) be written in vector form:

$$\vec{r}_x(u,v) = \left(\vec{c}_x \cdot \vec{\varphi}\right) = \sum_{\ell=0}^{n} c_{\ell,x}\varphi_\ell, \quad \vec{r}_y(u,v) = \left(\vec{c}_y \cdot \vec{\varphi}\right) = \sum_{\ell=0}^{n} c_{\ell,y}\varphi_\ell, \quad \vec{r}_z(u,v) = \left(\vec{c}_z \cdot \vec{\varphi}\right) = \sum_{\ell=0}^{n} c_{\ell,z}\varphi_\ell,$$

$$\vec{\varphi} = (\varphi_0, \ldots, \varphi_\ell, \ldots, \varphi_n)^T, \quad \varphi_\ell = \left(B_\ell^n(v)B_0^m(u)\langle w_{\ell 0}\rangle, \ldots, B_\ell^n(v)B_m^m(u)\langle w_{\ell m}\rangle\right), \quad \ell = \overline{0, n},$$

$$\vec{c}_x = (p_{0,x}, \ldots, p_{\ell,x}, \ldots, p_{n,x})^T, \quad \vec{c}_y = \left(p_{0,y}, \ldots, p_{\ell,y}, \ldots, p_{n,y}\right)^T, \quad \vec{c}_z = (p_{0,z}, \ldots, p_{\ell,z}, \ldots, p_{n,z})^T,$$

where $p_{\ell,x} = (p_{\ell 0,x}, \ldots, p_{\ell m,x})$, $p_{\ell,y} = \left(p_{\ell 0,y}, \ldots, p_{\ell m,y}\right)$, $p_{\ell,z} = (p_{\ell 0,z}, \ldots, p_{\ell m,z})$.

Let us assume that on any curvilinear face surface, $N \times M$ points are interpolation nodes, for which their Cartesian x_{ij}, y_{ij}, z_{ij} ($i = \overline{1,N}, j = \overline{1,M}$) coordinates are known (as well as their corresponding values of parameters u_{ij}, v_{ij}), listed in the order of their connection in the framework of control points of the face being constructed. Then using the coordinate values of the interpolation nodes x_{ij}, y_{ij}, z_{ij} (and u_{ij}, v_{ij}) and the formula for $\vec{r}(u,v)$, we can formulate a system of linear equations with the unknowns being the coordinates of the control points (the pole matrix $\vec{p}_{ij}$):

$$A\vec{c}_x = \vec{q}_x, \quad A\vec{c}_y = \vec{q}_y, \quad A\vec{c}_z = \vec{q}_z,$$

$$A = \begin{bmatrix} \varphi_0(u_1, v_1) & \ldots & \varphi_\ell(u_1, v_1) & \ldots & \varphi_n(u_1, v_1) \\ \ldots & \ldots & \ldots & \ldots & \ldots \\ \varphi_0(u_i, v_i) & \ldots & \varphi_\ell(u_i, v_i) & \ldots & \varphi_n(u_i, v_i) \\ \ldots & \ldots & \ldots & \ldots & \ldots \\ \varphi_0(u_{N\times M}, v_{N\times M}) & \ldots & \varphi_\ell(u_{N\times M}, v_{N\times M}) & \ldots & \varphi_n(u_{N\times M}, v_{N\times M}) \end{bmatrix},$$

$$\vec{c}_x = (p_{0,x}, \ldots, p_{\ell,x}, \ldots, p_{n,x})^T, \quad \vec{c}_y = \left(p_{0,y}, \ldots, p_{\ell,y}, \ldots, p_{n,y}\right)^T, \quad \vec{c}_z = (p_{0,z}, \ldots, p_{\ell,z}, \ldots, p_{n,z})^T,$$

$$\vec{q}_x = (x_1, \ldots, x_i, \ldots, x_{N\times M}), \quad \vec{q}_y = (y_1, \ldots, y_i, \ldots, y_{N\times M}), \quad \vec{q}_z = (z_1, \ldots, z_i, \ldots, z_{N\times M}),$$

where $N \times M = (n+1) \times (m+1)$ is a number of interpolation nodes on the curvilinear face; $(n+1) \times (m+1)$ is the number of unknowns for each component (x, y or z) of pole matrix $\vec{p}_{ij}$; $\vec{r}_s = (x_s, y_s, z_s)^T$ is its radius vector; the Cartesian coordinates of points (in number $N \times M$) on the curvilinear face are approximated by the Bezier surface; and u_s, v_s are parameter values (with a changing area $0 \leq u \leq 1, 0 \leq v \leq 1$), appropriate to specified points $\vec{r}_s$, where $s = \overline{1, N \times M}$, on the curvilinear face.

However, such a system of equations will in most cases be overdetermined. The least squares method [4] can be used to overcome this disadvantage:

$$A\vec{c_x} = \vec{q_x}, \; A\vec{c_y} = \vec{q_y}, \; A\vec{c_z} = \vec{q_z},$$

$$A = \begin{bmatrix} \sum_{s=1}^{N\times M} \varphi_0(u_s,v_s)\varphi_0(u_s,v_s) & \ldots & \sum_{s=1}^{N\times M} \varphi_0(u_s,v_s)\varphi_\ell(u_s,v_s) & \ldots & \sum_{s=1}^{N\times M} \varphi_0(u_s,v_s)\varphi_n(u_s,v_s) \\ \ldots & \ldots & \ldots & \ldots & \ldots \\ \sum_{s=1}^{N\times M} \varphi_i(u_s,v_s)\varphi_0(u_s,v_s) & \ldots & \sum_{s=1}^{N\times M} \varphi_i(u_s,v_s)\varphi_\ell(u_s,v_s) & \ldots & \sum_{s=1}^{N\times M} \varphi_i(u_s,v_s)\varphi_n(u_s,v_s) \\ \ldots & \ldots & \ldots & \ldots & \ldots \\ \sum_{s=1}^{N\times M} \varphi_n(u_s,v_s)\varphi_0(u_s,v_s) & \ldots & \sum_{s=1}^{N\times M} \varphi_n(u_s,v_s)\varphi_\ell(u_s,v_s) & \ldots & \sum_{s=1}^{N\times M} \varphi_n(u_s,v_s)\varphi_n(u_s,v_s) \end{bmatrix},$$

$$\vec{c_x} = (p_{0,x}, \ldots, p_{\ell,x}, \ldots, p_{n,x})^T, \; \vec{c_y} = \left(p_{0,y}, \ldots, p_{\ell,y}, \ldots, p_{n,y}\right)^T, \; \vec{c_z} = (p_{0,z}, \ldots, p_{\ell,z}, \ldots, p_{n,z})^T,$$

$$q_{k,x} = \sum_{s=1}^{N\times M} \varphi_k(u_s, v_s) \cdot x_s, \; q_{k,y} = \sum_{s=1}^{N\times M} \varphi_k(u_s, v_s) \cdot y_s, \; q_{k,z} = \sum_{s=1}^{N\times M} \varphi_k(u_s, v_s) \cdot z_s, \; k = \overline{0,n},$$

$$\vec{\varphi} = (\varphi_0, \ldots, \varphi_\ell, \ldots, \varphi_n)^T, \; \varphi_\ell = \left(B^n_\ell(v)B^m_0(u)\langle w_{\ell 0}\rangle, \ldots, B^n_\ell(v)B^m_m(u)\langle w_{\ell m}\rangle\right), \; \ell = \overline{0,n},$$

$$p_{\ell,x} = (p_{\ell 0,x}, \ldots, p_{\ell m,x}), \; p_{\ell,y} = \left(p_{\ell 0,y}, \ldots, p_{\ell m,y}\right), \; p_{\ell,z} = (p_{\ell 0,z}, \ldots, p_{\ell m,z}),$$

where $N \times M = (n+1) \times (m+1)$ is the number of interpolation nodes on the curvilinear face; $(n+1) \times (m+1)$ is the number of unknowns for each component (x, y or z) of pole matrix $\vec{p_{ij}}$; $\vec{r_s} = (x_s, y_s, z_s)^T$ are its radius vector and Cartesian coordinates of points (in number $N \times M$) on the curvilinear face, which is approximated by the Bezier surface; and u_s, v_s are parameter values (with a changing area $0 \leq u \leq 1, 0 \leq v \leq 1$), appropriate to specified points $\vec{r_s}$, where $s = \overline{1, N \times M}$ on the curvilinear face.

Using the found projective variant (Bezier surface) of each curvilinear surface of block-primitive faces, a surface grid of block-primitives can be constructed. Then operating on this surface grid and using the method of three-dimensional transfinite interpolation [5] as well as the quasi orthogonalization method, a bulk structured quasiorthogonal computational grid (consisting of grid surfaces whose nodes are numbered using parameters) inside the block-primitive is created. Then, as mentioned above, the constructed local (in block-primitive) computational grid is combined (Figure 3) into a single global unstructured grid with common node numbering. After that, an additional stage of its optimization (improvement—"regularization") with the assessment of its quality is applied.

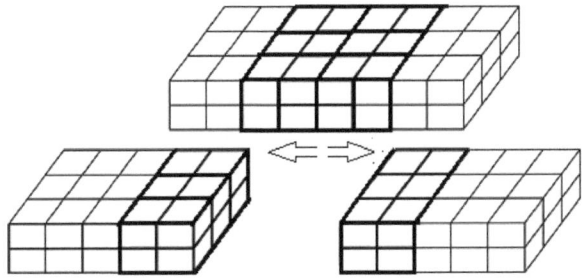

Figure 3. Formation of a single global unstructured grid.

For numerical adaptation (to the solution peculiarities) of the volumetric computational grid, the results of [6] or the principle of uniform distribution (equidistributional method) of the "adaptation" (weight) function w are used.

To give the bulk structured computational grid (generally speaking non-orthogonal) inside the block-primitive properties of quasiorthogonality, an approximate solution of the equation describing the longitudinal deformation of the plates is found in [7]. The initial approximation for the mock orthogonalization method is the computational grid obtained after the numerical adaptation step.

When describing the mock orthogonalization method, we introduce in the Cartesian coordinate system XYZ a rectangular parallelepiped $ABFEDCGH$, which has a continuously differentiable way to be mapped into a curvilinear parallelepiped (hexahedron) $A'B'F'E'D'C'G'H'$. The rectangular grid mapped to the domain forms $ABFEDCGH$, a smooth curvilinear grid in the domain $A'B'F'E'D'C'G'H'$.

Denote by $\vec{r}$ the radius vector in the XYZ coordinate system and introduce a vector $\vec{U} = \vec{r}^* - \vec{r}$ characterizing the displacement of points. Here, $\vec{r}$ and $\vec{r}^*$ are radius vectors of points of domains before $\vec{r} \in ABCD$ and after $\vec{r}^* \in A'B'F'E'D'C'G'H'$ transformation. To construct regular adaptive grids close to being orthogonal, the following equations are used to determine the displacement values U_x, U_y, U_z and to describe the longitudinal deformation of the plates [7]:

$$\frac{\partial}{\partial x}\left(\frac{\partial U_x}{\partial x}\right) + \frac{(1-\sigma)}{2}\frac{\partial}{\partial y}\left(\frac{\partial U_x}{\partial y}\right) + \frac{(1-\sigma)}{2}\frac{\partial}{\partial z}\left(\frac{\partial U_x}{\partial z}\right) + \frac{(1+\sigma)}{2}\left\{\frac{\partial}{\partial x}\left(\frac{\partial U_y}{\partial y}\right) + \frac{\partial}{\partial x}\left(\frac{\partial U_z}{\partial z}\right)\right\} +$$
$$+ \left\{\frac{\partial}{\partial x}\left(W\sqrt{\frac{g_{22}g_{33}}{g_{11}}}\frac{\partial U_x}{\partial x}\right) + \frac{\partial}{\partial y}\left(W\sqrt{\frac{g_{33}g_{11}}{g_{22}}}\frac{\partial U_x}{\partial y}\right) + \frac{\partial}{\partial z}\left(W\sqrt{\frac{g_{11}g_{22}}{g_{33}}}\frac{\partial U_x}{\partial z}\right)\right\} = 0,$$

$$\frac{\partial}{\partial y}\left(\frac{\partial U_y}{\partial y}\right) + \frac{(1-\sigma)}{2}\frac{\partial}{\partial x}\left(\frac{\partial U_y}{\partial x}\right) + \frac{(1-\sigma)}{2}\frac{\partial}{\partial z}\left(\frac{\partial U_y}{\partial z}\right) + \frac{(1+\sigma)}{2}\left\{\frac{\partial}{\partial y}\left(\frac{\partial U_x}{\partial x}\right) + \frac{\partial}{\partial y}\left(\frac{\partial U_z}{\partial z}\right)\right\} +$$
$$+ \left\{\frac{\partial}{\partial x}\left(W\sqrt{\frac{g_{22}g_{33}}{g_{11}}}\frac{\partial U_y}{\partial x}\right) + \frac{\partial}{\partial y}\left(W\sqrt{\frac{g_{33}g_{11}}{g_{22}}}\frac{\partial U_y}{\partial y}\right) + \frac{\partial}{\partial z}\left(W\sqrt{\frac{g_{11}g_{22}}{g_{33}}}\frac{\partial U_y}{\partial z}\right)\right\} = 0,$$

$$\frac{\partial}{\partial z}\left(\frac{\partial U_z}{\partial z}\right) + \frac{(1-\sigma)}{2}\frac{\partial}{\partial x}\left(\frac{\partial U_z}{\partial x}\right) + \frac{(1-\sigma)}{2}\frac{\partial}{\partial y}\left(\frac{\partial U_z}{\partial y}\right) + \frac{(1+\sigma)}{2}\left\{\frac{\partial}{\partial z}\left(\frac{\partial U_x}{\partial x}\right) + \frac{\partial}{\partial z}\left(\frac{\partial U_y}{\partial y}\right)\right\} +$$
$$+ \left\{\frac{\partial}{\partial x}\left(W\sqrt{\frac{g_{22}g_{33}}{g_{11}}}\frac{\partial U_z}{\partial x}\right) + \frac{\partial}{\partial y}\left(W\sqrt{\frac{g_{33}g_{11}}{g_{22}}}\frac{\partial U_z}{\partial y}\right) + \frac{\partial}{\partial z}\left(W\sqrt{\frac{g_{11}g_{22}}{g_{33}}}\frac{\partial U_z}{\partial z}\right)\right\} = 0,$$

The boundary conditions required to solve this system of equations are given as follows: $U_i|_\Gamma = r_i^*|_{\partial(A'B'F'E'D'C'G'H')} - r_i|_{\partial(ABFEDCGH)}$, $i \in \{x,y,z\}$, where the symbol ∂ means that the components of the radii of the vectors $\vec{r}$ and $\vec{r}^*$ are defined at the boundary of the corresponding domain.

The components of the covariant and contravariant metric tensor entering the system of equations are defined by the relations:

$$g_{ik} = \sum_{\alpha=1}^{3} \frac{\partial r'^\alpha}{\partial q^i}\frac{\partial r'^\alpha}{\partial q^k}, \quad \sum_{k=1}^{3} g_{ik}g^{kj} = \delta_i^j = \begin{cases} 1, i=j \\ 0, i \neq j \end{cases}, \quad q^1 = x, q^2 = y, q^3 = z.$$

The $\sigma \in [-1, 1]$ coefficient describes the ratio of transverse strain to longitudinal strain. The coefficient $W(x, y, z)$ is a control function used to achieve the desired degree of densification of the grid lines in the area of the strongest change in gas-dynamic functions or spatial boundaries.

Let us introduce vectors $\frac{\partial \vec{U}}{\partial \xi}, \frac{\partial \vec{U}}{\partial \eta}, \frac{\partial \vec{U}}{\partial \zeta}$ tangent to the grid lines in the spatial domain (x, y, z); then the control function can be formulated in the form

$$W(x,y,z) = 1+$$
$$+\beta \oint_{\Gamma_{\xi\eta}} \left\{\frac{\left|\frac{\partial \vec{U}}{\partial \xi}\right|\cdot\left|\frac{\partial \vec{U}}{\partial \eta}\right|}{\left|\frac{\partial \vec{U}}{\partial \xi}\times\frac{\partial \vec{U}}{\partial \eta}\right|}\right\}^2 d\Gamma_{\xi\eta} + \gamma \oint_{\Gamma_{\eta\zeta}} \left\{\frac{\left|\frac{\partial \vec{U}}{\partial \eta}\right|\cdot\left|\frac{\partial \vec{U}}{\partial \zeta}\right|}{\left|\frac{\partial \vec{U}}{\partial \eta}\times\frac{\partial \vec{U}}{\partial \zeta}\right|}\right\}^2 d\Gamma_{\eta\zeta} + \chi \oint_{\Gamma_{\xi\zeta}} \left\{\frac{\left|\frac{\partial \vec{U}}{\partial \xi}\right|\cdot\left|\frac{\partial \vec{U}}{\partial \zeta}\right|}{\left|\frac{\partial \vec{U}}{\partial \xi}\times\frac{\partial \vec{U}}{\partial \zeta}\right|}\right\}^2 \Gamma_{\zeta\zeta},$$

This kind of control function leads to the orthogonalization of relatively small cells. In the numerical construction of high aspect ratio grids, instead of contour integrals, the sum of expressions of the form $\left\{\frac{\left|\frac{\partial \vec{U}}{\partial \xi}\right|\cdot\left|\frac{\partial \vec{U}}{\partial \eta}\right|}{\left|\frac{\partial \vec{U}}{\partial \xi}\times\frac{\partial \vec{U}}{\partial \eta}\right|}\right\}^2$ or $\left\{\frac{\left|\frac{\partial \vec{U}}{\partial \eta}\right|\cdot\left|\frac{\partial \vec{U}}{\partial \zeta}\right|}{\left|\frac{\partial \vec{U}}{\partial \eta}\times\frac{\partial \vec{U}}{\partial \zeta}\right|}\right\}^2$, etc., and overall grid corners will be used.

To solve the problem $A\vec{U} = 0$, we used the method of establishment [8]. Step by "time" τ is found using the iterative method of a variational type.

3. A Mathematical Model for Determining the Individual Characteristics of a Solid-Propellant Rocket

This section considers the effect of a ballistic wave, resulting from the oncoming unperturbed airflow of the monoblock head part, on the thermophysical parameters of the down jet of air and combustion products flowing from the nozzle of a solid fuel rocket engine.

The numerical investigations of such kinds of flows can be performed on the basis of the solution of Navier–Stokes equations. The case of transition from Cartesian coordinates x^α to arbitrary curvilinear coordinates q^α while taking into account the absence of dependence of this transformation on time t is used for transformation. In this case, the system of Navier–Stokes equations of a compressible heat-conducting gas in arbitrary curvilinear coordinates q_1, q_2, q_3 takes the form [9]:

$$\frac{\partial}{\partial t}(J^{-1}\rho) + \frac{\partial}{\partial q^\alpha}(J^{-1}\rho v^\alpha) = 0,$$

$$\frac{\partial}{\partial t}(J^{-1}\rho v^i) + \frac{\partial}{\partial q^\alpha}(J^{-1}\rho v^\alpha v^i) + J^{-1}\Gamma^i_{\alpha\beta}\rho v^\alpha v^\beta + J^{-1}g^{i\alpha}\frac{\partial p}{\partial q^\alpha} -$$
$$-J^{-1}g^{i\alpha}\frac{\partial}{\partial q^\alpha}(\theta \, div(\vec{v})) - J^{-1}g^{i\beta}\left(\frac{1}{\sqrt{g}}\frac{\partial}{\partial q^\alpha}(\sqrt{g}A^\alpha_\beta) - \Gamma^\alpha_{\beta\ell}A^\ell_\alpha\right) - J^{-1}g^{\alpha\gamma}\left(\frac{\partial A^i_\gamma}{\partial q^\alpha} + \Gamma^i_{\ell\alpha}A^\ell_\gamma - \Gamma^\ell_{\gamma\alpha}A^i_\ell\right) = 0,$$

$$\frac{\partial}{\partial t}(J^{-1}\rho e) + \frac{\partial}{\partial q^\alpha}\left[J^{-1}(\rho v^\alpha e)\right] + \frac{J^{-1}P}{\sqrt{g}}\frac{\partial}{\partial q^i}(\sqrt{g}v^i) - J^{-1}\theta\left\{\frac{1}{\sqrt{g}}\frac{\partial}{\partial q^i}(\sqrt{g}v^i)\right\}^2 -$$
$$-\frac{J^{-1}A^\alpha_\ell A^\ell_\alpha}{\mu} - \frac{J^{-1}g_{i\ell}g^{\alpha\gamma}A^i_\gamma A^\ell_\alpha}{\mu} - g^{\alpha\beta}J^{-1}\frac{\partial}{\partial q^\alpha}\left(\lambda\frac{\partial T}{\partial q^\beta}\right) + g^{\alpha\beta}J^{-1}\Gamma^\ell_{\beta\alpha}\left(\lambda\frac{\partial T}{\partial q^\ell}\right) = 0$$

$$P^{i\alpha} = g^{i\alpha}P - g^{i\alpha}\left[\theta \, div(\vec{v})\right] - g^{i\beta}A^\alpha_\beta - g^{\alpha\gamma}A^i_\gamma, \quad A^\alpha_\beta = \mu(\partial v^\alpha/\partial x^\beta + \Gamma^\alpha_{k\beta}v^k).$$

where P, ρ and T are pressure, density and temperature; e and $\sum_{i=1}^{3}\frac{v_i^2}{2}$ are internal and kinetic energies of gas; $P^{\alpha\beta} = (P - \theta\nabla_\alpha v^\alpha)g^{\alpha\beta} - \mu(g^{\alpha\gamma}\nabla_\gamma v^\beta + g^{\beta\gamma}\nabla_\gamma v^\alpha)$ is stress tensor; $g^{\alpha\beta}$ is the contravariant metric tensor; v^i is the contravariant components of the velocity vector; $\theta = -\frac{2}{3}\mu$; μ is the shear viscosity; and λ is the heat transfer coefficient. In these expressions, repeated indices summation is assumed.

The reduced system of equations is supplemented by the initial conditions:

$$u(r,0) = 0, \; \rho(r,0) = \rho_o, e(r,0) = e_o.$$

The boundary conditions that determine the characteristics of the combustion products entering the engine chamber from the surface of a burning solid fuel have the form:

$$\vec{u}_s = u_w(\rho_T/\rho_s)\vec{n}, \rho_s = \frac{P}{RT_s}, e_s = \frac{RT_s}{(\gamma-1)}.$$

where u_s, ρ_s, T_s, e_s and R are the speed, density, temperature, internal energy and gas constant of incoming gaseous combustion products from the surface of solid fuel; ρ_T is the density of solid fuel; and u_w is the speed of movement of the surface of the fuel during its burnout. It is assumed that gas injection into the engine chamber occurs along the normal to the fuel surface. The burnup rate is known from experimentation or from calculations of the combustion kinetics [10]. It is given in the following form [11]:

$$u_w = u_{wo}P^\nu,$$

where u_{wo} is the value of the speed of movement of the burnable fuel boundary at pressure $P = 1$, and ν is the constant, depending on the type of fuel used.

On the stationary solid surfaces of the nozzle and the front bottom of the engine, the conditions of impermeability are set as $(\vec{u}\,\vec{n}) = 0$. At the boundary of the computational domain (behind the nozzle exit), through which the co-flow enters, the following gas-dynamic parameters are set: $\gamma = 1.4$, ρ_∞, P_∞, V_∞, where V_∞, ρ_∞ and P_∞ are the velocity, density and pressure of the gas entering through the boundary surface, respectively.

On the external (located at sufficiently large distances from the nozzle exit) surfaces of the computational domain, the free flow conditions are set as $\frac{\partial^2 \vec{f}}{\partial x_n^2} = 0$, where x_n is the coordinate normal to the boundary surface, and $\vec{f}$ is the vector of resulting variables.

Given what is known in the physical space, x, y, z coordinates of the grid nodes in the computational domain q_1, q_2, q_3, the metric coefficients can generally be found by numerical differentiation using the formulas [12].

The Christoffel symbols of the second kind are found using the formula $\Gamma^i_{jk} = \sum_{\ell=1}^{3} \frac{1}{2} g^{\ell i} \left(\frac{\partial g_{\ell j}}{\partial q^k} + \frac{\partial g_{\ell k}}{\partial q^j} - \frac{\partial g_{jk}}{\partial q^\ell} \right)$, and for the case of Euclidean physical space x, y, z, also using the formula $\Gamma^i_{jk} = \sum_{\alpha=1}^{3} \left[\left(\frac{\partial q^i}{\partial x^\alpha} \right) \left(\frac{\partial^2 x^\alpha}{\partial q^k \partial q^j} \right) \right]$.

4. Computational Method

To solve the gas-dynamic part of the system of equations, a nonlinear quasimonotone compact-polynomial difference scheme of higher-order accuracy [7,13–15], as well as a spatial splitting of Navier–Stokes equations [7] written in an arbitrary curvilinear coordinate system, were used. To calculate the flux vectors at the boundaries of the computational cell, the discontinuity calculation procedure formulated in [16] was applied. Other details of the nonlinear quasi-monotone compact polynomial difference scheme are given in [7,13]. The time step required to integrate the above difference scheme was chosen from the condition of the Courant–Friedrichs–Levy stability criterion.

The "hyperbolic" (convective) part of the computer model of targets was tested on a one-dimensional version of the Riemann problem (Soda problem) about the decay of an unstable discontinuity of a given configuration. A comparison of the exact solution and the approximate solution showed that the difference is not more than one percent [16]. Verification calculations were carried out to estimate the degree of attenuation of the reflected shockwave system and showed that the calculation error is within the experimental accuracy of the results and can reach a level of 10%. As an additional verification test, we considered flowing air around a wedge mated to a plate and a cone mated to a cylinder with the following oncoming flow parameters: pressure P = 2060 Pa, speed V = 1860 m/s, temperature T = 223 K and Mach number $M_\infty = 6$. These results are also in good agreement [12] with the above calculations (relative error of 0.4%). In addition, the methodology was tested with an example of a viscous jet flowing into a downstream gas stream [17] (relative error of 5%). The "thermal" ("parabolic") part of the model has been tested on some problems admitting exact analytical solutions: heating of a continuous medium [18] filling a flat semibounded space $r > 0$ by a heat flow through the left fixed boundary $r = 0$ (relative error less than 1.0%).

A composite two-block structured grid was invented, which was combined into a single computational grid. Block number one of the computational grid described the grid space of the combustion chamber, the nozzle block and the wake jet of combustion products. The characteristic size of the computational grid in the first block is 150 × 400 cells. The second block is located outside the solid propellant rocket monoblock and the wake (these two blocks are separated (for illustration) from each other by a black line in Figures 4–6). The characteristic size of the computational grid in this block is 350 × 550 cells. The calculation cells were thickened in the area of the boundary layer (the thickness of the boundary layer is several millimeters; the number of cells in the direction perpendicular to the SFRE surface is not less than 50) in the head part of the monoblock, at the cut of the combustion chamber nozzle and also in the mixing layers. The density gradient was used as a control (monitor) function.

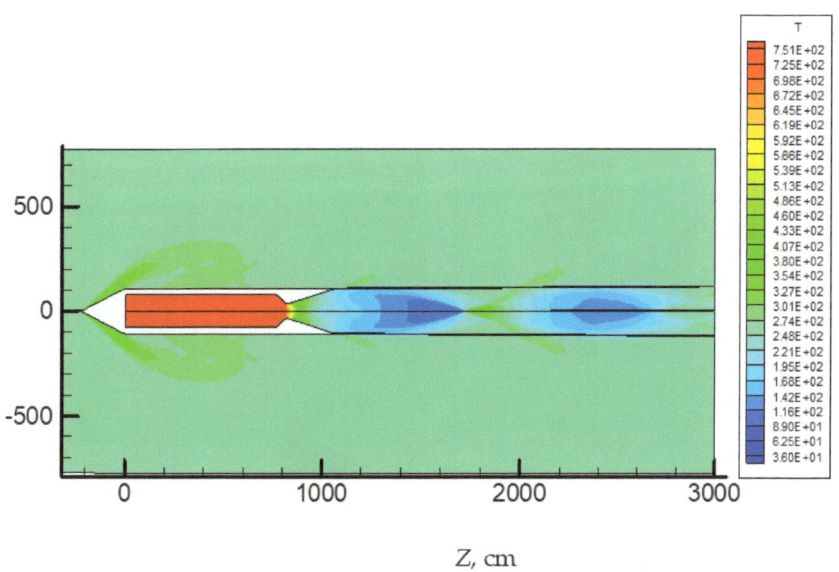

Figure 4. Spatial distribution of temperature T, K in the combustion products and the downpipe ($h = 25$ km, $n \approx 1$, $M_\infty \approx 2$, and $T_\infty = 270$ K).

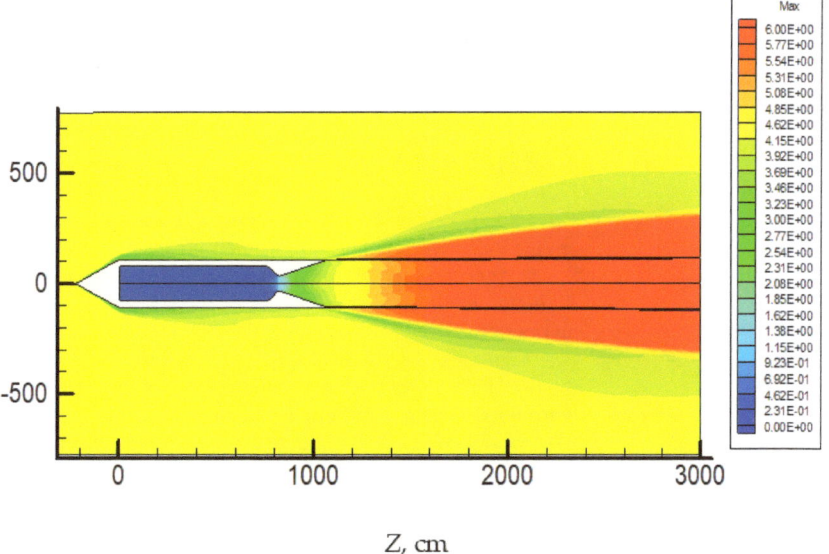

Figure 5. Spatial distribution of Mach number M in the combustion products and the down jet ($h = 55$ km, $n \approx 80$, $M = 4.4$, and $T_\infty = 270$ K).

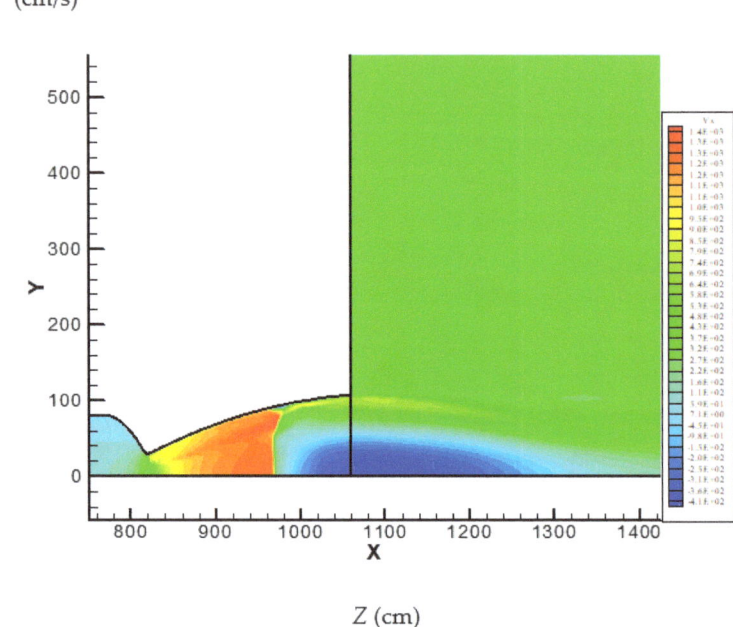

Figure 6. Spatial distribution of the longitudinal velocity in the combustion products and the wake air (Navier–Stokes equations, "elliptical" shape of the nozzle, h = 6 km).

5. Some Results of Calculations of Gas-Dynamic Parameters of a Jet Flowing into a Downstream Gas Stream

Based on the developed numerical codes [19–21] a numerical simulation of two trajectory points of the ARIAN 5 missile flight path was carried out: (1) W_∞ = 0.72 km/s, P_∞ = 0.036 at, T_∞ = 270 K, γ = 1.4, distance from the Earth's surface 25 km and (2) W_∞ = 1.5 km/s, P_∞ = 0.00065 at, h = 55 km). The prototype engine chosen was the solid propellant rocket engine P-85, which belongs to the medium class of solid propellant boosters of the European Space Agency [22], i.e., the monoblock consists of a cylinder with length Z_{noz} = 1060 cm, diameter equal to the diameter of the nozzle shear D_{noz} = 215 cm and a conical head with an opening angle of 54 degrees. The condensed phase was neglected [23].

Figures 4 and 5 show the spatial distributions of temperature T and Mach numbers for the first and second points of the trajectory of the ARIAN 5 rocket. The following notations were used: Mach numbers at nozzle cutoff $M_a = W_a/C_a = 4$ and in unperturbed flow $M_\infty = W_\infty/C_\infty$, adiabatic exponent γ and degree of inconsistency $n = P_a/P_\infty$ (where the indices a and ∞ correspond to the gas-dynamic parameters at nozzle cutoff and unperturbed flow).

Figure 4 shows spatial distributions of the temperature and Mach number corresponding to the first point of the monoblock flight path. In this case, a flow pattern corresponding to a small value of the degree of inconsistency (h = 25 km, n = 1) was realized. Here, due to a sufficiently large value of pressure in the down jet ($P_\infty \approx P_a$), the radial expansion of the central exhaust gas jet was strongly limited. This limitation lead to the falling of the densification jump on the jet axis (axial coordinate of drop region Z = 1700 cm—conic nozzle shape) with the following regular reflection from it; the temperature distribution was aligned along the jet axis, and the characteristic transverse size of the central jet was close to diameter of nozzle shear. In this case, the number of "barrels" increases (if we compare with the results of 55 km) and becomes more than one during interaction between the down jet and the central jet.

At high under-expanding (second point of the flight path; option $h = 55$ km, $n = 80$), the flow pattern shown in Figure 5 is realized. These figures illustrate the wave structure of a highly under-expanded jet flow into the cocurrent stream. From the given distributions, it can be seen that with sufficiently high values of the degree of under-expansion n near the exit edge of the nozzle and in the down jet of ambient air due to the collision of the expanding jet of the SFRE exhaust and the down jet, an oblique shock wave (SW) and a hanging SW falling on the jet axis, which is characterized by a regular reflection from the jet axis (the axial coordinate of the incident area $Z = 1700$ cm—"conical" nozzle shape), emerge. In this case, due to the fact that the size of the first barrel grows as $\sqrt{n}$, only the first "barrel" is observed, the size of which significantly exceeds the characteristic transverse size of the SFRE.

The calculations also show that there is a noticeable (second trajectory point in Figure 5) effect of the leading shock wave on the thermophysical parameters of the down jet of air and combustion products expiring from the nozzle of the solid propellant rocket engine.

It is known [24–28] that a decrease in the degree of non-design n below a certain value n_{cr} leads to the irregular reflection of the incident shock from the jet axis with the formation of a Y-shaped system of shocks, consisting of two oblique and one direct shocks. Spatial distributions of the Mach number, pressure and longitudinal velocity in combustion products and wake air corresponding to the first point of the ARIAN 5 flight trajectory (flight altitude 6 km), which are presented in Figures 6 and 7, illustrate this fact. In this group of calculations, the formation of "barrels" is not observed; the temperature along the jet axis is equalized and amounts to 600 K. The decrease in the degree of non-design is accompanied by an irregular reflection of the hanging shock from the jet axis with the formation of a figurative system of shocks, consisting of two oblique and one direct shocks. In these variants of calculations (altitude 6 km, degree of non-design $n = 0.7$), this shock system had a "standard" form, entered the supersonic part of the nozzle and led to the separation of the SFRE exhaust gas flow from the nozzle walls. At the same time, a zone of reverse currents formed behind the central shock wave, which has a toroidal shape [29].

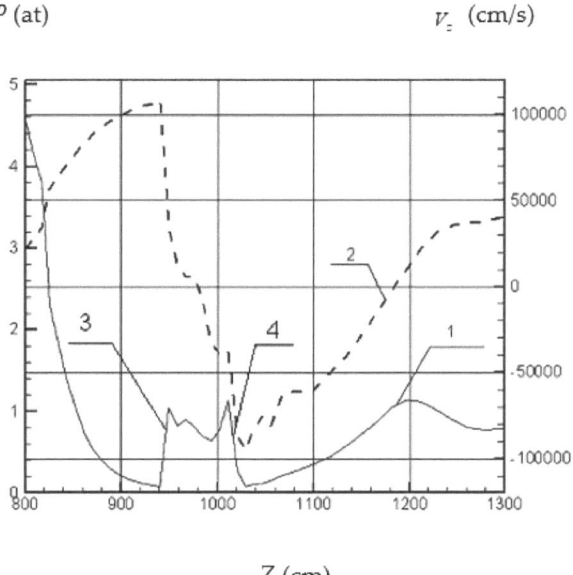

Figure 7. Distributions of pressure (1) and longitudinal velocity V_z (2) along the solid propellant rocket motor axis (conical shape of the nozzle, $h = 6$ km, M=0.9). (3) Main shock wave, (4) secondary shock wave.

The appearance of the reverse flow zone is mainly associated with a large positive pressure gradient (Figure 7, axial region ($1000 \leq z \leq 1200$ cm)) behind the nozzle exit [24], which occurs due to a sharp expansion of the wake jet towards the axis of the coaxially interacting jets (the pressure in the wake jet P_∞ is approximately twice the pressure at the nozzle exit P_a).

Wake jet expansion leads to the narrowing and hence the deceleration (with pressure increase to $P_T \approx P_\infty + \frac{\rho_\infty V_{\infty,z}^2}{2} \approx 1$; see Figure 7) of the jet flowing out through the solid propellant rocket nozzle exit, consisting of combustion products. This increase in pressure creates a positive gradient in the axial region ($1000 \leq z \leq 1200$ cm), which leads to the occurrence of a reverse flow (Figure 7, for $Z = 1000$ cm, $V_z = -1 \times 10^{-5}$ cm/s). At the same time, as can be seen from Figure 7, the equilibrium condition for the vortex flow is satisfied (the pressure inside the shock system (3); (4) is equal to the flow pressure in the stagnation zone P_T), and the vortex region spatially fixes its position.

Thus, apparently, a necessary condition for the occurrence of a vortex region in the nozzle apparatus behind the shock wave is the achievement in the stagnation zone (Figure 7, at $V_z \approx 0$) of the level of pressure values equal to the total pressure in the cocurrent air flow, i.e., $P \approx P_\infty + \frac{\rho_\infty V_{\infty,z}^2}{2}$. In this case, it is also necessary that the degree of non-design $n < 1$, determined at the nozzle exit, be located below a certain critical value n_{cr}.

In general, the structure of the gas flow in the SFRE nozzle block under the condition of the formation of a zone of reverse currents differs from the case of flow, when a Y-shaped system of shocks is formed inside the nozzle, and can be described as follows (Figure 6): the main shock wave resulting from the entry of a hanging shock wave into the nozzle apparatus; secondary SW or compression wave, which may appear due to the occurrence of a reverse flow at a large value of the positive pressure gradient in the stagnation zone; zone of reverse currents, located behind the system of jumps; and stagnation zone of the flow of combustion products of solid fuel, located behind the nozzle exit and responsible for the occurrence of a positive pressure gradient P.

The dimensions, shape and location of the reverse current zone are determined by the following factors:

* Ratio of velocities in the wake and central jets;
* Degree of unaccountability n;
* Geometry of the nozzle.

6. Conclusions

A numerical technique for constructing regular curvilinear adaptive grids in arbitrary domains is formulated. This technique makes it possible to construct an adaptive (to the boundaries of the computational zone and peculiarities of solving mathematical physics problems [30–36]) computational grid by solving elliptic partial derivative equations and with the help of special adaptation algorithms. On the basis of the developed numerical codes, numerical simulations of two points of the ARIAN 5 rocket flight trajectory were performed.

The features of the structure and spatial distributions of the gas-dynamic parameters of the exhaust viscous flow inside the nozzle and in their interaction with the cocurrent flow of the surrounding gas outside the nozzle apparatus were studied. Numerical solutions were obtained that describe the structure of wakes in relation to the flight conditions of the ARIAN 5 rocket. Numerical studies have revealed the emergence of a central zone of reverse currents, having a toroidal shape, inside the nozzle apparatus behind a Y-figurative system of jumps.

Author Contributions: Investigation, S.V.R. and A.Y.V.; methodology, software, V.V.K.; validation, V.V.K.; writing—original draft preparation, S.V.R. and V.V.K.; writing—review and editing, V.V.K., S.V.R. and A.Y.V.; visualization, V.V.K.; supervision, S.V.R. All authors have read and agreed to the published version of the manuscript.

Funding: This research received no external funding.

Institutional Review Board Statement: Not applicable.

Informed Consent Statement: Not applicable.

Data Availability Statement: No new data were created or analyzed in this study. Data sharing is not applicable to this article.

Conflicts of Interest: The authors declare no conflict of interest.

References

1. Sikirica, A.; Grbčić, L.; Alvir, M.; Kranjčević, L. Computational Efficiency Assessment of Adaptive Mesh Refinement for Turbulent Jets in Crossflow. *Mathematics* **2022**, *10*, 620. [CrossRef]
2. Cherfils, L.; Feireisl, E.; Michálek, M.; Miranville, A.; Petcu, M.; Pražák, D. The compressible Navier-Stokes-Cahn-Hilliard equations with dynamic boundary conditions. *Math. Models Methods Appl. Sci.* **2019**, *29*, 2557–2584. [CrossRef]
3. Zhou, S.-S.; Shah, N.A.; Dassios, I.; Saleem, S.; Nonlaopon, K. A comparative analysis of fractional-order gas dynamics equations via analytical techniques. *Mathematics* **2021**, *9*, 1735. [CrossRef]
4. Magnus, Y.; Katyshev, P.K.; Peresetsky, A.A. *Econometrics*; Starting Course: Moscow, Russia, 2007; 504p.
5. Hauser, J.; Xia, Y. *Modern Introduction to Grid Generation COSMASE*; Shortcourse Notes; EPF Lausanne: Lausanne, Switzerland, 1996.
6. Golovanov, N.N. *Geometric Modeling*; Fizmatlit: Moscow, Russia, 2002; 472p.
7. Ryzhkov, S.V.; Kuzenov, V.V. New realization method for calculating convective heat transfer near the hypersonic aircraft surface. *ZAMP* **2019**, *70*, 46. [CrossRef]
8. Samarskij, A.A.; Nikolaev, E.S. *Numerical Methods for Grid Equations, Methods for Solving Grid Equations*; Birkhauser: Basel, Switzerland, 1989; 424p.
9. Kovenia, V.M.; Ianenko, N.N. *Metod Rasshchepleniia v Zadachakh Gazovoi Dinamiki*; Nauka: Moscow, Russia, 1981; 304p.
10. Surzhikov, S.T.; Krier, H. Computational models of combustion of nonmetallized heterogeneous propellant. *High Temp.* **2003**, *41*, 95–128. [CrossRef]
11. Sorkin, R.E. *Theory of Intra-Chamber Processes in Rocket Systems on Solid Fuel*; Nauka: Moscow, Russia, 1983.
12. Golovachev, Y.P. *Numerical Simulation of Viscous Gas Flows in a Shock Layer*; Fizmatlit: Moscow, Russia, 1996.
13. Kuzenov, V.V.; Ryzhkov, S.V. Approximate method for calculating convective heat flux on the surface of bodies of simple geometric shapes. *J. Phys. Conf. Ser.* **2017**, *815*, 012024. [CrossRef]
14. Formalev, V.F.; Kolesnik, S.A.; Garibyan, B.A. Mathematical modeling of heat transfer in anisotropic plate with internal sinks. *AIP Conf. Proc.* **2019**, *2181*, 020003.
15. Kuzenov, V.V.; Ryzhkov, S.V. Evaluation of the possibility of ignition of a hydrogen–oxygen mixture by erosive flame of the impulse laser. *Laser Phys.* **2019**, *29*, 096001. [CrossRef]
16. Kulikovsky, A.G.; Pogorelov, N.V.; Semenov, A.Y. *Mathematical Issues of Numerical Solution of Hyperbolic Systems of Equations*; Fizmatlit: Moscow, Russia, 2001.
17. Kovalev, B.D.; Myshenkov, V.I. Calculation of a viscous supersonic jet flowing into a concurrent. *Sci. Notes TsAGI* **1978**, *9*, 125–130.
18. Samarskii, A.A.; Popov, I.P. *Raznostnye Metody Resheniia Zadach Gazovoi Dinamiki*; Editorial URSS: Moscow, Russia, 2009; 424p.
19. Kuzenov, V.V.; Ryzhkov, S.V. Approximate calculation of convective heat transfer near hypersonic aircraft surface. *J. Enhanc. Heat Transf.* **2018**, *25*, 181–193. [CrossRef]
20. Kuzenov, V.V.; Ryzhkov, S.V. Calculation of plasma dynamic parameters of the magneto-inertial fusion target with combined exposure. *Phys. Plasmas* **2019**, *26*, 092704. [CrossRef]
21. Ryzhkov, S.V.; Kuzenov, V.V. Analysis of the ideal gas flow over body of basic geometrical shape. *Int. J. Heat Mass Transf.* **2019**, *132*, 587–592. [CrossRef]
22. Uhrig, G.; Boury, D. Large Space Solid Rocket Propulsion in Europe. In Proceedings of the 34th AIAA/ASME/SAE/ASEE Joint Propulsion Conference and Exhibit, Cleveland, OH, USA, 13–15 July 1998.
23. Varaksin, A.Y. Two-phase flows with solid particles, droplets, and bubbles: Problems and research results. *High Temp.* **2020**, *58*, 595–614. [CrossRef]
24. Kuzenov, V.V.; Surzhikov, S.T. Numerical modeling of the internal ballistics of solid propellant rocket engines and the structure of wake jets. *IPMech RAS Prepr.* **2005**, *780*, 47.
25. Dulov, V.G.; Lukyanov, G.A. *Gas Dynamics of Outflow Processes*; Nauka: Novosibirsk, Russia, 1984.
26. Avduevsky, V.S.; Ashratov, E.A.; Ivanov, A.V.; Pirumov, U.G. *Supersonic Non-Isobaric Gas Jets*; Mechanical Engineering: Moscow, Russia, 1985.

27. Pirumov, U.G.; Roslyakov, G.S. *Gas Dynamics of Nozzles*; Higher School: Moscow, Russia, 1987.
28. Gribben, B.J.; Badcock, K.J.; Richards, B.E. Numerical Study of Shock-Reflection Hysteresis in an Underexpanded Jet. *AIAA J.* **2000**, *38*, 275–283. [CrossRef]
29. Varaksin, A.Y. Two-phase boundary layer of gas with solid particles. *High Temp.* **2020**, *58*, 716–732. [CrossRef]
30. Kuzenov, V.V.; Ryzhkov, S.V. Numerical simulation of the effect of laser radiation on matter in an external magnetic field. *J. Phys. Conf. Ser.* **2017**, *830*, 012124. [CrossRef]
31. Kuzenov, V.V.; Ryzhkov, S.V.; Frolko, P.A. Numerical simulation of the coaxial magneto-plasma accelerator and non-axisymmetric radio frequency discharge. *J. Phys. Conf. Ser.* **2017**, *830*, 012049. [CrossRef]
32. Varaksin, A.Y. Effect of macro-, micro- and nanoparticles on turbulence in a carrier gas. *Dokl. Phys.* **2021**, *66*, 72–75. [CrossRef]
33. N'Guessan, M.-A.; Massot, M.; Séries, L.; Tenaud, C. High order time integration and mesh adaptation with error control for incompressible Navier–Stokes and scalar transport resolution on dual grids. *J. Comput. Appl. Math.* **2021**, *387*, 112542. [CrossRef]
34. Valiyev, K.F.; Kraiko, A.N.; Tillyayeva, N.I. Simplification of Numerical and Analytical Tools for Sonic Boom Description. *Comput. Math. Math. Phys.* **2022**, *62*, 624–640. [CrossRef]
35. Arnold, A.; Geevers, S.; Perugia, I.; Ponomarev, D. An adaptive finite element method for high-frequency scattering problems with smoothly varying coefficients. *Comput. Math. Appl.* **2022**, *109*, 1–14. [CrossRef]
36. Nkemzi, B.; Jung, M. The Fourier-finite-element method for Poisson's equation in three-dimensional axisymmetric domains with edges: Computing the edge flux intensity functions. *J. Numer. Math.* **2020**, *28*, 75–98. [CrossRef]

Article

Simulations of Hypersonic Boundary-Layer Transition over a Flat Plate with the Spalart-Allmaras One-Equation BCM Transitional Model

Yu Chen * and Nick Gibbons

School of Mechanical and Mining Engineering, The University of Queensland, Brisbane, QLD 4072, Australia
* Correspondence: y.chen16@uq.net.au

Abstract: Transitional flow has a significant impact on vehicles operating at supersonic and hypersonic speeds. An economic way to simulate this problem is to use computational fluid dynamics (CFD) codes. However, not all CFD codes can solve transitional flows. This paper examines the ability of the Spalart–Allmaras one-equation BCM (SA-BCM) transitional model to solve hypersonic transitional flow, implemented in the open-source CFD code Eilmer. Its performance is validated via existing wind tunnel data. Eight different hypersonic flow conditions are applied. A flat plate model is built for the numerical tests. The results indicate that the existing SA-BCM model is sensitive to the freestream turbulence intensity and the grid size. It is not accurate in all the test cases, though the transitional length can be matched by tuning the freestream intensity. This is likely due to the intermittency term of the SA-BCM model not being appropriately calibrated for high-velocity flow, though if the model can be recalibrated it may be able to solve the general high-velocity flows. Although the current SA-BCM model is only accurate under certain flow conditions after one calibration process, it remains attractive to CFD applications. As a one-equation model, the SA-BCM model runs much faster than multiple-equation flow models.

Keywords: hypersonic; transitional flow; CFD; Eilmer

MSC: 65-04; 65-11; 65Z05

1. Introduction

The transition region in fluid dynamics refers to an area where a laminar flow is transforming to turbulent flow, typically in a boundary layer. Due to the difficulty of predicting the onset of transition, the uncertainty of this location can have a significant impact on engineering applications, affecting shock wave/boundary layer interactions, increasing the heat transfer rate, and impacting the separation of shear layers [1,2]. Accurate predictions of this phenomenon are, therefore, critical to the re-entry stage of reusable launch vehicles and scramjet-powered vehicles [3]. Transition also increases uncertainties in the prediction of the aerodynamics of wind turbine blades [4]. Turbulent transition is initiated by noise in the freestream flow, which comes from the surroundings via sound waves or vibrations, and interactions with the flow around an object of interest. Further downstream, the initially small noise gets amplified by instabilities, and eventually can trigger a chaotic turbulent breakdown. There exist many known instabilities, including those producing roughness, waviness, bluntness [5,6]. Other instabilities include Gortler, the first mode, the second mode, 3D cross flow, and the shock layer [7–10]. However, research into laminar–turbulent transition is often stymied by difficulties with conventional wind tunnel tests. Data can be disturbed by the high level of noise from the wind tunnel walls [5,11]. Furthermore, large differences between conventional-tunnel data and quiet-tunnel data may be expected [5].

To avoid the cost of physical experiments, computational fluid dynamics (CFD) is a popular method of analyzing fluid dynamics; however, the reliability of CFD results mainly depends on the solver types and flow models within. Most conventional turbulent flow models in CFD software (ANSYS 2022 R2; ANSYS, Inc.; Canonsburg, PA, USA, OpenFoam 6/7/8/9/10; The OpenFoam Foundation Ltd.; USA) are adapted from Reynolds-averaged Navier–Stokes (RANS) equations. One-equation models are one type of RANS model, and include the Spalart–Allmaras (SA) model and Bradshaw's model [12,13]. Two-equation models are another type, such as the $k - \varepsilon$ model, $k - \omega$ model, and Menter's Shear Stress Transport turbulence (SST) model [14–16]. The third type includes more complex stress-transport models, such as the Launder–Reece–Rodi (LRR) model [17]. Although these conventional models work well in specific cases, they are unable to predict boundary-layer transitional flow, or model the transition region in an accurate manner [12–22]. It should also be noted that direct numerical simulation (DNS) is able to solve this problem; nevertheless, the cost of computing resources is too high for it to be widely adopted [23,24], at least for engineering applications.

Many researchers have developed modifications of RANS models that work for transitional flow. These modifications draw on an improved understanding of the mechanisms of transition, such as bypass transition, K-type transition, and H-type transition [25,26]. It is known that secondary instability has a major impact on bypass transition, while other types of transition can be predicted by linear stability theory. Recent CFD studies have probed these phenomena using DNS methods [27–29]. Additionally, hypersonic boundary-layer transition has been studied by Mee [30] in a shock tunnel, finding that the length of a transition region increases with the flow velocity. In a hypersonic boundary layer, the transition problem is much more complex, due to the various types of interaction between vehicle surface and external flow [31]. Though these theories account for transition in some cases and to some degree, the full dynamics of transitional flow remain unexplained. Fully turbulent CFD models are commonly used without considering the transition region, which leads to inaccuracy. The economic way to solve transitional flow in CFD still needs improvement.

In this research, the Spalart–Allmaras one-equation Bas–Cakmakcioglu-modified (SA-BCM) transitional model [32] is built into the Eilmer open-source compressible flow code to solve hypersonic transitional flow, the equation of which is developed from the SA model [12]. The SA-BCM model has an intermittency factor to simulate transition and has been modified from the original SA-BC model to ensure Galilean invariance. Additionally, the one-equation model is easy to implement and runs faster than a multi-equation model. It has been reported that the model works well in predicting transition in low-velocity flows [32]. Nevertheless, its performance in hypersonic flow is unknown. This paper aims to validate the model by applying to existing flat-plate experimental data taken from He and Morgan's paper [33]. Eight flow cases have been chosen for comparison, and the transition onset points computed by the CFD are compared with their experimental counterparts. We find that the SA-BCM model can accurately solve cases with proper calibration. However, the calibrated values are limited to the flow condition they are developed on and cannot be generalized. It is also observed that the transition region in the SA-BCM model is quite sensitive to grid size.

2. Implementation and Testing Strategy

The following sections review the SA-BCM model and demonstrate how the flat plate simulation is developed. All the necessary configuration details are clarified. It also introduces a grid convergence study to ensure discretization errors have been appropriately minimized.

2.1. Review of SA-BCM Model

The SA-BCM model is a local-correlated one-equation model that was presented by Cakmakcioglu et al. in 2020. As a modified version of the SA-BC model, it has two key features compared to the original model. Primarily, it eliminates the lack of Galilean invariance. Secondly, it removes the Reynolds number within the equation. The model has an intermittency factor, γ_{BC}. The full SA-BCM model is illustrated in the following equations [32]:

$$\frac{\partial \tilde{v}}{\partial t} + u_j \frac{\partial \tilde{v}}{\partial x_j} = \gamma_{BC} C_{b1} \tilde{S} \tilde{v} - C_{w1} f_w \left(\frac{\tilde{v}}{d}\right) + \frac{1}{\sigma} \left[\frac{\partial}{\partial x_j}\left((v + \tilde{v})\frac{\partial \tilde{v}}{\partial x_j}\right) + C_{b2} \frac{\partial \tilde{v}}{\partial x_j} \frac{\partial \tilde{v}}{\partial x_j}\right] \quad (1)$$

$$\gamma_{BC} = 1 - exp\left(-\sqrt{Term1} - \sqrt{Term2}\right) \quad (2)$$

$$Term1 = \frac{max(Re_\theta - Re_{\theta c}, \ 0.0)}{\chi_1 Re_{\theta c}} \quad (3)$$

$$Term2 = max\left(\frac{\mu_t}{\chi_2 \mu}, \ 0.0\right) \quad (4)$$

$$Re_\theta = \frac{Re_{\theta v}}{2.193} \quad (5)$$

$$Re_{\theta v} = \frac{\rho d^2}{\mu}\Omega \quad (6)$$

$$Re_{\theta c} = 803.73(Tu_\infty + 0.6067)^{-1.027} \quad (7)$$

Additionally, χ_1 is 0.002 and χ_2 is 0.02 for all simulations. The value of χ_2 is calibrated from Schubauer and Klebanoff's flat-plate test [34]. μ_t is turbulent viscosity, accounting for the closure of the RANS equation. Other constants can be found in the original SA model, as listed in the following equations [12]:

$$C_{w1} = \frac{C_{b1}}{\kappa^2} + \frac{1 + C_{b2}}{\sigma} \quad (8)$$

$$f_w = g\left[\frac{1 + C_{w3}^6}{g^6 + C_{w3}^6}\right]^{\frac{1}{6}} \quad (9)$$

$$g = r + C_{w2}\left(r^6 - r\right) \quad (10)$$

$$r = min\left[\frac{\tilde{v}}{\tilde{S}\kappa^2 d^2}, 10\right] \quad (11)$$

$$\tilde{S} = \Omega + \frac{\tilde{v}}{\kappa^2 d^2} f_{v2} \quad (12)$$

$$f_{v2} = 1 - \frac{\chi}{1 + \chi f_{v1}} \quad (13)$$

$$\chi = \frac{\tilde{v}}{v} \quad (14)$$

$$f_{v1} = \frac{\chi^3}{\chi^3 + C_{v1}^3} \quad (15)$$

where C_{b1}, C_{b2}, σ, C_{v1}, C_{w2} and C_{w3} are model constants that are set to 0.1355, 0.622, $\frac{2}{3}$, 7.1, 0.3 and 2. κ is the von Karman constant, which is 0.41.

The original model was constructed in ANSYS and tested in an Eppler E387 aerofoil case and a 6:1 prolate spheroid case by Cakmakcioglu et al. [32]. The skin friction from the simulation is compared with experimental data. Aerofoil tests show the SA-BCM model results match closely with the measurements, as well as the $\gamma - Re_{\theta t}$ model. Although there are some deviations in the prolate spheroid case, it is still reasonable for a one-equation model to achieve accurate results. However, these tests are under low-velocity and low-

Re flow. The performance of the SA-BCM model to predict supersonic and hypersonic transitional flow is unclear.

2.2. Eilmer and Numerical Plate Model

The SA-BCM model tested in this work is implemented in Eilmer [35], an open-source computational fluid dynamics code developed at the University of Queensland to support research in hypersonic and high-temperature gas dynamics. Eilmer is a fluid simulation program which solves the physical quantities and chemical reactions of high-speed gas flow. It is written in the D programming language and uses an embedded Lua interpreter for configuration and run-time customization. Eilmer contains a wide range of customizable options, including gas models, turbulence models, and flux calculators. In this research, both the existing SA model and a laminar flow condition are compared with the SA-BCM model. The transitional flow model has been built into Eilmer by the first author. As shown in Appendix A, SA-BCM is available in the public repository for broader use.

To assess the performance of SA-BCM under high-velocity flow conditions, a flat-plate model from He and Morgan's experiments [33]—which were conducted in the T4 free-piston shock tunnel at the University of Queensland—is chosen for the test. The plate is 600 mm long and 300 mm wide with a 30° tapered edge. The CFD flow condition is initially aligned with one of their experimental conditions: s00 from Table 1 [33]. After successful implementation and calibration, seven other flow conditions are also tested. Additionally, the freestream kinematic viscosity is set to $\tilde{\nu}_{farfield} = 0.025\nu_\infty$, while the value is $\tilde{\nu}_{farfield} = 5\nu_\infty$ in the original SA model. Since the physical experiment was performed in a free-piston shock tunnel [33], the freestream turbulence intensity, Tu_∞, is chosen to meet the same shock-tunnel condition. Two studies have performed similar experiments in the same type of shock tunnel, where the freestream flow is around Mach 6 [36,37]. Based on those reports, the Tu_∞ value is set to 0.4% here. However, the value is not fixed and can be adjusted further to correct the model through the research. The turbulent Schmidt number is left to its default value of 0.75, while the turbulent Prandtl number (Pr) is adjusted to the dry air at low-pressure conditions [38]. The Pr for each simulation case is also listed in Table 1.

Table 1. Flow condition for the simulation [33].

Simulation Case	H_0 (MJ/kg)	T_∞ (K)	p_∞ (kPa)	M_∞	U_∞ (m/s)	Re_u ($\times 10^6$)	Re_t ($\times 10^6$)	Pr
s00	2.45	254	3.25	6.52	2100	4.99	1.28	0.719
s01	7.00	867	3.28	5.74	3360	1.25	0.65	0.694
s02	2.35	240	5.22	6.55	2060	10.30	1.74	0.723
s03	6.40	770	5.00	5.81	3150	2.60	1.03	0.688
s04	2.88	310	8.70	6.48	2200	9.56	1.63	0.705
s05	9.19	1257	9.60	5.47	3810	2.18	0.71	0.713
s06	3.17	347	18.30	6.30	2380	20.80	2.81	0.697
s07	10.10	1340	23.80	5.46	4050	4.30	1.33	0.717

An ideal air–gas model is applied for all the simulations, which does not consider the chemical reaction of the gas. To simplify the domain, only a 2D plate model is built (see Figure 1). The topology for the CFD grid consists of two blocks: blk0 is a blank block in front of the plate, and blk1 is the block that contains the plate, which is highlighted in yellow. The blank block is needed to simulate a stagnation point in the correct manner, although this does result in a minor increase in the computing resources required. The plate boundary BC is set to the fixed temperature of 300 K. Since the contact time between the gas and the plate is extremely short (in the order of milliseconds), it is assumed that no temperature change happens during the test. Flow comes in from the AF boundary and exits through the CD boundary. The height of the model is large enough to contain the entire shock from the stagnation to the end of the plate. As the shock is relatively weak in a flat-plate model, the grid structure is not adapted to the shock shape.

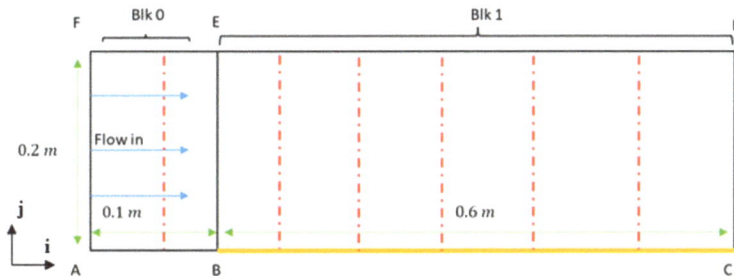

Figure 1. Demonstration of the flat-plate model.

Viscous effects are turned on to evaluate the interaction between the flow boundary layer and the plate surface. The details of the s00 simulation configuration script are demonstrated in Appendix B. A series of files are generated after the simulation which collect the flow quantities along the BC boundary. The data from the final timestep, after the simulation has converged, is then compared to the experimental measurements to verify the transition model [33]. The location of transition region is be determined via heat transfer. The overall results of each simulation are visualized via ParaView software (ParaView 5.6; Kitware; USA).

2.3. Simulation Configuration

All the different flow cases use the same configuration with the same structured grid, except the grid convergence study. During the grid convergence study, various cell sizes for the simulation grid are evaluated. All the simulations are run on the same hardware, as detailed in Table 2.

Table 2. Hardware information.

Hardware	Detail
CPU	AMD Ryzen 7 5800X
GPU	Nvidia GeForce RTX 3070Ti
Installed RAM	USCorsair LPX DDR4 $2 \times 16GB$
Installed Disk Space	Samsung PM9A1 $512GBSSD$
System	Ubuntu 20.04 LTS

Two cluster functions are used in the model. One is a fixed Roberts function that clusters to the BE boundary, improving the accuracy of the solution near the stagnation point. The cfx0 is in the block 0, and the cfx0 is in the block 1.

$$\text{cfx0} = \text{RobertsFunction:new}\{\text{end0} = \text{false}, \text{end1} = \text{true}, \beta = 1.1\} \quad (16)$$

$$\text{cfx1} = \text{RobertsFunction:new}\{\text{end0} = \text{true}, \text{end1} = \text{false}, \beta = 1.1\} \quad (17)$$

The second cluster function is based on a geometric series and is applied along the AC boundary to resolve the boundary layer.

$$\text{cfy} = \text{GeometricFunction} : \text{new}\{a = 0.001, r = 1.2, N = Nj_0\} \quad (18)$$

where 'a' defines the smallest cell size close to the surface that is the ratio of the height of the block. The growth rate of the cell size is defined by parameter 'r', while the N represents the quantities. The number of cells in different directions is represented by and Nj, while 0 and 1 mean the block number.

The final grid information is demonstrated in Table 3, and the special configuration of the Lua script of the plate model is shown in Table 4. To increase the simulation speed, the message passing interface (MPI) parallel strategy is implemented. blk0 and blk1 are equally divided into two and six blocks, respectively, via Eilmer's FBArray function. Thus, there are eight fluid blocks in total, which are calculated by eight separate processors in parallel. The time stepping scheme is set to the backward Euler method. A Courant–Friedrichs–Lewy (CFL) schedule is used, rather than a fixed CFL value. The maximum CFL value is set to twenty. As for the max simulation time, it is defined by the two times plate length, l_{BC}, divided by the freestream flow velocity, U_∞. Thus, the time is enough for the flow to pass the plate. AUSMDV is the chosen flux calculator in this simulation, which is relatively economical. It should be noticed that Prandtl number is adapted to different flow conditions, while Tu_∞ is adjusted to 1.6% in model calibration step to match the experimental results.

Table 3. Grid information.

Cell Size (m)	Ni_0	Nj_0	Ni_1	Nj_1	a	r	Max CFL
0.002	50	100	300	100	0.0001	1.2	20

Table 4. Details of the configuration in flat-plate Lua script.

Configuration Parameter	Value
config.dimensions	2
config.axisymmetric	false
config.viscous	true
config.report_invalid_cells	true
config.compute_loads	true
config.dt_loads	1×10^{-5}
config.flux_calculator	ausmdv
config.max_time	$2 \times \frac{l_{BC}}{U_\infty}$
config.max_step	5×10^5
config.dt_init	1×10^{-8}
config.cfl_schedule	$\{\{0.0, 0.5\}, \{5 \times 10^{-5}, 20.0\}\}$
config.dt_plot	config.max_time/10.0
For Turbulence Only	
config.turbulence_model	"spalart_allmaras" or "spalart_allmaras_bcm"
config.turbulence_prandtl_number	0.89 (default)
config.turbulence_schmidt_number	0.75 (default)
config.freestream_turbulent_intensity	0.4%

2.4. Grid Convergence Study Plan

A grid convergence study is conducted before simulating different flow cases to assure the CFD is appropriately resolved. There are three interesting issues to investigate. The first one is the general cell size of the model. At this stage, there is no cluster function along the BE boundary, and only a fixed geometric function is implemented along the AC boundary, as defined in Equation (19). The general cell size is maintained as a square shape. Four different cell sizes are assessed at this stage, as shown in Table 5. The cell size is the length of the cell. The actual nodes in each direction are the cell number plus one.

$$cfy = \text{RobertsFunction:new}\{end0 = true, end1 = false, beta = 1.02\} \qquad (19)$$

Table 5. Test of general cell size.

Case No.	Cell Size (m)	Ni_0	Nj_0	Ni_1	Nj_1
1	0.004	25	40	150	40
2	0.0025	40	80	240	80
3	0.002	50	100	300	100
4	0.001	100	200	600	200

The second interesting issue is the parameters of the geometric cluster function, defined in Equation (18). The grid convergence study aims to find out how the parameters 'a' and 'r' in the geometric function impact the convergence. Under this test, the general cell size is set to 0.002 m. 'a' is tested from 0.01 to 0.00004, while 'r' is tested from 1.05 to 1.2.

Finally, a separate convergence study investigates the effect of the CFL schedule. Since different time-stepping schemes are sensitive to the CFL value, the maximum CFL value in the CFL schedule is assessed in the grid convergence section. To simplify the test process, only the maximum CFL value is adjusted in the schedule. The results of the convergence study are presented in the next section. After completing the convergence study, the SA-BCM model is applied to other flow conditions using the coarsest grid that properly resolves the required gradients.

3. Results

This section illustrates the results of the grid convergence study, as well as the SA-BCM model calibration and simulations of different flow cases. At first, the flat plate model is verified in a grid convergence study. Secondly, the freestream turbulence intensity is calibrated with the s00 flow case, the value of which is eventually set to 1.4%. Finally, the model with the new freestream turbulence intensity value is assessed with eight widely different hypersonic flow conditions. For ease of comparison, a new coordinate 'x' is introduced, which ignores the blank block and starts from the front point B to point C in Figure 1. All the simulations are conducted with the 2D flat-plate model. This research mainly focuses on the heat transfer in the boundary layer, which can directly reflect the transition start point.

3.1. Results of Grid Convergence Study

This section presents three approaches to grid convergence. The first is general cell size. The second is the geometric cluster function, and the final one is the max CFL value in the CFL schedule, which affects the time-accurate solutions. All the convergence studies are based on the flow condition of the s00 case in Table 1, and all the cases use $Tu_\infty = 4\%$. The reason for selecting the specific Tu_∞ is because the lower value of Tu_∞ in some grids cannot turn on the turbulent effect of the SA-BCM model.

The resulting heat transfer along the plate surfaces with different general cell size is plotted in Figure 2. However, there is no evident sign of convergence of adjusting this variable. Additionally, the rising cell quantities dramatically increase the running time of a script. When the general cell size is reduced to 0.001 m, the running time costs over one hour. Since the most interested area is the boundary layer, the geometric cluster function should play a more important role. When the cell size is smaller than 0.001 m, it is also found that the setting conflicts with the geometric cluster function and can cause geometry distortion.

Next, two parameters of geometric function are investigated, which are 'a' and 'r' in Equation (18). At first, variations of the cell ratio 'a' are assessed, while the growth rate, 'r', is set to 1.2. 'a' is reduced from 0.01 to 0.00004, Figure 3. The convergence is observed when 'a' reaches 0.0001. At this value, the laminar region and turbulent region highly converge. However, there is still minor gap in the transition region, as shown in red circle in Figure 3. When 'a' starts from 0.01 to 0.0001, the running time rises from 3 min to 90 min. Considering the finiteness of computing resources, a = 0.0001 is chosen as sufficient for this research. In addition to the SA-BCM model, the result of the SA model also shows convergence, as presented by Figure A1.

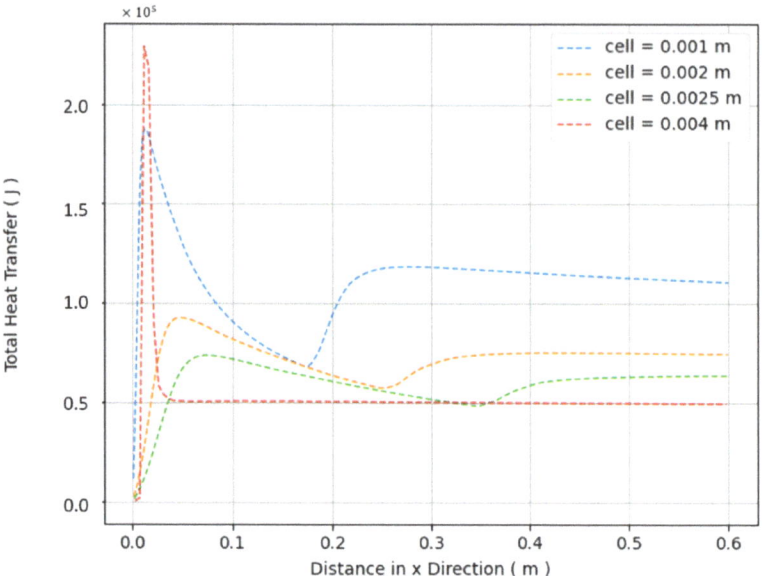

Figure 2. Grid convergence study of general cell size.

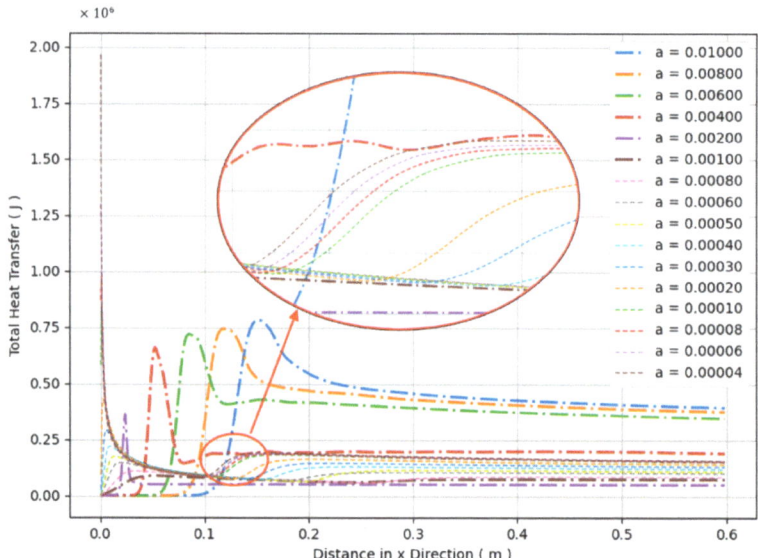

Figure 3. Grid convergence study of cell ratio 'a'.

Normally, the growth rate is not as important as the cell ratio to the boundary layer. This research investigates it regardless. For convenience, 'a' is set to 0.001 at this stage. The growth rate, 'r', varies from 1.05 to 1.35. The result indicates no evident effect of convergence, and the heat transfer function fluctuates like a sine function in the transition region (Figure 4). Therefore, the growth rate retains 1.2 for the later simulation.

Initially, the maximum CFL value was set to 50. However, instabilities are observed within the heat transfer graph in this case. After the max CFL value is reduced to twenty, the heat transfer function becomes much more stable. To figure out whether this configuration affects convergence, the value is reduced further, and the results are demonstrated in Figure 5. The difference among them is extremely small. Thus, the max CFL value, 20, is enough for this research. As a result, the grid information presented in Table 3 is used for the subsequent studies.

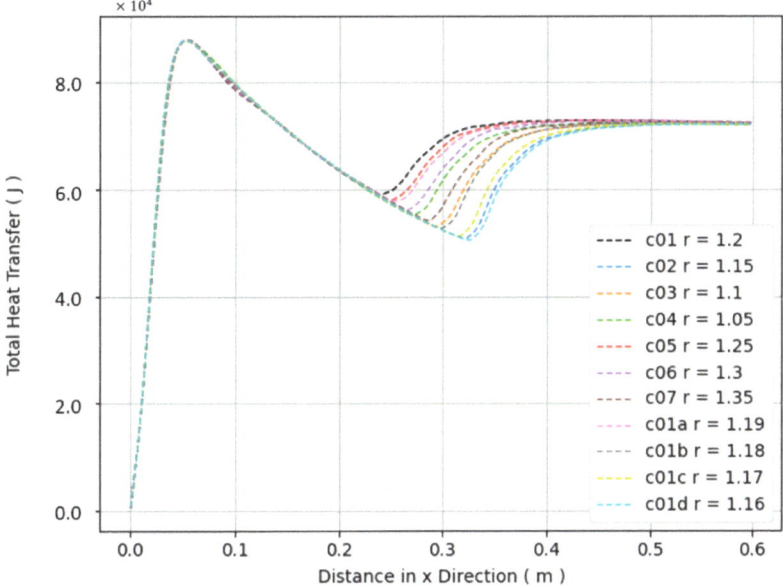

Figure 4. Grid convergence study of growth ratio 'r'.

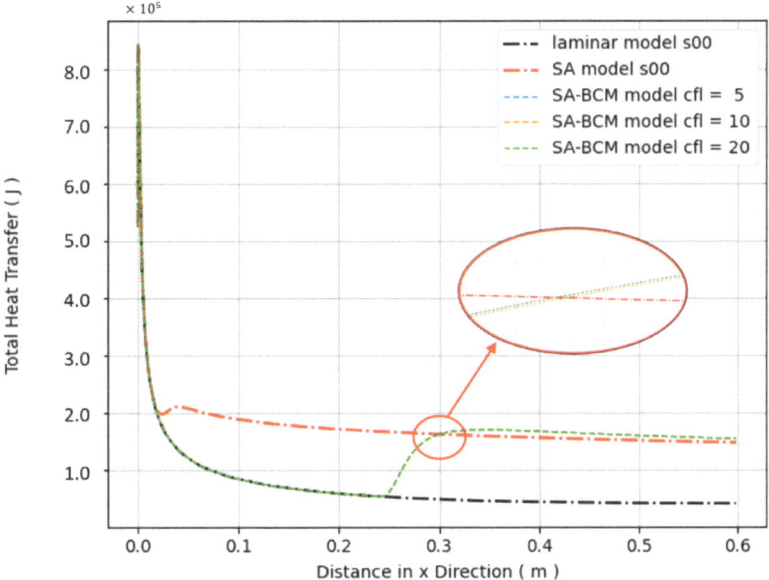

Figure 5. Grid convergence study of max CFL value.

3.2. SA-BCM Model Calibration

The flow condition s00 is applied, and the transition onset location is calibrated to He and Morgan's paper [33] by adjusting the applied freestream turbulence intensity assumed by the code. The final grid structure is shown in Figure 6. The comparison of different Tu_∞ values in the SA-BCM model is indicated in Figure 7. The performance of SA-BCM model is compared to the laminar model and the original fully turbulent SA model. There is a clear indication that the SA-BCM model transforms from the laminar model to the SA turbulent model. The transition onset point is found by comparing the SA-BCM model to the laminar model at 1% difference. The reference transition onset point is $x_t = 0.256$ m [33]. The deviation of each case is shown in Table 6. The total heat transfer q of each model at the transition point is also calculated. After that, the percentage difference between the SA model and the SA-BCM model in the fully turbulent region at $x = 0.5$ m is compared as well. The result indicates that the SA-BCM model has the least error compared to the experiment result, as $Tu_\infty = 1.6\%$. This value is used to evaluate the model in different flow conditions. It should also be noted that $Tu_\infty = 0.4\%$ is too small to turn on the turbulence and the SA-BCM result is exactly same as the laminar model.

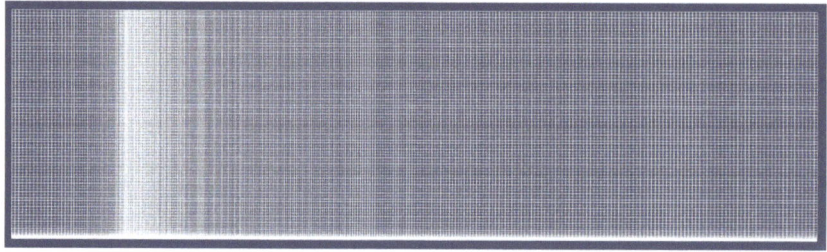

Figure 6. Grid of the flat plate.

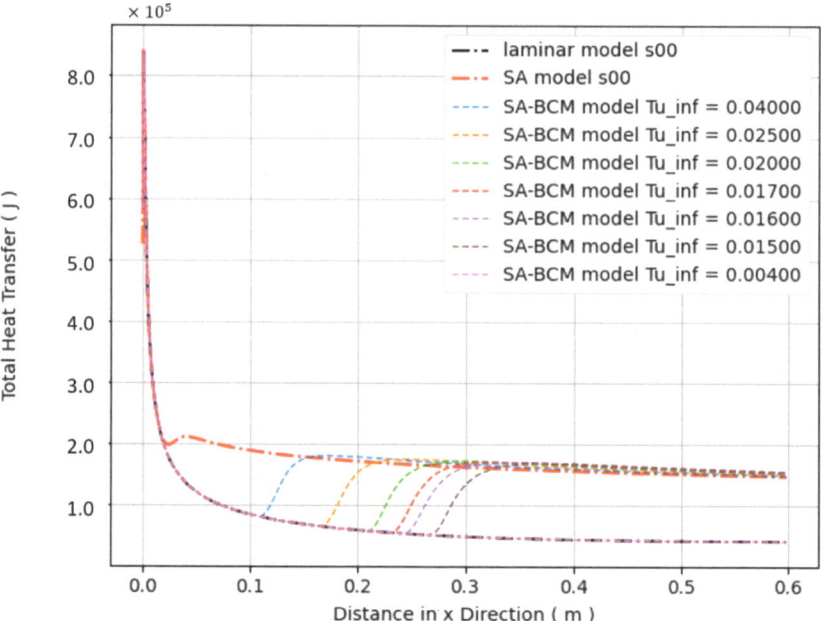

Figure 7. Calibration of freestream turbulence intensity.

Table 6. Comparison of the results of SA-BCM model with experiment data.

Tu_∞	Transition Onset Point x_t [1]	Error of x_t to Reference	q_{la} (J)	q_{sb} (J)	q_{sa} at $x = 0.5$ (J)	q_{sb} at $x = 0.5$ (J)	Difference
4.0%	0.111	−56.69%	8.08×10^4	8.29×10^4	1.52×10^5	1.54×10^5	1.60%
2.5%	0.168	−34.26%	6.53×10^4	6.69×10^4	1.52×10^5	1.57×10^5	3.19%
2.0%	0.213	−16.92%	5.80×10^4	6.06×10^4	1.52×10^5	1.58×10^5	4.47%
1.7%	0.234	−8.45%	5.53×10^4	5.74×10^4	1.52×10^5	1.60×10^5	5.24%
1.6%	0.246	−4.04%	5.40×10^4	5.53×10^4	1.52×10^5	1.60×10^5	5.66%
1.5%	0.269	5.13%	5.16×10^4	5.31×10^4	1.52×10^5	1.62×10^5	6.48%
0.4%	N/A	N/A	N/A	N/A	1.52×10^5	4.27×10^5	−71.84%

[1] The subscript t means transition onset point. The Laminar model and SA turbulent model are represented by *la* and *sa*. The notation *sb* means SA-BCM model.

3.3. Simulation of Different Flow Conditions

The simulation results of eight flow cases are presented in this section. The performance of the SA-BCM model is compared to a laminar model and a fully turbulent SA model in each case, plotted in Figure 8. As calibrated in the previous section, the SA-BCM model switches from laminar flow to turbulent flow smoothly in the s00 case. The evidence of transition is also visible in the flow profiles (Figures A2–A9). However, the results of the SA-BCM model are the same as the laminar model in the s01 case, and it fails again in the s03 case. The turbulent effects seem to be underestimated in the s05 case. Besides these, the SA-BCM model seems to work well in the other flow conditions. This study also investigates the error between the transition onset point of the simulation result and the experimental results of each flow case from He and Morgan [33] (Table 7). Additionally, the percentage error map against the flow Mach number is plotted in Figure 9. The y+ of the first cell of the flat plate in each case is demonstrated in Table 8. The maximum dx values of all the flow cases and different flow models are the same, which are 3.35×10^{-3} m. Similarly, the minimum dx is 5.84×10^{-4} m for all the simulations. Since it is a 2D model, there is no z direction.

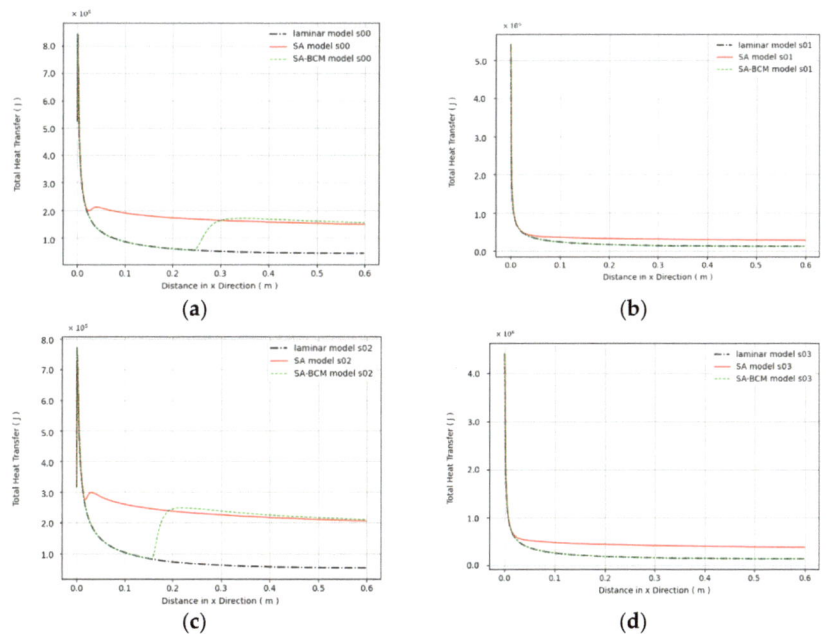

Figure 8. Cont.

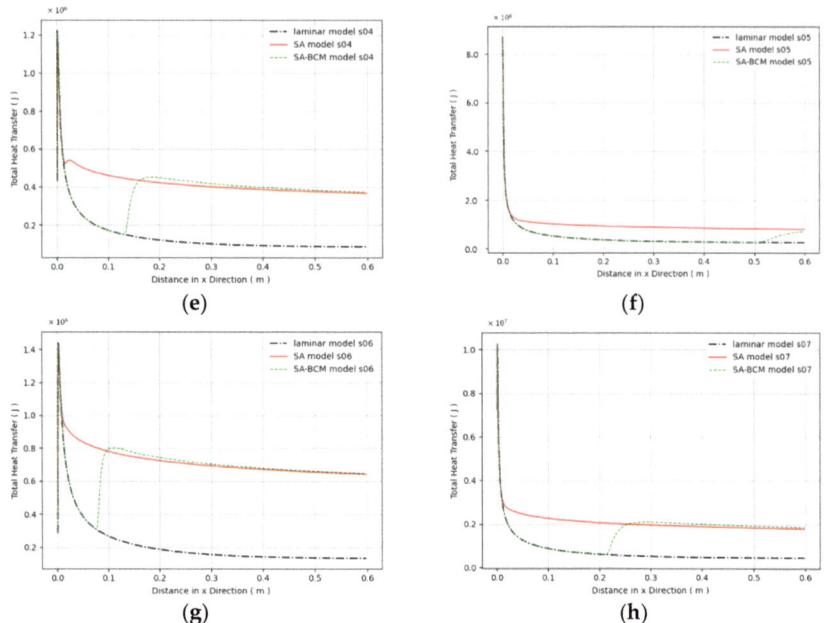

Figure 8. Flow model comparison: (**a**) s00 case; (**b**) s01 case; (**c**) s02 case; (**d**) s03 case; (**e**) s04 case; (**f**) s05 case; (**g**) s06 case; (**h**) s07 case.

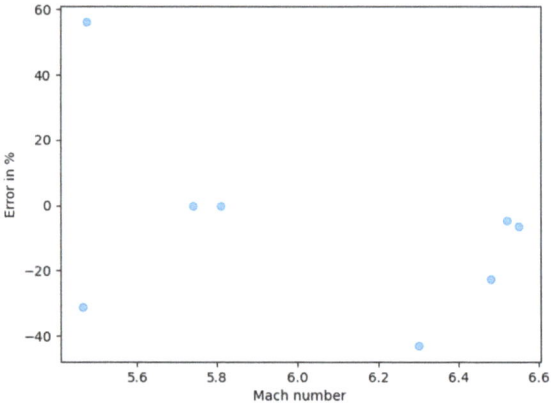

Figure 9. Error of different flow cases against Mach number.

Table 7. Transition onset locations under different flow cases.

Simulation Case	Reference x_t [33] (m)	Simulation x_t (m)	Error (%)
s00	0.256	0.245	−4.51
s01	0.520	N/A	N/A
s02	0.169	0.158	−6.27
s03	0.396	N/A	N/A
s04	0.171	0.132	−22.60
s05	0.326	0.508	56.12
s06	0.135	0.077	−43.07
s07	0.309	0.213	−31.17

Table 8. y+ of the first cell over the flat plate in each case.

Simulation Case	y+ of Laminar Model	y+ of SA Model	y+ of SA-BCM Model
s00	6.64	6.65	6.64
s01	2.87	2.87	2.87
s02	8.44	8.50	8.44
s03	3.88	3.88	3.88
s04	9.04	9.17	9.04
s05	3.84	3.84	3.84
s06	11.42	12.48	11.42
s07	5.77	5.78	5.77

4. Discussion

4.1. About the Grid Convergence Study

The grid convergence study has investigated three factors that impact the grid accuracy, including the general cell size in the freestream, the geometric cluster function along the plate surface, and the max CFL value used for the backward Euler stepping scheme. The results show that it is the parameter 'a' of the geometric cluster function that impacts the boundary flow most significantly. The second most important factor is the max CFL value in the CFL schedule. As explained by this research, it seems the max CFL value lower than twenty makes the simulation converge neatly in time, as compared to larger values where noise is observed.

The general cell size in the freestream area may possess less impact on the boundary flow, compared to the cell size in the boundary area. Additionally, too small overall cell size can conflict with the geometric cluster function and result in geometry distortion. Thus, it is recommended that the general grid size should be defined with caution when the geometric function is used. Despite this, the grid convergence reveals that the transition length predicted by the SA-BCM model is highly sensitive to the grid size. Even though the laminar region and turbulent region converges to a certain value, the transition region keeps fluctuating around some points (Figures 3 and 4).

Another concern is the y+ value in this study. The overall y+ value is quite high. When y+ is greater than five, the turbulent onset point may take place early [39]. Since s01, s03 and s05 cases possess relatively low y+, the transition of these three cases may be turned on slower than the others with higher y+. However, the grid convergence study indicates that further reduction in cell size along the boundary layer does not have much effect on the turbulent onset location when 'a' is less than 0.0002. On the contrary, this action can significantly increase the simulation time. While a = 0.00004, the simulation costs more than nine hours to run. Thus, the large y+ value should not account for the inaccuracy of this model. For the ease of simulating and adjusting codes at the development stage, configures with short running time are still preferred.

4.2. Performance of SA-BCM Model in Hypersonic Flow

The prediction of the transition onset location in the s00 flow condition shows good agreement with the shock tunnel experiment [33] after the modification of turbulence intensity in Table 6. When Tu_∞ is set to 1.6%, the most accurate transition onset location is obtained. The obtained transition onset location is $x_t = 0.246$ m, compared to $x_t = 0.256$ m in the experiment [33]. Figure 8a indicates that the SA-BCM model perfectly fits the laminar model before the transition and matches the SA turbulence model after transition. The laminar flow gradually changes into turbulent flow in the transition region. This evidence proves the ability of the SA-BCM model to potentially predict the hypersonic transitional flow, after appropriate calibration. The transition is also observed in the profiles of physical quantities of the flow. The laminar model has no turbulence, while the SA model generates turbulent viscosity at the leading edge of the plate. Only the SA-BCM model shows a transition from laminar flow to turbulent flow. This phenomenon is distinctive in μ_t and $\hat{v}$ profiles. As in μ_t profiles, there is no turbulence and the μ_t is completely missing in the boundary region of the laminar model, while μ_t starts from the stagnation point in the SA model. In the SA-BCM model, there is a delay before the beginning of the rise in μ_t. This delay indicates the flow is still laminar in that region.

However, the calibrated turbulence intensity disagrees with the experimental measurements of the T4 free-piston shock tunnel [36]. At a similar flow condition to s00 in a similar shock tunnel, Tu_∞ is around 0.4%, rather than 1.6%. One likely reason for this is that the measurement of turbulence intensity is not accurate. Another reason could be that the constant of $\Re_{\theta c}$ function in the SA-BCM model is not designed for hypersonic flow conditions. Moreover, this research finds that a higher Tu_∞ value may increase the running time of the simulations dramatically.

The performance of SA-BCM in different flow conditions is also unsatisfactory. The model fails to predict the transition in the s01 and s03 cases. One probable reason for this may be that Tu_∞ is too small to turn on the turbulence in the s01 and s03 cases. This hypothesis is supported by the s05 and s06 cases. In the s05 case, transition is observed near the end of the plate, while the transition occurs too early in the s06 case. Thus, the accuracy of the SA-BCM model is significantly affected by Tu_∞ in hypersonic flow. Additionally, the SA-BCM model can be accurate in different flow cases if the Tu_∞ is calibrated with different flow conditions. In this case, the flow model should be precise and able to adopt appropriate Tu_∞ in certain conditions. However, this may require a table of Tu_∞ to be built in the program and raise the programming complexity.

According to Table 7, it seems that the SA-BCM model with calibrated Tu_∞ from one flow condition is not accurate in other cases. As shown in Figure 9, the error in the SA-BCM model is unlikely to have a linear relationship with the Mach number. It may relate to the specific enthalpy and internal energy of the flow. This drawback introduces complexities into the use of the SA-BCM model, as it always requires calibrating in different flow conditions.

4.3. Tu_∞ and γ_{BC} in SA-BCM Model

The constant parameters in the SA-BCM model could lead the simulation to predict wrong results at high-velocity flow. Thus far, all the results indicate the error within the SA-BCM model relating to the Tu_∞ value. It seems the SA-BCM model gives invalid results due to the wrong Tu_∞. However, the similar hypersonic flow condition where Tu_∞ equals 0.4% is also used in two papers. One is in simulation with the $\gamma - Re_{\theta t}$ model and the $k - \omega - \gamma$ model [37]. Another one is tested with a one-equation γ model [40]. The second case defines a flat plate with an adiabatic condition, rather than fixed temperature. All these models work well with $Tu_\infty = 0.4\%$. As a result, the freestream turbulence intensity value is not the source of the misconduct of the SA-BCM model. Other parameters inside the γ_{BC} term may be relevant to the problem.

A deep look into the SA-BCM model shows that the constants are calibrated by the low-velocity test, and the χ_2 inside the γ_{BC} is calibrated from Schubauer and Klebanoff's flat-plate test [34]. The highest flow speed in those wind tunnel experiments was 42.7 m/s, which is extremely low compared to the simulation cases in this research. According to Table 1 [33], the lowest flow velocity is 2100 m/s in the s00 case. Thus, those constants can cause trouble in high-enthalpy and high-velocity flow. The effort of calibrating Tu_∞ is the compensation for the inaccurate constants within the SA-BCM model under high-velocity flow. If the constant inside the γ_{BC} model can be recalibrated with a new physical experimental result from supersonic or hypersonic flow tests, it may be possible to apply SA-BCM to general high-velocity flow problems.

4.4. Comparison with Modified $\gamma - Re_{\theta t}$ Model

The original $\gamma - Re_{\theta t}$ model, proposed by Menter et al. [39], is a two-equation model based on the LCTM concept. The model is widely adopted and has a few modified versions which are adapted to hypersonic flow problems [2,41–43]. After a few years, Menter et al. [44] announced a simplified one-equation γ model. The new model eliminates the lack of Galilean invariance and removes the transitional Reynold's number $Re_{\theta t}$ in the transport equation. In 2020, an improved one-equation γ model is proposed by Liu et al. [40]. Compared to the Menter's model [44], the key difference is that Re_{θ} and γ are modified to simulate high-speed transitional flow. The new γ considers the physical information of the flow. A new feature is the introduction of the Fr term based on Hao's research [45]. This replaced the $Re_{v,max}$ term in the original equation, which is not compatible with hypersonic boundary conditions [2]. Another important update is to add the $f(Tu_\infty)$ term, which is inspired by Yang et al. [46].

The improved one-equation γ model has been tested by Liu et al. [40] in a supersonic flat-plate case [47], a hypersonic flat-plate case [30], a slender-cone case [48], a X-51A forebody case [49], and a hypersonic inflatable aerodynamic decelerator case [50,51]. All the results indicate that the improved model has significantly increasing accuracy. Although the original model has problems with predicting the skin fraction along an adiabatic flat plate, the modified version can accurately predict the transition starting point and flow quantity [40]. This new modified model may have an advantage over the SA-BCM model based on accuracy. However, the SA-BCM model is not fully calibrated for hypersonic flow and the potential for this model is still uncertain. In practical programming, the software may need an additional equation to find the turbulent frequency, ω. Another transport equation is also needed to calculate the turbulent kinetic energy, k. As a result, this two-equation model is expected to cost much more in terms of computing resources than one-equation SA-BCM model.

5. Conclusions

This paper presents research into the performance of the SA-BCM turbulent transition model for high-velocity flow. The model is tested in a flat-plate CFD simulation with eight different flow conditions [33]. The SA-BCM model has the potential to predict the transition region in hypersonic conditions with calibrated Tu_∞. However, there are two evident shortcomings. Primarily, the heat transfer in the transition region is extremely sensitive to the local grid size. Even though the laminar region and the turbulent region of the SA-BCM model converged in our grid convergence study, the transition region may still be unstable. Secondly, the accuracy of the SA-BCM model relies on the precise tuning of Tu_∞. To increase the accuracy, different flow conditions may require a corresponding Tu_∞ value. As demonstrated in this research, a single Tu_∞ calibrated from the s00 case does not give accurate flow solutions in other flow conditions. As a result, this drawback restricts the application of the model.

It is the constant in γ_{BC} term that should account for the shortcomings, rather than Tu_∞. The original γ_{BC} term is calibrated with low-velocity flow data, which are unlikely to predict high-velocity flow in the correct manner. Adjusting Tu_∞ only compensates for some model constants, which cannot solve the intrinsic problems within the SA-BCM model. Although the application of this model is restricted by the Tu_∞ and γ_{BC} term, the SA-BCM is still accurate to use after the Tu_∞ has been calibrated. As a one-equation model, it is also fast to run and remains attractive to modern CFD. In conclusion, the performance of the SA-BCM model in hypersonic flow is summarized as follows:

- Possesses fast running speed;
- Has potential for industrial applications;
- Can partially solve hypersonic transitional flow;
- Requires calibration of Tu_∞ for complex flow conditions;
- Requires awareness that the transition region is sensitive to the grid;
- Needs recalibration of the model constants to solve intrinsic inaccuracy.

There are two recommendations for future research on this topic. One is to re-calibrate the γ_{BC} term and make it suitable for supersonic and hypersonic flows. This may require extra effort in physical experiments. Another is to replace the γ_{BC} term and combine the SA-BCM model with other transitional flow models. A practical way to do this may be to replace the γ_{BC} term with the intermittency factor from the modified one-equation γ

model [40]. However, this may cause other issues, as the one-equation γ model needs turbulent kinetic energy, k, and turbulent frequency, ω. This would, however, require hybridization with the k and ω calculated from the $k - \omega$ equations [15], which would somewhat increase the running time and would require new model development.

Author Contributions: Conceptualization, Y.C. and N.G.; methodology, Y.C.; software, Y.C. and N.G.; validation, Y.C.; formal analysis, Y.C.; investigation, Y.C.; resources, Y.C. and N.G.; data curation, Y.C.; writing—original draft preparation, Y.C.; writing—review and editing, Y.C. and N.G.; visualization, Y.C. All authors have read and agreed to the published version of the manuscript.

Funding: This research received no external funding.

Institutional Review Board Statement: Not applicable.

Informed Consent Statement: Not applicable.

Data Availability Statement: The data presented in this study are available on request from the corresponding authors. The Eilmer software can be found at: https://gdtk.uqcloud.net/ (accessed on 1 June 2022).

Conflicts of Interest: The authors declare no conflict of interest.

Abbreviations

d	distance to the wall (m)
H_0	specific enthalpy at stagnation point (J/kg)
k	turbulent kinetic energy (J/kg)
M	Mach number
p	freestream pressure (Pa)
Pr	Prandtl number
q	heat transfer (J)
Re_t	transition onset Reynolds number
Re_u	unit Reynolds number ($1/m$)
Re_v	vorticity Reynolds number
Re_θ	momentum thickness Reynolds number
T	freestream temperature (K)
Tu_∞	freestream turbulence intensity (%)
U	velocity (m/s)
γ	intermittency
κ	Von Karman constant
μ	dynamic viscosity (kg/ms)
ν	kinematic viscosity (m^2/s)
$\hat{\nu}$	turbulent kinematic viscosity (m^2/s)
ρ	density (kg/m^3)
ω	turbulent frequency
Ω	magnitude of vorticity
Subscripts	
0	stagnation quantity
∞	freestream quantity
t	transition onset
la	laminar model
sa	SA turbulent model
sb	SA-BCM model

Appendix A

```
/*
Spalart–Allmaras 'BCM' variant for transitional flows:

"A Revised One-Equation Transitional Model for External Aerodynamics",
Cakmakcioglu, S. C., Bas, O., Mura, R., and Kaynak, U.
AIAA Paper 2020-2706, June 2020, (10.2514/6.2020-2706)

@author: Yu Chen and Nick Gibbons
*/
class sabcmTurbulenceModel: saTurbulenceModel {
this (){
number Pr_t = GlobalConfig.turbulence_prandtl_number;
double Tu_inf = GlobalConfig.freestream_turbulent_intensity;
this(Pr_t, Tu_inf);
}

this (const JSONValue config){
number Pr_t = getJSONdouble(config, "turbulence_prandtl_number", 0.89);
double Tu_inf = getJSONdouble(config, "freestream_turbulent_intensity", 0.01);
this(Pr_t, Tu_inf);
}

this (sabcmTurbulenceModel other){
this(other.Pr_t, other.Tu_inf);
}

this (number Pr_t, double Tu_inf) {
this.Tu_inf = Tu_inf;
super(Pr_t);
}

@nogc override string modelName() const {return "spalart_allmaras_bcm";}

override sabcmTurbulenceModel dup() {
return new sabcmTurbulenceModel(this);
}

@nogc override
void source_terms(const FlowState fs,const FlowGradients grad, const number ybar,
const number dwall, const number L_min, const number L_max,
ref number[] source) const {
/*
Spalart–Allmaras Source Terms:
Notes:
- SA production term modified by Yu Chen
See: https://turbmodels.larc.nasa.gov/sa-bc_1eqn.html (Accessed on 1 March 2020)
*/

number nuhat = fs.turb [0];
number rho = fs.gas.rho;
number nu = fs.gas.mu/rho;
number chi = nuhat/nu;
number chi_cubed = chi*chi*chi;
number fv1 = chi_cubed/(chi_cubed + cv1_cubed);
number fv2 = 1.0-chi/(1.0 + chi*fv1);
number ft2 = 0.0; //no ft2 in sa-bcm
```

```
number nut = nuhat*fv1;

//additional parmeters for sa-bcm
number mu = fs.gas.mu;
number re_theta_c = 803.73*pow((Tu_inf*100.0 + 0.6067),−1.027);
number chi1 = 0.002;
number chi2 = 0.02;
number Omega = compute_Omega(grad);

number d = compute_d(nut,nu,grad.vel,dwall,L_min,L_max,fv1,fv2,ft2);
number Shat_by_nuhat = compute_Shat_mulitplied_by_nuhat(grad, nuhat, nu, d, fv1, fv2);

//additional parmeters for sa-bcm
number re_nu = rho*d*d/mu*Omega; //omega needs to be defined
number re_theta = re_nu/2.193;
number mu_t = turbulent_viscosity(fs, grad, ybar, dwall);
number term1 = fmax(re_theta-re_theta_c, 0.0)/(chi1 * re_theta_c);
number term2 = fmax(mu_t/(chi2*mu), 0.0); //mu_t needs to be defined
number gamma_bc = 1.0-exp(-sqrt(term1)-sqrt(term2));
number production = gamma_bc*rho*cb1*Shat_by_nuhat; //Different terms to sa mdoel

number r = compute_r(Shat_by_nuhat, nuhat, d);
number g = r + cw2*(pow(r,6.0)-r);
number fw = (1.0 + cw3_to_the_sixth)/(pow(g,6.0) + cw3_to_the_sixth);
fw = g*pow(fw, 1.0/6.0);
number destruction = rho*cw1*fw*nuhat*nuhat/d/d;

////No axisymmetric corrections terms in dS/dxi dS/dxi
number nuhat_gradient_squared = 0.0;
foreach(i; 0 .. 3) nuhat_gradient_squared+ = grad.turb [0][i]*grad.turb [0][i];
number dissipation = cb2/sigma*rho*nuhat_gradient_squared;

number T = production-destruction + dissipation;
source [0] = T;
return;
}//end source_terms()
private:
double Tu_inf;//freestream turbulence intensity
}
```

Appendix B

```
–General fluid config
config.title = "plate in ideal air, M = 6.52"
config.dimensions = 2
config.axisymmetric = false
config.viscous = true
config.report_invalid_cells = true
config.gasdynamic_update_scheme = "backward_euler"
config.cfl_schedule = {{0.0,0.5}, {50e−6,20.0}}
–Turbulent config
config.turbulence_model = "spalart_allmaras_bcm"
–Turbulence model: "none", "k_omega", "spalart_allmaras", "spalart_allmaras_edwards"
config.freestream_turbulent_intensity = 0.016

config.turbulence_prandtl_number = 0.719 –(default:0.89)
config.turbulence_schmidt_number = 0.75

–Flow conditions
```

```
nsp, nmodes, gm = setGasModel('ideal-air-gas-model.lua')

–Initial gas conditions
p_inf = 3.25e03–Pa
T_inf = 254.0–K
M_inf = 6.52

–Compute additional gas info
gas_inf = GasState:new{gm}
gas_inf.T = T_inf
gas_inf.p = p_inf
gm:updateThermoFromPT(gas_inf)

gm:updateSoundSpeed(gas_inf)
u_inf = M_inf*gas_inf.a
gm:updateTransCoeffs(gas_inf)

–Use updated gas properties to estimate turbulence quantities
turb_lam_viscosity_ratio = 0.025–From NASA SA-BCM model [0.015, 0.025]
nu_inf = gas_inf.mu/gas_inf.rho
nuhat_inf = turb_lam_viscosity_ratio*nu_inf

–Set flow conditions
inflow = FlowState:new{p = p_inf, T = T_inf, velx = u_inf,vely = 0.0, nuhat = nuhat_inf}

–Specify geometry
len = 0.6 –meter
h = 0.2 –meter
A = Vector3:new{x = 0.0, y = 0.0}
B = Vector3:new{x = 0.1, y = 0.0}
C = Vector3:new{x = len + B.x, y = 0.0}
D = Vector3:new{x = len + B.x, y = h}
E = Vector3:new{x = B.x, y = h}
F = Vector3:new{x = 0.0, y = h}

–Set boundary paths
AB = Line:new{p0 = A, p1 = B} –south
AF = Line:new{p0 = A, p1 = F} –west
BE = Line:new{p0 = B, p1 = E} –east/west
FE = Line:new{p0 = F, p1 = E} –north

BC = Line:new{p0 = B, p1 = C} –south
CD = Line:new{p0 = C, p1 = D} –east
ED = Line:new{p0 = E, p1 = D} –north

–Build patch, grid and block
ni0 = 50
nj0 = 100
ni1 = 300
nj1 = nj0

cfx0 = RobertsFunction:new{end0 = false, end1 = true, beta = 1.1}
cfx1 = RobertsFunction:new{end0 = true, end1 = false, beta = 1.1}
cfy = GeometricFunction:new{a = 0.0001, r = 1.2, N = nj0}

quad = {}
quad [0] = makePatch{north = FE, east = BE, south = AB, west = AF}
quad [1] = makePatch{north = ED, east = CD, south = BC, west = BE}
```

```
grid = {}
grid [0] = StructuredGrid:new{psurface = quad [0], niv = ni0 + 1, njv = nj0 + 1, cfList = {east = cfy,
west = cfy, north = cfx0, south = cfx0}}
grid [1] = StructuredGrid:new{psurface = quad [1], niv = ni1 + 1, njv = nj1 + 1, cfList = {east = cfy,
west = cfy, north = cfx1, south = cfx1}}

blk = {}

--mpi FBArrary
blk [0] = FBArray:new{grid = grid [0], initialState = inflow,nib = 2,njb = 1,
bcList = {west = InFlowBC_Supersonic:new{flowState = inflow},
north = OutFlowBC_Simple:new{},
east = OutFlowBC_Simple:new{}}
}
blk [1] = FBArray:new{grid = grid [1], initialState = inflow,nib = 6,njb = 1,
bcList = {north = OutFlowBC_Simple:new{},
east = OutFlowBC_Simple:new{},
south = WallBC_NoSlip_FixedT:new{Twall = T_inf,group = "loads"}}
}

identifyBlockConnections()

config.compute_loads = true
config.dt_loads = 1.0e−5

--Set some simulation parameters
config.flux_calculator = "ausmdv"
config.max_time = 2.0*len/u_inf
config.max_step = 500000
config.dt_init = 1.0e−8
config.dt_plot = config.max_time/10.0
```

Appendix C

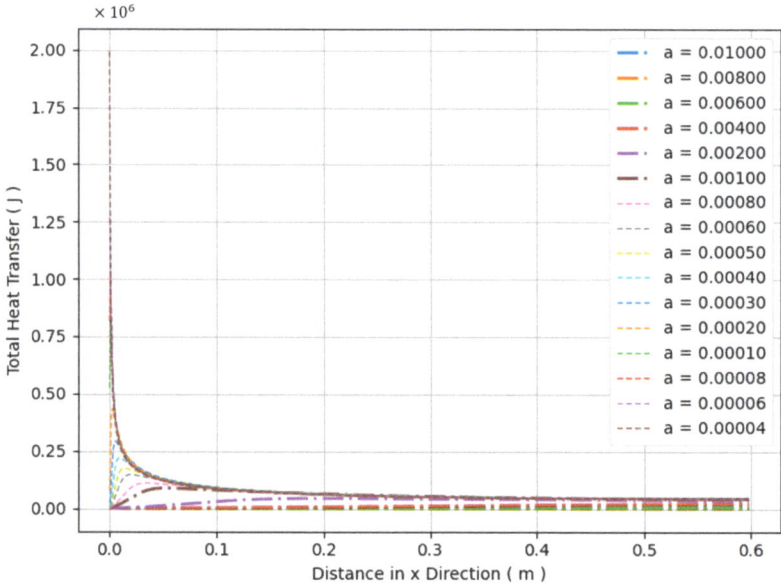

Figure A1. Grid convergence study of cell ratio 'a' in SA model.

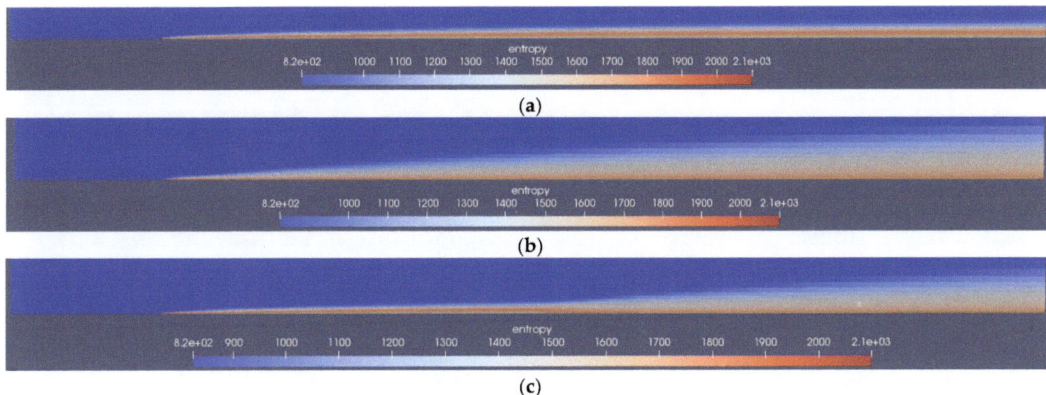

Figure A2. Entropy profile of s00: (**a**) laminar model; (**b**) SA model; (**c**) SA-BCM model.

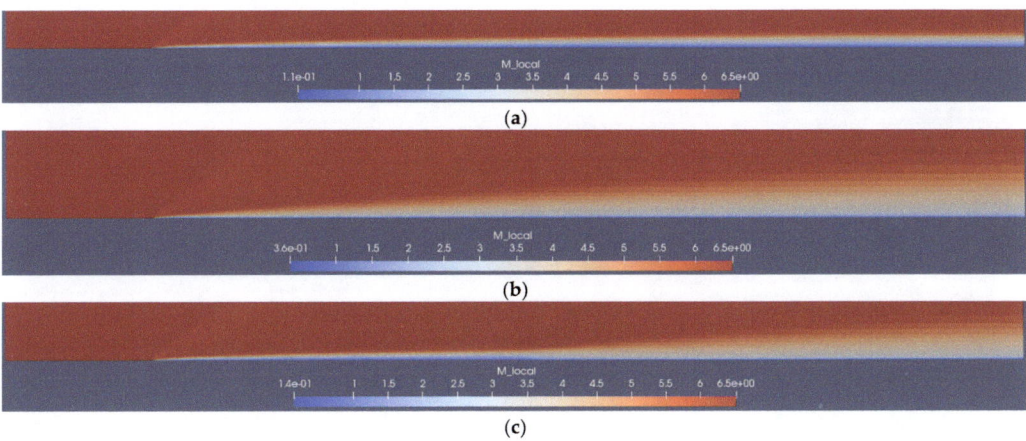

Figure A3. Local Mach number profile of s00: (**a**) laminar model; (**b**) SA model; (**c**) SA-BCM model.

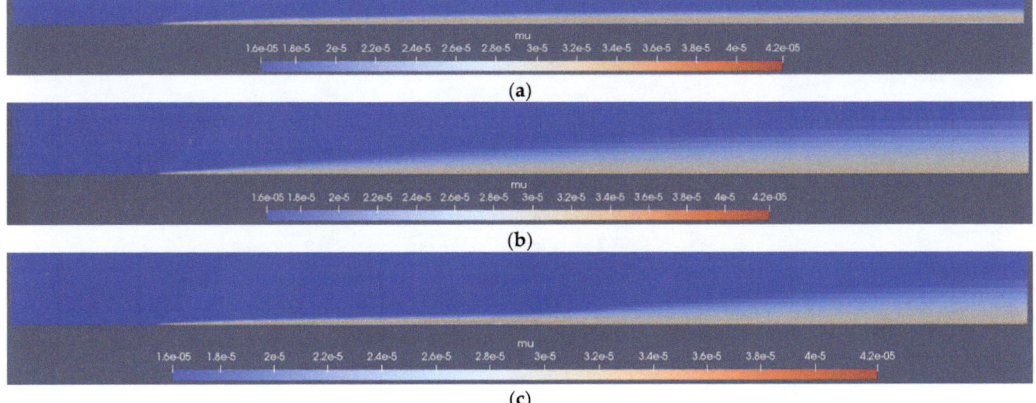

Figure A4. Dynamic viscosity profile of s00: (**a**) laminar model; (**b**) SA model; (**c**) SA-BCM model.

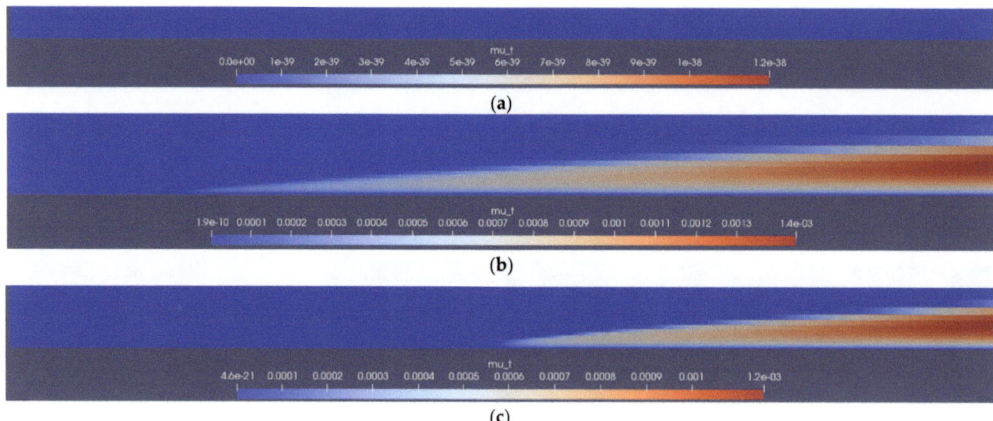

Figure A5. Turbulent onset dynamic viscosity profile of s00: (**a**) laminar model; (**b**) SA model; (**c**) SA-BCM model.

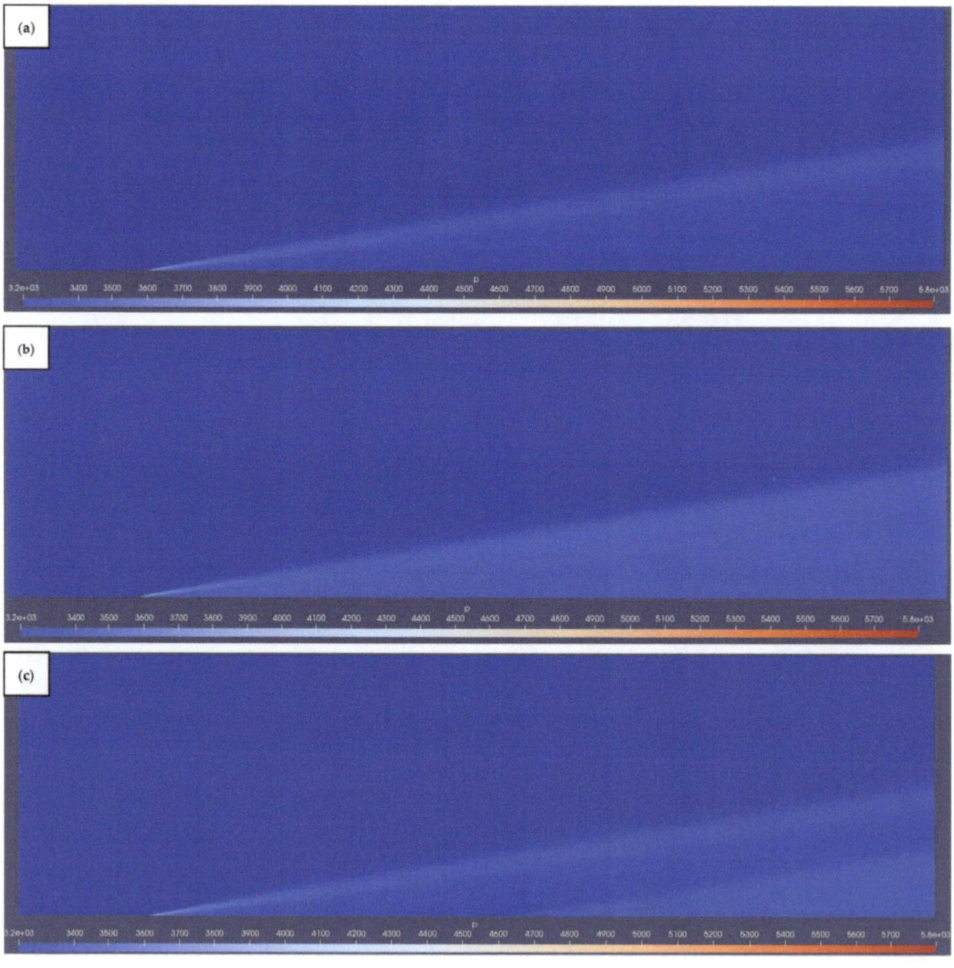

Figure A6. Pressure profile of s00: (**a**) laminar model; (**b**) SA model; (**c**) SA-BCM model.

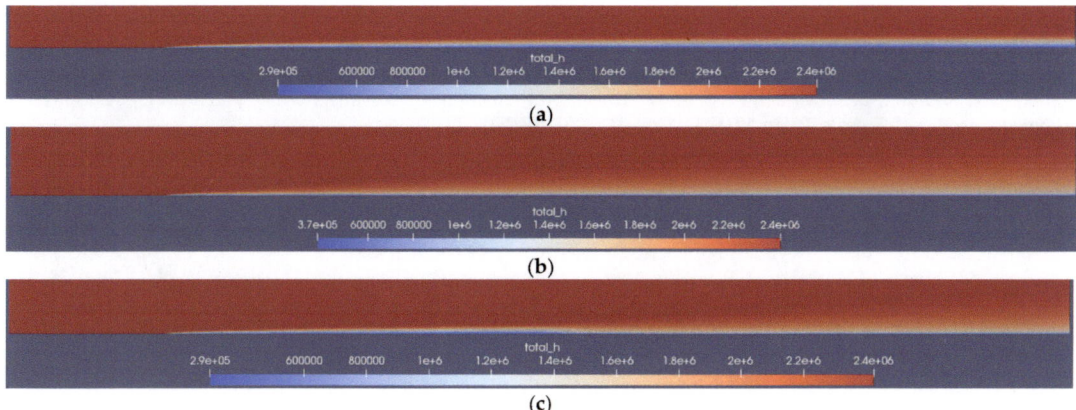

Figure A7. Total enthalpy of s00: (**a**) laminar model; (**b**) SA model; (**c**) SA-BCM model.

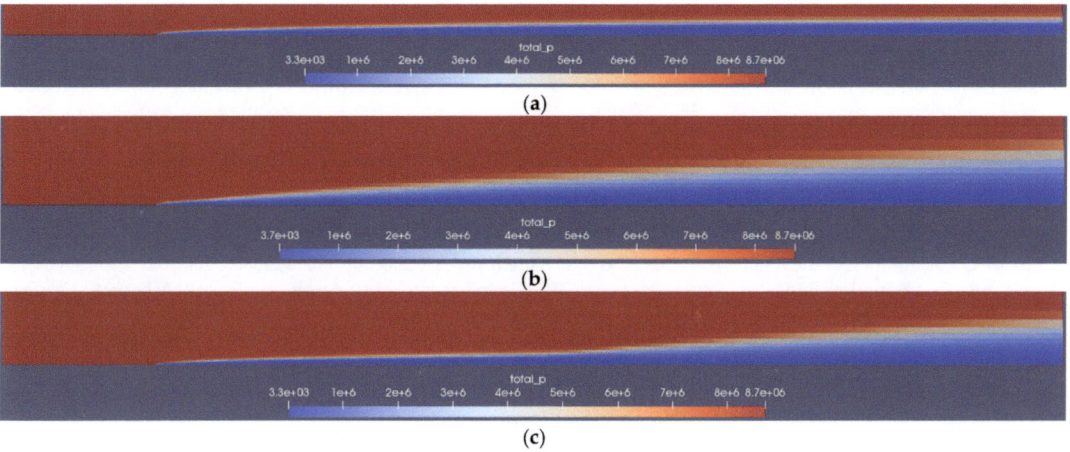

Figure A8. Total pressure profile of s00: (**a**) laminar model; (**b**) SA model; (**c**) SA-BCM model.

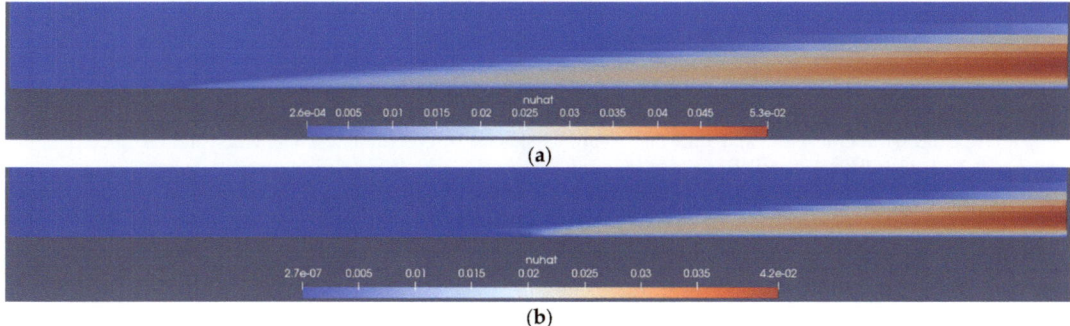

Figure A9. Nuhat profile of s00: (**a**) SA model; (**b**) SA-BCM model.

References

1. Schneider, S.P. Laminar-Turbulent Transition on Reentry Capsules and Planetary Probes. *J. Spacecr. Rocket.* **2006**, *43*, 1153–1173. [CrossRef]
2. Frauholz, S.; Reinartz, B.U.; Müller, S.; Behr, M. Transition Prediction for Scramjets Using γ-Reθt Model Coupled to Two Turbulence Models. *J. Propuls. Power* **2015**, *31*, 1404–1422. [CrossRef]
3. Sommer, S.C.; Compton, D.L.; Short, B.J.; Ames Research Center. *Free-Flight Measurements of Static and Dynamic Stability of Models of the Project Mercury Re-Entry Capsule at Mach Numbers 3 and 9.5*; National Aeronautics and Space Administration: Washington DC, USA, 1960.
4. Michna, J.; Rogowski, K.; Bangga, G.; Hansen, M.O.L. Accuracy of the Gamma Re-Theta Transition Model for Simulating the DU-91-W2-250 Airfoil at High Reynolds Numbers. *Energies* **2021**, *14*, 8224. [CrossRef]
5. Schneider, S.P. Effects of High-Speed Tunnel Noise on Laminar-Turbulent Transition. *J. Spacecr. Rocket.* **2001**, *38*, 323–333. [CrossRef]
6. Schneider, S.P. Hypersonic Laminar–Turbulent Transition on Circular Cones and Scramjet Forebodies. *Prog. Aerosp. Sci.* **2004**, *40*, 1–50. [CrossRef]
7. Saric, W.S. Görtler Vortices. *Annu. Rev. Fluid Mech.* **1994**, *26*, 379–409. [CrossRef]
8. Mack, L.M. *Boundary-Layer Linear Stability Theory*; California Inst of Tech Pasadena Jet Propulsion Lab: La Cañada Flintridge, CA, USA, 1984.
9. Reed, H.L.; Lin, R.-S. *Stability of Three-Dimensional Boundary Layers*; SAE: Warrendale, PA, USA, 1987.
10. Kundu, A.; Thangadurai, M.; Biswas, G. Investigation on Shear Layer Instabilities and Generation of Vortices during Shock Wave and Boundary Layer Interaction. *Comput. Fluids* **2021**, *224*, 104966. [CrossRef]
11. Beckwith, I.E.; Miller, C.G. Aerothermodynamics and Transition in High-Speed Wind Tunnels at NASA Langley. *Annu. Rev. Fluid Mech.* **1990**, *22*, 419–439. [CrossRef]
12. Spalart, P.; Allmaras, S. A One-Equation Turbulence Model for Aerodynamic Flows. In Proceedings of the 30th Aerospace Sciences Meeting and Exhibit, Reno, NV, USA, 6–9 January 1992; American Institute of Aeronautics and Astronautics: Reston, VA, USA, 1992.
13. Bradshaw, P.; Ferriss, D.H.; Atwell, N.P. Calculation of Boundary-Layer Development Using the Turbulent Energy Equation. *J. Fluid Mech.* **1967**, *28*, 593–616. [CrossRef]
14. Jones, W.P.; Launder, B.E. The Prediction of Laminarization with a Two-Equation Model of Turbulence. *Int. J. Heat Mass Transf.* **1972**, *15*, 301–314. [CrossRef]
15. Wilcox, D.C. Formulation of the K-w Turbulence Model Revisited. *AIAA J.* **2008**, *46*, 2823–2838. [CrossRef]
16. Menter, F.R. Two-Equation Eddy-Viscosity Turbulence Models for Engineering Applications. *AIAA J.* **1994**, *32*, 1598–1605. [CrossRef]
17. Launder, B.E.; Reece, G.J.; Rodi, W. Progress in the Development of a Reynolds-Stress Turbulence Closure. *J. Fluid Mech.* **1975**, *68*, 537–566. [CrossRef]
18. Crivellini, A.; D'Alessandro, V. Spalart–Allmaras Model Apparent Transition and RANS Simulations of Laminar Separation Bubbles on Airfoils. *Int. J. Heat Fluid Flow* **2014**, *47*, 70–83. [CrossRef]
19. Sai, V.A.; Lutfy, F.M. Analysis of the Baldwin-Barth and Spalart-Allmaras One-Equation Turbulence Model. *AIAA J.* **1995**, *33*, 1971–1974. [CrossRef]
20. Cebeci, T. *Analysis of Turbulent Flows with Computer Programs*; Elsevier Science & Technology: Oxford, UK, 2013; ISBN 978-0-08-098335-6.
21. Karvinen, A.; Ahlstedt, H. Comparison of Turbulence Models in Case of Three-Dimensional Diffuser. In Proceedings of the Open Source CFD International Conference 2008, Berlin, Germany, 4–5 December 2008.
22. Miroshnichenko, I.; Sheremet, M. Comparative Study of Standard $k-\varepsilon$ and $k-\omega$ Turbulence Models by Giving an Analysis of Turbulent Natural Convection in an Enclosure. *EPJ Web Conf.* **2015**, *82*, 01057. [CrossRef]
23. Rodi, W. DNS and LES of Some Engineering Flows. *Fluid Dyn. Res.* **2006**, *38*, 145–173. [CrossRef]
24. Yang, X.I.A.; Griffin, K.P. Grid-Point and Time-Step Requirements for Direct Numerical Simulation and Large-Eddy Simulation. *Phys. Fluids* **2021**, *33*, 015108. [CrossRef]
25. Kendall, J. Experiments on Boundary-Layer Receptivity to Freestream Turbulence. In Proceedings of the 36th AIAA Aerospace Sciences Meeting and Exhibit, Reno, NV, USA, 12–15 January 1998; American Institute of Aeronautics and Astronautics: Reston, VA, USA, 1998.
26. Klebanoff, P.S.; Tidstrom, K.D.; Sargent, L.M. The Three-Dimensional Nature of Boundary-Layer Instability. *J. Fluid Mech.* **1962**, *12*, 1–34. [CrossRef]
27. Zhao, Y.; Lei, C.; Patterson, J.C. The K-Type and H-Type Transitions of Natural Convection Boundary Layers. *J. Fluid Mech.* **2017**, *824*, 352–387. [CrossRef]
28. Sayadi, T.; Hamman, C.W.; Moin, P. *Direct Numerical Simulation of H-Type and K-Type Transition to Turbulence*; Center for Turbulence Research Annual Research Briefs; NASA Ames: Mountain View, CA, USA, 2011; pp. 109–121.
29. Xu, J.; Liu, J.; Mughal, S.; Yu, P.; Bai, J. Secondary Instability of Mack Mode Disturbances in Hypersonic Boundary Layers over Micro-Porous Surface. *Phys. Fluids* **2020**, *32*, 044105. [CrossRef]

30. Mee, D.J. Boundary-Layer Transition Measurements in Hypervelocity Flows in a Shock Tunnel. *AIAA J.* **2002**, *40*, 1542–1548. [CrossRef]
31. Anderson, J.D. *Hypersonic and High-Temperature Gas Dynamics*, 3rd ed.; American Institute of Aeronautics & Astronautics: Reston, VA, USA, 2019; ISBN 978-1-62410-645-3.
32. Cakmakcioglu, S.C.; Bas, O.; Mura, R.; Kaynak, U. A Revised One-Equation Transitional Model for External Aerodynamics. In Proceedings of the AIAA AVIATION 2020 FORUM, Virtual Event, 15–19 June 2020; American Institute of Aeronautics and Astronautics: Reston, VA, USA, 2020.
33. He, Y.; Morgan, R.G. Transition of Compressible High Enthalpy Boundary Layer Flow over a Flat Plate. *Aeronaut. J.* **1994**, *98*, 25–34. [CrossRef]
34. Schubauer, G.B.; Klebanoff, P.S. *Contributions on the Mechanics of Boundary-Layer Transition*; National Advisory Committee For Aeronautics; NACA: Washington, DC, USA, 1955.
35. Gibbons, N.N.; Damm, K.A.; Jacobs, P.A.; Gollan, R.J. Eilmer: An Open-Source Multi-Physics Hypersonic Flow Solver. *arXiv* **2022**, arXiv:2206.01386.
36. Papp, J.L.; Dash, S.M. Rapid Engineering Approach to Modeling Hypersonic Laminar-To-Turbulent Transitional Flows. *J. Spacecr. Rocket.* **2005**, *42*, 467–475. [CrossRef]
37. Zhao, Y.; Yan, C.; Liu, H.; Zhang, K. Uncertainty and Sensitivity Analysis of Flow Parameters for Transition Models on Hypersonic Flows. *Int. J. Heat Mass Transf.* **2019**, *135*, 1286–1299. [CrossRef]
38. Rogers, G.F.C.; Mayhew, Y.R. *Thermodynamic and Transport Properties of Fluids: SI Units*, 5th ed.; reprinted; SI units; Blackwell: Oxford, UK, 2003; ISBN 978-0-631-19703-4.
39. Menter, F.R.; Langtry, R.B.; Likki, S.R.; Suzen, Y.B.; Huang, P.G.; Völker, S. A Correlation-Based Transition Model Using Local Variables—Part I: Model Formulation. *J. Turbomach.* **2006**, *128*, 413. [CrossRef]
40. Liu, Z.; Yan, C.; Cai, F.; Yu, J.; Lu, Y. An Improved Local Correlation-Based Intermittency Transition Model Appropriate for High-Speed Flow Heat Transfer. *Aerosp. Sci. Technol.* **2020**, *106*, 106122. [CrossRef]
41. Krause, M.; Behr, M.; Ballmann, J. Modeling of Transition Effects in Hypersonic Intake Flows Using a Correlation-Based Intermittency Model. In Proceedings of the 15th AIAA International Space Planes and Hypersonic Systems and Technologies Conference, Dayton, OH, USA, 28 April–1 May 2008; American Institute of Aeronautics and Astronautics: Reston, VA, USA, 2008.
42. You, Y.; Luedeke, H.; Eggers, T.; Hannemann, K. Application of the Y-Reot Transition Model in High Speed Flows. In Proceedings of the 18th AIAA/3AF International Space Planes and Hypersonic Systems and Technologies Conference, Tours, France, 24–28 September 2012; American Institute of Aeronautics and Astronautics: Reston, VA, USA, 2012.
43. de Rosa, D.; Catalano, P. RANS Simulations of Transitional Flow by γ Model. *Int. J. Comput. Fluid Dyn.* **2019**, *33*, 407–420. [CrossRef]
44. Menter, F.R.; Smirnov, P.E.; Liu, T.; Avancha, R. A One-Equation Local Correlation-Based Transition Model. *Flow Turbul. Combust.* **2015**, *95*, 583–619. [CrossRef]
45. Hao, Z.; Yan, C.; Qin, Y.; Zhou, L. Improved γ-Reθt Model for Heat Transfer Prediction of Hypersonic Boundary Layer Transition. *Int. J. Heat Mass Transf.* **2017**, *107*, 329–338. [CrossRef]
46. Yang, M.; Xiao, Z. Distributed Roughness Induced Transition on Wind-Turbine Airfoils Simulated by Four-Equation k-ω-γ-Ar Transition Model. *Renew. Energy* **2019**, *135*, 1166–1177. [CrossRef]
47. Pirozzoli, S.; Grasso, F.; Gatski, T.B. Direct Numerical Simulation and Analysis of a Spatially Evolving Supersonic Turbulent Boundary Layer at M=2.25. *Phys. Fluids* **2004**, *16*, 530–545. [CrossRef]
48. Horvath, T.; Berry, S.; Hollis, B.; Singer, B.; Chang, C.-L. Boundary Layer Transition on Slender Cones in Conventional and Low Disturbance Mach 6 Wind Tunnels. In Proceedings of the 32nd AIAA Fluid Dynamics Conference and Exhibit, St. Louis, MO, USA, 24–26 June 2002; American Institute of Aeronautics and Astronautics: Reston, VA, USA, 2012.
49. Borg, M.; Schneider, S. Effect of Freestream Noise on Instability and Transition for the X-51A Lee Side. In Proceedings of the 47th AIAA Aerospace Sciences Meeting including The New Horizons Forum and Aerospace Exposition, Orlando, FL, USA, 5–8 January 2009; American Institute of Aeronautics and Astronautics: Reston, VA, USA, 2009.
50. Hollis, B.R.; Hollingsworth, K.E. *Experimental Study of Hypersonic Inflatable Aerodynamic Decelerator (HIAD) Aeroshell with Axisymmetric Surface Deflection Patterns*; NASA: Washington, DC, USA, 2017.
51. Hollis, B.R. Surface Heating and Boundary-Layer Transition on a Hypersonic Inflatable Aerodynamic Decelerator. *J. Spacecr. Rocket.* **2018**, *55*, 856–876. [CrossRef]

Article

The Effect of Adhesion on Indentation Behavior of Various Smart Materials

Qinghui Luo [1], Yueting Zhou [1,*], Lihua Wang [1] and Shenghu Ding [2]

[1] School of Aerospace Engineering and Applied Mechanics, Tongji University, 100 Zhangwu Road, Shanghai 200092, China
[2] School of Mathematics and Statistics, Ningxia University, Yinchuan 750021, China
* Correspondence: zhouyt@tongji.edu.cn

Abstract: The nanoindentation technique plays a significant role in characterizing the mechanical properties of materials at nanoscale, where the adhesion effect becomes very prominent due to the high surface-to-volume ratio. For this paper, the classical adhesion theories were generalized to study the contact behaviors of various piezoelectric materials indented by conical punches with different electric properties. With the use of the Hankel integral transform, dual integral equations, and superposing principle, the closed-form solutions of the physical fields for the Johnson-Kendall-Roberts (JKR) and Maugis-Dugdale (M-D) models were obtained, respectively. The contribution of the electrical energy to the energy release rate under the conducting punch was taken into consideration. The relationships between the contact radius, the indentation load, and the indentation depth were set up using the total energy method for the JKR model and the Griffith energy balance for the M-D model, respectively. Numerical results indicate that increasing the half cone angle of the conical punch enhances the adhesion effect, which can significantly affect the accuracy of the results of characterization in nanoindentation tests. It was found that the effect of electric potential on adhesion behaviors is sensitive to different material properties, which are not revealed in the existing studies of axisymmetric adhesive contact of piezoelectric materials and multiferroic composite materials. The load-displacement curves under conical punches with different half cone angles have very different slopes. These results indicate that the half cone angle has a prominent effect on the characterization of mechanical properties of piezoelectric solids in nanoindentation tests.

Keywords: piezoelectric materials; conical punch; adhesive contact; analytical solution

MSC: 74E10; 74G05; 74G65; 74M15

Citation: Luo, Q.; Zhou, Y.; Wang, L.; Ding, S. The Effect of Adhesion on Indentation Behavior of Various Smart Materials. *Mathematics* 2022, 10, 4511. https://doi.org/10.3390/math10234511

Academic Editor: Denis N. Sidorov

Received: 19 October 2022
Accepted: 25 November 2022
Published: 29 November 2022

Publisher's Note: MDPI stays neutral with regard to jurisdictional claims in published maps and institutional affiliations.

Copyright: © 2022 by the authors. Licensee MDPI, Basel, Switzerland. This article is an open access article distributed under the terms and conditions of the Creative Commons Attribution (CC BY) license (https://creativecommons.org/licenses/by/4.0/).

1. Introduction

As typical functional materials, piezoelectric materials have received increasingly wide applications in a variety of smart structures and devices, such as transducers [1], sensors [2], actuators [3], generators [4], energy harvest devices [5], and so on. It is essential for these various applications to accurately characterize the electric and mechanical properties of piezoelectric materials for realizing effective quality control and performance prediction [6,7]. In order to achieve these goals, many intelligent artificial algorithms, such as the genetic algorithm [7–10], and soft computing tools, such as neural networks [11,12], have been used. The nanoindentation technique, also known as instrumented indentation, has become one of the most widely used testing techniques for evaluating the mechanical properties of a variety of materials [13,14], including the traditional stiff piezoelectric ceramics, such as polycrystalline lead zirconate titanate (PZT), barium titanate (BaTiO$_3$), etc., and the new soft piezoelectric materials with low elastic modulus, such as polyvinylidene fluoride (PVDF). However, soft materials always display obvious and strong adhesion effects in nanoindentation experiments, which have significant influence on the results of characterization [15,16].

Adhesion is a phenomenon which describes the tendency of different surfaces or particles to cling to one another. The adhesion effect plays a significant role in micro/nanoscale contact behaviors owing to the high surface-to-volume ratio [17–19]. During the nanoindentation testing technique, the sample is pressed by a small indenter tip, and the force and displacement are continuously measured as a function of time with high accuracy and precision. The recorded indentation force-displacement curves are often viewed as the 'fingerprints' of the tested materials, which can be analyzed to evaluate their mechanical properties. However, there always exists an obvious adhesion effect between the nanoindenter tip and the soft sample, which can lead to inaccurate estimation of the mechanical properties, such as the elastic modulus and hardness values. For example, it has been verified by [20] that contact stiffness in the presence of adhesion effect is always smaller than the counterpart value in the absence of the adhesion effect at the same indentation depth, while for the same indentation force, the results are the opposite. Therefore, the adhesion effect should be considered to avoid obtaining incorrect results during the nanoindentation testing of soft materials.

Contact problems are not only very common in nature but also a key issue in practical engineering. Whether discussing traditional indentation or nanoindentation technique, their theoretical foundations are both in contact mechanics [13]. During the past few years, the contact mechanics of piezoelectric materials have received comprehensive and rapid development through theoretical deductions, numerical simulations, and experimental observations. Various contact problems have received considerable attention and been widely studied by many investigators, including the indentation problems under some typical indenter profiles [21–31], the frictionless contact problems [32–41], the frictional contact problems [42–47], the fretting contact problems [48–50] and the dynamic contact problems [51,52]. During nanoindentation tests, sharp indenter is widely used due to its higher resolution and the simplicity of the procedure [15]. As a typical sharp punch, the contact behaviors of piezoelectric materials indented by a conical punch have been widely investigated by many scholars. Chen et al. [21] studied the frictionless indentation problem of a piezoelectric solid punched by a rigid conical punch. Ding et al. [53] analyzed the frictional contact behavior between a piezoelectric solid and a rigid conical punch. Giannakopoulos and Suresh [22] developed a general theory for the axisymmetric indentation problem of transversely isotropic piezoelectric materials by using the Hankel integral transform technique. The closed-form solutions of physical quantities under the action of the rigid conducting and insulating conical punches were obtained, which later were generalized to piezoelectric film with finite thickness by [25,54]. Sridhar et al. [23] conducted an experimental investigation into the mechanical and electrical responses of piezoelectric solids indented by a rigid conducting conical punch with zero electric potential. Makagon et al. [24] analyzed the sliding frictional contact behavior between a piezoelectric solid and a rigid conical punch. Yang [26] obtained the general solutions of the piezoelectric solids punched by a rigid indenter with axisymmetric arbitrary profile and presented the closed-form solutions of the stress and electric displacement fields in the case of a rigid conical punch.

It is worth noting that the aforementioned works only focus on the macroscale contact behaviors of piezoelectric materials, and the influence of the adhesion effect was not taken into consideration. With the increasingly broad applications of piezoelectric materials in various micro-electro-mechanical systems (MEMS) devices, where the adhesion effect becomes very prominent due to the high surface-to volume ratio [17], the contact problems of piezoelectric materials at the micro/nanoscale have been studied by some researchers in the past few years. Chen and Yu [55] first extended the classical JKR model [56] and the M-D model [57] to study the adhesion behaviors of piezoelectric materials. The results indicated that the coupling effect between adhesion and piezoelectric effects lead to much more complicated adhesion behaviors than in the pure elastic case. Rogowski and Kalinski [58] studied the adhesion behaviors of a piezoelectric solid indented by a rigid circular punch and demonstrated the explicit expression of contact stresses, displacement outside the contact zone, and electric physical quantities. Guo and Jin [59] established a generalized JKR model to study the adhesive contact problem between a piezoelectric solid and a rigid cylinder with constant electric potential. It was found that piezoelectric materials can be used to realize reversible adhesion. Jin et al. [60] developed the JKR-type adhesive contact model for the piezoelectric solid punched by a rigid indenter with an axisymmetric power-law profile. It is worth pointing out that all of the aforementioned works involved only single layer piezoelectric materials. However, layered structures have been widely used in various MEMS devices and structures [1,61]. To this end, the adhesion behaviors of layered piezoelectric structures were studied [62–64], which are helpful for revealing the adhesion mechanism of MEMS involving piezoelectric solids.

As typical multi-functional materials, multiferroic composite materials have been widely used in a variety of MEMS smart structures [65–67] due to their multi-field coupling effect. The contact behaviors of multiferroic composite media at micro/nanoscale have attracted some attention from researchers. Recently, with the use of the superposition principle and generalized potential theory, Wu et al. [68] first generalized the classical adhesive contact theories to multiferroic composite materials. They established corresponding JKR and M-D models for the multiferroic half-space under a spherical indenter with four different electric and magnetic properties. It was found that the electric potential and magnetic potential can be used to adjust the adhesion behaviors. More recently, Wu and Li [69] studied the frictionless adhesive contact behaviors between a rigid conical punch and a multiferroic half-space using the same approach. They found that the pull-off force can be adjusted by altering the half cone angle of the conical punch.

It is worth mentioning that the adhesion behaviors of multiferroic composite materials discussed in the above-mentioned two works [68,69] involved only one kind of material (i.e., $BaTiO_3$-$CoFe_2O_4$). Although the effects of the electric potential and the half cone angle of the conical punch on adhesion behaviors were discussed, whether these effects are dependent on different material properties is unclear. However, the nanoindentation technique has been widely used in characterizing the mechanical and electric properties of various piezoelectric materials [70–72]. For the two-dimensional adhesive contact of piezoelectric materials indent by a rigid cylinder, it has been verified that different types of piezoelectric materials share entirely different adhesion behaviors under an electric load [60], which reveals that the effect of the electric load on adhesion behaviors is sensitive to material properties. For the indentation problem of purely elastic materials under a conical punch, the existing results indicate that the half cone angle can significantly affect the calculation of mechanical properties in nanoindentation tests [15]. For the indentation behaviors of various piezoelectric materials indented by a rigid conical punch, it is unclear whether the effects of the electric potential and the half cone angle on adhesion behaviors are sensitive to different material properties, or whether the half cone angle has a significant effect on the characterization of mechanical properties of piezoelectric materials in nanoindentation tests. The current work is devoted to answer these queries.

It is well known that the classical adhesion theories include the JKR model [56], the DMT model [73], the M-D model [57] and the double-Hertz (D-H) model [74]. The M-D and D-H models are regarded as more general theories than the JKR and DMT models, since both the M-D and D-H models are applicable to the arbitrary Tabor parameter [75], whose applicable scope can vary between soft materials and extremely hard materials. The JKR and DMT models can be described as two limit cases derived from the M-D model, which thus can be used to verify the correctness of the M-D model. The JKR model is the most widely used theory in nanoindentation experiments due to its convenience and reasonability [16,76,77]. Based on the above considerations, the classical JKR and M-D models were generalized in the present study to investigate the adhesive contact behaviors of various piezoelectric materials indented by conical punches with different electric properties. Numerical analysis indicated that the effect of the electric potential on adhesion behaviors is sensitive to different material properties, while the effect of the half cone angle on adhesion behaviors is insensitive to different material properties, which are not revealed in the existing studies into piezoelectric materials [60] and multiferroic composite materials [68,69]. Increasing the half cone angle can significantly enhance the adhesion effect, which suggests to us that a conical punch with a small half cone angle should be adopted in nanoindentation tests to reduce the effect of adhesion and improve the accuracy of characterization results. Furthermore, it was found that the load-displacement curves under conical punches with different half cone angles have very different slopes, which indicates that the half cone angle can significantly affect the characterization of mechanical properties of piezoelectric solids in nanoindentation tests.

2. Problem Description and Formulation
2.1. Problem Description

As shown in Figure 1, consider the axisymmetric frictionless adhesive contact problem of a transversely isotropic piezoelectric solid indented by a rigid conical punch with a constant electric potential, ϕ_0, which is acted on by an indentation force, P. The cylindrical coordinate (r, θ, z) is set up at the surface of the piezoelectric solid. The half cone angle of the rigid conical punch is denoted as α, and the contact radius is a, while h stands for the indentation depth and $p(r)$ represents the adhesion force. The piezoelectric solid is polarized with the positive z-axis.

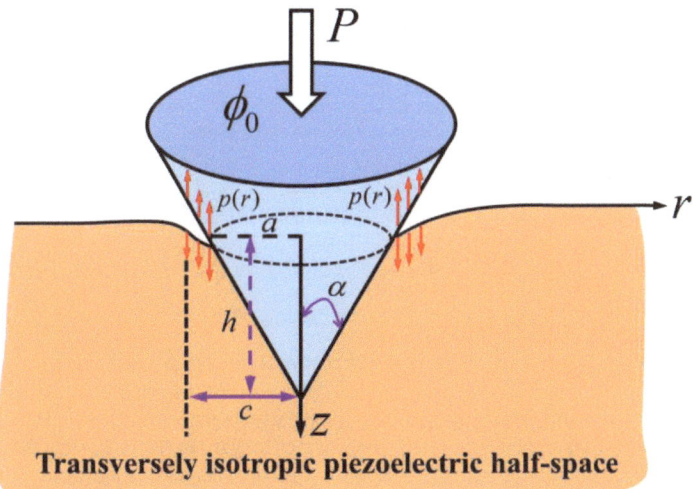

Figure 1. Schematic illustration of a piezoelectric solid in adhesive contact with a rigid conical punch under a normal force, P (negative when tensile). ϕ_0 denotes the constant electric potential; a, h, α, and $p(r)$ stand for the contact radius, the indentation depth, the half cone angle of the rigid conical punch, and the adhesion force, respectively. The poling direction of the piezoelectric solid corresponds with the positive z-axis.

2.2. Governing Equations

In the absence of body forces and body charges, the equilibrium equations and Gauss equation can be given as

$$\begin{aligned} \frac{\partial \sigma_{rr}}{\partial r} + \frac{\partial \sigma_{rz}}{\partial z} + \frac{\sigma_{rr} - \sigma_{\theta\theta}}{r} &= 0, \\ \frac{\partial \sigma_{rz}}{\partial r} + \frac{\partial \sigma_{zz}}{\partial z} + \frac{\sigma_{rz}}{r} &= 0, \\ \frac{\partial D_r}{\partial r} + \frac{D_r}{r} + \frac{\partial D_z}{\partial z} &= 0, \end{aligned} \quad (1)$$

where σ_{ij} and D_i denote the stress and electric displacement components, respectively.

In the cylindrical coordinates system, the constitutive equations can be expressed as

$$\begin{aligned}
\sigma_{rr} &= c_{11}\varepsilon_{rr} + c_{12}\varepsilon_{\theta\theta} + c_{13}\varepsilon_{zz} - e_{31}E_z, \\
\sigma_{\theta\theta} &= c_{12}\varepsilon_{rr} + c_{11}\varepsilon_{\theta\theta} + c_{13}\varepsilon_{zz} - e_{31}E_z, \\
\sigma_{zz} &= c_{13}(\varepsilon_{rr} + \varepsilon_{\theta\theta}) + c_{33}\varepsilon_{zz} - e_{33}E_z, \\
\sigma_{rz} &= 2c_{44}\varepsilon_{rz} - e_{15}E_r, \\
D_r &= 2e_{15}\varepsilon_{rz} + \in_{11} E_r, \\
D_z &= e_{31}(\varepsilon_{rr} + \varepsilon_{\theta\theta}) + e_{33}\varepsilon_{zz} + \in_{33} E_z,
\end{aligned} \qquad (2)$$

where c_{ij}, e_{ij}, and $\in_{ij}$ represent the elastic, piezoelectric, and dielectric constants, respectively. Both ε_{ij} and E_i denote the strain and electric field components, respectively. The strain and electric field can be expressed by the mechanical displacements u_r, u_z, and the electric potential, ϕ, via the following relations:

$$\begin{aligned}
\varepsilon_{rr} &= \tfrac{\partial u_r}{\partial r},\ \varepsilon_{\theta\theta} = \tfrac{u_r}{r},\ \varepsilon_{zz} = \tfrac{\partial u_z}{\partial z}, \\
2\varepsilon_{rz} &= \tfrac{\partial u_r}{\partial z} + \tfrac{\partial u_z}{\partial r},\ E_r = -\tfrac{\partial \phi}{\partial r},\ E_z = -\tfrac{\partial \phi}{\partial z}.
\end{aligned} \qquad (3)$$

Through substitution of Equations (2) and (3) into Equation (1), one can obtain the following governing equations:

$$\begin{aligned}
&c_{11}\left(\tfrac{\partial^2 u_r}{\partial r^2} + \tfrac{1}{r}\tfrac{\partial u_r}{\partial r} - \tfrac{u_r}{r^2}\right) + c_{44}\tfrac{\partial^2 u_r}{\partial z^2} + (c_{13}+c_{44})\tfrac{\partial^2 u_z}{\partial r\partial z} + (e_{31}+e_{15})\tfrac{\partial^2 \phi}{\partial r\partial z} = 0, \\
&(c_{13}+c_{44})\left(\tfrac{\partial^2 u_r}{\partial r\partial z} + \tfrac{1}{r}\tfrac{\partial u_r}{\partial z}\right) + c_{44}\left(\tfrac{\partial^2 u_z}{\partial r^2} + \tfrac{1}{r}\tfrac{\partial u_z}{\partial r}\right) + c_{33}\tfrac{\partial^2 u_z}{\partial z^2} \\
&+ e_{15}\left(\tfrac{\partial^2 \phi}{\partial r^2} + \tfrac{1}{r}\tfrac{\partial \phi}{\partial r}\right) + e_{33}\tfrac{\partial^2 \phi}{\partial z^2} = 0, \\
&(e_{31}+e_{15})\left(\tfrac{\partial^2 u_r}{\partial r\partial z} + \tfrac{1}{r}\tfrac{\partial u_r}{\partial z}\right) + e_{15}\left(\tfrac{\partial^2 u_z}{\partial r^2} + \tfrac{1}{r}\tfrac{\partial u_z}{\partial r}\right) + e_{33}\tfrac{\partial^2 u_z}{\partial z^2} \\
&- \in_{11}\left(\tfrac{\partial^2 \phi}{\partial r^2} + \tfrac{1}{r}\tfrac{\partial \phi}{\partial r}\right) - \in_{33}\tfrac{\partial^2 \phi}{\partial z^2} = 0.
\end{aligned} \qquad (4)$$

2.3. General Solutions

The results shown in Equation (4) are the governing equations with respect to the mechanical displacement components and the electric potential. By solving Equation (4) and substituting the solutions into Equations (2) and (3), one can obtain the corresponding components of stress and electric displacement. Using the Hankel integral transform, and considering the frictionless contact boundary condition, the general solutions of the surface normal displacement, surface normal stress, and electric displacement can be obtained as follows [25]:

$$\begin{aligned}
u_z(r,0) &= \int_0^\infty [M_1 A_1(\xi) + M_2 A_2(\xi)]\xi J_0(\xi r)d\xi, \\
\phi(r,0) &= \int_0^\infty [M_3 A_1(\xi) + M_4 A_2(\xi)]\xi J_0(\xi r)d\xi, \\
\sigma_{zz}(r,0) &= \int_0^\infty [M_5 A_1(\xi) + M_6 A_2(\xi)]\xi^2 J_0(\xi r)d\xi, \\
D_z(r,0) &= \int_0^\infty [M_7 A_1(\xi) + M_8 A_2(\xi)]\xi^2 J_0(\xi r)d\xi,
\end{aligned} \qquad (5)$$

where $M_i (i = 1, 2, \ldots, 8)$ represent the material constants related to the material properties of piezoelectric materials, whose explicit expressions were given by Appendix (A.8) in [25]; $A_i(\xi)$ $(i = 1, 2)$ denote the undetermined constants that can be obtained with use of the corresponding boundary conditions; and $J_0(\xi r)$ denotes the Bessel function of the first kind of zero order. In order to obtain the general solutions shown in Equation (5), the regularity condition of the piezoelectric solid at infinity is considered, i.e., $u_r, u_z, \phi \to 0$, $\sqrt{r^2 + z^2} \to 0$.

For the frictionless contact problem between a piezoelectric solid and a rigid axisymmetric punch with arbitrary profile, whose shape function can be denoted as $f(r)$, the solutions of the surface mechanical displacement, stress, and electric displacement of the piezoelectric solid can be obtained with use of Equation (5) and the corresponding boundary conditions. It is worth mentioning that the electrical boundary conditions for conducting and insulating indenters are different.

First, whether for the conducting or insulating indenter, the mechanical boundary conditions can be described as

$$\begin{cases} u_z(r,0) = h - f(r), & 0 \leq r \leq a, \\ \sigma_{zz}(r,0) = 0, & r > a, \end{cases} \quad (6)$$

where h, $f(r)$, and a stand for the indentation depth, the shape function of the punch, and the contact radius, respectively. For the three typical indenters (the flat-ended cylindrical, the conical, and the spherical punches), the shape functions are denoted as

$$f(r) = \begin{cases} 0, & (0 \leq r \leq a) \text{ (flat-endedcircular punch)}, \\ r \cot \alpha, & (0 \leq r \leq a) \text{ (conical punch)}, \\ r^2/(2R), & (0 \leq r \leq a) \text{ (spherical punch)}. \end{cases} \quad (7)$$

For the electrically conducting indenter, the electrical boundary conditions are given as

$$\begin{cases} \phi(r,0) = \phi_0, & 0 \leq r \leq a, \\ D_z(r,0) = 0, & r > a, \end{cases} \quad (8)$$

where ϕ_0 is a constant denoting the constant electric potential.

For the electrically insulating indenter, the corresponding electrical boundary condition is expressed as

$$D_z(r,0) = 0, \quad r \geq 0. \quad (9)$$

In addition, for both the conducting and insulating indenters, the following equilibrium condition should be satisfied:

$$P = -2\pi \int_0^a r \sigma_{zz}(r,0) dr, \quad (10)$$

where P is the indentation load. For the conducting indenter, one can further obtain

$$Q = -2\pi \int_0^a r D_z(r,0) dr, \quad (11)$$

where Q stands for the total electric charge.

3. The Solution of the JKR Model

In this section, the classical JKR model [56] is generalized to investigate the adhesive contact problem of a piezoelectric solid indented by a rigid conical punch.

3.1. Boundary Conditions for the JKR Model

In the classical JKR model, only the adhesion force within the contact area was taken into consideration. According to the different electric properties of the indenters, the mixed boundary conditions for the conducting and insulating punches can be described as follows:

Case I: electrically conducting punch

$$\begin{aligned} u_z(r,0) &= h - r \cot \alpha, \quad \phi(r,0) = \phi_0, & 0 \leq r < a, \\ \sigma_{zz}(r,0) &= D_z(r,0) = 0, & r > a, \\ \sigma_{rz}(r,0) &= 0, & r \geq 0. \end{aligned} \quad (12)$$

Case II: electrically insulating punch

$$\begin{aligned} u_z(r,0) &= h - r\cot\alpha, & 0 \leq r < a, \\ \sigma_{zz}(r,0) &= 0, & r > a, \\ \sigma_{zr}(r,0) &= D_z(r,0) = 0, & r \geq 0. \end{aligned} \quad (13)$$

Referring to the establishment process of the classical JKR model, the solutions for piezoelectric materials can be derived by superposing the corresponding piezoelectric Hertz contact solution under the conical punch, and the Boussinesq contact solution under the flat-ended circular punch, as shown in Figure 2a,b. Using the general solutions presented in Equation (5) and combining the corresponding boundary conditions shown in Equations (12) and (13), one can obtain the closed-form analytical solutions of the contact problems of the piezoelectric solid indented by the rigid conical punch and flat-ended cylindrical punch, respectively. For the convenience of subsequent analysis, the solutions of the above-mentioned two subproblems are listed in Appendices A and B.

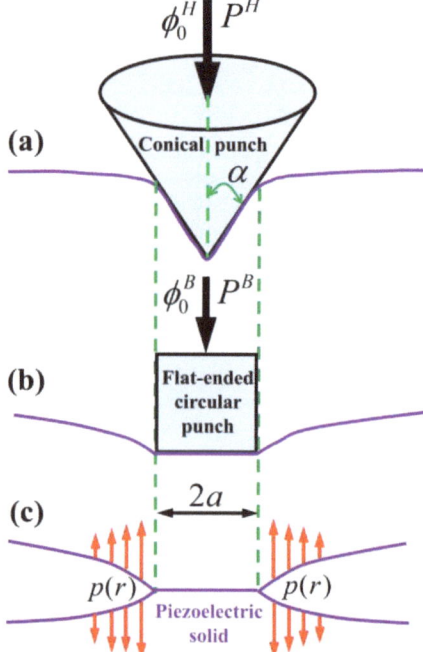

Figure 2. Illustration of the M-D model of a conical punch on a piezoelectric solid: (**a**) Hertz piezoelectric contact for a conical punch. (**b**) Boussinesq piezoelectric contact for a flat-ended circular punch. (**c**) An axisymmetric external crack in an infinite piezoelectric body.

3.2. The Solution of Case I: Electrically Conducting Punch

Using the Hertz solutions in Equations (A2)–(A6) and the corresponding Boussinesq solutions in Equations (A14)–(A18), the solutions of the JKR model for a piezoelectric solid indented by a rigid conducting conical punch can be obtained as

$$h^{JKR} = \frac{\pi a}{4}\cot\alpha - B_3\phi_0 + \frac{P}{4B_4 a}, \quad (14)$$

$$\sigma_{zz}^{JKR}(r,0) = -B_4\cot\alpha\cosh^{-1}\left(\frac{a}{r}\right) + \frac{\pi a^2 B_4\cot\alpha - P}{2\pi a\sqrt{a^2 - r^2}}, \quad (15)$$

$$D_z^{JKR}(r,0) = \frac{2B_5(B_6+B_3)\phi_0}{\pi\sqrt{a^2-r^2}} - B_5 \cot\alpha \cosh^{-1}\left(\frac{a}{r}\right) + \frac{B_5}{B_4}\frac{\pi a^2 B_4 \cot\alpha - P}{2\pi a\sqrt{a^2-r^2}}, \tag{16}$$

$$u_z^{JKR}(r,0) = \begin{cases} h^{JKR} - r\cot\alpha, & 0 \le r \le a, \\ \frac{2}{\pi}h^{JKR}\sin^{-1}\left(\frac{a}{r}\right) + \left(\sqrt{r^2-a^2}-r\right)\cot\alpha, & r > a, \end{cases} \tag{17}$$

$$\phi^{JKR}(r,0) = \begin{cases} \phi_0, & 0 \le r \le a, \\ \frac{2}{\pi}\phi_0 \sin^{-1}\left(\frac{a}{r}\right), & r > a. \end{cases} \tag{18}$$

According to the establishment procedure of the classical JKR model, the total energy method should be adopted to obtain the relationship between the indentation force and contact radius. The total free energy of the contact system can be expressed as

$$U_T = U_E + U_D + U_P + U_S, \tag{19}$$

where U_T, U_E, U_D, U_P, and U_S denote the total free energy, the elastic strain energy, the electrostatic field energy, the mechanical energy, and the surface energy of the contact system, respectively, which are defined as

$$U_E = -\frac{1}{2}\int_0^{2\pi}\int_0^a \sigma_{zz}^{JKR}(r,0)u_z^{JKR}(r,0)\,rdrd\theta, \tag{20}$$

$$U_D = -\frac{1}{2}\int_0^{2\pi}\int_0^a D_z^{JKR}(r,0)\phi^{JKR}(r,0)rdrd\theta, \tag{21}$$

$$U_P = -Ph^{JKR},\ U_S = -\pi a^2 \Delta\gamma, \tag{22}$$

where $\Delta\gamma$ is the surface energy denoting the work of adhesion for per unit area needed to separate two contacting objects from equilibrium state to infinity.

Substituting Equations (14)–(18) into Equations (20)–(22) yields that

$$\begin{aligned}U_E &= \frac{P^2}{8B_4 a} + \frac{\pi^2 \cot^2\alpha B_4 a^3}{24} - \frac{PB_3\phi_0}{2},\ U_D = \frac{B_5}{2B_4}P\phi_0 - 2B_5(B_6+B_3)a\phi_0^2,\\ U_P &= -\frac{\pi\cot\alpha}{4}Pa - \frac{P^2}{4aB_4} + PB_3\phi_0.\end{aligned} \tag{23}$$

In order to obtain the results presented in Equation (23), the following integral results were utilized [69]:

$$\begin{aligned}&\int_0^a \frac{r}{\sqrt{a^2-r^2}}dr = a,\ \int_0^a \frac{r^2}{\sqrt{a^2-r^2}}dr = \frac{\pi}{4}a^2,\\ &\int_0^a r\cosh^{-1}\frac{a}{r}dr = \frac{1}{2}a^2,\ \int_0^a r^2\cosh^{-1}\frac{a}{r}dr = \frac{\pi a^3}{12}.\end{aligned} \tag{24}$$

The equilibrium state of the contact system should satisfy the following condition:

$$\left.\frac{\partial U_T}{\partial a}\right|_P = 0, \tag{25}$$

By substituting Equation (23) into Equation (19) and then inserting the corresponding result into Equation (25), one can obtain

$$P = \pi\cot\alpha B_4 a^2 \pm 4a\sqrt{\pi B_4 \Delta\gamma a + B_4 B_5(B_6+B_3)\phi_0^2}. \tag{26}$$

The stable equilibrium state of the contact system should satisfy the condition $\frac{\partial^2 U_T}{\partial a^2} > 0$, in which case

$$P^{JKR} = \pi B_4 a^2 \cot\alpha - 4a\sqrt{\pi B_4 \Delta\gamma a + B_4 B_5 (B_6 + B_3)\phi_0^2}. \tag{27}$$

If the rigid conical punch has zero electric potential (i.e., $\phi_0 = 0$), Equation (27) degenerates into the following form:

$$P = \pi \cot\alpha B_4 a^2 - 4a\sqrt{\pi B_4 \Delta\gamma a}, \tag{28}$$

which is the same as the result of Equation (3.16) obtained in [60].

When a piezoelectric material degenerates into a isotropic elastic solid, considering $B_4 = E^*/2$ (where E^* denotes the equivalent elastic modulus), Equation (28) can be rewritten as

$$P = \frac{\pi \cot\alpha E^*}{2} a^2 - \sqrt{8\pi E^* \Delta\gamma a^3}, \tag{29}$$

which is in agreement with the result of Equation (17) derived from [78].

By substituting Equation (27) into Equations (14)–(16), one can obtain

$$\begin{aligned}
h^{JKR} &= \tfrac{\pi a}{2}\cot\alpha - B_3\phi_0 - \tfrac{1}{B_4}\sqrt{B_4\pi\Delta\gamma a + B_4 B_5(B_6+B_3)\phi_0^2},\\
\sigma_{zz}^{JKR}(r,0) &= -B_4\cot\alpha\cosh^{-1}\tfrac{a}{r} + \tfrac{2}{\pi}\sqrt{\tfrac{\pi B_4\Delta\gamma a + B_4 B_5(B_6+B_3)\phi_0^2}{a^2-r^2}},\\
D_z^{JKR}(r,0) &= \tfrac{2B_5(B_6+B_3)\phi_0}{\pi\sqrt{a^2-r^2}} - B_5\cot\alpha\cosh^{-1}\tfrac{a}{r}\\
&+ \tfrac{2B_5}{\pi B_4}\sqrt{\tfrac{\pi B_4\Delta\gamma a + B_4 B_5(B_6+B_3)\phi_0^2}{a^2-r^2}}.
\end{aligned} \tag{30}$$

In adhesive contact problems, the pull-off force is regarded as the maximum external pulling force needed to separate two contacting objects, which is a vital physical quantity. In order to obtain the explicit expression of the pull-off force, one must consider the following condition:

$$\frac{dP}{da} = 0. \tag{31}$$

Inserting Equation (27) into Equation (31) yields

$$\chi_1 a^3 + \chi_2 a^2 + \chi_3 a + \chi_4 = 0, \tag{32}$$

where

$$\begin{aligned}
\chi_1 &= \pi^3 B_4^3 \cot^2\alpha\Delta\gamma,\ \chi_2 = \pi^2 B_4^3 B_5(B_6+B_3)\cot^2\alpha\phi_0^2 - 9\pi^2 B_4^2 \Delta\gamma^2,\\
\chi_3 &= -12\pi B_4^2 B_5(B_6+B_3)\Delta\gamma\phi_0^2,\ \chi_4 = -4B^2\phi_0^4.
\end{aligned} \tag{33}$$

Using the Cardans formula, one can derive

$$\Delta = \left(\tfrac{q}{2}\right)^2 + \left(\tfrac{p}{3}\right)^3 = -\tfrac{4B^3\phi_0^6}{B_4^4\pi^6\cot^2\alpha}\left(\tfrac{B^2\phi_0^4}{27\Delta\gamma^4} + \tfrac{B\phi_0^2}{3\Delta\gamma^2} + \tfrac{1}{\cot^4\alpha}\right), \tag{34}$$

where $B = B_4 B_5(B_6+B_3)$, and p and q are defined as

$$p = \frac{\chi_3}{\chi_1} - \frac{\chi_2^2}{3\chi_1^2},\ q = \frac{\chi_4}{\chi_1} + \frac{2\chi_2^3}{27\chi_1^3} - \frac{\chi_2\chi_3}{3\chi_1^2}. \tag{35}$$

The numerical results indicate that $B > 0$ for several common piezoelectric materials (e.g., PZT-4, PZT-5A, BaTiO$_3$, and Ba$_{0.917}$Ca$_{0.083}$TiO$_3$); hence, one can obtain that $\Delta < 0$, and Equation (32) has three real roots given as follows:

$$a_1 = \frac{2\sqrt{-3p}}{3}\cos\frac{\beta}{3} - \frac{1}{3}\left(\frac{BB_4^2\pi^2\cot^2\alpha\phi_0^2 - 9\pi^2 B_4^2\Delta\gamma^2}{\pi^3 B_4^3\cot^2\alpha\Delta\gamma}\right),$$

$$a_2 = -\frac{\sqrt{-3p}}{3}\left(\cos\frac{\beta}{3} - \sqrt{3}\sin\frac{\beta}{3}\right) - \frac{1}{3}\left(\frac{BB_4^2\pi^2\cot^2\alpha\phi_0^2 - 9\pi^2 B_4^2\Delta\gamma^2}{\pi^3 B_4^3\cot^2\alpha\Delta\gamma}\right), \quad (36)$$

$$a_3 = -\frac{\sqrt{-3p}}{3}\left(\cos\frac{\beta}{3} + \sqrt{3}\sin\frac{\beta}{3}\right) - \frac{1}{3}\left(\frac{BB_4^2\pi^2\cot^2\alpha\phi_0^2 - 9\pi^2 B_4^2\Delta\gamma^2}{\pi^3 B_4^3\cot^2\alpha\Delta\gamma}\right),$$

where

$$\beta = \arccos\left(-\frac{3q\sqrt{-3p}}{2p^2}\right), \quad 0 \leq \beta \leq \pi. \quad (37)$$

From Equation (37), one can find that $0 \leq \beta/3 \leq \pi/3$. Therefore, the three roots in Equation (36) satisfy the following orders

$$a_3 \leq a_2 \leq a_1. \quad (38)$$

In addition, from Equation (36), one can obtain the following relation:

$$\begin{aligned}
a_1 &= \frac{2\sqrt{-3p}}{3}\cos\frac{\beta}{3} - \frac{1}{3}\left(\frac{BB_4^2\pi^2\cot^2\alpha\phi_0^2 - 9\pi^2 B_4^2\Delta\gamma^2}{\pi^3 B_4^3\cot^2\alpha\Delta\gamma}\right) \\
&\geq \frac{\sqrt{-3p}}{3} - \frac{1}{3}\left(\frac{BB_4^2\pi^2\cot^2\alpha\phi_0^2 - 9\pi^2 B_4^2\Delta\gamma^2}{\pi^3 B_4^3\cot^2\alpha\Delta\gamma}\right) \\
&= \frac{1}{3}\left[\sqrt{\frac{36B\phi_0^2}{\pi^2 B_4^2\cot^2\alpha} + \left(\frac{BB_4^2\pi^2\cot^2\alpha\phi_0^2 - 9\pi^2 B_4^2\Delta\gamma^2}{\pi^3 B_4^3\cot^2\alpha\Delta\gamma}\right)^2}\right. \\
&\quad \left. - \frac{BB_4^2\pi^2\cot^2\alpha\phi_0^2 - 9\pi^2 B_4^2\Delta\gamma^2}{\pi^3 B_4^3\cot^2\alpha\Delta\gamma}\right] \geq 0,
\end{aligned} \quad (39)$$

$$\begin{aligned}
a_3 &= -\frac{\sqrt{-3p}}{3}\left(\cos\frac{\beta}{3} + \sqrt{3}\sin\frac{\beta}{3}\right) - \frac{1}{3}\left(\frac{BB_4^2\pi^2\cot^2\alpha\phi_0^2 - 9\pi^2 B_4^2\Delta\gamma^2}{\pi^3 B_4^3\cot^2\alpha\Delta\gamma}\right) \\
&\leq -\frac{\sqrt{-3p}}{3} - \frac{1}{3}\left(\frac{BB_4^2\pi^2\cot^2\alpha\phi_0^2 - 9\pi^2 B_4^2\Delta\gamma^2}{\pi^3 B_4^3\cot^2\alpha\Delta\gamma}\right) \\
&= -\frac{1}{3}\left[\sqrt{\frac{36B\phi_0^2}{\pi^2 B_4^2\cot^2\alpha} + \left(\frac{BB_4^2\pi^2\cot^2\alpha\phi_0^2 - 9\pi^2 B_4^2\Delta\gamma^2}{\pi^3 B_4^3\cot^2\alpha\Delta\gamma}\right)^2}\right. \\
&\quad \left. + \frac{BB_4^2\pi^2\cot^2\alpha\phi_0^2 - 9\pi^2 B_4^2\Delta\gamma^2}{\pi^3 B_4^3\cot^2\alpha\Delta\gamma}\right] < 0.
\end{aligned} \quad (40)$$

It should be noted that the contact radius a should be a non-negative real quantity. Therefore, a_1 should be selected as the critical contact radius at the pull-off moment. One can obtain

$$P_{\text{pull-off}} = \pi\cot\alpha B_4 a_{\text{pull-off}}^2 - 4a_{\text{pull-off}}\sqrt{\pi B_4\Delta\gamma a_{\text{pull-off}} + B_4 B_5(B_6 + B_3)\phi_0^2}, \quad (41)$$

where

$$a_{\text{pull-off}} = a_1 = \frac{2\sqrt{-3p}}{3}\cos\frac{\beta}{3} - \frac{1}{3}\left(\frac{BB_4^2\pi^2\cot^2\alpha\phi_0^2 - 9\pi^2 B_4^2\Delta\gamma^2}{\pi^3 B_4^3\cot^2\alpha\Delta\gamma}\right). \quad (42)$$

By adopting the same solution procedures as those of Case I, one can also obtain the JKR solutions for Case II, and the solutions of Case II have similar mathematical structures to Case I. The corresponding solutions for Case II are presented in Appendix C.

4. The Solution of M-D Model

In this section, the classical M-D model is generalized to investigate the adhesive contact behaviors of a piezoelectric solid indented by a rigid conical punch. The adhesive contact problem in classical M-D adhesion theory was divided into three subproblems, i.e., the Hertz contact problem, the Boussinesq contact problem, and the external circular crack problem, as shown in Figure 2. This solution approach will also be adopted here to establish the M-D adhesive contact model for piezoelectric materials.

4.1. Boundary Conditions for the M-D Model

In the classical M-D model [57], the sophisticated adhesion force is simplified as a constant in an annular zone by using the Dugdale model [79]. In this case, the boundary conditions for the two cases of the M-D model can be expressed as follows:

Case I: electrically conducting punch

$$\sigma_{zz}(r,0) = \begin{cases} \sigma_0, & a < r < c, \\ 0, & c < r < \infty, \end{cases}$$
$$u_z(r,0) = h - r\cot\alpha, \quad \phi(r,0) = \phi_0, \quad 0 \leq r < a,$$
$$D_z(r,0) = 0, \quad r > a,$$
$$\sigma_{zr}(r,0) = 0, \quad r \geq 0. \tag{43}$$

Case II: electrically insulating punch

$$\sigma_{zz}(r,0) = \begin{cases} \sigma_0, & a < r < c, \\ 0, & c < r < \infty, \end{cases}$$
$$u_z(r,0) = h - r\cot\alpha, \quad 0 \leq r < a,$$
$$\sigma_{zr}(r,0) = D_z(r,0) = 0, \quad r \geq 0. \tag{44}$$

Note that in Equations (43) and (44), σ_0 denotes the constant adhesion force outside of the contact region, which is the theoretical adhesion strength of the material.

Using the general solutions obtained in Equation (5) and combining the corresponding boundary conditions presented in Equations (43) and (44), the solutions of the three subproblems can be obtained. The corresponding Hertz contact solutions and the Boussinesq contact solutions are presented in Appendices A and B, respectively. The solutions of the axisymmetric external circular crack problem in an infinite piezoelectric solid are given in Appendix E.

4.2. The Solution of Case I: Electrically Conducting Punch

The JKR solutions under a rigid conducting conical punch are presented in Section 4. Introducing the following stress and electric displacement intensity factors:

$$K_I = \frac{P_1 - P}{2a\sqrt{\pi a}}, \quad K_D = \frac{2B_5(B_6 + B_3)\phi_0}{\sqrt{\pi a}}, \tag{45}$$

where P_1 denotes the corresponding apparent Hertz load, then Equations (14)–(16) can be rewritten as follows:

$$h^{JKR} = \frac{\pi a}{2}\cot\alpha - B_3\phi_0 - \frac{\sqrt{\pi a}K_I}{2B_4}, \tag{46}$$

$$\sigma_{zz}^{JKR}(r,0) = -B_4\cot\alpha\cosh^{-1}\frac{a}{r} + \frac{K_I}{\sqrt{\pi a}}\frac{a}{\sqrt{a^2-r^2}}, \quad 0 \leq r < a. \tag{47}$$

$$D_z^{JKR}(r,0) = \sqrt{\frac{a}{\pi}}\frac{K_D}{\sqrt{a^2-r^2}} - B_5\cot\alpha\cosh^{-1}\frac{a}{r} + \frac{B_5}{B_4}\sqrt{\frac{a}{\pi}}\frac{K_I}{\sqrt{a^2-r^2}},\ 0 \le r < a. \quad (48)$$

Substituting Equation (46) into Equation (17), one can obtain

$$u_z^{JKR}(r,0) = \begin{cases} \frac{\pi a}{2}\cot\alpha - B_3\phi_0 - \frac{\sqrt{\pi a}K_I}{2B_4} - r\cot\alpha, & 0 \le r < a, \\ -\sqrt{\frac{a}{\pi}}\frac{K_I}{B_4}\sin^{-1}\frac{a}{r} + \frac{2}{\pi}\left(\frac{\pi a}{2}\cot\alpha - B_3\phi_0\right)\sin^{-1}\frac{a}{r} \\ +\left(\sqrt{r^2-a^2}-r\right)\cot\alpha, & r > a. \end{cases} \quad (49)$$

Using Equations (18) and (49), the discontinuity of the displacement and the electric potential outside the contact region can be defined as

$$\begin{aligned}\left[u_z^{JKR}(r,0)\right] &= f\left(\tfrac{r}{a}\right) - \delta + u_z(r,0) \\ &= \frac{K_I\sqrt{\pi a}}{B_4\pi}\cos^{-1}\frac{a}{r} + \left(\frac{2B_3\phi_0}{\pi} - a\cot\alpha\right)\cos^{-1}\frac{a}{r} + \sqrt{r^2-a^2}\cot\alpha,\ r > a,\end{aligned} \quad (50)$$

and

$$\left[\phi^{JKR}(r,0)\right] = \frac{2}{\pi}\phi_0\sin^{-1}\frac{a}{r} - \phi_0 = -\frac{2\phi_0}{\pi}\cos^{-1}\frac{a}{r},\ r > a, \quad (51)$$

respectively.

The solutions of the external circular crack subjected to constant normal pressure, p_0, at the crack surfaces are presented in Appendix E. By inserting $p_0 = -\sigma_0$ into Equation (A111) and Equations (A114)–(A117) and combining the result in Equation (A91), one can obtain

$$\sigma_{zz}(r,0) = \begin{cases} \frac{K_m}{\sqrt{\pi a}}\frac{a}{\sqrt{a^2-r^2}} + \frac{2\sigma_0}{\pi}\tan^{-1}\sqrt{\frac{c^2-a^2}{a^2-r^2}}, & r < a, \\ \sigma_0, & a < r < c, \end{cases} \quad (52)$$

$$D_z(r,0) = \frac{B_5}{B_4\pi}\frac{K_m\sqrt{\pi a} + 2\sigma_0\sqrt{c^2-a^2}}{\sqrt{a^2-r^2}},\ r < a, \quad (53)$$

$$\begin{aligned}u_T &= -\frac{2\sigma_0}{B_1\pi a}\left[\sqrt{(c^2-a^2)(r^2-a^2)} - ac^2\int_a^{\min(r,c)}\frac{\sqrt{r^2-t^2}}{t^2\sqrt{c^2-t^2}}dt\right] \\ &+ \frac{K_m\sqrt{\pi a} + 2\sigma_0\sqrt{c^2-a^2}}{B_4\pi}\cos^{-1}\frac{a}{r},\ r > a,\end{aligned} \quad (54)$$

$$\phi_T = -\frac{2B_2\sigma_0}{B_1\pi a}\left[\sqrt{(c^2-a^2)(r^2-a^2)} - ac^2\int_a^{\min(r,c)}\frac{\sqrt{r^2-t^2}}{t^2\sqrt{c^2-t^2}}dt\right],\ r > a, \quad (55)$$

$$\delta' = \frac{\sigma_0}{2B_4}\left(\frac{c^2}{a}\cos^{-1}\frac{a}{c} - \sqrt{c^2-a^2}\right), \quad (56)$$

where

$$K_m = -\frac{\sigma_0}{\sqrt{\pi a}}\left(\sqrt{c^2-a^2} + \frac{c^2}{a}\cos^{-1}\frac{a}{c}\right). \quad (57)$$

By superposing Equations (47) and (48) and Equations (52) and (53), one can determine that

$$\sigma_{zz}^{M-D}(r,0) = \begin{cases} -B_4\cot\alpha\cosh^{-1}\frac{a}{r} + \frac{a}{\sqrt{\pi a}}\frac{K_I+K_m}{\sqrt{a^2-r^2}} \\ +\frac{2\sigma_0}{\pi}\tan^{-1}\sqrt{\frac{c^2-a^2}{a^2-r^2}},\ r < a, \\ \sigma_0,\ a < r < c. \end{cases} \quad (58)$$

$$D_z^{M-D}(r,0) = \frac{K_D}{\sqrt{\pi a}} \frac{a}{\sqrt{a^2-r^2}} - B_5 \cot\alpha \cosh^{-1}\frac{a}{r}$$
$$+ \frac{B_5}{B_4} \frac{K_I+K_m}{\sqrt{\pi a}} \frac{a}{\sqrt{a^2-r^2}} + \frac{2B_5\sigma_0}{B_4\pi}\sqrt{\frac{c^2-a^2}{a^2-r^2}}, r < a. \tag{59}$$

According to the classical M-D theory [57], in order to eliminate the stress singularity at the fringe of the contact zone, the following continuity condition should be satisfied:

$$K_I + K_m = 0 \Rightarrow K_I = \frac{P_1 - P}{2a\sqrt{\pi a}} = -K_m = \frac{\sigma_0}{\sqrt{\pi a}}\left(\sqrt{c^2-a^2} + \frac{c^2}{a}\cos^{-1}\frac{a}{c}\right). \tag{60}$$

From Equation (60), one can obtain

$$P = P_1 - 2\sigma_0 a\left(\sqrt{c^2-a^2} + \frac{c^2}{a}\cos^{-1}\frac{a}{c}\right)$$
$$= \pi a^2 B_4 \cot\alpha - 2\sigma_0 a\left(\sqrt{c^2-a^2} + \frac{c^2}{a}\cos^{-1}\frac{a}{c}\right). \tag{61}$$

Using the continuity condition in Equation (60), Equations (58) and (59) can be simplified as

$$\sigma_{zz}^{M-D}(r,0) = \begin{cases} -B_4 \cot\alpha \cosh^{-1}\frac{a}{r} + \frac{2\sigma_0}{\pi}\tan^{-1}\sqrt{\frac{c^2-a^2}{a^2-r^2}}, & r < a, \\ \sigma_0, & a < r < c. \end{cases} \tag{62}$$

and

$$D_z^{M-D}(r,0) = \frac{K_D}{\sqrt{\pi a}}\frac{a}{\sqrt{a^2-r^2}} - B_5 \cot\alpha \cosh^{-1}\frac{a}{r} + \frac{2B_5\sigma_0}{B_4\pi}\sqrt{\frac{c^2-a^2}{a^2-r^2}}, r < a, \tag{63}$$

respectively.

For the indentation depth, by superposing Equations (14) and (56) and combining the result presented in Equation (61), one can obtain

$$h^{M-D} = \frac{\pi a}{2}\cot\alpha - \frac{\sigma_0}{B_4}\sqrt{c^2-a^2} - B_3\phi_0. \tag{64}$$

Using Equations (50) and (54), and considering the continuity condition in Equation (60), the discontinuity displacement outside the contact region can be obtained as

$$[u_z^{M-D}(r,0)] = \left(\frac{2B_3\phi_0}{\pi} - a\cot\alpha\right)\cos^{-1}\frac{a}{r}$$
$$+\sqrt{r^2-a^2}\cot\alpha + \frac{2\sigma_0\sqrt{c^2-a^2}}{\pi B_4}\cos^{-1}\frac{a}{r} \tag{65}$$
$$-\frac{2\sigma_0}{B_1\pi a}\left[\sqrt{(c^2-a^2)(r^2-a^2)} - ac^2\int_a^{\min(r,c)}\frac{\sqrt{r^2-t^2}}{t^2\sqrt{c^2-t^2}}dt\right].$$

The discontinuity of the displacement can be given as

$$\delta_t = [u_z^{M-D}(c,0)] = \left[\sqrt{m^2-1} - \cos^{-1}\left(\frac{1}{m}\right)\right]a\cot\alpha$$
$$+\frac{2B_3\phi_0}{\pi}\cos^{-1}\left(\frac{1}{m}\right) + \frac{2\sigma_0 a}{\pi}\left[\frac{1}{B_4}\sqrt{m^2-1}\cos^{-1}\left(\frac{1}{m}\right) - \frac{1}{B_1}(m-1)\right], \tag{66}$$

where $m = c/a$.

By superposing Equations (51) and (55), the discontinuity of electric potential can be derived as

$$[\phi^{M-D}(r,0)] = -\frac{2\phi_0}{\pi}\cos^{-1}\frac{a}{r}$$
$$-\frac{2B_2\sigma_0}{B_1\pi a}\left[\sqrt{(c^2-a^2)(r^2-a^2)} - ac^2\int_a^{\min(r,c)}\frac{\sqrt{r^2-t^2}}{t^2\sqrt{c^2-t^2}}dt\right]. \tag{67}$$

where $a < r < c$, one can determine that

$$\left[\phi^{M-D}(r,0)\right] = -\frac{2\phi_0}{\pi}\cos^{-1}\frac{a}{r} \\ -\frac{2B_2\sigma_0}{B_1\pi a}\left[\sqrt{(c^2-a^2)(r^2-a^2)} - ac^2\int_a^r \frac{\sqrt{r^2-t^2}}{t^2\sqrt{c^2-t^2}}dt\right]. \tag{68}$$

by virtue of the following integral results [57]:

$$\int_a^r \frac{\sqrt{r^2-t^2}}{t^2\sqrt{c^2-t^2}}dt = \frac{1}{a}\sqrt{\frac{r^2-a^2}{c^2-a^2}} - \frac{1}{c}E(\zeta,t), \tag{69}$$

where

$$E(\zeta,t) = \int_0^\zeta \sqrt{1-t^2\sin^2\theta}\,d\theta \tag{70}$$

is the elliptic integral of the second kind, and

$$\zeta = \arcsin\left(\frac{c}{r}\sqrt{\frac{r^2-a^2}{c^2-a^2}}\right), \quad t = \frac{r}{c}. \tag{71}$$

Equation (68) can be simplified as

$$\left[\phi^{M-D}(r,0)\right] = -\frac{2\phi_0}{\pi}\cos^{-1}\frac{a}{r} \\ -\frac{2B_2\sigma_0}{B_1\pi a}\left[\sqrt{(c^2-a^2)(r^2-a^2)} - c^2\sqrt{\frac{r^2-a^2}{c^2-a^2}} + acE(\zeta,t)\right]. \tag{72}$$

When $\rho_0 \to 0$, from Equations (63) and (72), one can determine that

$$D_z^{M-D}(a-\rho_0,0) \approx \frac{2B_5(B_6+B_3)\phi_0}{\pi\sqrt{2a\rho_0}} + \frac{B_5}{B_4}\frac{2\sigma_0}{\pi}\sqrt{\frac{c^2-a^2}{2a\rho_0}}. \tag{73}$$

$$\left[\phi^{M-D}(a+\rho_0,0)\right] \approx -\frac{2\phi_0}{\pi}\cos^{-1}\frac{a}{a+\rho_0} \\ -\frac{2B_2\sigma_0}{B_1\pi a}\left[\sqrt{(c^2-a^2)2a\rho_0} - c^2\sqrt{\frac{2a\rho_0}{c^2-a^2}} + acE(\zeta,t)\right]. \tag{74}$$

In the case of $\rho_0 \to 0$, using the following results [68]:

$$\cos^{-1}\frac{a}{a+\rho_0} \approx \sqrt{\frac{2\rho_0}{a}}, \quad E(\zeta,t) \approx \frac{\sqrt{2a\rho_0}}{c}\left(\frac{a}{\sqrt{c^2-a^2}} + \frac{\sqrt{c^2-a^2}}{a}\right), \tag{75}$$

Equation (74) can be simplified as

$$\left[\phi^{M-D}(a+\rho_0,0)\right] = -\frac{2}{\pi}\left(\phi_0 + \frac{B_2}{B_1}\sigma_0\sqrt{c^2-a^2}\right)\sqrt{\frac{2\rho_0}{a}}. \tag{76}$$

Using the virtual crack closure integral technique [68,69], the energy release rate of the piezoelectric solid can be calculated as

$$G = \sigma_0\delta_t + \lim_{\delta\to 0}\frac{1}{\delta}\int_0^\delta \frac{1}{2}D_z^{M-D}(a-\rho_0,0)\left[\phi^{M-D}(a+\delta-\rho_0,0)\right]d\rho_0. \tag{77}$$

By substituting Equations (73) and (76) into Equation (77), and using the following integral result [80]:

$$\lim_{\delta\to 0}\frac{1}{\delta}\int_0^\delta \sqrt{\frac{\delta-\rho_0}{\rho_0}}d\rho_0 = \frac{\pi}{2}, \tag{78}$$

the energy release rate can be derived as

$$\begin{aligned}G =& \left[\sqrt{m^2-1}-\cos^{-1}\left(\tfrac{1}{m}\right)\right]\sigma_0 a\cot\alpha + \tfrac{2B_3\phi_0\sigma_0}{\pi}\cos^{-1}\left(\tfrac{1}{m}\right) \\ &+\tfrac{2\sigma_0^2 a}{\pi}\left[\tfrac{1}{B_4}\sqrt{m^2-1}\cos^{-1}\left(\tfrac{1}{m}\right)-\tfrac{1}{B_1}(m-1)\right]-\tfrac{B_5(B_3+B_6)\phi_0^2}{\pi a} \\ &-\tfrac{1}{\pi}\left[\tfrac{B_5}{B_4}+\tfrac{B_2 B_5(B_3+B_6)}{B_1}\right]\phi_0\sigma_0\sqrt{m^2-1}-\tfrac{B_2 B_5}{B_1 B_4}\tfrac{\sigma_0^2 a}{\pi}(m^2-1).\end{aligned} \quad (79)$$

Using the Griffith energy balance criterion, one can determine that

$$\begin{aligned}&\left[\sqrt{m^2-1}-\cos^{-1}\left(\tfrac{1}{m}\right)\right]\sigma_0 a\cot\alpha + \tfrac{2B_3\phi_0\sigma_0}{\pi}\cos^{-1}\left(\tfrac{1}{m}\right) \\ &+\tfrac{2\sigma_0^2 a}{\pi}\left[\tfrac{1}{B_4}\sqrt{m^2-1}\cos^{-1}\left(\tfrac{1}{m}\right)-\tfrac{1}{B_1}(m-1)\right]-\tfrac{B_5(B_3+B_6)\phi_0^2}{\pi a} \\ &-\tfrac{1}{\pi}\left[\tfrac{B_5}{B_4}+\tfrac{B_2 B_5(B_3+B_6)}{B_1}\right]\phi_0\sigma_0\sqrt{m^2-1}-\tfrac{B_2 B_5}{B_1 B_4}\tfrac{\sigma_0^2 a}{\pi}(m^2-1)=\Delta\gamma,\end{aligned} \quad (80)$$

where $\Delta\gamma$ denotes the work of adhesion.

The correctness of the above results can be verified by checking whether the corresponding JKR solutions obtained in Section 3.2 can be derived as the limit case from them, and the detailed procedures can be found in Appendix F. This verified method was also adopted in the classical M-D theory [81].

By adopting the same solution procedures as those of Case I, one can also obtain the corresponding solutions for Case II, and the solutions of Case II have the similar mathematical structures to Case I. The corresponding solutions for Case II are presented in Appendix D.

5. Numerical Results and Discussion

In this section, the effects of the electric potential, the half cone angle of the conical punch, and different material properties on the adhesion behaviors will be revealed. In the following numerical analysis, the corresponding numerical results were computed by Mathematica software. The material properties of the four different piezoelectric materials examined here are listed in Table 1. For the sake of convenience, the following dimensionless physical parameters are defined:

$$P^* = P\big/\left(\tfrac{\Delta\gamma^2}{B_4}\right),\ a^* = a\big/\left(\tfrac{\Delta\gamma}{B_4}\right),\ h^* = h\big/\left(\tfrac{\Delta\gamma}{B_4}\right),\\ \phi^* = B_3\phi_0\big/\left(\tfrac{\Delta\gamma}{B_4}\right),\ m = \tfrac{c}{a},\ \lambda = \tfrac{\sigma_0}{B_4}. \quad (81)$$

5.1. JKR Solutions

Based on the JKR theory, the variations of the dimensionless contact radius, a^*, with the dimensionless indentation force, P^*, for the four different piezoelectric materials are shown in Figure 3. From Figure 3a, one can see that the electric potential has a prominent effect on the adhesive contact behavior. For the electrically conducting punch, the pull-off force increases with the electric potential. In the case of $Ba_{0.917}Ca_{0.083}TiO_3$, as the dimensionless electric potential, ϕ^*, increases from 0 to 3, the corresponding pull-off force increases by about six times, which indicates that the adhesion effect can be strengthened by applying electric potential. This conclusion is in good agreement with the experimental results derived by [82]. Furthermore, the above result also suggests that as typical functional materials, piezoelectric materials offer a new approach to achieve reversible adhesion.

Table 1. Material constants of the four piezoelectric materials.

	PZT-4	PZT-5A	BaTiO$_3$	(Ba$_{0.917}$Ca$_{0.083}$)TiO$_3$
Elastic coefficients (GPa)				
c_{11}	139.00	121.00	150.00	158.00
c_{33}	115.00	111.00	146.00	150.00
c_{44}	25.60	21.10	44.00	45.00
c_{12}	77.80	75.40	66.00	69.00
c_{13}	74.30	75.20	66.00	67.50
Piezoelectric coefficients (C/m^2)				
e_{31}	−5.200	−5.400	−4.350	−3.100
e_{33}	15.10	15.80	17.50	13.50
e_{15}	12.70	12.30	11.40	10.90
Dielectric constants (10^{-9} F/m)				
$\in_{11}$	6.461	8.107	9.868	8.850
$\in_{33}$	5.620	7.346	11.151	8.054
Material coefficients				
B_1 (GPa)	56.41	47.88	70.68	71.48
B_2 (10^9 V/m)	1.246	1.0196	0.8645	0.8787
B_3 (10^{-10} m/V)	2.501	3.035	1.668	1.312
B_4 (GPa)	43.00	36.56	61.77	64.09
B_5 (C/m^2)	10.756	11.097	10.302	8.411
B_6 (10^{-10} m/V)	8.027	9.807	11.567	11.381

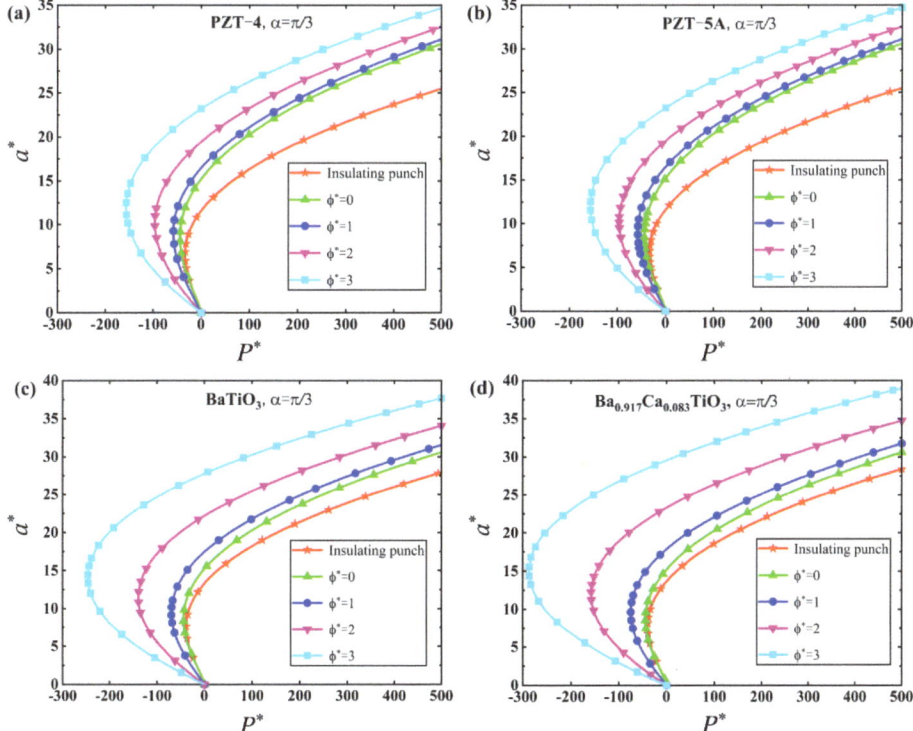

Figure 3. The dimensionless contact radius, a^*, as a function of the dimensionless indentation force, P^*, at a fixed value of $\alpha = \pi/3$ for the JKR model. (**a**) PZT-4. (**b**) PZT-5A. (**c**) BaTiO$_3$. (**d**) Ba$_{0.917}$Ca$_{0.083}$TiO$_3$.

For a given indentation force, one can determine from Figure 3 that the larger the exerted electric potential, the larger the contact radius, which reveals that it is easier to obtain a larger contact area for a conducting punch with higher electric potential. It is worth noting that the $P^* - a^*$ curves of the insulating punch are always below the corresponding curves for the conducting punch. This result indicates that the minimum pull-off force is obtained for the insulating punch, and for a given indentation force, the contact radius under the action of the insulating punch is always smaller than the counterpart value induced by the conducting punch. In addition, comparing the results displayed in Figure 3a–d, one can determine that under the action of the same electric potential, the adhesion strengthening effect induced by the electric potential for the BaTiO$_3$ and Ba$_{0.917}$Ca$_{0.083}$TiO$_3$ was more prominent than that for the PZT-4 and PZT-5A, which stems from different material properties between them. This reveals that the effect of the electric potential on the $a^* \sim P^*$ curve is sensitive to different material properties, which was not suggested in the existing studies on piezoelectric materials [60] and multiferroic composite materials [68,69].

Figures 4 and 5 display the effect of the half cone angle of the rigid conical punch on the adhesion behaviors of the four different piezoelectric materials. It can be seen in Figure 4 that whether for the insulating punch or the conducting punch with zero electric potential, the pull-off force increases with the half cone angle of the rigid conical punch. For a given indentation force, the larger the half cone angle, the larger the contact radius. It is worth mentioning that the curves of the conducting punch with zero electric potential are always above the corresponding curves for the insulating punch, which indicates that for conical punches with the same half cone angle, the contact radius induced by the conducting punch is always larger than the counterpart value under the insulating punch when both of them are subjected to the same indentation force.

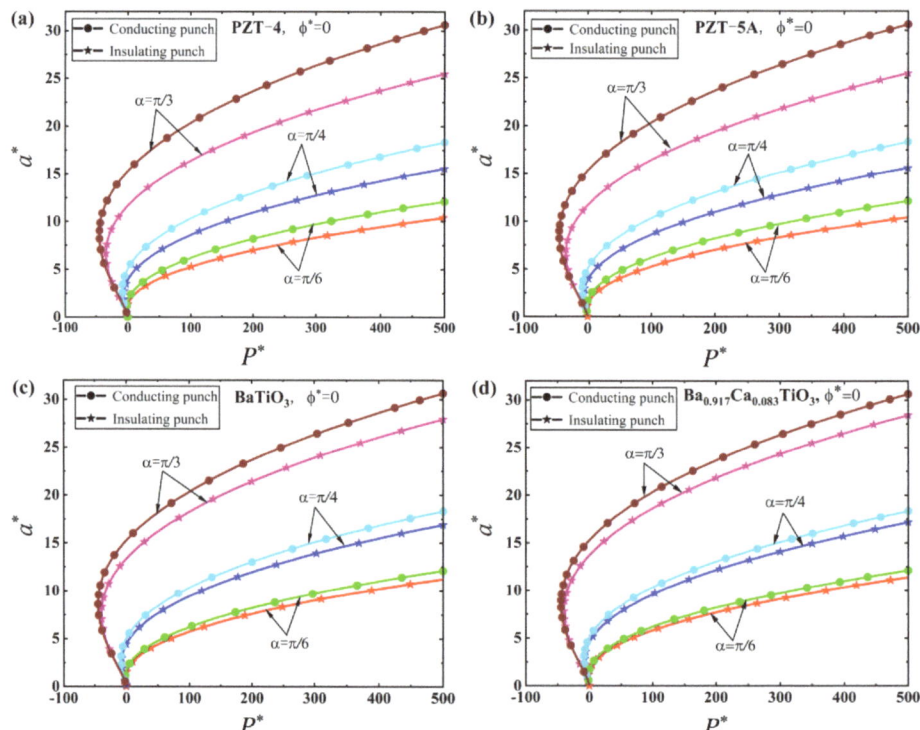

Figure 4. Variation of the dimensionless contact radius, a^*, with the dimensionless indentation force, P^*, at the different values of $\alpha = \pi/6, \pi/4$ and $\pi/3$ for the conducting punch with zero electric potential and insulating punch. (**a**) PZT-4. (**b**) PZT-5A. (**c**) BaTiO$_3$. (**d**) Ba$_{0.917}$Ca$_{0.083}$TiO$_3$.

According to the results presented in Figures 3 and 4, one can find that increasing the electric potential or increasing the half cone angle of the conical punch can enhance the adhesion effect. Therefore, it can be found from Figures 4 and 5 that the pull-off force and the contact radius under the action of the same indentation force for a conducting punch with non-zero electric potential are obviously larger than the counterpart values induced by a conducting punch with zero potential. Furthermore, one can see from Figure 5 that for the conducting punch with non-zero electric potential, the adhesion strengthening effect induced by increasing the half cone angle was very prominent. For example, for the PZT-4 subjected to the dimensionless electric potential $\phi^* = 2$, as the half cone angle of the conical punch changes from $\pi/6$ to $\pi/3$, the pull-off force of the contact system increases by about seven times, which suggests to us that a conical punch with a small cone angle should be adopted in nanoindentation tests in order to reduce the effect of adhesion on the results of characterization. From Figures 4 and 5, one can determine that the $a^* \sim P^*$ curves for the four different piezoelectric materials examined here are not very distinct, which reveals that the effect of the half cone angle on the adhesion behavior is insensitive to the material properties. This conclusion was obtained for the first time in our work and was not given in the existing studies on piezoelectric materials [60] and multiferroic composite materials [68,69].

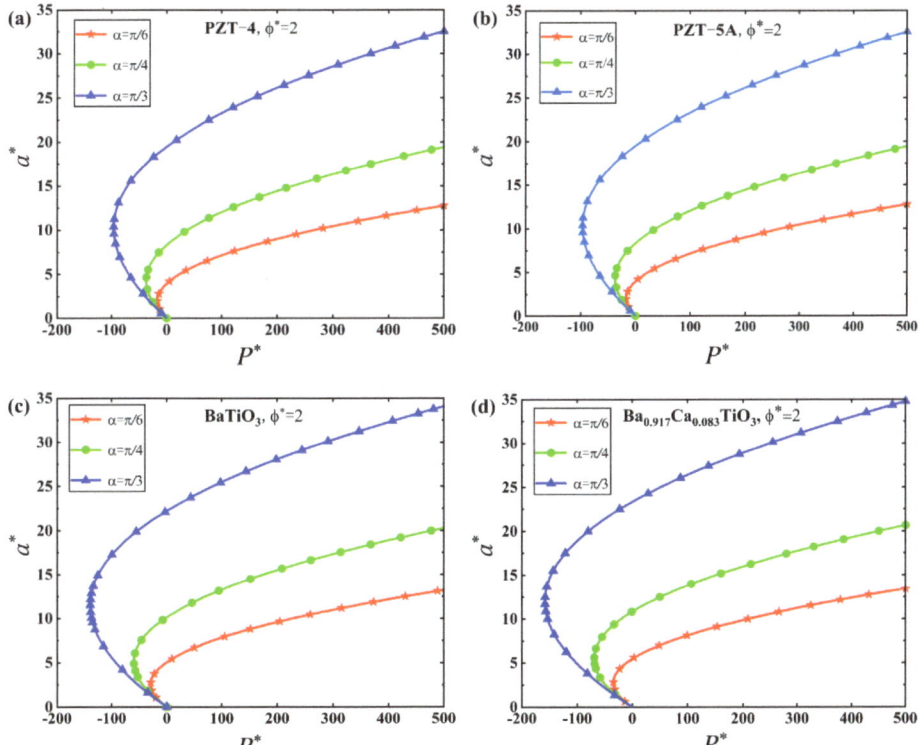

Figure 5. Variation of the dimensionless contact radius, a^*, with the dimensionless indentation force, P^*, at the different values of $\alpha = \pi/6, \pi/4$ and $\pi/3$ for the conducting punch with non-zero electric potential ($\phi^* = 2$). (**a**) PZT-4. (**b**) PZT-5A. (**c**) BaTiO$_3$. (**d**) Ba$_{0.917}$Ca$_{0.083}$TiO$_3$.

The scanning probe microscope and nanoindentation technique play significant roles in characterizing the mechanical properties of various materials. During the nanoindentation testing technique, the sample is pressed by a small indenter tip and the force and displacement are continuously measured as a function of time with high accuracy and precision, which can be used to evaluate the mechanical properties of the materials. Therefore, the indentation force-displacement curve $P^* \sim h^*$ is the key theoretical foundation of the nanoindentation technique. When a piezoelectric solid is indented by a rigid conducting or insulating conical punch, the dimensionless indentation force, P^*, as a function of the dimensionless indentation depth, h^*, for the four different piezoelectric materials is shown in Figure 6. We found that the pull-off force of the conducting punch under force control increases with increases in the electric potential. The sign of the electric potential has little effect on the magnitude of pull-off force. Furthermore, one may notice that the critical indentation depth at the pull-off moment in the case of a negative electric potential is always larger than the counterpart value when the punch is subjected to positive electric potential.

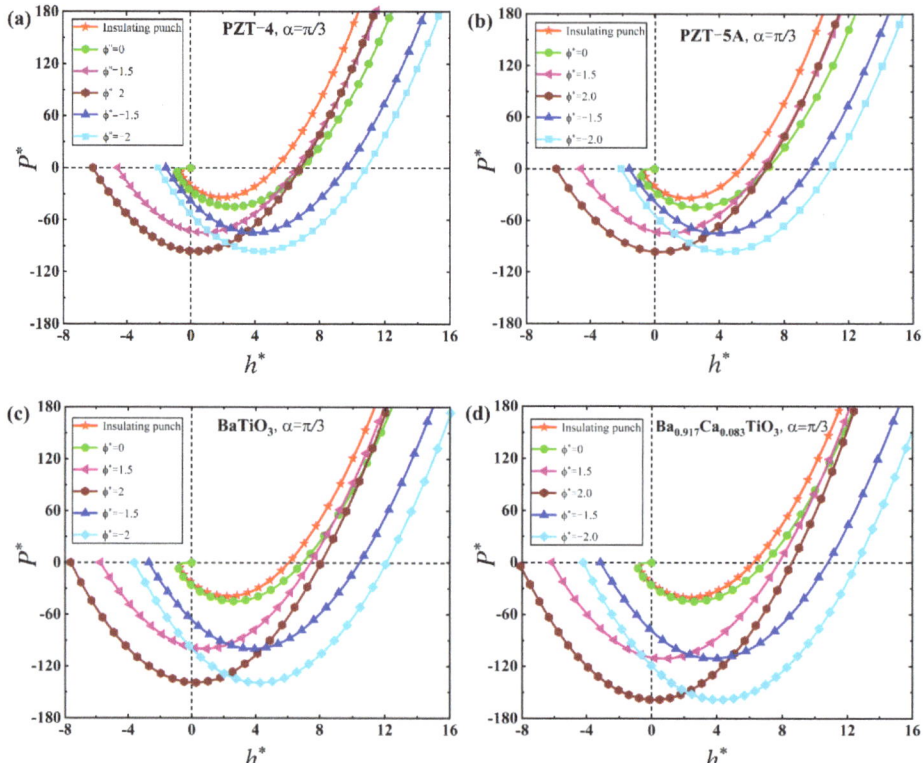

Figure 6. The dimensionless indentation force, P^*, as a function of the dimensionless indentation depth, h^*, at a fixed value of $\alpha = \pi/3$ for the JKR model. (**a**) PZT-4. (**b**) PZT-5A. (**c**) BaTiO$_3$. (**d**) Ba$_{0.917}$Ca$_{0.083}$TiO$_3$.

It can be seen from Figure 6 that the $P^* \sim h^*$ curves of the conducting punch are always below the corresponding curves of the insulating punch, which yields two main conclusions. First, the pull-off force under force control for the conducting punch is always larger than the counterpart value of the insulating punch, which is consistent with the conclusions derived from Figures 3 and 4. Second, for a given indentation force, the indentation depth under the action of the insulating punch is always smaller than the counterpart value for the conducting punch. In contrast, for a given indentation depth, the indentation force exerted on the insulating punch is larger than the counterpart value applied to the conducting punch. The above results can serve as the theoretical foundation for the nanoindentation technique in characterizing the mechanical and adhesion properties of piezoelectric materials. By comparing the results shown in Figure 6a–d, one can conclude that the effect of the electric potential on the adhesion behaviors of $BaTiO_3$ and $Ba_{0.917}Ca_{0.083}TiO_3$ was more prominent than that on PZT-4 and PZT-5A, which is attributed to the different material properties of the four piezoelectric materials examined here. This also reveals that the effect of the electric potential on $P^* \sim h^*$ curve is largely dependent on different material properties, which was not derived in the existing studies on piezoelectric materials [60] and multiferroic composite materials [68,69].

Figures 7 and 8 present the effect of the half cone angle of a conical punch on the variation of the dimensionless indentation force, P^*, with the dimensionless indentation depth, h^*. One can see in Figure 7 that the pull-off force increases with the half cone angle for both the insulating and conducting conical punches, which is consistent with the conclusions obtained from Figures 4 and 5. It is noteworthy that the $P^* \sim h^*$ curve lies almost entirely on the positive semi-axis of P^* for the very sharp punch (i.e., $\alpha \leq \pi/6$), which suggests that the adhesion effect is very weak in this case. Therefore, a conical punch with a small half cone angle should be adopted in nanoindentation tests, as this can weaken the adhesion effect and improve the accuracy of the results of characterization.

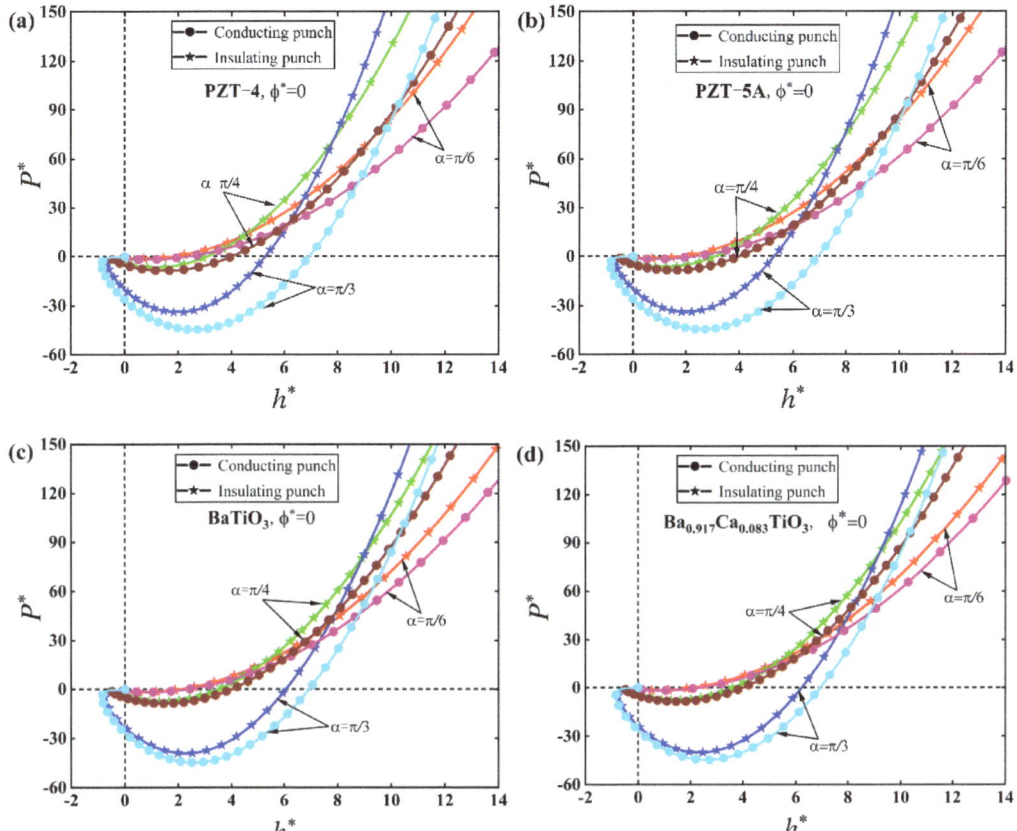

Figure 7. Variation of the dimensionless indentation force, P^*, with the dimensionless indentation depth h^* at the different values of $\alpha = \pi/6, \pi/4$ and $\pi/3$ for the conducting punch with zero electric potential and the insulating punch. (**a**) PZT-4. (**b**) PZT-5A. (**c**) $BaTiO_3$. (**d**) $Ba_{0.917}Ca_{0.083}TiO_3$.

For the conducting punch with non-zero electric potential, the results shown in Figure 8 reveal that the adhesion strengthening effect induced by increasing the half cone angle of the conical punch becomes more prominent. It can be seen in Figures 7 and 8 that the $P^* \sim h^*$ curves for the four different piezoelectric materials examined here are very similar, which suggests that the effect of the half cone angle on the load-displacement curves is insensitive to material properties, which was not revealed in the existing studies on piezoelectric materials [60] and multiferroic composite materials [68,69]. Furthermore, one can see from Figure 7 that the load-displacement curves under the conical indenters with different half cone angles have very different slopes, which indicates that the half cone angle can significantly affect the characterization of mechanical properties in nanoindentation tests.

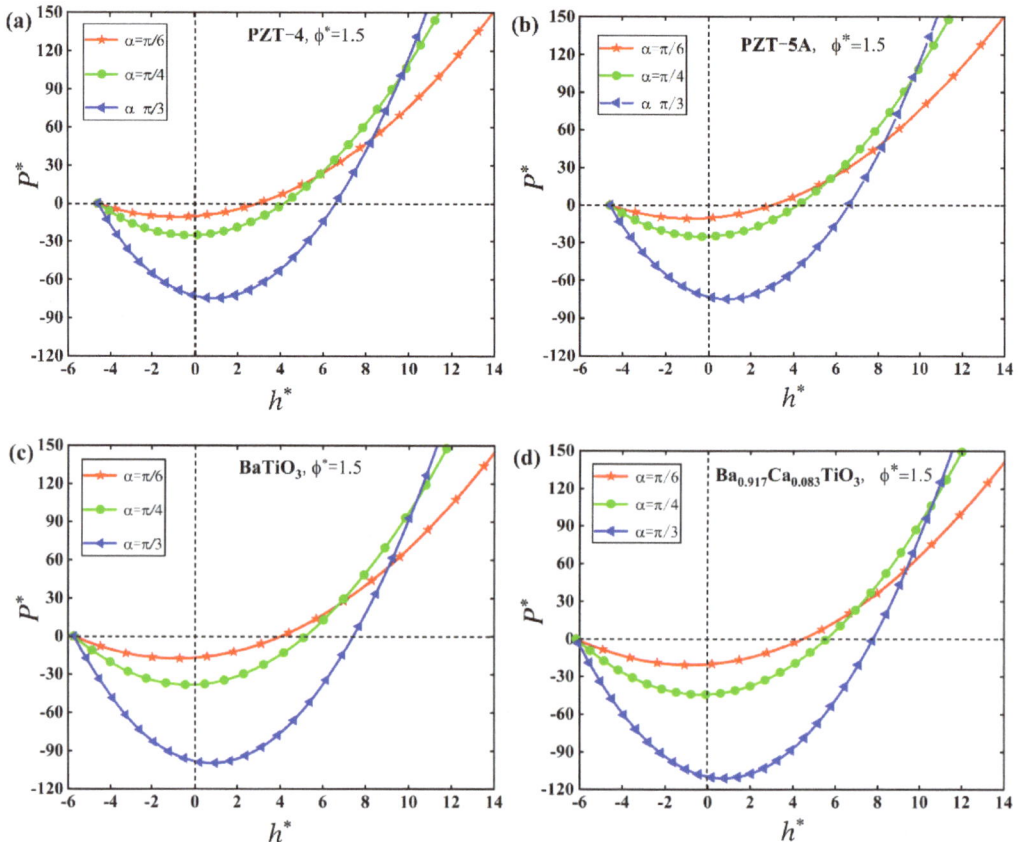

Figure 8. The dimensionless indentation force, P^*, as a function of the dimensionless indentation, h^*, at the different values of $\alpha = \pi/6, \pi/4$ and $\pi/3$ for the conducting punch with non-zero electric potential ($\phi^* = 1.5$). (**a**) PZT-4. (**b**) PZT-5A. (**c**) BaTiO$_3$. (**d**) Ba$_{0.917}$Ca$_{0.083}$TiO$_3$.

Figure 9 illustrates the influence of the dimensionless electric potential, ϕ^*, on the variation of the dimensionless contact radius, a^*, with the dimensionless indentation depth, h^*. The results reveal that the electric potential has a prominent effect on the relation between the contact radius and the indentation depth. It is worth noting that the $a^* \sim h^*$ curves for the conducting punch are always above the corresponding curve for the insulating punch, which indicates that for a given indentation depth, the contact radius under the action of the conducting punch is always larger than the counterpart value of the insulating punch. Furthermore, for the insulating punch and the conducting punch with zero electric potential, one can determine that the critical contact radius at pull-off moment is a finite value under displacement control. In contrast, the pull-off moment happens when the contact radius decreases to zero for the conducting punch. However, the correctness of these conclusions should be verified by corresponding experimental studies in the future.

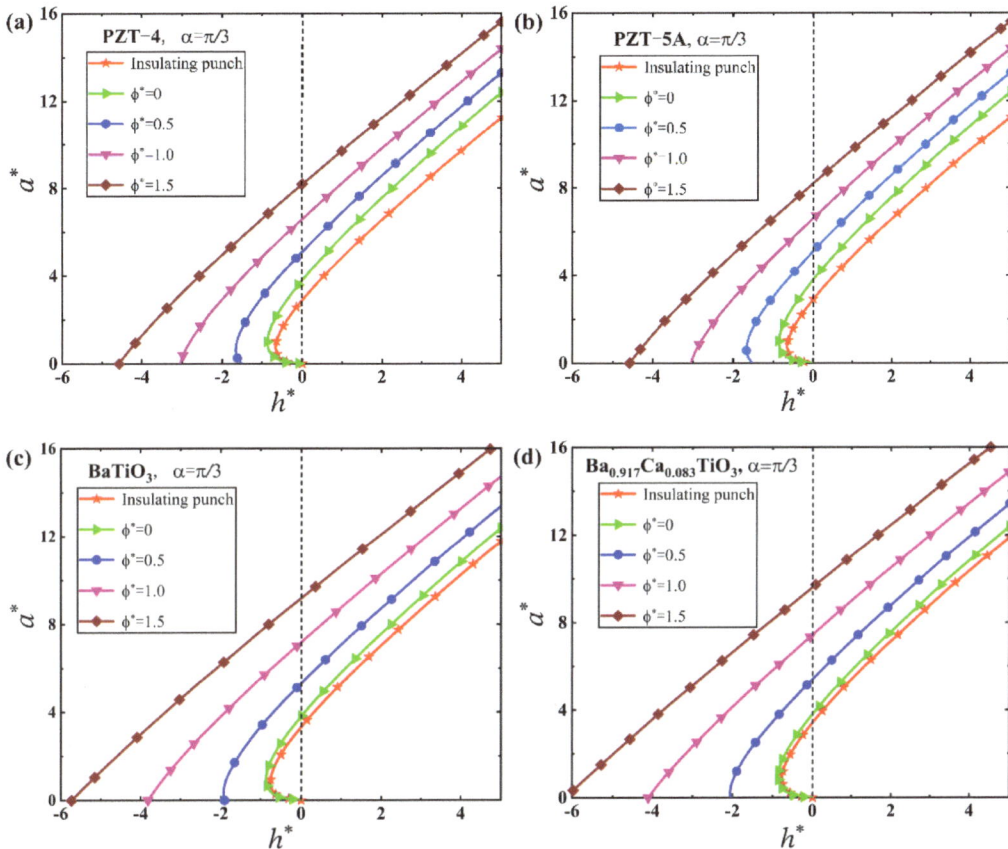

Figure 9. The dimensionless contact radius, a^*, as a function of the dimensionless indentation depth, h^*, at a fixed value of $\alpha = \pi/3$ for the JKR model. (**a**) PZT-4. (**b**) PZT-5A. (**c**) BaTiO$_3$. (**d**) Ba$_{0.917}$Ca$_{0.083}$TiO$_3$.

The effect of the half cone angle on the variation of the dimensionless contact radius as a function of the dimensionless indentation depth is shown in Figures 10 and 11. It can be seen in Figure 10 that for a given indentation depth, the larger the half cone angle, the larger the contact radius for both the insulating and conducting punches, which is easy to understand. In the case of a punch with the same half cone angle and indentation depth, the contact radius for the conducting punch is always larger than the counterpart value for the insulating punch, and the difference between them increases with increases in the half cone angle. By comparing the results displayed in Figures 10 and 11, one can determine that the half cone angle has a more prominent effect on the variation of the dimensionless contact radius with the dimensionless indentation depth when a piezoelectric solid is indented by a conducting punch with non-zero electric potential. Furthermore, the $a^* \sim h^*$ curves for the four different piezoelectric materials presented in Figures 10 and 11 are very similar, which also means that the effect of the half cone angle on the relation between the contact radius and indentation depth is insensitive to material properties.

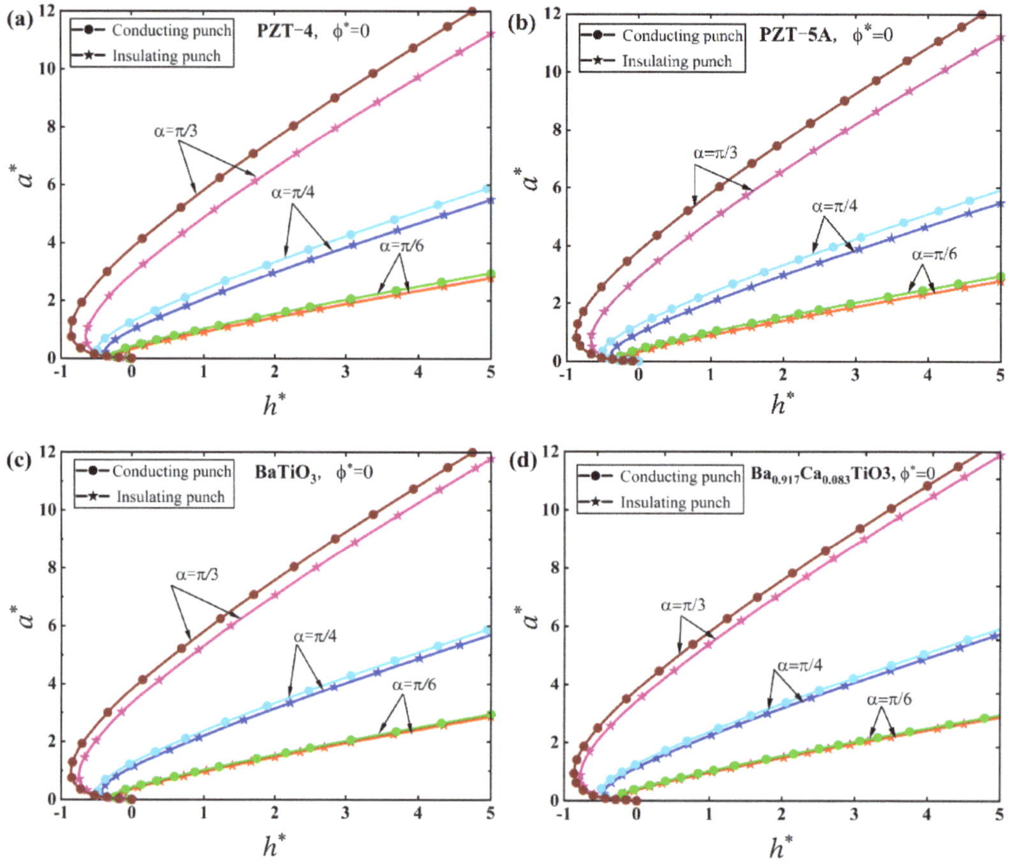

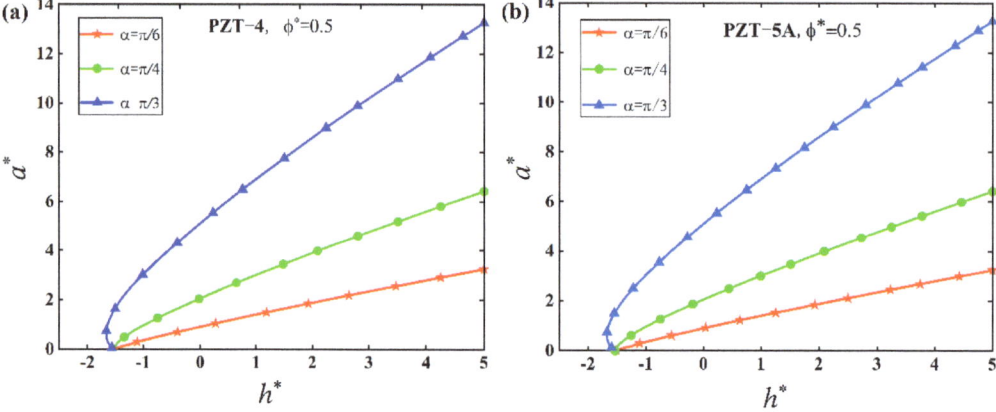

Figure 10. Variation of the dimensionless contact radius, a^*, with the dimensionless indentation depth, h^*, at the different values of $\alpha = \pi/6, \pi/4$ and $\pi/3$ for the conducting punch with zero electric potential and the insulating punch. (**a**) PZT-4. (**b**) PZT-5A. (**c**) BaTiO$_3$. (**d**) Ba$_{0.917}$Ca$_{0.083}$TiO$_3$.

Figure 11. *Cont.*

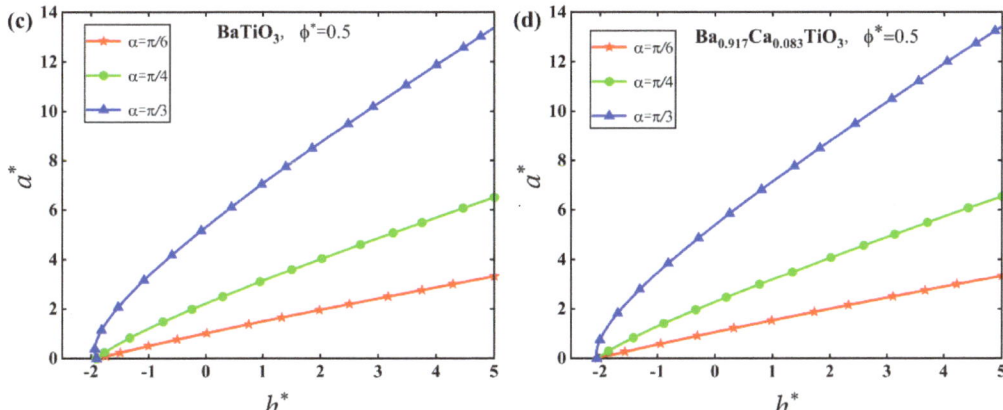

Figure 11. Variation of the dimensionless contact radius, a^*, with the dimensionless indentation depth, h^*, at different values of $\alpha = \pi/6, \pi/4$ and $\pi/3$ for the conducting punch with non-zero electric potential ($\phi^* = 0.5$). (**a**) PZT-4. (**b**) PZT-5A. (**c**) BaTiO$_3$. (**d**) Ba$_{0.917}$Ca$_{0.083}$TiO$_3$.

Figure 12 presents the effect of the electric potential on the pull-off force of different piezoelectric adhesion systems. It can be seen in Figure 12 that the electric potential has a very significant effect on the pull-off force of the piezoelectric adhesion system. For the four different piezoelectric materials considered here, the dimensionless pull-off force increases by more than two times as the absolute value of the dimensionless electric potential increases from 0 to 2. This result embodies the adhesion strengthening effect induced by the electric potential, which is in agreement with the experimental result given by [82]. In addition, one can also determine that the pull-off force for the conducting punch is always larger than the counterpart value of the insulating punch. The variation of the dimensionless pull-off force as a function of the half cone angle of the conical punch is shown in Figure 13. The results reveal that the magnitude of the pull-off force increases with the half cone angle and finally approaches infinity in the limit case $\alpha = \pi/2$, which is consistent with the result given by a multiferroic half-space indented by a rigid conical punch [69]. In the limit case of $\alpha = \pi/2$, the rigid conical punch becomes the semi-infinite rigid punch. By comparing the results presented in Figure 13a–d, one can conclude that the effect of the half cone angle on the pull-off force is insensitive to the material properties.

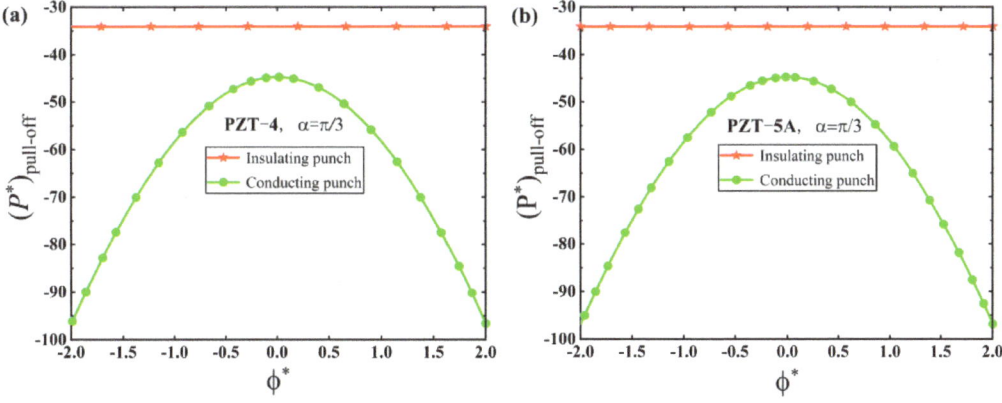

Figure 12. *Cont.*

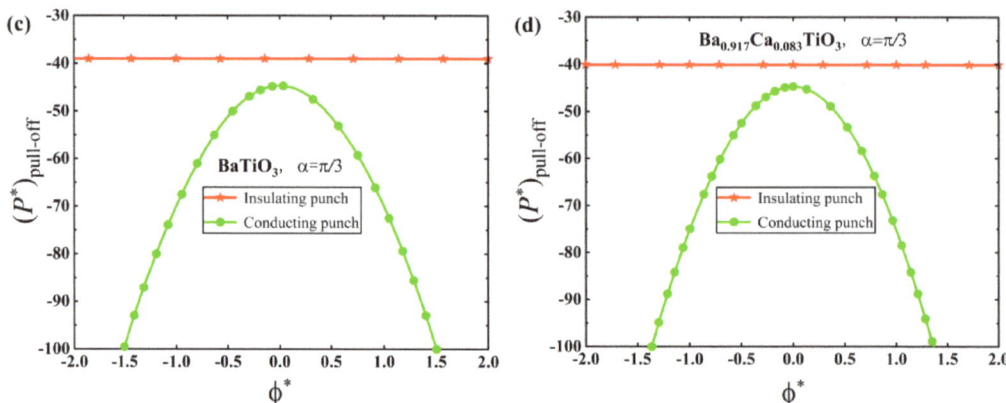

Figure 12. Variation of the dimensionless pull-off force, $P^*_{\text{pull-off}}$, with the dimensionless electric potential, ϕ^*, at a fixed value of $\alpha = \pi/3$. (**a**) PZT-4. (**b**) PZT-5A. (**c**) BaTiO$_3$. (**d**) Ba$_{0.917}$Ca$_{0.083}$TiO$_3$.

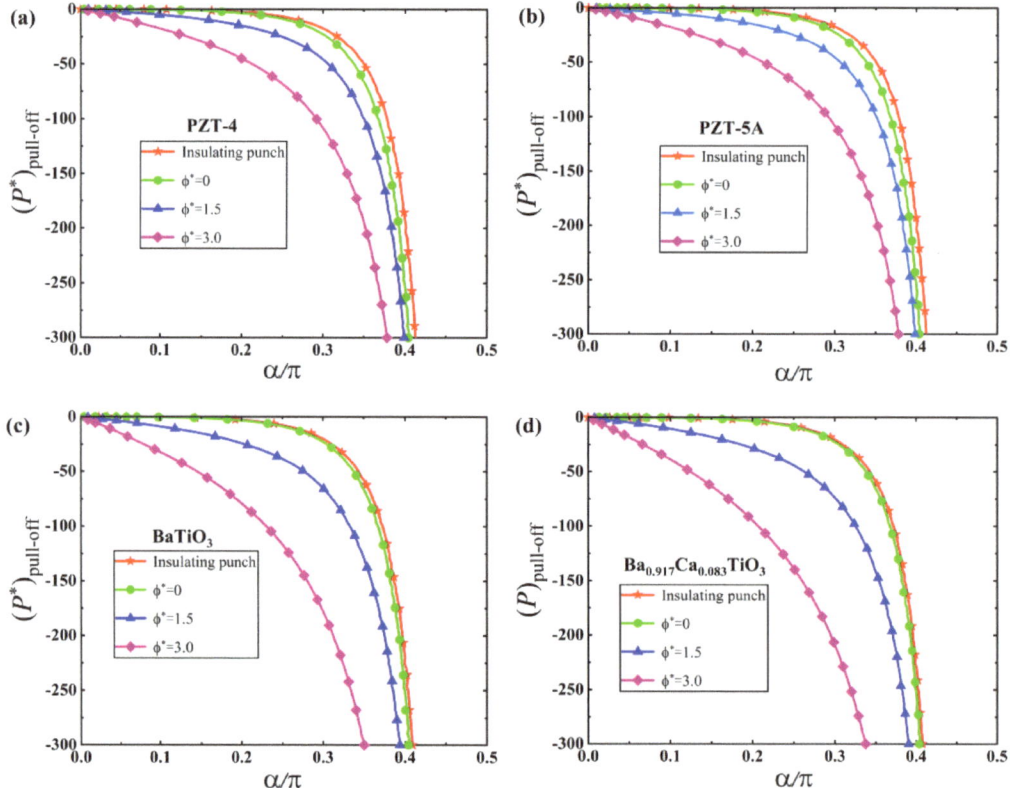

Figure 13. The dimensionless pull-off force, $P^*_{\text{pull-off}}$, as a function of the half cone angle of the rigid conical punch, α/π, for the JKR model. (**a**) PZT-4. (**b**) PZT-5A. (**c**) BaTiO$_3$. (**d**) Ba$_{0.917}$Ca$_{0.083}$TiO$_3$.

5.2. M-D Solutions

Figure 14 displays the variation of the dimensionless parameter $m = c/a$ as a function of the dimensionless contact radius, a^*, for the M-D model. It is shown that the transition parameter, λ, and the dimensionless electric potential, ϕ^*, have significant effects on the physical quantity, m, whose value reflects the size of the cohesive zone. The results presented in Figure 14a indicate that the dimensionless parameter, m, diminishes as the transition parameter, λ, and the dimensionless contact radius, a^*, increase. When the transition parameter, λ, increases, which can be understood as the adhesion force increasing, then the dimensionless parameter, m, decreases, i.e., the cohesive zone outside the contact region diminishes. In Figure 14b, one can see that for a given transition parameter, λ, and a dimensionless contact radius, a^*, the larger the electric potential, the larger the value of m is, which reveals that the adhesion effect can be strengthened by applying the electric potential.

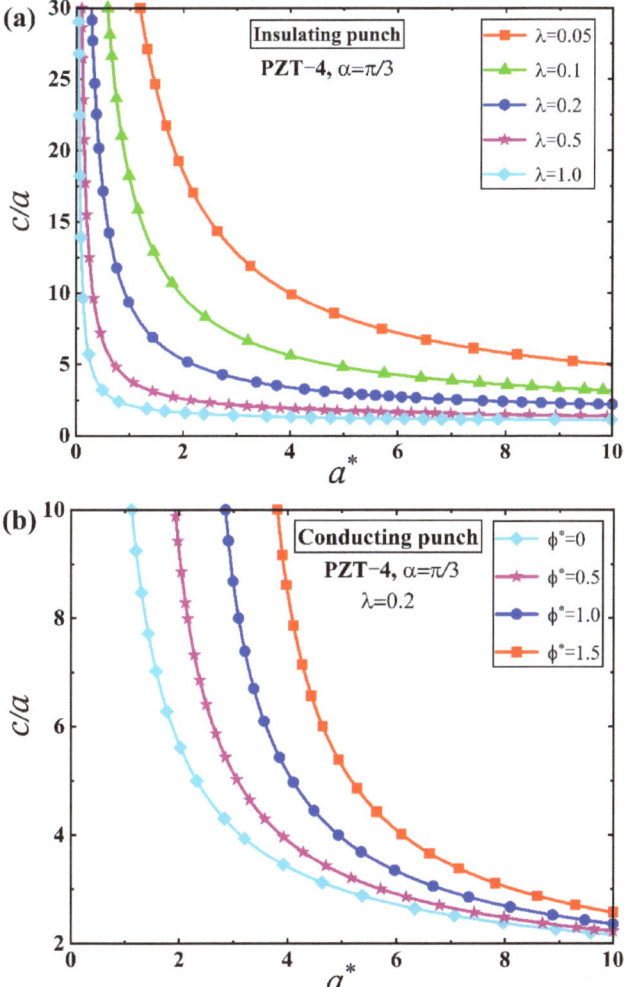

Figure 14. Variation of c/a with the dimensionless contact radius, a^*. (**a**) The effect of the transition parameter, λ. (**b**) The effect of the dimensionless electric potential, ϕ^*.

Figures 15 and 16 illustrate the variation of the dimensionless contact radius, a^*, with the dimensionless indentation force, P^*, under the action of the insulating punch and the conducting punch with non-zero electric potential based on the M-D model, respectively. It can be found that for both the insulating punch and the conducting punch with non-zero electric potential, as the transition parameter, λ, increases from 0.1 to 2.0, the $a^* \sim P^*$ curve for the M-D model then can be approximated by the corresponding curve in the JKR model. This suggests that the $a^* \sim P^*$ curve in the JKR model can be regarded as the limit case of the corresponding solution for the M-D model, which has been verified by theoretical derivation in Appendix F.

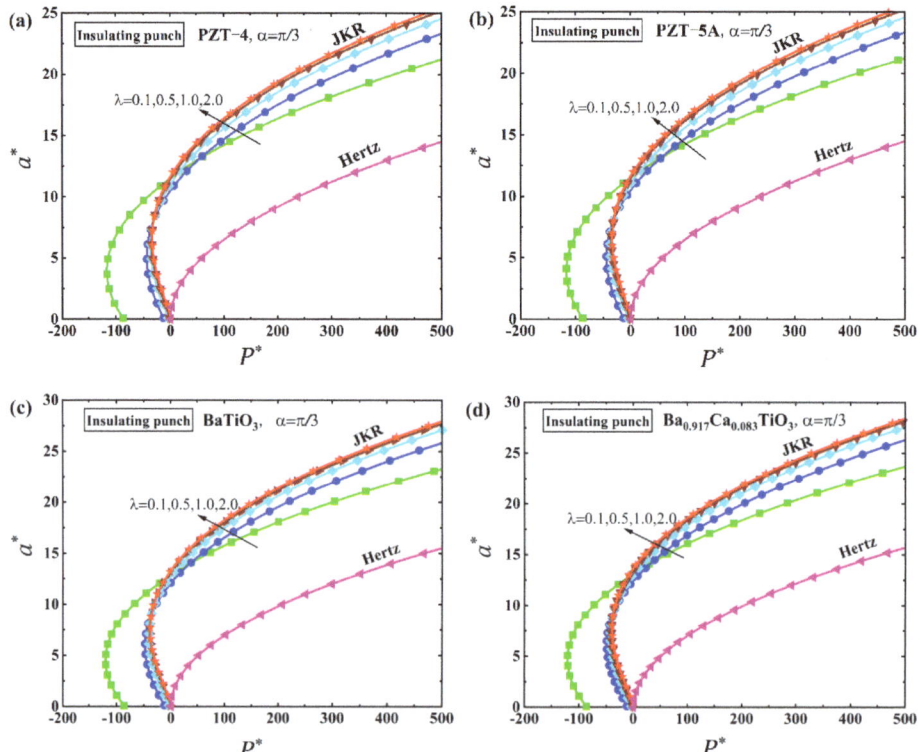

Figure 15. The dimensionless contact radius, a^*, as a function of the dimensionless indentation force, P^*, under the action of an insulating punch for the M-D model. (**a**) PZT-4. (**b**) PZT-5A. (**c**) BaTiO$_3$. (**d**) Ba$_{0.917}$Ca$_{0.083}$TiO$_3$.

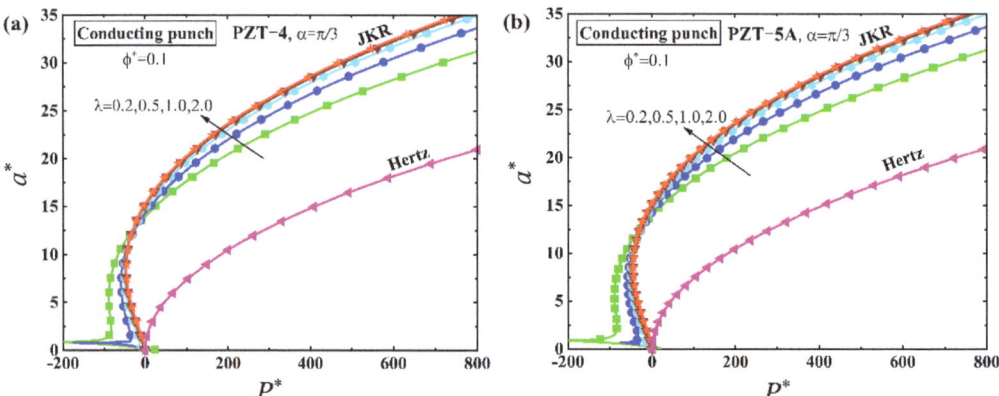

Figure 16. *Cont.*

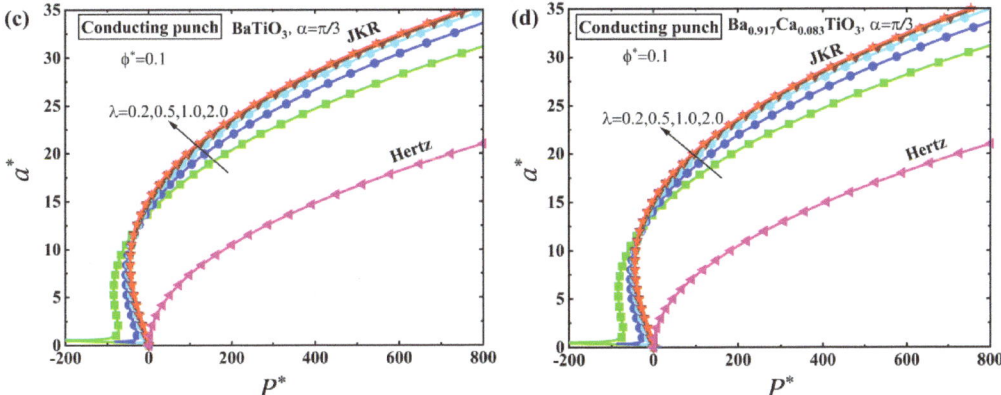

Figure 16. The dimensionless indentation force, P^*, as a function of the dimensionless indentation depth, h^*, under the action of a conducting punch for the M-D model. (**a**) PZT-4. (**b**) PZT-5A. (**c**) BaTiO$_3$. (**d**) Ba$_{0.917}$Ca$_{0.083}$TiO$_3$.

The variations of the dimensionless indentation force, P^*, with the dimensionless indentation depth, h^*, for the insulating punch and the conducting punch with a constant electric potential are shown in Figures 17 and 18, respectively. It is seen that for both the insulating punch and the conducting punch with non-zero electric potential, when the transition parameter, λ, changes from 0.2 to 2.0, the $P^* \sim h^*$ curves for the M-D model can be approximated by the corresponding curves in the JKR model. Similarly, the $a^* \sim h^*$ curves for the M-D model can also be replaced by the corresponding results in the JKR model when the transition parameter changes from 0.2 to 2.0, as shown in Figures 19 and 20. This reveals that the JKR solutions can be regarded as the limit case, which can be degenerated from the corresponding solutions in M-D model. This conclusion has also been verified through rigorous theoretical derivation in Appendix F.

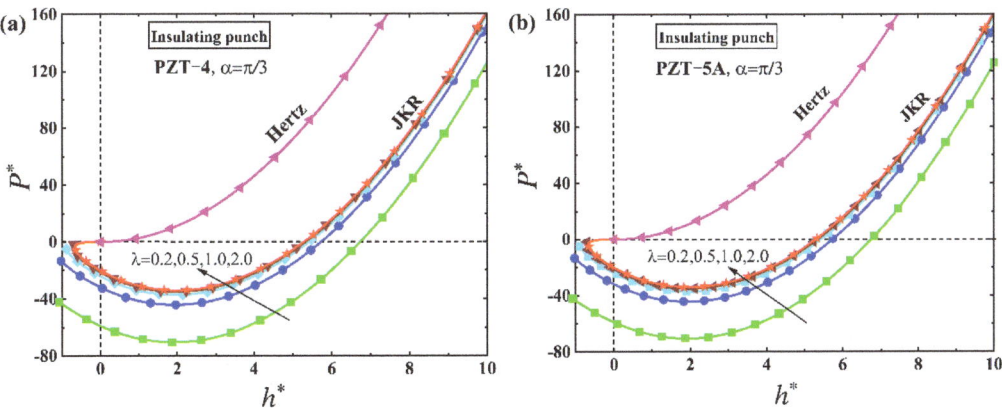

Figure 17. *Cont.*

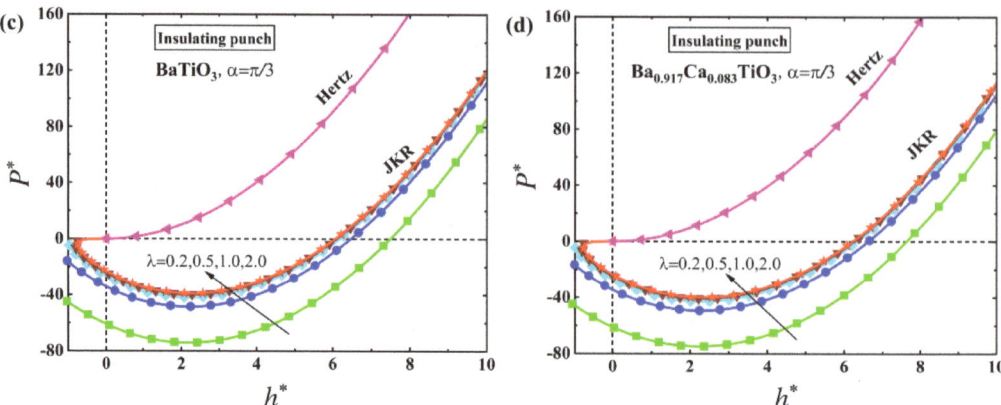

Figure 17. The dimensionless indentation force, P^*, as a function of the dimensionless indentation depth, h^*, under the action of an insulating punch for the M-D model. (**a**) PZT-4. (**b**) PZT-5A. (**c**) BaTiO$_3$. (**d**) Ba$_{0.917}$Ca$_{0.083}$TiO$_3$.

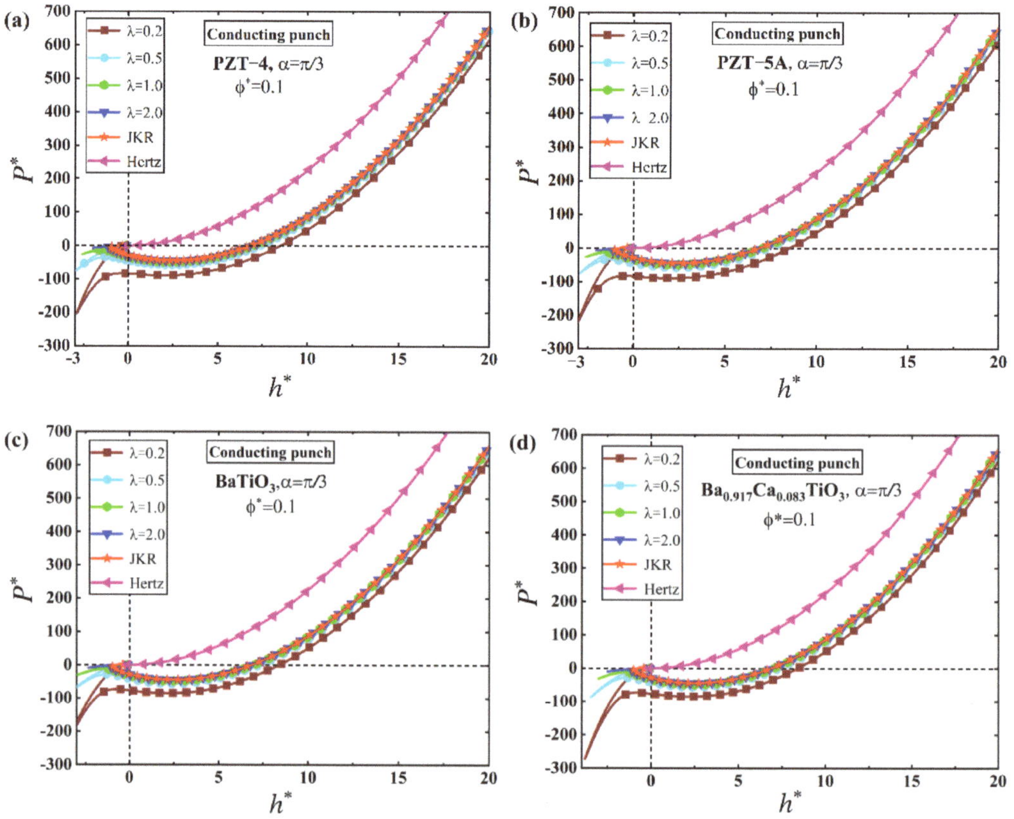

Figure 18. The dimensionless indentation force, P^*, as a function of the dimensionless indentation depth, h^*, under the action of a conducting punch for the M-D model. (**a**) PZT-4. (**b**) PZT-5A. (**c**) BaTiO$_3$. (**d**) Ba$_{0.917}$Ca$_{0.083}$TiO$_3$.

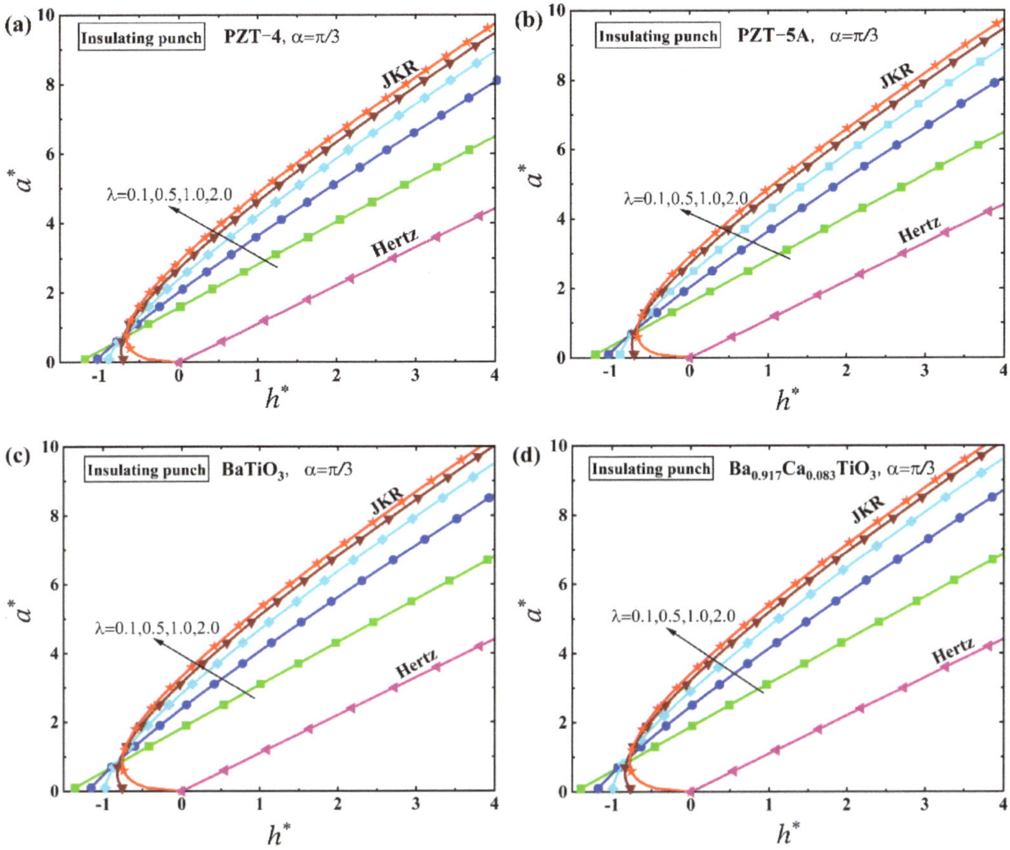

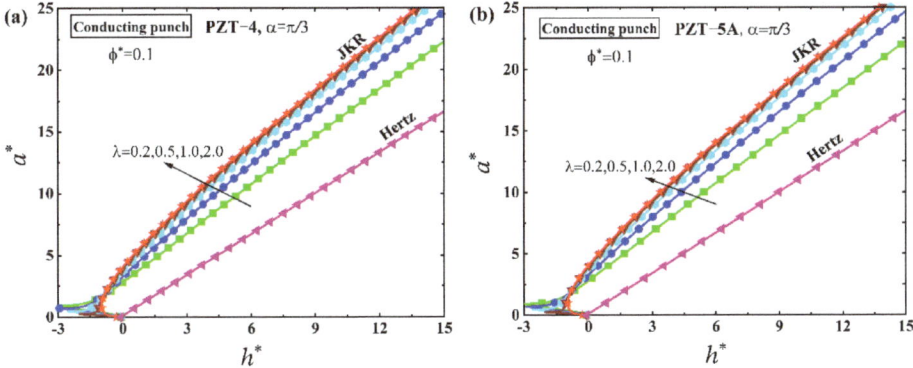

Figure 19. The dimensionless contact radius, a^*, as a function of the dimensionless indentation depth, h^*, under the action of an insulating punch for the M-D model. (**a**) PZT-4. (**b**) PZT-5A. (**c**) BaTiO$_3$. (**d**) Ba$_{0.917}$Ca$_{0.083}$TiO$_3$.

Figure 20. *Cont.*

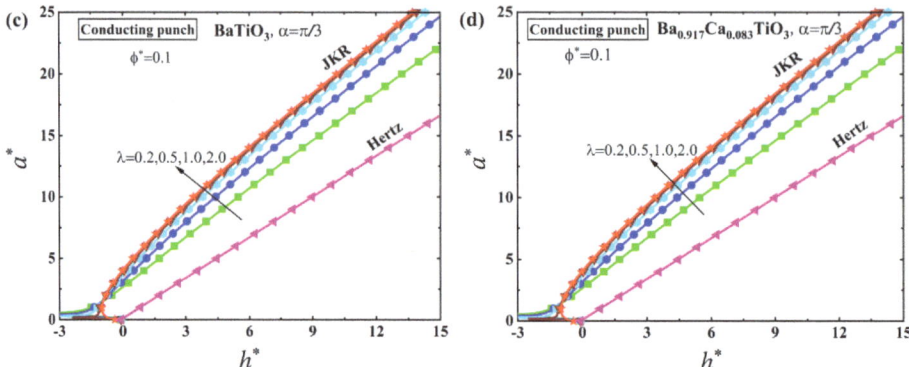

Figure 20. The dimensionless contact radius, a^*, as a function of the dimensionless indentation depth, h^*, under the action of a conducting punch for the M-D model. (**a**) PZT-4. (**b**) PZT-5A. (**c**) BaTiO$_3$. (**d**) Ba$_{0.917}$Ca$_{0.083}$TiO$_3$.

6. Conclusions

The adhesive contact problem between a rigid conical punch and a transversely isotropic piezoelectric solid was studied in this work. The classical adhesion theories were extended to investigate the contact behaviors of various piezoelectric materials indented by conical punches with different electric properties. The closed-form solutions for the JKR and M-D models were obtained by virtue of the Hankel integral transform, dual integral equations, and the superposing principle. The contribution of the electrical energy to the energy release rate under the conducting punch was taken into consideration. The relationships between the contact radius, the indentation load, and the indentation depth were established using the total energy method for the JKR model and the Griffith energy balance for the M-D model. The main conclusions can be summarized as follows:

(1) The adhesion effect between the tip of the conical punch and the piezoelectric solid can be enhanced by increasing the electric potential and the half cone angle of the punch, which suggests that a conical punch with a small half cone angle should be adopted in nanoindentation tests in order to reduce the effect of adhesion and improve the accuracy of characterization results.

(2) The effect of electric potential on adhesion behaviors is sensitive to different material properties, while the effect of the half cone angle of the conical punch on adhesion behaviors is insensitive to different material properties. These conclusions were made for the first time in this work.

(3) The load-displacement curves under the conical punch with different half cone angles have very different slopes, which indicates that the half cone angle of the conical punch can significantly affect the characterization of mechanical properties of piezoelectric solids in nanoindentation tests.

The results obtained from this paper can not only serve as the theoretical foundation for nanoindentation tests in characterizing the material properties of piezoelectric solids, but also offer new approaches to achieving reversible adhesion.

Author Contributions: Conceptualization, Y.Z., L.W. and S.D.; Methodology, Q.L. and Y.Z.; Investigation, Q.L.; Writing—original draft, Q.L.; Writing—review & editing, Q.L., Y.Z., L.W. and S.D.; Funding acquisition, Y.Z. All authors have read and agreed to the published version of the manuscript.

Funding: This work was supported by the National Natural Science Foundation of China (11972257, 12272269, 11832014 and 11472193), the China Scholarship Council (CSC), and the Fundamental Research Funds for the Central Universities (22120180223).

Conflicts of Interest: The authors declare no conflict of interest.

Appendix A. The Hertz Contact Solution

For the Hertz contact problem of a piezoelectric solid indented by a rigid punch, the analytical solutions of the full fields were obtained by [25]. For the convenience of referring and using, the corresponding results are presented in this section. The explicit expressions of the material constants $B_i (i = 1, 2, \ldots, 6)$ involved in this section and the following sections (Appendices B–E) are given as follows [25]:

$$B_1 = \frac{M_6 M_7 - M_5 M_8}{M_1 M_8 - M_2 M_7}, \quad B_2 = \frac{M_3 M_8 - M_4 M_7}{M_1 M_8 - M_2 M_7}, \quad B_3 = \frac{M_1 M_6 - M_2 M_5}{M_4 M_5 - M_3 M_6},$$
$$B_4 = \frac{M_6 M_3 - M_5 M_4}{M_1 M_4 - M_2 M_3}, \quad B_5 = \frac{M_3 M_8 - M_4 M_7}{M_1 M_4 - M_2 M_3}, \quad B_6 = \frac{M_1 M_8 - M_2 M_7}{M_3 M_8 - M_4 M_7}, \tag{A1}$$

where the explicit expressions of $M_i (i = 1, 2, \ldots, 8)$ can be found in Equation (A8) of [25].

Case I: electrically conducting punch

For the electrically conducting punch, the Hertz contact solutions can be obtained using the following equations:

$$\sigma_{zz}^H(r, 0) = -B_4 \cot \alpha \cosh^{-1} \frac{a}{r}, \tag{A2}$$

$$D_z^H(r, 0) = -B_5 \left[\cot \alpha \cosh^{-1} \frac{a}{r} - \frac{2(B_3 + B_6)\phi_0}{\pi \sqrt{a^2 - r^2}} \right], \tag{A3}$$

$$h^H = \frac{\pi}{2} a \cot \alpha - B_3 \phi_0, \quad P^H = B_4 \pi a^2 \cot \alpha, \tag{A4}$$

$$u_z^H(r, 0) = \begin{cases} h^H - r \cot \alpha, & 0 \leq r \leq a, \\ \frac{2h^H}{\pi} \sin^{-1} \frac{a}{r} + \cot \alpha \left(\sqrt{r^2 - a^2} - r \right), & r > a, \end{cases} \tag{A5}$$

$$\phi^H(r, 0) = \begin{cases} \phi_0, & 0 \leq r \leq a, \\ \frac{2\phi_0}{\pi} \sin^{-1} \frac{a}{r}, & r > a, \end{cases} \tag{A6}$$

$$[u_z^H(r, 0)] = f(r) - \delta + u_z^H(r, 0)$$
$$= \left(\frac{2 B_3 \phi_0}{\pi} - a \cot \alpha \right) \cos^{-1} \frac{a}{r} + \sqrt{r^2 - a^2} \cot \alpha, \quad r > a, \tag{A7}$$

$$\left[\phi^H(r, 0)\right] = \phi^H(r, 0) - \phi_0 = -\frac{2\phi_0}{\pi} \cos^{-1} \frac{a}{r}, \quad r > a. \tag{A8}$$

Case II: electrically insulating punch

When the rigid conical punch is electrically insulating, the corresponding solutions can be defined as

$$\sigma_{zz}^H(r, 0) = -B_1 \cot \alpha \cosh^{-1} \frac{a}{r}, \quad 0 \leq r < a \tag{A9}$$

$$h^H = \frac{\pi a \cot \alpha}{2}, \quad P^H = \pi a^2 B_1 \cot \alpha, \tag{A10}$$

$$u_z^H(r, 0) = \begin{cases} h^H - r \cot \alpha, & 0 \leq r \leq a, \\ \frac{2h^H}{\pi} \left(\sqrt{\frac{r^2}{a^2} - 1} - \frac{r}{a} + \sin^{-1} \frac{a}{r} \right), & r > a, \end{cases} \tag{A11}$$

$$\phi^H(r, 0) = \begin{cases} B_2 (h^H - r \cot \alpha), & 0 \leq r \leq a, \\ \frac{2 B_2 h^H}{\pi} \left(\sqrt{\frac{r^2}{a^2} - 1} - \frac{r}{a} + \sin^{-1} \frac{a}{r} \right), & r > a. \end{cases} \tag{A12}$$

$$\left[u_z^H(r,0)\right] = \sqrt{r^2 - a^2}\cot\alpha - a\cot\alpha \cos^{-1}\frac{a}{r}. \tag{A13}$$

Appendix B. The Boussinesq Contact Solution

For the Boussinesq contact problem, the corresponding solutions can be obtained as follows:

Case I: electrically conducting punch

$$\sigma_{zz}^B(r,0) = -\frac{P^B}{2\pi a\sqrt{a^2 - r^2}}, \quad r < a, \tag{A14}$$

$$D_z^B(r,0) = -\frac{2B_5(h^B - B_6\phi_0)}{\pi\sqrt{a^2 - r^2}}, \quad r < a, \tag{A15}$$

$$P^B = 4aB_4(h^B + B_3\phi_0), \tag{A16}$$

$$u_z^B(r,0) = \begin{cases} h^B, & r \leq a, \\ \frac{2h^B}{\pi}\sin^{-1}\frac{a}{r}, & r > a, \end{cases} \tag{A17}$$

$$\phi^B(r,0) = \begin{cases} \phi_0, & r \leq a, \\ \frac{2\phi_0}{\pi}\sin^{-1}\frac{a}{r}, & r > a. \end{cases} \tag{A18}$$

Case II: electrically insulating punch

$$\sigma_{zz}^B(r,0) = -\frac{P^B}{2\pi a\sqrt{a^2 - r^2}}, \quad r < a, \tag{A19}$$

$$P^B = 4aB_1h^B, \tag{A20}$$

$$u_z^B(r,0) = \begin{cases} h^B, & r \leq a, \\ \frac{2h^B}{\pi}\sin^{-1}\frac{a}{r}, & r > a, \end{cases} \tag{A21}$$

$$\phi^B(r,0) = \begin{cases} B_2h^B, & r \leq a, \\ \frac{2B_2h^B}{\pi}\sin^{-1}\frac{a}{r}, & r > a. \end{cases} \tag{A22}$$

Appendix C. The Solutions of the JKR Model for Case II

When the conical punch is electrically insulating, by superposing the Hertz contact solutions from Equations (A9)–(A13) and the Boussinesq contact solutions from Equations (A19)–(A22), one can determine that

$$h^{JKR} = \frac{\pi a \cot\alpha}{4} + \frac{P}{4B_1 a}, \tag{A23}$$

$$\sigma_{zz}^{JKR}(r,0) = -B_1\cot\alpha\cosh^{-1}\frac{a}{r} + \frac{B_1\cot\alpha \pi a^2 - P}{2\pi a\sqrt{a^2 - r^2}}, \tag{A24}$$

$$u_z^{JKR}(r,0) = \begin{cases} h^{JKR} - r\cot\alpha, & r \leq a, \\ \frac{2}{\pi}h^{JKR}\sin^{-1}\frac{a}{r} + \left(\sqrt{r^2 - a^2} - r\right)\cot\alpha, & r > a, \end{cases} \tag{A25}$$

$$\phi^{JKR}(r,0) = \begin{cases} B_2(h^{JKR} - r\cot\alpha), & r \leq a, \\ B_2\left[\frac{2}{\pi}h^{JKR}\sin^{-1}\frac{a}{r} + \left(\sqrt{r^2 - a^2} - r\right)\cot\alpha\right], & r > a, \end{cases} \tag{A26}$$

$$\begin{aligned}\left[u_z^{JKR}(r,0)\right] &= f(r) - h^{JKR} + u_z^{JKR}(r,0) \\ &= \sqrt{r^2 - a^2}\cot\alpha - \frac{2}{\pi}h^{JKR}\cos^{-1}\frac{a}{r}, \quad r > a.\end{aligned} \quad (A27)$$

For the rigid insulating indenter, the contribution of the electrical energy to the total free energy of the contact system is nil due to the lack of electric displacement within the contact region. Under these circumstances, the total free energy, U_T, is composed of three parts, including the elastic strain energy, U_E, the mechanical potential energy, U_P and the surface energy, U_S. As such, one can deduce that

$$U_T = U_E + U_P + U_S, \quad (A28)$$

They can be calculated as

$$U_E = -\frac{1}{2}\int_0^{2\pi}\int_0^a \sigma_{zz}(r,\theta,0)u_z^{JKR}(r,\theta,0)\,rdrd\theta = \frac{B_1\pi^2\cot^2\alpha a^3}{24} + \frac{P^2}{8B_1 a}, \quad (A29)$$

$$U_P = -\frac{\pi\cot\alpha}{4}Pa - \frac{P^2}{4B_1 a}, \quad (A30)$$

$$U_S = -\pi a^2 \Delta\gamma, \quad (A31)$$

In order to obtain the result in Equation (A29), the integral results shown in Equation (24) were used.

The equilibrium state of the contact system should satisfy the following condition:

$$\left.\frac{\partial U_T}{\partial a}\right|_P = 0. \quad (A32)$$

By inserting the results presented in Equations (A28)–(A31) into Equation (A32), one can obtain

$$P = \pi B_1 \cot\alpha\, a^2 \pm 4\sqrt{\pi\Delta\gamma B_1 a^3}. \quad (A33)$$

The stable equilibrium state of the contact system should satisfy the condition $\frac{\partial^2 U_T}{\partial a^2} > 0$, then one can determine that

$$P = \pi B_1 \cot\alpha\, a^2 - 4\sqrt{\pi\Delta\gamma B_1 a^3}. \quad (A34)$$

When piezoelectric materials degenerate into isotropic elastic solids, i.e., $B_1 = E^*/2$ (E^* is the equivalent elastic modulus), Equation (A34) can be rewritten as

$$P = \frac{\pi E^* \cot\alpha}{2}a^2 - \sqrt{8\pi\Delta\gamma E^* a^3}, \quad (A35)$$

which is the same as the result of Equation (17) obtained in [78].

Considering the following condition:

$$\frac{dP}{da} = 0, \quad (A36)$$

substituting Equation (A34) into Equation (A36) yields

$$a_{\text{pull-off}} = \frac{9\Delta\gamma}{\pi B_1 \cot^2\alpha}, \quad (A37)$$

which is the critical contact radius at the pull-off moment. By inserting this result into Equation (A34), one can define the explicit expression of the pull-off force as

$$P_{\text{pull-off}} = -\frac{27\Delta\gamma^2}{\pi B_1 \cot^3 \alpha}. \tag{A38}$$

If the piezoelectric materials degenerate into isotropic elastic solids, one can obtain

$$P_{\text{pull-off}} = -\frac{54\Delta\gamma^2}{\pi E^* \cot^3 \alpha}, \tag{A39}$$

This result is consistent with that of Equation (16) defined in [78].

Appendix D. The Solutions of the M-D Model for Case II

The JKR solutions for a piezoelectric solid indented by a rigid insulating conical punch are presented in Equations (A23)–(A27). If we define that

$$K_I = \lim_{r \to a} \sqrt{2\pi(a-r)} \sigma_{zz}(r,0) = \frac{P^H - P}{2a\sqrt{\pi a}}, \tag{A40}$$

where P^H is the apparent Hertz load, then the stress distribution in Equation (A24) can be rewritten as follows:

$$\sigma_{zz}^{JKR}(r,0) = -B_1 \cot \alpha \cos h^{-1} \frac{a}{r} + \frac{K_I}{\sqrt{\pi a}} \frac{a}{\sqrt{a^2 - r^2}}. \tag{A41}$$

The solutions of the external circular crack subjected to a uniform pressure, p_0, on the crack surfaces are presented in Appendix E. By substituting $p_0 = -\sigma_0$ into Equations (A98), (A102), and (A106), one can obtain

$$\sigma_{zz}(r,0) = \begin{cases} \frac{K_m}{\sqrt{\pi a}} \frac{a}{\sqrt{a^2 - r^2}} + \frac{2\sigma_0}{\pi} \tan^{-1} \sqrt{\frac{c^2 - a^2}{a^2 - r^2}}, & r < a, \\ \sigma_0, & a < r < c, \end{cases} \tag{A42}$$

$$u_T = -\frac{2\sigma_0}{B_1 \pi} \left[\sqrt{c^2 - a^2} \left(\sqrt{\frac{r^2}{a^2} - 1} - \cos^{-1} \frac{a}{r} \right) - c^2 \int_a^{\min(r,c)} \frac{\sqrt{r^2 - t^2}}{t^2 \sqrt{c^2 - t^2}} dt \right] \\ + \frac{K_m \sqrt{\pi a}}{B_1 \pi} \cos^{-1} \frac{a}{r}, \quad r > a, \tag{A43}$$

$$\delta' = \frac{\sigma_0 a}{2B_1} \left(\frac{c^2}{a^2} \cos^{-1} \frac{a}{c} - \sqrt{\frac{c^2}{a^2} - 1} \right), \tag{A44}$$

where

$$K_m = -\frac{\sigma_0}{\sqrt{\pi a}} \left(\sqrt{c^2 - a^2} + \frac{c^2}{a} \cos^{-1} \frac{a}{c} \right). \tag{A45}$$

Superposing Equations (A41) and (A42) yields

$$\sigma_{zz}^{M-D}(r,0) = \begin{cases} \frac{K_m + K_I}{\sqrt{\pi a}} \frac{a}{\sqrt{a^2 - r^2}} - B_1 \cot \alpha \cos h^{-1} \frac{a}{r} \\ + \frac{2\sigma_0}{\pi} \tan^{-1} \sqrt{\frac{c^2 - a^2}{a^2 - r^2}} & r < a, \\ \sigma_0, & a < r < c. \end{cases} \tag{A46}$$

According to the classical M-D theory [57], in order to eliminate the stress singularity at the contact periphery, the following condition should be satisfied:

$$K_I + K_m = 0 \Rightarrow K_I = -K_m \Rightarrow \frac{P^H - P}{2a\sqrt{\pi a}} = \frac{\sigma_0}{\sqrt{\pi a}} \left(\sqrt{c^2 - a^2} + \frac{c^2}{a} \cos^{-1} \frac{a}{c} \right). \tag{A47}$$

From Equation (A47), one can obtain

$$P^{M-D} = P^H - 2\sigma_0 a\left(\sqrt{c^2 - a^2} + \frac{c^2}{a}\cos^{-1}\frac{a}{c}\right)$$
$$= B_1 \cot\alpha \pi a^2 - 2\sigma_0 a\left(\sqrt{c^2 - a^2} + \frac{c^2}{a}\cos^{-1}\frac{a}{c}\right). \quad (A48)$$

Using the continuity condition in Equation (A47), the stress distribution given by Equation (A46) can be simplified as follows:

$$\sigma_{zz}^{M-D}(r,0) = \begin{cases} -B_1 \cot\alpha \cosh^{-1}\frac{a}{r} + \frac{2\sigma_0}{\pi}\tan^{-1}\sqrt{\frac{c^2-a^2}{a^2-r^2}}, & r < a, \\ \sigma_0, & a < r < c. \end{cases} \quad (A49)$$

By adding Equation (A23) to Equation (A28) and using the result in Equation (A48), one obtains

$$h^{M-D} = \frac{\pi a \cot\alpha}{4} + \frac{P}{4B_1 a} + \frac{\sigma_0 a}{2B_1}\left(\frac{c^2}{a^2}\cos^{-1}\frac{a}{c} - \sqrt{\frac{c^2}{a^2} - 1}\right)$$
$$= \frac{\pi a \cot\alpha}{2} - \frac{\sigma_0}{B_1}\sqrt{c^2 - a^2}. \quad (A50)$$

Using the result in Equation (A40), Equation (A23) can be rewritten as

$$h^{JKR} = \frac{\pi a \cot\alpha}{2} - \frac{K_I \sqrt{\pi a}}{2B_1}. \quad (A51)$$

Inserting Equation (A51) into Equation (A27), one can obtain

$$\left[u_z^{JKR}(r,0)\right] = \sqrt{r^2 - a^2}\cot\alpha - a\cot\alpha\cos^{-1}\frac{a}{r}$$
$$+ \frac{K_I \sqrt{\pi a}}{B_1 \pi}\cos^{-1}\frac{a}{r}, \quad r > a. \quad (A52)$$

By superposing Equation (A43) and (A52), considering the continuity condition in Equation (A47), one obtains

$$\left[u_z^{M-D}(r,0)\right] = \sqrt{r^2 - a^2}\cot\alpha - a\cot\alpha\cos^{-1}\frac{a}{r}$$
$$- \frac{2\sigma_0}{B_1 \pi}\left[\sqrt{c^2 - a^2}\left(\sqrt{\frac{r^2}{a^2} - 1} - \cos^{-1}\frac{a}{r}\right) - c^2 \int_a^{\min(r,c)} \frac{\sqrt{r^2-t^2}}{t^2\sqrt{c^2-t^2}}dt\right], \quad r > a. \quad (A53)$$

Using Equation (A53), the discontinuity displacement can be defined as

$$\delta_t = \left[u_z^{M-D}(c,0)\right] = \left(\sqrt{m^2 - 1} - \cos^{-1}\frac{1}{m}\right)a\cot\alpha$$
$$+ \frac{2\sigma_0 a}{B_1 \pi}\left(\sqrt{m^2 - 1}\cos^{-1}\frac{1}{m} - m + 1\right), \quad (A54)$$

where $m = c/a$.

Using the relation in Equation (A121), Equation (A54) can be rewritten as

$$\delta_t = \left(\sqrt{m^2 - 1} - \tan^{-1}\sqrt{m^2 - 1}\right)a\cot\alpha$$
$$+ \frac{2\sigma_0 a}{B_1 \pi}\left(\sqrt{m^2 - 1}\tan^{-1}\sqrt{m^2 - 1} - m + 1\right). \quad (A55)$$

When the complicated adhesion force is simplified by using the Dugdale cohesive model [79], one can obtain the following relation:

$$J = G = \sigma_0 \delta_t = \Delta\gamma, \quad (A56)$$

where J, G and $\Delta\gamma$ denote the J-integral, energy release rate and work of adhesion, respectively.

By substituting Equation (A55) into Equation (A56), one can obtain

$$\left(\sqrt{m^2-1}-\tan^{-1}\sqrt{m^2-1}\right)\sigma_0 a \cot\alpha \\ + \frac{2\sigma_0^2 a}{B_1 \pi}\left(\sqrt{m^2-1}\tan^{-1}\sqrt{m^2-1}-m+1\right) = \Delta\gamma. \tag{A57}$$

In the subsequent analysis, the correctness of these solutions will be verified by checking whether the corresponding JKR solutions presented in Appendix C can be degenerated as the limiting case from the M-D solutions obtained in this section.

First, from Equation (A47), one can obtain

$$K_I = \frac{\sigma_0}{\sqrt{\pi a}}\left(\sqrt{c^2-a^2}+\frac{c^2}{a}\cos^{-1}\frac{a}{c}\right) = \frac{\sigma_0 a}{\sqrt{\pi a}}\left(\sqrt{m^2-1}+m^2\cos^{-1}\frac{1}{m}\right). \tag{A58}$$

Using the relation in Equation (A121), Equation (A58) can be rewritten as

$$\frac{K_I\sqrt{\pi a}}{\sigma_0 a} = \sqrt{m^2-1}+m^2\tan^{-1}\sqrt{m^2-1}. \tag{A59}$$

When $m \to 1$, $\tan^{-1}\sqrt{m^2-1} \sim \sqrt{m^2-1}$, then

$$\frac{K_I\sqrt{\pi a}}{\sigma_0 a} \approx 2\sqrt{m^2-1}. \tag{A60}$$

Using Equation (A60), the stress distribution in Equation (A49) can be expressed as follows:

$$\sigma_{zz}^{M-D}(\rho,0) = \begin{cases} -B_1 \cot\alpha\cosh^{-1}\frac{1}{\rho}+\frac{2\sigma_0}{\pi}\tan^{-1}\sqrt{\frac{m^2-1}{1-\rho^2}}, & \rho < 1, \\ \sigma_0, & 1 < \rho < m, \end{cases} \tag{A61}$$

where $\rho = r/a$.

It can be seen in Equation (A60) that $m \to 1$ as $\sigma_0 \to \infty$. Under these circumstances, Equation (A61) can be simplified as follows:

$$\sigma_{zz}(\rho,0) = -B_1 \cot\alpha\cosh^{-1}\frac{1}{\rho}+\frac{K_I}{\sqrt{\pi a}}\frac{1}{\sqrt{1-\rho^2}}, \quad \rho < 1, \tag{A62}$$

which is consistent with the corresponding JKR solution presented in Equation (A24).

From Equation (A59), one can find that $\sigma_0 \to 0$ as $m \to \infty$, and as such, Equation (A61) degenerates into the following form:

$$\sigma_{zz}(r,0) = -B_1 \cot\alpha\cosh^{-1}\frac{a}{r}, \quad r < a, \tag{A63}$$

which is in agreement with the corresponding Hertz solution obtained in Equation (A9).

The discontinuity displacement outside the contact region in Equation (A53) can be expressed as follows:

$$[u_z^{M-D}(r,0)] = \sqrt{r^2-a^2}\cot\alpha - a\cot\alpha\cos^{-1}\frac{a}{r} \\ -\frac{2\sigma_0 a}{B_1 \pi}\left[\sqrt{m^2-1}\left(\sqrt{\frac{r^2}{a^2}-1}-\cos^{-1}\frac{a}{r}\right) - m^2\int_1^{\min(\rho,m)}\frac{\sqrt{\rho^2-t^2}}{t^2\sqrt{m^2-t^2}}dt\right]. \tag{A64}$$

As $m \to \infty$, Equation (A64) can be simplified as [57]:

$$[u_z(r,0)] = \sqrt{r^2-a^2}\cot\alpha - a\cot\alpha\cos^{-1}\frac{a}{r}, \tag{A65}$$

which is the same as the corresponding Hertz solution shown in Equation (A13).

When $m \to 1$, Equation (A65) can be expressed as follows:

$$[u_z^{M-D}(r,0)] = \sqrt{r^2 - a^2} \cot\alpha - a\cot\alpha \cos^{-1}\frac{a}{r} + \frac{2\sigma_0 a\sqrt{m^2-1}}{B_1\pi}\cos^{-1}\frac{a}{r}$$
$$- \frac{2\sigma_0 a}{B_1\pi}\left[\sqrt{m^2-1}\sqrt{\frac{r^2}{a^2}-1} - m^2 \int_1^{\min(\rho,m)} \frac{\sqrt{\rho^2-t^2}}{t^2\sqrt{m^2-t^2}}dt\right], \; r > a. \tag{A66}$$

Substituting Equation (A60) into Equation (A66) yields

$$[u_z^{M-D}(r,0)] = \sqrt{r^2 - a^2}\cot\alpha - a\cot\alpha\cos^{-1}\frac{a}{r} + \frac{K_I\sqrt{\pi a}}{B_1\pi}\cos^{-1}\frac{a}{r}$$
$$- \frac{2\sigma_0 a}{B_1\pi}\left[\sqrt{m^2-1}\sqrt{\frac{r^2}{a^2}-1} - m^2\int_1^{\min(\rho,m)}\frac{\sqrt{\rho^2-t^2}}{t^2\sqrt{m^2-t^2}}dt\right], \; r > a. \tag{A67}$$

Using the integral result in Equation (A128), Equation (A67) can be simplified as

$$[u_z(r,0)] = \sqrt{r^2-a^2}\cot\alpha - a\cot\alpha\cos^{-1}\frac{a}{r} + \frac{K_I\sqrt{\pi a}}{B_1\pi}\cos^{-1}\frac{a}{r}, \; r > a, \tag{A68}$$

which is consistent with the corresponding JKR solution obtained in Equation (A27).

By virtue of the relation in Equation (A132), the indentation depth in Equation (A50) can be expressed as

$$h^{M-D} = \frac{\pi a \cot\alpha}{4} + \frac{P}{4B_1 a} + \frac{\sigma_0 a}{2B_1}\left(m^2 \tan^{-1}\sqrt{m^2-1} - \sqrt{m^2-1}\right). \tag{A69}$$

From Equation (A47), one can obtain the following result:

$$\sigma_0 a = \frac{B_1 \pi a^2 \cot\alpha - P}{2a\left(\sqrt{m^2-1} + m^2\tan^{-1}\sqrt{m^2-1}\right)}. \tag{A70}$$

By substituting Equation (A70) into Equation (A69), one can obtain

$$h^{M-D} = \frac{\pi a \cot\alpha}{4} + \frac{P}{4B_1 a}$$
$$+ \frac{B_1 \pi a^2 \cot\alpha - P}{4B_1 a}\frac{m^2\tan^{-1}\sqrt{m^2-1}-\sqrt{m^2-1}}{m^2\tan^{-1}\sqrt{m^2-1}+\sqrt{m^2-1}}. \tag{A71}$$

When $m \to 1$, by combining the results obtained in Equation (A134), Equation (A71) can be simplified as

$$h = \frac{\pi a \cot\alpha}{4} + \frac{P}{4B_1 a}, \tag{A72}$$

which is the same as the corresponding JKR solution presented in Equation (A23).

When $m \to \infty$, Equation (A71) can be simplified as:

$$h = \frac{\pi a \cot\alpha}{2}, \tag{A73}$$

which is identical to the Hertz solution obtained in Equation (A10).

The energy release rate can be derived from Equation (A56) as follows:

$$G = \left(\sqrt{m^2-1} - \tan^{-1}\sqrt{m^2-1}\right)\sigma_0 a \cot\alpha$$
$$+ \frac{2\sigma_0^2 a}{B_1\pi}\left(\sqrt{m^2-1}\tan^{-1}\sqrt{m^2-1} - m + 1\right). \tag{A74}$$

Inserting Equation (A70) into Equation (A74) yields

$$G = \frac{(P^H-P)\cot\alpha}{2a} \frac{\sqrt{m^2-1}-\tan^{-1}\sqrt{m^2-1}}{\sqrt{m^2-1}+m^2\tan^{-1}\sqrt{m^2-1}} \\ + \frac{(P^H-P)^2}{2\pi B_1 a^3} \frac{\sqrt{m^2-1}\tan^{-1}\sqrt{m^2-1}-m+1}{\left(\sqrt{m^2-1}+m^2\tan^{-1}\sqrt{m^2-1}\right)^2}. \tag{A75}$$

In the limit case, as $m \to 1$, letting $m = 1+\varepsilon$ and using the result in Equation (A144), one can obtain

$$G \approx \frac{(P^H - P)^2}{16\pi B_1 a^3}. \tag{A76}$$

Using the energy balance relation, one can obtain

$$P = P^H \pm 4\sqrt{\pi B_1 \Delta\gamma a^3}. \tag{A77}$$

Considering the stable equilibrium condition of the contact system, one can determine that

$$P = P^H - 4\sqrt{\pi B_1 \Delta\gamma a^3} = B_1 \cot\alpha \pi a^2 - 4\sqrt{\pi B_1 \Delta\gamma a^3}, \tag{A78}$$

which is in agreement with the corresponding JKR solution obtained in Equation (A34).

Therefore, the above results indicate that the JKR solutions of a piezoelectric solid indented by a rigid insulating conical punch can be regarded as the limiting case, which can be degenerated from the corresponding M-D solutions. The correctness of the corresponding solutions is verified.

Appendix E. External Circular Crack Problem

In this section, we will investigate the external circular crack problem in an infinite piezoelectric solid, as shown in Figure A1. The prescribed normal pressure, $p(r)$, is symmetrically exerted on the upper and lower crack surfaces. The considered problem can be formulated by

$$\begin{cases} u_z(r,0) = 0, \phi(r,0) = 0, & 0 \leq r \leq a, \\ \sigma_{zz}(r,0) = -p(r), D_z(r,0) = 0, & r > a, \\ \sigma_{rz}(r,0) = 0, & r \geq 0. \end{cases} \tag{A79}$$

It should be noted that $p(r)$ is positive for compression and negative for tension.

The general solutions of the axisymmetric problem for the piezoelectric solids are presented in Equation (5). By substituting Equation (5) into Equation (A79), one can obtain

$$\begin{cases} \int_0^\infty A_1(\xi)\xi J_0(\xi r)d\xi = 0, & 0 < r < a, \\ \int_0^\infty A_1(\xi)\xi^2 J_0(\xi r)d\xi = -\frac{M_8 p(r)}{M_5 M_8 - M_6 M_7}, & r > a, \end{cases} \tag{A80}$$

$$\begin{cases} \int_0^\infty A_2(\xi)\xi J_0(\xi r)d\xi = 0, & 0 < r < a, \\ \int_0^\infty A_2(\xi)\xi^2 J_0(\xi r)d\xi = \frac{M_7 p(r)}{M_5 M_8 - M_6 M_7}, & r > a. \end{cases} \tag{A81}$$

Equations (A80) and (A81) are a pair of dual integral equations with respect to the undetermined constants $A_1(\xi)$ and $A_2(\xi)$. The explicit expressions of $A_1(\xi)$ and $A_2(\xi)$ can be obtained by solving Equations (A80) and (A81) using the same method adopted in [83,84], and then, by inserting the corresponding solutions into Equation (5), one can obtain the solutions for the external circular crack problem. In order to save space, the detailed solution procedures are omitted here, and we only present the final results as follows:

$$\begin{cases} u_z(r,0) = \frac{2}{B_1 \pi} \int_a^r \frac{g(t)}{\sqrt{r^2-t^2}} dt, & r > a, \\ \phi(r,0) = \frac{B_2}{B_1} \frac{2}{\pi} \int_a^r \frac{g(t)}{\sqrt{r^2-t^2}} dt, & r > a, \\ \sigma_{zz}(r,0) = \frac{2}{\pi} \left[\frac{g(a)}{\sqrt{a^2-r^2}} + \int_a^\infty \frac{g'(t)}{\sqrt{t^2-r^2}} dt \right], & r < a, \\ D_z(r,0) = 0, & r \geq 0, \end{cases} \quad (A82)$$

where B_1 and B_2 are material constants defined in Equation (A1), and

$$g(t) = \int_t^\infty \frac{sp(s)}{\sqrt{s^2 - t^2}} ds. \quad (A83)$$

When the surface of external crack is subjected to the prescribed uniform pressure, p_0, one has the following equation from [81]:

$$g(t) = \int_t^\infty \frac{sp(s)}{\sqrt{s^2 - t^2}} ds = \begin{cases} p_0 \sqrt{c^2 - t^2}, & a < t < c, \\ 0, & t \geq c, \end{cases} \quad (A84)$$

and one can the determine that

$$g'(t) = \begin{cases} -\frac{p_0 t}{\sqrt{c^2-t^2}}, & a < t < c, \\ 0, & t \geq c. \end{cases} \quad (A85)$$

Inserting Equations (A84) and (A85) into (82)$_3$ yields

$$\sigma_{zz}(r,0) = \frac{2p_0}{\pi} \left(\sqrt{\frac{c^2 - a^2}{a^2 - r^2}} - \tan^{-1} \sqrt{\frac{c^2 - a^2}{a^2 - r^2}} \right), \; r < a, \quad (A86)$$

and the stress distribution at the crack surface can obtained as

$$\sigma_{zz}(r,0) = \begin{cases} \frac{2p_0}{\pi} \left(\sqrt{\frac{c^2-a^2}{a^2-r^2}} - \tan^{-1} \sqrt{\frac{c^2-a^2}{a^2-r^2}} \right), & r < a, \\ -p_0, & a < r < c, \\ 0, & r > c. \end{cases} \quad (A87)$$

By substituting of Equation (A84) into Equations (A82)$_1$ and (A82)$_2$, can obtain

$$u_z(r,0) = \frac{2p_0}{B_1 \pi} \left[\frac{\sqrt{c^2 - a^2}\sqrt{r^2 - a^2}}{a} - c^2 \int_a^{\min(r,c)} \frac{\sqrt{r^2 - t^2}}{t^2 \sqrt{c^2 - t^2}} dt \right], \; r > a, \quad (A88)$$

$$\phi(r,0) = \frac{B_2}{B_1} \frac{2p_0}{\pi} \left[\frac{\sqrt{c^2 - a^2}\sqrt{r^2 - a^2}}{a} - c^2 \int_a^{\min(r,c)} \frac{\sqrt{r^2 - t^2}}{t^2 \sqrt{c^2 - t^2}} dt \right], \; r > a. \quad (A89)$$

respectively.

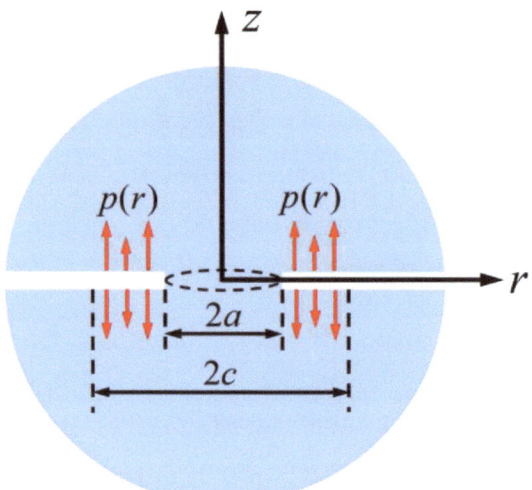

Figure A1. Schematic illustration of an external circular crack contained in an infinite transversely isotropic piezoelectric solid.

It is worth noting that the stresses at the crack surface are not self-equilibrated since the force

$$\int_0^a \sigma_{zz}(r,0) 2\pi r dr = p_0 \pi (c^2 - a^2) - 2p_0 a^2 \left[\frac{c^2}{a^2} \cos^{-1}\left(\frac{a}{c}\right) - \sqrt{\frac{c^2}{a^2} - 1} \right] \tag{A90}$$

does not equilibrate with the force $p_0 \pi (c^2 - a^2)$ exerted on the crack surface. Therefore, an additional force of

$$P' = 2p_0 a^2 \left[\frac{c^2}{a^2} \cos^{-1}\left(\frac{a}{c}\right) - \sqrt{\frac{c^2}{a^2} - 1} \right] > 0 \tag{A91}$$

is thus exerted at infinity which permits $u_z(r, \infty)$ to be zero.

In order to satisfy the force equilibrium condition, keeping the radius, a, constant, exerting the force $-P'$ (tensile force) at infinity, which will give rise to a displacement like the Boussinesq flat punch and introduce in the ligament a stress distribution. According to the different electric properties of the punch, two cases will be discussed separately in the following:

Case (a): superposing the solutions of a rigid insulating circular punch

The solutions to the Boussinesq problem under the action of a rigid insulating circular punch are presented in Equations (A19)–(A22). By inserting $-P'$ into Equations (A19)–(A22), one can obtain

$$\sigma_{zz}^B(r,0) = \frac{P'}{2\pi a \sqrt{a^2 - r^2}}, \quad r < a, \tag{A92}$$

$$h^B = -\frac{P'}{4B_1 a}, \tag{A93}$$

$$u_z^B(r,0) = \begin{cases} -\frac{P'}{4B_1 a}, & 0 \le r \le a, \\ -\frac{P'}{2B_1 \pi a} \sin^{-1}\left(\frac{a}{r}\right), & r > a, \end{cases} \tag{A94}$$

$$\phi^B(r,0) = \begin{cases} -\frac{B_2 P'}{4B_1 a}, & 0 \leq r \leq a, \\ -\frac{B_2 P'}{2B_1 \pi a}\sin^{-1}\left(\frac{a}{r}\right), & r > a. \end{cases} \quad \text{(A95)}$$

By superposing Equations (A87)$_1$ and (A92), and combining the results in Equation (A91), one obtains

$$\sigma_{zz}(r,0) = \frac{K_m}{\sqrt{\pi a}}\frac{a}{\sqrt{a^2-r^2}} - \frac{2p_0}{\pi}\tan^{-1}\sqrt{\frac{c^2-a^2}{a^2-r^2}}, \quad r < a, \quad \text{(A96)}$$

where

$$K_m = \frac{p_0}{\sqrt{\pi a}}\left[\sqrt{c^2-a^2} + \frac{c^2}{a}\cos^{-1}\left(\frac{a}{c}\right)\right]. \quad \text{(A97)}$$

By considering Equations (A87) and (A96), the stress distribution of the circular external crack subjected to the uniform pressure, p_0, on crack surfaces can be defined as

$$\sigma_{zz}(r,0) = \begin{cases} \frac{K_m}{\sqrt{\pi a}}\frac{a}{\sqrt{a^2-r^2}} - \frac{2p_0}{\pi}\tan^{-1}\sqrt{\frac{c^2-a^2}{a^2-r^2}}, & r < a, \\ -p_0, & a < r < c, \\ 0, & r > c. \end{cases} \quad \text{(A98)}$$

By substituting Equation (A91) into Equations (A94) and (A95), one can obtain

$$u_z^B(r,0) = \begin{cases} -\frac{p_0 a}{2B_1}\left[\frac{c^2}{a^2}\cos^{-1}\left(\frac{a}{c}\right) - \sqrt{\frac{c^2}{a^2}-1}\right], & 0 \leq r \leq a, \\ -\frac{p_0 a}{B_1 \pi}\left[\frac{c^2}{a^2}\cos^{-1}\left(\frac{a}{c}\right) - \sqrt{\frac{c^2}{a^2}-1}\right]\sin^{-1}\left(\frac{a}{r}\right), & r > a. \end{cases} \quad \text{(A99)}$$

$$\phi^B(r,0) = \begin{cases} -\frac{B_2 p_0 a}{2B_1}\left[\frac{c^2}{a^2}\cos^{-1}\left(\frac{a}{c}\right) - \sqrt{\frac{c^2}{a^2}-1}\right], & 0 \leq r \leq a, \\ -\frac{B_2 p_0 a}{B_1 \pi}\left[\frac{c^2}{a^2}\cos^{-1}\left(\frac{a}{c}\right) - \sqrt{\frac{c^2}{a^2}-1}\right]\sin^{-1}\left(\frac{a}{r}\right), & r > a. \end{cases} \quad \text{(A100)}$$

respectively.

In Boussinesq's theory, the profile of the surface is given by [81]:

$$u_B = -\frac{p_0 a}{B_1 \pi}\left[\frac{c^2}{a^2}\cos^{-1}\left(\frac{a}{c}\right) - \sqrt{\frac{c^2}{a^2}-1}\right]\sin^{-1}\left(\frac{a}{r}\right), \quad r \geq a, \quad \text{(A101)}$$

and the "penetration" of the punch is defined by

$$\delta_B = -\frac{p_0 a}{2B_1}\left[\frac{c^2}{a^2}\cos^{-1}\left(\frac{a}{c}\right) - \sqrt{\frac{c^2}{a^2}-1}\right] < 0. \quad \text{(A102)}$$

Taking the origin of displacement at the tip of the crack, one has

$$u_z'(r,0) = \delta_B - u_B, \quad \text{(A103)}$$

Substitution of Equations (A101) and (A102) into Equation (A103) yields

$$u_z'(r,0) = \frac{p_0 a}{B_1 \pi}\left(\sqrt{\frac{c^2}{a^2}-1} - \frac{c^2}{a^2}\cos^{-1}\frac{a}{c}\right)\cos^{-1}\frac{a}{r} < 0. \quad \text{(A104)}$$

Similarly, one can obtain

$$\phi'(r,0) = \frac{B_2 p_0 a}{B_1 \pi}\left(\sqrt{\frac{c^2}{a^2}-1} - \frac{c^2}{a^2}\cos^{-1}\frac{a}{c}\right)\cos^{-1}\frac{a}{r} < 0. \tag{A105}$$

Adding the displacement and electric potential shown in Equations (A104) and (A105) to the corresponding results given by Equations (A88) and (A89), respectively, we obtain

$$u_T = u_z(r,0) - u_z'$$
$$= \frac{2p_0}{B_1 \pi}\left[\sqrt{c^2-a^2}\left(\sqrt{\frac{r^2}{a^2}-1}-\cos^{-1}\frac{a}{r}\right) - c^2\int_a^{\min(r,c)}\frac{\sqrt{r^2-t^2}}{t^2\sqrt{c^2-t^2}}dt\right] \tag{A106}$$
$$+ \frac{K_m\sqrt{\pi a}}{B_1 \pi}\cos^{-1}\frac{a}{r},$$

$$\phi_T = \phi(r,0) - \phi'$$
$$= \frac{2B_2 p_0}{B_1 \pi}\left[\sqrt{c^2-a^2}\left(\sqrt{\frac{r^2}{a^2}-1}-\cos^{-1}\frac{a}{r}\right) - c^2\int_a^{\min(r,c)}\frac{\sqrt{r^2-t^2}}{t^2\sqrt{c^2-t^2}}dt\right] \tag{A107}$$
$$+ \frac{B_2 K_m \sqrt{\pi a}}{B_1 \pi}\cos^{-1}\frac{a}{r}.$$

When a piezoelectric material degenerates into an isotropic elastic solid, $B_1 = E^*/2 = E/2(1-\nu^2)$ (where E and ν are the elastic modulus and the Poisson's ratio of the isotropic elastic material, respectively), Equation (A106) can be rewritten as

$$u_T = 4\frac{1-\nu^2}{\pi E}p_0\left[\sqrt{c^2-a^2}\left(\sqrt{\frac{r^2}{a^2}-1}-\cos^{-1}\frac{a}{r}\right) - c^2\int_a^{\min(r,c)}\frac{\sqrt{r^2-t^2}}{t^2\sqrt{c^2-t^2}}dt\right] \tag{A108}$$
$$+ \frac{1-\nu^2}{\pi E}K_m\sqrt{\pi a}\cos^{-1}\frac{a}{r},$$

which is the same as the result of Equation (3.150) obtained in [81].

Case (b): superposing the solutions of a rigid conducting circular punch

The solutions to the Boussinesq problem under the action of a rigid conducting circular punch are given by Equations (A14)–(A18). For a rigid conducting circular punch with zero electric potential (i.e., $\phi_0 = 0$), substituting $-P'$ into Equations (A14)–(A18) yields

$$\sigma_{zz}^B(r,0) = \frac{P'}{2\pi a\sqrt{a^2-r^2}}, \tag{A109}$$

$$D_z^B(r,0) = \frac{B_5}{B_4}\frac{P'}{2\pi a\sqrt{a^2-r^2}}, \tag{A110}$$

$$h^B = -\frac{P'}{4aB_4}, \tag{A111}$$

$$u_z^B(r,0) = \begin{cases} -\frac{P'}{4aB_4}, & 0 \le r \le a, \\ -\frac{P'}{2\pi a B_4}\sin^{-1}\left(\frac{a}{r}\right), & r > a, \end{cases} \tag{A112}$$

$$\phi^B(r,0) = 0, \quad r \ge 0. \tag{A113}$$

By adding the stress distribution given by Equations (A87)–(A109) and combining the result of Equation (A91), one can obtain

$$\sigma_{zz}(r,0) = \begin{cases} \frac{K_m}{\sqrt{\pi a}}\frac{a}{\sqrt{a^2-r^2}} - \frac{2p_0}{\pi}\tan^{-1}\sqrt{\frac{c^2-a^2}{a^2-r^2}}, & r < a, \\ -p_0, & a < r < c, \\ 0, & r > c, \end{cases} \tag{A114}$$

which are the same as the results given by Equation (A98).

Inserting Equation (A91) into Equation (A110) yields

$$D_z(r,0) = \frac{B_5}{B_4} \frac{K_m\sqrt{\pi a} - 2p_0\sqrt{c^2 - a^2}}{\pi\sqrt{a^2 - r^2}}, \ r < a, \tag{A115}$$

where K_m is defined by Equation (A97).

By adopting the same solution procedures as those of Equations (A101)–(A107), the crack opening displacement and the discontinuity of the electric potential under the action of $-P'$ can be defined as

$$\begin{aligned} u_T &= \frac{2p_0}{B_1\pi a}\left[\sqrt{(c^2-a^2)(r^2-a^2)} - ac^2\int_a^{\min(r,c)} \frac{\sqrt{r^2-t^2}}{t^2\sqrt{c^2-t^2}}dt\right] \\ &+ \frac{K_m\sqrt{\pi a} - 2p_0\sqrt{c^2-a^2}}{B_4\pi}\cos^{-1}\frac{a}{r}, \ r > a. \end{aligned} \tag{A116}$$

$$\phi_T = \frac{B_2}{B_1}\frac{2p_0}{\pi a}\left[\sqrt{(c^2-a^2)(r^2-a^2)} - ac^2\int_a^{\min(r,c)}\frac{\sqrt{r^2-t^2}}{t^2\sqrt{c^2-t^2}}dt\right], \ r > a. \tag{A117}$$

Appendix F. Verification of the Results in Section 4.2

In this section, the correctness of the results obtained in Section 4.2 will be verified, which was achieved by checking whether the corresponding JKR solutions presented in Section 3.2 can be degenerated as the limiting cases of the M-D solutions obtained in Section 4.2.

First, Equations (62) and (63) can be rewritten in the following forms:

$$\sigma_{zz}^{M-D}(\rho,0) = \begin{cases} -B_4\cot\alpha\cosh^{-1}\frac{1}{\rho} + \frac{2\sigma_0}{\pi}\tan^{-1}\sqrt{\frac{m^2-1}{1-\rho^2}}, & \rho < 1, \\ \sigma_0, & 1 < \rho < m, \end{cases} \tag{A118}$$

$$D_z^{M-D}(\rho,0) = \frac{2B_5(B_6+B_3)\phi_0}{\pi a\sqrt{1-\rho^2}} - B_5\cot\alpha\cosh^{-1}\frac{1}{\rho} + \frac{B_5}{B_4}\frac{2\sigma_0}{\pi}\sqrt{\frac{m^2-1}{1-\rho^2}}, \ \rho < 1, \tag{A119}$$

where $\rho = r/a, m = c/a$.

From Equation (60), one can obtain

$$K_I = \frac{\sigma_0 a}{\sqrt{\pi a}}\left(\sqrt{m^2-1} + m^2\cos^{-1}\frac{1}{m}\right). \tag{A120}$$

Using the following relation from [81]:

$$\cos^{-1}\left(\frac{1}{m}\right) = \tan^{-1}\sqrt{m^2-1}, \ m > 0, \tag{A121}$$

Equation (A120) can be expressed as

$$\frac{K_I\sqrt{\pi a}}{\sigma_0 a} = \sqrt{m^2-1} + m^2\tan^{-1}\sqrt{m^2-1}. \tag{A122}$$

When $m \to 1$, considering the relation $\tan^{-1}\sqrt{m^2-1} \sim \sqrt{m^2-1}$, one can determine that

$$\frac{K_I\sqrt{\pi a}}{\sigma_0 a} \approx 2\sqrt{m^2-1}. \tag{A123}$$

Substituting Equation (A123) into Equations (A118) and (A119) yields

$$\begin{cases} \sigma_{zz}(\rho,0) = -B_4 \cot\alpha \cosh^{-1}\frac{1}{\rho} + \frac{K_I}{\sqrt{\pi a}}\frac{1}{\sqrt{1-\rho^2}}, & \rho < 1, \\ D_z(\rho,0) = \frac{2B_5(B_6+B_3)\phi_0}{\pi a\sqrt{1-\rho^2}} - B_5 \cot\alpha \cosh^{-1}\frac{1}{\rho} + \frac{B_5}{B_4}\frac{K_I}{\sqrt{\pi a}}\frac{1}{\sqrt{1-\rho^2}}, & \rho < 1, \end{cases} \quad (A124)$$

which are consistent with the JKR solutions obtained in Equations (47) and (48).

When $m \to \infty$, from Equation (A122), one can determine that $\sigma_0 \to 0$. In this case, Equations (62) and (63) can be simplified as

$$\begin{cases} \sigma_{zz}(\rho,0) = -B_4 \cot\alpha \cosh^{-1}\frac{1}{\rho}, & \rho < 1, \\ D_z(\rho,0) = \frac{2B_5(B_6+B_3)\phi_0}{\pi a\sqrt{1-\rho^2}} - B_5 \cot\alpha \cosh^{-1}\frac{1}{\rho}, & \rho < 1, \end{cases} \quad (A125)$$

which are the same as the corresponding Hertz solutions presented in Equations (A2) and (A3).

For the discontinuity displacement outside the contact region, $\sigma_0 \to 0$ as $m \to \infty$, and Equation (65) degenerates into the following form:

$$[u_z(r,0)] = \left(\frac{2B_3\phi_0}{\pi} - a\cot\alpha\right)\cos^{-1}\frac{a}{r} + \sqrt{r^2 - a^2}\cot\alpha, \quad r > a, \quad (A126)$$

which is consistent with the Hertz solution presented in Equation (A7).

When $m \to 1$, using the relation in Equation (A123), Equation (65) can be simplified as follows:

$$[u_z(r,0)] = \left(\frac{2B_3\phi_0}{\pi} - a\cot\alpha\right)\cos^{-1}\frac{a}{r} + \sqrt{r^2-a^2}\cot\alpha + \frac{K_I\sqrt{\pi a}}{B_4\pi}\cos^{-1}\frac{a}{r} \\ - \frac{2\sigma_0 a}{B_1\pi}\left[\sqrt{(m^2-1)(\rho^2-1)} - m^2\int_1^{\min(\rho,m)}\frac{\sqrt{\rho^2-t^2}}{t^2\sqrt{m^2-t^2}}dt\right], \quad r > a. \quad (A127)$$

Considering the following integral result [81]:

$$\lim_{m\to 1}\left(m^2\int_1^m \frac{\sqrt{\rho^2-t^2}}{t^2\sqrt{m^2-t^2}}dt\right) = \lim_{m\to 1}\left(m^2\sqrt{\rho^2-\xi^2}\int_1^m \frac{dt}{t^2\sqrt{m^2-t^2}}\right) \\ = \lim_{m\to 1}\sqrt{\rho^2-\xi^2}\sqrt{m^2-1} = \sqrt{(m^2-1)(\rho^2-1)}. \quad (A128)$$

By inserting Equation (A128) into Equation (A127), one can obtain

$$[u_z(r,0)] = \left(\frac{2B_3\phi_0}{\pi} - a\cot\alpha\right)\cos^{-1}\frac{a}{r} + \sqrt{r^2-a^2}\cot\alpha \\ + \frac{K_I\sqrt{\pi a}}{B_4\pi}\cos^{-1}\frac{a}{r}, \quad r > a, \quad (A129)$$

which is the same as the corresponding JKR solution presented in Equation (50).

From the results given by Equations (A126) and (A128), one can determine that for both $m \to \infty$ and $m \to 1$, Equation (67) can be simplified as follows:

$$[\phi(r,0)] = -\frac{2\phi_0}{\pi}\cos^{-1}\frac{a}{r}, \quad r > a, \quad (A130)$$

which is consistent with the Hertz solution and the JKR solution obtained in Equations (A8) and (51), respectively.

For the indentation depth, superposing Equations (14) and (56) yields

$$h^{M-D} = \frac{\pi a}{4}\cot\alpha + \frac{P}{4B_4 a} - B_3\phi_0 + \frac{\sigma_0 a}{2B_4}\left(m^2\tan^{-1}\sqrt{m^2-1} - \sqrt{m^2-1}\right). \quad (A131)$$

Using Equations (45) and (A122), one can determine that

$$\sigma_0 a = \frac{B_4 \pi a^2 \cot\alpha - P}{2a\left(\sqrt{m^2-1} + m^2 \tan^{-1}\sqrt{m^2-1}\right)}. \tag{A132}$$

Substituting Equation (A132) into Equation (A131) yields

$$h^{M-D} = \frac{\pi a}{4}\cot\alpha + \frac{P}{4B_4 a} - B_3\phi_0 \\ + \frac{m^2 \tan^{-1}\sqrt{m^2-1} - \sqrt{m^2-1}}{m^2 \tan^{-1}\sqrt{m^2-1} + \sqrt{m^2-1}} \cdot \frac{B_4 \pi a^2 \cot\alpha - P}{4B_4 a}. \tag{A133}$$

As $m \to 1$,

$$\frac{m^2 \tan^{-1}\sqrt{m^2-1} - \sqrt{m^2-1}}{m^2 \tan^{-1}\sqrt{m^2-1} + \sqrt{m^2-1}} \approx \frac{\sqrt{m^2-1} - \sqrt{m^2-1}}{2\sqrt{m^2-1}} = 0, \tag{A134}$$

and as such, Equation (A133) can be simplified as

$$h = \frac{\pi a}{4}\cot\alpha + \frac{P}{4B_4 a} - B_3\phi_0, \tag{A135}$$

which is consistent with the corresponding JKR solution obtained in Equation (14).

When $m \to \infty$, it can be determined that

$$\frac{m^2 \tan^{-1}\sqrt{m^2-1} - \sqrt{m^2-1}}{m^2 \tan^{-1}\sqrt{m^2-1} + \sqrt{m^2-1}} \approx \frac{\pi m^2/2 - \sqrt{m^2-1}}{\pi m^2/2 + \sqrt{m^2-1}} \approx 1, \tag{A136}$$

then one can determine that

$$h = \frac{\pi a}{2}\cot\alpha - B_3\phi_0, \tag{A137}$$

which is the same as the Hertz solution presented in Equation (A4).

Using the relation given by Equation (A121), the energy release rate obtained in Equation (79) can be expressed in the following form:

$$G = \left(\sqrt{m^2-1} - \tan^{-1}\sqrt{m^2-1}\right)\sigma_0 a \cot\alpha + \frac{2B_3\phi_0\sigma_0}{\pi}\tan^{-1}\sqrt{m^2-1} \\ + \frac{2\sigma_0^2 a}{\pi B_4}\left[\sqrt{m^2-1}\tan^{-1}\sqrt{m^2-1} - \frac{B_4}{B_1}(m-1)\right] - \frac{B_5(B_3+B_6)\phi_0^2}{\pi a} \\ - \frac{1}{\pi}\left[\frac{B_5}{B_4} + \frac{B_2 B_5(B_3+B_6)}{B_1}\right]\phi_0\sigma_0\sqrt{m^2-1} - \frac{B_2 B_5}{B_1 B_4}\frac{\sigma_0^2 a}{\pi}(m^2-1). \tag{A138}$$

Substitution of Equation (A132) into Equation (A138) yields

$$G = \frac{\cot\alpha(P^H - P)\left(\sqrt{m^2-1} - \tan^{-1}\sqrt{m^2-1}\right)}{2a\left(\sqrt{m^2-1} + m^2 \tan^{-1}\sqrt{m^2-1}\right)} \\ + \left\{B_3 \tan^{-1}\sqrt{m^2-1} - \frac{1}{2}\left[\frac{B_5}{B_4} + \frac{B_2 B_5(B_3+B_6)}{B_1}\right]\sqrt{m^2-1}\right\} \times \\ \frac{(P^H - P)\phi_0}{\pi a^2\left(\sqrt{m^2-1} + m^2 \tan^{-1}\sqrt{m^2-1}\right)} - \frac{B_2 B_5}{4\pi B_1 B_4 a^3}\frac{(P^H-P)^2(m^2-1)}{\sqrt{m^2-1} + m^2\tan^{-1}\sqrt{m^2-1}} \\ + \frac{(P^H-P)^2}{2\pi B_4 a^3}\frac{\sqrt{m^2-1}\tan^{-1}\sqrt{m^2-1} - \frac{B_4}{B_1}(m-1)}{\left(\sqrt{m^2-1} + m^2 \tan^{-1}\sqrt{m^2-1}\right)^2} - \frac{B_5(B_3+B_6)\phi_0^2}{\pi a}. \tag{A139}$$

When $m \to 1$, using the relation $\tan^{-1}\sqrt{m^2-1} \sim \sqrt{m^2-1}$, Equation (A139) can be simplified as

$$G = \left\{B_3 - \frac{1}{2}\left[\frac{B_5}{B_4} + \frac{B_2 B_5(B_3+B_6)}{B_1}\right]\right\} \frac{(P^H-P)\phi_0}{2\pi a^2}$$
$$+ \frac{(P^H-P)^2}{2\pi B_4 a^3} \frac{\sqrt{m^2-1}\tan^{-1}\sqrt{m^2-1} - \frac{B_4}{B_1}(m-1)}{\left(\sqrt{m^2-1}+m^2\tan^{-1}\sqrt{m^2-1}\right)^2} - \frac{B_5(B_3+B_6)\phi_0^2}{\pi a}. \quad (A140)$$

For several common piezoelectric materials (e.g., PZT-4, PZT-5A, BaTiO$_3$ and Ba$_a$Ca$_b$TiO$_3$), the numerical results indicate that

$$B_3 \approx \frac{1}{2}\left[\frac{B_5}{B_4} + \frac{B_2 B_5(B_3+B_6)}{B_1}\right], \quad \frac{B_4}{B_1} \approx 1. \quad (A141)$$

Using the above results, Equation (A140) can be further simplified as

$$G = \frac{(P^H-P)^2}{2\pi B_4 a^3} \frac{\sqrt{m^2-1}\tan^{-1}\sqrt{m^2-1} - m + 1}{\left(\sqrt{m^2-1}+m^2\tan^{-1}\sqrt{m^2-1}\right)^2} - \frac{B_5(B_3+B_6)\phi_0^2}{\pi a}. \quad (A142)$$

As $m \to 1$, letting $m = 1 + \varepsilon$, one can obtain [81]:

$$\tan^{-1}\sqrt{m^2-1} \approx \sqrt{2\varepsilon}\left(1 - \frac{5\varepsilon}{12}\right), \quad (A143)$$

and as such,

$$\sqrt{m^2-1}\tan^{-1}\sqrt{m^2-1} - m + 1 \approx 2\varepsilon, \quad \sqrt{m^2-1}+m^2\tan^{-1}\sqrt{m^2-1} \approx 2\sqrt{2\varepsilon}. \quad (A144)$$

Inserting Equation (A144) into Equation (A142) yields

$$G = \frac{(P^H-P)^2}{16\pi B_4 a^3} - \frac{B_5(B_3+B_6)\phi_0^2}{\pi a}. \quad (A145)$$

Using the energy balance relation as presented in Equation (80), one can determine that

$$P = P^H \pm 4a\sqrt{\pi B_4 a \Delta \gamma + B_4 B_5(B_3+B_6)\phi_0^2}. \quad (A146)$$

Combining the stable equilibrium condition of the contact system, we can determine that

$$P = P^H - 4a\sqrt{\pi B_4 a \Delta \gamma + B_4 B_5(B_3+B_6)\phi_0^2}. \quad (A147)$$

Substituting Equation (A4)$_2$ into Equation (A147) yields

$$P = \pi B_4 a^2 \cot\alpha - 4a\sqrt{\pi B_4 a \Delta \gamma + B_4 B_5(B_3+B_6)\phi_0^2}, \quad (A148)$$

which is the same as the corresponding JKR solution obtained in Equation (27).

Therefore, the above results indicate that the JKR solutions of a piezoelectric solid under the action of a rigid conducting conical punch can be regarded as the limiting case, which can be degenerated from the corresponding M-D solutions. The correctness of the corresponding solutions is verified.

References

1. Zhao, C.; Knisely, K.E.; Colesa, D.J.; Pfingst, B.E.; Raphael, Y.; Grosh, K. Voltage readout from a piezoelectric intracochlear acoustic transducer implanted in a living guinea pig. *Sci. Rep.* **2019**, *9*, 3711. [CrossRef] [PubMed]
2. Ejeian, F.; Azadi, S.; Razmjou, A.; Orooji, Y.; Kottapalli, A.; Warkiani, M.E.; Asadnia, M. Design and applications of MEMS flow sensors: A review. *Sens. Actuators A Phys.* **2019**, *295*, 483–502. [CrossRef]
3. Murray, C.; McCoul, D.; Sollier, E.; Ruggiero, T.; Niu, X.; Pei, Q.; Di Carlo, D. Electro-adaptive microfluidics for active tuning of channel geometry using polymer actuators. *Microfluid. Nanofluidics* **2012**, *14*, 345–358. [CrossRef]
4. Deng, W.; Zhou, Y.; Libanori, A.; Chen, G.; Yang, W.; Chen, J. Piezoelectric nanogenerators for personalized healthcare. *Chem. Soc. Rev.* **2022**, *51*, 3380–3435. [CrossRef] [PubMed]
5. Kim, S.-G.; Priya, S.; Kanno, I. Piezoelectric MEMS for energy harvesting. *MRS Bull.* **2012**, *37*, 1039–1050. [CrossRef]
6. Awada, A.; Younes, R.; Ilinca, A. Optimized Active Control of a Smart Cantilever Beam Using Genetic Algorithm. *Designs* **2022**, *6*, 36. [CrossRef]
7. Wang, Z.; Qin, X.; Zhang, S.; Bai, J.; Li, J.; Yu, G. Optimal Shape Control of Piezoelectric Intelligent Structure Based on Genetic Algorithm. *Adv. Mater. Sci. Eng.* **2017**, *2017*, 6702183. [CrossRef]
8. Mangaiyarkarasi, P.; Lakshmi, P. Numerical and experimental analysis of piezoelectric vibration energy harvester in IoT based F-SEPS application using optimization techniques. *Microsyst. Technol.* **2021**, *27*, 2955–2979. [CrossRef]
9. Fountas, N.A.; Vaxevanidis, N.M. Optimization of abrasive flow nano-finishing processes by adopting artificial viral intelligence. *J. Manuf. Mater. Process.* **2021**, *5*, 22. [CrossRef]
10. Nabavi, S.; Zhang, L. Frequency Tuning and Efficiency Improvement of Piezoelectric MEMS Vibration Energy Harvesters. *J. Microelectromech. Syst.* **2018**, *28*, 77–87. [CrossRef]
11. Abdeljaber, O.; Avci, O.; Inman, D.J. Active vibration control of flexible cantilever plates using piezoelectric materials and artificial neural networks. *J. Sound Vib.* **2016**, *363*, 33–53. [CrossRef]
12. Abolhasani, M.M.; Shirvanimoghaddam, K.; Khayyam, H.; Moosavi, S.M.; Zohdi, N.; Naebe, M. Towards predicting the piezoelectricity and physiochemical properties of the electrospun P(VDF-TrFE) nanogenrators using an artificial neural network. *Polym. Test.* **2018**, *66*, 178–188. [CrossRef]
13. Kachanov, M.; Kalinin, S. Nanoelectromechanics of piezoelectric indentation and applications to scanning probe microscopies of ferroelectric materials. *Philos. Mag.* **2005**, *85*, 1017–1051.
14. Carrillo, F.; Gupta, S.; Balooch, M.; Marshall, S.J.; Marshall, G.W.; Pruitt, L.; Puttlitz, C.M. Nanoindentation of polydimethylsiloxane elastomers: Effect of crosslinking, work of adhesion, and fluid environment on elastic modulus. *J. Mater. Res.* **2011**, *20*, 2820–2830. [CrossRef]
15. Lin, Z.; Yu, Z.; Wei, Y. Measurement of nanoindentation properties of polymers considering adhesion effects between AFM sharp indenter and material. *J. Adhes. Sci. Technol.* **2020**, *34*, 1591–1608. [CrossRef]
16. Kohn, J.C.; Ebenstein, D. Eliminating adhesion errors in nanoindentation of compliant polymers and hydrogels. *J. Mech. Behav. Biomed. Mater.* **2013**, *20*, 316–326. [CrossRef]
17. Zhao, Y.P.; Wang, L.S.; Yu, T.X. Mechanics of adhesion in MEMS—A review. *J. Adhes. Sci. Technol.* **2003**, *17*, 519–546. [CrossRef]
18. Zhou, S.A. On forces in microelectromechanical systems. *Int. J. Eng. Sci.* **2003**, *41*, 313–335. [CrossRef]
19. Lim, A.E.; Lam, Y.C. Vertical Squeezing Route Taylor Flow with Angled Microchannel Junctions. *Ind. Eng. Chem. Res.* **2021**, *60*, 14307–14317. [CrossRef]
20. Yang, F.Q. Effect of adhesion energy on the contact stiffness in nanoindentation. *J. Mater. Res.* **2006**, *21*, 2683–2688. [CrossRef]
21. Chen, W.-Q.; Shioya, T.; Ding, H.-J. The Elasto-Electric Field for a Rigid Conical Punch on a Transversely Isotropic Piezoelectric Half-Space. *J. Appl. Mech.* **1999**, *66*, 764–771. [CrossRef]
22. Giannakopoulos, A.; Suresh, S. Theory of indentation of piezoelectric materials. *Acta Mater.* **1999**, *47*, 2153–2164. [CrossRef]
23. Sridhar, S.; Giannakopoulos, A.E.; Suresh, S. Mechanical and electrical responses of piezoelectric solids to conical indentation. *J. Appl. Phys.* **2000**, *87*, 8451–8456. [CrossRef]
24. Makagon, A.; Kachanov, M.; Kalinin, S.V.; Karapetian, E. Indentation of spherical and conical punches into piezoelectric half-space with frictional sliding: Applications to scanning probe microscopy. *Phys. Rev. B* **2007**, *76*, 064115. [CrossRef]
25. Wang, J.H.; Chen, C.Q.; Lu, T.J. Indentation responses of piezoelectric films. *J. Mech. Phys. Solids* **2008**, *56*, 3331–3351. [CrossRef]
26. Yang, F. Analysis of the axisymmetric indentation of a semi-infinite piezoelectric material: The evaluation of the contact stiffness and the effective piezoelectric constant. *J. Appl. Phys.* **2008**, *103*, 074115. [CrossRef]
27. Kamble, S.N.; Kubair, D.V.; Ramamurty, U. Indentation strength of a piezoelectric ceramic: Experiments and simulations. *J. Mater. Res.* **2009**, *24*, 926–935. [CrossRef]
28. Liu, M.; Yang, F.Q. Orientation effect on the Boussinesq indentation of a transversely isotropic piezoelectric material. *Int. J. Solids Struct.* **2013**, *50*, 2542–2547. [CrossRef]
29. Berndt, E.A.; Sevostianov, I. Action of a smooth flat charged punch on the piezoelectric half-space possessing symmetry of class 6. *Int. J. Eng. Sci.* **2016**, *103*, 77–96. [CrossRef]
30. Rodríguez-Tembleque, L.; Sáez, A.; Aliabadi, M. Indentation response of piezoelectric films under frictional contact. *Int. J. Eng. Sci.* **2016**, *107*, 36–53. [CrossRef]
31. Hou, P.F.; Zhang, W.H. 3D Axisymmetric exact solutions of the piezo-coating sensors for coating/substrate system under charged conical contact. *Int. J. Solids Struct.* **2019**, *185–186*, 342–364. [CrossRef]

32. Guillermo, R.; Paul, H. Frictionless contact in a layered piezoelectric half-space. *Smart Mater. Struct.* **2003**, *12*, 612–625.
33. Hao, T.H. Exact solution of a flat smooth punch on a piezoelectric half plane. *Mech. Res. Commun.* **2003**, *30*, 455–461.
34. Guillermo, R. Frictionless contact in a layered piezoelectric medium characterized by complex eigenvalues. *Smart Mater. Struct.* **2006**, *15*, 1287–1295.
35. Wang, B.L.; Han, J.C.; Du, S.Y.; Zhang, H.Y.; Sun, Y.G. Electromechanical behaviour of a finite piezoelectric layer under a flat punch. *Int. J. Solids Struct.* **2008**, *45*, 6384–6398. [CrossRef]
36. Zhou, Y.T.; Lee, K.Y. New, real fundamental solutions to the transient thermal contact problem in a piezoelectric strip under the coupling actions of a rigid punch and a convective heat supply. *Int. J. Solids Struct.* **2011**, *48*, 2706–2717. [CrossRef]
37. Zhou, Y.-T.; Lee, K.Y. Theory of moving contact of anisotropic piezoelectric materials via real fundamental solutions approach. *Eur. J. Mech. A Solids* **2012**, *35*, 22–36. [CrossRef]
38. Zhou, Y.-T.; Zhong, Z. Application of dual series equations to wavy contact between piezoelectric materials and an elastic solid. *Int. J. Appl. Mech.* **2014**, *6*, 1450046. [CrossRef]
39. Zhou, Y.-T.; Zhong, Z. The interaction of two rigid semi-cylinders over anisotropic piezoelectric materials by the generalized Almansi theorem. *Smart Mater. Struct.* **2015**, *24*, 085011. [CrossRef]
40. Çömez, İ.; Güler, M.A.; El-Borgi, S. Continuous and discontinuous contact problems of a homogeneous piezoelectric layer pressed by a conducting rigid flat punch. *Acta Mech.* **2019**, *231*, 957–976. [CrossRef]
41. Su, J.; Ke, L.-L.; Wang, Y.-S. Elastohydrodynamic lubrication line contact of piezoelectric materials. *Int. J. Mech. Sci.* **2019**, *163*, 105145. [CrossRef]
42. Fan, H.; Sze, K.-Y.; Yang, W. Two-dimensional contact on a piezoelectric half-space. *Int. J. Solids Struct.* **1996**, *33*, 1305–1315. [CrossRef]
43. Zhou, Y.T.; Lee, K.Y. Thermo-electro-mechanical contact behavior of a finite piezoelectric layer under a sliding punch with frictional heat generation. *J. Mech. Phys. Solids* **2011**, *59*, 1037–1061. [CrossRef]
44. Zhou, Y.T.; Lee, K.Y. Exact solutions of the 2-D frictional sliding contact problem of electrically insulated triangular and cylindrical punches on piezoelectric materials. *Zamm-Z. Angew. Math. Phys.* **2013**, *93*, 217–232. [CrossRef]
45. Li, X.; Zhou, Y.-T.; Zhong, Z. On the analytical solution for sliding contact of piezoelectric materials subjected to a flat or parabolic indenter. *Z. Angew. Math. Phys.* **2014**, *66*, 473–495. [CrossRef]
46. Ma, J.; Ke, L.-L.; Wang, Y.-S. Electro-mechanical sliding frictional contact of a piezoelectric half-plane under a rigid conducting punch. *Appl. Math. Model.* **2014**, *38*, 5471–5489. [CrossRef]
47. Zhou, Y.-T.; Lee, K.Y. Investigation of frictional sliding contact problems of triangular and cylindrical punches on monoclinic piezoelectric materials. *Mech. Mater.* **2014**, *69*, 237–250. [CrossRef]
48. Su, J.; Ke, L.-L.; Wang, Y.-S. Two-dimensional fretting contact analysis of piezoelectric materials. *Int. J. Solids Struct.* **2015**, *73-74*, 41–54. [CrossRef]
49. Su, J.; Ke, L.-L.; Wang, Y.-S. Two-dimensional fretting contact of piezoelectric materials under a rigid conducting cylindrical punch. *J. Mech. Mater. Struct.* **2016**, *11*, 535–558. [CrossRef]
50. Shu, Y.-J.; Ke, L.-L.; Su, J.; Wang, Y.-S. Experimental Investigation on Fretting Wear Behavior of Piezoceramics under Sphere-on-Flat Contact. *Tribol. Trans.* **2020**, *63*, 971–985. [CrossRef]
51. Lv, X.; Ke, L.-L.; Su, J.; Tian, J.-Y. Axisymmetric contact vibration analysis of a rigid spherical punch on a piezoelectric half-space. *Int. J. Solids Struct.* **2020**, *210–211*, 224–236. [CrossRef]
52. Lv, X.; Su, J.; Tian, J.-Y.; Ke, L.-L. Dynamic contact response of an elastic sphere on a piezoelectric half-space. *Appl. Math. Model.* **2021**, *100*, 16–32. [CrossRef]
53. Ding, H.-J.; Hou, P.-F.; Guo, F.-L. The elastic and electric fields for three-dimensional contact for transversely isotropic piezoelectric materials. *Int. J. Solids Struct.* **2000**, *37*, 3201–3229. [CrossRef]
54. Wu, Y.F.; Yu, H.Y.; Chen, W.Q. Mechanics of indentation for piezoelectric thin films on elastic substrate. *Int. J. Solids Struct.* **2012**, *49*, 95–110. [CrossRef]
55. Chen, Z.-R.; Yu, S.-W. Micro-scale adhesive contact of a spherical rigid punch on a piezoelectric half-space. *Compos. Sci. Technol.* **2005**, *65*, 1372–1381. [CrossRef]
56. Johnson, K.L.; Kendall, K.; Roberts, A.D. Surface energy and the contact of elastic solids. *Proc. R. Soc. A Math. Phys. Eng. Sci.* **1971**, *324*, 301–313.
57. Maugis, D. Adhesion of spheres: The JKR-DMT transition using a Dugdale model. *J. Colloid Interface Sci.* **1992**, *150*, 243–269. [CrossRef]
58. Rogowski, B.; Kaliński, W. The adhesive contact problem for a piezoelectric half-space. *Int. J. Press. Vessel. Pip.* **2007**, *84*, 502–511. [CrossRef]
59. Guo, X.; Jin, F. A generalized JKR-model for two-dimensional adhesive contact of transversely isotropic piezoelectric half-space. *Int. J. Solids Struct.* **2009**, *46*, 3607–3619. [CrossRef]
60. Jin, F.; Yan, S.P.; Guo, X.; Wang, X.Y. On the contact and adhesion of a piezoelectric half-space under a rigid punch with an axisymmetric power-law profile. *Mech. Mater.* **2018**, *129*, 189–197. [CrossRef]
61. Kanda, K.; Hirai, S.; Fujita, T.; Maenaka, K. Piezoelectric MEMS with multilayered Pb(Zr,Ti)O$_3$ thin films for energy harvesting. *Sens. Actuators A Phys.* **2018**, *281*, 229–235. [CrossRef]

62. Zhou, Y.-T.; Luo, Q.-H. Asymmetric non-slipping adhesion behavior of layered piezoelectric structures. *Int. J. Mech. Sci.* **2022**, *224*, 107330. [CrossRef]
63. Luo, Q.-H.; Zhou, Y.-T. Adhesive contact behavior between piezoelectric and elastic materials with a mismatch strain. *Acta Mech.* **2022**, *233*, 617–639. [CrossRef]
64. Luo, Q.-H.; Zhou, Y.-T. Adhesive behavior of transversely isotropic piezoelectric bimaterials. *Int. J. Solids Struct.* **2021**, *236–237*, 111360. [CrossRef]
65. Shirbani, M.M.; Shishesaz, M.; Hajnayeb, A.; Sedighi, H.M. Coupled magneto-electro-mechanical lumped parameter model for a novel vibration-based magneto-electro-elastic energy harvesting systems. *Phys. E Low-Dimens. Syst. Nanostruct.* **2017**, *90*, 158–169. [CrossRef]
66. Shishesaz, M.; Shirbani, M.M.; Sedighi, H.M.; Hajnayeb, A. Design and analytical modeling of magneto-electro-mechanical characteristics of a novel magneto-electro-elastic vibration-based energy harvesting system. *J. Sound Vib.* **2018**, *425*, 149–169. [CrossRef]
67. Skrzypacz, P.; Ellis, G.; He, J.H.; He, C.H. Dynamic pull-in and oscillations of current-carrying filaments in magnetic micro-electro-mechanical system. *Commun. Nonlinear Sci. Numer. Simul.* **2022**, *109*, 106350. [CrossRef]
68. Wu, F.; Li, X.-Y.; Zheng, R.-F.; Kang, G.-Z. Theory of adhesive contact on multi-ferroic composite materials: Spherical indenter. *Int. J. Eng. Sci.* **2018**, *134*, 77–116. [CrossRef]
69. Wu, F.; Li, C. Theory of adhesive contact on multi-ferroic composite materials: Conical indenter. *Int. J. Solids Struct.* **2021**, *233*, 111217. [CrossRef]
70. Rar, A.; Pharr, G.M.; Oliver, W.C.; Karapetian, E.; Kalinin, S.V. Piezoelectric nanoindentation. *J. Mater. Res.* **2006**, *21*, 552–556. [CrossRef]
71. Pan, K.; Liu, Y.Y.; Xie, S.H.; Liu, Y.M.; Li, J.Y. The electromechanics of piezoresponse force microscopy for a transversely isotropic piezoelectric medium. *Acta Mater.* **2013**, *61*, 7020–7033. [CrossRef]
72. Broitman, E.; Soomro, M.Y.; Lu, J.; Willander, M.; Hultman, L. Nanoscale piezoelectric response of ZnO nanowires measured using a nanoindentation technique. *Phys. Chem. Chem. Phys.* **2013**, *15*, 11113–11118. [CrossRef]
73. Derjaguin, B.; Muller, V.; Toporov, Y. Effect of contact deformations on the adhesion of particles. *J. Colloid Interface Sci.* **1975**, *53*, 314–326. [CrossRef]
74. Greenwood, J.A.; Johnson, K.L. An alternative to the Maugis model of adhesion between elastic spheres. *J. Phys. D Appl. Phys.* **1998**, *31*, 3279–3290. [CrossRef]
75. Tabor, D. Surface forces and surface interactions. *J. Colloid Interface Sci.* **1977**, *58*, 3–14. [CrossRef]
76. Ganser, C.; Czibula, C.; Tscharnuter, D.; Schoberl, T.; Teichert, C.; Hirn, U. Combining adhesive contact mechanics with a viscoelastic material model to probe local material properties by AFM. *Soft Matter* **2017**, *14*, 140–150. [CrossRef]
77. Argatov, I.; Mishuris, G. Cylindrical lateral depth-sensing indentation of anisotropic elastic tissues: Effects of adhesion and incompressibility. *J. Adhes.* **2017**, *94*, 583–596. [CrossRef]
78. Vallet, D.; Barquins, M. Adhesive contact and kinetics of adherence of a rigid conical punch on an elastic half-space (natural rubber). *Int. J. Adhes. Adhes.* **2002**, *22*, 41–46. [CrossRef]
79. Dugdale, D.S. Yielding of stress sheets containing slits. *J. Mech. Phys. Solids* **1960**, *8*, 100–104. [CrossRef]
80. Suo, Z.G.; Kuo, C.M.; Barnett, D.M.; Willis, J.R. Fracture mechanics for piezoelectric ceramics. *J. Mech. Phys. Solids* **1992**, *40*, 739–765. [CrossRef]
81. Maugis, D. *Contact, Adhesion and Rupture of Elastic Solids*; Springer: Berlin/Heidelberg, Germany, 2000.
82. Cacucciolo, V.; Shea, H.; Carbone, G. Peeling in electroadhesion soft grippers. *Extreme Mech. Lett.* **2021**, *50*, 101529. [CrossRef]
83. Lowengrub, M.; Sneddon, I.N. The distribution of stress in the vicinity of an external crack in an infinite elastic solid. *Int. J. Eng. Sci.* **1965**, *3*, 451–460. [CrossRef]
84. Sneddon, I.N. The elementary solution of dual integral equation. *Glasg. Math. J.* **1960**, *4*, 108–110. [CrossRef]

Article

A Collapse Strength Model for a 7″ Crescent-Worn Casing Connection Considering Sealing Integrity

Xing Zhou [1], Qinfeng Di [1], Xiaoliang Wang [2], Dakun Luo [1], Feng Chen [3,*] and Wenchang Wang [1,*]

[1] School of Mechanics and Engineering Science, Shanghai University, Shanghai 200444, China
[2] CNPC Tarim Oilfield Company, Korla 841000, China
[3] School of Mechatronics Engineering and Automation, Shanghai University, Shanghai 200444, China
* Correspondence: chenfeng536@shu.edu.cn (F.C.); vincentw@shu.edu.cn (W.W.); Tel.: +86-5633-3256 (F.C.)

Abstract: Collapse failure under external pressure is one of the common failure forms of casing. Much research has been performed on the casing body, but few on the threaded connection, in view of the general belief that the threaded connection has a thicker wall and larger collapse strength than the casing body. However, under external pressure, the sealing capacity of a worn casing connection will decrease due to deformation of the sealing structure, so the influence of sealing ability should be considered to determine the collapse strength of casing. In this paper, we established a three-dimensional finite element model of a 7″ crescent-worn casing connection and calculated the collapse strength of the connection under different wear depths. Meanwhile, the stress distribution characteristics on the sealing surface were obtained and the influence of wear on the sealing performance of the casing connection under external pressure was analyzed. The results showed that when the wear rate exceeds a certain value, the collapse strength of the connection based on sealing integrity was lower than that of the casing body. Based on these, a collapse strength model for a 7″ crescent-worn casing connection considering sealing integrity was developed and a safety evaluation method of the collapse strength of the worn casing string was proposed.

Keywords: collapse strength; casing connection; crescent wear; sealing integrity; finite element method

MSC: 74S05

1. Introduction

In recent years, the cessation of production and the abandonment of oil and gas wells due to wellbore integrity damage frequently occurs, and the problem of wellbore integrity has attracted more attention [1–5]. The wellbore system involves tubing, casing, wellhead, packer, and more. Among them, the casing string is an important downhole tool to protect the borehole, reinforce the wellbore, isolate the oil, gas, and water layers, and seal various complex formation; it is also the key barrier of wellbore integrity. Therefore, its failure will pose a serious threat to production safety. Unfortunately, such failures do exist and are more likely to take place when casing wear takes place, which is caused by the friction between the down-hole tubular string and wellbore wall in complex structure wells [6].

Collapse is one of the common failure modes of the casing string under the action of external pressure. There are a lot of researchers working on the mechanism of casing collapse. Both analytical [7–12] and finite element methods [13–16] have been employed to carry out various studies on casing collapse, leading to the development of a relatively rigorous theoretical system and mature technical methods. However, most of these works focus on the casing body, treating the casing as a uniform round pipe. In fact, the casing string is not only composed of the casing body, but also threaded connections, which connect thousands of meters of casing together and could be the main failure location of the casing string. According to field statistics, 64% of casing failure accidents take place at threaded connections and some wells even reach 86% [17]. In addition, the failed

connections found on the field have serious wear phenomenon [18], but little attention has been paid to the strength of casing connections. One of the reasons is that the threaded connection has a larger wall thickness compared to the casing body, giving people an impression that the collapse strength of the connection is greater than that of the casing body. The other reason is that the structure of the connection is too complex to analyze. The engaged surface of the pin and box is a three-dimensional spiral surface, which involves strong nonlinearities, making it difficult to carry out the relevant research in depth. In addition, it should be noted that compared to the casing body, the threaded connection has a sealing problem. Chen et al. [19] established a three-dimensional finite element model of the casing connection and studied the distribution characteristics of contact stress on the joint sealing surface under complex loads. Xu [4] studied the contact pressure on the sealing surface by an analytical method. The current research on connection sealing are mostly about the contact stress on the sealing surface, but the criterion of seal failure caused by the change of contact stress is not given; the wear phenomenon and how to measure the mechanical properties of the connection under the condition of considering the integrity of the seal are not unified. Under the action of external load, the worn casing connection will have a larger structural deformation and this affects the sealing performance; it is thus necessary to consider the sealing performance when determining the collapse strength. However, this problem has not been received enough attention so far. In this paper, the finite element method was used to calculate the collapse strength of a worn 7″ casing connection. Based on the accuracy verification of the model and simulation algorithm, a three-dimensional finite element model of the worn casing connection was proposed to evaluate the collapse strength and the mechanical characteristics of the sealing surface of crescent-worn casing connections. Then, the influence of wear on the sealing integrity was discussed; the collapse strength considering the sealing integrity of the worn casing connection was also assessed using a sealing criterion. Finally, the partition evaluation diagram of collapse strength of the 7″ worn casing connection was obtained considering the sealing integrity when wear rates of the casing body and the connection are different.

2. The Calculation Formula of Collapse Strength for Worn Casing and Verification of Finite Element Model

2.1. The Calculation Formula of Collapse Strength for Worn Casing

According to the theory of elasticity, the collapse strength formula of the eccentric-worn casing body can be derived as [20]:

$$P_s = -\frac{Y_p(a^2+b^2)\left[(a^2+b^2-c^2)^2 - 4a^2b^2\right]}{2b^2\left[(b^2-c^2)^2 - a^2(a-2c)^2\right]} \tag{1}$$

where Y_P is the yield strength of casing, MPa; $b = \frac{D_c}{2}$, D_c is the outer diameter of casing, mm; and $a = b - \frac{t_{max}+t_{min}}{2}$, $c = \frac{t_{max}-t_{min}}{2}$ with t_{max} and t_{min} denoting, respectively, the maximum and minimum wall thickness of casing, mm.

The collapse strength formula of the crescent-worn casing body can be expressed as [20]:

$$P_{yw} = P_s \left(\frac{d}{D_i+\delta}\right)^{\left(\frac{\delta}{t}\right)} \tag{2}$$

where P_{yw} is the collapse strength of crescent-worn casing, MPa; d is the diameter of drill pipe causing casing wear, mm; D_i is the inner diameter of casing, mm; δ is the wear depth, mm; and t is the thickness of wall, mm.

2.2. Finite Element Calculation of Collapse Strength for Crescent-Worn Casing

Figure 1a shows a three-dimensional model of 7″ (ϕ 177.8 mm × 12.65 mm) crescent-worn casing body. The simulation results will be compared with Formula (2) in Section 2.1 so as to verify the reliability of the finite element model. In Figure 1b, R1 represents the radius of drill pipe causing casing wear, which is taken as 44.5 mm in this paper. The model has a total of 107,870 nodes and 80,100 elements. The element type is C3D8I, and the mesh is evenly distributed. The crescent internal wear of 0~4 mm was considered; the influence of wear depth on stress characteristics of casing under external pressure was calculated by ABAQUS 6.14. The density, elastic modulus, and Poisson's ratio of the casing material are 7850 kg/m^3, 210 GPa and 0.29, respectively.

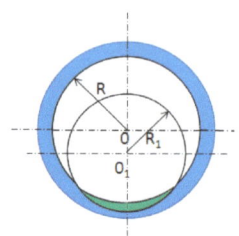

(**a**) Mesh model of casing body   (**b**) Schematic diagram of crescent-worn casing

Figure 1. Three-dimensional finite element model of casing body.

The results of the finite element method and the analytical solution calculated by Formula (2) were compared in Table 1. The results show that the minimum relative error is only 1.14% (occurring at 1 mm worn), the maximum relative error is 5.39% (occurring at 2 mm worn), and the average of relative error is 3.86%. The relative error is the absolute value of the error between Formula (2) and the finite element simulation results under the same wear condition. The above results show that the finite element results are in good agreement with the results by Formula (2), which verifies the accuracy of the finite element model.

Table 1. Comparison of results by Formula (2) and finite element method for casing body.

Wear depth/mm	0	1	2	3	4
Results by formula (2)/MPa	97.13	85.23	73.33	61.54	50.00
Finite element results/MPa	99.78	86.20	69.38	58.29	47.61
Relative error	2.72%	1.14%	5.39%	5.29%	4.77%

3. Calculation of Collapse Strength of Crescent-Worn Casing Connection

Figure 2 depicts a three-dimensional finite element model of casing connection with P110 steel grade. The specific geometric parameters of casing connection are given in Table 2.

Figure 2. Three-dimensional finite element model of casing connection.

Table 2. Geometric parameters of casing connection.

Parameter	Value/Type
Thread profile	Buttress
Pitch	5.08 mm
Thread taper	1:16
Sealing structure	The ball to the cone Cone taper of 1:16 Radius of the ball 18 mm
Outer diameter of the connection	194.5 mm
Outer diameter of casing body	177.8 mm
Inner diameter of casing body	152.5 mm

An eight-node hexahedron element was selected to calculate the deformation of above model. The total number of nodes and elements are 604,572 and 495,530, respectively. The mesh was refined in the stress-concentrated parts such as thread teeth and sealing surface. Material properties are the same as those in Section 2.2. The crescent wear was established on the inner wall of the casing connection, and the wear depth was also 0~4 mm.

To be clear, in this study, the calculation of the casing connection is based on the following assumptions:

(1) The basic physical quantities of the box and pin are continuously distributed, such as stress, strain, and displacement;
(2) The material of the pin and box of the casing connection adopts the assumption of uniformity and isotropy;
(3) Under the action of external force, the casing connection deformation is elastic deformation before the yield load, and plastic deformation after the yield load, without considering the viscosity, creep, and other effects.

The load was applied by establishing the coupling form of distributing nodes on the end surface of the pin; the constraint was imposed by establishing the coupling form of the kinematical node at the end surface of the box, as shown in Figure 3. Load cases are shown in Table 3.

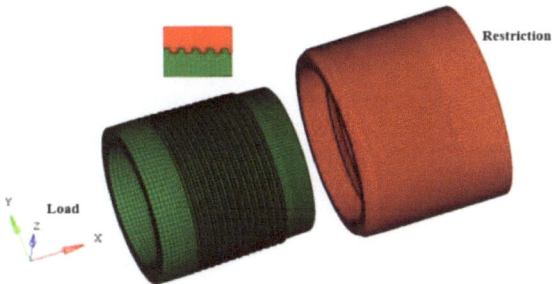

Figure 3. Boundary conditions.

Table 3. Load cases.

Load Cases	Magnitude
Step 1: Make-up	9.49 kN·m
Step 2: External pressure	200 MPa

For the convenience of the following description, the section diagram of the connection is given below and the key parts are marked in red boxes, as shown in the Figure 4. In the figure, zone I represents the engagement area of thread teeth, and zone II represents the sealing surface. The red and white symbols in the zone I and zone II are the locations of the two critical nodes A1 and A2 in the analysis below, and their function and selection will be explained below.

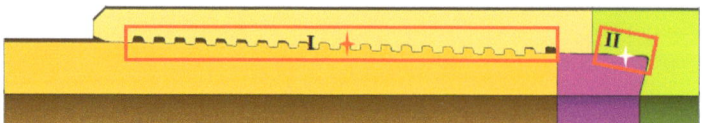

Figure 4. The section diagram of connection.

In order to reveal the influence of wear depth on the collapse strength of the casing connection, the von Mises stress curve at a node where the stress is relatively concentrated on the engagement area of thread teeth (corresponding to the red symbol of zone I in Figure 4) was plotted with the change of external pressure during the increase of wear depth, as shown in Figure 5. For simplicity, it is referred to as node A1 below.

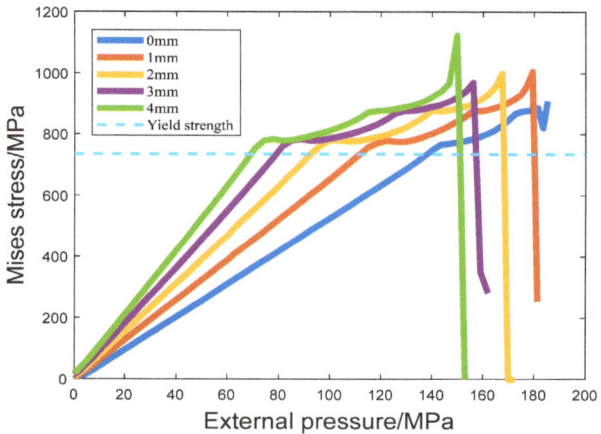

Figure 5. Curve of stress variation with load at node A1.

The external pressure corresponding to the stress reaching the yield strength is getting smaller with increased wear depth, as shown by the blue dotted line in Figure 5. It is widely known that if a small load increment causes a large increment of the maximum von Mises stress in the finite element calculation, it indicates that the casing connection has lost the ability to resist a further increase of external pressure and the corresponding von Mises stress can be regarded as the collapse strength of the casing connection. The collapse strength of the crescent-worn casing connection is 125.9 MPa, 103.8 MPa, 88.8 MPa, 74.1 MPa, and 63.5 MPa, corresponding to the wear depth of 0mm, 1mm, 2mm, 3mm, and 4mm, respectively. In other words, when crescent wear takes place, the collapse strength of the connection decreases with the increased wear depth. It can be found that under the same wear condition, the collapse strength of the casing connection is slightly greater than that of the casing body shown in Table 1. This is because the connection is engaged together through the pin and box, and the overall thickness of the connection after engagement is greater than the casing body.

However, wear reduces the collapse strength of the casing connection. When the wear depth reaches 4 mm, the collapse strength of the crescent-worn connection decreases by 49.6% compared with that of the unworn connection. That is to say, when the wear rate reaches about 30%, the collapse strength of the connection is reduced by nearly half. In this case, the casing connection is more likely to collapse, which greatly increases the risk of wellbore integrity damage.

Through curve fitting, the relationship between wear rate and the collapse strength of the crescent-worn casing connection can be obtained:

$$P_{cj} = -196.6\zeta^3 + 362\zeta^2 - 291\zeta + 125.6 \qquad (3)$$

where ζ is the wear rate, defined as the ratio of wear depth δ to original wall thickness t; and P_{cj} is the collapse strength of the connection with crescent-worn, MPa.

Figure 6 shows the collapse strength of the worn connection considering the sealing integrity calculated based on the finite element solution and fitting curve drawn by the formula (3).

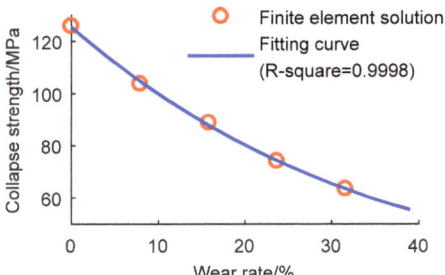

Figure 6. The finite element calculation results and fitting curve.

4. Influence of Wear Depth on Sealing Performance of Connection

Formula (3) is the collapse strength model only considering strength characteristics. However, a very important fact should be recognized, which is that casing connection is not a real thick-wall casing body due to the engagement of the pin and box. Not only its strength but also its sealing performance should be paid attention to under the external pressure. When the casing connection deforms greatly under external load, sealing failure may occur and the integrity of the casing string may be problematic. Therefore, it is more practical to study the casing collapse strength considering the sealing integrity.

Similarly, for the convenience of subsequent analysis and explanation, the diagrams of the critical path are given below, as shown in the Figure 7. Figure 7a shows the complete connection and the circumferential path on the sealing surface (corresponding to zone II in Figure 4). It should be noted that the circumferential path is a ring of sealing ring composed of the node where the maximum contact stress is located along the axial direction on the sealing surface. Figure 7b shows only the sealing ring of the sealing surface in the connection.

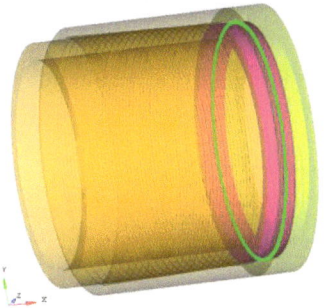

(**a**) Location of circumferential path   (**b**) Circumferential path and axial path

Figure 7. Critical path.

4.1. Axial Distribution Characteristics of Stress on Sealing Surface

The casing connection studied in this paper adopts a sphere-cone sealing structure, as shown in Figure 8. The sealing is realized by a radial interference fit of the sealing surface and the sealing performance is mainly reflected in the distribution of contact stress on the sealing surface.

Figure 8. Sealing structure of the casing connection.

A higher contact stress and a larger contact width are the two important features of an excellent sealing performance in the elastic range. The stress on the sealing surface has greatly exceeded the elastic limit. Meanwhile, there is plastic deformation which is helpful to the sealing performance in a certain range. Therefore, it is difficult to accurately describe the micro channel on the sealing surface, which increases the difficulty of evaluating the sealing performance of the sealing surface. In view of both elastic and plastic deformation, fluid leakage will appear in the direction of small leakage resistance, so the fluid leakage resistance is also affected by the contact stress and contact width of the sealing surface. The contact pressure along the axial path on the wear side of the sealing surface was selected (as shown in Figure 7) to analyze the variation of stress characteristics with different wear depths. The simulation results of the model showed that the width of the sealing surface of the connection corresponding to different wear depths are the same (3.75 mm); thus, only the contact stress on the sealing surface is discussed below.

The node with the maximum contact stress on the sealing surface was taken from the axial path (the intersection of the green-color circumferential path and the black-color axial path is shown in Figure 7b); for simplicity, it is referred to as node A2. Node A2 is the node of maximum stress on the axial path and the critical node for sealing the connection; its location is in the marked white symbol of zone II in Figure 4. It can be said that the value of contact stress at A2 node determines the sealing quality of the connection, as shown in Figure 9. The change of contact stress at this point with external pressure was observed under different wear depths, as shown in Figure 10.

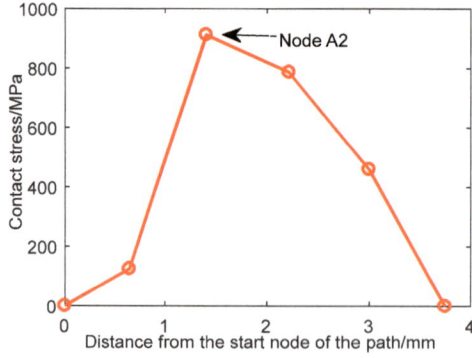

Figure 9. Axial distribution characteristics of stress on sealing surface.

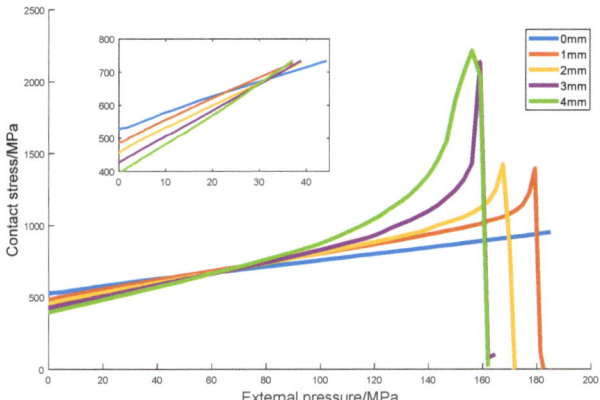

Figure 10. Change of contact stress on node A2 with external pressure and partially enlarged diagram.

As can be seen from Figure 10, with the increase of external pressure, the contact stress on the sealing surface of the casing connection increases gently at first (in the elastic stage), then increases sharply (in the plastic stage), finally dropping rapidly to zero, at which time-step a structural plastic failure has occurred (as shown in Figure 11). The partially enlarged diagram in Figure 10 shows that the contact stress on the sealing surface of the pretightening connection decreases with the increased wear depth when the external pressure is zero. With the gradual increase of external pressure, the connections with different wear depths reach the yield strength successively. The calculation results show that a greater wear depth corresponds to a smaller external pressure when the contact stress reaches the yield strength—that is, the sealing integrity of the connection decreases.

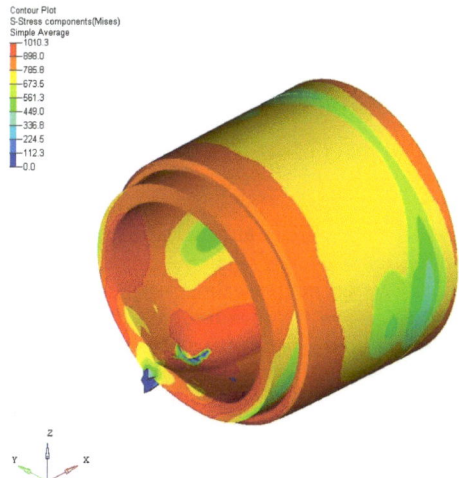

Figure 11. Structural plastic failure occurred in casing connection.

In order to illustrate the influence of wear on the sealing performance of the connection, the collapse strength of each model calculated in Section 3 was taken as the dividing line of elastic–plastic, and the average contact stress on the sealing surface of the crescent-worn connection at the elastic stage was obtained, as shown in Table 4.

It can be found that the average contact stress on the sealing surface of the crescent-worn casing connection decreases gradually with increased wear depth. When the wear depth reaches 4 mm, the average contact stress on the sealing surface is reduced by 16.5%, which reduces the sealing performance of the connection to a certain degree.

Table 4. Average contact stress of node A2 at elastic stage.

Wear depth/mm	0	1	2	3	4
Average contact stress/MPa	593.81	562.04	542.93	520.98	495.67

4.2. Circumferential Distribution Characteristics of Stress on Sealing Surface

In order to observe the circumferential distribution of contact stress along the sealing surface of the worn connection in the process of increasing external pressure, the circumferential contact stress along the ring (corresponding to the green-color ring in Figure 7a) on the sealing surface was extracted and expressed in Figure 12.

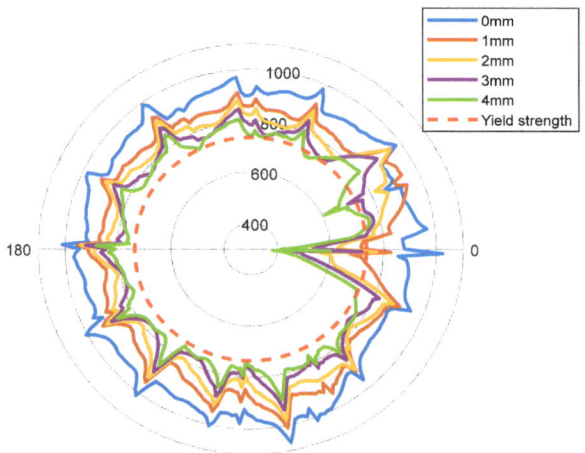

Figure 12. Contact stress distribution on the circumferential path under different wear depths.

It can be found that the stress characteristics along the circumferential path show irregular fluctuations corresponding to each wear depth, which is mainly due to the nonlinear contact characteristics caused by the helix angle of the threaded teeth. With the increase of wear depth, the circumferential contact stress on the sealing surface is gradually decreased, and the contact stress along the circumferential becomes more uneven, which will have an adverse effect on the sealing performance.

As shown in Table 5, the maximum contact stress, minimum contact stress, and average contact stress on the circumferential path decrease gradually with increased wear depth, and when the wear depth reaches 4 mm, they decrease by 16.2%, 54.9%, and 18.6%, respectively, compared with the unworn connection.

The calculation results show that the maximum contact stress and average contact stress decrease slightly whereas the minimum contact stress decreases greatly. The minimum contact stress on the unworn connection is 845.0 MPa, slightly greater than the yield strength of the material. When the wear depth is 1 mm, the minimum contact stress has decreased to 674.8 MPa, which is lower than the yield strength of the material. With the increase of the wear depth, the minimum contact stress further decreases. When the wear depth is 4 mm, the minimum contact stress decreases by more than half compared with the unworn connection, which is much lower than the yield strength of the material.

Although the maximum contact stress and the average contact stress are both greater than the yield strength under different wear depths, it seems that the connection has reliable sealing performance. Since the contact stress along the circumferential path taken in this paper is the maximum value along the axial path on the whole sealing surface, the minimum contact stress on the circumferential path in Table 5 is also the maximum contact stress on the axial path where the point is located. Therefore, the minimum contact stress is too much lower than the yield strength of the material, indicating that there may be a leakage channel along the axial path at this position, resulting in connection seal failure. By observing the node of the minimum contact stress on the circumferential path, it was found that the minimum contact stress occurred on the side where the wear occurred under different wear depths, which also proves that the wear has a strong destructive effect on the sealing integrity of the connection.

Table 5. Contact stress on circumferential path.

Wear/mm	0	1	2	3	4
Maximum contact stress/MPa	1068.6	1010.1	976.5	937.9	896.0
Minimum contact stress/MPa	845.0	674.8	560.8	452.4	381.5
Average contact stress/MPa	926.8	865.9	825.5	785.0	754.5

4.3. Collapse Strength of Worn Casing Connection Considering Sealing Performance

According to the analysis in Section 4.2, the occurrence of wear reduces the contact stress on the sealing surface of the casing connection and increases the uneven distribution along the circumferential direction, which obviously has an adverse effect on the sealing performance of the connection. Although the worn connection has not been collapsed and sealing failure may have occurred, the obtained collapse strength will be divorced from reality and will have no practical value only considering the collapse strength of the connection without paying attention to the reduction of its sealing performance. Therefore, a calculation model of the collapse strength of the casing connection considering sealing integrity should be proposed.

Based on the theory of sealing contact energy [21], the flow resistance preventing gas from passing through metal to the metal sealing structure can be characterized by some integral value of contact stress on effective contact width.

When gas seal index W_a > critical gas seal index W_{ac}, there is no Leakage;

When gas seal index W_a < critical gas seal index W_{ac}, leakage takes place.

Murtagian's experimental results show that the gas seal index of the metal sealing structure with a sphere-cone can be expressed as [22]:

$$W_a = \int_0^L P^n e(l) \mathrm{d}l \tag{4}$$

P_e is the contact stress along the axial path of the wear side of the sealing surface corresponding to the moment of collapse failure occurs, MPa; l is the contact width of the sealing surface, mm; and n is set to 1.2 when sealing compound is used—otherwise, it is set to 1.4.

The critical gas seal index obtained through the experiment test can be expressed as [22]:

$$W_{ac} = 1.84 \times \left(\frac{P_{gas}}{P_{atm}}\right)^{1.177} \tag{5}$$

P_{gas} is gas pressure that needs to be sealed, MPa; and P_{atm} is atmospheric pressure, MPa.

Equations (4) and (5) can be used to obtain the maximum gas pressure in the casing with reliable sealing, which is equivalent to the collapse strength corresponding to seal failure under the action of external pressure.

Atmospheric pressure is 0.1 MPa. The collapse strength of the worn connection calculated based on this is 104.7 MPa, 81.8 MPa, 64.4 MPa, 56.0 MPa, and 48.0 MPa, respectively, corresponding to the wear depth of 0 mm, 1 mm, 2 mm, 3 mm, and 4 mm, respectively. Considering the sealing integrity, the relationship between the collapse strength and wear depth of the connection is similar to that of the casing body; that is, with the increase of wear depth, the collapse strength decreases gradually, but the corresponding value decreases slightly. According to the calculated results, the polynomial relationship between wear rate ζ and the collapse strength of the casing connection considering sealing integrity is formulated as follows:

$$P_{cs} = -403.91\zeta^3 + 638.39\zeta^2 - 339.15\zeta + 104.67 \qquad (6)$$

Figure 13 shows the collapse strength of the worn connection considering the sealing integrity calculated based on the finite element solution and fitting curve. Compared with the results in Section 3, the collapse strength of the connection is greatly reduced after considering the sealing integrity.

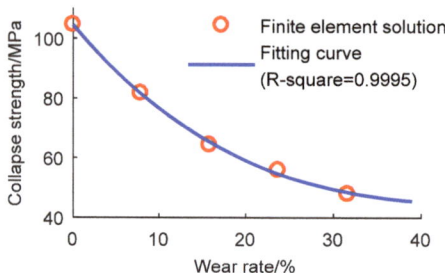

Figure 13. Finite element calculation results and fitting curve.

5. Discussion

In engineering practice, the sealing integrity of the threaded connection is evaluated by the leakage rate. Leakage rate refers to the leakage rate of medium fluid per second through the sealed interface under standard test conditions. For metal–metal seals, according to the requirements of the threaded connection test procedure of tubing/casing (ISO 13679), the gas leakage rate during the test is less than 0.9 cm^3/15 min, which is an indicator of good sealing [23]. However, in this study, it is not very possible to quantitatively calculate the leakage rate of the casing connection under wear condition or the collapse strength under critical leakage rate. Therefore, the seal integrity in this article refers to that idea that when the casing string (including casing body and threaded connection) is worn at different degrees, the collapse strength considering the sealing integrity is calculated based on the contact energy theory of the metal seal. This evaluation method considering the sealing integrity of connections makes up for the shortcomings of the current research which only pays attention to the collapse strength in the casing string and ignores the sealing failure of connection. As the weak part of the casing string, the threaded connection is the common site of failure due to a seal problem, so the entire casing string can be considered safe when the safety of the threaded connection is guaranteed.

Figure 14 shows the corresponding casing body collapse strength P_{cb}, casing connection collapse strength P_{cj}, and casing connection collapse strength considering sealing integrity P_{cs}. For an unworn connection, the collapse strength is 129.50 MPa, and the collapse strength of the connection considering sealing integrity is 104.74 MPa. For an unworn casing body, its collapse strength is 97.13 MPa, which is lower than connection. At this point, the collapse strength of the connection can be calculated according to the casing body, which is consistent with the current understanding that the collapse strength of the connection is much larger than the casing body.

When the casing body and the connection have the same wear depth, the above conclusion is also established if the sealing integrity is not considered. However, when the wear rate exceeds 5.5% (corresponding to the wear depth of 0.69 mm), the collapse strength of the connection considering sealing integrity is smaller than the casing body. If the wear depth of the connection and the casing body is different, it can also be judged by Figure 14 to determine the minimum collapse strength of the casing string.

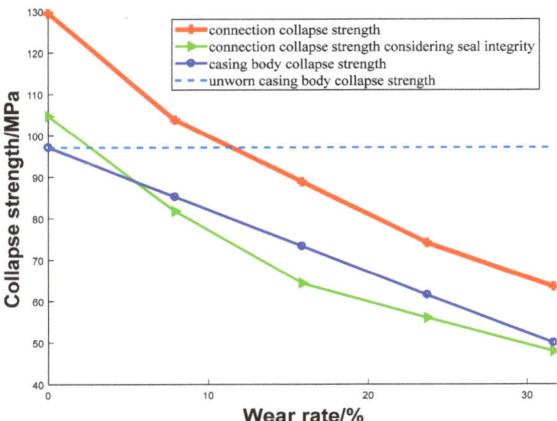

Figure 14. Collapse strength of casing body and connection under different wear depths.

For both the casing body and the connection, with the deepening of wear, the collapse strength will decrease in different degrees. Without wear, the finite element calculation result in Section 2.2 was compared with the full-scale collapse test data of a casing body of the same size (ϕ 177.80 mm × 12.65 mm P110) in [24]: the experimental result was 99.1 MPa, which was very close to the 99.8 MPa calculated by the model in this paper. For the casing connection, we compared it with the experimental data, which is equivalent to two layers of casing body with a larger wall thickness. In the experiment [25], for P110 steel casing, when the diameter–thickness ratio Dc/t is less than 14 (the corresponding diameter-to-thickness ratio Dc/t in the model of an equivalent casing is 9.3), the collapse strength is greater than 124.1 MPa (18,000 psi); this is consistent with the 125.9 MPa calculated for the unworn connection in Section 3. However, when considering the sealing integrity of the connection, the collapse strength of the unworn connection is only 104.7 MPa, a decrease of 16.8%, indicating that when considering the sealing integrity, the effective collapse strength of the connection cannot reach the expectation, which is consistent with the current understanding. That is to say, if only considering the connection strength, the connection may have had a seal failure while the structure was intact; if wear is taken into account, the effective collapse strength of the connection is even lower.

In actual working conditions, the wear depth of the casing body and the connection are often different, and the wear condition of the connection is usually more serious. Therefore, it is necessary to discuss the collapse strength of the casing body and the connection when the wear is not synchronous.

Considering the sealing performance of the connection, the difference of the collapse strength of the connection and casing body with wear rate is shown in Figure 15. The meaning of this figure is the relative strength relationship between the collapse strength of the connection and the casing body when their wear rate changes, respectively. As shown in the Figure 15, the grey plane gives a zero datum; above the datum plane is the area where the collapse strength of the casing connection is higher than that of the casing body when the wear rate changes, respectively; below the datum plane is the area where the collapse strength of the casing connection is lower than that of the casing body.

Generally, the wear of the connection is more serious; that is, the wear rate of the connection is greater than that of the casing body. Due to the thicker wall of the connection, only the collapse strength of the casing body is usually considered. However, from the perspective of wellbore integrity, not only the collapse strength under the influence of wear but also the sealing integrity of the casing string should be considered to make the risk assessment of the casing string collapse more practical.

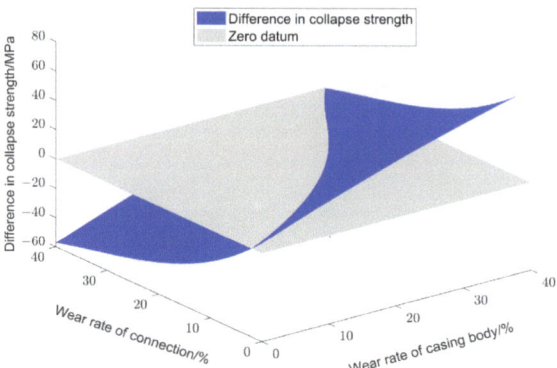

Figure 15. The difference of collapse strength between connection and body varies with wear rate.

A projection of Figure 15 on the XY plane can be used to obtain the collapse strength of the casing body and connection based on the sealing integrity, as shown in Figure 16. Using ζ_p to represent the wear rate of the casing body and ζ_c to represent the wear rate of the connection, the expression of the red and green areas in Figure 16 can be obtained by polynomial fitting as follows:

$$\begin{cases} \zeta_c \geq 0.01565\zeta_p{}^2 + 0.3136\zeta_p + 2.744 & \text{(red area)} \\ \zeta_c < 0.01565\zeta_p{}^2 + 0.3136\zeta_p + 2.744 & \text{(green area)} \end{cases} \quad (7)$$

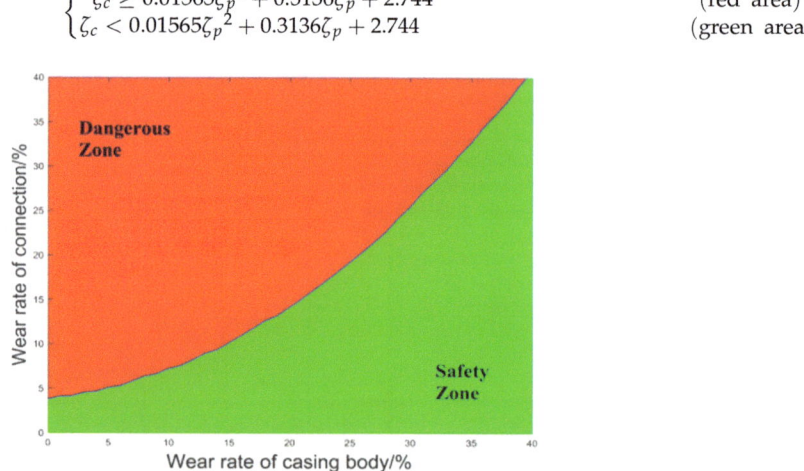

Figure 16. Partition evaluation of collapse strength of casing string based on sealing integrity.

The green area in Figure 16 shows that the collapse strength of the connection is higher than that of the body under different wear rates. Based on the above considerations, this area is defined as a "safe area". Since the collapse strength of the connection is greater than that of the body under the corresponding wear rate of the "safety zone", it is only necessary to evaluate the impact of wear on the collapse strength of the casing body according to Formula (2) to protect the whole casing string from collapse and leakage. The red area in Figure 16 shows that the collapse strength of the casing connection is lower than that of the body; this area is defined as a "dangerous area". Under the corresponding wear rate of the "dangerous area", the impact of wear on the collapse strength of the casing string should be evaluated according to Formula (6) based on the connection.

6. Conclusions

In this article, we established the finite element model of a 7″ crescent-worn casing threaded connection. In addition to studying the effect of wear on the collapse strength traditionally, we also proposed an evaluation method of the worn casing connection with consideration of seal safety. According to the study above, we reached the following conclusions:

(1) Under external pressure, the contact stress on the sealing surface of the worn casing connection will decrease significantly, increasing the risk of leakage of the connection.

(2) The collapse strength of the connection without considering sealing integrity is greater than that of the casing body under the same wear condition, which is consistent with the current understanding.

(3) The collapse strength of the connection may be less than the casing body when considering the sealing integrity. For the 7″ casing in this paper, the collapse strength of the connection is smaller than the casing body when the wear rate exceeds 5.5% for gas seal conditions.

(4) Since the casing body and connection often have different wear depths, an evaluation model of the collapse strength of the worn casing connection considering the sealing integrity was developed, which can determine the wear depth at which the collapse strength of the connection is lower than that of the casing body.

Author Contributions: Conceptualization, Q.D. and F.C.; methodology, X.Z., F.C. and D.L.; software, X.Z. and F.C.; validation, X.W., W.W. and Q.D.; formal analysis, X.Z. and F.C.; investigation, D.L. and X.W.; resources, W.W.; data curation, Q.D.; writing—original draft preparation, X.Z. and F.C.; writing—review and editing, Q.D., F.C. and W.W.; visualization, X.Z. and D.L.; supervision, W.W. and Q.D. All authors have read and agreed to the published version of the manuscript.

Funding: This research was supported by the National Natural Science Foundation of China (52174003, U1663205, 51804194, 51704191).

Institutional Review Board Statement: Not applicable.

Informed Consent Statement: Not applicable.

Data Availability Statement: The data presented in this article are available upon reasonable request from the corresponding author.

Conflicts of Interest: The authors declare no conflict of interest.

References

1. Smith, L.; Milanovic, D. The total control of well integrity management. In Proceedings of the Abu Dhabi International Petroleum Exhibition and Conference, Abu Dhabi, United Arab Emirates, 3–6 November 2008; p. SPE117121.
2. Annandale, A.; Conway, R.; Copping, S. A systematic approach to well integrity management. In Proceedings of the SPE Digital Energy Conference & Exhibition, Houston, TX, USA, 7–8 April 2009; p. SPE123201.
3. Buchmiller, D.; Rengard, O.; Haug, L.T.; Horte, T.; Grytoyr, G.; Katla, E. Advancements in structural well integrity design and operation. In Proceedings of the Offshore Technology Conference, Houston, TX, USA, 30 April–3 May 2012; p. SPE23278.
4. Xu, H. Study on Joint Strength and Sealing Theory for Casing and Tubing Premium Connection. Ph.D. Thesis, Southwest Petroleum University, Chengdu, China, 2015.
5. Liu, K. Research on Well Integrity of Horizontal Shale Gas Well with Hydraulic Fracturing. Ph.D. Thesis, China University of Petroleum, Beijing, China, 2019.
6. Chen, L. Analysis of the Rub-Impact and Its Induced Wear Characteristics of Drill String on Casing. Master's Thesis, Shanghai University, Shanghai, China, 2019.
7. Li, H. *China Pipe Engineering*; Petroleum Industry Press: Beijing, China, 1999.
8. Clinedinst, W.O. *A Rational Expression for the Critical Collapsing Pressure of Pipe under External Pressure*; American Petroleum Institute: Chicago, IL, USA, 1963; pp. 383–391.
9. Mimura, H.; Mimaki, T.; Tamano, T. *Finite Element Analysis of Collapse Strength of Casing*; Nippon Steel Corporation: Tokyo, Japan, 1987.
10. Qiu, W.; Zhao, H. Analysis of casing extrusion. *Acta Pet. Sin.* **1995**, *16*, 99–107.
11. Gong, W. Application of trigonometric series to calculate critical external pressure of circular pipe with uneven wall thickness. *Oil Drill. Prod. Technol.* **1990**, *12*, 1–10.
12. Huang, W.; Gao, D. A theoretical study of the critical external pressure for casing collapse. *J. Nat. Gas Sci. Eng.* **2015**, *12*, 290–297. [CrossRef]

13. Huang, X.; Mihsein, M.; Kibble, K.; Hall, R. Collapse strength analysis of casing design using finite element method. *Int. J. Press. Vessel. Pip.* **2000**, *77*, 359–367. [CrossRef]
14. Berger, A.; Fleckenstein, W.W.; Eustes, A.W.; Thonhauser, G. Effect of eccentricity, voids, cement channels, and pore pressure decline on collapse resistance of casing. In Proceedings of the SPE Annual Technical Conference and Exhibition, Houston, TX, USA, 26–29 September 2004.
15. Chen, Z.; Zhu, W.; Di, Q. Effects of eccentricity of casing on collapse resistance in non-uniform in-situ stresses. *J. Shanghai Univ. (Nat. Sci. Ed.)* **2012**, *18*, 83–86.
16. Jin, C.; Qian, F.; Feng, F. Effect of variable drill pipe sizes on casing wear collapse strength. *J. Pet. Sci. Eng.* **2020**, *12*, 195. [CrossRef]
17. Cai, X.; Gao, L. Current development situation of the special threaded connection for tubing/casing. *Welded Pipe Tube* **2008**, *4*, 41–44+94.
18. Wang, N. Analysis of 3D Mechanical Characteristics of Special Threaded Joints of Worn Tubing. Master's Thesis, Shanghai University, Shanghai, China, 2020.
19. Chen, W.; Di, Q.; Zhang, H.; Chen, F.; Wang, W. The sealing mechanism of tubing and casing premium threaded connections under complex loads. *J. Pet. Sci. Eng.* **2018**, *171*, 724–730. [CrossRef]
20. Liang, E. Test on Wear Rule and Prediction on Wear Degree of Casing in Deep Wells and Extended Reach Wells. Ph.D. Thesis, Yanshan University, Qinhuangdao, China, 2012.
21. Xu, H.; Yang, B.; Shi, T.; Zhang, Z. Analysis of influencing hermetic seal performance with a spherical-conical surface and special screw threads. *J. Southwest Pet. Univ. (Nat. Sci. Ed.)* **2017**, *39*, 162–166.
22. Murtagian, G.R.; Fanelli, V.; Villasante, J.A.; Johnson, D.H.; Ernst, H.A. Sealability of stationary metal-to-metal seal. *J. Tribol.* **2004**, *126*, 591–596. [CrossRef]
23. ISO 13679; Petroleum and Natural Gas Industries—Procedures for Testing Casing and Tubing Connection. IX-ISO: Geneva, Switzerland, 2019.
24. Lou, Q.; Du, W.; Han, X.L.; Li, D.F.; Zhang, G.L. Analysis on the influence factors of casing collapse resistance strength. *Adv. Mater. Res.* **2012**, *415–417*, 2121–2125. [CrossRef]
25. Brechan, B.; Kornberg, E.; Sangesland, S.; Dale, S.I. Well integrity model- klever&tamano collapse. In Proceedings of the SPE/IADC Middle East Drilling Technology Conference and Exhibition, Abu Dhabi, United Arab Emirates, 29–31 January 2018.

Disclaimer/Publisher's Note: The statements, opinions and data contained in all publications are solely those of the individual author(s) and contributor(s) and not of MDPI and/or the editor(s). MDPI and/or the editor(s) disclaim responsibility for any injury to people or property resulting from any ideas, methods, instructions or products referred to in the content.

Article

Weighted Radial Basis Collocation Method for the Nonlinear Inverse Helmholtz Problems

Minghao Hu, Lihua Wang *, Fan Yang and Yueting Zhou

School of Aerospace Engineering and Applied Mechanics, Tongji University, Shanghai 200092, China
* Correspondence: lhwang@tongji.edu.cn

Abstract: In this paper, a meshfree weighted radial basis collocation method associated with the Newton's iteration method is introduced to solve the nonlinear inverse Helmholtz problems for identifying the parameter. All the measurement data can be included in the least-squares solution, which can avoid the iteration calculations for comparing the solutions with part of the measurement data in the Galerkin-based methods. Appropriate weights are imposed on the boundary conditions and measurement conditions to balance the errors, which leads to the high accuracy and optimal convergence for solving the inverse problems. Moreover, it is quite easy to extend the solution process of the one-dimensional inverse problem to high-dimensional inverse problem. Nonlinear numerical examples include one-, two- and three-dimensional inverse Helmholtz problems of constant and varying parameter identification in regular and irregular domains and show the high accuracy and exponential convergence of the presented method.

Keywords: weighted radial basis collocation method; Newton's iteration method; nonlinear; inverse Helmholtz problems; parameter identification

MSC: 65D12; 65N21

1. Introduction

The Helmholtz equation can represent many physical and engineering problems, such as structural vibration [1], wave scattering [2], acoustics [3], electromagnetic problem and heat conduction [4], etc. However, in many engineering applications, the physical parameters are unknown or the boundary conditions are incomplete due to some technical difficulties associated with data acquisition. Therefore, studying the inverse Helmholtz problems has attracted much attention in the past decades, which includes the parameter inversion problems with unknown wave numbers, boundary inversion problems with unknown boundary conditions, and so on.

Many numerical methods have been proposed for the inverse Helmholtz problems; for example, the finite difference method (FDM) [5] and finite element method (FEM) [6]. FDM is very convenient for solving problems with regular boundaries, but it is hard to deal with irregular regions. FEM can handle the problems of complex geometry. However, the high gradients between the elements are not continuous, which affect the accuracy of the high gradients; remeshing is required for solving the nonlinear problems, which reduces the efficiency. Moreover, Onishi et al. [7] noticed that the FEM solution for the inverse Cauchy problem cannot converge. After that, meshfree methods became a kind of popular method, since the mesh distortion and remeshing can be avoided. In addition, meshfree methods can achieve high accuracy and convergence to solve general scientific and engineering problems. Typical meshfree methods include the element free Galerkin method (EFGM) [8], reproduced kernel particle method (RKPM) [9], finite point method (FPM) [10], point interpolation method (PIM) [11], radial basis collocation method (RBCM) [12], stabilized collocation method [13,14], etc.

Among many meshfree methods, RBCM, which is based on the radial basis functions (RBFs) approximation and strong form collocation, has attracted special attention because of its high accuracy and simple implementation [15–17]. Dehghan and Shokri [18] utilized the RBFs with a collocation method for solving a one-dimensional wave equation with an integral condition, which demonstrated that the accuracy of this method is superior to the FDM. Further, Wang et al. [19] investigated the stability, dispersion and eigenvalue analysis of RBCM in detail for one to three-dimensional wave propagation. Moreover, RBCM has been reported to perform well in the boundary value problems [20–23], incompressible elasticity [24], fluid–structure interaction [25], composite materials [26–30], heat transfer problem [31], fracture problems [32], etc.

For solving the Helmholtz problems, Hon and Chen [33] employed the boundary knot method (BKM) for the 2D and 3D Helmholtz problems under complicated domains with irregular boundaries. Marin and Lesnic [34,35] applied the method of fundamental solutions (MFS) to the Cauchy problem associated with Helmholtz-type equations. For the inverse Helmholtz problems, Jin and Zheng [36] proposed an efficient and stable numerical scheme based on the method of fundamental solutions to solve the inverse problems associated with the Helmholtz equations. Hon and Wei [37] developed the fundamental solution based on the RBFs to solve the inverse heat conduction problem. In addition, Shojaei et al. [38–40] used the fundamental solution based on EBFs to solve the Helmholtz-type problems. Based on the RBFs approximation and the method of particular solutions, Li et al. [41] solved the nonhomogeneous backward heat conduction problems. Yu et al. [42] improved the regularization method for the ill-posed backward heat conduction problem in the eigenvalue analysis. Most of the aforementioned methods for the direct or inverse Helmholtz problems are based on the fundamental solutions, which are hard to be acquired for the complex problems. Moreover, nonlinear analysis is always a difficult part for the analysis of Helmholtz problems.

In this paper, a weighted radial basis collocation method (WRBCM) [20,43–45], which has been well applied for the boundary value problems [20] and inverse wave propagation problems [43–45], is introduced for the nonlinear inverse Helmholtz problems of wave number identification. For the first time, appropriate weights that should be imposed on the boundary conditions and measurement conditions are derived for the inverse Helmholtz problems. Error analysis and convergence studies demonstrated in the numerical examples demonstrate the good accuracy and optimal convergence of the presented method.

2. Approximation of Radial Basis Functions

For the approximation, consider a closed problem domain $\overline{\Omega}$, which is discretized by a group of source points $(\mathbf{x}_1, \mathbf{x}_2, \cdots, \mathbf{x}_{N_s})$, where N_s is the number of source points. A function $u(\mathbf{x})$ defined in this problem domain can be approximated by the radial basis function (RBF) approximation, as follows

$$u(\mathbf{x}) \approx \widetilde{u}(\mathbf{x}) = \sum_{I=1}^{N_s} \varphi_I(\mathbf{x}) d_I \quad (1)$$

where $\widetilde{u}(\mathbf{x})$ is the approximation function, $\varphi_I(\mathbf{x})$ is the utilized RBF, and d_I is the node coefficient. RBFs represent a group of functions where the function values are only depending on the radial distance. One of the most popular RBFs is called the Multiquadric (MQ) RBF, which was proposed by Hardy [46,47], and it can be expressed as

$$\varphi_I(\mathbf{x}) = \left(r_I^2 + c^2\right)^{\xi - \frac{3}{2}}, \xi = 1, 2, 3, \ldots \quad (2)$$

where $r_I = |\mathbf{x} - \mathbf{x}_I|$ denotes the Euclidean distance between collocation point $\mathbf{x}$ and source point $\mathbf{x}_I$, c is the shape parameter controlling the shape of the function, and ξ is the parameter representing different forms of the MQ function. When $\xi = 1, 2, 3$, the RBF is called the reciprocal (or inverse) MQ RBF, linear MQ RBF and cubic MQ RBF, respectively. Another representative RBF proposed by Krige [48] is called the Gaussian RBF as follows

$$\varphi_I(\mathbf{x}) = exp\left(-\frac{r_I^2}{c^2}\right) \quad (3)$$

In comparison, the Gaussian RBF is more local than MQs, for which it works better for the problems with locality properties.

In this work, the reciprocal MQ is employed for the approximation. To evaluate the convergence property, Madych and Nelson [49] provided the error estimate for MQs as

$$\left|\left|u - \tilde{u}\right|\right|_{L^\infty(\Omega)} \leq C\eta^{c/h}\left|\left|u\right|\right|_l \quad (4)$$

Here, C is a generic constant, h is the characteristic nodal distance, $\eta \in (0,1)$ is a real number independent of c and h, and $||u||_l$ is the induced form defined in [49].

3. Formulations for the Inverse Helmholtz Problem of Identifying Parameter

3.1. Discretization of the Governing Equation as Well as Boundary Conditions and Known Conditions

The governing equation for the inverse Helmholtz problem of unknown parameter can be expressed as

$$\Delta u(\mathbf{x}) + k(\mathbf{x})u(\mathbf{x}) = f(\mathbf{x}), \mathbf{x} \in \Omega \quad (5)$$

with the boundary conditions

$$B^h u(\mathbf{x}) = h(\mathbf{x}), \mathbf{x} \in \Gamma_h \quad (6)$$

$$B^g u(\mathbf{x}) = g(\mathbf{x}), \mathbf{x} \in \Gamma_g \quad (7)$$

and the known conditions obtained from measurement data

$$A u(\mathbf{x}) = b(\mathbf{x}), \mathbf{x} \in \Pi \quad (8)$$

where Ω, Γ_h and Γ_g define the problem domain, Neumann boundary and Dirichlet boundary, respectively, and $\Omega \cup \Gamma_g \cup \Gamma_h = \overline{\Omega}$. Π is a subdomain with known conditions from the measurement data, and $\Pi \in \overline{\Omega}$. Δ is the Laplace operator in Ω. B^g is the spatial boundary operator on Γ_g. B^h is the spatial boundary operator on Γ_h. A is the spatial differential operator in Π. Furthermore, u is the problem unknown, k presents the unknown parameter, which denotes the wave number, and f is the source term. The known terms of the Neumann and Dirichlet boundary conditions are represented by h and g, respectively. The known term of the measurement data is denoted by b.

The approximated function denoted as $\tilde{u} \approx u$ and approximated parameter denoted as $\tilde{k} \approx k$ take the following form

$$u \approx \tilde{u} = \mathbf{\Phi}^T(\mathbf{x})\mathbf{d} \quad (9)$$

$$k(\mathbf{x}) \approx \tilde{k}(\mathbf{x}) = \mathbf{\Phi}^T(\mathbf{x})\overline{\mathbf{d}} \quad (10)$$

where

$$\mathbf{\Phi}^T(\mathbf{x}) = [\varphi_1, \varphi_2, \cdots, \varphi_{N_s}] \quad (11)$$

$$\mathbf{d} = [d_1, d_2, \cdots, d_{N_s}]^T \quad (12)$$

$$\overline{\mathbf{d}} = \left[\overline{d}_1, \overline{d}_2, \cdots, \overline{d}_{N_s}\right]^T \quad (13)$$

Substituting the approximations (9) and (10) into Equations (5)–(8) renders

$$\Delta\mathbf{\Phi}^{\mathrm{T}}(\mathbf{x})\mathbf{d} + \mathbf{\Phi}^{\mathrm{T}}(\mathbf{x})\overline{\mathbf{d}}\mathbf{\Phi}^{\mathrm{T}}(\mathbf{x})\mathbf{d} = f(\mathbf{x}), \quad \mathbf{x} \in \Omega \tag{14}$$

$$B^h\mathbf{\Phi}^{\mathrm{T}}(\mathbf{x})\mathbf{d} = h(\mathbf{x}), \quad \mathbf{x} \in \Gamma_h \tag{15}$$

$$B^g\mathbf{\Phi}^{\mathrm{T}}(\mathbf{x})\mathbf{d} = g(\mathbf{x}), \quad \mathbf{x} \in \Gamma_g \tag{16}$$

$$A\mathbf{\Phi}^{\mathrm{T}}(\mathbf{x})\mathbf{d} = b(\mathbf{x}), \quad \mathbf{x} \in \Pi \tag{17}$$

Let $\{\mathbf{p}_I\}_{I=1}^{N_p} \subseteq \Omega$, $\{\mathbf{q}_I\}_{I=1}^{N_q} \subseteq \Gamma_h$, $\{\mathbf{r}_I\}_{I=1}^{N_r} \subseteq \Gamma_g$ and $\{\mathbf{a}_I\}_{I=1}^{N_a} \subseteq \Pi$ be the collocation points in the domain Ω, on Neumann boundary Γ_h, on Dirichlet boundary Γ_g and in the subdomain with known conditions Π, respectively. Here N_p, N_q, N_r and N_a are the correspondent numbers of collocation points. The total number of collocation points is $N_c = N_p + N_q + N_r + N_a$. Evaluating the strong form Equations (14)–(17) at the collocation points in the problem domain, on the boundaries and in the subdomain associated with measurement data, we can obtain

$$\Delta\mathbf{\Phi}^{\mathrm{T}}(\mathbf{p})\mathbf{d} + \mathbf{\Phi}^{\mathrm{T}}(\mathbf{p})\overline{\mathbf{d}}\mathbf{\Phi}^{\mathrm{T}}(\mathbf{p})\mathbf{d} = f(\mathbf{p}), \quad \mathbf{p} \in \Omega \tag{18}$$

$$B^h\mathbf{\Phi}^{\mathrm{T}}(\mathbf{q})\mathbf{d} = h(\mathbf{q}), \quad \mathbf{q} \in \Gamma_h \tag{19}$$

$$B^g\mathbf{\Phi}^{\mathrm{T}}(\mathbf{r})\mathbf{d} = g(\mathbf{r}), \quad \mathbf{r} \in \Gamma_g \tag{20}$$

$$A\mathbf{\Phi}^{\mathrm{T}}(\mathbf{a})\mathbf{d} = b(\mathbf{a}), \quad \mathbf{a} \in \Pi \tag{21}$$

For solving the nonlinear Equation (18), the Newton's iteration method can be employed for the iterative solutions. For Equations (18)–(21), Newton's iteration equation is given as

$$\mathbf{J}^n\left(\mathbf{D}^{n+1} - \mathbf{D}^n\right) = \mathbf{F}^n \tag{22}$$

where

$$\mathbf{J}^n = [\mathbf{J}_1^n, \mathbf{J}_2^n, \mathbf{J}_3^n, \mathbf{J}_4^n]^{\mathrm{T}} \tag{23}$$

$$\mathbf{J}_1^n = \begin{bmatrix} \Delta\mathbf{\Phi}^{\mathrm{T}}(\mathbf{p}_1) + \mathbf{\Phi}^{\mathrm{T}}(\mathbf{p}_1)\overline{\mathbf{d}}^n\,\mathbf{\Phi}^{\mathrm{T}}(\mathbf{p}_1) & \mathbf{\Phi}^{\mathrm{T}}(\mathbf{p}_1)\left(\mathbf{\Phi}^{\mathrm{T}}(\mathbf{p}_1)\mathbf{d}^n\right) \\ \Delta\mathbf{\Phi}^{\mathrm{T}}(\mathbf{p}_2) + \mathbf{\Phi}^{\mathrm{T}}(\mathbf{p}_2)\overline{\mathbf{d}}^n\,\mathbf{\Phi}^{\mathrm{T}}(\mathbf{p}_2) & \mathbf{\Phi}^{\mathrm{T}}(\mathbf{p}_2)\left(\mathbf{\Phi}^{\mathrm{T}}(\mathbf{p}_2)\mathbf{d}^n\right) \\ \vdots & \vdots \\ \Delta\mathbf{\Phi}^{\mathrm{T}}\left(\mathbf{p}_{N_p}\right) + \mathbf{\Phi}^{\mathrm{T}}\left(\mathbf{p}_{N_p}\right)\overline{\mathbf{d}}^n\,\mathbf{\Phi}^{\mathrm{T}}\left(\mathbf{p}_{N_p}\right) & \mathbf{\Phi}^{\mathrm{T}}\left(\mathbf{p}_{N_p}\right)\left(\mathbf{\Phi}^{\mathrm{T}}\left(\mathbf{p}_{N_p}\right)\mathbf{d}^n\right) \end{bmatrix}, \tag{24}$$

$$\mathbf{J}_2^n = \begin{bmatrix} B^h\mathbf{\Phi}^{\mathrm{T}}(\mathbf{q}_1) & 0 \\ B^h\mathbf{\Phi}^{\mathrm{T}}(\mathbf{q}_2) & 0 \\ \vdots & \vdots \\ B^h\mathbf{\Phi}^{\mathrm{T}}\left(\mathbf{q}_{N_q}\right) & 0 \end{bmatrix}, \quad \mathbf{J}_3^n = \begin{bmatrix} B^g\mathbf{\Phi}^{\mathrm{T}}(\mathbf{r}_1) & 0 \\ B^g\mathbf{\Phi}^{\mathrm{T}}(\mathbf{r}_2) & 0 \\ \vdots & \vdots \\ B^g\mathbf{\Phi}^{\mathrm{T}}(\mathbf{r}_{N_r}) & 0 \end{bmatrix}, \quad \mathbf{J}_4^n = \begin{bmatrix} A\mathbf{\Phi}^{\mathrm{T}}(\mathbf{a}_1) & 0 \\ A\mathbf{\Phi}^{\mathrm{T}}(\mathbf{a}_2) & 0 \\ \vdots & \vdots \\ A\mathbf{\Phi}^{\mathrm{T}}(\mathbf{a}_{N_a}) & 0 \end{bmatrix}$$

$$\mathbf{D}^{n+1} = \left[d_1^{n+1}, d_2^{n+1}, \cdots, d_{N_s}^{n+1}, \overline{d}_1^{n+1}, \overline{d}_2^{n+1}, \cdots, \overline{d}_{N_s}^{n+1}\right]^{\mathrm{T}} \tag{25}$$

$$\mathbf{F}^n = [-\mathbf{F}_1^n, -\mathbf{F}_2^n, -\mathbf{F}_3^n, -\mathbf{F}_4^n]^{\mathrm{T}} \tag{26}$$

$$\mathbf{F}_1^n = \begin{bmatrix} \Delta\mathbf{\Phi}^T(\mathbf{p}_1)\mathbf{d}^n + \mathbf{\Phi}^T(\mathbf{p}_1)\overline{\mathbf{d}}^{-n}\left(\mathbf{\Phi}^T(\mathbf{p}_1)\mathbf{d}^n\right) - f(\mathbf{p}_1) \\ \Delta\mathbf{\Phi}^T(\mathbf{p}_2)\mathbf{d}^n + \mathbf{\Phi}^T(\mathbf{p}_2)\overline{\mathbf{d}}^{-n}\left(\mathbf{\Phi}^T(\mathbf{p}_2)\mathbf{d}^n\right) - f(\mathbf{p}_2) \\ \vdots \\ \Delta\mathbf{\Phi}^T\left(\mathbf{p}_{N_p}\right)\mathbf{d}^n + \mathbf{\Phi}^T\left(\mathbf{p}_{N_p}\right)\overline{\mathbf{d}}^{-n}\left(\mathbf{\Phi}^T\left(\mathbf{p}_{N_p}\right)\mathbf{d}^n\right) - f\left(\mathbf{p}_{N_p}\right) \end{bmatrix}, \quad \mathbf{F}_2^n = \begin{bmatrix} B^h\mathbf{\Phi}^T(\mathbf{q}_1)\mathbf{d}^n - h(\mathbf{q}_1) \\ B^h\mathbf{\Phi}^T(\mathbf{q}_2)\mathbf{d}^n - h(\mathbf{q}_2) \\ \vdots \\ B^h\mathbf{\Phi}^T\left(\mathbf{q}_{N_q}\right)\mathbf{d}^n - h\left(\mathbf{q}_{N_q}\right) \end{bmatrix},$$

$$\mathbf{F}_3^n = \begin{bmatrix} B^g\mathbf{\Phi}^T(\mathbf{r}_1)\mathbf{d}^n - g(\mathbf{r}_1) \\ B^g\mathbf{\Phi}^T(\mathbf{r}_2)\mathbf{d}^n - g(\mathbf{r}_2) \\ \vdots \\ B^g\mathbf{\Phi}^T(\mathbf{r}_{N_r})\mathbf{d}^n - g(\mathbf{r}_{N_r}) \end{bmatrix}, \quad \mathbf{F}_4^n = \begin{bmatrix} A\mathbf{\Phi}^T(\mathbf{a}_1)\mathbf{d}^n - b(\mathbf{a}_1) \\ A\mathbf{\Phi}^T(\mathbf{a}_2)\mathbf{d}^n - b(\mathbf{a}_2) \\ \vdots \\ A\mathbf{\Phi}^T(\mathbf{a}_{N_a})\mathbf{d}^n - b(\mathbf{a}_{N_a}) \end{bmatrix} \tag{27}$$

Here, $\mathbf{D}^n$ is a column vector of $2N_s \times 1$, $\mathbf{F}^n = \mathbf{F}(\mathbf{D}^n)$ is a column vector of $N_c \times 1$, $\mathbf{J}^n = \mathbf{J}(\mathbf{D}^n)$ is a column vector of $N_c \times (2N_s)$ and $N_c = N_p + N_q + N_r + N_a$. According to Equation (22), the unknown coefficients in the $n+1$ time step can be achieved based on the solutions of n time step as below

$$\mathbf{D}^{n+1} = \mathbf{J}^n \backslash \mathbf{F}^n + \mathbf{D}^n \tag{28}$$

in which $\backslash$ denoted the left division. Given an initial guess $\mathbf{D}^0$, we can obtain $\mathbf{D}^1, \mathbf{D}^2, \cdots, \mathbf{D}^{n+1}$ according to Equation (28), until the error $\|\mathbf{D}^{n+1} - \mathbf{D}^n\|_2$ is less than the given error bound.

3.2. Least-Squares Solution

The collocation method is equivalent to the least-squares method with integration quadratures [20]. The least-squares method is to seek the solution $\tilde{u} \in U$, where U is the admissible space spanned by the RBFs, such that

$$E\left(\tilde{\mathbf{u}}\right) = \min_{\mathbf{v} \in U} E(\mathbf{v}) \tag{29}$$

where

$$\mathbf{v} = \begin{bmatrix} \tilde{u} \\ \tilde{k} \end{bmatrix} \tag{30}$$

The least-squares functional $E(\mathbf{v})$ is denoted as

$$E(\mathbf{v}) = \tfrac{1}{2}\int_\Omega (\mathbf{L}\mathbf{v} - \mathbf{f})^T(\mathbf{L}\mathbf{v} - \mathbf{f})d\Omega + \tfrac{1}{2}\int_{\Gamma_h}\left(\mathbf{B}^h\mathbf{v} - \mathbf{h}\right)^T\left(\mathbf{B}^h\mathbf{v} - \mathbf{h}\right)d\Gamma \\ + \tfrac{1}{2}\int_{\Gamma_g}(\mathbf{B}^g\mathbf{v} - \mathbf{h})^T(\mathbf{B}^g\mathbf{v} - \mathbf{h})d\Gamma + \tfrac{1}{2}\int_\Pi (\mathbf{A}\mathbf{v} - \mathbf{b})^T(\mathbf{A}\mathbf{v} - \mathbf{b})d\Pi \tag{31}$$

and

$$E(\mathbf{v}^{n+1}) = \tfrac{1}{2}\int_\Omega \left(\mathbf{L}\mathbf{v}^{n+1} - \overline{\mathbf{f}}^{-n+1}\right)^T\left(\mathbf{L}\mathbf{v}^{n+1} - \overline{\mathbf{f}}^{-n+1}\right)d\Omega + \tfrac{1}{2}\int_{\Gamma_h}\left(\mathbf{B}^h\mathbf{v}^{n+1} - \mathbf{h}\right)^T\left(\mathbf{B}^h\mathbf{v}^{n+1} - \mathbf{h}\right)d\Gamma \\ + \tfrac{1}{2}\int_{\Gamma_g}(\mathbf{B}^g\mathbf{v}^{n+1} - \mathbf{h})^T(\mathbf{B}^g\mathbf{v}^{n+1} - \mathbf{h})d\Gamma + \tfrac{1}{2}\int_\Pi (\mathbf{A}\mathbf{v}^{n+1} - \mathbf{b})^T(\mathbf{A}\mathbf{v}^{n+1} - \mathbf{b})d\Pi \tag{32}$$

in which

$$\mathbf{L} = \begin{bmatrix} \Delta & u \end{bmatrix}, \quad \mathbf{B}^h = \begin{bmatrix} B^h \\ 0 \end{bmatrix}, \quad \mathbf{B}^g = \begin{bmatrix} B^g \\ 0 \end{bmatrix}, \quad \mathbf{A} = \begin{bmatrix} A \\ 0 \end{bmatrix}, \tag{33}$$

$$\mathbf{L}\mathbf{v}^{n+1} = \begin{bmatrix} \Delta + k^n & u^n \end{bmatrix}\begin{bmatrix} u^{n+1} \\ k^{n+1} \end{bmatrix}, \quad \overline{\mathbf{f}}^{-n+1} = \mathbf{f} + \mathbf{u}^n(\mathbf{k}^n)^T \tag{34}$$

Define a norm

$$\|\mathbf{v}^{n+1}\|_H = \left(\|\mathbf{L}\mathbf{v}^{n+1}\|_{0,\Omega}^2 + \|\mathbf{v}^{n+1}\|_{1,\Omega}^2 + \|\mathbf{B}^h\mathbf{v}^{n+1}\|_{0,\Gamma_h}^2 + \|\mathbf{B}^g\mathbf{v}^{n+1}\|_{0,\Gamma_g}^2 + \|\mathbf{A}\mathbf{v}^{n+1}\|_{0,\Pi}^2\right)^{\frac{1}{2}} \tag{35}$$

By using the Lax-Milgram lemma [50], we can achieve the error estimate as follows

$$\begin{aligned}\|\mathbf{u}^{n+1} - \widetilde{\mathbf{u}}^{n+1}\|_H &\leq C \inf_{\mathbf{v}\in U}\|\mathbf{u}^{n+1} - \mathbf{v}^{n+1}\|_H \\ &\leq C_1\|\mathbf{L}\mathbf{v}^{n+1} - \mathbf{f}\|_{0,\Omega} + C_2\|\mathbf{u}^{n+1} - \mathbf{v}^{n+1}\|_{1,\Omega} + C_3\|\mathbf{B}^h\mathbf{v}^{n+1} - \mathbf{h}\|_{0,\Gamma_h} \\ &\quad + C_4\|\mathbf{B}^g\mathbf{v}^{n+1} - \mathbf{g}\|_{0,\Gamma_g} + C_5\|\mathbf{A}\mathbf{v}^{n+1} - \mathbf{b}\|_{0,\Pi}\end{aligned} \tag{36}$$

In the inverse Helmholtz problem, $B^h = \frac{\partial}{\partial n}$, $B^g = 1$, $A = 1$, where n denotes the outer normal of the boundary, and we have the following error estimate

$$\begin{aligned}\|u^{n+1} - \widetilde{u}^{n+1}\|_H &\leq \overline{C}_1\|C_{11}\Delta(u^{n+1} - v^{n+1}) + C_{12}(u^{n+1} - v^{n+1})\|_{0,\Omega} + \overline{C}_2\|\tfrac{\partial u^{n+1}}{\partial n} - \tfrac{\partial v^{n+1}}{\partial n}\|_{0,\Gamma_h} + \overline{C}_3\|(u^{n+1} - v^{n+1})\|_{0,\Gamma_g} \\ &\leq +\overline{C}_4\|u^{n+1} - v^{n+1}\|_{0,\Pi} + \overline{C}_5\|u^{n+1} - v^{n+1}\|_{2,\Omega} + \overline{C}_6\|u^{n+1} - v^{n+1}\|_{0,\Omega} \\ &\quad + \overline{C}_2\|\tfrac{\partial u^{n+1}}{\partial n} - \tfrac{\partial v^{n+1}}{\partial n}\|_{0,\Gamma_h} + \overline{C}_3\|(u^{n+1} - v^{n+1})\|_{0,\Gamma_g} + \overline{C}_4\|u^{n+1} - v^{n+1}\|_{0,\Pi} \\ &:= E_\Omega + E_{\Gamma^h} + E_{\Gamma^g} + E_\Pi\end{aligned} \tag{37}$$

Since the errors are not balanced in the domain as well as the subdomain and on the boundaries, some weights should be introduced on the boundary and known measurement conditions. The weighted least-squares functional can be expressed by

$$\begin{aligned}\widetilde{E}(\mathbf{v}^{n+1}) &= \tfrac{1}{2}\int_\Omega \left(\mathbf{L}\mathbf{v}^{n+1} - \overline{\mathbf{f}}\right)^T \left(\mathbf{L}\mathbf{v}^{n+1} - \overline{\mathbf{f}}\right) d\Omega + \tfrac{w^h}{2}\int_{\Gamma_h}\left(\mathbf{B}^h\mathbf{v}^{n+1} - \mathbf{h}\right)^T\left(\mathbf{B}^h\mathbf{v}^{n+1} - \mathbf{h}\right)d\Gamma \\ &\quad + \tfrac{w^g}{2}\int_{\Gamma_g}\left(\mathbf{B}^g\mathbf{v}^{n+1} - \mathbf{h}\right)^T\left(\mathbf{B}^g\mathbf{v}^{n+1} - \mathbf{h}\right)d\Gamma + \tfrac{w^a}{2}\int_\Pi\left(\mathbf{A}\mathbf{v}^{n+1} - \mathbf{b}\right)^T\left(\mathbf{A}\mathbf{v}^{n+1} - \mathbf{b}\right)d\Pi\end{aligned} \tag{38}$$

To seek an optimal solution $\widetilde{\mathbf{u}}$ satisfying

$$\widetilde{E}\left(\widetilde{\mathbf{u}}^{n+1}\right) = \min_{\mathbf{v}\in U}\widetilde{E}\left(\mathbf{v}^{n+1}\right) \tag{39}$$

Accordingly, a modified norm should be considered

$$\|\mathbf{v}^{n+1}\|_B = \left(\|\mathbf{L}\mathbf{v}^{n+1}\|_{0,\Omega}^2 + \|\mathbf{v}^{n+1}\|_{1,\Omega}^2 + w^h\|\mathbf{B}^h\mathbf{v}^{n+1}\|_{0,\Gamma^h}^2 + w^g\|\mathbf{B}^g\mathbf{v}^{n+1}\|_{0,\Gamma^g}^2 + w^a\|\mathbf{A}\mathbf{v}^{n+1}\|_{0,\Pi}^2\right)^{\frac{1}{2}} \tag{40}$$

A corresponding error estimate is given as

$$\begin{aligned}\|\mathbf{u}^{n+1} - \widetilde{\mathbf{u}}^{n+1}\|_B &\leq \widetilde{C}\inf_{\mathbf{v}\in U}\|\mathbf{u}^{n+1} - \mathbf{v}^{n+1}\|_B \\ &\leq \widetilde{C}_1\|\mathbf{L}\mathbf{v}^{n+1} - \mathbf{f}\|_{0,\Omega} + \widetilde{C}_2\|\mathbf{u}^{n+1} - \mathbf{v}^{n+1}\|_{1,\Omega} + \widetilde{C}_3\sqrt{w^h}\|\mathbf{B}^h\mathbf{v}^{n+1} - \mathbf{h}\|_{0,\Gamma_h} \\ &\quad + \widetilde{C}_4\sqrt{w^g}\|\mathbf{B}^g\mathbf{v}^{n+1} - \mathbf{g}\|_{0,\Gamma_g} + \widetilde{C}_5\sqrt{w^a}\|\mathbf{A}\mathbf{v}^{n+1} - \mathbf{b}\|_{0,\Pi}\end{aligned} \tag{41}$$

For the inverse Helmholtz problem, we can obtain the following error estimate

$$\begin{aligned}\|u^{n+1} - \widetilde{u}^{n+1}\|_B &\leq \widehat{C}_1\|u^{n+1} - v^{n+1}\|_{2,\Omega} + \widehat{C}_2\|u^{n+1} - v^{n+1}\|_{0,\Omega} + \widehat{C}_3\sqrt{w^h}\|\tfrac{\partial u^{n+1}}{\partial n} - \tfrac{\partial v^{n+1}}{\partial n}\|_{0,\Gamma_h} \\ &\quad + \widehat{C}_4\sqrt{w^g}\|(u^{n+1} - v^{n+1})\|_{0,\Gamma_g} + \widehat{C}_5\sqrt{w^a}\|u^{n+1} - v^{n+1}\|_{0,\Pi}\end{aligned} \tag{42}$$

There exist the following inverse inequalities [50]

$$\|\eta\|_{k,\Omega} \leq CN_s^{k-l}\|\eta\|_{l,\Omega'}, \quad k > l \quad \forall \eta \in U \tag{43}$$

$$\left\|\frac{\partial \eta}{\partial n}\right\|_{0,\Gamma^h} \leq C\|\eta\|_{2,\Omega}, \quad \forall \eta \in U \tag{44}$$

$$\|\eta\|_{0,\Gamma^g} \leq C\|\eta\|_{1,\Omega}, \quad \forall \eta \in U \tag{45}$$

Then, we achieve

$$\begin{aligned}\|u^{n+1} - \tilde{u}^{n+1}\|_B &\leq \hat{C}_1 N_s \|u^{n+1} - v^{n+1}\|_{1,\Omega} + \hat{C}_2 N_s \sqrt{w^h}\|u^{n+1} - v^{n+1}\|_{1,\Omega} \\ &+ \hat{C}_3 \sqrt{w^g}\|u^{n+1} - v^{n+1}\|_{1,\Omega} + \hat{C}_4 \sqrt{w^a}\|u^{n+1} - v^{n+1}\|_{1,\Omega}\end{aligned} \tag{46}$$

According to Equation (46), to minimize the weighted functional in Equation (38) for balancing errors, the following weights should be introduced

$$\sqrt{w^h} \approx O(1), \quad \sqrt{w^g} \approx \sqrt{w^a} \approx O(N_s) \tag{47}$$

Introducing the approximations in Equations (9) and (10) into Equation (31), the discrete form of Equation (31) can be written as

$$\begin{aligned}E(\mathbf{D}^{n+1}) = &\tfrac{1}{2}\sum_{I=1}^{N_p} \left(\mathbf{L}\boldsymbol{\Phi}^{\mathrm{T}}(\mathbf{p}_I)\mathbf{D}^{n+1} - \mathbf{f}^{-n+1}\right)^{\mathrm{T}} \left(\mathbf{L}\boldsymbol{\Phi}^{\mathrm{T}}(\mathbf{p}_I)\mathbf{D}^{n+1} - \mathbf{f}^{-n+1}\right) \\ &+ \tfrac{1}{2}\sum_{I=1}^{N_q} \left(\mathbf{B}^h\boldsymbol{\Phi}^{\mathrm{T}}(\mathbf{q}_I)\mathbf{D}^{n+1} - \mathbf{h}\right)^{\mathrm{T}} \left(\mathbf{B}^h\boldsymbol{\Phi}^{\mathrm{T}}(\mathbf{q}_I)\mathbf{D}^{n+1} - \mathbf{h}\right) \\ &+ \tfrac{1}{2}\sum_{I=1}^{N_r} \left(\mathbf{B}^g\boldsymbol{\Phi}^{\mathrm{T}}(\mathbf{r}_I)\mathbf{D}^{n+1} - \mathbf{g}\right)^{\mathrm{T}} \left(\mathbf{B}^g\boldsymbol{\Phi}^{\mathrm{T}}(\mathbf{r}_I)\mathbf{D}^{n+1} - \mathbf{g}\right) \\ &+ \tfrac{1}{2}\sum_{I=1}^{N_a} \left(\mathbf{A}\boldsymbol{\Phi}^{\mathrm{T}}(\mathbf{r}_I)\mathbf{D}^{n+1} - \mathbf{b}\right)^{\mathrm{T}} \left(\mathbf{A}\boldsymbol{\Phi}^{\mathrm{T}}(\mathbf{r}_I)\mathbf{D}^{n+1} - \mathbf{b}\right)\end{aligned} \tag{48}$$

By imposing the corresponding weights on the boundary and known conditions, the corresponding discrete form of Equation (38)

$$\begin{aligned}\widetilde{E}(\mathbf{D}^{n+1}) = &\tfrac{1}{2}\sum_{I=1}^{N_p} \left(\mathbf{L}\boldsymbol{\Phi}^{\mathrm{T}}(\mathbf{p}_I)\mathbf{D}^{n+1} - \mathbf{f}^{-n+1}\right)^{\mathrm{T}} \left(\mathbf{L}\boldsymbol{\Phi}^{\mathrm{T}}(\mathbf{p}_I)\mathbf{D}^{n+1} - \mathbf{f}^{-n+1}\right) \\ &+ \tfrac{w^h}{2}\sum_{I=1}^{N_q} \left(\mathbf{B}^h\boldsymbol{\Phi}^{\mathrm{T}}(\mathbf{q}_I)\mathbf{D}^{n+1} - \mathbf{h}\right)^{\mathrm{T}} \left(\mathbf{B}^h\boldsymbol{\Phi}^{\mathrm{T}}(\mathbf{q}_I)\mathbf{D}^{n+1} - \mathbf{h}\right) \\ &+ \tfrac{w^g}{2}\sum_{I=1}^{N_r} \left(\mathbf{B}^g\boldsymbol{\Phi}^{\mathrm{T}}(\mathbf{r}_I)\mathbf{D}^{n+1} - \mathbf{g}\right)^{\mathrm{T}} \left(\mathbf{B}^g\boldsymbol{\Phi}^{\mathrm{T}}(\mathbf{r}_I)\mathbf{D}^{n+1} - \mathbf{g}\right) \\ &+ \tfrac{w^a}{2}\sum_{I=1}^{N_a} \left(\mathbf{A}\boldsymbol{\Phi}^{\mathrm{T}}(\mathbf{r}_I)\mathbf{D}^{n+1} - \mathbf{b}\right)^{\mathrm{T}} \left(\mathbf{A}\boldsymbol{\Phi}^{\mathrm{T}}(\mathbf{r}_I)\mathbf{D}^{n+1} - \mathbf{b}\right)\end{aligned} \tag{49}$$

Minimization $\widetilde{E}(\mathbf{a})$ in Equation (49) gives the following weighted discrete linear equations

$$\begin{bmatrix}\mathbf{J}_1^n \\ \sqrt{w^h}\mathbf{J}_2^n \\ \sqrt{w^g}\mathbf{J}_3^n \\ \sqrt{w^a}\mathbf{J}_4^n\end{bmatrix}(\mathbf{D}^{n+1} - \mathbf{D}^n) = \begin{bmatrix}\mathbf{F}_1^n \\ \sqrt{w^h}\mathbf{F}_2^n \\ \sqrt{w^g}\mathbf{F}_3^n \\ \sqrt{w^a}\mathbf{F}_4^n\end{bmatrix} \tag{50}$$

4. Numerical Solutions of Some Representative Examples

4.1. One-Dimensional Inverse Helmholtz Problem of Constant Parameter Identification

Consider a one-dimensional (1D) Helmholtz equation of identifying the wave number as follows

$$\frac{\partial u^2(x)}{\partial x^2} + ku(x) = 0, 0 < x < 1 \tag{51}$$

$$u = 0, \quad x = 0; \quad u = 1, \quad x = 1 \tag{52}$$

and an additional known condition is given as

$$u(0.5) = \sin 1 / \sin 2 \tag{53}$$

where k is an unknown wave number. The analytical solutions are $u(x) = \sin 2x / \sin 2$, $k = 4$.

Figure 1 presents the influence of shape parameter c on accuracy and stability when $N_s = 31$. The blue dotted line represents the L2 norm of u, and the red dot dash line represents the condition number of the stiffness matrix. It can be observed that with the increase in the shape parameter, the accuracy increases obviously at the beginning and gradually reaches the peak. However, the condition number of the stiffness matrix is always increasing with the growth of the shape parameter, which means that the stability is decreasing. Therefore, the criterion for selecting the optimal shape parameter is to increase the accuracy as much as possible until the condition number of the stiffness matrix dramatically affects the solution. The optimal shape parameter can be selected at the intersection of the two lines displayed in Figure 1. The value of shape parameter c is chosen to be 1.1, 0.8 and 0.65, which corresponds to $N_s = 11, 21$ and 31, respectively. Figures 2 and 3 present the solution $u(x)$ and the corresponding error $u - \tilde{u}$ as well as the convergence of WRBCM in the 1D parameter identification inverse Helmholtz problem under different discretizations, which demonstrate the good accuracy and exponential convergence of the proposed method. The weights imposed on the Dirichlet boundary and measurement conditions are $\sqrt{w^g} \approx \sqrt{w^a} \approx 10$ which agree well with the mathematical derivation presented in Equation (47). Figure 4 shows that the corresponding error of WRBCM after adding weights on the boundary is much lower than RBCM. The iteration processes of wave number k are shown in Figure 5, in which the error bound is set to be 10^{-10}. The results demonstrate that the iteration solutions converge quite fast. The convergence of the wave number is displayed in Figure 6, which indicates that the solutions of the identified parameter can also achieve exponential convergence. Convergence studies presented in Figures 3 and 6 demonstrate that the proposed WRBCM can acquire optimal convergences for both the unknown and parameter solutions in the 1D inverse Helmholtz problem. Since WRBCM is a global method, it can be observed from Figure 7 that the condition number of the stiffness matrix will increase with the refinement of the discrete points.

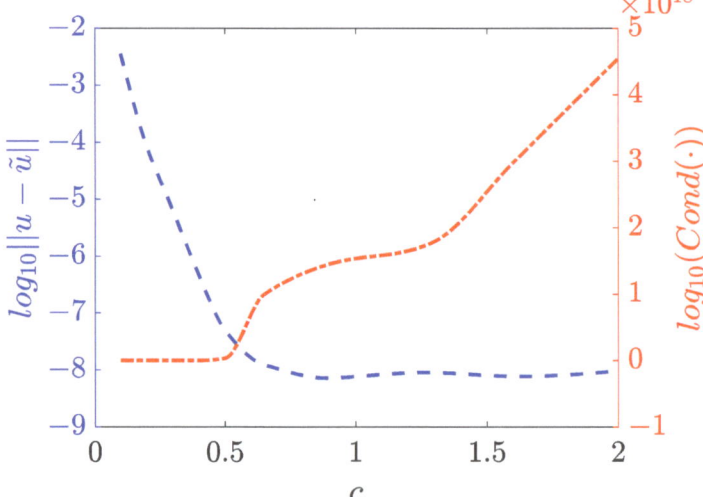

Figure 1. Variation of accuracy and condition number of the stiffness matrix with shape parameter c when $N_s = 31$.

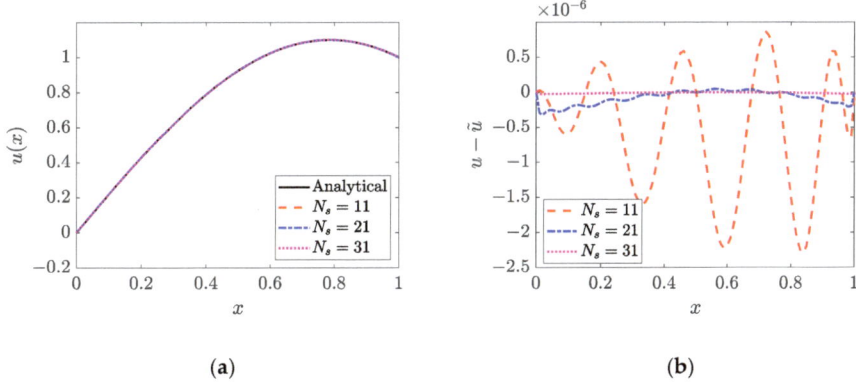

Figure 2. Solution and corresponding error for the 1D constant parameter identification problem: (**a**) solution; (**b**) corresponding error.

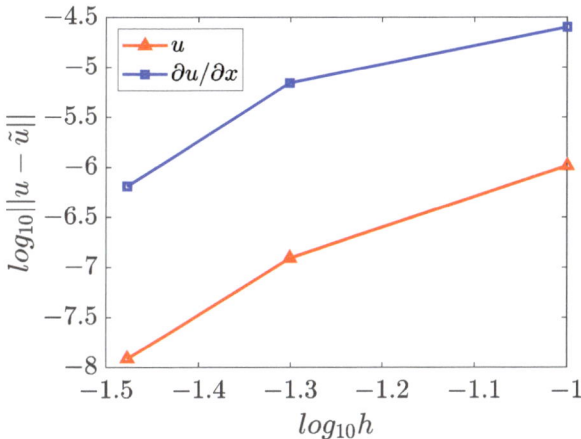

Figure 3. Convergence of the solutions for the 1D constant parameter identification problem.

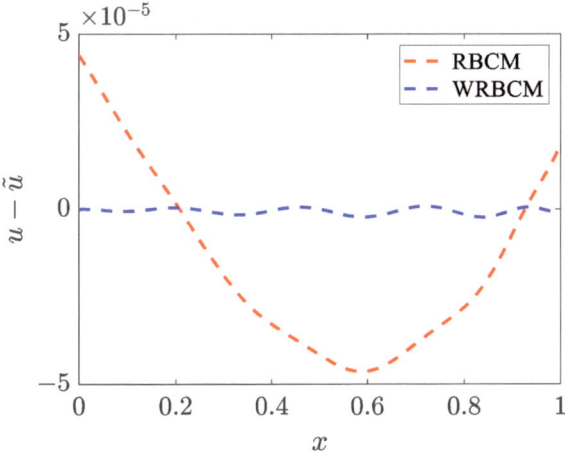

Figure 4. Solution comparison between RBCM and WRBCM for the 1D constant parameter identification problem.

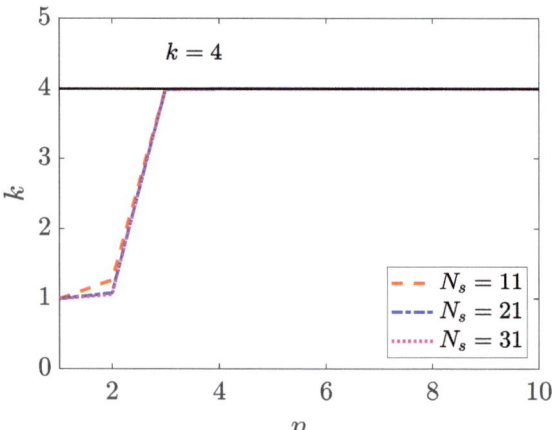

Figure 5. Variation of wave number k with iteration steps for the 1D constant parameter identification problem.

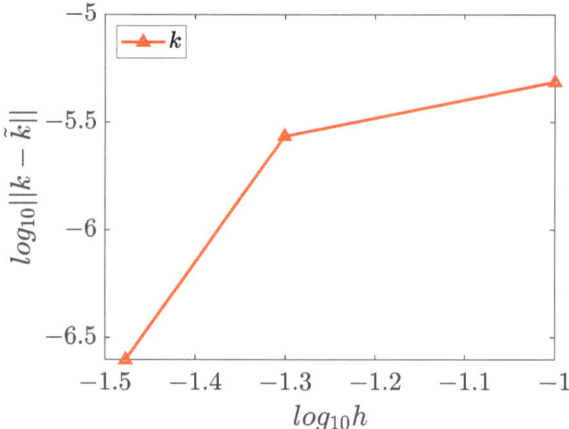

Figure 6. Convergence of wave number for the 1D constant parameter identification problem.

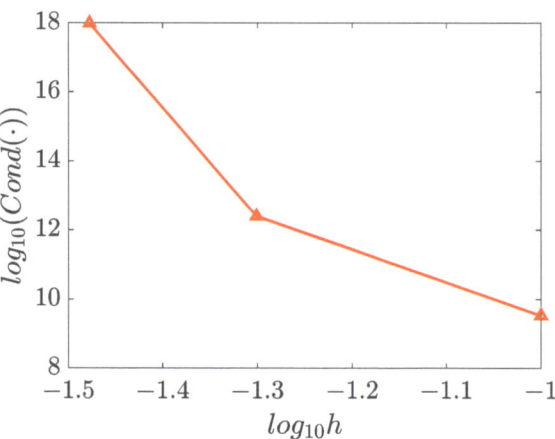

Figure 7. Condition number of stiffness matrix for the 1D constant parameter identification problem.

4.2. Two-Dimensional Inverse Helmholtz Problem of Constant Parameter Identification in Irregular Geometry

In this example, we study a two-dimensional (2D) inverse Helmholtz problem in irregular domain, as shown in Figure 8.

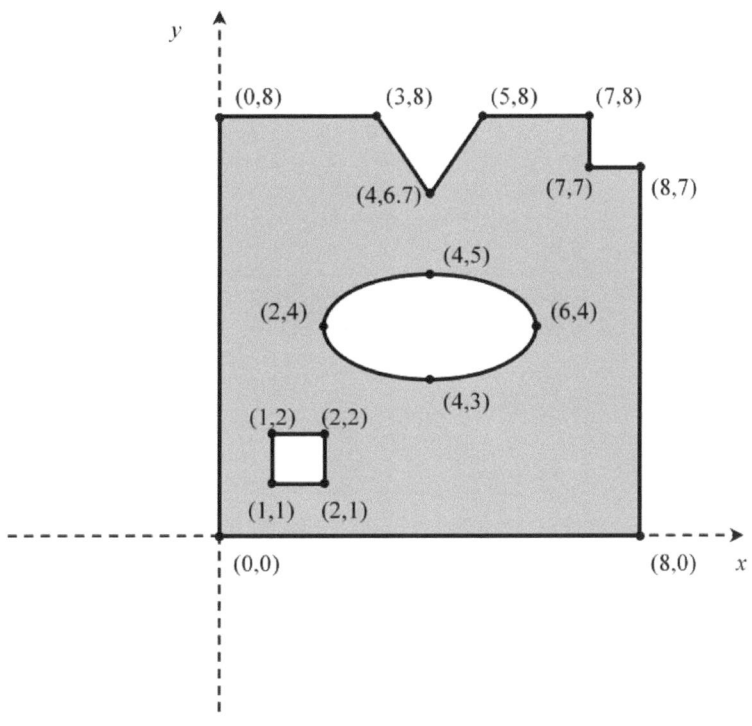

Figure 8. Configuration of 2D irregular geometry [33].

The governing equation and boundary conditions are given as follows

$$\frac{\partial^2 u}{\partial x^2} + \frac{\partial^2 u}{\partial y^2} + k^2 u = 0, \text{ in } \Omega \tag{54}$$

$$\frac{\partial u}{\partial x} = \cos(x)\sin(y), \quad \text{on } x = 0, y \in [0,8] \tag{55}$$

$$\frac{\partial u}{\partial y} = \sin(x)\cos(y), \quad \text{on } y = 0, x \in [0,8] \tag{56}$$

$$u(x,y) = \sin(x)\sin(y), \quad \text{on } \Gamma_g \tag{57}$$

where $\Gamma_g = \bigcup_{i=1}^{11} \Gamma_g^i$ and

$$\begin{aligned}
&\Gamma_g^1 = \{x = 8, y \in [0,7]\}, \quad \Gamma_g^2 = \{y = 8, x \in [0,3] \cup [5,7]\}, \quad \Gamma_g^3 = \{x = 7, y \in [7,8]\}, \\
&\Gamma_g^4 = \{y = 7, x \in [7,8]\}, \quad \Gamma_g^5 = \{1.3x + y - 11.9 = 0, x \in [3,4], y \in [6.7,8]\}, \\
&\Gamma_g^6 = \{1.3x - y + 1.5 = 0, x \in [4,5], y \in [6.7,8]\}, \quad \Gamma_g^7 = \left\{ \frac{(x-4)^2}{4} + (y-4)^2 = 1, x \in [2,6], y \in [3,5] \right\} \\
&\Gamma_g^8 = \{x = 1, y \in [1,2]\}, \quad \Gamma_g^9 = \{x = 2, y \in [1,2]\}, \quad \Gamma_g^{10} = \{y = 1, x \in [1,2]\}, \quad \Gamma_g^{11} = \{y = 2, x \in [1,2]\}
\end{aligned} \tag{58}$$

An additional known condition is presented as

$$u(x,4) = \sin(x)\sin(4), \quad \text{on } \Pi \tag{59}$$

where $\Pi = \{y = 4, x \in [0,2] \cup [6,8]\}$. The analytical solution is $u(x,y) = \sin(x)\sin(y)$ and the wave number that needs to be determined is $k = \sqrt{2}$. The error bound is set to be 10^{-10} for the iteration solutions. The weights imposed on the Dirichlet and measurement boundary conditions for this example are $\sqrt{w^g} \approx \sqrt{w^a} \approx 100$, and for the Neumann boundary condition is $\sqrt{w^h} \approx 1$. The value of the shape parameter c is chosen to be 4, 2.2, 2 for the three discretization schemes, respectively.

Figures 9 and 10 display the solutions of u as well as its corresponding errors and the boundary errors under the discretization of $N_s = 11 \times 11$, 21×21 and 31×31, respectively. The errors are decreasing with refinement, which demonstrate that the proposed method can converge well in this inverse problem of the irregular domain. This is also illustrated in Figure 11, where the solutions converge exponentially. Figure 12 shows the iteration process of the unknown wave number, which indicates that this method can converge for the identification very quickly. The convergence of the identified wave number is exhibited in Figure 13. The solutions show that the exponential convergence can also be obtained for the unknown wave number identification. Figure 14 presents the condition number under different discretizations, where the condition number increases with the decrease in the node distance.

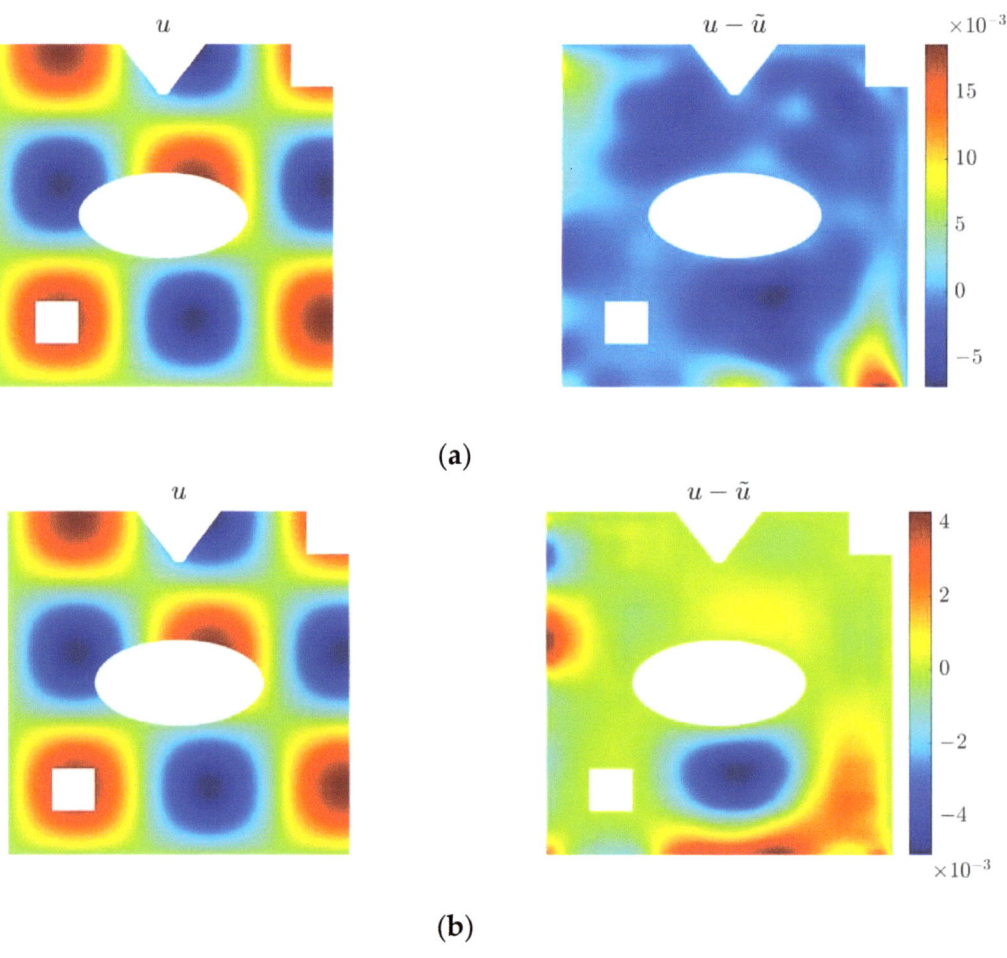

Figure 9. *Cont.*

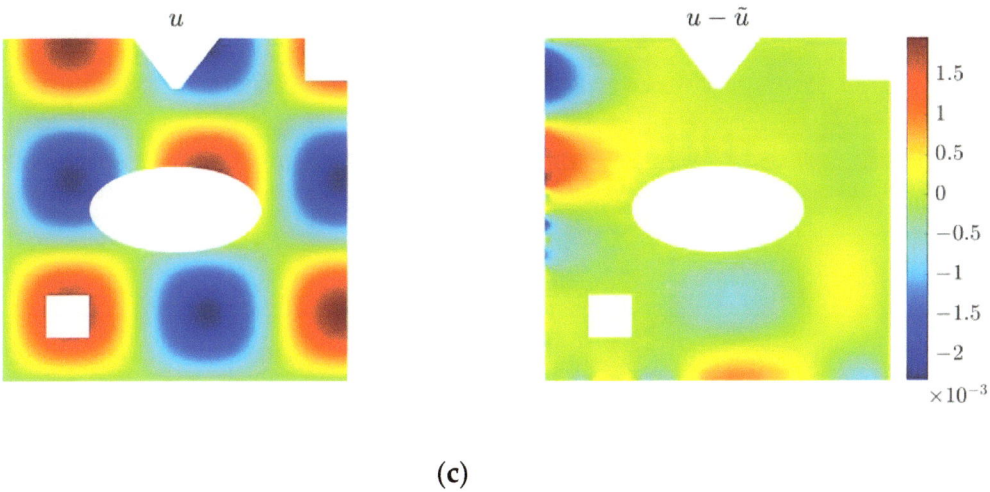

(c)

Figure 9. Solution and corresponding error for the 2D constant parameter identification problem in irregular geometry under different discretizations: (**a**) $N_s = 11 \times 11$; (**b**) $N_s = 21 \times 21$; (**c**) $N_s = 31 \times 31$.

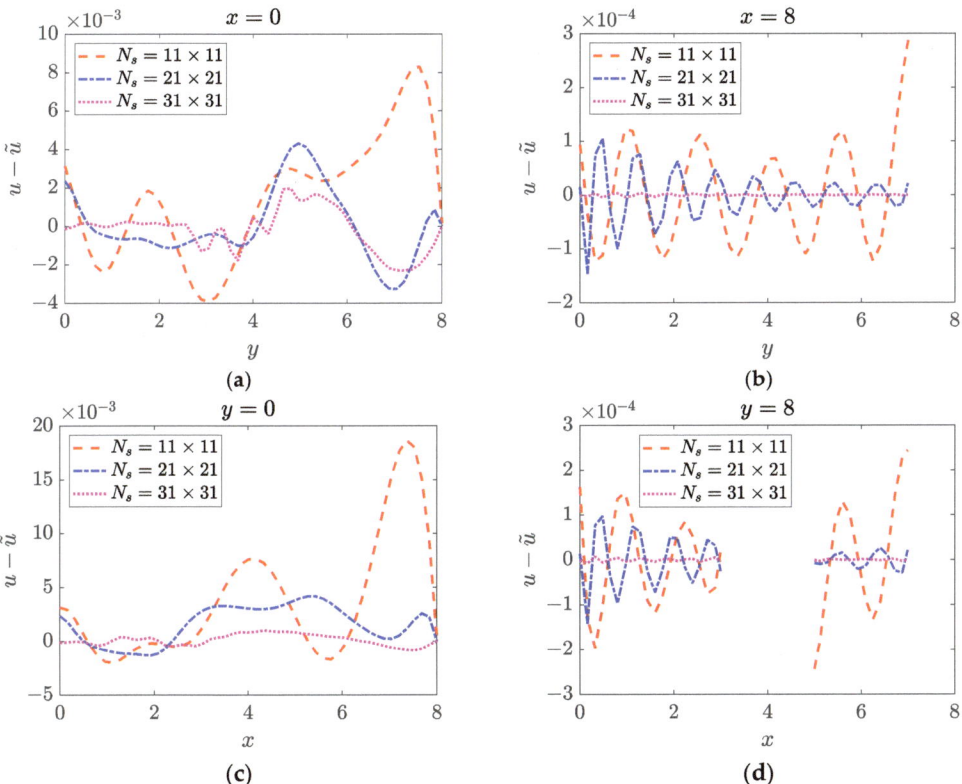

Figure 10. Boundary solutions for the 2D constant parameter identification problem in irregular geometry: (**a**) $x = 0$; (**b**) $x = 8$; (**c**) $y = 0$; (**d**) $y = 8$.

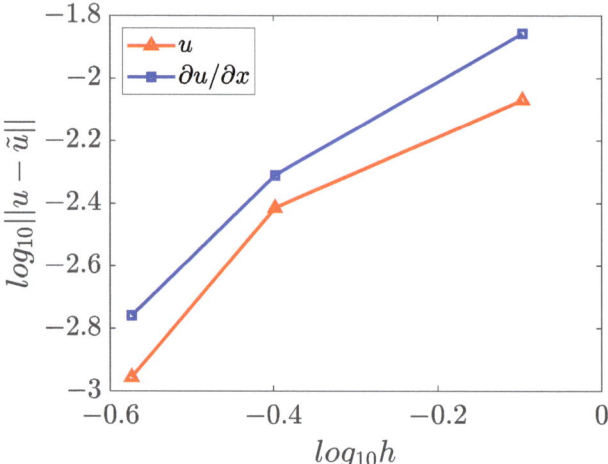

Figure 11. Convergence of the solutions for the 2D constant parameter identification problem in irregular geometry.

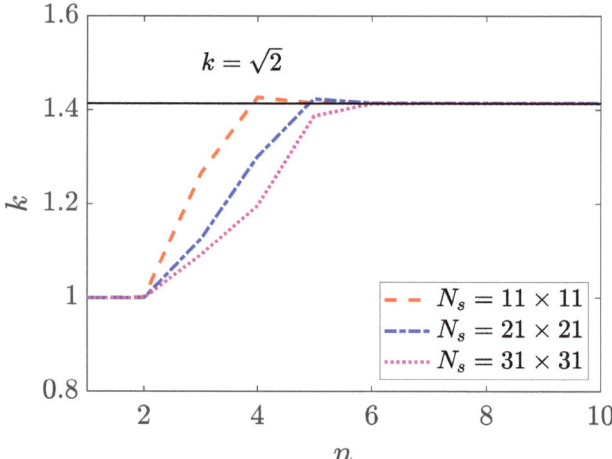

Figure 12. Variation of wave number k with iteration steps for the 2D constant parameter identification problem in irregular geometry.

4.3. Two-Dimensional Inverse Helmholtz Problem of Parameter Identification

After studying two examples of constant parameter identification, we further investigate a 2D inverse Helmholtz problem for identifying the varying parameter. The governing equation associated with boundary conditions can be expressed by

$$-\Delta u(x,y) + k(x,y)u(x,y) = 2\sin x \cos y + \frac{x^2 \sin x \cos y}{2}, \text{ in } \Omega, \quad (60)$$

$$u(x,y) = 0, \quad \text{on } \Gamma_g \quad (61)$$

The given known condition is

$$u(x,0) = \sin x, \quad \text{on } \Pi \quad (62)$$

The problem domain is $\Omega = [0, \pi] \times [-\frac{\pi}{2}, \frac{\pi}{2}]$. $\Gamma_g = \partial\Omega$ denotes the Dirichlet boundary and $\Pi = \{y = 0, x \in [0, \pi]\}$ represents the subdomain for the measurement condition. The analytical solution for this problem is $u(x, y) = \sin x \cos y$, and the parameter that needs to be recognized is given as $k(x, y) = x^2/2$. The weights imposed on the boundary conditions are $\sqrt{w^g} \approx \sqrt{w^a} \approx 100$. The value of shape parameter c is chosen to be 3, 1.3, 0.85 for the three discretizations, respectively.

The numerical solutions for u and k are presented in Figures 15–17, which demonstrate that the WRBCM can also achieve a high accuracy for solving the inverse Helmholtz problem of the varying parameter identification. The convergence studies for u and k are exhibited in Figures 18 and 19, respectively. These indicate that for the varying parameter identification problem, the WRBCM can also acquire the exponential convergence for both the solutions and the identified parameter. The condition number of the stiffness matrix is shown in Figure 20, and a similar conclusion can be achieved, as in example 1 and 2.

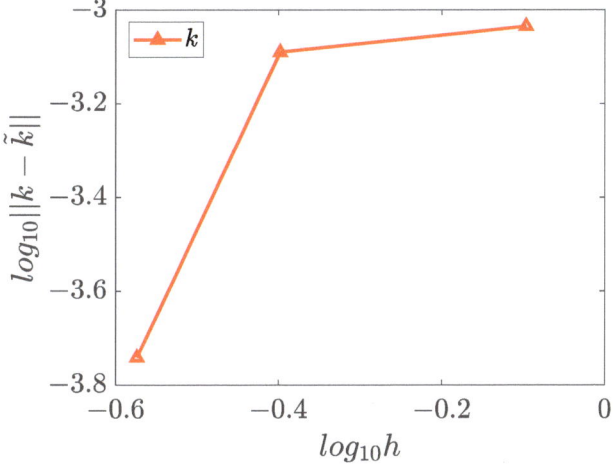

Figure 13. Convergence of wave number for the 2D constant parameter identification problem in irregular geometry.

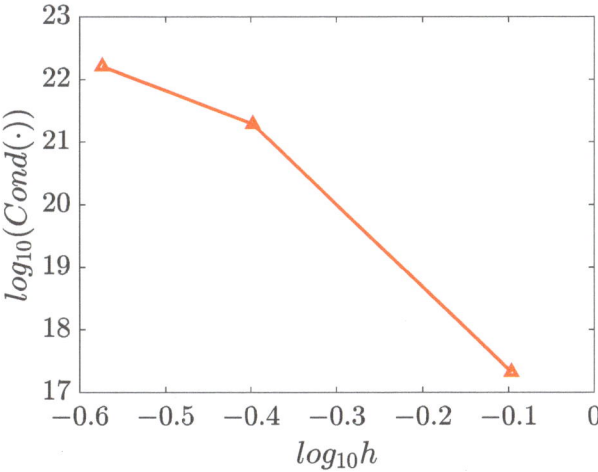

Figure 14. Condition number of stiffness matrix for the 2D constant parameter identification problem in irregular geometry.

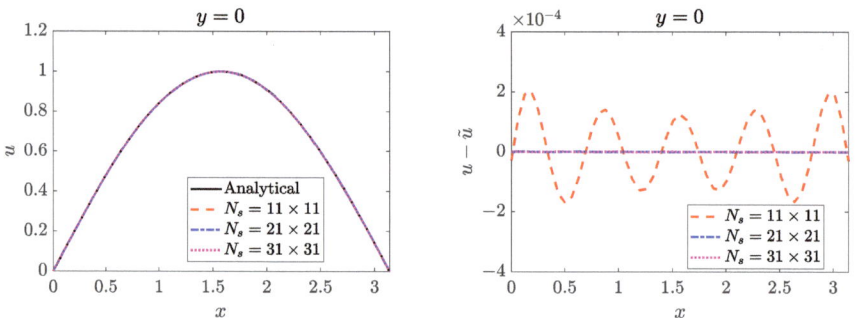

Figure 15. Solution and corresponding error for the 2D varying parameter identification problem.

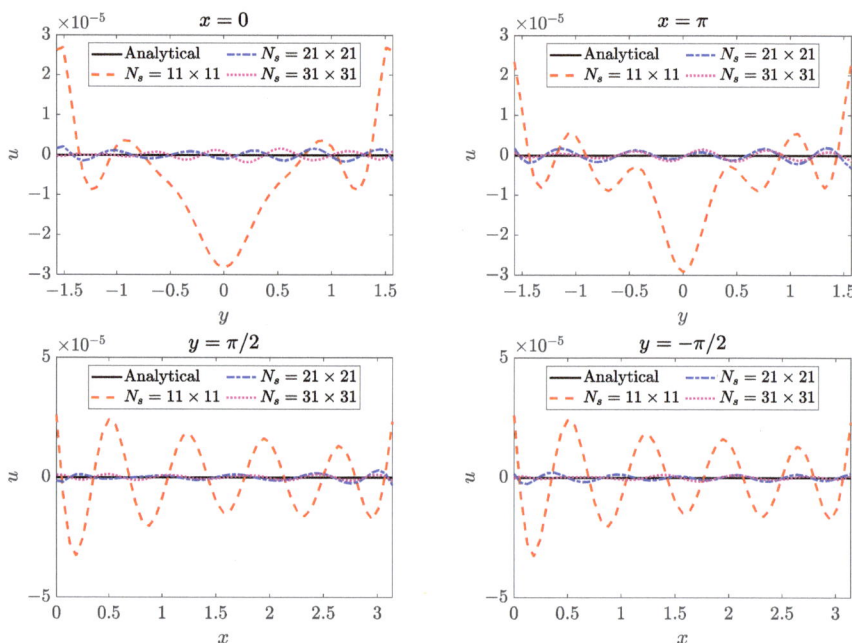

Figure 16. Boundary solutions for the 2D varying parameter identification problem.

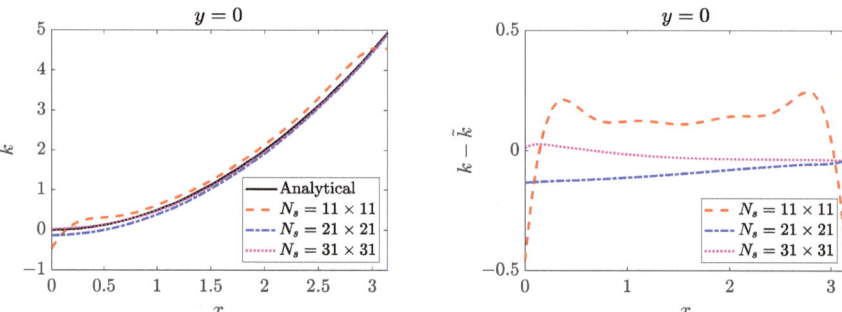

Figure 17. Solution and corresponding error of wave number k for the 2D varying parameter identification problem.

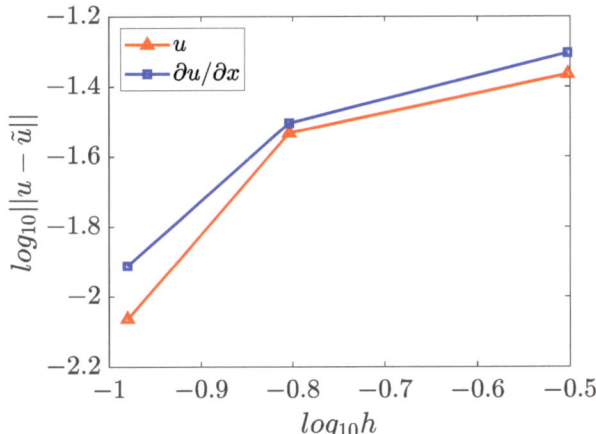

Figure 18. Convergence of the solutions for the 2D varying parameter identification problem.

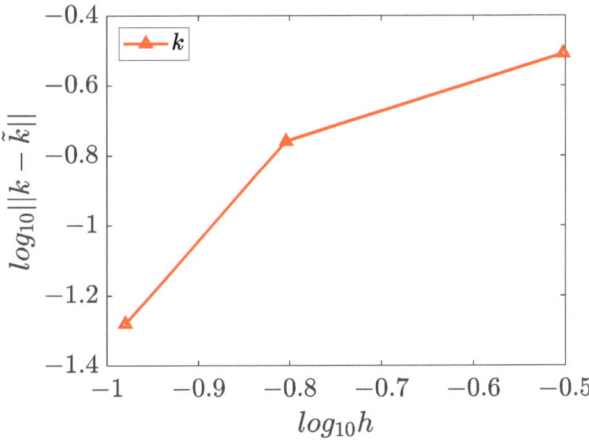

Figure 19. Convergence of wave number for the 2D varying parameter identification problem.

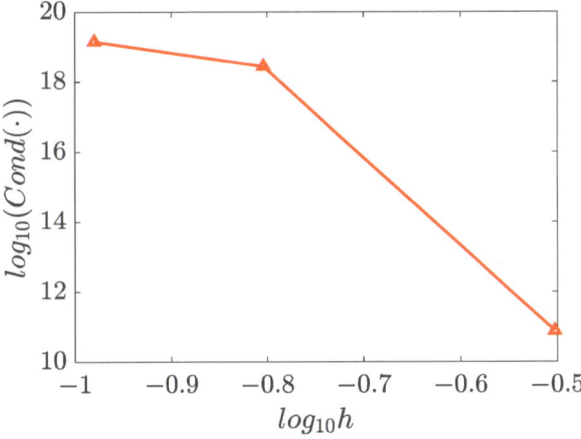

Figure 20. Condition number of stiffness matrix for the 2D varying parameter identification problem.

4.4. Three-Dimensional Inverse Helmholtz Problem of Parameter Identification in Cubic Domain

Next, a three-dimensional (3D) inverse Helmholtz problem of varying parameter identification in cubic domain is studied. The governing equation is described by

$$\frac{\partial^2 u}{\partial x^2} + \frac{\partial^2 u}{\partial y^2} + \frac{\partial^2 u}{\partial z^2} + k(x,y,z)u = \left(x^2 + y/2 + z\right)(\sin x + \sin y + \sin z), \text{ in } \Omega \tag{63}$$

$$u(x,y,z) = \sin(x) + \sin(y) + \sin(z), \quad \text{on } \Gamma_g \tag{64}$$

The measurement condition on a plane is expressed as

$$u(0.5, y, z) = \sin(0.5) + \sin(y) + \sin(z), \quad \text{in } \Pi \tag{65}$$

where $\Omega = [0,1] \times [0,1] \times [0,1]$, $\Gamma_g = \partial \Omega$ and $\Pi = \{x = 0.5, y \in [0,1], z \in [0,1]\}$. The analytical solution and the identified parameter are given by

$$\begin{aligned} u(x,y,z) &= \sin(x) + \sin(y) + \sin(z) \\ k(x,y,z) &= x^2 + \tfrac{1}{2}y + z + 1 \end{aligned} \tag{66}$$

The weights for the boundary conditions are selected as $\sqrt{w^g} \approx \sqrt{w^a} \approx 100$, and the shape parameter is 3.3, 2.5, 1.7 for the three different discretizations, respectively.

Since the shape functions of RBFs are only depending on the radial distance from the origin, it is quite easy and straightforward to extend 1D problems to 2D and 3D problems. Once again, high accuracy can be obtained for solving the problem unknowns u and k, as shown in Figures 21 and 22, and exponential convergence can also be obtained for this 3D problem in cubic domain, as presented in Figures 23–25 indicates that the WRBCM possesses high accuracy on the boundaries when proper weights are imposed on the boundary conditions during the solutions. Figure 26 presents the condition number of stiffness matrix for the 3D inverse problem. Once again, the refinement of the discretization increases the condition number, which has a negative effect on the stability.

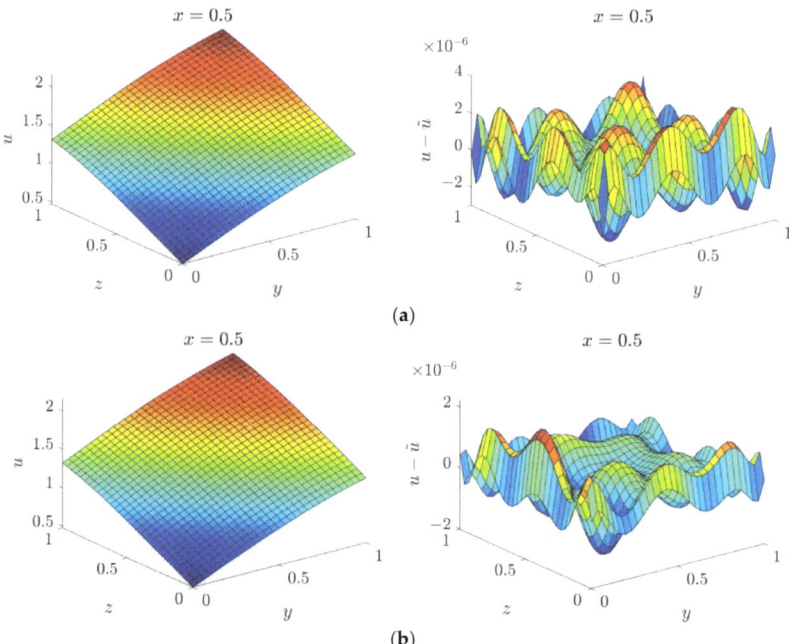

Figure 21. Cont.

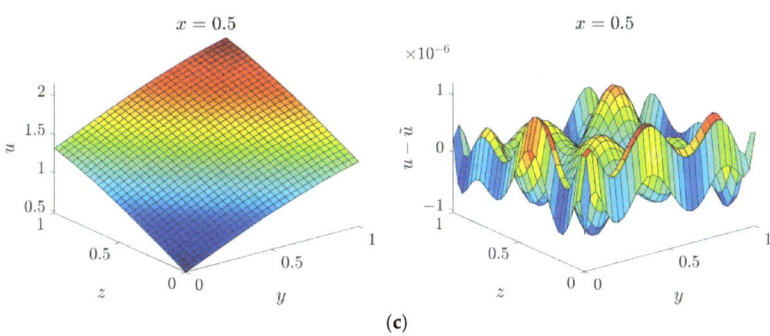

(c)

Figure 21. Solution and corresponding error for the 3D parameter identification problem in cubic domain under different discretizations: (**a**) $N_s = 7 \times 7 \times 7$; (**b**) $N_s = 9 \times 9 \times 9$; (**c**) $N_s = 11 \times 11 \times 11$.

(a)

(b)

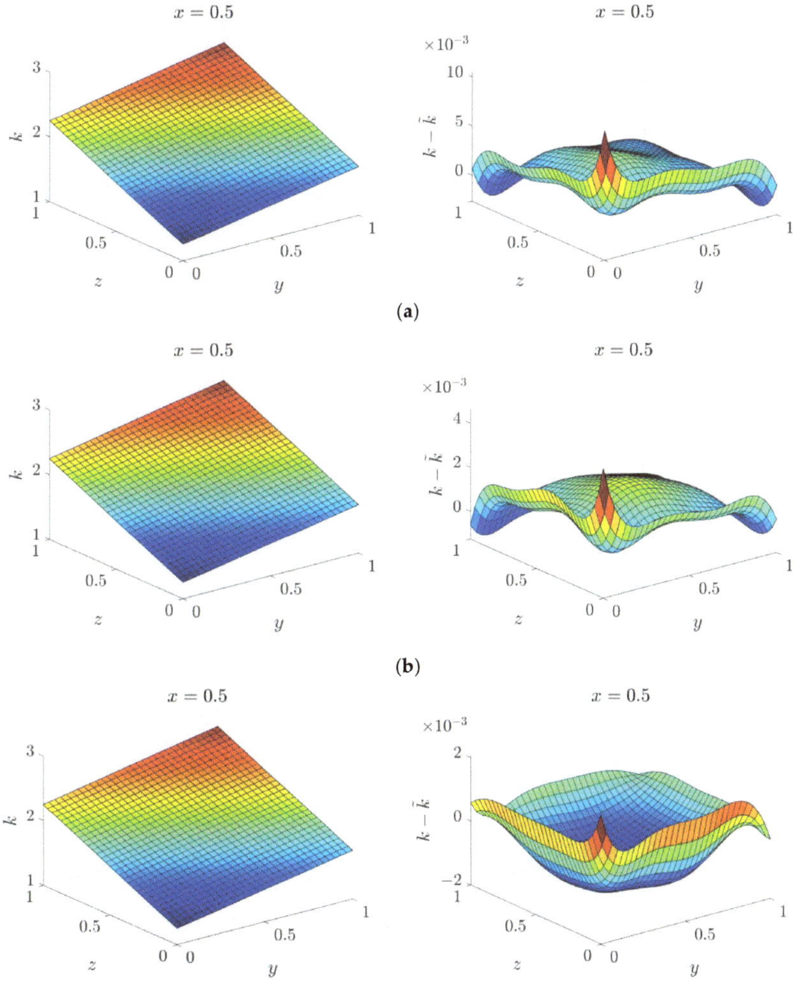

(c)

Figure 22. Solution of wave number k for the 3D parameter identification problem in cubic domain under different discretizations: (**a**) $N_s = 7 \times 7 \times 7$; (**b**) $N_s = 9 \times 9 \times 9$; (**c**) $N_s = 11 \times 11 \times 11$.

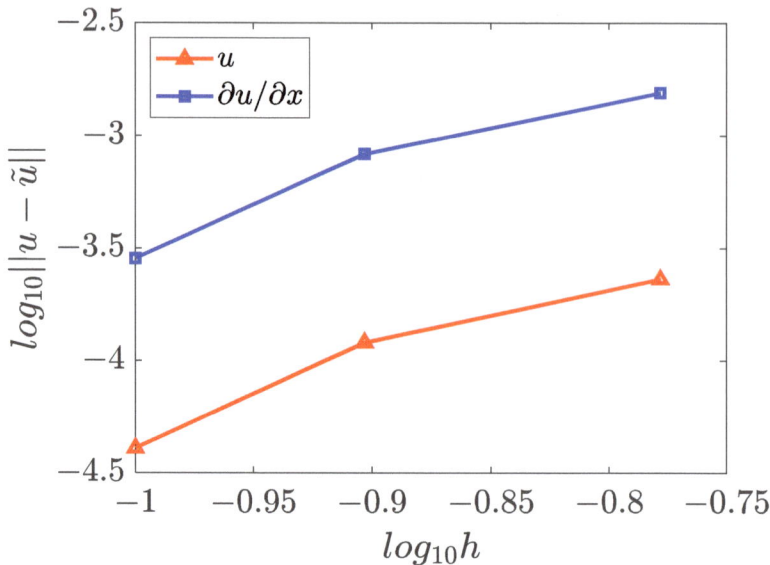

Figure 23. Convergence of the solutions for the 3D parameter identification problem in cubic domain.

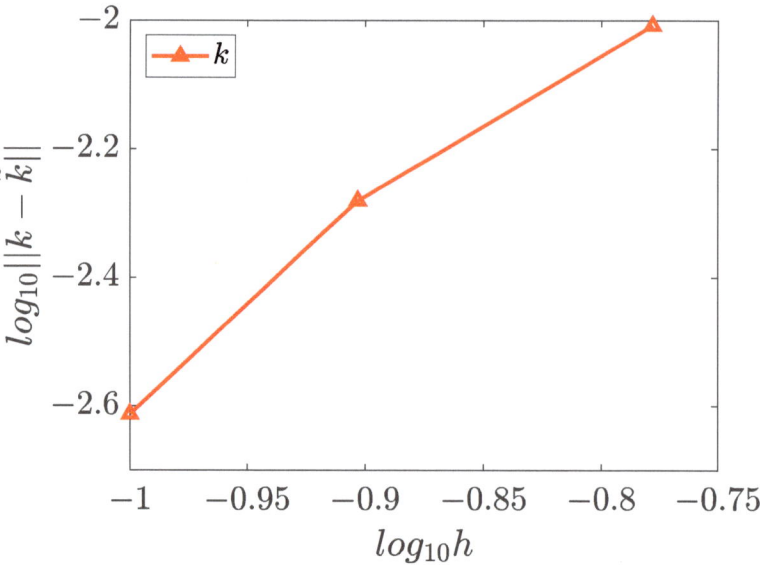

Figure 24. Convergence of wave number for the 3D parameter identification problem in cubic domain.

4.5. Three-Dimensional Inverse Helmholtz Problem of Parameter Identification in Spherical Domain

We further consider another three-dimensional inverse Helmholtz problem of the parameter identification in spherical domain. The governing equation and boundary conditions are given as

$$\frac{\partial^2 u}{\partial x^2} + \frac{\partial^2 u}{\partial y^2} + \frac{\partial^2 u}{\partial z^2} + k(x,y,z)u = \left(\frac{1}{2}x + y^2 - z\right)\sin(x)\cos(y)\cos(z), \text{ in } \Omega \quad (67)$$

$$u(x,y,z) = \sin(x)\cos(y)\cos(z), \text{ on } \Gamma_g \tag{68}$$

where $\Omega = \{x^2 + y^2 + z^2 < 1, x \in (-1,1), y \in (-1,1), z \in (-1,1)\}$, and $\Gamma_g = \{x^2 + y^2 + z^2 = 1, x \in [-1,1], y \in [-1,1], z \in [-1,1]\}$. The measurement condition is given, as follows

$$u(x,0,z) = \sin(x)\cos(z), \text{ on } \Pi \tag{69}$$

The analytical solution is expressed by

$$u(x,y,z) = \sin(x)\cos(y)\cos(z) \tag{70}$$

and the wave number that needs to be identified is

$$k(x,y,z) = \frac{1}{2}x + y^2 - z + 3 \tag{71}$$

Further, the weights imposed on the boundary conditions are provided as $\sqrt{w^g} \approx \sqrt{w^a} \approx 100$. The shape parameter is 2.5, 2 and 1.5, respectively.

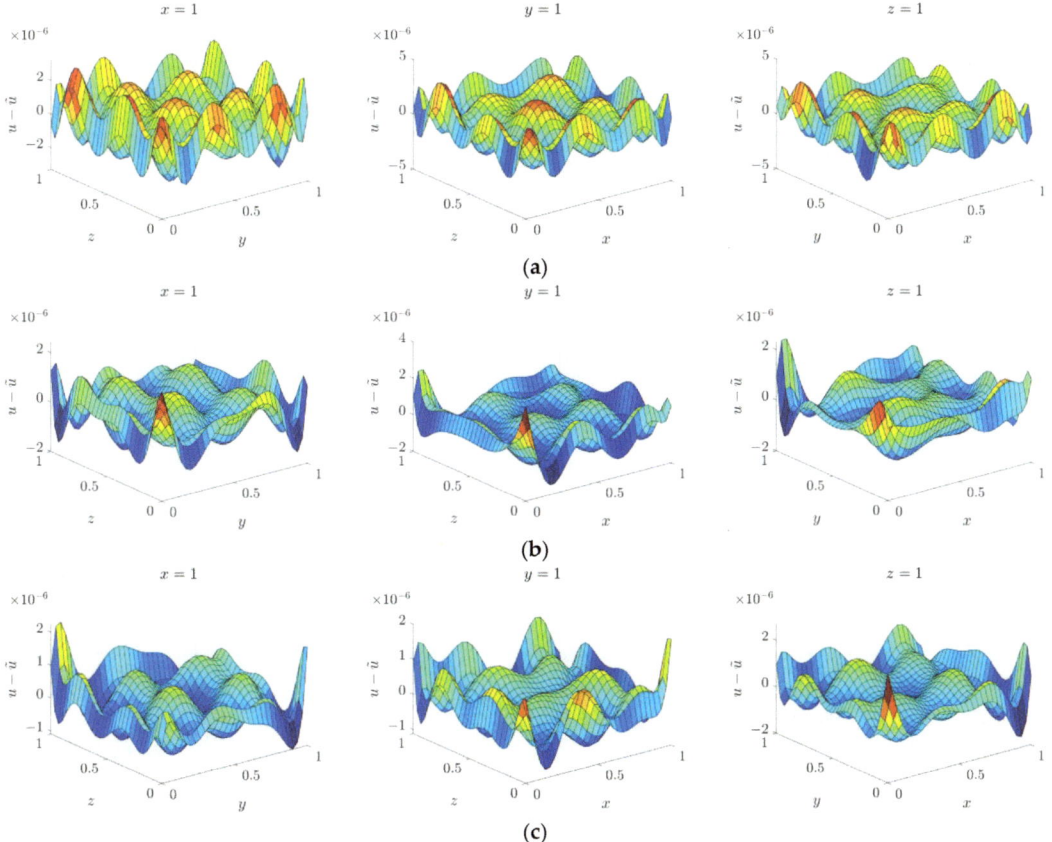

Figure 25. Errors of boundary solutions for the 3D parameter identification problem in cubic domain under different discretizations: (**a**) $N_s = 7 \times 7 \times 7$; (**b**) $N_s = 9 \times 9 \times 9$; (**c**) $N_s = 11 \times 11 \times 11$.

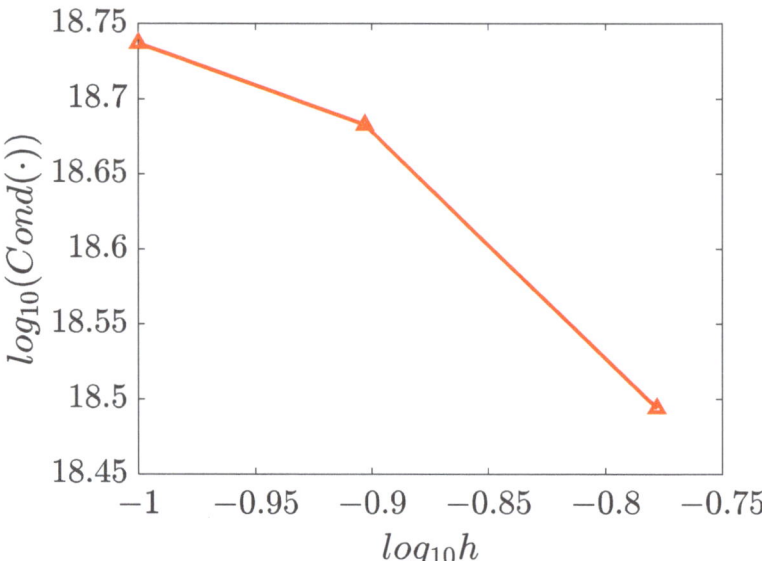

Figure 26. Condition number of stiffness matrix for the 3D parameter identification problem in cubic domain.

The numerical solutions and boundary solutions of u are displayed in Figures 27 and 28, and the solutions of k are presented in Figure 29. The results state that the WRBCM can obtain a high accuracy not only for the solution of the problem unknown u but also for the solution of the identified parameter k. Moreover, high accuracy can also be achieved on the boundaries by imposing the appropriate weights. The convergence studies of u and k are shown in Figures 30 and 31, which indicate that both solutions of u and k can receive exponential convergence. These results demonstrate that the WRBCM is a very good candidate for solving the nonlinear inverse Helmholtz problem of parameter identifications. Figure 32 displays the condition number for the 3D inverse problem in a spherical domain, and the condition number also follows the rules presented in the former examples.

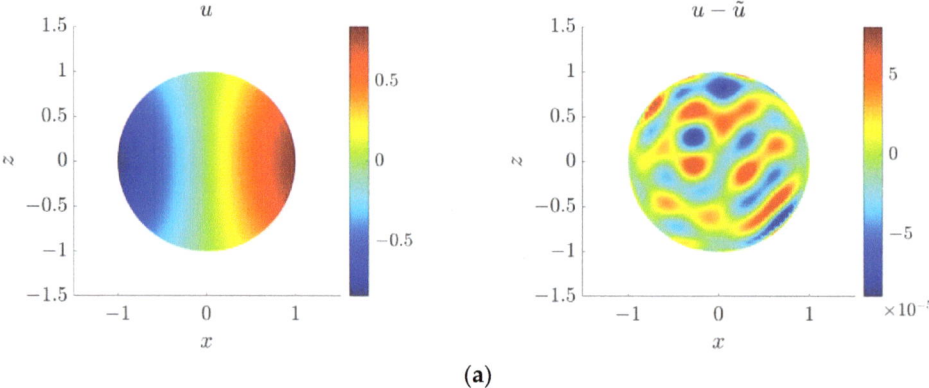

(a)

Figure 27. *Cont.*

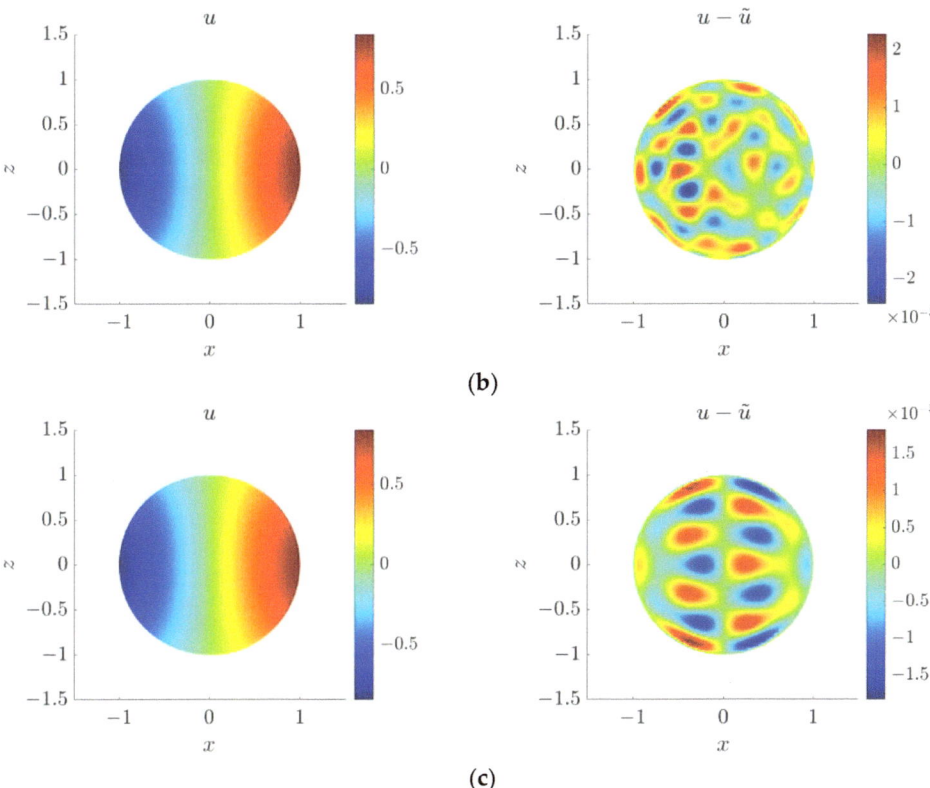

Figure 27. Solution and corresponding error at $y = 0$ for the 3D parameter identification problem in spherical domain under different discretizations: (**a**) $N_s = 7 \times 7 \times 7$; (**b**) $N_s = 9 \times 9 \times 9$; (**c**) $N_s = 11 \times 11 \times 11$.

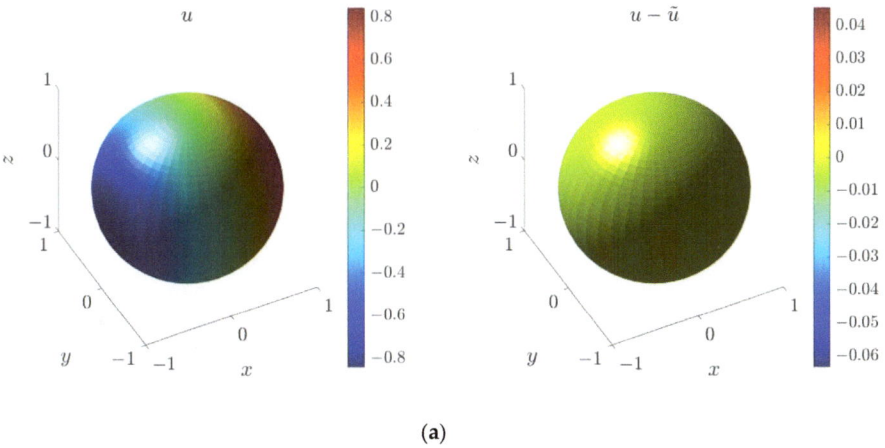

(**a**)

Figure 28. *Cont.*

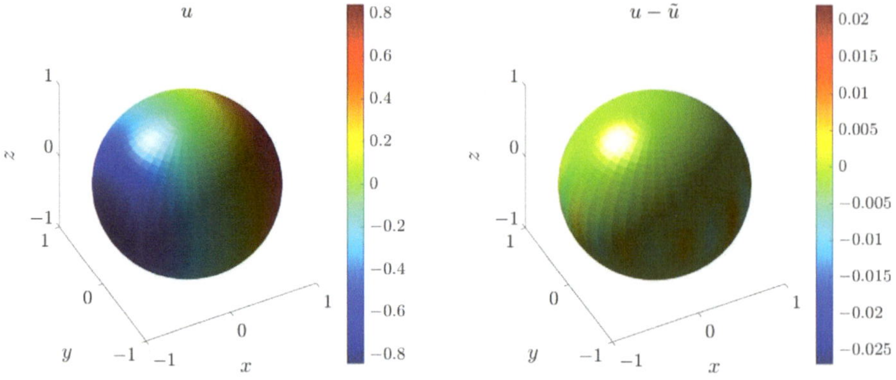

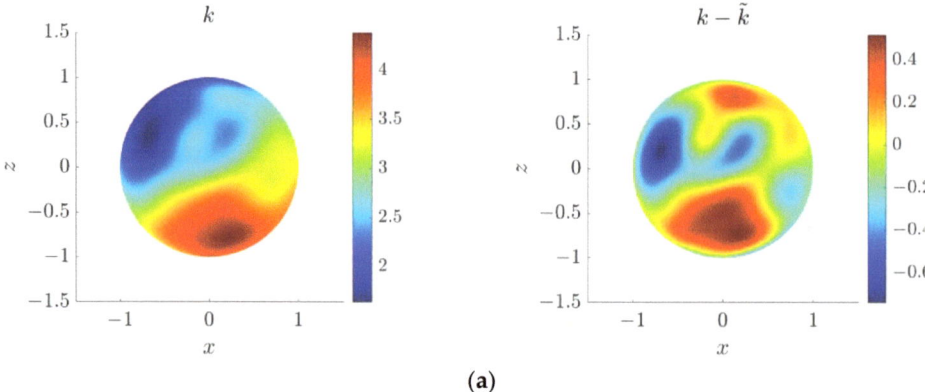

Figure 28. Boundary solution for the 3D parameter identification problem in spherical domain under different discretizations: (**a**) $N_s = 7 \times 7 \times 7$; (**b**) $N_s = 9 \times 9 \times 9$; (**c**) $N_s = 11 \times 11 \times 11$.

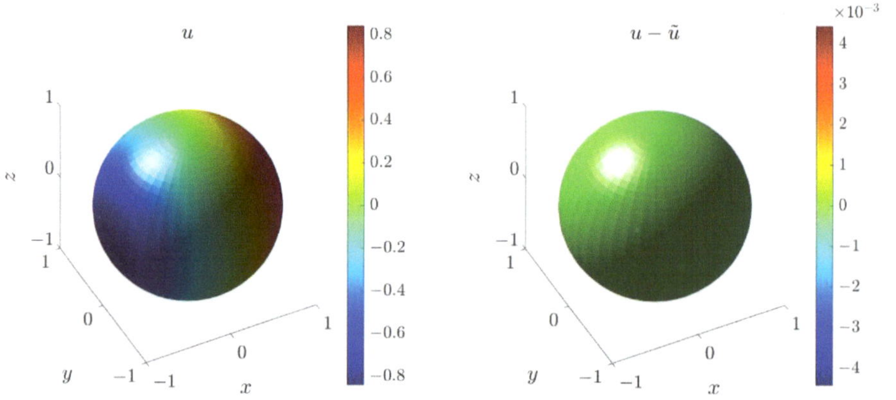

Figure 29. *Cont.*

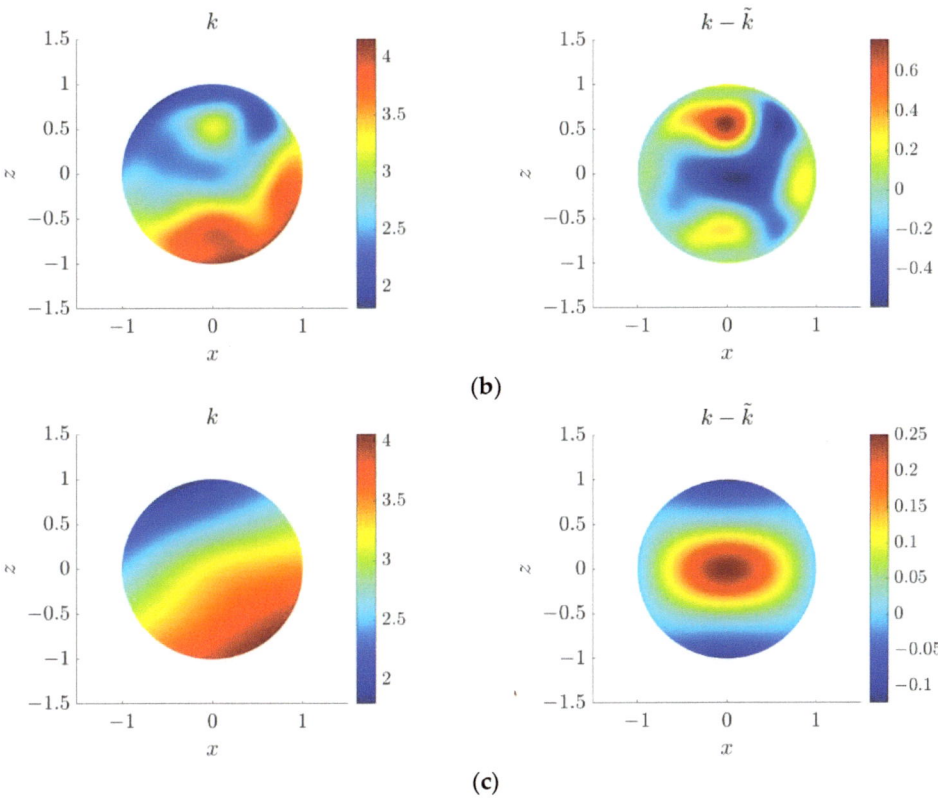

Figure 29. Solution and corresponding error of wave number k for the 3D parameter identification problem in spherical domain under different discretizations: (**a**) $N_s = 7 \times 7 \times 7$; (**b**) $N_s = 9 \times 9 \times 9$; (**c**) $N_s = 11 \times 11 \times 11$.

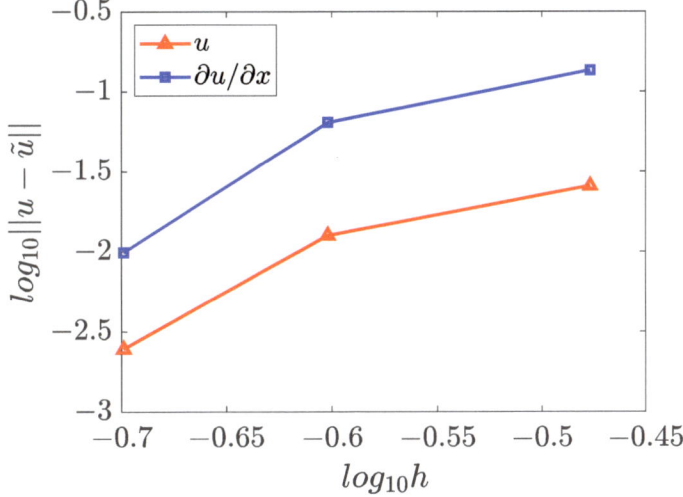

Figure 30. Convergence of the solutions for the 3D parameter identification problem in spherical domain.

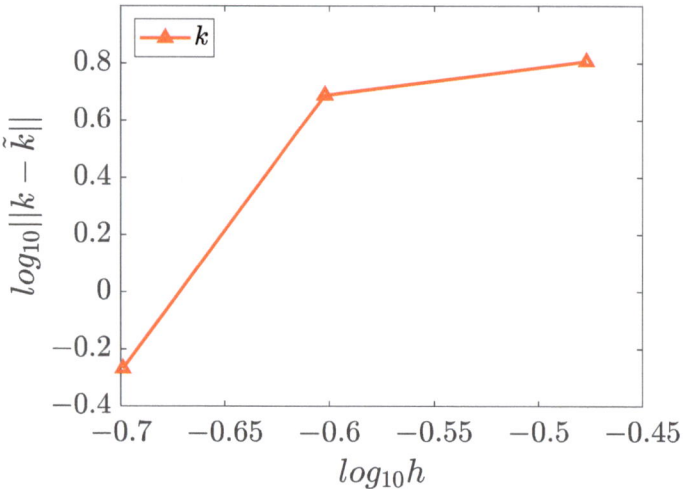

Figure 31. Convergence of wave number for the 3D parameter identification problem in spherical domain.

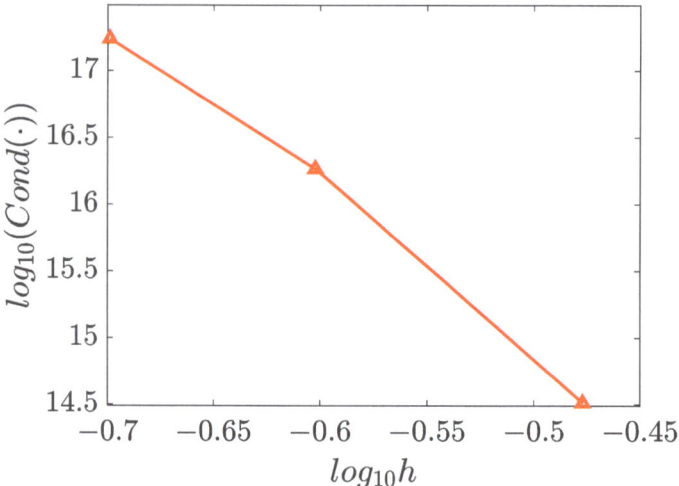

Figure 32. Condition number of stiffness matrix for the 3D parameter identification problem in spherical domain.

5. Conclusions

In this paper, a strong form weighted radial basis collocation method (WRBCM) combined with Newton's iteration method is proposed to solve the nonlinear inverse Helmholtz problems of parameter identification. The radial basis collocation method (RBCM) using MQ-RBF possesses exponential convergence. Proper weights that should be imposed on the Neumann and Dirichlet boundary conditions as well as measurement conditions for achieving high accuracy and optimal convergence are mathematically derived. In the numerical examples, we investigate the influences of shape parameter on the accuracy and stability. Choosing an appropriate shape parameter can balance the solution accuracy and the condition number of the stiffness matrix, which affect the stability of the numerical solution. WRBCM is compared with the traditional RBCM in accuracy, and the solutions indicate that by adding proper weights on the boundary, the solution accuracy can be significantly improved. Numerical examples demonstrate that the proposed WRBCM can work well for 1D, 2D and 3D problems, and also has good performances on the inverse problem in both regular and irregular domains. We will extend this method for solving the inverse Helmholtz problems of other types, for example, boundary identification or source identification, etc., in the future work.

Author Contributions: Conceptualization, L.W.; methodology, M.H.; software, M.H.; validation, M.H.; formal analysis, L.W.; investigation, M.H.; resources, L.W.; data curation, L.W.; writing—original draft preparation, M.H.; writing—review and editing, L.W.; visualization, M.H.; supervision, F.Y. and Y.Z.; project administration, L.W.; funding acquisition, L.W. All authors have read and agreed to the published version of the manuscript.

Funding: This research was funded by National Natural Science Foundation of China, grant number 11972261, 12272270 and the Fundamental Research Funds for the Central Universities. The APC was funded by National Natural Science Foundation of China, grant number 11972261.

Data Availability Statement: Data is contained within the article or supplementary material.

Acknowledgments: All individuals included in this section have consented to the acknowledgement.

Conflicts of Interest: The authors declare no conflict of interest.

References

1. Beskos, D.E. Boundary element methods in dynamic analysis: Part II (1986–1996). *Appl. Mech. Rev.* **1997**, *50*, 149–197. [CrossRef]
2. Hall, W.S.; Mao, X.Q. A boundary element investigation of irregular frequencies in electromagnetic scattering. *Eng. Anal. Bound. Elem.* **1995**, *16*, 245–252. [CrossRef]
3. Chen, J.T.; Wong, F.C. Dual formulation of multiple reciprocity method for the acoustic mode of a cavity with a thin partition. *J. Sound Vib.* **1998**, *217*, 75–95. [CrossRef]
4. Wood, A.S.; Tupholme, G.E.; Bhatti, M.I.H.; Heggs, P.J. Steady-state heat transfer through extended plane surfaces. *Int. Commun. Heat Mass Transf.* **1995**, *22*, 99–109. [CrossRef]
5. Shojaei, A.; Galvanetto, U.; Rabczuk, T.; Jenabi, A.; Zaccariotto, M. A generalized finite difference method based on the Peridynamic differential operator for the solution of problems in bounded and unbounded domains. *Comput. Methods Appl. Mech. Eng.* **2019**, *343*, 100–126. [CrossRef]
6. Zienkiewicz, O.C. Achievements and some unsolved problems of the finite element method. *Int. J. Numer. Methods Eng.* **2000**, *47*, 9–28. [CrossRef]
7. Onishi, K.; Kobayashi, K.; Ohura, Y. Numerical solution of a boundary inverse problem for the Laplace equation. *Theor. Appl. Mech.* **1996**, *45*, 257–264.
8. Belytschko, T.; Krongauz, Y.; Organ, D.; Fleming, M.; Krysl, P. Meshless methods: An overview and recent developments. *Comput. Methods Appl. Mech. Eng.* **1996**, *139*, 3–47. [CrossRef]
9. Liu, W.K.; Chen, Y.; Jun, S.; Chen, J.S.; Belytschko, T.; Pan, C.; Uras, R.A.; Chang, C. Overview and applications of the reproducing kernel particle methods. *Arch. Comput. Methods Eng.* **1996**, *3*, 3–80. [CrossRef]
10. Oñate, E.; Perazzo, F.; Miquel, J. A finite point method for elasticity problems. *Comput. Struct.* **2001**, *79*, 2151–2163. [CrossRef]
11. Liu, G.R.; Gu, Y. A point interpolation method for two-dimensional solids. *Int. J. Numer. Methods Eng.* **2001**, *50*, 937–951. [CrossRef]
12. Cheng, A.D.; Cabral, J.J.S.P. Direct solution of ill-posed boundary value problems by radial basis function collocation method. *Int. J. Numer. Methods Eng.* **2005**, *64*, 45–64. [CrossRef]
13. Wang, L.; Qian, Z. A meshfree stabilized collocation method (SCM) based on reproducing kernel approximation. *Comput. Methods Appl. Mech. Eng.* **2020**, *371*, 113303. [CrossRef]
14. Wang, L.; Hu, M.; Zhong, Z.; Yang, F. Stabilized Lagrange Interpolation Collocation Method: A meshfree method incorporating the advantages of finite element method. *Comput. Methods Appl. Mech. Eng.* **2023**, *404*, 115780. [CrossRef]
15. Wang, L. Radial basis functions methods for boundary value problems: Performance comparison. *Eng. Anal. Bound. Elem.* **2017**, *84*, 191–205. [CrossRef]
16. Wang, L.; Liu, Y.; Zhou, Y.; Yang, F. Static and dynamic analysis of thin functionally graded shell with in-plane material inhomogeneity. *Int. J. Mech. Sci.* **2021**, *193*, 106165. [CrossRef]
17. Liu, Z.; Xu, Q. A Multiscale RBF Collocation Method for the Numerical Solution of Partial Differential Equations. *Mathematics* **2019**, *7*, 964. [CrossRef]
18. Dehghan, M.; Shokri, A. A meshless method for numerical solution of the one-dimensional wave equation with an integral condition using radial basis functions. *Numer. Algorithms* **2009**, *52*, 461–477. [CrossRef]
19. Wang, L.; Chu, F.; Zhong, Z. Study of radial basis collocation method for wave propagation. *Eng. Anal. Bound. Elem.* **2013**, *37*, 453–463. [CrossRef]

20. Hu, H.Y.; Chen, J.S.; Hu, W. Weighted radial basis collocation method for boundary value problems. *Int. J. Numer. Methods Eng.* **2007**, *69*, 2736–2757. [CrossRef]
21. Zhang, X.; Song, K.Z.; Lu, M.W.; Liu, X. Meshless methods based on collocation with radial basis functions. *Comput. Mech.* **2000**, *26*, 333–343. [CrossRef]
22. Liu, X.; Liu, G.R.; Tai, K.; Lam, K. Radial point interpolation collocation method (RPICM) for partial differential equations. *Comput. Math. Appl.* **2005**, *50*, 1425–1442. [CrossRef]
23. Chen, J.S.; Hillman, M.; Chi, S.W. Meshfree methods: Progress made after 20 years. *J. Eng. Mech.* **2017**, *143*, 04017001. [CrossRef]
24. Wang, L.; Zhong, Z. Radial basis collocation method for nearly incompressible elasticity. *J. Eng. Mech.* **2013**, *139*, 439–451. [CrossRef]
25. Zheng, H.; Zhang, C.; Wang, Y.; Chen, W.; Sladek, J.; Sladek, V. A local RBF collocation method for band structure computations of 2D solid/fluid and fluid/solid phononic crystals. *Int. J. Numer. Methods Eng.* **2017**, *110*, 467–500. [CrossRef]
26. Ferreira, A.J.M.; Roque, C.M.C.; Jorge, R.M.N. Free vibration analysis of symmetric laminated composite plates by FSDT and radial basis functions. *Comput. Methods Appl. Mech. Eng.* **2005**, *194*, 4265–4278. [CrossRef]
27. Ferreira, A.J.M.; Fasshauer, G.E. Computation of natural frequencies of shear deformable beams and plates by an RBF-pseudospectral method. *Comput. Methods Appl. Mech. Eng.* **2006**, *196*, 134–146. [CrossRef]
28. Chu, F.; Wang, L.; Zhong, Z.; He, J. Hermite radial basis collocation method for vibration of functionally graded plates with in-plane material inhomogeneity. *Comput. Struct.* **2014**, *142*, 79–89. [CrossRef]
29. Ferreira, A.J.M.; Carrera, E.; Cinefra, M.; Roque, C.M.C.; Polit, O. Analysis of laminated shells by a sinusoidal shear deformation theory and radial basis functions collocation, accounting for through-the-thickness deformations. *Compos. Part B Eng.* **2011**, *42*, 1276–1284. [CrossRef]
30. Chen, J.S.; Wang, L.; Hu, H.Y.; Chi, S.W. Subdomain radial basis collocation method for heterogeneous media. *Int. J. Numer. Methods Eng.* **2009**, *80*, 163–190. [CrossRef]
31. Zerroukat, M.; Power, H.; Chen, C. A numerical method for heat transfer problems using collocation and radial basis functions. *Int. J. Numer. Methods Eng.* **1998**, *42*, 1263–1278. [CrossRef]
32. Wang, L.; Chen, J.S.; Hu, H.Y. Subdomain radial basis collocation method for fracture mechanics. *Int. J. Numer. Methods Eng.* **2010**, *83*, 851–876. [CrossRef]
33. Hon, Y.C.; Chen, W. Boundary knot method for 2D and 3D Helmholtz and convection–diffusion problems under complicated geometry. *Int. J. Numer. Methods Eng.* **2003**, *56*, 1931–1948. [CrossRef]
34. Marin, L.; Lesnic, D. The method of fundamental solutions for the Cauchy problem associated with two-dimensional Helmholtz-type equations. *Comput. Struct.* **2005**, *83*, 267–278. [CrossRef]
35. Marin, L. A meshless method for the numerical solution of the Cauchy problem associated with three-dimensional Helmholtz-type equations. *Appl. Math. Comput.* **2005**, *165*, 355–374. [CrossRef]
36. Jin, B.; Zheng, Y. A meshless method for some inverse problems associated with the Helmholtz equation. *Comput. Methods Appl. Mech. Eng.* **2006**, *195*, 2270–2288. [CrossRef]
37. Hon, Y.C.; Wei, T. A fundamental solution method for inverse heat conduction problem. *Eng. Anal. Bound. Elem.* **2004**, *28*, 489–495. [CrossRef]
38. Shojaei, A.; Boroomand, B.; Soleimanifar, E. A meshless method for unbounded acoustic problems. *J. Acoust. Soc. Am.* **2016**, *139*, 2613–2623. [CrossRef]
39. Shojaei, A.; Hermann, A.; Seleson, P.; Cyron, C.J. Dirichlet absorbing boundary conditions for classical and peridynamic diffusion-type models. *Comput. Mech.* **2020**, *66*, 773–793. [CrossRef]
40. Hermann, A.; Shojaei, A.; Steglich, D.; Höche, D.; Zeller-Plumhoff, B.; Cyron, C.J. Combining peridynamic and finite element simulations to capture the corrosion of degradable bone implants and to predict their residual strength. *Int. J. Mech. Sci.* **2022**, *220*, 107143. [CrossRef]
41. Li, M.; Jiang, T.; Hon, Y.C. A meshless method based on RBFs method for nonhomogeneous backward heat conduction problem. *Eng. Anal. Bound. Elem.* **2010**, *34*, 785–792. [CrossRef]
42. Yu, Y.; Luo, X.; Zhang, H.; Zhang, Q. The Solution of Backward Heat Conduction Problem with Piecewise Linear Heat Transfer Coefficient. *Mathematics* **2019**, *7*, 388. [CrossRef]
43. Wang, L.; Wang, Z.; Qian, Z. A meshfree method for inverse wave propagation using collocation and radial basis functions. *Comput. Methods Appl. Mech. Eng.* **2017**, *322*, 311–350. [CrossRef]
44. Wang, L.; Wang, Z.; Qian, Z.; Gao, Y.; Zhou, Y. Direct collocation method for identifying the initial conditions in the inverse wave problem using radial basis functions. *Inverse Probl. Sci. Eng.* **2018**, *26*, 1695–1727. [CrossRef]
45. Wang, L.; Qian, Z.; Wang, Z.; Gao, Y.; Peng, Y. An efficient radial basis collocation method for the boundary condition identification of the inverse wave problem. *Int. J. Appl. Mech.* **2018**, *10*, 1850010. [CrossRef]
46. Hardy, R.L. Multiquadric equations of topography and other irregular surfaces. *J. Geophys. Res.* **1971**, *76*, 1905–1915. [CrossRef]
47. Hardy, R.L. Research results in the application of multiquadratic equations to surveying and mapping problems. *Surv. Mapp.* **1975**, *35*, 321–332.
48. Krige, D.G. A statistical approach to some basic mine valuation problems on the Witwatersrand. *J. South. Afr. Inst. Min. Metall.* **1951**, *52*, 119–139.

49. Madych, W.R.; Nelson, S.A. Multivariate interpolation and conditionally positive definite functions. II. *Math. Comput.* **1990**, *54*, 211–230. [CrossRef]
50. Li, Z.C.; Lu, T.T.; Hu, H.Y.; Cheng, A.H. *Trefftz and Collocation Methods*; WIT Press: Boston, MA, USA, 2008.

Disclaimer/Publisher's Note: The statements, opinions and data contained in all publications are solely those of the individual author(s) and contributor(s) and not of MDPI and/or the editor(s). MDPI and/or the editor(s) disclaim responsibility for any injury to people or property resulting from any ideas, methods, instructions or products referred to in the content.

Article

Enhancing the Heat Transfer Due to Hybrid Nanofluid Flow Induced by a Porous Rotary Disk with Hall and Heat Generation Effects

Naif Abdulaziz M. Alkuhayli [1,2]

[1] School of Computing and Mathematical Sciences, University of Leicester, Leicester LE1 7RH, UK; nama8@leicester.ac.uk or naalkuhayli@ju.edu.sa
[2] Mathematics Department, College of Science, Jouf University, P.O. Box 2014, Sakaka 72388, Saudi Arabia

Abstract: A study of hybrid-nanofluid flow induced by the uniform rotation of a circular porous disk is presented for the purpose of facilitating the heat transfer rate. The Hall and Ohmic heating effects resulting from an applied magnetic field and the source of heat generation/absorption are also considered to see their impact on flow behavior and enhancing the heat transfer rate. The physical problem under the given configuration is reduced to a set of nonlinear partial differential equations using the conservation laws. Similarity transformations are adopted to obtain a system of ordinary differential equations which are further solved using the Shooting Method. Results are presented via graphs and tables thereby analyzing the heat transfer mechanism against different variations of physical parameters. Outcomes indicate that the wall suction plays a vital role in determining the behavior of different parameters on the velocity components. It is notable that the wall suction results in a considerable reduction in all the velocity components. The enhanced Hartman number yields a growth in the radial velocity and a decay in the axial velocity. Moreover, consequences of all parametric effects on the temperature largely depend upon the heat generation/absorption.

Keywords: magnetohydrodynamics; porous disk; hall currents; ohmic heating; heat generation; wall suction; shooting method

MSC: 35Qxx; 65Nxx; 49M37; 74A15; 35Q30

1. Introduction

The poor thermal characteristics of orthodox fluids have been a concern for engineers for a long time. Different methods were proposed and tested to enhance the performance of orthodox heat transfer fluids. During the last decade of the 20th century, Choi and Eastman [1] came up with the novel idea of suspending nanometer-sized metallic particles in the convectional fluids to enhance thermal performance of such fluids. This novelty proved to be more than helpful in a number of ways and the solutions resulting from the inclusion of nanoparticles in base fluids were termed as 'nanofluids'. The nanofluids caught the attention of researchers from all over the globe due to their unique thermophysical and chemical properties, hence their wide-spread applications are found in different domains of engineering. To name a few, they include biomedical engineering, domestic and industrial cooling/heating systems, the IT and automobile industry, modern drug delivery systems, etc., that find several applications for nanofluids. Such diverse properties and wide-spread applications are the reasons behind the extensive research that is being carried out on nanofluids. Some analytical and numerical studies on fluid/nanofluid flows are shown through references [2–8].

Hybrid nanofluids are an advanced type of nanofluid obtained by mixing at least two types of nanoparticles in a single fluid. Such mixing helps to attain unique thermal/chemical properties which are difficult to obtain otherwise. Recently, the flow of hybrid nanofluids is being studied by many motivated researchers. Lund et al. [9] performed a stability analysis of hybrid nanofluids consisting of copper-alumina nanoparticles flowing over a shrinking surface. Sindhu et al. [10] analyzed the flow of hybrid nanofluids through a micro channel by incorporating the shape factors of the nanoparticles. Natural convection for hybrid nanofluids flowing through a porous medium has been investigated by Izadi et al. [11]. Abbasi et al. [12] performed a thermodynamic analysis of the electro-osmotic flow of hybrid nanofluids.

Flows produced by rotary disks are important due to their applications in many industrial processes as most industrial appliances are constituted of rotating parts submerged in fluids. Pioneering analysis presenting the modelling and analysis of such flows came from a classical study by Von Kármán [13]. In this study, he proved that the velocity components as well as pressure depend only upon the axial coordinate and hence similarity transformations were used to obtain the solutions. A similar methodology was used by several researchers to examine such flows under different flow configurations. Another comprehensive study presenting an insight into flow over rotating disks is presented by Brady and Durlofsky [14]. Andersson and Korte [15] studied the MHD flow of power-law fluid whereas Turkyilmazoglu [16] and Rashidi et al. [17] analyzed the flow and the entropy generation, respectively, of nanofluids while considering the rotary disks. Abdel-Wahed and Emam [18] examined MHD flow considering a rotating disk with Hall effects. The flow of nanofluids generated by a rotating porous disk was studied by Uddin et al. [19]. In another study, Turkyilmazoglu [20] analyzed the heat transfer and fluid flow due to rotating as well as vertically moving disks. Some recent studies in this regard can be seen through references [21,22].

Low thermal productivity of fluids is a main cause for several heat-transport mechanisms in engineering applications including engines, transformers, microwave tubes, heat exchangers, oils and lubricants, etc. It is well known that the materials that have high thermal conductivity (for example, copper, graphene, aluminum, etc.) are considered speedy exchangers of heat. Animasaun et al. [23] presented a detailed analysis of numerous self-similar flows emphasizing the dynamics of nanofluids, thereby listing the nanomaterials with high thermal conductivity for their more effective use in energy transfer. Asim and Siddiqui [24] analyzed a comprehensive perspective on properties of fundamental hydrothermal and heat and mass transfer of hybrid nanofluids. Heat transfer in rotating flows is an interesting area of research where there are enormous applications in the manufacturing of crystal growth, computer storage devices, thermal power generation and gas turbine motors. The literature review suggests that not much has been said about the hybrid nanofluid flow generated by a rotating porous disk despite having multiple applications in engineering and medical sciences. This study aims to fill that gap. It is well established that the contribution of hybrid nanofluids expedites the heat transfer rate, as is evident from the literature [25–28] whereas suction/injection facilitates keeping the temperature under control despite the heat generation. Thus, the novelty of the underlying problem lies in the fact that it analyzes heat transfer rate from fluid to the wall and vice versa due to the concentration of hybrid nanoparticles, suction/injection and heat generation and absorption for assisting the heat transportation. The nanoparticles consist of copper and titanium dioxide suspended in water, whereas the Lorentz force generated by a uniform magnetic field and its effects, i.e., the Hall and Ohmic heating is also assumed. Heat generation/absorption is also accounted for to present a detailed insight into the heat transfer phenomenon. Similarity transformations are adopted to reduce the nonlinear system of PDEs to a system of ODEs. Solutions are obtained using the numerical shooting method and results are presented in graphical and tabular form for analysis. For validation purposes, a comparison of the reduced case of the present study with previously available results is presented and a good agreement was noted.

The underlying article is arranged in the following prospects: Section 2 details the mathematical equations related to flow geometry with dimensional and non-dimensional settings whereas Section 3 briefly explains the adopted methodology for obtaining the flow parameters. The results and discussions are in Section 4 whilst key findings are provided in Section 5.

2. Governing Equations

Consider the steady flow of a hybrid-nanofluid induced by a uniformly rotating disk as shown by Figure 1. The disk is considered porous and rotating with a uniform angular velocity ω. The cylindrical coordinate system '$(r, \Theta, z)'$ has been adopted in a way that the disk rotates in $z = 0$ plane and a hybrid nanofluid fills the space $z \geq 0$. The hybrid-nanofluid is composed of copper and titanium dioxide nanoparticles suspended in water. The disk and ambient are held at constant temperatures T_w and T_∞, respectively.

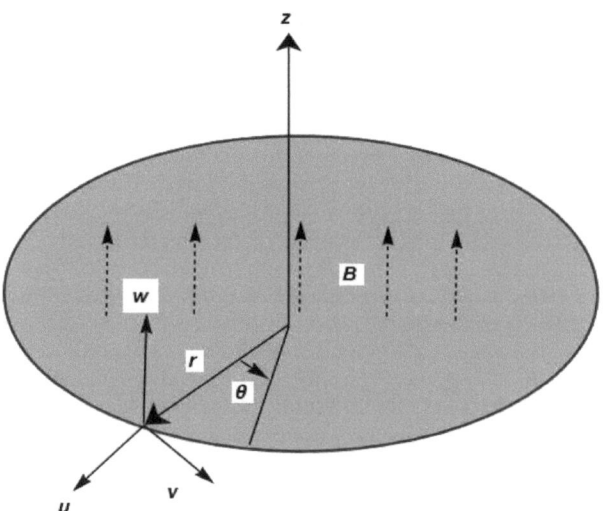

Figure 1. A rotating disk.

Rotation of the disk generates a 3D flow governed by the velocity field '$\overline{V} = [u(r,\Theta,z), v(r,\Theta,z), w(r,\Theta,z)]'$. Because of the radial symmetry, the variations in flow are considered independent of Θ. Mathematical forms of conservation of mass, momentum and energy for present flow configuration are given as:

$$\frac{1}{r}\frac{\partial}{\partial r}(ur) + \frac{\partial w}{\partial z} = 0, \tag{1}$$

$$\rho_{hnf}\left(u\frac{\partial u}{\partial r} + w\frac{\partial u}{\partial z} - \frac{v^2}{r}\right) = -\frac{\partial p}{\partial r} + \mu_{hnf}\left(\frac{\partial^2 u}{\partial r^2} + \frac{1}{r}\frac{\partial u}{\partial r} + \frac{\partial^2 u}{\partial z^2} - \frac{u}{r^2}\right) + F_r, \tag{2}$$

$$\rho_{hnf}\left(u\frac{\partial v}{\partial r} + w\frac{\partial v}{\partial z} + \frac{uv}{r}\right) = \mu_{hnf}\left(\frac{\partial^2 v}{\partial r^2} + \frac{1}{r}\frac{\partial v}{\partial r} + \frac{\partial^2 v}{\partial z^2} - \frac{v}{r^2}\right) + F_\Theta, \tag{3}$$

$$\rho_{hnf}\left(u\frac{\partial w}{\partial r} + w\frac{\partial w}{\partial z}\right) = -\frac{\partial p}{\partial z} + \mu_{hnf}\left(\frac{\partial^2 w}{\partial r^2} + \frac{1}{r}\frac{\partial w}{\partial r} + \frac{\partial^2 w}{\partial z^2}\right) + F_z, \tag{4}$$

$$(\rho C_p)_{hnf}\left(u\frac{\partial T}{\partial r} + w\frac{\partial T}{\partial z}\right) = k_{hnf}\left(\frac{\partial^2 T}{\partial r^2} + \frac{1}{r}\frac{\partial T}{\partial r} + \frac{\partial^2 T}{\partial z^2}\right) + \frac{1}{\sigma_{hnf}}\overline{J}.\overline{J} + \delta. \tag{5}$$

Here the subscript 'hnf' stands for hybrid nanofluid and ρ, p, μ, C_p, k, $\sigma\left(=\frac{1}{E}\right)$, δ and $\overline{J}$ denote the density, pressure, viscosity, specific heat, thermal conductivity and electric conductivity denoting the rate of charge flow, dimensional heat generation/absorption and current density, respectively. Effective quantities for hybrid nanofluid are given as follows [10–12]:

$$\begin{cases} \rho_{hnf} = \rho_{TiO_2}\phi_{TiO_2} + (1+(-\phi_{Cu}-\phi_{TiO_2}))\rho_f + \rho_{Cu}\phi_{Cu}, \\ \frac{\mu_{hnf}}{\mu_f} = (1-(\phi_{Cu}+\phi_{TiO_2}))^{-2.5}, \\ (\rho C_p)_{hnf} = (\rho C_p)_{Cu}\phi_{Cu} + (1+(-\phi_{Cu}-\phi_{TiO_2}))(\rho C_p)_f + (\rho C_p)_{TiO_2}\phi_{TiO_2}, \\ \frac{k_{hnf}}{k_f} = \frac{\left(\frac{\phi_{Cu}k_{Cu}+\phi_{TiO_2}k_{TiO_2}}{\phi_{Cu}+\phi_{TiO_2}}\right)-2(\phi_{Cu}+\phi_{TiO_2})k_f+2k_f+2(\phi_{Cu}k_{Cu}+\phi_{TiO_2}k_{TiO_2})}{\left(\frac{k_{Cu}\phi_{Cu}+\phi_{TiO_2}k_{TiO_2}}{\phi_{Cu}+\phi_{TiO_2}}\right)-(\phi_{Cu}k_{Cu}+\phi_{TiO_2}k_{TiO_2})+k_f(2+(\phi_{Cu}+\phi_{TiO_2}))} \end{cases} \quad (6)$$

Here the subscript 'f' stands for the base fluid, water in this case. The thermophysical parametric values for the nanoparticles and the base fluids considered herein are provided by Table 1 [4,16] whereas units of ρ, k, C_p, and σ are kgm^{-3}, Wm^{-1}k^{-1}, Jkg^{-1}K^{-1}, and Sm^{-1}, respectively.

Table 1. Thermo-physical properties of nanoparticles and water.

Material	ρ	k	C_p	σ
Copper	8933	401	385.0	5.96×10^7
Water	997.1	0.613	4179	0.05
Titanium dioxide	4250	8.9538	686.2	1.0×10^{-12}

The Lorentz force ($\overline{F} = [F_r, F_\theta, F_z] = \overline{J} \times \overline{B}$) generated due to a magnetic field of the form $\overline{B} = [0,0,B_0]$ is computed using the generalized Ohms law as follows:

$$\overline{J} = \sigma_{hnf}\left[\overline{E} + \overline{V}\times\overline{B} - \frac{(\overline{J}\times\overline{B})}{en_e}\right]. \quad (7)$$

Here e and n_e denote 'charge of electron' and 'number density of free electrons'. It is relevant to mention that the free electron density determines the electrical conductivity of metal which is inserted via Ohm's law. This also refers to the whole solution considering the nanofluids in general. The source of number density is a modified Ohm's law for Hall effects. However, an explicit expression of number density is not used here because it is considered to be a part of a generalized Ohm's law which is further non-dimensionalized. The comprehensive details of the set of formulae for various materials can be seen in [29].

Moreover, $\overline{E}$ is applied to an electric field which in the present scenario is considered zero. In the absence of an electric field, for the velocity and magnetic field under consideration, the Lorentz force takes the form:

$$\overline{F} = \left[\frac{A_1 B_0^2}{A_1^2 m^2+1}(-u+mA_1 v)\sigma_f, -\frac{\sigma_f B_0^2}{A_1^2 m^2+1}(mA_1 u+v), 0\right]. \quad (8)$$

Here $m = \frac{B_0 \sigma_f}{n_e \cdot e}$ is the Hall parameter and the form of A_1 having the electric conductivity for hybrid nanofluid consisting of copper and titanium dioxide nanoparticles suspended in water is given as:

$$A_1 = 1 + \frac{3\left(\frac{\sigma_{TiO_2}\phi_{TiO_2}+\sigma_{Cu}\phi_{Cu}}{\sigma_f}\right) - 3(\phi_{TiO_2}+\phi_{Cu})}{\left(\frac{\sigma_{TiO_2}\phi_{TiO_2}+\sigma_{Cu}\phi_{Cu}}{\sigma_f(\phi_{TiO_2}+\phi_{Cu})}+2\right) - \left(\frac{\sigma_{TiO_2}\phi_{TiO_2}+\sigma_{Cu}\phi_{Cu}}{\sigma_f}\right) - (\phi_{TiO_2}+\phi_{Cu})}.$$

Here ϕ indicates the 'volume fraction of nanoparticles' and subscripts f, cu and TiO_2 represent fluid (water), copper and titanium oxide, respectively.

Equations (1)–(5) subject to Equations (7) and (8) take the following form:

$$\frac{1}{r}\frac{\partial}{\partial r}(ur) + \frac{\partial w}{\partial z} = 0, \quad (9)$$

$$\rho_{hnf}\left(u\frac{\partial u}{\partial r} + w\frac{\partial u}{\partial z} - \frac{v^2}{r}\right) = -\frac{\partial p}{\partial r} + \mu_{hnf}\left(\frac{\partial^2 u}{\partial r^2} + \frac{1}{r}\frac{\partial u}{\partial r} + \frac{\partial^2 u}{\partial z^2} - \frac{u}{r^2}\right) \\ - \frac{A_1 \sigma_f B_0^2}{A_1^2 m^2 + 1}(u - mA_1 v), \quad (10)$$

$$\rho_{hnf}\left(u\frac{\partial v}{\partial r} + w\frac{\partial v}{\partial z} + \frac{uv}{r}\right) = \mu_{hnf}\left(\frac{\partial^2 v}{\partial r^2} + \frac{1}{r}\frac{\partial v}{\partial r} + \frac{\partial^2 v}{\partial z^2} - \frac{v}{r^2}\right) \\ - \frac{\sigma_f B_0^2}{A_1^2 m^2 + 1}(mA_1 u + v), \quad (11)$$

$$\rho_{hnf}\left(u\frac{\partial w}{\partial r} + w\frac{\partial w}{\partial z}\right) = -\frac{\partial p}{\partial z} + \mu_{hnf}\left(\frac{\partial^2 w}{\partial r^2} + \frac{1}{r}\frac{\partial w}{\partial r} + \frac{\partial^2 w}{\partial z^2}\right), \quad (12)$$

$$(\rho C_p)_{hnf}\left(u\frac{\partial T}{\partial r} + w\frac{\partial T}{\partial z}\right) = k_{hnf}\left(\frac{\partial^2 T}{\partial r^2} + \frac{1}{r}\frac{\partial T}{\partial r} + \frac{\partial^2 T}{\partial z^2}\right) \\ + \frac{\sigma_f B_0^2}{A_1^2 m^2 + 1}\{(u - mA_1 v)^2 + (mA_1 u + v)^2\} + \delta. \quad (13)$$

The boundary conditions for present flow with 'suction/injection' at the face of the porous rotating disk are stated as below:

$$u = 0, \ v = r\omega, \ w = \overline{v}_w, \ T = T_w, \quad \text{at } z = 0, \quad (14)$$

$$u = 0, \ v = 0, \ w = 0, \ T = 0, \quad \text{as } z \to \infty. \quad (15)$$

Here $\overline{v}_w$ is the constant value of axial velocity at the boundary of the porous disk. Following the deductions of Kármán, and considering the velocity components to be dependent upon 'z', the following similarity transformations are considered [12,14,16]:

$$\eta = z\left(\frac{\omega}{v_f}\right)^{\frac{1}{2}}, \ (u,v,w) = \left(r\omega F(\eta), r\omega G(\eta), \left(\omega v_f\right)^{\frac{1}{2}} H(\eta)\right), \\ (p, T) = (p_\infty - \omega\mu_f p(\eta), T_\infty + (T_w - T_\infty)\theta(\eta)). \quad (16)$$

Here η is introduced as a dimensionless variable and $F(\eta)$, $G(\eta)$ and $H(\eta)$ are dimensionless functions of η considered in radial, azimuthal and axial directions, respectively. As quoted, the use of similarity transformations reduces our governing equations to a system of ODEs as follows:

$$H'(\eta) + 2F(\eta) = 0 \quad (17)$$

$$A_2 F''(\eta) = \frac{A_1 M}{A_1^2 m^2 + 1}(F(\eta) - mA_1 G(\eta)) + A_3(F^2(\eta) + H(\eta)F'(\eta) - G^2(\eta)) \quad (18)$$

$$A_2 G''(\eta) - \frac{A_1 M}{A_1^2 m^2 + 1}(G(\eta) + mA_1 F(\eta)) - A_3(2F(\eta)G(\eta) + H(\eta)G'(\eta)) = 0, \quad (19)$$

$$H''(\eta) - P'(\eta) - H(\eta)H'(\eta) = 0, \quad (20)$$

$$A_4 \theta''(\eta) + \frac{PrEcA_1 M}{A_1^2 m^2 + 1}\left\{(F(\eta) - mA_1 G(\eta))^2 + (G(\eta) + mA_1 F(\eta))^2\right\} \\ - PrA_5 H(\eta)\theta'(\eta) + Pr\epsilon = 0. \quad (21)$$

M, Pr, Ec and ϵ, respectively, denote the Hartman number, the Prandtl number, the Eckert number, and dimensionless heat generation/absorption, given as:

$$M = \frac{\sigma_f B_0^2}{\rho_f \omega}, \ Pr = \frac{v_f(\rho C_p)_f}{K_f}, \ Ec = \frac{\rho_f r^2 \omega^2}{(\rho C_p)_f (T_w - T_\infty)}, \epsilon = \frac{\delta}{\omega v_f}. \quad (22)$$

and the $A_i s$ appearing are given as:

$$A_2 = (1 - (\phi_{Cu} + \phi_{TiO_2}))^{-2.5},$$
$$A_3 = \rho_{TiO_2}\phi_{TiO_2} + (1 + (-\phi_{Cu} - \phi_{TiO_2}))\rho_f + \rho_{Cu}\phi_{Cu},$$
$$A_4 = \frac{\left(\frac{\phi_{Cu}k_{Cu} + \phi_{TiO_2}k_{TiO_2}}{\phi_{Cu} + \phi_{TiO_2}}\right) - 2(\phi_{Cu}+\phi_{TiO_2})k_f + 2k_f + 2(\phi_{Cu}k_{Cu}+\phi_{TiO_2}k_{TiO_2})}{\left(\frac{k_{Cu}\phi_{Cu}+\phi_{TiO_2}k_{TiO_2}}{\phi_{Cu}+\phi_{TiO_2}}\right) - (\phi_{Cu}k_{Cu}+\phi_{TiO_2}k_{TiO_2}) + k_f(2 + (\phi_{Cu}+\phi_{TiO_2}))}, \quad (23)$$
$$A_5 = (\rho C_p)_{hnf} = (\rho Cp)_{Cu}\phi_{Cu} + (1 + (-\phi_{Cu} - \phi_{TiO_2})).$$

In view of such considerations, the dimensionless boundary conditions for current flow pattern are assumed as follows:

$$F(\eta) = 0, \ H(\eta) = v_w, \ G(\eta) = 1, \ \theta(\eta) = 1 \ at \ \eta = 0, \quad (24)$$

and

$$F(\eta) = G(\eta) = \theta(\eta) = 0 \ as \ \eta \to \infty \quad (25)$$

The 'local skin friction coefficients' (C_i, where $i = F, G, H$ denotes skin friction coefficient for that specific component of velocity) and 'heat transfer rate at the wall' ($A_4\theta'(0)$) are important quantities of interest and hence are included in the analysis.

3. Shooting Method

The nonlinear-coupled system of Equations (17)–(21) subject to boundary conditions (24) and (25) are difficult to solve exactly. Hence, the shooting method is adopted to obtain the solutions of said system of equations in Mathematica. The shooting method is usually employed by considering the boundary conditions as a multivariate function of initial conditions at some point. Therefore, as a first step, the boundary value problem is transformed to finding the initial conditions via an initial guess that offers a solution to the problem in a convenient manner. In the next step, the Runge–Kutta method is employed to target the other boundary and then the results are matched for the first initial guess. This process is continued until the acceptable solution with minimum error is achieved. Here, the step size is effectively taken to be 0.01 for all numerical computations. Numerical solutions are compiled in the form of graphical illustrations and are presented for physical analysis of the results in the subsequent section.

4. Results and Discussions

This section aims to analyze the obtained results via graphical and tabular illustrations. Plots of velocity components and temperature profile for variations in embedded parameters are presented and analyzed. To avoid repetition, only graphs of effective quantities of interest are included. Moreover, values of thermophysical quantities are taken as provided via Table 1, whereas '$Pr = 6.2, M = 1, m = 0.5, Ec = 0.5, \epsilon = 0.5$, and $v_w = -1$' unless stated otherwise. It is important to note that the flow behavior is discussed in detail for pertinent parameters as stated, since the flow parameters in dimensional and non-dimensional settings are related to each other through Equations (6), (16), (22) and (24). A variation in flow behavior due to varying physical parameters can be viewed through graphical and tabular analysis to be explained subsequently. Further reasoning and justification can be extracted through parametric relations stated via Equations (6), (16), (22) and (24).

To verify the validation of present results, a comparison of the reduced case of the present study is provided with previously available studies via Table 2. It is noted that present results are in excellent agreement with previous results reported by Rashidi et al. [17] and Uddin et al. [19] in qualitative manner. Quantitatively, a difference of up to 10^{-2} is noted in the results, which is mainly due to the consideration of different viscosity models considered herein.

Table 2. Comparison with previously reported results [17,19].

ϵ	v_w	Rashidi et al. [17]	Uddin et al. [19]	$F'(0)$ for Present Study
0	0	0.309237	0.309236	0.309254
	−1	0.251039	0.251038	0.256351
	−2	0.188718	0.188715	0.197141

4.1. Analysis of Dimensionless Velocity

Figures 2–16 are plotted to examine the effects of variations in wall suction, the Hartman number, the Hall parameter and the nanoparticles' volume fraction of both nanoparticles on the radial, azimuthal and axial velocity components. Figure 2 indicates that the radial velocity decreases with an increase in wall suction. This figure also highlights the fact that flows induced by a rigid rotating disk possess larger axial velocities compared to a porous disk. The azimuthal velocity tends to decrease with increasing wall suction parameters (see Figure 3). Such a decrease is less significant when compared with that of radial velocity. Notable and uniform reduction in the axial velocity is observed for enhanced wall suction (see Figure 4).

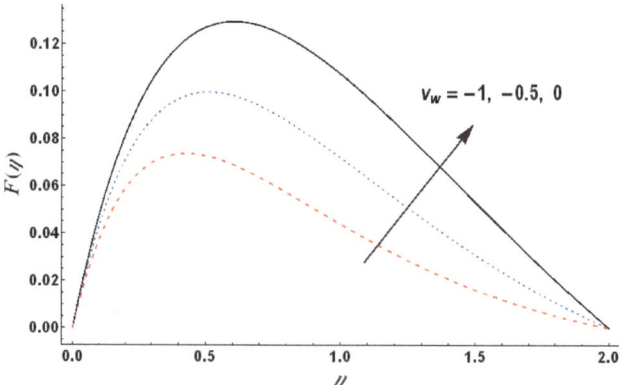

Figure 2. Wall suction versus dimensionless radial velocity.

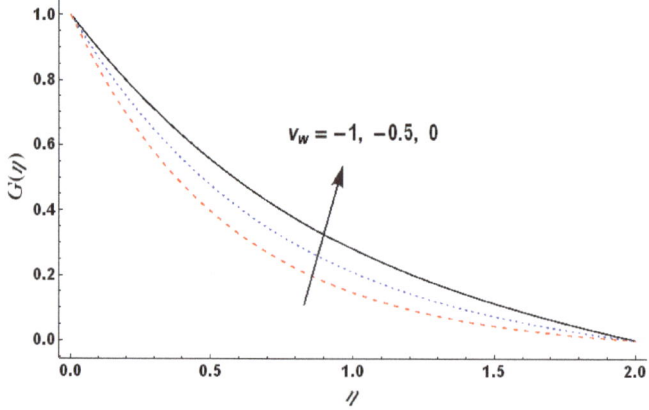

Figure 3. Wall suction versus the dimensionless azimuthal velocity.

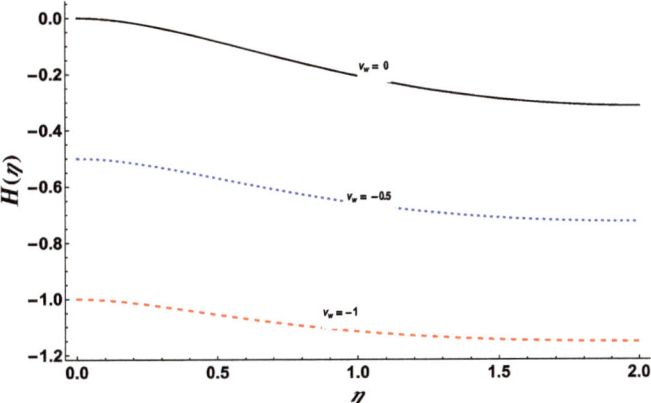

Figure 4. Wall suction versus the dimensionless axial velocity.

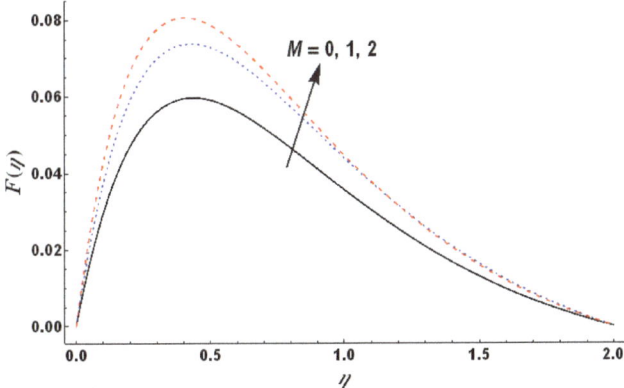

Figure 5. Hartman number versus the dimensionless radial velocity.

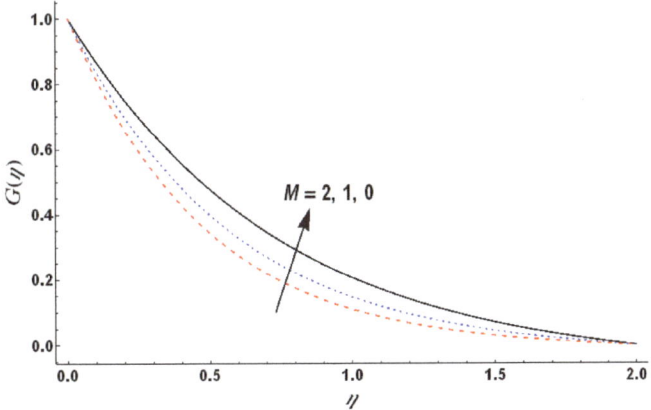

Figure 6. Hartman number versus the dimensionless azimuthal velocity.

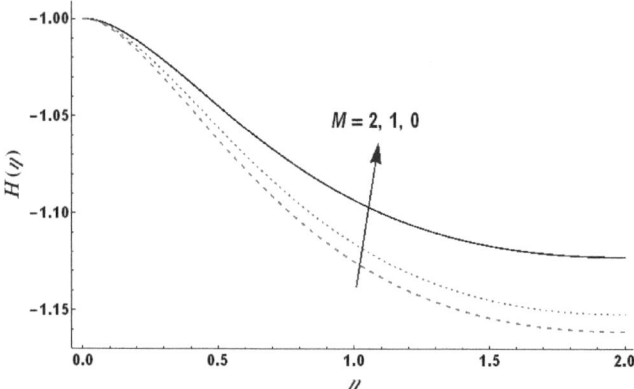

Figure 7. Hartman number versus the dimensionless axial velocity.

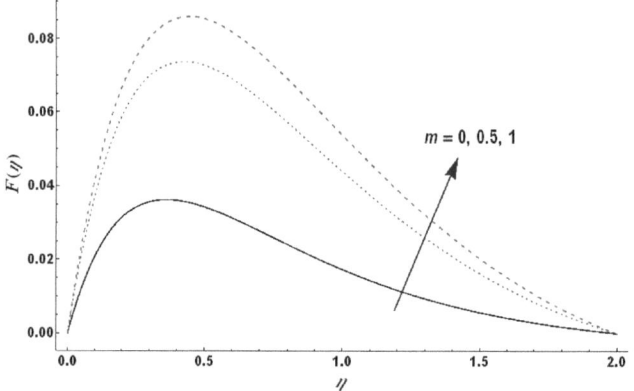

Figure 8. Hall parameter versus the dimensionless radial velocity.

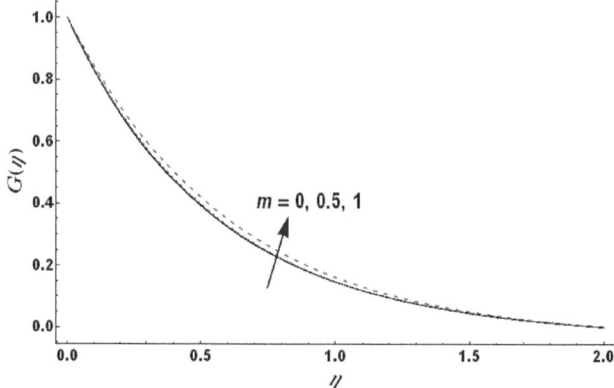

Figure 9. Hall parameter versus the dimensionless azimuthal velocity.

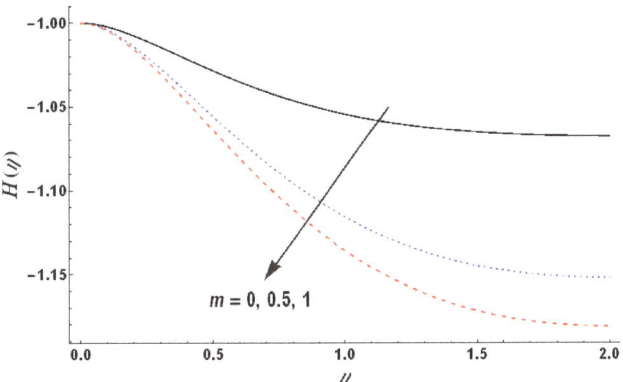

Figure 10. Hall parameter versus the dimensionless axial velocity.

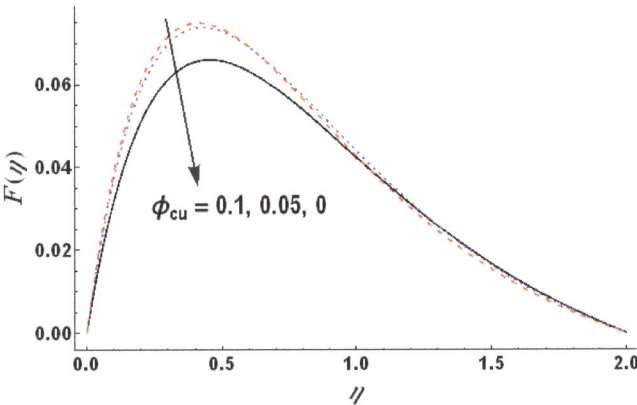

Figure 11. Volume fraction of copper nanoparticles versus the dimensionless radial velocity.

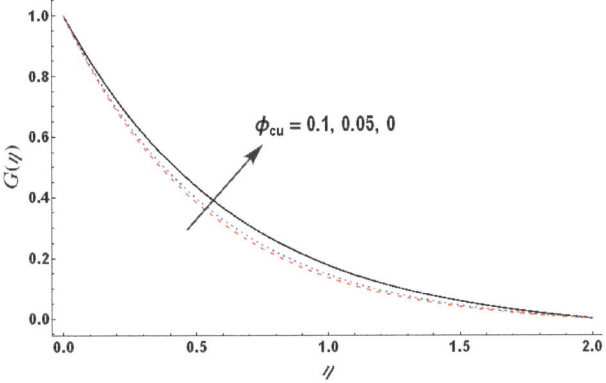

Figure 12. Volume fraction of copper nanoparticles versus the dimensionless azimuthal velocity.

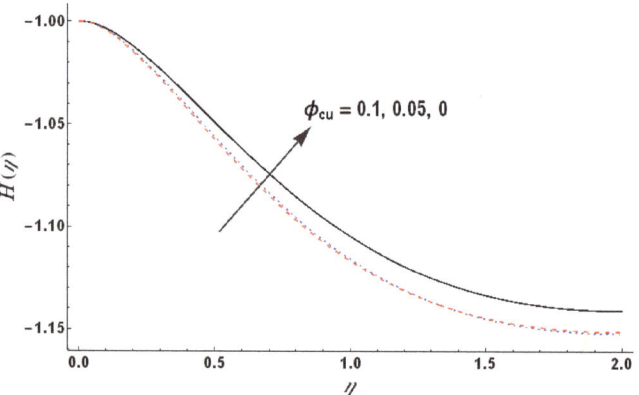

Figure 13. Volume fraction of copper nanoparticles versus the dimensionless axial velocity.

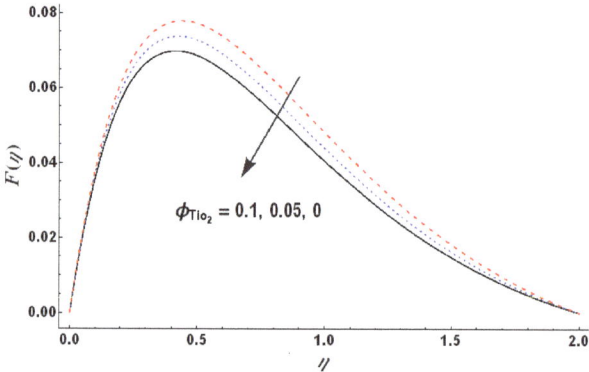

Figure 14. Volume fraction of Titanium dioxide nanoparticles versus the dimensionless radial velocity.

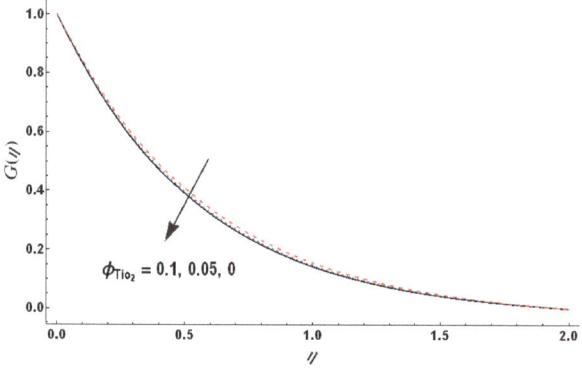

Figure 15. Volume fraction of Titanium dioxide nanoparticles versus the dimensionless azimuthal velocity.

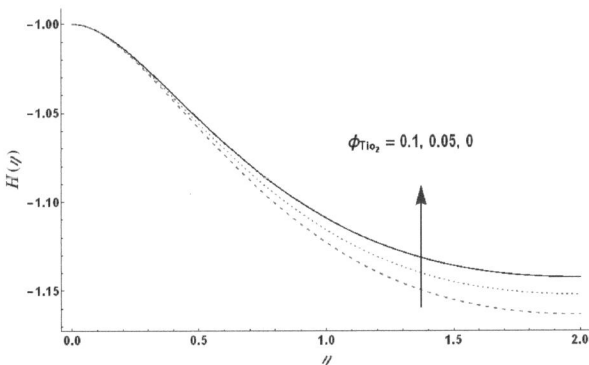

Figure 16. Volume fraction of Titanium dioxide nanoparticles versus the dimensionless axial velocity.

An increased Hartman number tends to enhance the radial velocity (see Figure 5) and such an increase is significant near the porous disk. Figures 6 and 7 show that the azimuthal as well as axial velocity components decrease with an increase in the Hartman number (M). Such a decrease in $H(\eta)$ becomes larger as the distance from the disk increases. The effects of the Hall parameter (m) on the velocity components are analyzed through Figures 8–10. It is noted via these figures that both the radial and azimuthal velocities show an increasing trend for an increase in m. Such an increase is large for the radial velocity and small in the case of the azimuthal velocity. The axial velocity on the other hand decreases significantly for an increase in m. The effects of the volume fractions of copper and titanium dioxide nanoparticles on the velocity components are studied via Figures 11–16. These figures demonstrate that the radial velocity increases with an increase in the nanoparticles' volume fraction of both types of nanoparticles. Such an increase is noted to be uniform for an increase in titanium dioxide nanoparticles. The axial velocity is noted to decrease with an increase in the nanoparticles' volume fraction of both types of nanoparticles and again such a decrease is noted to be uniform for the titanium dioxide nanoparticles. The azimuthal velocity, on the other hand, demonstrates the opposite behavior for the two types of nanoparticles.

4.2. Analysis of Dimensionless Temperature

Figures 17–23 have been plotted to study the behavior of dimensionless temperature (θ) for variations in different embedded parameters. It is worth noting that the heat generation/absorption plays a key role on the impact of all parameters. Even a small value of heat generation parameters becomes influential due to the Prandtl number (say $\epsilon = 0.2$). Figure 17 shows that the temperature decreases with an increase in wall suction for the case of heat generation. This fact indicates that wall suction facilitates the cooling down of the rotating fluid and can help in keeping the temperature under control despite the heat generation. An increase in the value of the Hartman number increases the temperature which is mainly due to the consideration of Ohmic heating (see Figure 18). On the other hand, an increase in the values of the Hall parameter reduces the temperature. Figures 20 and 21 indicate that the dimensionless temperature of hybrid nanofluid increases with an increase in the volume fraction of both type of nanoparticles for the case of heat absorption as well as for minute heat generation ($\epsilon = 0.2 - 0.4$). This role of nanoparticles is reversed for larger heat generation with the fluid, i.e., an increase in the nanoparticles' volume fraction reduces the dimensionless temperature (see Figure 22). This observation highlights the role of nanoparticles in facilitating the heat transfer from fluid to the wall and vice versa. Figure 23 depicts the dimensionless temperature for the cases of heat generation, no heat generation/absorption and heat absorption. This figure shows that temperature profile changes significantly for changes in ϵ.

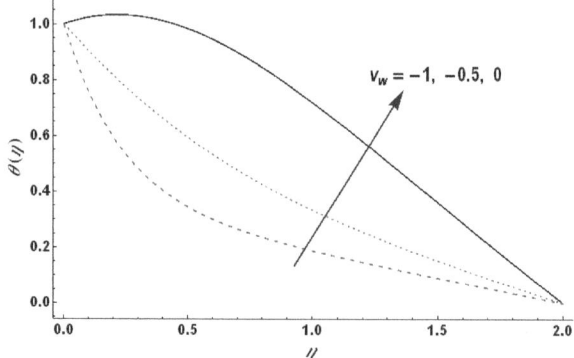

Figure 17. Wall suction versus the dimensionless temperature.

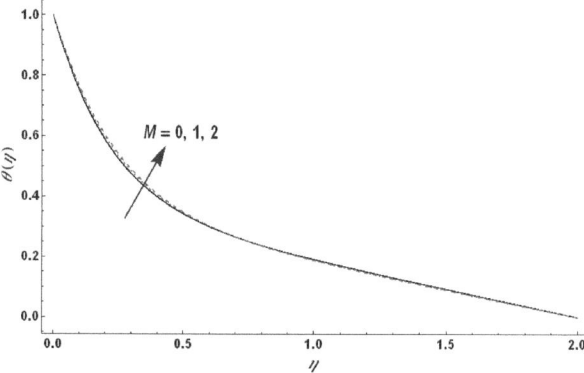

Figure 18. Hartman number versus the dimensionless temperature.

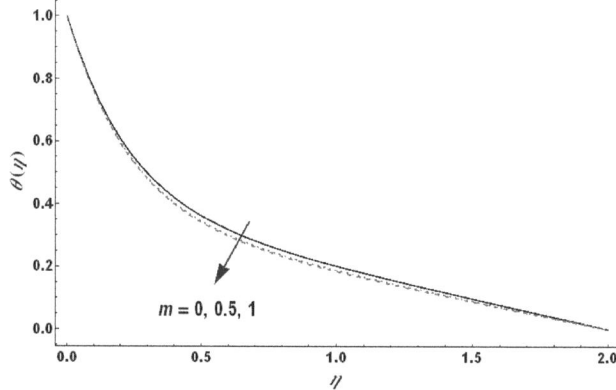

Figure 19. Hall parameter versus the dimensionless temperature.

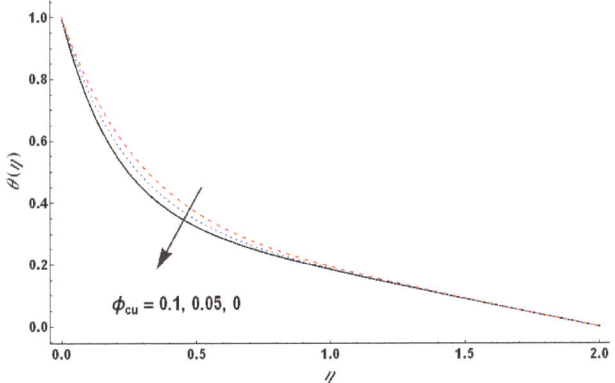

Figure 20. Volume fraction of copper nanoparticles versus the dimensionless temperature for $\epsilon = 0.2$.

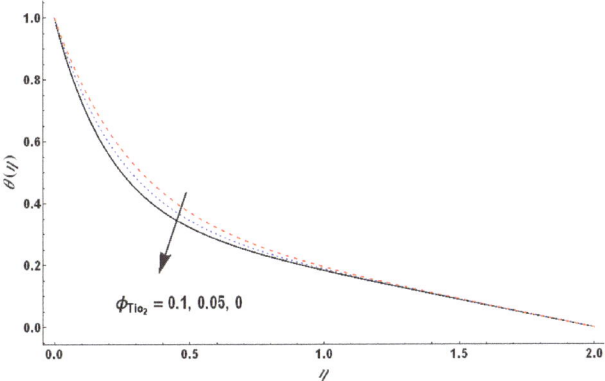

Figure 21. Volume fraction of Titanium dioxide nanoparticles versus the dimensionless temperature.

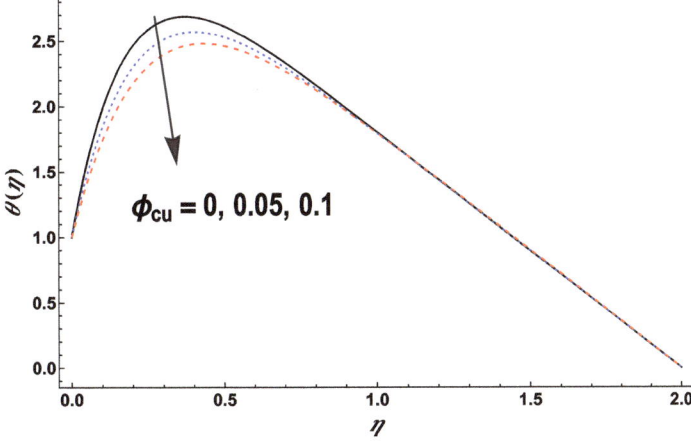

Figure 22. Volume fraction of copper nanoparticles versus the dimensionless temperature for $\epsilon = 2$.

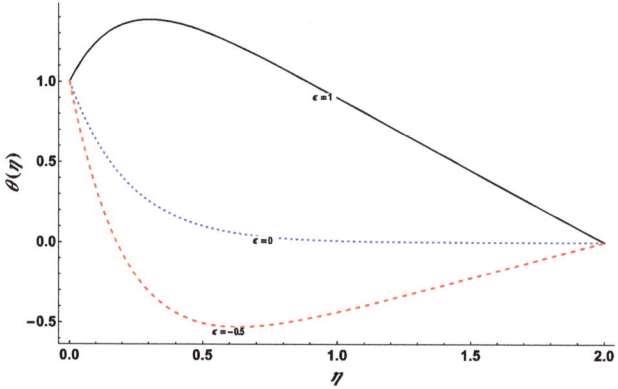

Figure 23. Heat generation/absorption versus the dimensionless temperature.

The numerical values of local skin friction and the rate of heat transfer at the boundary for variations in the nanoparticles' volume fraction of both types of nanoparticles and wall suction are given via Tables 3 and 4. It is noted via these tables that an increase in the volume fraction of nanoparticles results in an increase in the skin friction coefficients. It is a noteworthy fact that the impact of copper nanoparticles on such increase is large compared to that of titanium dioxide nanoparticles. On the other hand, such an increase is relatively uniform for the case of TiO_2 nanoparticles. The skin friction coefficient in the radial direction decreases whereas it increases with a decrease in the value of v_w along the azimuthal direction. Here the positive value of v_w indicates the case of minute injection.

Table 3. Local skin friction coefficients for variations in different parameters.

ϕ_{cu}	ϕ_{TiO_2}	v_w	$A_2 F'(0)$	$-A_2 G'(0)$
0.0	0.05	−1	0.448061	1.82267
0.05			0.614161	2.31676
0.1			0.745451	2.76917
0.05	0.0		0.521083	2.06778
	0.05		0.614161	2.31676
	0.1		0.721574	2.57965
	0.05	0.5	0.731593	1.07797
		0.0	0.721085	1.4041
		−0.5	0.679381	1.81585

Table 4. Local heat transfer coefficient for variations in different parameters.

ϕ_{cu}	ϕ_{TiO_2}	v_w	ϵ	$-A_4 \theta'(0)$
0.0	0.05	−1	0.5	0.749743
0.05				0.781668
0.1				0.800912
0.05	0.0			0.795555
	0.05			0.781668
	0.1			0.771571

Table 4. *Cont.*

ϕ_{Cu}	ϕ_{TiO_2}	v_w	ϵ	$-A_4\theta'(0)$
	0.05	0.5		−1.48757
		0.0		−2.18461
		−0.05		−1.33788
		−1.0	0.5	0.781668
			0.0	5.94662
			−0.5	11.1116

The amount of heat transfer at the wall boosts with the rise in nanoparticles' volume fraction of both nanoparticles for positive values of ϵ. Variation in the values of heat transfer at the wall depends on the heat generation/absorption as nanoparticles only facilitate the heat transfer. The amount of heat transfer at the boundary increases as one moves from the case of heat generation to heat absorption.

5. Conclusions

The heat transfer analysis for flow of hybrid nanofluid composed of copper and titanium dioxide nanoparticles suspended in water induced by the uniform rotation of a circular porous disk has been analyzed. The Hall and Ohmic heating effects along with heat generation/absorption have been considered. The main outcomes of this study are summarized below:

- Wall suction results in a considerable reduction in all the velocity components.
- An increase in the values of the Hartman number result in an increase in the radial and a reduction in the axial velocity.
- An increase in the values of the Hall parameter result in a slight increase in the azimuthal velocity. The effects of titanium dioxide nanoparticles on the velocity components are uniform compared to that of the copper nanoparticles.
- The consequences of physical parameters versus the dimensionless temperature largely depend upon the heat generation/absorption.

To see further aspects of this study, various experimental analyses report different empirical relationships for the apparent viscosity and thermal conductivity of nanofluids. Therefore, it will be useful to analyze the flow of nanofluids due to the rotating disk using different models for the apparent viscosity and thermal conductivity. Furthermore, in various engineering phenomena, the flux on a rotating disk is influenced by the impact of external magnetic flux. Thus, analyzing the response of base fluid with the concentration of various types of nanoparticle nanofluids under the influence of a magnetic field can also be considered.

Funding: This research received no external funding.

Data Availability Statement: No new data were created or analyzed in this study. Data sharing is not applicable to this article.

Conflicts of Interest: The author declares no conflict of interest. The funders had no role in the design of the study; in the collection, analyses, or interpretation of data; in the writing of the manuscript; or in the decision to publish the results.

References

1. Choi, S.U.S.; Eastman, J.A. Enhancing thermal conductivity of fluids with nanoparticles. In Proceedings of the ASME International Mechanical Engineering Congress & Exposition, San Francisco, CA, USA, 12–17 November 1995.
2. Buongiorno, J. Convective transport in nanofluids. *ASME J. Heat Transf.* **2006**, *128*, 240–250. [CrossRef]
3. Tiwari, R.K.; Das, M.K. Heat transfer augmentation in a two-sided lid-driven differentially heated square cavity utilizing nanofluids. *Int. J. Heat Mass Transf.* **2007**, *50*, 2002–2018. [CrossRef]

4. Iqbal, J.; Abbasi, F.M.; Shehzad, S.A. Heat transportation in peristalsis of Carreau-Yasuda nanofluid through a curved geometry with radial magnetic field. *Int. Commun. Heat Mass Transf.* **2020**, *117*, 104774. [CrossRef]
5. Abbasi, F.M.; Gul, M.; Shehzad, S.A. Effectiveness of temperature-dependent properties of Au, Ag, Fe_3O_4, Cu nanoparticles in peristalsis of nanofluids. *Int. Commun. Heat Mass Transf.* **2020**, *116*, 104651. [CrossRef]
6. Saba; Abbasi, F.M.; Shehzad, S.A. Magnetized peristaltic transportation of Boron-Nitride and Ethylene-Glycol nanofluid through a curved channel. *Chem. Phys. Lett.* **2022**, *803*, 139860. [CrossRef]
7. Rasheed, A.; Nawaz, R.; Khan, S.A.; Hanif, H.; Wahab, A. Numerical study of a thin film flow of fourth grade fluid. *Int. J. Numer. Methods Heat Fluid Flow* **2015**, *25*, 929–940. [CrossRef]
8. Akbar, T.; Nawaz, R.; Kamran, M.; Rasheed, A. MHD flow analysis of second grade fluids in porous media with prescribed vorticity. *AIP Adv.* **2015**, *5*, 117133. [CrossRef]
9. Lund, L.A.; Omar, Z.; Khan, I.; Seikh, A.H.; Sherif, E.S.M.; Nisar, K.S. Stability analysis and multiple solution of $Cu–Al_2O_3/H_2O$ nanofluid contains hybrid nanomaterials over a shrinking surface in the presence of viscous dissipation. *J. Mater. Res. Technol.* **2020**, *9*, 421–432. [CrossRef]
10. Sindhu, S.; Gireesha, B.J.; Sowmya, G.; Makinde, O.D. Hybrid nanoliquid flow through a microchannel with particle shape factor, slip and convective regime. *Int. J. Numer. Methods Heat Fluid Flow* **2022**, *32*, 3388–3410. [CrossRef]
11. Izadi, M.; Sheremet, M.A.; Mehryan, S. Natural convection of a hybrid nanofluid affected by an inclined periodic magnetic field within a porous medium. *Chin. J. Phys.* **2020**, *65*, 447–458. [CrossRef]
12. Abbasi, F.M.; Zahid, U.M.; Akbar, Y.; Saba; Hamida, M.B.B. Thermodynamic analysis of electroosmosis regulated peristaltic motion of Fe_3O_4–Cu/H_2O hybrid nanofluid. *Int. J. Mod. Phys. B* **2022**, *36*, 2250060. [CrossRef]
13. Von Kármán, T. Uber laminare und turbulente reibung. *ZAMM J. Appl. Math. Mech.* **1921**, *1*, 233–252. [CrossRef]
14. Brady, J.F.; Durlofsky, L. On rotating disk flow. *J. Fluid Mech.* **1987**, *175*, 363–394. [CrossRef]
15. Andersson, H.I.; de Korte, E. MHD flow of a power-law fluid over a rotating disk. *Eur. J. Mech. B/Fluids* **2002**, *21*, 317–324. [CrossRef]
16. Turkyilmazoglu, M. Nanofluid flow and heat transfer due to a rotating disk. *Comput. Fluids* **2014**, *94*, 139–146. [CrossRef]
17. Rashidi, M.M.; Abelman, S.; Freidooni Mehr, N. Entropy generation in steady MHD flow due to a rotating porous disk in a nanofluid. *Int. J. Heat Mass Transf.* **2013**, *62*, 515–525. [CrossRef]
18. Abdel-Wahed, M.S.; Emam, T.G. Effect of Joule heating and Hall current on MHD flow of a nanofluid due to a rotating disk with viscous dissipation. *Therm. Sci.* **2016**, *22*, 857–870. [CrossRef]
19. Uddin, Z.; Asthana, R.; Awasthi, M.K.; Gupta, S. Steady MHD Flow of Nano-Fluids over a Rotating Porous Disk in the Presence of Heat Generation/Absorption: A Numerical Study using PSO. *J. Appl. Fluid Mech.* **2017**, *10*, 871–879. [CrossRef]
20. Turkyilmazoglua, M. Fluid flow and heat transfer over a rotating and vertically moving disk. *Phys. Fluids* **2018**, *30*, 063605. [CrossRef]
21. Sharma, K.; Vijay, N.; Mabood, F.; Badruddin, I. Numerical simulation of heat and mass transfer in magnetic nanofluid flow by a rotating disk with variable fluid properties. *Int. Commun. Heat Mass Transf.* **2022**, *133*, 105977. [CrossRef]
22. Kumar, S.; Sharma, K. Entropy optimized radiative heat transfer of hybrid nanofluid over vertical moving rotating disk with partial slip. *Chin. J. Phys.* **2022**, *77*, 861–873. [CrossRef]
23. Animasaun, I.L.; Shah, N.A.; Wakif, A.; Mahanthesh, B.; Sivaraj, R.; Koriko, O.K. *Ratio of Momentum Diffusivity to Thermal Diffusivity: Introduction, Meta-analysis, and Scrutinization*, 1st ed.; Chapman and Hall/CRC: Boca Raton, FL, USA, 2022. [CrossRef]
24. Asim, M.; Siddiqui, F.R. Hybrid Nanofluids—Next-Generation Fluids for Spray-Cooling-Based Thermal Management of High-Heat-Flux Devices. *Nanomaterials* **2022**, *12*, 507. [CrossRef] [PubMed]
25. Saranya, S.; Al-Mdallal, Q.M.; Javed, S. Shifted, Legendre Collocation Method for the Solution of Unsteady Viscous-Ohmic Dissipative Hybrid Ferrofluid Flow over a Cylinder. *Nanomaterials* **2021**, *11*, 1512. [CrossRef]
26. Saranya, S.; Baranyi, L.; Al-Mdallal, Q.M. Free convection flow of hybrid ferrofluid past a heated spinning cone. *Therm. Sci. Eng. Prog.* **2021**, *32*, 101335. [CrossRef]
27. Animasaun, I.L.; Al-Mdallal, Q.M.; Khan, U.; Alshomrani, A.S. Unsteady Water-Based Ternary Hybrid Nanofluids on Wedges by Bioconvection and Wall Stretching Velocity: Thermal Analysis and Scrutinization of Small and Larger Magnitudes of the Thermal Conductivity of Nanoparticles. *Mathematics* **2022**, *10*, 4309. [CrossRef]
28. Kanimozhi, B.; Muthtamilselvan, M.; Al-Mdallal, Q.M.; Abdalla, B. Combined Marangoni and Buoyancy Convection in a Porous Annular Cavity Filled with Ag-MgO/Water Hybrid Nanofluid. *Curr. Nanosci.* **2023**, *19*, 4–14. [CrossRef]
29. Manohara, S.R.; Hanagodimath, S.M.; Thind, K.S.; Gerward, L. On the effective atomic number and electron density: A comprehensive set of formulas for all types of materials and energies above 1keV. *Nucl. Instrum. Methods Phys. Res. Sect. B Beam Interact. Mater. At.* **2008**, *266*, 3906–3912. [CrossRef]

Disclaimer/Publisher's Note: The statements, opinions and data contained in all publications are solely those of the individual author(s) and contributor(s) and not of MDPI and/or the editor(s). MDPI and/or the editor(s) disclaim responsibility for any injury to people or property resulting from any ideas, methods, instructions or products referred to in the content.

Article

Magnetohydrodynamic Bioconvective Flow of Williamson Nanofluid over a Moving Inclined Plate Embedded in a Porous Medium

Amir Abbas [1], Radhika Khandelwal [2], Hafeez Ahmad [3], Asifa Ilyas [4], Liaqat Ali [5], Kaouther Ghachem [6], Walid Hassen [7] and Lioua Kolsi [8,*]

1. Department of Mathematics, Faculty of Science, University of Gujrat, Sub-Campus, Mandi Bahauddin 50400, Pakistan
2. Department of Mathematics, IIS (Deemed to be University), Jaipur 302020, India
3. Department of Statistics, School of Quantitive Sciences, University of Utara Malaysia, Sintok 06010, Malaysia
4. Department of Mathematic, Faculty of Science, University of Sargodha, Sargodha 40100, Pakistan
5. School of Sciences, Xi'an Technological University, Xi'an 710021, China
6. Department of Industrial Engineering and Systems, College of Engineering, Princess Nourah Bint Abdulrahman University, P.O. Box 84428, Riyadh 11671, Saudi Arabia
7. Laboratory of Metrology and Energy Systems, National Engineering School, Energy Engineering Department, University of Monastir, Monastir 5000, Tunisia
8. Department of Mechanical Engineering, College of Engineering, University of Ha'il, Ha'il City 81451, Saudi Arabia
* Correspondence: l.kolsi@uoh.edu.sa

Abstract: Research interest in nanotechnology is growing due to its diversified engineering and medical applications. Due to the importance of bioconvection in biotechnology and various biological systems, scientists have made significant contributions in the last ten years. The present study is focusing on the investigation of the magnetohydrodynamics (MHD) bioconvective heat transfer of a Williamson nanofluid past an inclined moving plate embedded in a porous medium. The partial differential equations governing the considered configuration are established, then transformed into ordinary differential equations using suitable similarity transformations. The variables corresponding to the velocity, temperature, nanoparticle volume fraction, and density of motile micro-organisms along with their gradients, are computed using the bvp4c-MATLAB built-in numerical solver. Results showed the rising of the buoyancy ration parameter leads to an increase in the flow velocity. It has been also observed that the flow intensity becomes more important with an increase in the Weissenberg number, and the opposite occurs with an increase in the bioconvective Rayleigh number. As an effect of the Brownian motion, a random fluid particle's motion is encountered.

Keywords: Williamson-fluid; porous-medium; moving-inclined-plate; nano-fluid; incompressible-fluid; bioconvection; gyrotactic-micro-organisms

MSC: 76R10

1. Introduction

Recently, nanofluids have been used in several engineering, biological, and medical applications due to their enhanced properties, such as magnetic, wetting, electrical, optical, and thermal properties that led to important improvements in their performances. Nanometer-sized particles are extremely useful in modern technology by improving the thermal conductivity of Newtonian and non-Newtonian fluids. Nanofluids are engineered by suspending nanosized particles in classical fluids, such as water, ethylene, oil, etc. The carbides, carbon nanotubes, oxides, and metals are used to make nanoparticles. The earliest investigations on thermal conductivity enhancement were performed by Masuda et al. [1]

in 1993. In 1995, Choi and Eastman [2], for the first time, introduced the term nanofluid to mention this new type of heat transfer fluid, which is characterized by higher thermal conductivities compared to usual fluids. The study conducted by Buongiorno [3] showed that the most effective heat transfer occurs at a nanoparticle's volume fraction of 5%. The same author developed an analytical model [4] for convective transport in nanofluids in which Brownian motion and the thermophoresis effect are taken into account. The major aim of the development of the nanofluids is to obtain the highest thermal conductivity using lower nanoparticle concentrations to avoid the sedimentation of the nanoparticles in the base fluids. The process of thermophoretic transportation and mixed convection flow across the surface of a sphere was the primary objective of the recent work of Abbas et al. [5]. Using nonlinear coupled partial differential equations, a mathematical model was developed to investigate the properties of heating and fluid flow. Ashraf et al. [6] focused on the physical behavior of the mixed effects of heat generation and absorption in the flow models. Abbas et al. [7] investigated the physical behavior of mixed-convection flow around a sphere's surface caused by the combined effects of temperature-dependent viscosity and thermophoretic motion. Ashraf et al. [8] investigated the impact of thermophoretic mobility and temperature-dependent thermal conductivity on natural convection flow around a sphere's surface at various circumferential locations. With the aid of suitable nondimensional variables, the modeled nonlinear governing partial differential has been turned into a dimensionless form. Abbas et al. [9] examined how thermal radiation and thermophoretic motion interact to create a constant, compressible, two-dimensional mixed-convection flow of an optic-dense gray fluid, and it is described by them. Ashraf et al. [10] studied the effect of thermophoretic motion and viscous dissipation on the two-dimensional fluid around a sphere. The phenomenon of mixed convection flow under the influence of exothermic catalytic chemical reactions over the curved surface was the focus of the work of Ahmad et al. [11], which considered the constant, exothermic chemical reaction-assisted, two-dimensional, incompressible, and mixed convective fluid flow.

Bioconvection is induced by the swimming of motile micro-organisms, leading to an increase in the density of the fluid. The gyrotactic micro-organisms are characterized as nanomaterials. When nanoparticles and mobile micro-organisms communicate, buoyancy forces cause bioconvection. Gyrotactic micro-organisms are only used in this context to stabilize the nanoparticles so that they can suspend efficiently in the base fluid. If the microfluidic device is created for bioapplications, the joule heating produced by active mixtures may harm biological samples. Bioconvection has the potential to improve nanofluid stability as well as mass transfer and mixing, particularly in microvolumes. Thus, the nanofluid and bioconvection combination may be a solution for cutting-edge microfluidic devices. The bioconvection in a horizontal layer is filled with a nanofluid, and the gyrotactic micro-organisms were explored by Kuznetsov [12]. In a nanofluid, convection is intended to be induced or enhanced using micro-organisms. An analysis of the mixed convection flow of a nanofluid over a stretching surface with a uniform free stream in the presence of both nanoparticles and gyrotactic micro-organisms was performed by Xu and Pop [13]. The effects of solar radiation on water-based nanofluid flow in the presence of gyrotactic micro-organisms past a permeable surface were examined by Acharya et al. [14]. Akbar et al. [15] looked at the combined impact of Brownian motion, thermophoresis, and magnetic field bioconvection on free convective 2D steady incompressible fluid over a stretching sheet with gyrotactic micro-organisms. The study was performed under consideration of the effect of a magnetic field perpendicular to the sheet. Later, Shen et al. [16] investigated the bioconvective heat transfer of steady incompressible viscous nanofluid flow over a stretching sheet that contained gyrotactic micro-organisms under the effect of velocity slip, radiation, and temperature jump. In order to explore the thermally and magnetically coupled stress nanoparticle flow, Khan et al. [17] established a theoretical bioconvection model that included narrative flow properties, such as activation energy, chemical reaction, and radiation aspects. The periodically porous, stretched shape was used to organize the accelerated flow. Xia et al. [18] analyzed the bioconvective flow of the incompressible, steady Eyring Powell nanofluid above a stretched, permeable cylindrical surface. In this study, magnetic field, viscous dissipation, and thermal radiation were also taken into account. Shi et al. [19] studied the transient MHD bioconvection flow of a nanofluid over a stretched sheet. Heat absorption/emitting, binary chemical reactions, and the thermal radiation effect were also considered. Yang et al. [20] investigated the natural convection of a second-grade bionanofluid between vertical parallel plates. Hayat et al. [21] studied the bioconvection heat transfer with a gyrotactic micro-organism of a Prandtl-Eyring nanofluid over a stretching sheet under the combined effects of thermal radiation and viscous dissipation. Khan et al. [22] examined the Darcy–Forchhiemer accelerating the flow of Eyring–Powell nanofluid over an oscillating surface while considering thermal radiations and gyrotactic micro-organisms effects. Effects of the Cattaneo–Christov theory and nonuniform heat source/sink phenomenon were also considered. In [23], the bioconvective heat transfer brought on by gyrotactic micro-organisms swimming in a nanofluid flowing across an unstable, curved stretched sheet was investigated, and the nonlinear partial differential equations were modified using local similarity transformations. With the excision/accretion of the leading edge, an inquiry for temperature variations with Cattaneo–Christov features and self-motivated bioconvective micro-organisms submerged in the water-based nanofluid was observed by Ali [24].

Many industrial and engineering applications involve the flow and heat transfer of the boundary layer over continuous solid surfaces. For example, materials produced by extrusion processes and heat-treated materials moving between feed and wind-up rolls or on a conveyor belt have the characteristics of a moving continuous surface. Sakiadis [25] initiated the study of boundary layer flow over a flat surface at a constant speed, and many researchers successively investigated various kinds of boundary layer flow due to a continuously moving or stretching surface. Erickson et al. [26] extended Sakiadis' problem to the scenario in which either suction or injection is permitted through the moving wall and took into account its effects on flow and heat transfer in the boundary layer. Crane [27] conducted a study for a boundary layer flow caused by a flat stretching surface whose velocity is proportional to the separation from the leading edge of the slit, in contrast to Sakiadis' work [25]. Ali et al. [28] examined the combined effects of bioconvection and magnetic field on boundary layer magnetohydrodynamic unsteady Sakiadis and Blasius flow of nanofluid with accretion/ablation of the leading edge. In addition, the convective boundary conditions, the Biot number, heat radiation, chemical reactions, and other impacts were seen. Abbas et al. [29] provided the analysis of fluid flow and heat transfer with temperature-dependent density, a magnetic field, and thermal radiation effects over an inclined moving plate. According to Abbas et al. [30], heat and mass transport in a third-grade fluid with the Darcy–Forchheimer relationship over an inclined, exponentially expanding surface imbedded in a porous medium were affected by the interaction of a linear chemical process and the Lorentz force. Abbas et al. [31] analyzed the Casson fluid flow and heat transfer under temperature-dependent thermal conductivity and thermal radiation along the exponentially stretching sheet. In a third-grade fluid with Darcy–Forchheimer relationship influence over an exponentially inclined stretched sheet embedded in a porous medium, Abbas et al. [32] studied the thermal-diffusion and diffusion-thermo impacts on heat and mass transmission.

Due to their widespread use in various industrial applications, such as polymer melting, blood polymers, drilling mud, fruit juice, certain oils and greases, and suspensions, non-Newtonian fluids have attracted the interest of several researchers and engineers. It is difficult to create a single model that takes into account all of the rheological properties of non-Newtonian fluids. To address these issues, academics created various models, such as Maxwell's fluid and Burger's fluid. Williamson fluid is a type of viscoelastic liquid. The use of Williamson nanofluid in industrial and manufacturing processes has had significant effects. Researchers have recently shown a strong interest in researching the fluid's characteristics to improve its applications. The Williamson fluid model is one of the best for non-Newtonian fluids since it takes maximum and minimum viscosities into account. It is extremely helpful for pseudoplastic fluids. Non-Newtonian fluids are applied in many different fields, such as ice cream paste, plasma mechanics, biothermal engineering, and blood circulation. Electronics, cancer chemotherapy, paper production, chemistry, medicine administration, lubricants, hydropower generation, and nuclear energy facilities are just a few industries that frequently use non-Newtonian fluids. Prasannakumara et al. [33] proposed a study on the impact of chemical reactions on Williamson nanofluid flow and studied the heat and mass transfer parts of a horizontally stretched surface sunk in a porous medium. The flow was taken in the impact of nonlinear thermal radiation. However, here, Bhatti et al. [34] discussed the upshot of thermal radiation and thermos-diffusion on the Williamson nanofluid above a porous stretched sheet. Zaman et al. [35] discussed the MHD bioconvective flow of the Williamson fluid. This fluid flow was analyzed for gyrotactic micro-organisms under Newtonian order and thermal radiation effects. Ali et al. [36] discussed the flow of 2D unsteady bioconvective non-Newtonian nanofluids. To understand the flow specimen, a carron nanofluid was considered that obtains micro-organisms and by using Darcy–Forchheimer law, porous systems were examined. Yahya et al. [37] examined the thermal properties of the Williamson Sutterby nanofluid flow passing through the Darcy–Forchheimer porous medium under the impact of the Cattaneo–Christov heat flux, convective boundary, and radiation heat flux. Self-driven micro-organisms and the electromagnetic field were also considered. Abbas et al. [38] investigated the behavior of heat transfer and magnetohydrodynamic Williamson nanofluid flow across a nonlinear stretched sheet embedded in a porous medium. The effects of heat generation and viscous dissipation were considered in that current work. Awan et al. [39] studied the heat and mass transfer processes under the chemical reaction and motile micro-organisms on the stretched sheet by encountering the Williamson nanofluid flow along with the thermal radiation influence.

The research community has considered magneto-hydrodynamic flow with diverse fluid parameters in great detail. The study of magnetic field effects has profound effects on physics, chemistry, and engineering. A wide range of technical devices, including magnetohydrodynamic (MHD) producers, pumps, bearings, and boundary layer processes, are impacted by the interaction between the flow of the electrically conducting fluid and the magnetic field. Numerous applications, including geophysics and magnetohydrodynamic power generation, have led to a tremendous amount of research on the different fluid properties, together with numerous geometries and distinct flow conditions. Abbas et al. [40] conducted research on the impact of magnetohydrodynamics on third-grade fluid flow past an inclined, exponentially extending sheet fixed in a porous medium under the influence of the Darcy–Forchheimer equation. Similar studies were carried out in [41–45]. Qayyum et al. [46] analyzed the nonlinear convective flow of Jeffrey nanofluid on a nonlinear convectively heated stretching sheet. They encountered nonlinear thermal radiation, heat production/absorption, and chemical reactions. Narsimulu et al. [47] investigated the steady two-dimensional flow of Carreau fluid that contains both nanoparticles and motile micro-organisms across a nonlinear stretching surface.

Numerous industrial operations, such as petroleum extraction, enhanced oil recovery, filtration procedures, chemical industry separation procedures, packed bed reactions, and many others, involve heat transfer in non-Newtonian fluid flows via a porous medium. Vasudev et al. [48] explored the interaction of heat transfer with peristaltic pumping of a Williamson fluid through a porous material in a planar channel. Some other relevant studies on porous media saturated with Williamson fluids can be found in the literature [49–55].

From the above-described literature survey, it has been observed that several works on bioconvection heat transfer in different Newtonian and non-Newtonian fluids along diverse geometries have been performed. In the current study, the bioconvective heat transfer of Williamson nanofluid having motile gyrotactic micro-organisms with magnetohydrodynamic effect along an inclined moving plate embedded in a porous medium is considered. To the best of our knowledge, no one has carried out such a study before this attempt. The whole process is modeled using differential equations and then solved by the built-in numerical solver bvp4c. The solutions to the physical variables are portrayed and shown in the coming sections.

2. Problem Formulation:

The studied configuration consists of a steady, two-dimensional, viscous, incompressible, bioconvective, and magnetohydrodynamic flow of Williamson nanofluid. The fluid flow is induced by the movement of a plate at a constant velocity $u = U_w$ at $y = 0$. The plate is inclined at an angle of inclination $\alpha = \pi/6$ and is confined within the domain $y \geq 0$. The considered geometry is embedded in a porous medium. Additionally, the nanoparticles are saturated with the self-propelled gyrotactic micro-organisms. It is assumed that the presence of nanoparticles has no effect on the swimming behavior of the micro-organism. Here, the suspension of nanoparticles is stable and does not agglomerate in the fluid. To avoid the bioconvective instability due to the enhanced suspension's viscosity, nanoparticle suspension in the base fluid has to be diluted. A magnetic field normal to the flow direction having a magnitude B_o is applied. The coordinates pointing in the flow direction and normal to the fluid flow directions are denoted by x and y, respectively. The corresponding velocity components are u and v (see Figure 1). By following [16,33,35], the law of conservation of mass, momentum equation, energy equation, nanoparticle volume fraction equation, and motile micro-organisms' equation, respectively, are given below:

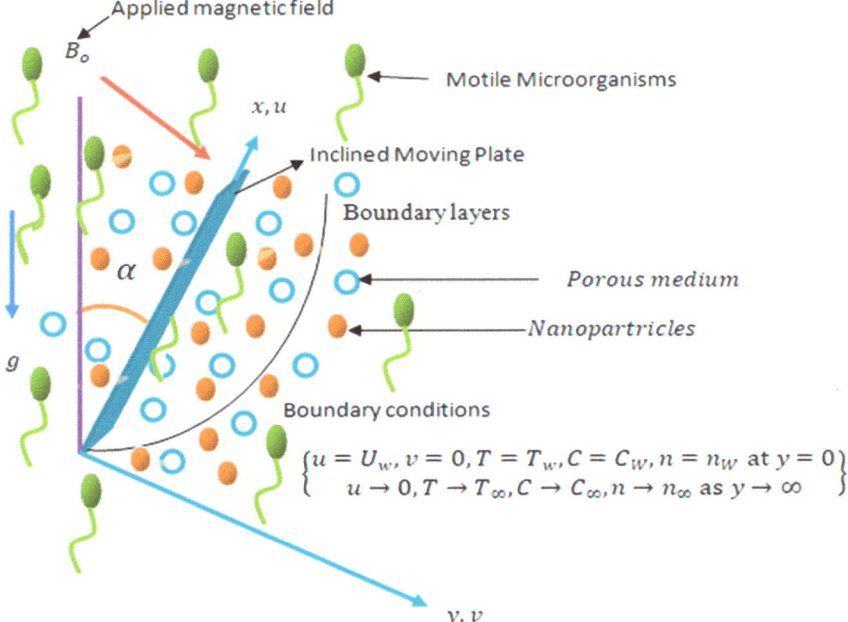

Figure 1. Flow configuration and coordinate system.

$$\frac{\partial u}{\partial x} + \frac{\partial v}{\partial y} = 0 \tag{1}$$

$$u\frac{\partial u}{\partial x} + v\frac{\partial u}{\partial y} = \frac{\mu}{\rho_f}\frac{\partial^2 u}{\partial y^2}$$
$$+ \left[\frac{(1-C_\infty)\rho_{f_\infty}\beta(T-T_\infty)}{\rho_f}\right.$$
$$\left. - \frac{\left[\left(\rho_p - \rho_{f_\infty}\right)(C-C_\infty) + (n-n_\infty)\left(\rho_{m_\infty} - \rho_f\right)\right]}{\rho_f}\right]g\cos\alpha - \frac{\sigma B_0^2 u}{\rho_f} + \sqrt{2}v\Gamma\frac{\partial u}{\partial y}\frac{\partial^2 u}{\partial y^2} \tag{2}$$
$$- \frac{v}{K_o}u,$$

$$u\frac{\partial T}{\partial x} + v\frac{\partial T}{\partial y} = \frac{\kappa}{c_p}\frac{\partial}{\partial y}\left[\frac{1}{\rho_f}\frac{\partial T}{\partial y}\right] + \tau\left[D_B\frac{\partial T}{\partial y}\frac{\partial C}{\partial y} + \frac{D_T}{T_w - T_\infty}\left(\frac{\partial T}{\partial y}\right)^2\right] \tag{3}$$

$$u\frac{\partial C}{\partial x} + v\frac{\partial C}{\partial y} = D_B\frac{\partial^2 C}{\partial y^2} + \frac{D_T}{T_w - T_\infty}\frac{\partial^2 T}{\partial y^2} \tag{4}$$

$$u\frac{\partial n}{\partial x} + v\frac{\partial n}{\partial y} = D_n\frac{\partial^2 n}{\partial y^2} - \frac{bW_c}{C_w - C_\infty}\frac{\partial\left(C\frac{\partial C}{\partial y}\right)}{\partial y} \tag{5}$$

The governing boundary conditions are:

$$u = U_w,\ v = 0,\ T = T_w,\ C = C_W,\ n = n_W\ \text{at}\ y = 0$$
$$u \to 0,\ T \to T_\infty,\ C \to C_\infty,\ n \to n_\infty\ \text{as}\ y \to \infty \tag{6}$$

In Equations (1)–(6), the symbols $u, v, T, T_W, T_\infty, C, C_W, C_\infty, n, n_W, n_\infty$ represent the velocity components in the x-direction, velocity component in the y-direction, fluid temperature, surface temperature, ambient temperature, fluid concentration, wall concentration, ambient concentration, fluid motile micro-organisms, surface motile micro-organisms, and ambient motile micro-organisms, respectively. The notations $v = \left(\frac{\mu}{\rho}\right)_f$, $\mu, \Gamma, \sigma, B_0, \rho_f, g, \beta, \rho_p, \gamma, \rho_m, K_o, k_f, (\rho C_P)_p, \tau = \frac{(\rho C_P)_p}{(\rho C_P)_f}, D_B, D_T, b, W_C, \alpha$, and D_n denote kinematic viscosity, dynamic viscosity, Williamson variable, electrical conductivity, magnetic field strength, fluid density, gravitational force, volumetric expansion, particle density, average volume of a micro-organisms, micro-organism density, porosity of the porous medium, thermal conductivity, fluid heat capacity, particle heat capacity, ratio between particle heat capacity to fluid heat capacity, Brownian motion coefficient, thermophoretic coefficient, chemotaxis constant, maximum cell swimming speed, angle of inclination of the inclined moving plate, and micro-organism diffusion coefficient, respectively. Here, the product bW_C is assumed to be constant.

3. Solution Methodology

This section is dedicated to elaborating on the solution methodology of the governing equations (Equations (1)–(5)) with boundary conditions (Equation (6)). In this section, the procedure to convert the partial differential equations into ordinary differential equations, the solution technique, and the computing tool used for the solution of flow equations are presented.

3.1. Similarity Variable Formulation:

In this subsection, the method and variables used for the transformation of partial differential equations to ordinary differential equations are described. The nonlinear and coupled partial differential equations are not easy to solve directly. Thus, the set of partial differential equations is converted into ordinary differential equations by using the similarity variables given in Equation (7).

$$\eta = \sqrt{\frac{U_w}{vx}}y, u = U_w f'(\eta), v = \frac{1}{2}\sqrt{\frac{U_w v}{x}}(\eta f' - f), \theta(\eta) = \frac{T - T_\infty}{T_w - T_\infty}, \phi(\eta) = \frac{C - C_\infty}{C_w - C_\infty}, \chi(\eta) = \frac{n - n_\infty}{n_w - n_\infty} \quad (7)$$

where, η, U_w, f, θ, ϕ, and χ are the similarity variable, velocity of the moving inclined plate, dimensionless temperature, dimensionless nanoparticle volume fraction, and dimensionless motile micro-organism function, respectively. By using the similarity variables presented in Equation (7) in Equations (1)–(5) with boundary conditions (6), the equation of continuity is satisfied automatically, and the reduced forms of the approximate forms of the momentum equation, energy equation, nanoparticles equation, and motile micro-organism equation become as follows:

$$-\frac{1}{2}ff'' = f''' + \lambda[1 - Nr\,\phi - Rb\,\chi]\cos\alpha + Wef''f''' - (K_p + M)f' \quad (8)$$

$$\theta'' + \frac{1}{2}Prf\theta' + PrNb\theta'\phi' + PrN_t\theta'^2 = 0, \quad (9)$$

$$\phi'' + \frac{1}{2}Scf\phi' + \frac{Nt}{Nb}\theta'' = 0, \quad (10)$$

$$\chi'' + \frac{1}{2}Sc_n f\chi' - Pe[\chi'\phi' + (\chi + 1)\phi''] = 0, \quad (11)$$

and the transformed boundary conditions are:

$$f' = 1, f = 0, \theta = 1, \phi = 1, \chi = 1 \text{ at } \eta = 0, f' = 0, \theta = 0, \phi = 0, \chi = 0 \text{ at } \eta \to \infty. \quad (12)$$

where, $\lambda = \frac{Gr}{Re_x^2}$ is the mixed convection parameter, $Nr = \frac{(\rho_p - \rho_{f\infty})\Delta C_w}{\rho_{f\infty}\beta(1 - C_\infty)\Delta T_w}$ is the buoyancy ratio parameter, $Rb = \frac{\gamma(\rho_{m\infty} - \rho_f)\Delta n_w}{\rho_{f\infty}\beta\Delta T_w(1 - C_\infty)}$ is the bioconvection Rayleigh number, $We = \frac{\Gamma x\sqrt{2U_w^3}}{\sqrt{v}}$ is the Weissenberg number, $K_p = \frac{v}{K_0 U_w}$ is the permeability parameter, $M = \frac{\sigma B_0^2}{U_w \rho_f}$ is the magnetic parameter, $Pr = \frac{v}{\kappa_f/(\rho C_p)_f}$ is the Prandtl number, $Nb = \frac{\tau D_B(C_w - C_\infty)}{v}$ is the Brownian motion parameter, $Nt = \frac{\tau D_T}{v}$, is the thermophoresis parameter, $Sc = \frac{v}{D_B}$ is the Schmidt number, $Sc_n = \frac{v}{D_n}$ is the bioconvective Schmidt number, $Pe = \frac{bWe}{D_n}$ is the bioconvective Peclet number, $Gr = \frac{g(1 - C_\infty)\rho_f \beta(T_w - T_\infty)x^3}{v^2}$ is the thermal Grashof number, and $Gr^* = \frac{g(\rho_p - \rho_f)(C_w - C_\infty)x^3}{v^2}$ is the solutal Grahsof number.

3.2. Numerical Technique

It is not obvious how to easily get the exact results of an extremely nonlinear coupled ordinary differential equation. Thus, the transformed equations are solved to get the estimated results by utilizing Matlab's built-in numerical solver, BVP4C. In the computation, $\eta\infty = 20.0$ is taken, and the axis is set according to the clear figure visibility. The Numerical Solver bvp4c is a finite difference code that implements the three-stage Lobato formula. This is a collocation formula, and the collocation polynomial a C^1 continuous solution that is of fourth-order accuracy and uniformly distributed in the interval of integration.

The residual of the continuous solution is the foundation for mesh selection and error control. The collocation method divides the integration interval into smaller intervals using a mesh of the points. The collocation condition and global system of algebraic equations caused by the boundary conditions applied to all of the subintervals are solved by the solver to get a numerical solution. The numerical solution's error is estimated by the solver for each subinterval. The solver adjusts the mesh and repeats the procedure if the solution does not meet the tolerance criteria. The starting mesh points must be supplied, along with a rough approximation of the solution at each mesh point. When the results produced by this numerical method in the current work are compared to those that have already been published, it is clear that there is excellent agreement between the two sets of results, demonstrating the accuracy and validity of the present results. The system of ODEs given in Equations (8)–(11) alone, with imposed boundary conditions presented in Equation (12), is first transformed into first order and then put into the MATLAB built-in function for a numerical solution. We set equations as below:

$$f = F(1),\ f' = F(2), f'' = F(3), \theta = F(4), \theta' = F(5),\ \phi = F(6),\ \phi' = F(7), \chi = F(8),\ \chi' = F(9) \tag{13}$$

$$FF1 = \{-\lambda[1 - Nr*F(6) - Rb*F(8)]*\cos(\alpha) + (K_P + M)*F(2)\}/(1 + We) \tag{14}$$

$$FF2 = -\frac{Pr}{2}*F(1)*F(5) - *Pr*F(5)*F(7) - Pr*Nt*(F(5))^2 \tag{15}$$

$$FF3 = -\frac{Sc}{2}F(1)*F(7) - \left(-\frac{Nt}{Nb}\right)*FF2 \tag{16}$$

$$FF4 = -\frac{Sc_n}{2}F(1)*F(9) + Pe*[\chi'\phi' + (\chi+1)FF3]$$

Boundary conditions

$$\begin{aligned} F(1) = 0,\ F(2) = 1,\ F(4) = 1,\ F(6) = 1, F(8) = 1, \\ F(2) \to 0, F(4) \to 0, F(6) \to 0, F(8) \to 0. \end{aligned} \tag{17}$$

The obtained solutions are presented and discussed with physical interpretation in the next section.

4. Results and Discussion

In this section obtained numerical solutions for velocity distribution $f'(\eta)$, temperature distribution $\theta(\eta)$, concentration distribution $\phi(\eta)$, and density of motile micro-organisms $\chi(\eta)$ along skin friction $f''(0)$, heat transfer rate $\theta'(0)$, mass transfer rate $\phi'(0)$, and rat of motile organisms $\chi'(0)$ are portrayed and discussed in detail. The physical parameters involved in the current model are the buoyancy ratio parameter Nr, magnetic parameter M, Brownian motion parameter Nb, thermophoresis parameter Nt, bioconvection Rayleigh number Rb, Weissenberg number W_e, angle of inclination α, Pradntl number Pr, Schimidt number Sc, and bioconvection Schmidt number Sc_n, and permeability parameter K_P.

4.1. Effects of Physical Parameters on Velocity Distribution

Effects of the buoyancy ratio parameter Nr on the velocity profile is demonstrated in Figure 2a, it can be noticed that with the rising of Nr, the velocity profile is decreased, and the maximum value is achieved at $Nr = 0.1$ and a minimum value is obtained at $Nr = 0.7$. Figure 3a is plotted to evaluate the influence of the magnetic parameter. It is seen that as M increases, the velocity magnitude decreases. The interaction between the applied magnetic field and the flowing electrically conductive fluid generates a body force called the Lorentz force. By increasing M, the produced Lorentz force becomes more important, and causes a damping effect, leading to a reduction in the flow intensity. In fact, from Figure 3a, it is visible that velocity decreases by increasing the magnetic parameter M. In Figure 4a, the effects of Nb are drawn. The Brownian motion leads greater fluid velocity, as it is presented in Figure 4a. Figure 5a illustrates the effect of Nt on velocity distribution. The graph shows that f' is enhanced as Nt is raised. This fact is physically due to the decrease in the viscosity of Nt that leads to the increase in fluid velocity. Figure 6a shows the effective relationship between the velocity distribution and the bioconvective Rayleigh number Rb. It can be observed that with the increases in the bioconvective Rayleigh number, the velocity decreases. Figure 7a presents the effects of e on f'. It is observed that the fluid velocity increases when We increases. An opposite behavior occurs when Kp is increased (Figure 8a).

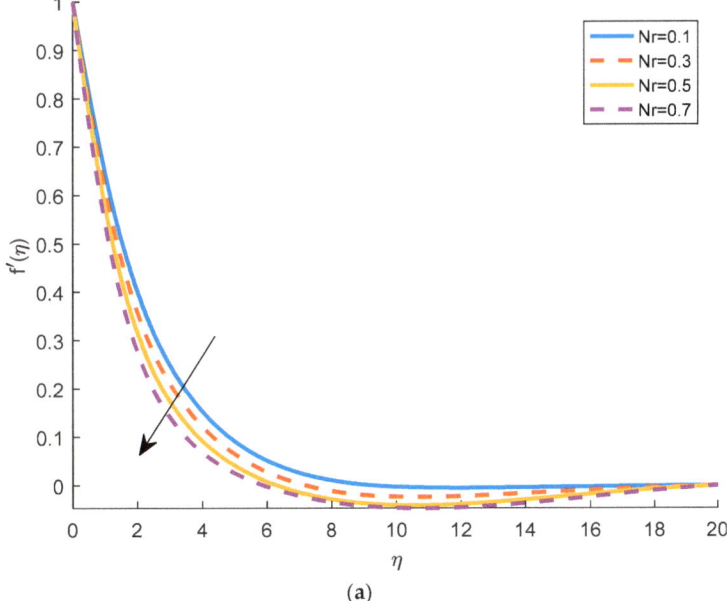

(a)

Figure 2. *Cont.*

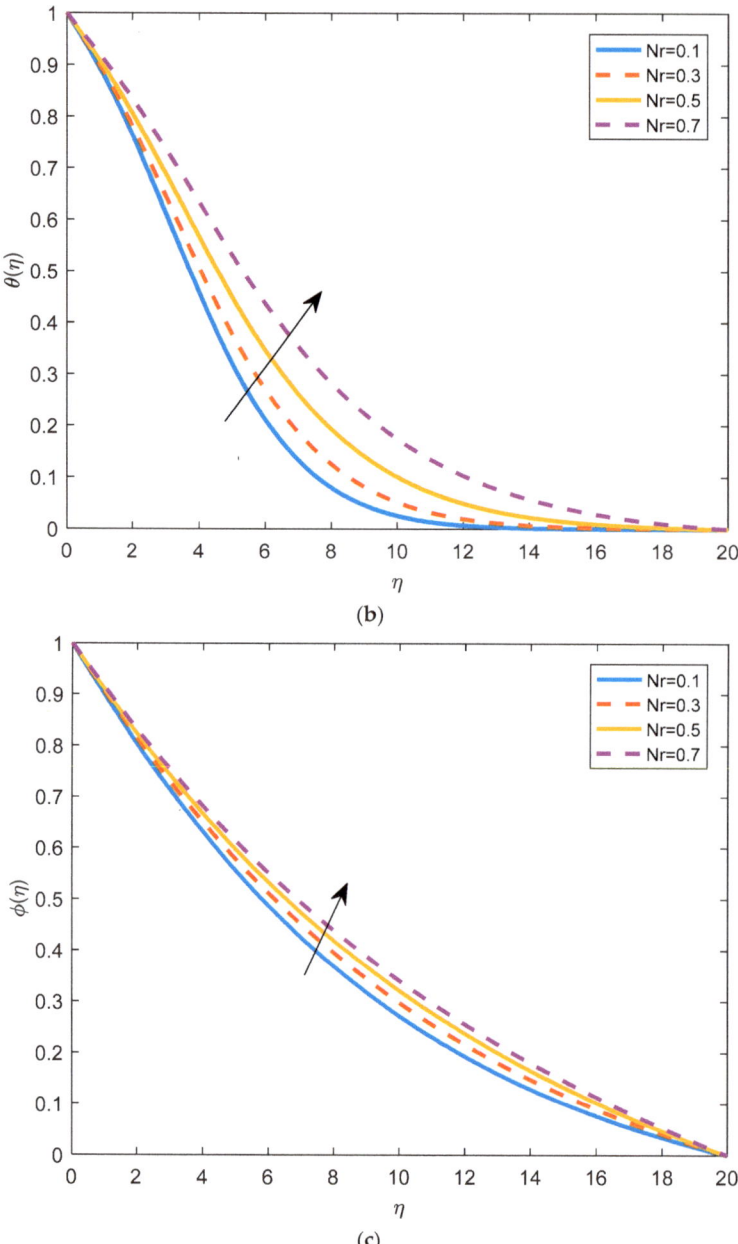

Figure 2. *Cont.*

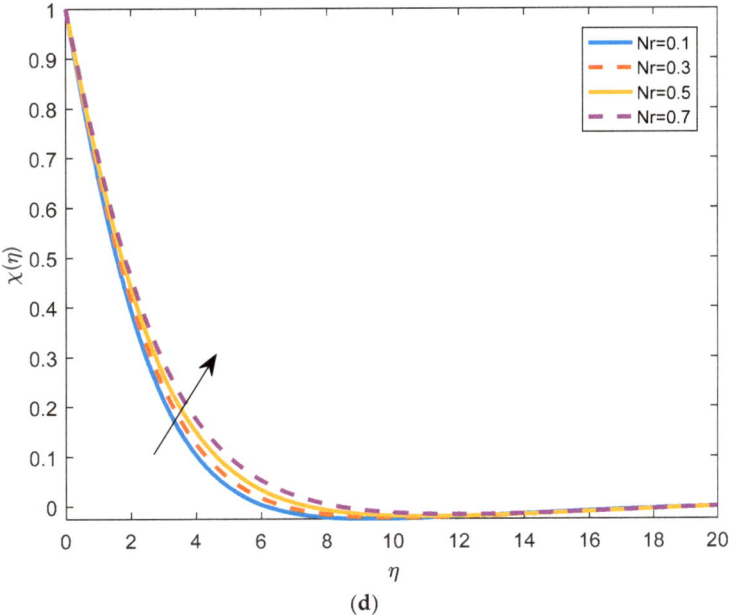

(d)

Figure 2. (**a**): Velocity distribution for various Nr when $M = 0.1$, $Rb = 0.1$, $Nt = 0.1$, $Nb = 2.0$, $\Pr = 1.5$, $W_e = 0.2$, $\lambda = 0.2$, $Sc = 0.5$, $Sc_n = 0.5$, $Pe = 1.0$, $K_p = 0.1$ at $\alpha = \pi/6$. (**b**): Temperature distribution for various Nr when $M = 0.1$, $Rb = 0.1$, $Nt = 0.1$, $Nb = 2.0$, $\Pr = 1.5$, $W_e = 0.2$, $\lambda = 0.2$, $Sc = 0.5$, $Sc_n = 0.5$, $Pe = 1.0$, $K_p = 0.1$ at $\alpha = \pi/6$. (**c**): Concentration distribution for various Nr when $M = 0.1$, $R_b = 0.1$, $N_t = 0.1$, $N_b = 2.0$, $\Pr = 1.5$, $W_e = 0.2$, $\lambda = 0.2$, $Sc = 0.5$, $Sc_n = 0.5$, $Pe = 1.0$, $K_P = 0.1$ at $\alpha = \pi/6$. (**d**): Density of motile micro-organisms for various Nr when $M = 0.1$, $Rb = 0.1$, $Nt = 0.1$, $Nb = 2.0$, $\Pr = 1.5$, $W_e = 0.2$, $\lambda = 0.2$, $Sc = 0.5$, $Sc_n = 0.5$, $Pe = 1.0$, $K_p = 0.1$ at $\alpha = \pi/6$.

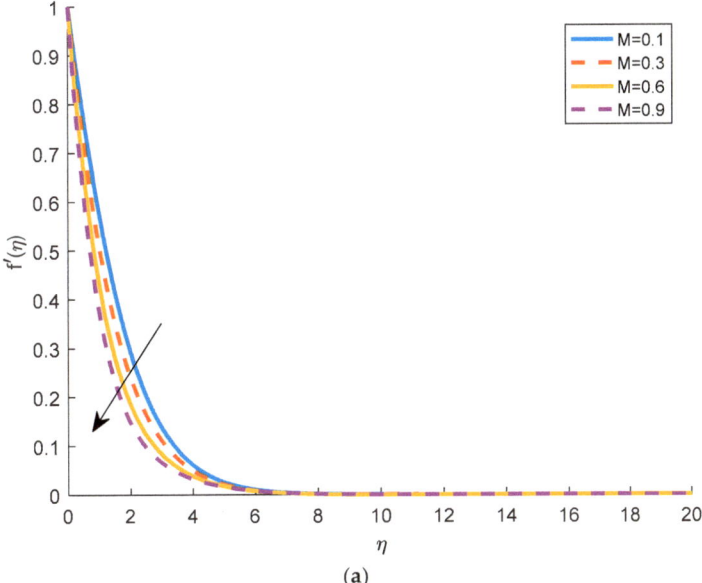

(a)

Figure 3. *Cont.*

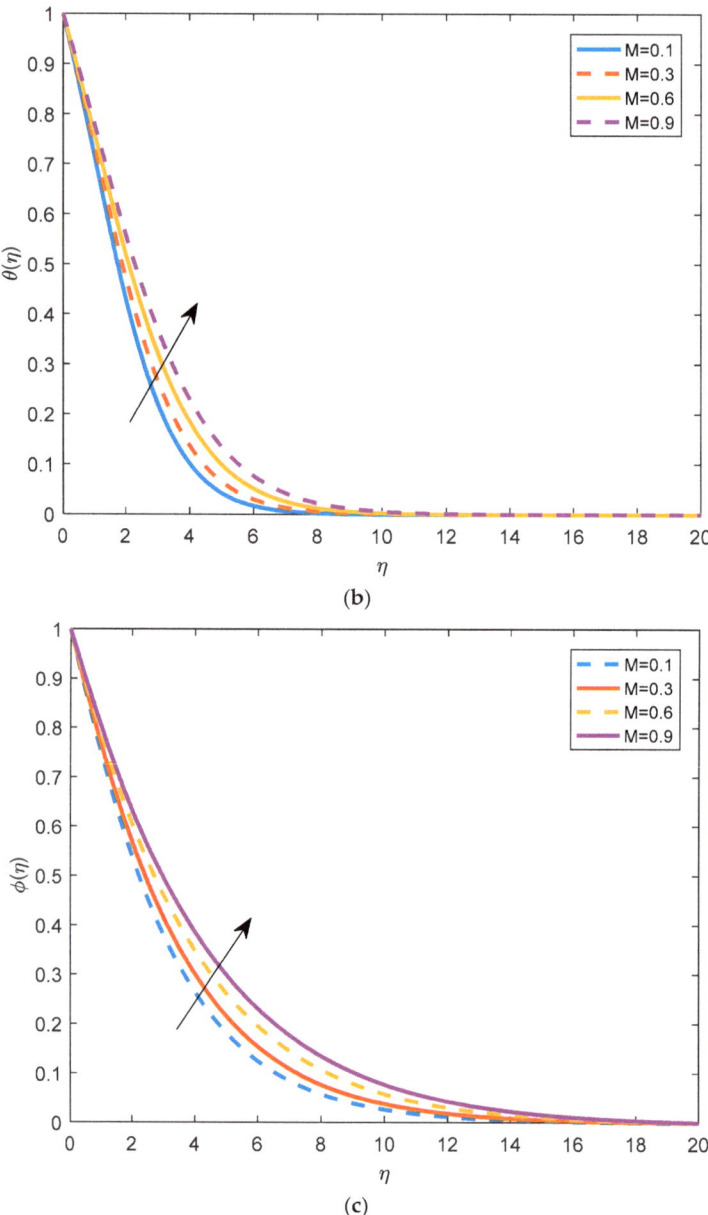

Figure 3. *Cont.*

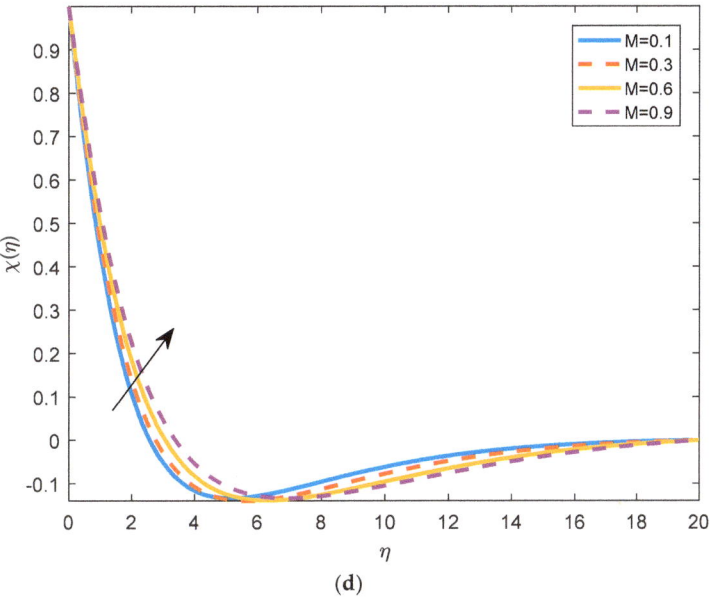

(d)

Figure 3. (**a**): Velocity distribution for various M when $Rb = 0.1$, $Nt = 0.1$, $Nb = 2.0$, $Pr = 1.5$, $W_e = 0.2$, $\lambda = 0.2$, $Sc = 0.5$, $Sc_n = 0.5$, $Pe = 1.0$, $K_p = 0.1$ at $\alpha = \pi/6$. (**b**): Temperature distribution for various M when $Rb = 0.1$, $Nt = 0.1$, $Nb = 2.0$, $Pr = 1.5$, $W_e = 0.2$, $\lambda = 0.2$, $Sc = 0.5$, $Sc_n = 0.5$, $Pe = 1.0$, $K_p = 0.1$ at $\alpha = \pi/6$. (**c**): Concentration distribution for various M when $Rb = 0.1$, $Nt = 0.1$, $Nb = 2.0$, $Pr = 1.5$, $W_e = 0.2$, $\lambda = 0.2$, $Sc = 0.5$, $Sc_n = 0.5$, $Pe = 1.0$, $K_p = 0.1$ at $\alpha = \pi/6$. (**d**): density of motile micro-organisms for various M when $R_b = 0.1$, $N_t = 0.1$, $N_b = 2.0$, $Pr = 1.5$, $W_e = 0.2$, $\lambda = 0.2$, $Sc = 0.5$, $Sc_n = 0.5$, $Pe = 1.0$, $K_p = 0.1$ at $\alpha = \pi/6$.

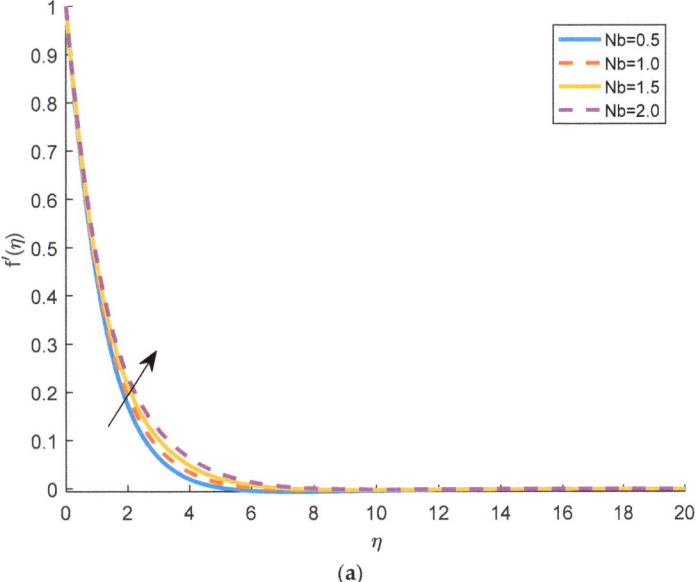

(a)

Figure 4. *Cont.*

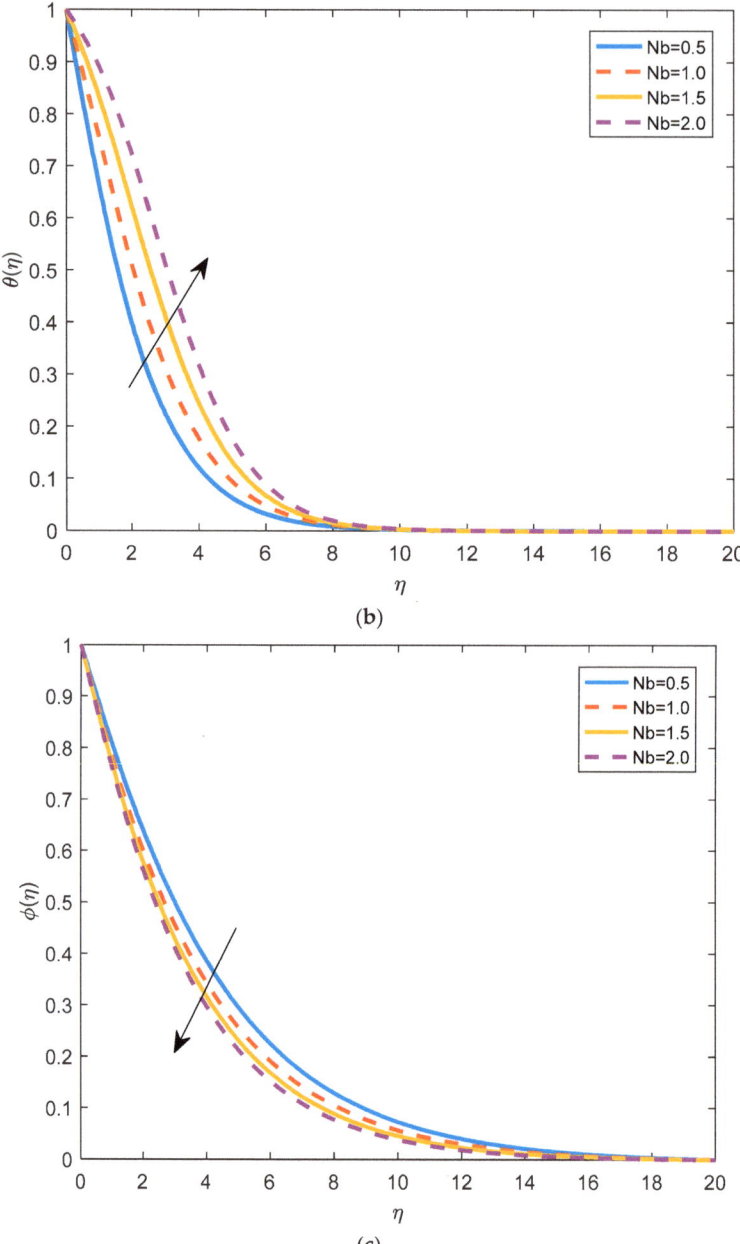

Figure 4. *Cont.*

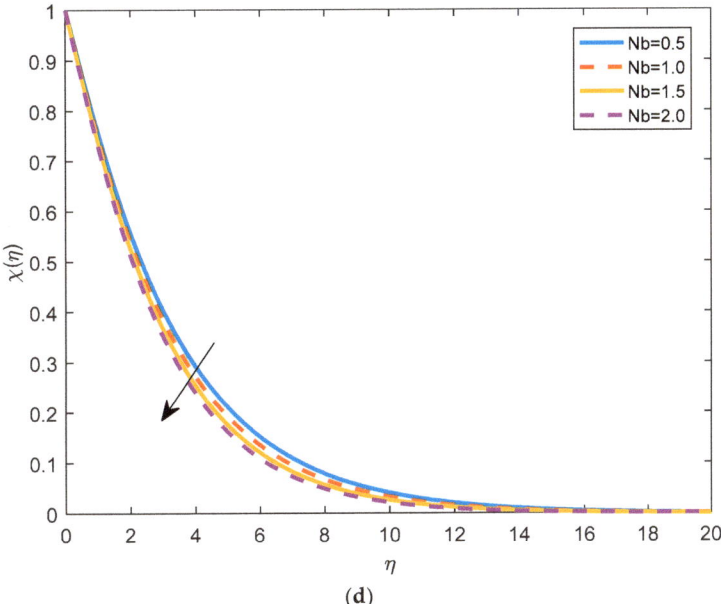

(d)

Figure 4. (**a**): Velocity distribution for various Nb when $R_b = 0.1$, $Nt = 0.1$, $M = 0.1$, $Pr = 1.5$, $W_e = 0.2$, $\lambda = 0.2$, $Sc = 0.5$, $Sc_n = 0.5$, $Pe = 1.0$, $K_p = 0.5$ at $\alpha = \pi/6$. (**b**): Temperature distribution for various Nb when $Rb = 0.1$, $Nt = 0.1$, $M = 0.1$, $Pr = 1.5$, $W_e = 0.2$, $\lambda = 0.2$, $Sc = 0.5$, $Sc_n = 0.5$, $Pe = 1.0$, $K_p = 0.5$ at $\alpha = \pi/6$. (**c**): Concentration distribution for various Nb when $Rb = 0.1$, $Nt = 0.1$, $M = 0.1$, $Pr = 1.5$, $W_e = 0.2$, $\lambda = 0.2$, $Sc = 0.5$, $Sc_n = 0.5$, $Pe = 1.0$, $K_p = 0.5$ at $\alpha = \pi/6$. (**d**): Density of motile micro-organisms for various Nb when $Rb = 0.1$, $Nt = 0.1$, $M = 0.1$, $Pr = 1.5$, $W_e = 0.2$, $\lambda = 0.2$, $Sc = 0.5$, $Sc_n = 0.5$, $Pe = 1.0$, $K_p = 0.5$ at $\alpha = \pi/6$.

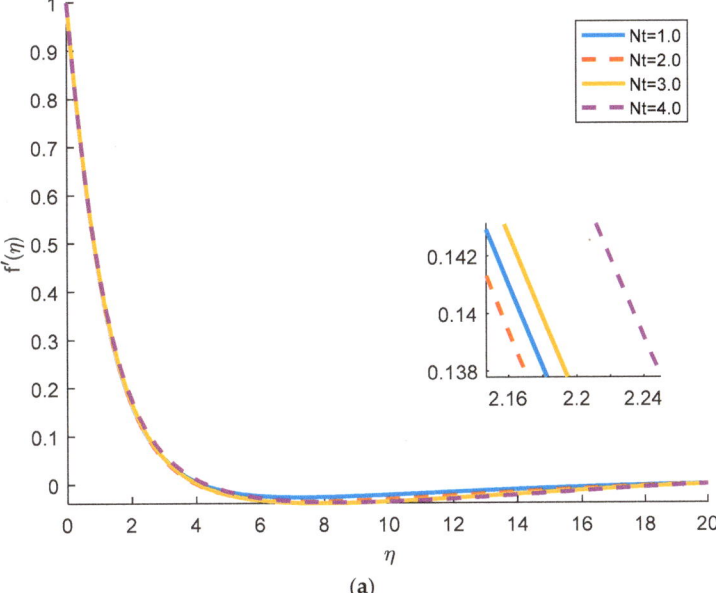

(a)

Figure 5. *Cont.*

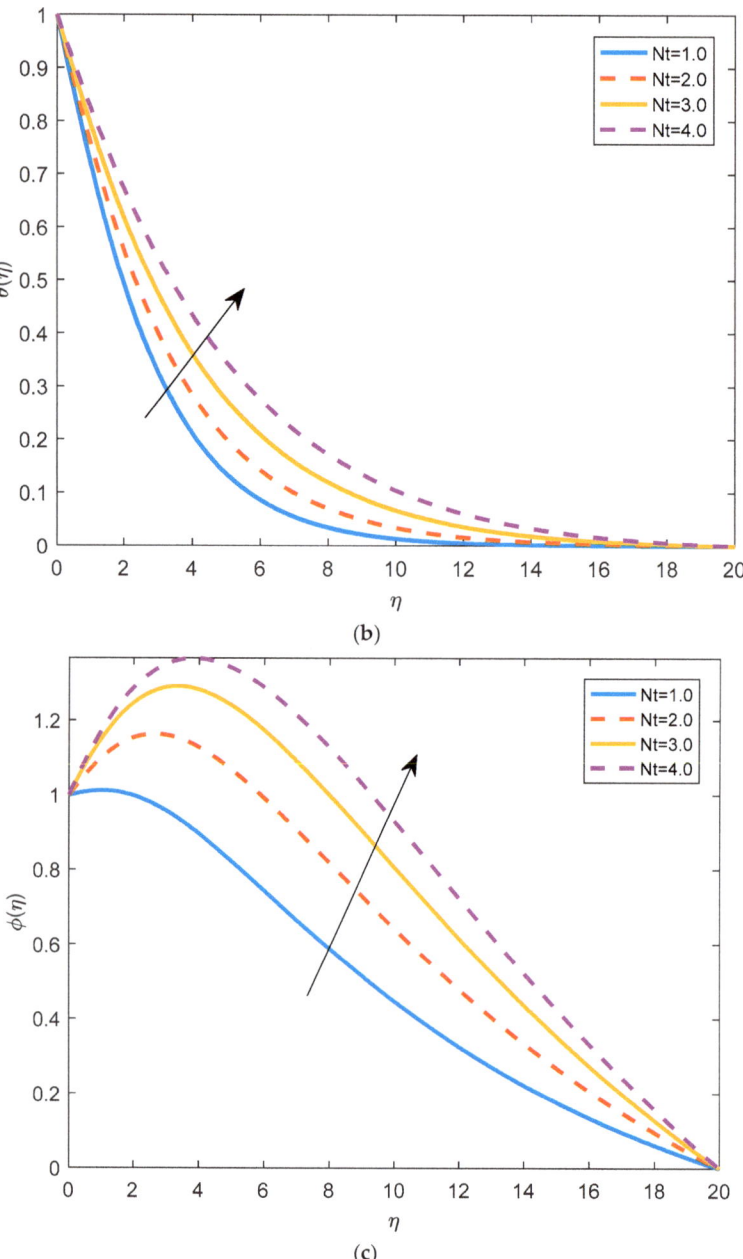

Figure 5. *Cont.*

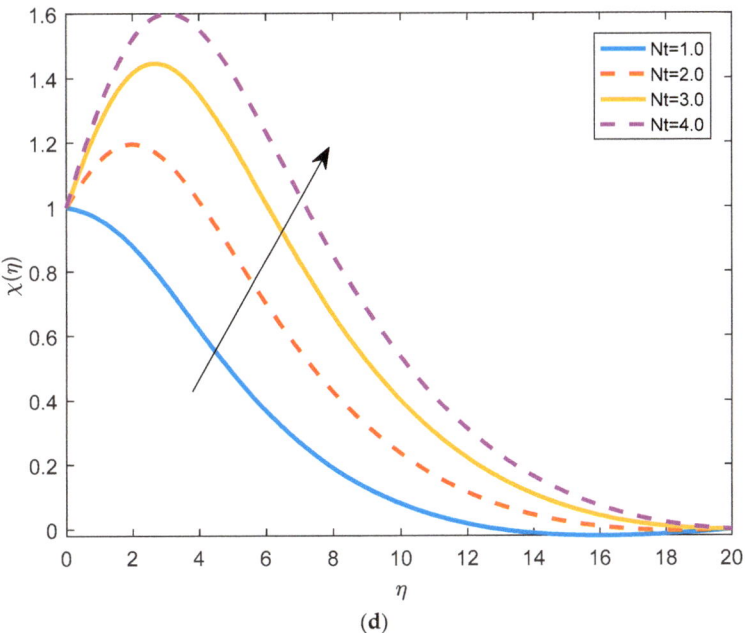

(d)

Figure 5. (**a**): Velocity distribution for various Nt when $Rb = 0.1$, $Nb = 2.0$, M = 0.1, Pr = 1.5, $W_e = 0.2$, $\lambda = 0.2$, Sc = 0.2, $Sc_n = 0.2$, Pe = 1.0, $K_p = 0.5$ at $\alpha = \pi/6$. (**b**): Temperature distribution for various Nt when $Rb = 0.1$, $Nb = 2.0$, M = 0.1, Pr = 1.5, $W_e = 0.2$, $\lambda = 0.2$, Sc = 0.2, $Sc_n = 0.2$, Pe = 1.0, $K_p = 0.5$ at $\alpha = \pi/6$. (**c**): Concentration distribution for various Nt when $Rb = 0.1$, $Nb = 2.0$, M = 0.1, Pr = 1.5, $W_e = 0.2$, $\lambda = 0.2$, Sc = 0.2, $Sc_n = 0.2$, Pe = 1.0, $K_p = 0.5$ at $\alpha = \pi/6$. (**d**): Density of motile micro-organisms for various Nt when $Rb = 0.1$, $Nb = 2.0$, M = 0.1, Pr =1.5, $W_e = 0.2$, $\lambda = 0.2$, Sc = 0.2, $Sc_n = 0.2$, Pe = 1.0, $K_p = 0.5$ at $\alpha = \pi/6$.

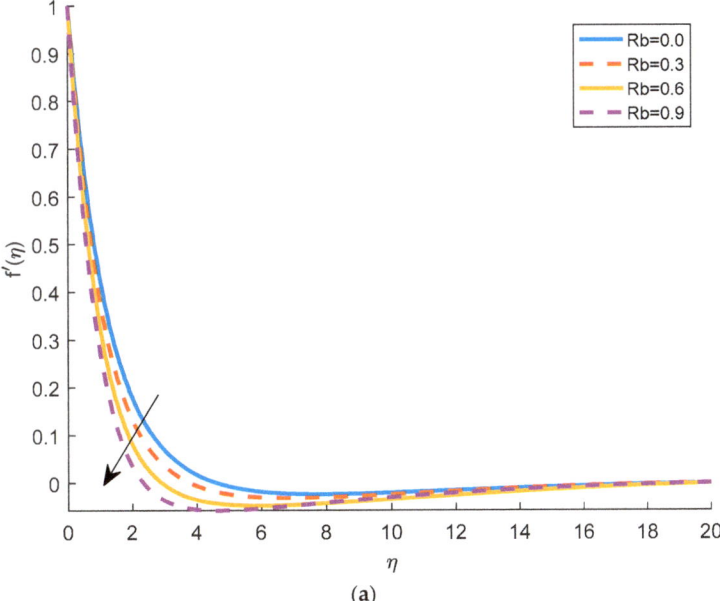

(a)

Figure 6. *Cont.*

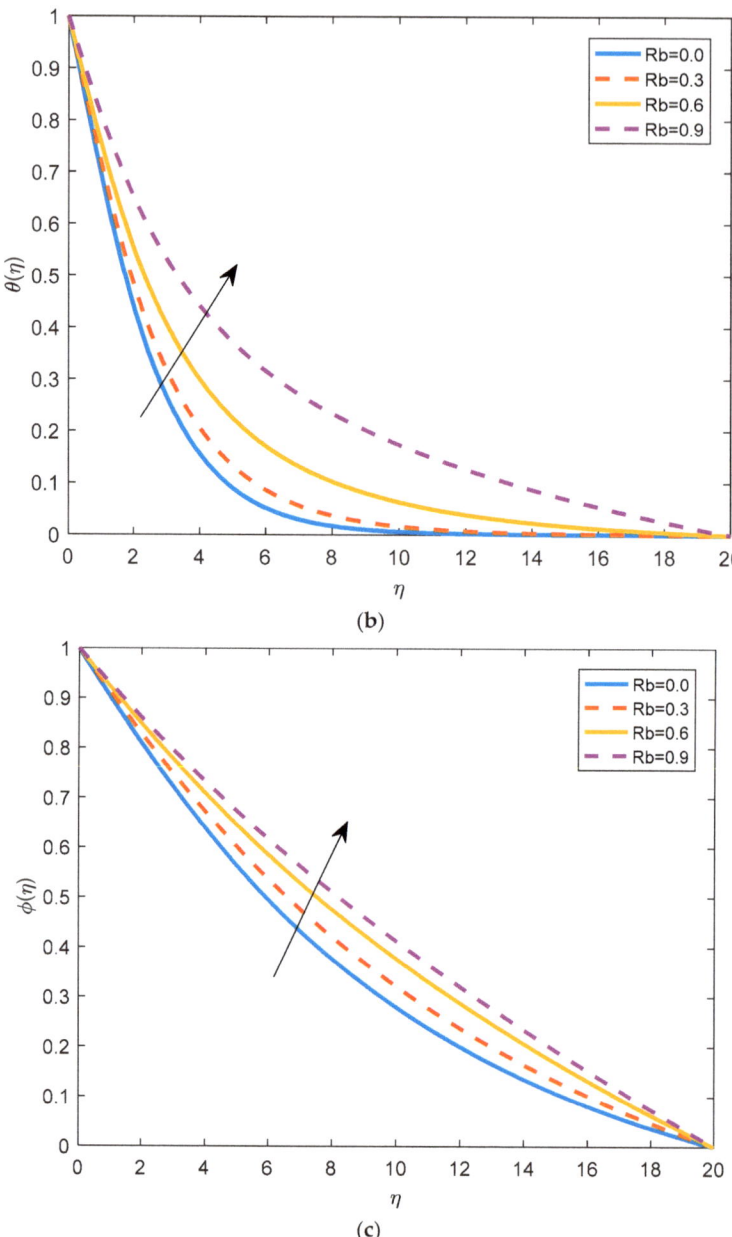

Figure 6. *Cont.*

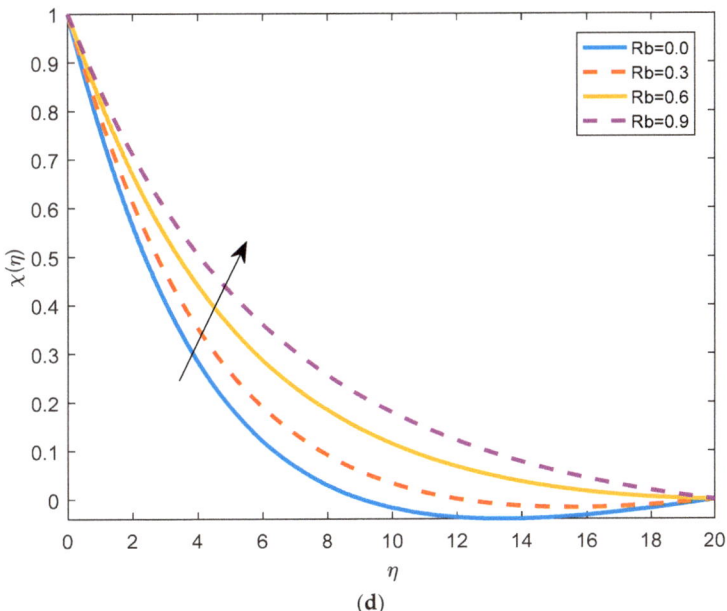

(d)

Figure 6. (**a**): Velocity distribution for various Rb when $Nt = 0.1$, $Nb = 2.0$, M = 0.1, Pr = 1.5, $W_e = 0.2$, $\lambda = 0.2$, Sc = 0.2, $Sc_n = 0.2$, Pe = 1.0, $K_p = 0.5$ at $\alpha = \pi/6$. (**b**): Temperature distribution for various Rb when $Nt = 0.1$, $Nb = 2.0$, M = 0.1, Pr =1.5, $W_e = 0.2$, $\lambda = 0.2$, Sc = 0.2, $Sc_n = 0.2$, Pe = 1.0, $K_p = 0.5$ at $\alpha = \pi/6$. (**c**): Concentration distribution for various Rb when $Nt = 0.1$, $Nb = 2.0$, M = 0.1, Pr = 1.5, $W_e = 0.2$, $\lambda = 0.2$, Sc = 0.2, $Sc_n = 0.2$, Pe = 1.0, $K_P = 0.5$ at $\alpha = \pi/6$. (**d**): Density of motile micro-organisms for various Rb when $N_t = 0.1$, $N_b = 2.0$, M = 0.1, Pr =1.5, $W_e = 0.2$, $\lambda = 0.2$, Sc = 0.2, $Sc_n = 0.2$, Pe = 1.0, $K_p = 0.5$ at $\alpha = \pi/6$.

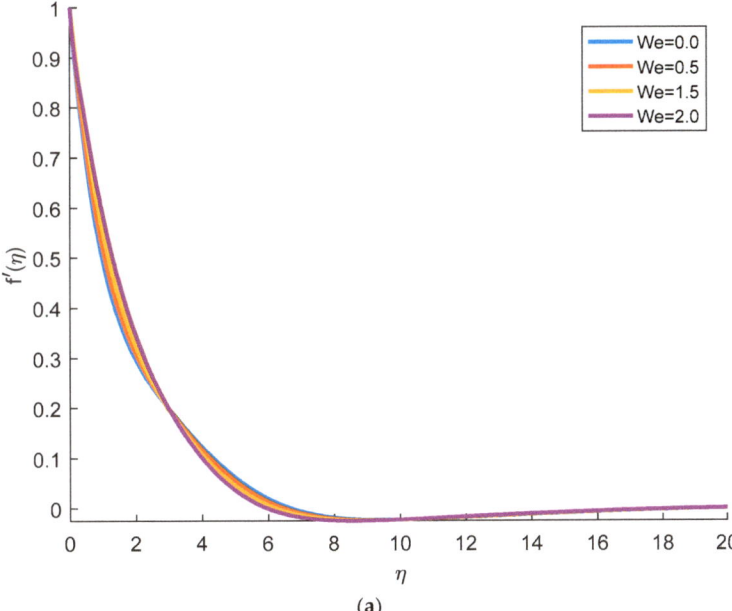

(a)

Figure 7. *Cont.*

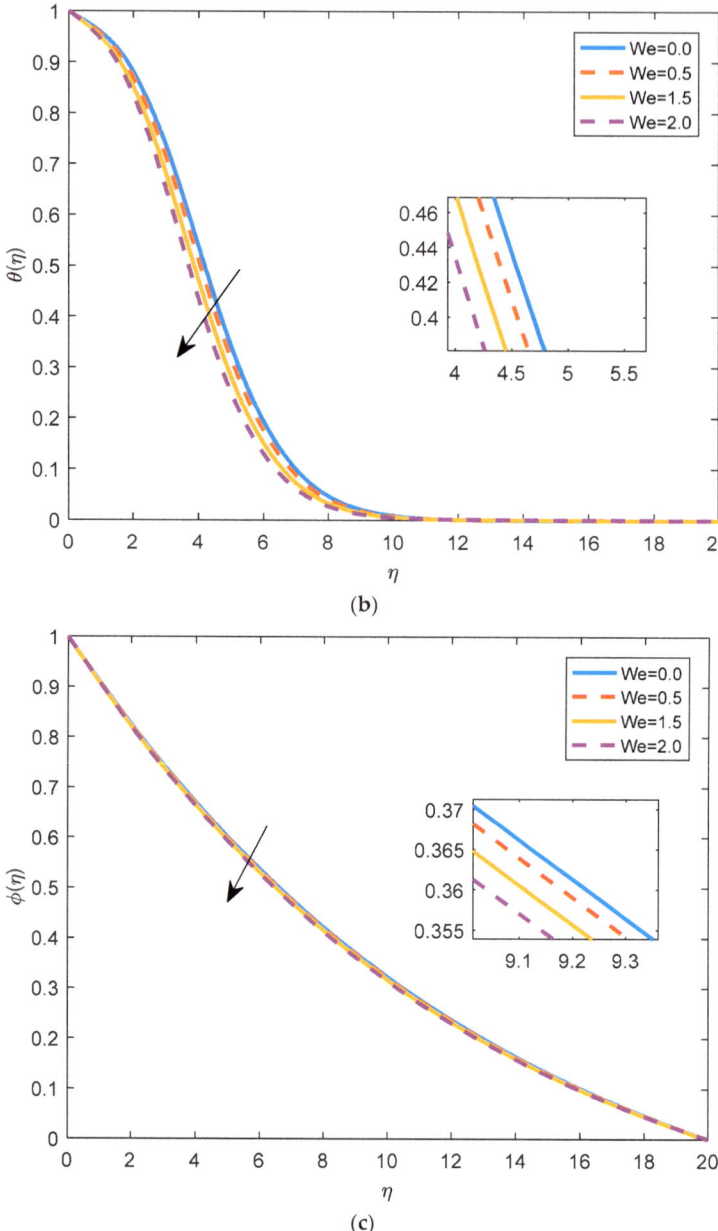

Figure 7. *Cont.*

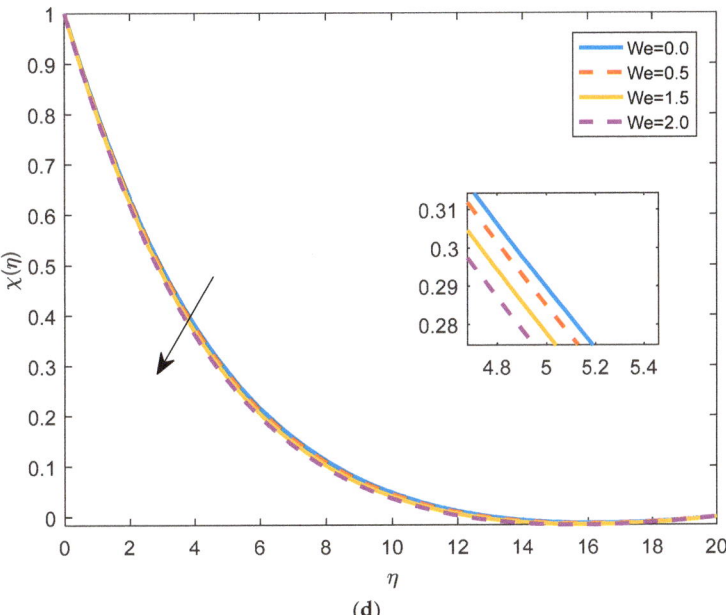

(d)

Figure 7. (**a**): Velocity distribution for various W_e when $Nt = 0.1$, $Nb = 2.0$, $M = 1.0$, $Pr = 1.5$, $R_b = 0.1$, $\lambda = 0.2$, $Sc = 0.5$, $Sc_n = 0.5$, $Pe = 1.0$, $K_p = 0.5$ at $\alpha = \pi/6$. (**b**): Temperature distribution for various W_e when $Nt = 0.1$, $Nb = 2.0$, $M = 1.0$, $Pr = 1.5$, $Rb = 0.1$, $\lambda = 0.2$, $Sc = 0.5$, $Sc_n = 0.5$, $Pe = 1.0$, $K_p = 0.5$ at $\alpha = \pi/6$. (**c**): Concentration distribution for various W_e when $Nt = 0.1$, $Nb = 2.0$, $M = 1.0$, $Pr = 1.5$, $Rb = 0.1$, $\lambda = 0.2$, $Sc = 0.5$, $Sc_n = 0.5$, $Pe = 1.0$, $K_p = 0.5$ at $\alpha = \pi/6$. (**d**): Density of motile micro-organisms for various W_e when $Nt = 0.1$, $Nb = 2.0$, $M = 1.0$, $Pr = 1.5$, $Rb = 0.1$, $\lambda = 0.2$, $Sc = 0.5$, $Sc_n = 0.5$, $Pe = 1.0$, $K_p = 0.5$ at $\alpha = \pi/6$.

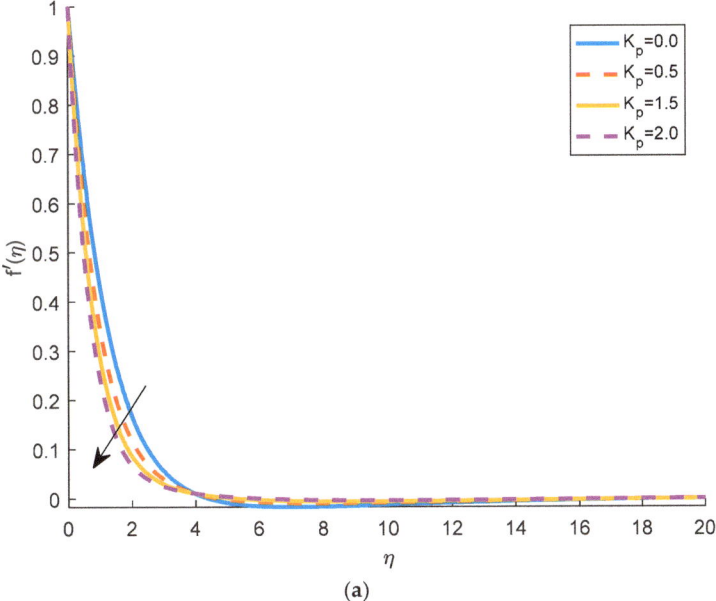

(a)

Figure 8. *Cont.*

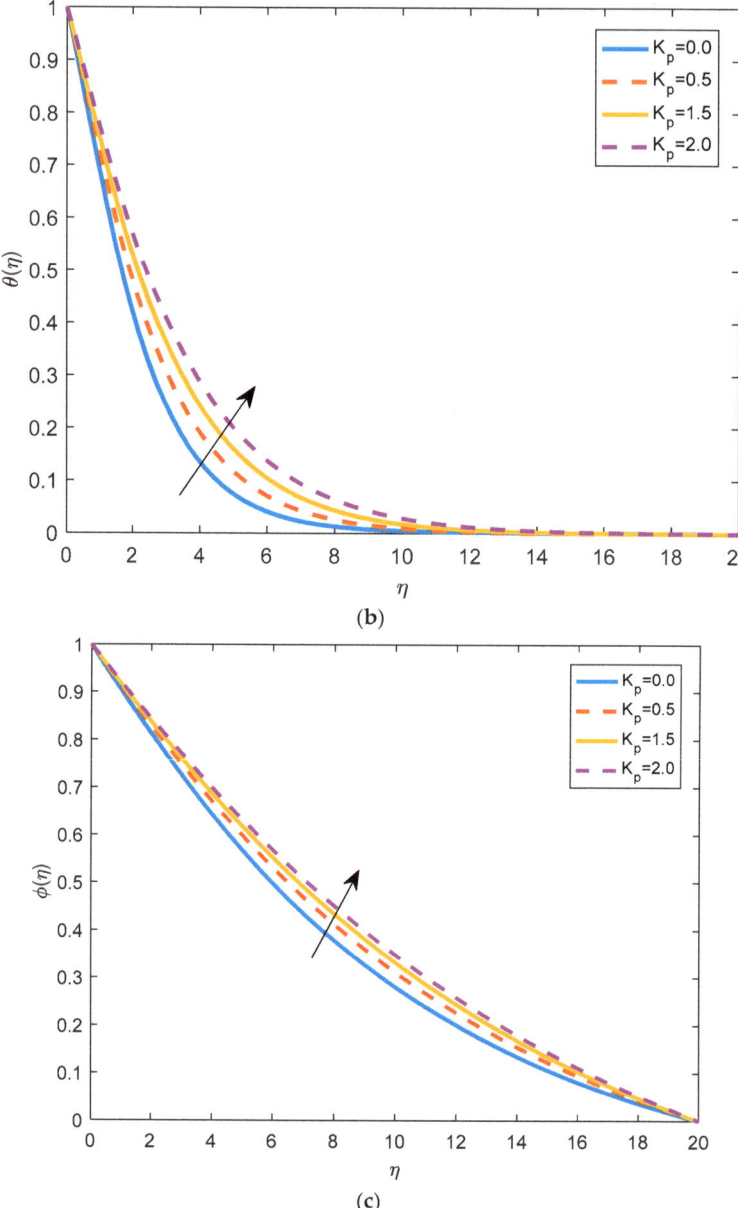

Figure 8. *Cont.*

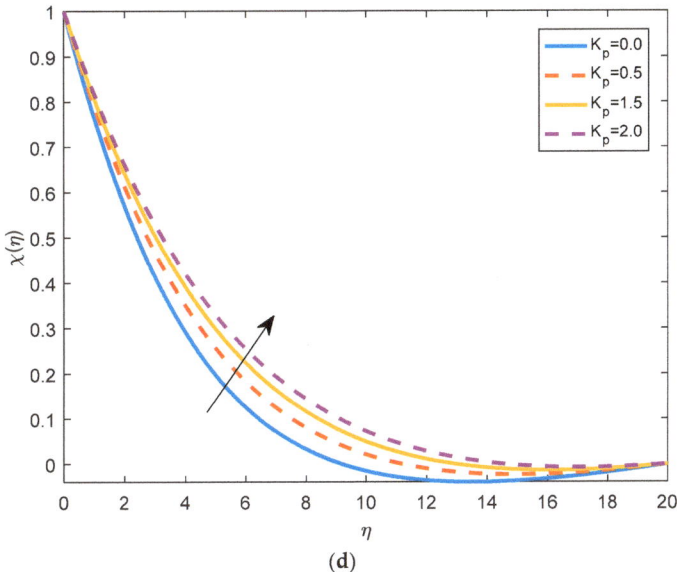

(d)

Figure 8. (**a**): Velocity distribution for porosity parameter K_p when Nt = 0.1, Nb = 2.0, M = 1.0, Pr = 1.5, Rb = 0.1, λ = 0.2, Sc = 0.5, Sc_n = 0.5, Pe = 1.0, W_e = 0.2 at $\alpha = \pi/6$. (**b**): Temperature distribution for various porosity parameter K_p when Nt = 0.1, Nb = 2.0, M = 1.0, Pr = 1.5, Rb = 0.1, λ = 0.2, Sc = 0.5, Sc_n = 0.5, Pe = 1.0 W_e = 0.2 at $\alpha = \pi/6$. (**c**): Concentration distribution for K_p when Nt = 0.1, Nb = 2.0, M = 1.0, Pr = 1.5, Rb = 0.1, λ = 0.2, Sc = 0.5, Sc_n = 0.5, Pe = 1.0 W_e = 0.2 at $\alpha = \pi/6$. (**d**): Density of motile micro-organisms for various K_p when Nt = 0.1, Nb = 2.0, M = 1.0, Pr = 1.5, Rb = 0.1, λ = 0.2, Sc = 0.5, Sc_n = 0.5, Pe = 1.0 W_e = 0.2 at $\alpha = \pi/6$.

4.2. Effects of Physical Parameters on Temperature Distribution

The impact of the buoyancy ratio parameter on the temperature profile is displayed in Figure 2b, it is clear from the variations that with the increase in Nr, the temperature of the fluid increases. The effect of the applied magnetic field on the temperature field is illustrated in Figure 3b. It can be concluded that by increasing the value of M the temperature becomes higher. This trend is physically justified by the fact that the increase in the intensity of the magnetic field augments the resistance to flow that causes the increase in the temperature of the fluid. Figure 4b is plotted to understand the impact of the Brownian motion on the temperature field. The fluid particles' random movement is driven by the stronger Brownian motion (higher values of Nb). Significant heat is produced as a result of this erratic movement, which leads to a rise in temperature. Similarly, from Figure 5b, it can be noticed that the fluid temperature increases by increasing the thermophoresis parameter Nt. This is due to the fact that heated particles are drawn away from hot surfaces and toward colder areas by the thermophoresis force, causing an increase in the liquid temperature inside the boundary layer. The effect of the Rayleigh number on the temperature is depicted in Figure 6b. The analysis of this figure shows that the temperature increases with the increasing value of Rb. However, on the other side, an opposite behavior occurs with the increase in the Weissenberg number (Figure 7b). Heating effect is directly proportional to the permeability K_p; it implies that with the increasing values of K_p, temperature becomes higher, as observed in Figure 8b.

4.3. Effects of Physical Parameters on Nanoparticles Concentration

Figure 2c describes the concentration profiles for various values of the buoyancy parameter Nr. Concentrations are higher for larger values of Nr. Similarly, as presented in Figure 3c, the same impact is encountered when the magnetic field magnitude is increased.

Figure 4c illustrates the impact of Brownian motion (Nb) on the concentration profile $\phi(\eta)$. The concentrations are lower for higher values of Nb. The effects of Nt on nanoparticles concentration are shown in Figure 5c. It should be mentioned that the thermal conductivity increases with increasing Nt. This is the major reason that leads to the higher concentrations, as presented in Figure 5c. At higher values of the thermophoresis parameter, the concentration also increases. Figure 6c is plotted to investigate the effect of the Rayleigh number (Rb) on the concentration profile. It is clear that the increase in concentration is proportional to Rb values. Contrary, the Weissenberg parameter (W_e) has an opposite impact as shown in Figure 7c. In fact, from Figure 7c, it can be seen that the concentration becomes lower with higher (W_e). As presented in Figure 8c, the permeability parameter K_p has a direct effect on the concentration distribution and with the increment of K_p, the concentration values increase.

4.4. Effects of Physical Parameters on the Density of Motile Microorganisms

Figure 2d presents the influence of the buoyancy parameter on the density of motile micro-organisms. It can be noticed that the density of motile micro-organisms increases with the lowering of Nr. The magnetic parameter also has the same impact on the density of motile micro-organisms as shown in Figure 3d. Figure 3d shows that the density increases at higher values of M. The density of motile micro-organisms has an opposite behavior to the Brownian motion effect. In fact, Figure 4d shows that the values of motile micro-organisms decrease with higher values of Nb. Figure 5d illustrates the motile micro-organisms' profiles for the various values of the thermophoresis parameter. It is noticed that it increases with Nt when other dimensionless parameters are kept constant. Similarly, the increase in the Rayleigh number (Rb) leads to higher values of the density of motile micro-organisms (Figure 6d). Whereas the density of motile micro-organisms decreases with the increase in the Weissenberg parameter (W_e) as illustrated in Figure 7d. Figure 8d shows that the density of the motile micro-organisms is directly proportional to K_p.

4.5. Effect of Pertinent Parameters on Skin Friction, Rate of Heat Transfer, Rate of Mass Transfer, and Rate of Motile Organisms

Tables 1 and 2 are presented to illustrate the physical behavior of the skin friction, rate of heat transfer, rate of mass transfer, and rate of motile organisms for the mixed convection parameter and the bioconvection Peclet number, respectively. From Table 1, it is noticed that the heat transfer rate has an increasing trend, but the remaining quantities are showing a decreasing trend. Table 2 indicates that the bioconvective Peclet number reduces the rates of mass transfer and the motile organism, but the skin friction and rate of heat transfer increase accordingly.

Table 1. Physical behavior of $(a) f''(0)$ $(b) - \theta'(0)$ $(c) - \phi'(0)$ $(d) - \chi'(0)$ at angle $\pi/6$ when $Nr = 0.2$, $Rb = 0.1$ $K_P = 0.5$ $M = 0.1$ $W_e = 0.2$, $Pr = 3.0$, $Nt = 0.1$, $Nb = 2$, $Sc = 0.2$, $Scn = 0.2$, $Pe = 1$.

λ	$f''(0)$	$-\theta'(0)$	$-\phi'(0)$	$-\chi'(0)$
0.1	0.84342	0.38469	0.08851	0.23197
1.0	0.55897	0.46628	0.05885	0.14685
2.0	0.26238	0.49037	0.05462	0.13256
3.0	0.03197	0.48689	0.07111	0.17407

Table 2. Physical behavior of $(a)f''(0)(b) - \theta'(0)(c) - \phi'(0)(d) - \chi'(0)$ at angle $\pi/6$ when $Nr = 0.2$, $Rb = 0.1$ $K_P = 0.5$, $M = 0.1$ $W_e = 0.2$, $Pr = 3.0$, $Nt = 0.1$, $Nb = 2$, $Sc = 0.2$, $Scn = 0.2$, $\lambda = 0.2$.

Pe	$f''(0)$	$-\theta'(0)$	$-\phi'(0)$	$-\chi'(0)$
0.1	0.81186	0.40318	0.08193	0.11090
1.0	0.80805	0.396523	0.08511	0.22353
2.0	0.80498	0.393091	0.08741	0.36484
3.0	0.80198	0.39013	0.08921	0.51773

5. Conclusions

The present study is intended to investigate the magnetohydrodynamics effects on the bioconvective heat transfer of a Williamson nanofluid with gyrotactic micro-organisms over a moving inclined plate embedded in a porous medium. The main findings can be highlighted as follows:

- With the increase in Nr, the velocity profile decreases. It is seen that, as the magnetic parameter increases, the fluid velocity decreases. The Brownian motion causes the intensification of the flow by increasing the fluid velocity. This fact is physically true, in fact, as Nt increases, the viscosity decreases, and the fluid velocity increases. It is also observed that with the increment of bioconvection Rayleigh number, the velocity goes down.
- By increasing the magnetic parameter, the temperature increases. In fact, the increase M enhances the resistance within the fluid and causes higher fluid temperatures. The temperature of the fluid increases by increasing the thermophoresis parameter. The heating effect is directly proportional to the permeability parameter.
- Concentration of the profile boosts up by taking larger values of the buoyancy ratio parameter. Brownian motion, thermophoresis, and permeability parameters increase the nanoparticles' concentration.
- The density of motile micro-organism increases with the buoyancy ratio parameter and the bioconvective Rayleigh number and decreases with the Brownian motion parameter.
- The skin friction and heat transfer rate decrease with the mixed convection parameter and bioconvection Peclet number.
- The graphical results satisfy the given boundary conditions asymptotically.

Author Contributions: Conceptualization, A.A., R.K., H.A., L.A., K.G. and L.K.; Methodology, A.A., R.K., H.A., A.I., K.G., W.H. and L.K.; Software, A.A.; Formal analysis, R.K., A.I., L.A., K.G. and W.H.; Investigation, A.A., R.K. and K.G.; Writing—original draft, A.A., R.K., H.A., A.I., L.A., K.G., W.H. and L.K.; Writing—review & editing, R.K., H.A., A.I., L.A., K.G., W.H. and L.K.; Visualization, A.A.; Supervision, L.K.; Project administration, K.G.; Funding acquisition, K.G. All authors have read and agreed to the published version of the manuscript.

Funding: Princess Nourah bint Abdulrahman University Researchers Supporting Project number (PNURSP2023R41), Princess Nourah bint Abdulrahman University, Riyadh, Saudi Arabia.

Institutional Review Board Statement: Not applicable.

Informed Consent Statement: Not applicable.

Data Availability Statement: Not applicable.

Conflicts of Interest: The authors declare no conflict of interest.

References

1. Masuda, H.; Ebata, A.; Teramae, K. Alteration of thermal conductivity and viscosity of liquid by dispersing ultra-fine particles. Dispersion of Al2O3, SiO2 and TiO2 ultra-fine particles. *Netsu Bussei* **1993**, *7*, 227–233. [CrossRef]
2. Choi, S.U.; Eastman, J.A. *Enhancing Thermal Conductivity of Fluids with Nanoparticles*; Argonne Natl. Lab. (ANL): Argonne, IL, USA, 1995; Volume 231, pp. 99–106.
3. Buongiorno, J.; Hu, W. Nanofluid coolants for advanced nuclear power plants. *Proc. ICAPP* **2005**, *5*, 15–19.
4. Buongiorno, J. Convective Transport in Nanofluids. *J. Heat Transf.* **2006**, *128*, 240–245. [CrossRef]
5. Abbas, A.; Ashraf, M.; Chu, Y.M.; Zia, S.; Khan, I.; Nisar, K.S. Computational study of the coupled mechanism of thermophoretic transportation and mixed convection flow around the surface of a sphere. *Molecules* **2020**, *25*, 2694. [CrossRef]
6. Ashraf, M.; Abbas, A.; Zia, S.; Chu, Y.M.; Khan, I.; Nisar, K.S. Computational analysis of the effect of nano particle material motion on mixed convection flow in the presence of heat generation and absorption. *CMC-Comput. Mater. Contin.* **2020**, *65*, 1809–1823. [CrossRef]
7. Abbas, A.; Ashraf, M. Combined effects of variable viscosity and thermophoretic transportation on mixed convection flow around the surface of a sphere. *Therm. Sci.* **2020**, *24*, 4089–4101. [CrossRef]
8. Ashraf, M.; Abbas, A.; Ali, A.; Shah, Z.; Alrabaiah, H.; Bonyah, E. Numerical simulation of the combined effects of thermophoretic motion and variable thermal conductivity on free convection heat transfer. *AIP Adv.* **2020**, *10*, 085005. [CrossRef]
9. Abbas, A.; Ashraf, M.; Chamkha, A.J. Combined effects of thermal radiation and thermophoretic motion on mixed convection boundary layer flow. *Alex. Eng. J.* **2021**, *60*, 3243–3252. [CrossRef]
10. Ashraf, M.; Abbas, A.; Oztop, H.F.; Nisar, K.S.; Khan, I. Computations of mixed convection slip flow around the surface of a sphere: Effects of thermophoretic transportation and viscous dissipation. *Heat Transf.* **2021**, *50*, 7349–7362. [CrossRef]
11. Ahmad, U.; Ashraf, M.; Abbas, A.; Rashad, A.M.; Nabwey, H.A. Mixed convection flow along a curved surface in the presence of exothermic catalytic chemical reaction. *Sci. Rep.* **2021**, *11*, 12907. [CrossRef] [PubMed]
12. Kuznetsov, A.V. The onset of nanofluid bioconvection in a suspension containing both nanoparticles and gyrotactic microorganisms. *Int. Commun. Heat Mass Transf.* **2010**, *37*, 1421–1425. [CrossRef]
13. Xu, H.; Pop, I. Mixed convection flow of a nanofluid over a stretching surface with uniform free stream in the presence of both nanoparticles and gyrotactic microorganisms. *Int. J. Heat Mass Transf.* **2014**, *75*, 610–623. [CrossRef]
14. Acharya, N.; Das, K.; Kundu, P.K. Framing the effects of solar radiation on magneto-hydrodynamics bioconvection nanofluid flow in presence of gyrotactic microorganisms. *J. Mol. Liq.* **2016**, *222*, 28–37. [CrossRef]
15. Akbar, N.S.; Khan, Z.H. Magnetic field analysis in a suspension of gyrotactic microorganisms and nanoparticles over a stretching surface. *J. Magn. Magn. Mater.* **2016**, *410*, 72–80. [CrossRef]
16. Shen, B.; Zheng, L.; Zhang, C.; Zhang, X. Bioconvection heat transfer of a nanofluid over a stretching sheet with velocity slip and temperature jump. *Therm. Sci.* **2017**, *21*, 2347–2356. [CrossRef]
17. Khan, S.U.; Al-Khaled, K.; Aldabesh, A.; Awais, M.; Tlili, I. Bioconvection flow in accelerated couple stress nanoparticles with activation energy: Bio-fuel applications. *Sci. Rep.* **2021**, *11*, 3331. [CrossRef]
18. Xia, W.F.; Haq, F.; Saleem, M.; Khan, M.I.; Khan, S.U.; Chu, Y.M. Irreversibility analysis in natural bio-convective flow of Eyring-Powell nanofluid subject to activation energy and gyrotactic microorganisms. *Ain Shams Eng. J.* **2021**, *12*, 4063–4074. [CrossRef]
19. Shi, Q.H.; Hamid, A.; Khan, M.I.; Kumar, R.N.; Gowda, R.P.; Prasannakumara, B.C.; Shah, N.A.; Khan, S.U.; Chung, J.D. Numerical study of bio-convection flow of magneto-cross nanofluid containing gyrotactic microorganisms with activation energy. *Sci. Rep.* **2021**, *11*, 16030. [CrossRef]
20. Yang, D.; Ullah, S.; Tanveer, M.; Farid, S.; Rehman, M.I.U.; Shah, N.A.; Chung, J.D. Thermal transport of natural convection flow of second grade bio-nanofluid in a vertical channel. *Case Stud. Therm. Eng.* **2021**, *28*, 101377. [CrossRef]
21. Hayat, T.; Ullah, I.; Muhammad, K.; Alsaedi, A. Gyrotactic microorganism and bio-convection during flow of Prandtl-Eyring nanomaterial. *Nonlinear Eng.* **2021**, *10*, 201–212. [CrossRef]
22. Khan, S.U.; Irfan, M.; Khan, M.I.; Abbasi, A.; Rahman, S.U.; Niazi, U.M.; Farooq, S. Bio-convective Darcy-Forchheimer oscillating thermal flow of Eyring-Powell nanofluid subject to exponential heat source/sink and modified Cattaneo–Christov model applications. *J. Indian Chem. Soc.* **2022**, *99*, 100399. [CrossRef]
23. Saranya, S.; Ragupathi, P.; Al-Mdallal, Q. Analysis of bio-convective heat transfer over an unsteady curved stretching sheet using the shifted Legendre collocation method. *Case Stud. Therm. Eng.* **2022**, *39*, 102433. [CrossRef]
24. Ali, L.; Ali, B.; Ghori, M.B. Melting effect on Cattaneo–Christov and thermal radiation features for aligned MHD nanofluid flow comprising microorganisms to leading edge: FEM approach. *Comput. Math. Appl.* **2022**, *109*, 260–269. [CrossRef]
25. Sakiadis, B.C. Boundary-layer behavior on continuous solid surfaces: II. The boundary layer on a continuous flat surface. *Ai Ch E J.* **1961**, *7*, 221–225. [CrossRef]
26. Erickson, L.E.; Fan, L.T.; Fox, V.G. Heat and mass transfer on moving continuous flat plate with suction or injection. *Ind. Eng. Chem. Fundam.* **1966**, *5*, 19–25. [CrossRef]
27. Crane, L.J. Flow past a stretching plate. *Z. Angew. Math. Phys. ZAMP* **1970**, *21*, 645–647. [CrossRef]
28. Ali, L.; Ali, B.; Liu, X.; Ahmed, S.; Shah, M.A. Analysis of bio-convective MHD Blasius and Sakiadis flow with Cattaneo-Christov heat flux model and chemical reaction. *Chin. J. Phys.* **2022**, *77*, 1963–1975. [CrossRef]

29. Abbas, A.; Ijaz, I.; Ashraf, M.; Ahmad, H. Combined effects of variable density and thermal radiation on MHD Sakiadis flow. *Case Stud. Therm. Eng.* **2021**, *28*, 101640. [CrossRef]
30. Abbas, A.; Shafqat, R.; Jeelani, M.B.; Alharthi, N.H. Significance of chemical reaction and Lorentz force on third-grade fluid flow and heat transfer with Darcy–Forchheimer law over an inclined exponentially stretching sheet embedded in a porous medium. *Symmetry* **2022**, *14*, 779. [CrossRef]
31. Abbas, A.; Noreen, A.; Ali, M.A.; Ashraf, M.; Alzahrani, E.; Marzouki, R.; Goodarzi, M. Solar radiation over a roof in the presence of temperature-dependent thermal conductivity of a Casson flow for energy saving in buildings. *Sustain. Energy Technol. Assess.* **2022**, *53*, 102606. [CrossRef]
32. Abbas, A.; Shafqat, R.; Jeelani, M.B.; Alharthi, N.H. Convective heat and mass transfer in third-grade fluid with Darcy–Forchheimer relation in the presence of thermal-diffusion and diffusion-thermo effects over an exponentially inclined stretching sheet surrounded by a porous medium: A CFD study. *Processes* **2022**, *10*, 776. [CrossRef]
33. Prasannakumara, B.C.; Gireesha, B.J.; Gorla, R.S.; Krishnamurthy, M.R. Effects of chemical reaction and nonlinear thermal radiation on Williamson nanofluid slip flow over a stretching sheet embedded in a porous medium. *J. Aerosp. Eng.* **2016**, *29*, 04016019. [CrossRef]
34. Bhatti, M.M.; Rashidi, M.M. Effects of thermo-diffusion and thermal radiation on Williamson nanofluid over a porous shrinking/stretching sheet. *J. Mol. Liq.* **2016**, *221*, 567–573. [CrossRef]
35. Zaman, S.; Gul, M. Magnetohydrodynamic bioconvective flow of Williamson nanofluid containing gyrotactic microorganisms subjected to thermal radiation and Newtonian conditions. *J. Theor. Biol.* **2019**, *479*, 22–28. [CrossRef]
36. Li, Y.X.; Al-Khaled, K.; Khan, S.U.; Sun, T.C.; Khan, M.I.; Malik, M.Y. Bio-convective Darcy-Forchheimer periodically accelerated flow of non-Newtonian nanofluid with Cattaneo–Christov and Prandtl effective approach. *Case Stud. Therm. Eng.* **2021**, *26*, 101102. [CrossRef]
37. Yahya, A.U.; Salamat, N.; Habib, D.; Ali, B.; Hussain, S.; Abdal, S. Implication of Bio-convection and Cattaneo-Christov heat flux on Williamson Sutter by nanofluid transportation caused by a stretching surface with convective boundary. *Chin. J. Phys.* **2021**, *73*, 706–718. [CrossRef]
38. Abbas, A.; Jeelani, M.B.; Alnahdi, A.S.; Ilyas, A. MHD Williamson Nanofluid Fluid Flow and Heat Transfer Past a Non-Linear Stretching Sheet Implanted in a Porous Medium: Effects of Heat Generation and Viscous Dissipation. *Processes* **2022**, *10*, 1221. [CrossRef]
39. Awan, A.U.; Shah, S.A.A.; Ali, B. Bio-convection effects on Williamson nanofluid flow with exponential heat source and motile microorganism over a stretching sheet. *Chin. J. Phys.* **2022**, *77*, 2795–2810. [CrossRef]
40. Abbas, A.; Jeelani, M.B.; Alharthi, N.H. Magnetohydrodynamic effects on third-grade fluid flow and heat transfer with darcy–forchheimer law over an inclined exponentially stretching sheet embedded in a porous medium. *Magnetochemistry* **2022**, *8*, 61. [CrossRef]
41. Ashraf, M.; Ilyas, A.; Ullah, Z.; Abbas, A. Periodic magnetohydrodynamic mixed convection flow along a cone embedded in a porous medium with variable surface temperature. *Ann. Nucl. Energy* **2022**, *175*, 109218. [CrossRef]
42. Abbas, A.; Ahmad, H.; Mumtaz, M.; Ilyas, A.; Hussan, M. MHD dissipative micropolar fluid flow past stretching sheet with heat generation and slip effects. *Waves Random Complex Media* **2022**, 1–15. [CrossRef]
43. Abbas, A.; Jeelani, M.B.; Alharthi, N.H. Darcy–Forchheimer Relation Influence on MHD Dissipative Third-Grade Fluid Flow and Heat Transfer in Porous Medium with Joule Heating Effects: A Numerical Approach. *Processes* **2022**, *10*, 906. [CrossRef]
44. Ali, L.; Ali, B.; Liu, X.; Iqbal, T.; Zulqarnain, R.M.; Javid, M. A comparative study of unsteady MHD Falkner–Skan wedge flow for non-Newtonian nanofluids considering thermal radiation and activation energy. *Chin. J. Phys.* **2022**, *77*, 1625–1638. [CrossRef]
45. Ali, L.; Wang, Y.; Ali, B.; Liu, X.; Din, A.; Al Mdallal, Q. The function of nanoparticle's diameter and Darcy-Forchheimer flow over a cylinder with effect of magnetic field and thermal radiation. *Case Stud. Therm. Eng.* **2021**, *28*, 101392. [CrossRef]
46. Qayyum, S.; Hayat, T.; Alsaedi, A.; Ahmad, B. Magnetohydrodynamic (MHD) nonlinear convective flow of Jeffrey nanofluid over a nonlinear stretching surface with variable thickness and chemical reaction. *Int. J. Mech. Sci.* **2017**, *134*, 306–314. [CrossRef]
47. Narsimulu, G.; Gopal, D.; Udaikumar, R. Numerical approach for enhanced mass transfer of bio-convection on magneto-hydrodynamic Carreau fluid flow through a nonlinear stretching surface. *Mater. Today Proc.* **2022**, *49*, 2267–2275. [CrossRef]
48. Vasudev, C.; Rao, U.R.; Reddy, M.S.; Rao, G.P. Peristaltic pumping of Williamson fluid through a porous medium in a horizontal channel with heat transfer. *Am. J. Sci. Ind. Res.* **2010**, *1*, 656–666. [CrossRef]
49. Eldabe, N.T.; Elogail, M.A.; Elshaboury, S.M.; Hasan, A.A. Hall effects on the peristaltic transport of Williamson fluid through a porous medium with heat and mass transfer. *Appl. Math. Model.* **2016**, *40*, 315–328.
50. Khan, M.I.; Alzahrani, F.; Hobiny, A.; Ali, Z. Modeling of Cattaneo-Christov double diffusions (CCDD) in Williamson nanomaterial slip flow subject to porous medium. *J. Mater. Res. Technol.* **2020**, *9*, 6172–6177. [CrossRef]
51. Bhatti, M.M.; Arain, M.B.; Zeeshan, A.; Ellahi, R.; Doranehgard, M.H. Swimming of Gyrotactic Microorganism in MHD Williamson nanofluid flow between rotating circular plates embedded in porous medium: Application of thermal energy storage. *J. Energy Storage* **2022**, *45*, 103511. [CrossRef]
52. Mishra, P.; Kumar, D.; Kumar, J.; Abdel-Aty, A.H.; Park, C.; Yahia, I.S. Analysis of MHD Williamson micropolar fluid flow in non-Darcian porous media with variable thermal conductivity. *Case Stud. Therm. Eng.* **2022**, *36*, 102195. [CrossRef]
53. Rajput, G.R.; Jadhav, B.P.; Patil, V.S.; Salunkhe, S.N. Effects of nonlinear thermal radiation over magnetized stagnation point flow of Williamson fluid in porous media driven by stretching sheet. *Heat Transf.* **2021**, *50*, 2543–2557. [CrossRef]

54. Reddy, Y.D.; Mebarek-Oudina, F.; Goud, B.S.; Ismail, A.I. Radiation, velocity and thermal slips effect toward MHD boundary layer flow through heat and mass transport of Williamson nanofluid with porous medium. *Arab. J. Sci. Eng.* **2022**, *47*, 16355–16369. [CrossRef]
55. Yousef, N.S.; Megahed, A.M.; Ghoneim, N.I.; Elsafi, M.; Fares, E. Chemical reaction impact on MHD dissipative Casson-Williamson nanofluid flow over a slippery stretching sheet through porous medium. *Alex. Eng. J.* **2022**, *61*, 10161–10170. [CrossRef]

Disclaimer/Publisher's Note: The statements, opinions and data contained in all publications are solely those of the individual author(s) and contributor(s) and not of MDPI and/or the editor(s). MDPI and/or the editor(s) disclaim responsibility for any injury to people or property resulting from any ideas, methods, instructions or products referred to in the content.

Article

A Novel Monte Carlo Method to Calculate the Thermal Conductivity in Nanoscale Thermoelectric Phononic Crystals Based on Universal Effective Medium Theory

Zhizhong Yan [1,2,*] and Ercong Cheng [1]

[1] School of Mathematics and Statistics, Beijing Institute of Technology, Beijing 100081, China
[2] Beijing Key Laboratory on MCAACI, Beijing Institute of Technology, Beijing 100081, China
* Correspondence: zzyan@bit.edu.cn; Fax: +86-10-68913829

Abstract: Thermal reduction by enhancing heat-generation phonon scattering can improve thermoelectric performance. In this paper, the phonon transport subjected to internal heat generation in two-dimensional nanoscale thermoelectric phononic crystals is investigated by a novel Monte Carlo method based on the universal effective medium theory, called the MCBU method. The present approach is validated. Compared with the universal effective medium theory method, the MCBU method is easier to implement. More importantly, the deviation of the computation time between the two methods can be ignored. With almost the same time cost, the present method can accurately calculate the effective thermal conductivity of complex geometric structures that cannot be calculated by the effective medium theory. The influences of porosity, temperature, pore shape and material parameters on thermal conductivity are discussed in detail. This study offers useful methods and suggestions for fabricating these materials with heat isolation and reduction.

Keywords: Monte Carlo method; Boltzmann transport equation; thermoelectric phononic crystal; thermal conductivity; universal effective medium theory

MSC: 80M31

1. Introduction

In the past decades, nanotechnology has been used more and more widely in thermoelectric devices, which makes the study of heat conduction theory extremely important. Generally, the phonon Boltzmann transport equation (BTE) can characterize thermal transport well in nanostructures. In order to solve the BTE, researchers have made a lot of progress [1–8]. The Gray model is commonly used [2]; however, solving the BTE in this way sometimes leads to inaccurate solutions that cannot be ignored. The different lattice Boltzmann methods have also been developed by the methods mentioned in references [3–6]. However, the lattice Boltzmann methods still have some shortcomings. For example, they are used for non-physical prediction in the ballistic state [5,6]. There is another method that can directly solve the BTE by using the finite difference method, namely the discrete ordinate method [7]. However, in addition to requiring a large amount of memory to solve the equation, this method also shows a slow convergence near the diffusion limit. Moreover, the discrete unified gas dynamics scheme [8] has been proven to be effective and deliver high-precision for low-dimensional thermal phonon transport, but it has not been used to solve the BTE in three-dimensional geometry. The state-space strategies are the basis of the novel theory of control and its advantage is the characterization of approaches of importance through the BTE in favoring transport functions. However, for this method, in the previous duration the processes were sufficient for them with only one differential equation for a reasonably low order [9]. The main step of the finite element method for solving the BTE is obtaining the equations of motion for the finite elements [10]. However, this method is very time consuming and it cannot handle the infinite domain problems well. So far, the Monte Carlo (MC) simulation has been proved to be an efficient method for solving the BTE. Two typical MC methods are used, of which the ensemble MC method is employed to calculate the effective thermal conductivity in many kinds of nanostructures, for example, silicon structures [11,12] and even composites [13,14]. The other method, the phonon tracing MC method, simulates the trajectories of phonons independently which reduces the computation time greatly [15,16]. Therefore, both the ensemble MC and the phonon tracing MC are suitable methods used for phonon transport in many kinds of nanostructures with a larger size, and they can also solve the BTE with high accuracy and minimum calculation time [1].

Recently, Yu-Chao Hua and Bing-Yang Cao proposed an efficient two-step Monte Carlo method for heat conduction in nanostructures [1]. However, it is difficult to calculate the effective thermal conductivity of complex structures with different pore shapes. Effective medium theory (EMT) is a widely used analytical method to study the optical responses of subwavelength periodic structures [17–19] and it can achieve similar functions of the whole system by defining the average value of materials with effective parameters [20]. The Maxwell-Garnett theory and the Bruggeman EMT are based on the material characteristics of each component in the mixture, which play an important role in effective medium methods. The composition of dielectric materials usually shows different structural properties. To calculate the thermal conductivity of these materials, EMT should be a favored method; for a given material and geometric structure, the EMT method can calculate the thermal conductivity by achieving the functions of the given system [21]. Due to these characteristics of EMT, it has many applications in electrical conductivity and related issues [22–26].

At nanoscale, the size characteristics of phononic crystals are very close to or even smaller than the mean free path (MFP) of phonons, and the heat conduction no longer obeys the Fourier law. Therefore, in order to deeply understand phonon transport in thermoelectric phononic crystals, the correct models and methods are required to simulate the phonon transport. The EMT method can effectively calculate the effective thermal conductivity, and the value of the effective thermal conductivity only depends on the porosity. However, the EMT method is not the best method to calculate the effective thermal conductivity of complex geometry. The MC method mainly calculates the effective thermal conductivity through the MC model, which can reduce the calculation time without damaging the accuracy. However, this method still has problems in calculating the effective thermal conductivity of complex pore shapes. The general effective medium theory can calculate the effective thermal conductivity of different pore shapes by implementing the suppression function. Therefore, we combine the MC method with the general effective medium theory method to develop a novel method for calculating the effective thermal conductivity of complex pore shapes as effectively as these two methods. In this paper, a novel Monte Carlo method based on the universal effective medium theory is developed to calculate the thermal conductivity in nanoscale thermoelectric phononic crystals with complex geometries, which is the creativity point in this paper. The outline of this paper is as follows. In Section 2, the method description is introduced. In addition, the numerical experiments are conducted to numerically illustrate some properties of the present method in Section 3, followed by a summary in Section 4. In this paper, the MCBU method is compared with the EMT method and it is found that the MCBU method can effectively and accurately calculate the effective thermal conductivity of different geometric shapes, while the EMT method cannot deal with it well, which is the main focus of this paper.

2. Method Description

2.1. Geometric Model

In this paper, a nanoporous phononic crystal is considered. First, a schematic diagram of phononic crystals is shown in Figure 1. In order to reduce calculation resources, the whole phononic crystal is divided into several unit cells, in which the pore shape of each unit cell is rectangular. The heat flux is parallel to the plane of the crystal for transmission.

The two-dimensional (2D) view of the geometry is also shown in Figure 1b. The model illustrates phonon activities during the transport process where a temperature difference is applied between two boundaries along the *x*-direction. Phonons are emitted from the hot temperature boundaries, diffusive reflection occurs when the phonon meets the inner surface of the unit cell hole, and specular reflection occurs when it encounters the boundary of the unit cell, as shown in Figure 1b. In the present work, when calculating the effective thermal conductivity of a nanostructure with different pore shapes, such as circle pores, rhombus pores and triangle pores, we can replace the rectangle pores of the schematic diagram of phononic crystals shown in Figure 1 can be replaced with the above shapes.

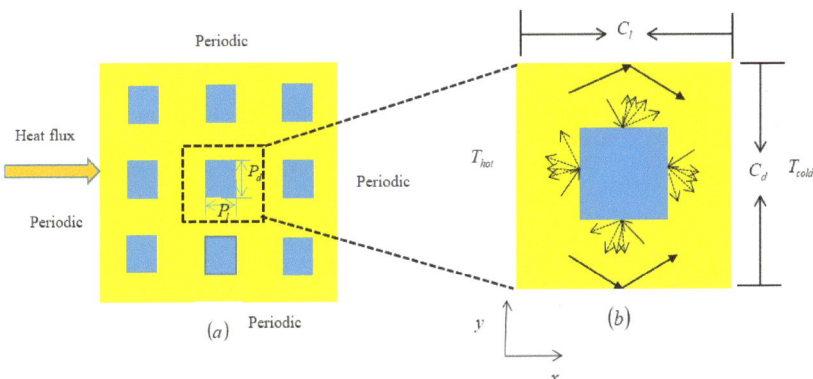

Figure 1. The sketch for nanoporous phononic crystals. (**a**) In-plane heat flux view. (**b**) Geometric model for the unit cell of heat flux under in-plane condition.

2.2. Boltzmann Transport Equation

The BTE can be used to model phonon behavior in phononic crystals. In a lattice, without external force, the BTE equation is expressed as

$$\frac{\partial f(t,\mathbf{r},\mathbf{k})}{\partial t} + \mathbf{v} \cdot \nabla f(t,\mathbf{r},\mathbf{k}) = \left(\frac{\partial f(t,\mathbf{r},\mathbf{k})}{\partial t}\right)_{scatter} \tag{1}$$

Equation (1) in ref. [25] is related to the variation of distribution function $f(t, \mathbf{r}, \mathbf{k})$, and $f(t, \mathbf{r}, \mathbf{k})$ is a function which is dependent on time t, phonon position $\mathbf{r}$ and phonon wave $\mathbf{k}$. The phonon group velocity $\mathbf{v}$ is $\mathbf{v} = \nabla_\mathbf{k} \omega$. The left side of Equation (1) represents the drift term of phonons in the phononic crystals. The right side of the equation describes the scattering term of phonons and phonons, impurities and boundaries.

2.3. Thermal Conductivity in Phononic Crystals Based on Universal Effective Medium Theory

In this section, in order to calculate the effective thermal conductivity in phononic crystals with complex geometric parameters, the effective thermal conductivity in nanoscale thermoelectric phononic crystals will be calculated by using the MCBU method.

First, we can develop the phonon BTE into anisotropic-MFP-BTE [27–35]:

$$F_{ml} \cdot \nabla \Delta T_{ml}^{(n)} + \Delta T_{ml}^{(n)} = \sum_{m'l'} \alpha_{m'l'} \Delta T_{m'l'}^{(n-1)} \tag{2}$$

where $F_{ml} = \Lambda_m \hat{S}_l$ and $\hat{S}_l = \sin(\phi_l)\,\hat{x} + \cos(\phi_l)\hat{y}$.

Then the effective thermal conductivity is given as follows:

$$k_{eff} = -\frac{L}{\Delta TA} \int J \cdot \hat{n} dS \tag{3}$$

where A is the surface area, L is the periodicity, $\hat{n} = \hat{x}$, ΔT is the pseudo-temperature, J is the heat flux and it can be described by

$$J = \frac{C_v \Lambda v_j}{4\pi} \frac{dT}{dx} A \int_0^{2\pi} \int_{-1}^{1} (\exp(-\frac{L_{rp}}{\Lambda\sqrt{1-\mu^2}}) - 1)\mu^2 d\mu d\varphi$$
$$= \frac{C_v \Lambda v_j}{3} \frac{dT}{dx} A^2 \frac{3}{4\pi A} \int_0^{2\pi} \int_{-1}^{1} (\exp(-\frac{L_{rp}}{\Lambda\sqrt{1-\mu^2}}) - 1)\mu^2 d\mu d\varphi \quad (4)$$
$$= -\frac{C_v \Lambda v_j}{3} \frac{dT}{dx} A^2 S(\overline{\Lambda}_{bulk,j}).$$

where C_v is the heat capacity, v_j is the velocity, L_{rp} is the length from the point r to the point p at pore boundaries, Λ is the intrinsic MFP, $S(\overline{\Lambda}_{bulk,j})$ is the suppression function. Then we can obtain the effective thermal conductivity by substituting Equation (4) into Equation (3) as follows:

$$k_{eff} = -\frac{L}{\Lambda TA} \int -\frac{C_v \Lambda v_j}{3} \frac{dT}{dx} A^2 S(\overline{\Lambda}_{bulk,j}) \cdot \hat{n} dS$$
$$= \int L \frac{C_v \Lambda v_j}{3} A S(\overline{\Lambda}_{bulk,j}) \cdot \hat{n} dS \quad (5)$$
$$= \int k_{bulk}(\Lambda) S(\overline{\Lambda}_{bulk,j}, L) d\Lambda$$

where $S(\overline{\Lambda}_{bulk,j}, L)$ is the suppression function which can describe the degree of reduction of heat transport with respect to the bulk for a given intrinsic MFP.

Integrating $\int k_{bulk}(\Lambda) S(\overline{\Lambda}_{bulk,j}, L) d\Lambda$ by parts and substituting it into Equation (5), we can obtain the following formula:

$$k_{eff} = k_{bulk}[S(\infty) - \int_0^\infty \frac{1}{1 + \frac{\Lambda_0}{\Lambda}} \frac{\partial S(\Lambda)}{\partial \Lambda} d\Lambda] \quad (6)$$

To obtain the final equation, we take $S(\infty) = S(0) + \int_0^\infty \frac{\partial S(\Lambda)}{\partial \Lambda} d\Lambda$ and $S(\Lambda) = \frac{S(\Lambda \to 0)}{1 + \frac{\Lambda}{L_c}}$ into Equation (6):

$$\frac{k_{eff}}{k_{bulk}} = S(0) + \int_0^\infty (1 - \frac{1}{1 + \frac{\Lambda_0}{\Lambda}}) \frac{\partial S(\Lambda)}{\partial \Lambda} d\Lambda$$
$$= S(0) - S(0) \int_0^\infty \frac{\Lambda_0}{\Lambda + \Lambda_0} \frac{L_c}{(L_c + \Lambda)^2} d\Lambda \quad (7)$$
$$= S(0)[1 - \int_0^\infty \frac{\Lambda_0}{\Lambda + \Lambda_0} \frac{L_c}{(L_c + \Lambda)^2} d\Lambda]$$
$$= S(0)\left[1 - \Lambda_0 L_c \frac{1}{L_c^2 + \Lambda_0(\Lambda_0 - 2L_c)} \left(-\ln\left(\frac{\Lambda_0}{L_c}\right) + (\Lambda_0 - 2L_c)/L_c + 1\right)\right]$$

Then Equation (7) is the final equation of the effective thermal conductivity.

Where Λ_0 is the medium MFP of the thermal conductivity distribution, L_c is the mean light-of-sight between phonon scattering events with the nanostructure. Then we obtain the effective thermal conductivity in terms of the Monte Carlo method combined with the universal effective medium theory.

The graphic below describes the sequence of processing steps and the parameters used:

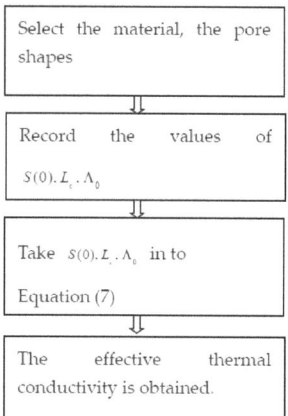

3. Results and Discussions

In this section, the accuracy of the MCBU method is checked and the results are compared with those of the two-step MC method and the MC model in Reference [1]. The two-step MC method calculates the thermal conductivity through the formula $\frac{k_{eff\_limit}}{k_{bulk}} = \frac{3\Delta L}{4l_0}\frac{p_0}{1-p_i}$, where ΔL is the length of simulation unit, l_0 is the average MFP and p_0 is the initial phonon transmittance, p_i is the internal phonon transmittance. The MC model calculates the thermal conductivity through the formula $\frac{k_{eff,po}}{k_{bulk}} = 1 - \frac{3}{\pi R_p^2(\varepsilon^{-1}-1)}\int_{R_p}^{\frac{R_p}{\sqrt{\varepsilon}}} r\,dr \int_0^{2\pi}\int_0^1 \exp(-\frac{L_{rp}}{l_0\sqrt{1-\mu^2}})\mu^2 d\mu d\varphi$, where R_p is the pore radius and ε is the porosity.

The deviation between p_0 and p_i can be ignored. Therefore, when calculating the effective thermal conductivity by the two-step MC method, p_i can be replaced by p_0. Figure 2 illustrates the effective thermal conductivity varying with L_c. It is found that the effective thermal conductivity increases with increasing L_c, and the results obtained by the MCBU method agree well with those predicted by the two-step MC method; the deviation between them decreases with increasing L_c. In addition, the results obtained by the two methods are both slightly less than those obtained by the MC model, and approach the value predicted by the MC model.

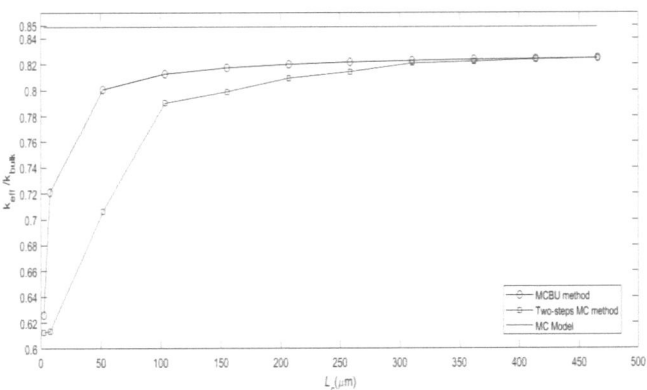

Figure 2. The effective thermal conductivity computed using the MCBU method, the two-step MC method and the MC model.

In the following, numerical experiments are conducted to show the effectiveness of the MCBU method, and the comparison between the MCBU method and effective medium theory (EMT) method is discussed in detail. First, the results are illustrated in Table 1 and Figure 3. In Table 1, k_s is denoted as the thermal conductivity of rectangle pores in the MCBU method, k_m as the thermal conductivity of the EMT method; and t_s is denoted as the computation time of the MCBU method, and t_m as the computation time of the EMT method. From Table 1, we can see that the MCBU method is consistent with the EMT method with a deviation of less than 12%. In the AlN with rectangular pore shape, when the porosity is 0.35 and 0.4, the MCBU method is consistent with the EMT method, with a deviation of about 3%. In addition, the deviation of the computation time between the two methods can be ignored. Figure 3 shows that the effective thermal conductivity decreases with the increase of porosity, and the deviation between the MCBU method and EMT method in rectangular and circular holes decreases sharply with the increase of porosity. For triangular and rhombic pores, the deviation between the two methods decreases with the decrease of porosity. With the change of pore shapes, the same value is obtained by using the EMT method, which indicates that the EMT method may have some problems in calculating the effective thermal conductivity of complex geometric pore shapes. Therefore, when calculating the effective thermal conductivity of pores with complex geometry, the MCBU method is a more suitable and quicker method.

Table 1. The effective thermal conductivity in material made of AlN, at 300 k, with the comparison of the EMT method and the MCBU method.

Φ	k_s	k_m	$\left|\frac{k_m - k_s}{k_m}\right|$ (%)	$|t_s - t_m|$ (s)
0.05	0.8170	0.9048	9.7%	3.35×10^{-3}
0.10	0.7241	0.8182	11.5%	3.19×10^{-3}
0.15	0.6707	0.7391	9.3%	3.30×10^{-3}
0.20	0.5962	0.6667	10.6%	3.31×10^{-3}
0.25	0.5486	0.6000	8.6%	3.21×10^{-3}
0.30	0.5093	0.5385	5.4%	3.19×10^{-3}
0.35	0.4675	0.4815	2.9%	3.29×10^{-3}
0.40	0.4403	0.4286	2.7%	3.33×10^{-3}

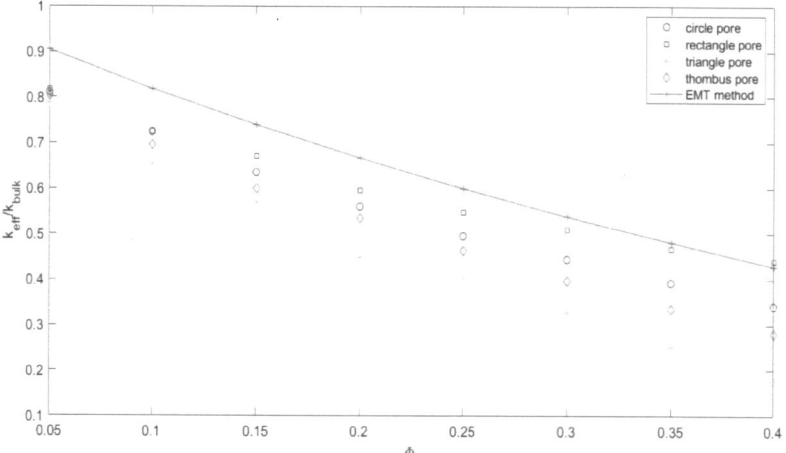

Figure 3. The effective thermal conductivity with two methods in AlN, at 300 k.

Next, based on other influencing factors, we compare the results between the MCBU method and the EMT method in detail. From Table 2, we can conclude that when the characteristic MFP Λ_0 is equal to 0.1 till 0.35, the effective thermal conductivity of rectangular pores is consistent with the EMT method, with a deviation of less than 20%, or even less than 5%. In addition, we find that the calculation time deviation between the two methods can be ignored, which shows the superiority of our method. In other words, it can accurately calculate more complex geometry than the effective medium theory in almost the same time. Figure 4 illustrates that the effective thermal conductivity calculated by the EMT method does not change with the changing of pore shapes and Λ_0. Moreover, from Figure 4, we can conclude that at the porosity of 0.25, the effective thermal conductivity in four kinds of shapes decreases with the increase of the characteristic MFP, and the deviation between the MCBU method and the EMT method decreases when the characteristic MFP decreases. In this figure, the effective thermal conductivity of rectangle pores is the closest to the EMT method.

Table 2. The effective thermal conductivity of rectangle pores compared with the EMT method.

Λ_0 (μm)	k_s	k_m	$\frac{k_m - k_s}{k_m}$ (%)	Deviation of the Computation Time (s)
0.1	0.5782	0.6000	3.6%	3.31×10^{-3}
0.15	0.5531	0.6000	7.8%	3.21×10^{-3}
0.20	0.5324	0.6000	11.3%	3.29×10^{-3}
0.25	0.5148	0.6000	14.2%	3.31×10^{-3}
0.30	0.4994	0.6000	16.8%	3.30×10^{-3}
0.35	0.4856	0.6000	19.1%	3.32×10^{-3}

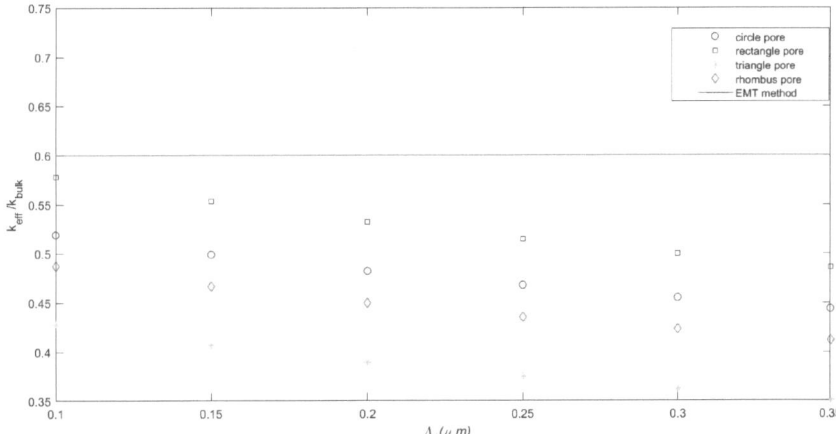

Figure 4. The effective thermal conductivity with the EMT method and the MCBU method with the changes of Λ_0.

Then, we analyze the influence of $S(0)$ on the effective thermal conductivity in AlN, at 300k, and compare the results between MCBU method and the EMT method. From Table 3, we can conclude that the MCBU method is consistent with the effective medium theory method. With the increase of $S(0)$, the deviation will be less than 15%. In addition, we can see that the difference in calculation time between the two methods can be ignored, which again shows the superiority of our method. Figure 5 illustrates that the effective thermal conductivity in four kinds of pore shapes calculated by the MCBU method, and the effective thermal conductivity calculated by the EMT method increases with the increase of $S(0)$ and the deviation between the MCBU method and the EMT method decreases with the increase of $S(0)$.

Table 3. The effective thermal conductivity in circle pores compared with the effective medium theory method.

$S(0)$	k_c	k_m	$\frac{k_m - k_c}{k_m}$ (%)	Deviation of the Computation Time (s)
0.3	0.2321	0.2987	22.3%	3.21×10^{-3}
0.4	0.3227	0.3986	19.0%	3.22×10^{-3}
0.5	0.4150	0.5038	17.6%	3.19×10^{-3}
0.6	0.5084	0.6000	15.3%	3.30×10^{-3}
0.7	0.6027	0.7007	13.9%	3.33×10^{-3}
0.8	0.6976	0.8018	12.8%	3.31×10^{-3}
0.9	0.7930	0.9000	11.9%	3.30×10^{-3}

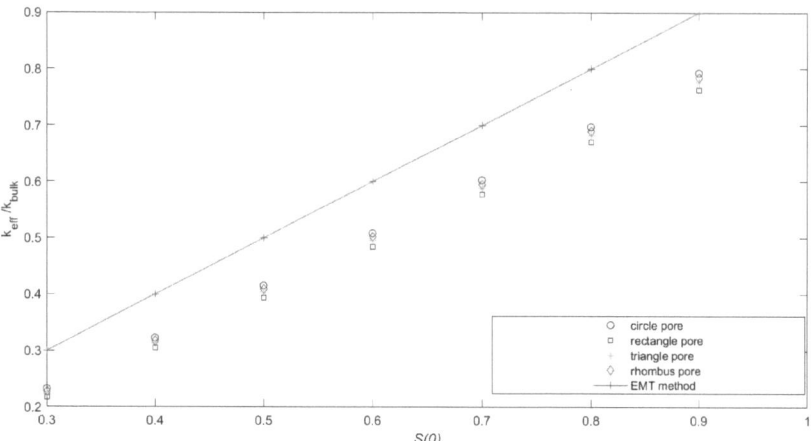

Figure 5. The effective thermal conductivity with the EMT method and the MCBU method with the changes of $S(0)$.

In the following, we analyze the influence of L_c/L on the effective thermal conductivity in AlN, at 300 k, with four kinds of pore shapes and compare the results of the MCBU method and the EMT method. As shown in Table 4, the MCBU method agrees with the EMT method with a deviation between them of less than 20%. Except for the cases where L_c/L equals to 1.8 and 2.0, the deviation between the two methods decreases with the increase of L_c/L, and when $L_c/L \geq 1.7$, the deviation between the two methods is less than 16.2%. From Figure 6, we can see that the two curves increase with the increase of L_c/L.

Table 4. The effective thermal conductivity in circle pores compared with the EMT method.

L_c/L	k_c	k_m	$\frac{k_m - k_c}{k_m}$ (%)	Deviation of the Computation Time (s)
1.5	0.3691	0.4493	17.8%	3.21×10^{-3}
1.6	0.3969	0.4815	17.6%	3.22×10^{-3}
1.7	0.4331	0.5152	15.9%	3.17×10^{-3}
1.8	0.4611	0.5504	16.2%	3.39×10^{-3}
1.9	0.4892	0.5748	15.0%	3.22×10^{-3}
2.0	0.5174	0.6129	15.6%	3.10×10^{-3}

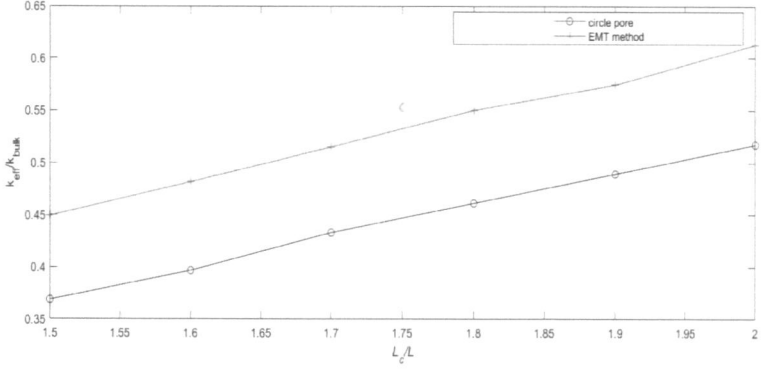

Figure 6. The effective thermal conductivity with the EMT method and the MCBU method with the changes of L_c/L in circle pores.

Then we calculate the effective thermal conductivity in rectangle pores and compare it with the EMT method. From Table 5, we can conclude that the MCBU method agrees with the EMT method with the deviation between them being less than 18%, and except for the cases where L_c/L equals to 1.6 and 1.7, the deviation between the two methods decreases with the increase of L_c/L and when $1.9 \leq L_c/L \leq 2.0$, the deviation between the two methods is less than 16%. Compared with Table 4, we can conclude that k_s is larger than k_c for all the values of L_c/L. From Figure 7, we can conclude that the two curves increase with the increase of L_c/L.

Table 5. The effective thermal conductivity in rectangle pores compared with the EMT method.

L_c/L	k_s	k_m	$\frac{k_m - k_s}{k_m}$ (%)	Deviation of the Computation Time (s)
1.5	0.5496	0.6667	17.6%	3.21×10^{-3}
1.6	0.5953	0.7241	17.8%	3.26×10^{-3}
1.7	0.6330	0.7544	16.1%	3.37×10^{-3}
1.8	0.6791	0.8182	17.0%	3.19×10^{-3}
1.9	0.7170	0.8519	15.8%	3.14×10^{-3}
2.0	0.7549	0.8868	14.9%	3.19×10^{-3}

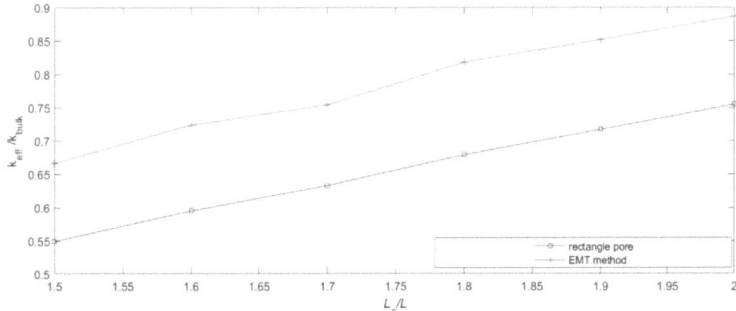

Figure 7. The effective thermal conductivity with the EMT method and the MCBU method with the changes of L_c/L in rectangle pores.

Next, we calculate the effective thermal conductivity in triangle pores and compare it with the EMT and we denote k_t as the thermal conductivity of the MCBU method and k_m as the thermal conductivity of the EMT method. From Table 6 and Figure 8, we can conclude that the effective thermal conductivity increases with the increase of L_c/L. From Table 6, we can conclude that MCBU method agrees with the EMT method with the deviation between them less than 18% and except for the cases where L_c/L equals to 1.6, the deviation between the two methods decreases with the increase of L_c/L and when $1.9 \leq L_c/L \leq 2.0$, the deviation between the two method is less than 15%. Compared with Tables 4–6, we have $k_c < k_t < k_s$ for all the values of L_c/L.

Table 6. The effective thermal conductivity in triangle pores compared with the EMT method.

L_c/L	k_t	k_m	$\frac{k_m - k_t}{k_m}$ (%)	Deviation of the Computation Time (s)
1.5	0.4511	0.5504	18.0%	3.22×10^{-3}
1.6	0.4878	0.5873	16.9%	3.16×10^{-3}
1.7	0.5164	0.6260	17.6%	3.30×10^{-3}
1.8	0.5533	0.6667	17.0%	3.11×10^{-3}
1.9	0.5904	0.6949	15.0%	3.09×10^{-3}
2.0	0.6192	0.7241	14.5%	3.19×10^{-3}

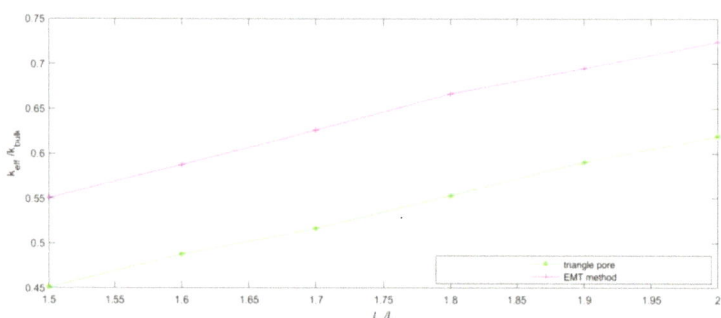

Figure 8. The effective thermal conductivity with the EMT method and the MCBU method with the changes of L_c/L in triangle pores.

Last, we calculate the effective thermal conductivity in rhombus pores and compare it with the EMT and we denote k_r as the thermal conductivity of the MCBU method and k_m as the thermal conductivity of the EMT method. From Table 7 and Figure 9, we can see that the effective thermal conductivity increases with the increase of L_c/L, and from Table 7, we can conclude that the MCBU method agrees with the EMT method with the deviation between them less than 19% and except for this, cases where L_c/L equals to 1.7, the deviation between the two methods decreases with the increase of L_c/L and when $1.7 \leq L_c/L \leq 2.0$, the deviation between the two method is less than 16.6%. Compared with Tables 4–6, we can conclude that $k_c < k_r < k_t < k_s$ for all the values of L_c/L.

Table 7. The effective thermal conductivity in rhombus pores compared with the EMT method.

L_c/L	k_r	k_m	$\frac{k_m-k_r}{k_m}$ (%)	Deviation of the Computation Time (s)
1.5	0.4183	0.5152	18.8%	3.32×10^{-3}
1.6	0.4548	0.5504	17.4%	3.26×10^{-3}
1.7	0.4831	0.5748	16.0%	3.27×10^{-3}
1.8	0.5114	0.6129	16.6%	3.31×10^{-3}
1.9	0.5483	0.6529	16.0%	3.39×10^{-3}
2.0	0.5768	0.6807	15.3%	3.30×10^{-3}

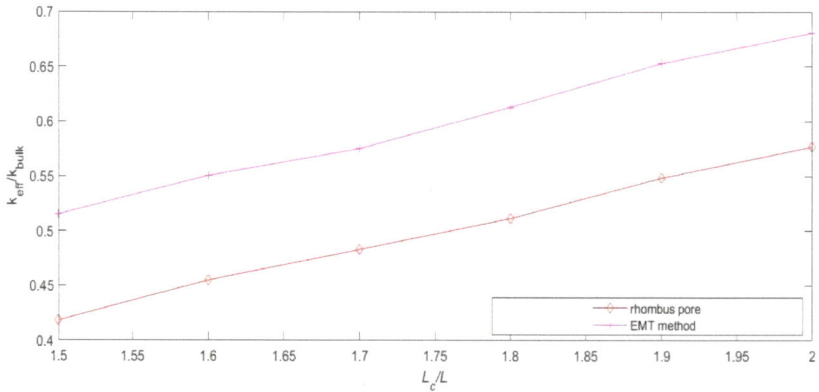

Figure 9. The effective thermal conductivity with the EMT method and the MCBU method in rhombus pores with changes of L_c/L.

Finally, a detailed analysis of influences of geometric parameters is conducted and discussed. In previous studies, the influences of porosity on thermal conductivity have been studied. However, little work has been done on the effects of different porosities on periodic nanoscale structures. In this paper, the effects of porosities on periodic nanostructures in different pore shapes are studied and shown in Figure 10. The black line denotes the circle pores, the blue line denotes the rectangle pores, the green line denotes the triangle pores and the red line denotes the rhombus pores. From Figure 10, it can be observed that the effective thermal conductivity decreases when the porosity increases and this is because the greater the porosity, the more loss of the heat flux passthrough to the material. The effective thermal conductivity of the triangle pore shapes is the most affected and it decreases most rapidly with the increase of the porosity. The thermal conductivity of the rectangle pore shapes is the least affected. With the increase of the porosity, the effective thermal conductivity of the rectangle pores decreases the slowest, followed by the circle pores and the rhombus pores. Let k_c, k_s, k_t, k_r be the effective thermal conductivity of circle pores, rectangle pores, triangle pores, and rhombus pores, respectively. It is clear that under the same porosity and the same temperature, we always have $k_s > k_c > k_r > k_t$ as shown in Figure 10.

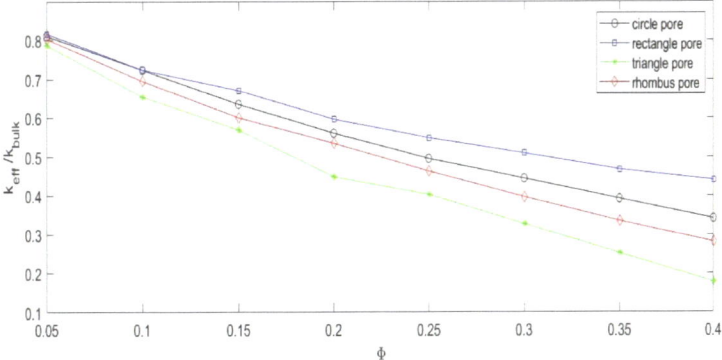

Figure 10. The effective thermal conductivity for four kinds of pore shapes at 300 k, AlN.

To evaluate the influence of the temperature, we calculate the effective thermal conductivity in different temperatures. When the temperature increases, no matter what the shape of the pore and the porosity, the effective thermal conductivity increases too. Without the loss of generality, we calculated the effective thermal conductivity with square shapes in at 200 k, 300 k, 400 k and 500 k, respectively, as shown in Figure 11. From this figure, we can conclude that at the same temperature, the trend of the effective thermal conductivity is dropping while the porosity is increasing and under the same porosity, the trend of conductivity is increasing while the temperature increasing. That is because when the temperature increases, the heat flux increases too and that causes the effective thermal conductivity increase.

To study the influence of the materials, we calculate the effective thermal conductivity with different pore shapes in four materials: AlAs, AlN, GaAs and Si. Without the loss of generality, we calculate the effective thermal conductivity in rectangle shapes in at 300 k. As shown in Figure 12, we can see that under the same porosity and the same temperature, the effective thermal conductivity in material made of AlN is the highest while, at the same time, the effective thermal conductivity in material made of Si is the lowest; the effective thermal conductivity in material made of GaAs is higher than that made of AlAs. Moreover, the thermal conductivity in material made of AlN and GaAs differs slightly but the conductivity in materials made of Si is significantly lower than the former, and this conclusion will not change with the change of the pore shapes. From this result, we can say that in materials made of AlN, there will be less loss of heat flux while in materials made of Si, there will be more loss of heat flux.

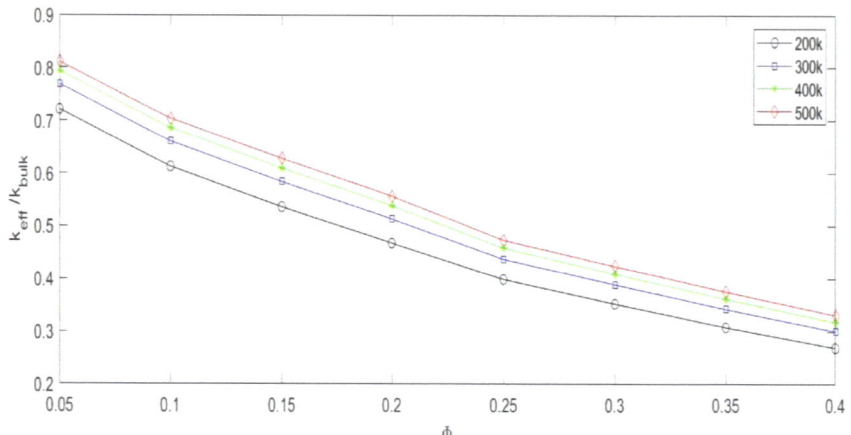

Figure 11. The effective thermal conductivity in square pores with different temperatures for AlAs.

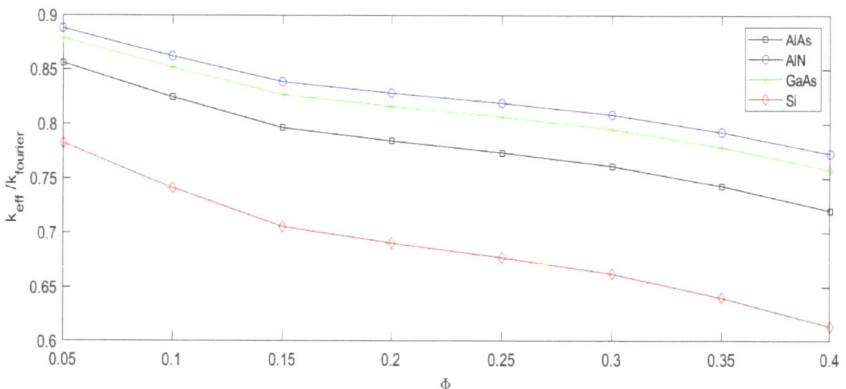

Figure 12. The effective thermal conductivity in rectangle pores with different materials, at 300 k.

In order to evaluate the influence of the location of pore shapes, we calculate the effective thermal conductivity in material made of AlAs for two kinds of rectangles. For one kind of rectangle, we set the parameter as $P_l = 2P_d$ which means the aspect ratio of the rectangle is 2 and for the other kind of the rectangle, we set the parameter as $P_d = 2P_l$ which means the aspect ratio of the rectangle is 0.5, as shown in Figure 13. From this figure, it can be clearly seen that the effective thermal conductivity of the rectangle with $P_l = 2P_d$ structure is always higher than the rectangle with $P_d = 2P_l$ structure and the gap between the two line widens with the growth of the porosity. From this result, we can see that the locations of the pores block the heat flux through the materials, changing the direction of the heat flux and affecting the effective thermal conductivity.

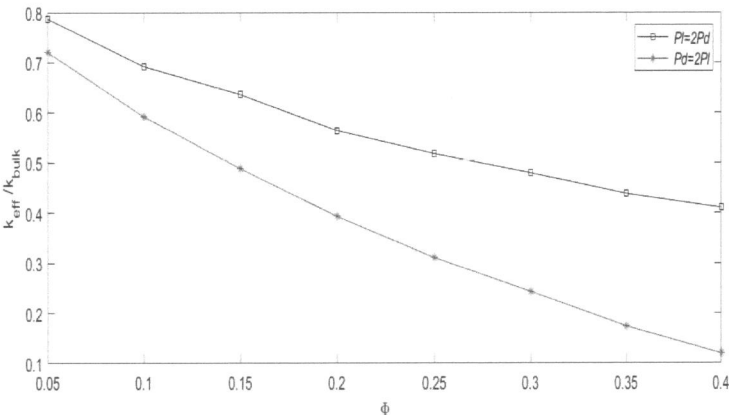

Figure 13. Rectangle pores with the length along the abscissa.

4. Conclusions

The EMT is a widely used method to predict the thermal conductivity in nanostructures. However, the thermal conductivity of different pore shapes cannot be described well. In the present work, a novel MC method is developed to overcome this deficiency. Several numerical experiments have been conducted to verify the present MCBU method. The MUBU method estimates the results well. The following conclusions can be obtained:

1. Λ_0, $S(0)$, L_c are the main parameters which can influence the effective thermal conductivity which is calculated by the MCBU method. The effective thermal conductivity decreases with the increases of Λ_0 and the effective thermal conductivity increases with the increases of the $S(0)$, L_c, respectively.
2. Pore shapes and porosity can influence the effective thermal conductivity. For the same porosity, the effective thermal conductivity in rectangle pores is always higher than circle pores, triangle pores and rhombus pores. At the same time, the effective thermal conductivity in triangle pores is the lowest compared to other pores. For the same pore shape, the effective thermal conductivity decreases with the increases of porosity.
3. The MCBU method can agree well with the EMT method with the same time requirements and the MCBU can calculate the effective thermal conductivity in complex pore shapes more accurately.

The MCBU method can efficiently calculate the thermal conductivity of different pore shapes. Although it can calculate the thermal conductivity of regular pore shapes, such as circle, rectangle, triangle and rhombus, it still has some limitations. To date, little work has been done on irregular pore shapes. The future research direction is to develop a method to calculate the effective thermal conductivity with irregular pore shapes, or try to cut irregular pore shapes into relatively regular shapes. In this way, a new method can be obtained to calculate the effective thermal conductivity with irregular and arbitrary pore shapes.

Author Contributions: Writing—original draft, E.C.; Writing—review & editing, Z.Y. All authors have read and agreed to the published version of the manuscript.

Funding: This research was funded by the National Natural Science Foundation of China (Grants 11002026, 11372039), the Beijing Natural Science Foundation (Grant 3133039), and the Scientific Research Foundation for the Returned (Grant 20121832001).

Acknowledgments: The authors gratefully acknowledge the support by the National Natural Science Foundation of China (Grants 11002026, 11372039), the Beijing Natural Science Foundation (Grant 3133039), and the Scientific Research Foundation for the Returned (Grant 20121832001).

Conflicts of Interest: The authors declare no conflict of interest.

Nomenclature

F_{ml}	A term which depends on Λ_m and $\hat{S}_l$
Λ_m	Phonon mean free path
$\Delta T_{ml}^{(n)}$	Pseudo-temperature
$\alpha_{m'l'}$	A coefficient in Equation (2)
$\hat{S}_l$	Phonon direction function
J	Heat flux
A	Surface area
L	Periodicity
$\hat{n}$	Direction vector
C_v	Heat capacity
v_j	Velocity
L_{rp}	The length from the point r to the point p at pore boundaries
Λ	Intrinsic MFP
$S(\overline{\Lambda}_{bulk,j})$	Suppression function
Λ_0	Medium MFP
L_c	The mean light-of-sight between phonon scattering events with nanostructure
p_0	The initial phonon transmittance
p_i	The internal phonon transmittance
ΔL	The length of simulation unit
l_0	The average MFP
R_p	Pore radius
Φ	Porosity
t_s	Computation time of the MCBU method
t_m	Computation time of the EMT method
k_m	Effective thermal conductivity of the EMT method
k_s	Effective thermal conductivity of rectangle pore in the MCBU method
k_c	Effective thermal conductivity of circle pore in the MCBU method
k_t	Effective thermal conductivity of triangle pore in the MCBU method
k_r	Effective thermal conductivity of rhombus pore in the MCBU method
P_l	The length of the rectangle
P_d	The width of the rectangle

References

1. Hua, Y.-C.; Cao, B.-Y. An efficient two-step Monte Carlo method for heat conduction in nanostructures. *J. Comput. Phys.* **2017**, *342*, 253–266. [CrossRef]
2. Wang, D.; Qu, Z.; Ma, Y. An enhanced Gray model for nondiffusive heat conduction solved by implicit lattice Boltzmann method. *Int. J. Heat Mass Transf.* **2016**, *94*, 411–418. [CrossRef]
3. Fučík, R.; Straka, R. Equivalent finite difference and partial differential equations for the lattice Boltzmann method. *Comput. Math. Appl.* **2021**, *90*, 96–103. [CrossRef]
4. Gibanov, N.S.; Rashidi, M.M.; Sheremet, M. Comparative analysis of the lattice Boltzmann method and the finite difference technique of thermal convection in closed domains with heaters. *Int. J. Numer. Methods Heat Fluid Flow* **2022**, *32*. [CrossRef]
5. Chattopadhyay, A.; Pattamatta, A. A Comparative Study of Submicron Phonon Transport Using the Boltzmann Transport Equation and the Lattice Boltzmann Method. *Numer. Heat Transf. Part B Fundam.* **2014**, *66*, 360–379. [CrossRef]
6. Guo, Y.; Wang, M. Lattice Boltzmann modeling of phonon transport. *J. Comput. Phys.* **2016**, *315*, 1–15. [CrossRef]
7. Cheng, W.; Alkurdi, A.; Chapuis, P.-O. Coupling Mesoscopic Boltzmann Transport Equation and Macroscopic Heat Diffusion Equation for Multiscale Phonon Heat Conduction. *Nanoscale Microscale Thermophys. Eng.* **2020**, *24*, 150–167. [CrossRef]
8. Yang, Z.; Liu, S.; Zhuo, C.; Zhong, C. Pseudopotential-based discrete unified gas kinetic scheme for modeling multiphase fluid flows. *Adv. Aerodyn.* **2022**, *4*, 1–26. [CrossRef]
9. Abouelregal, A.E.; Marin, M. The Response of Nanobeams with Temperature-Dependent Properties Using State-Space Method via Modified Couple Stress Theory. *Symmetry* **2020**, *12*, 1276. [CrossRef]
10. Scutaru, M.L.; Vlase, S.; Marin, M.; Modrea, A. New analytical method based on dynamic response of planar mechanical elastic systems. *Bound. Value Probl.* **2020**, *2020*, 104. [CrossRef]
11. Jean, V.; Fumeron, S.; Termentzidis, K.; Tutashkonko, S.; Lacroix, D. Monte Carlo simulations of phonon transport in nanoporous silicon and germanium. *J. Appl. Phys.* **2014**, *115*, 024304. [CrossRef]

12. Wolf, S.; Neophytou, N.; Kosina, H. Thermal conductivity of silicon nanomeshes: Effects of porosity and roughness. *J. Appl. Phys.* **2014**, *115*, 204306. [CrossRef]
13. Jeng, M.-S.; Yang, R.; Song, D.; Chen, G. Modeling the Thermal Conductivity and Phonon Transport in Nanoparticle Composites Using Monte Carlo Simulation. *J. Heat Transf.* **2008**, *130*, 042410. [CrossRef]
14. Péraud, J.; Hadjiconstantinou, N. Efficient simulation of multidimensional phonon transport using energy-based variance-reduced Monte Carlo formulations. *Phys. Rev. B* **2021**, *84*, 205331. [CrossRef]
15. Tang, D.-S.; Cao, B.-Y. Ballistic thermal wave propagation along nanowires modeled using phonon Monte Carlo simulations. *Appl. Therm. Eng.* **2017**, *117*, 609–616. [CrossRef]
16. Tang, D.-S.; Hua, Y.-C.; Cao, B.-Y. Thermal wave propagation through nanofilms in ballistic-diffusive regime by Monte Carlo simulations. *Int. J. Therm. Sci.* **2016**, *109*, 81–89. [CrossRef]
17. Wen, Z.; Xu, H.; Zhao, W.; Zhou, Z.; Li, X.; Li, S.; Zhou, J.; Sun, Y.; Dai, N.; Hao, J. Nonlocal effective-medium theory for periodic multilayered metamaterials. *J. Opt.* **2021**, *23*, 065103. [CrossRef]
18. Tang, S.; Zhu, B.; Jia, M.; He, Q.; Sun, S.; Mei, Y.; Zhou, L. Effective-medium theory for one-dimensional gratings. *Phys. Rev. B* **2015**, *91*, 174201. [CrossRef]
19. Liu, T.; Ma, S.; Yang, B.; Xiao, S.; Zhou, L. Effective-medium theory for multilayer metamaterials: Role of near-field corrections. *Phys. Rev. B* **2020**, *102*, 174208. [CrossRef]
20. Hao, Z.; Zhuang, Y.; Chen, Y.; Liu, Y.; Chen, H. Effective medium theory of checkboard structures in the long-wavelength limit. *Chin. Opt. Lett.* **2020**, *18*, 072401. [CrossRef]
21. Hosseini, S.A.; Khanniche, S.; Greaney, P.A.; Romano, G. Universal effective medium theory to predict the thermal conductivity in nanostructured materials. *Int. J. Heat Mass Transf.* **2021**, *183*, 122040. [CrossRef]
22. Lin, S.; Liu, Y.; Cai, Z.; Zhao, C. High-Throughput Screening of Aperiodic Superlattices Based on Atomistic Simulation-Informed Effective Medium Theory and Genetic Algorithm. *Int. J. Heat Mass Transf.* **2023**, *202*. [CrossRef]
23. Meng, Q.; Bai, Z.; Diao, H.; Liu, H. Effective Medium Theory for Embedded Obstacles in Elasticity with Applications to Inverse Problems. *SIAM J. Appl. Math.* **2022**, *82*, 720–749. [CrossRef]
24. Kilany, A.; Abo-Dahab, S.; Abd-Alla, A.; Aboelnour, N. Photothermal and void effect of a semiconductor rotational medium based on Lord-Shulman theory. *Mech. Based Des. Struct. Mach.* **2022**, *50*, 2555–2568. [CrossRef]
25. Li, J.; Li, Y.; Wang, W.; Li, L.; Qiu, C.-W. Effective medium theory for thermal scattering off rotating structures. *Opt. Express* **2020**, *28*, 25894. [CrossRef] [PubMed]
26. Qin, F.; Peng, M.; Estevez, D.; Brosseau, C. Electromagnetic composites: From effective medium theories to metamaterials. *J. Appl. Phys.* **2022**, *132*, 101101. [CrossRef]
27. Liang, Q.; He, Y.-L.; Ren, Q.; Zhou, Y.-P.; Xie, T. A detailed study on phonon transport in thin silicon membranes with phononic crystal nanostructures. *Appl. Energy* **2018**, *227*, 731–741. [CrossRef]
28. Hua, Y.; Cao, B.-Y. Interface-based two-way tuning of the in-plane thermal transport in nanofilms. *J. Appl. Phys.* **2018**, *123*, 114304. [CrossRef]
29. Majumdar, A. Microscale Heat Conduction in Dielectric Thin Films. *J. Heat Transf.* **1993**, *115*, 7–16. [CrossRef]
30. Zeng, Y.; Marconnet, A. Reevaluating the suppression function for phonon transport in nanostructures by Monte Carlo techniques. *J. Appl. Phys.* **2019**, *125*, 034301. [CrossRef]
31. Hua, Y.-C.; Cao, B.-Y. Cross-plane heat conduction in nanoporous silicon thin films by phonon Boltzmann transport equation and Monte Carlo simulations. *Appl. Therm. Eng.* **2017**, *111*, 1401–1408. [CrossRef]
32. Lee, J.; Lee, W.; Wehmeyer, G.; Dhuey, S.; Olynick, D.L.; Cabrini, S.; Dames, C.; Urban, J.J.; Yang, P. Investigation of phonon coherence and backscattering using silicon nanomeshes. *Nat. Commun.* **2017**, *8*, 14054. [CrossRef]
33. Péraud, J.-P.M.; Hadjiconstantinou, N.G. An alternative approach to efficient simulation of micro/nanoscale phonon transport. *Appl. Phys. Lett.* **2012**, *101*, 153114. [CrossRef]
34. Schleeh, J.; Mateos, J.; Íñiguez-de-la-Torre, I.; Wadefalk, N.; Nilsson, P.A.; Grahn, J.; Minnich, A. Phonon black-body radiation limit for heat dissipation in electronics. *Nat. Mater.* **2014**, *14*, 187–192. [CrossRef] [PubMed]
35. Ravichandran, N.K.; Minnich, A.J. Coherent and incoherent thermal transport in nanomeshes. *Phys. Rev. B* **2014**, *89*, 205432. [CrossRef]

Disclaimer/Publisher's Note: The statements, opinions and data contained in all publications are solely those of the individual author(s) and contributor(s) and not of MDPI and/or the editor(s). MDPI and/or the editor(s) disclaim responsibility for any injury to people or property resulting from any ideas, methods, instructions or products referred to in the content.

Article

LLE-NET: A Low-Light Image Enhancement Algorithm Based on Curve Estimation

Xiujie Cao * and Jingjun Yu

School of Mechanical Engineering and Automation, Beihang University, Beijing 100191, China; jjyu@buaa.edu.cn
* Correspondence: caoxiujie@buaa.edu.cn

Abstract: Low-light image enhancement is very significant for vision tasks. We introduce Low-light Image Enhancement via Deep Learning Network (LLE-NET), which employs a deep network to estimate curve parameters. Cubic curves and gamma correction are employed for enhancing low-light images. Our research trains a lightweight network to estimate the parameters that determine the correction curve. By the results of the deep learning network, accurate correction curves are confirmed, which are used for the per-pixel correction of RGB channels. The image enhanced by our models closely resembles the input image. To further accelerate the inferring speed of the low-light enhancement model, a low-light enhancement model based on gamma correction is proposed with one iteration. LLE-NET exhibits remarkable inference speed, achieving 400 fps on a single GPU for images sized $640 \times 480 \times 3$ while maintaining pleasing enhancement quality. The enhancement model based on gamma correction attains an impressive inference speed of 800 fps for images sized $640 \times 480 \times 3$ on a single GPU.

Keywords: low-light image enhancement; curve enhancement; zero-reference learning

MSC: 03C30

1. Introduction

Recently, there has been significant development in image-based applications due to continuous development in image-processing algorithms and camera sensors [1]. However, the acquired images are often under-exposed due to inevitable environmental, or technical factors [2], including scene conditions, inadequate illumination or suboptimal camera parameters [3]. Low-light images consistently exhibit low contrast and visibility, presenting challenges for human perception and various high-level visual tasks [4,5], such as object detection [6], object segmentation [7], and object tracking [8]. Low-light image enhancement has a wide range of applications, and reliable low-light image enhancement techniques can improve the visual effects of application scenarios. Enhancing low-light images can effectively enhance the performance of visual simultaneous localization and mapping (SLAM) in low-light underwater conditions [9]. Low-light image enhancement can be used in imaged-based 3D reconstruction in low-light conditions [10]. Enhancing low-light images for lane detection under low-light environments plays a significant role in advanced driver assistance systems (ADAS) [11]. Therefore, the exploration of low-light image enhancement has emerged as a challenging and dynamically evolving research domain [12].

The aims of low-light image enhancement are to enhance the visibility and contrast of low-light images [13]. Numerous conventional methods for enhancing low-light images have been implemented [14,15]. Conventional processing methods typically depend on specific statistical models and assumptions, such as the Retinex model [15] and histogram equalization [16]. Nevertheless, these techniques necessitate parameter adjustments tailored to varying application scenarios, and the imprecise statistical models can easily introduce excessive artifacts [13]. Traditional methods work well for low-contrast images (such as overall darker images); however, they often do not take into account the effects

Citation: Cao, X.; Yu, J. LLE-NET: A Low-Light Image Enhancement Algorithm Based on Curve Estimation. *Mathematics* **2024**, *12*, 1228. https://doi.org/10.3390/math12081228

Academic Editors: Lihua Wang, Benny Y. C. Hon and Sheng-Wei Chi

Received: 18 March 2024
Revised: 13 April 2024
Accepted: 15 April 2024
Published: 19 April 2024

Copyright: © 2024 by the authors. Licensee MDPI, Basel, Switzerland. This article is an open access article distributed under the terms and conditions of the Creative Commons Attribution (CC BY) license (https://creativecommons.org/licenses/by/4.0/).

of spatially varing illumination, leading to an unbalanced intensity distribution in local areas [17]. In recent years, a plethora of deep-learning models have surfaced for tasks related to enhancing low-light images. In comparison to conventional methods, these deep-learning approaches offer superior accuracy, robustness, and speed [18]. Despite the substantial performance enhancements brought about by learning-based approaches, a new issue has arisen known as learning bias. This refers to the phenomenon wherein the enhancement results are heavily influenced by the characteristics of the training dataset. In other words, the enhancement effect of low-light image enhancement algorithms using supervised learning is influenced by the low-light image training dataset. The creation of paired low-light image training datasets involves significant subjective factors. To mitigate this constraint, recent exploration has focused on unsupervised learning models utilizing unpaired data. The aim is to develop robust algorithms capable of maintaining generality across diverse real-world scenarios, thus obviating the need for paired data [17]. While learning-based methods often yield satisfactory results, many of them demand substantial computational resources and entail long inference times. Consequently, their suitability for real-time systems or mobile applications is limited [19].

In tasks such as object detection and visual SLAM, low-light image enhancement algorithms based on deep learning commonly serve as preprocessing algorithms for real-time tasks. Thus, low-light image enhancement demands high real-time processing speeds. The bright areas in the enhanced image should be kept from overexposure, and the brightness in dark areas should be increased. The enhanced image should have minimal color distortion. Visual SLAM algorithms are often applied in various application scenarios; hence, it is desired that the low-light enhancement algorithms minimize the influence of paired datasets as much as possible. Therefore, we are looking for low-light image enhancement algorithms that are better suited for image preprocessing in visual tasks related to visual SLAM, with an emphasis on reducing dependency on paired datasets.

Our motivations. To address the problem of image enhancement in low-light environments for visual SLAM, we have designed a low-light image enhancement network. Firstly, in order to improve the algorithm's adaptability to different scenes, we prioritize using a Zero-shot low-light image enhancement method, avoiding the use of paired training datasets. Secondly, to enhance the inference speed of low-light image enhancement and better meet the real-time requirements of visual SLAM, we have designed a low-light image enhancement method based on gamma correction [20]. Furthermore, to achieve better low-light image enhancement results, we propose a cubic curve enhancement method based on multiple iterations. To fulfill SLAM requirements, our method ensures a close resemblance between the enhanced image and the original input to maintain accuracy.

Our contributions. Our model is inspired by Zero-DCE [21] and LUT-GCE [22]. Different from the Zero-DCE algorithm, we abandon the method of estimating curve parameter maps, and instead, we use a deep-learning network to predict the control parameters of enhancement curves. Unlike LUT-GCE, we improved the network architecture, redesigned the loss function, and additionally introduced a gamma correction-based enhancement method. In comparison to existing open-source deep learning algorithms for enhancing low-light images, our method demonstrates superior performance in both inference speed and resemblance.

Our primary contributions are outlined below:

- A low-light image enhancement model(LLE-NET) based on curve estimation is proposed which estimates the control parameters of enhancement curves. LLE-NET eliminates the need for paired training data, mitigating the risk of overfitting and demonstrating strong generalization across diverse lighting conditions.
- Cubic curves and gamma correction are used in this enhancement method. If computing power permits, using a cubic enhancement curve can achieve fine results. If the computational burden is heavy, a method based on gamma correction for low-light image enhancement can be chosen.

- We conduct extensive experiments to validate the effectiveness of LLE-NET across a wide range of comparison methods and affirm its efficacy.

2. Related Work

In this section, a concise overview of previous works related to low-light image enhancement is introduced, including traditional methods and learning-based methods.

2.1. Traditional Enhancement Methods

Histogram Equalization (HE) is one of the simplest and most commonly used techniques for enhancing low-light images [23]. HE simplifies global statistics by utilizing statistical information across all pixel values, representing them in terms of the density of pixel values [19,24]. Brithness Preserving Bi-Histogram Equalization(BPBHE) was proposed to address the issue of the flattening effect observed in HE methods [25]. Recently, the enhancement of images using HE has been formulated as an optimization problem [23,26]. Gamma correction is applied to color space components with the aim of enhancing contrast [27]. A contrast-limited adaptive histogram equalization (CLAHE) with color correction based on normalized gamma transformation in the Lab color space is suggested for enhancing low-light images [28].

Retinex theory-based methods for enhancing low-light images have attracted significant attention [4,29]. The Retinex model decomposes low-light images into reflection and illumination components [12]. A multi-scale Retinex-based approach utilizing the illumination components is employed for enhancing image contrast [30]. A multi-scale Retinex with color restoration (MSRCR) technique is suggested to address image degradation under foggy weather conditions [31]. An enhanced Retinex algorithm is proposed for enhancing low-light images, addressing issues such as local halo blurring [32].

These traditional methods lack adaptability and may result in significant noise, as well as over- and/or under-enhancement in their outcomes [29]. Global HE methods are based on the grayscale content of the entire image and modify pixels through a transformation function, which can easily lead to local overexposure. Local HE methods consider the equalization of neighborhood pixels by using their histogram intensity statistics. The original image is divided into various sub-blocks in the form of squares or rectangles. Histogram equalization transformation functions are computed at each position by calculating the histogram of neighborhood points, resulting in a checkerboard effect in the enhanced image [23]. Retinex theory-based methods are prone to unnatural and overexposure effects, presenting a challenge in adaptability across various scenes [4]. Furthermore, the computational cost of Retinex algorithms that use traditional iterative optimization for adjusting a single image is high, hindering their application in real-time conditions. Consequently, many deep learning algorithms that improve upon Retinex have been proposed.

2.2. Learning-Based Methods

Recently, learning-based approaches for various vision tasks have been developed. Current low-light image enhancement methods using deep learning can be categorized into four groups: supervised learning, unsupervised learning, semi-supervised learning, and zero-shot learning methods [12].

Supervised learning methods have shown considerable advancements in low-light image enhancement. MBLLEN [33] leverages multi-branch fusion to extract diverse features across various levels, generating the final output image. The SID dataset is obtained by varying the ISO settings while maintaining constant the position of the camera [6,34]. These datasets are often constructed through subjective retouching processes or artificial adjustments of camera parameters [17]. Low-light images are often affected by changes in illumination, color distortion, and noise, making it challenging to determine a singular well-lit reference ground. Consequently, the preference for an enhanced image often varies depending on the user's choice. Obtaining a true paired image dataset is difficult due to these variations. To mitigate the requirement for extensive training data, large-scale paired low-light datasets are synthesized using efficient low-light simulation techniques. An attention-guided low-light image enhancement approach is proposed, utilizing the synthesized paired simulation dataset [20]. The deep-learning enhancement methods based on Retinex are implemented, such as RetinexNet [35], RUAS [29], KinD [36], SCI [37]. The method based on the exposure prediction model (EPIM) and feature extraction module (FEM) is proposed using hybrid feature weighted fusion strategy [38].

To mitigate the impact of paired training data, unsupervised generative adversarial networks, such as CycleGAN [39] and EnlightenGAN [40] are proposed, eliminating the need for paired low-light image datasets. However, unsupervised GAN-based methods typically require a meticulous selection of unpaired training data. The method based on multi-objective grey wolf optimization is proposed without the need for low-light and normal images as training data [41].

In contrast, zero-shot learning approaches circumvent the need for pre-training and can directly enhance images from input low-light images. Zero-DCE [21] employs pixel-wise and uses high-order curve estimation to dynamically adjust the dynamic range of an input image. RRDNet [42] decomposes the input image into three components, illumination, reflection, and noise. Algorithms based on multi-objective grey wolf optimization introduce transformer structures and attention-guided mechanisms, resulting in larger model sizes compared to Zero-DCE [21], thus leading to poor real-time performance. To expedite inference speed, a single convolutional layer model (SCLM) utilizing effective structural re-parameterization techniques is proposed [19].

Algorithms for low-light image enhancement using supervised learning are often influenced by the training dataset, but they generally perform better in environments similar to the training set. In contrast, unsupervised learning-based low-light image enhancement algorithms avoid the influence of datasets, but many of these algorithms have a heavy computational burden, making them unsuitable for real-time applications, such as EnlightenGAN [40] and the method based on multi-objective grey wolf optimization [41]. The advantage of Zero-shot algorithms is that they avoid the constraint of paired datasets, but the drawback is that they may produce less detailed enhanced images due to the lack of constraints from paired datasets. In practice, current deep learning algorithms have their own strengths and weaknesses based on different evaluation metrics. Generally, evaluations are conducted based on actual application scenarios, such as the requirement for high real-time performance or high enhancement quality. While learning-based methods have delivered satisfactory outcomes, ensuring short inference times is crucial for real-time applications.

3. Proposed Method

The framework of LLE-NET is shown in Figure 1. To accelerate the inference speed, we initially resize the input image to a consistent size $3 \times 128 \times 128$ pixels using downsampling. Then the resized image is put into the LLE-NET model which predicts Low-light Enhancement curves (LE-curve) trainable parameters. The number of output results predicted by LLE-NET is correlated with the iteration count. Next, the RGB channels of the input image are sequentially enhanced based on the LE-curve defined by the predicted parameters. If the iteration count is greater than 1, the result of the last iterative enhancement image is used as input, and iterative enhancement is performed again using the parameters estimated by LLE-NET until the number of iterations n is reached. We will provide a detailed introduction to the LE-curve, the LLE-NET framework, and the definition of non-reference loss function.

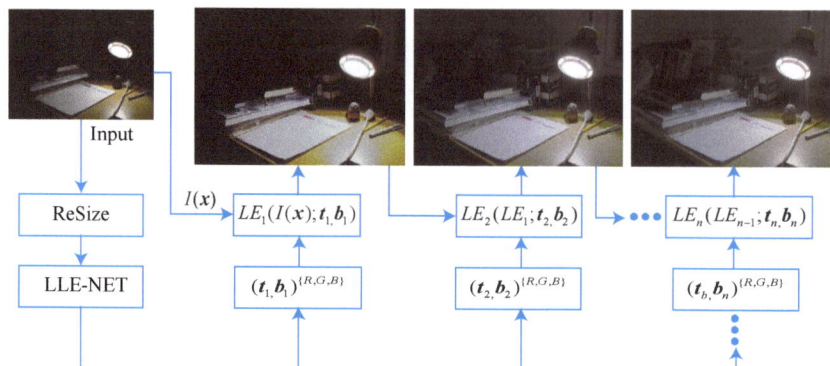

Figure 1. Framework of LLE-NET. LLE-NET is designed to predict parameters for Light-Enhancement curves(LE-curve). LE-curves are applied to iteratively enhance a given image.

3.1. Low-Light Enhancement Curve

According to the requirements of histogram equalization, if the transformation curve exhibits the following characteristics, it can be utilized as an enhancement curve. Zero-DCE [21] and LUT-GCE [22] have already demonstrated their feasibility.

(1) The enhancement curve is required to be a continuously ascending function to maintain the contrast between adjacent pixels.
(2) After normalizing the image, each enhanced pixel value should be confined within the range of [0, 1] to prevent overflow truncation.
(3) The transformation function should aim for simplicity while remaining differentiable for efficient backpropagation.

We use the cubic curve from reference [22]. The definition of a cubic transformation curve is

$$LE(I(x); a, t, b, h) = a(I(x) - t)^3 + bI(x) + h, \qquad (1)$$

where $LE(I(x); a, t, b, h)$ represents the enhanced images of the provided input $I(x)$, x denotes the image pixel, $I(x)$ is the corresponding pixel value, a, t, b and h are trainable curve parameters. If a, t, b and h are given, the cubic curve will be fully defined.

With the constraints $LE(0) = 0$ and $LE(1) = 1$, we can derive

$$LE = \begin{cases} -at^3 + h = 0 & I(x) = 0 \\ a(1-t)^3 + b + h = 1 & I(x) = 1 \end{cases}. \qquad (2)$$

Furthermore, it can be obtained as formula

$$\begin{cases} a = \frac{(1-b)}{(1-t)^3 + t^3} \\ h = \frac{t^3(1-b)}{(1-t)^3 + t^3} \end{cases}. \qquad (3)$$

By computing the derivative of Equation (1), we can obtain that

$$LE'(I(x); a, t, b, h) = 3a(I(x) - t)^2 + b. \qquad (4)$$

When we set $a \geq 0$ and $b \geq 0$, it ensures that the derivative function values are greater than 0. Equation (1) maintains monotonicity to retain the contrast between adjacent pixels.

Next we can reformulate the cubic curve Equation (1) as (5), where $t, b \in [0, 1]$ are trainable curve parameters.

$$LE(I(x); t, b) = \frac{(1-b)(I(x) - t)^3}{(1-t)^3 + t^3} + bI(x) + \frac{t^3(1-b)}{(1-t)^3 + t^3} \tag{5}$$

The LE-curve defined in Equation (1) can be iteratively applied to improve enhancement outcomes in difficult low-light conditions. Equation (6) defines the iterative formula, where n represents the number of iterations. When n is equal to 1, Equation (6) can be degraded to Equation (1).

$$LE_{c,n}(LE_{c,n-1}; a_n, t_n, b_n, h_n) = a_n(LE_{c,n-1} - t_n)^3 + b_n LE_{c,n-1} + h_n \tag{6}$$

Only using variables (t, b), Equation (6) can be reformulated as Equation (7).

$$LE_{c,n}(LE_{c,n-1}; t_n, b_n) = \frac{(1-b_n)(LE_{c,n-1} - t_n)^3}{(1-t_n)^3 + t_n^3} + b_n LE_{c,n-1} + \frac{t_n^3(1-b_n)}{(1-t_n)^3 + t_n^3} \tag{7}$$

To accelerate inference speed, if we set n as equal to 1 using a cubic curve as the enhancement curve, the brightness and contrast of the enhanced image are not very good. So, we cannot simply accelerate the inference speed by reducing the number of iterations as conducted in the Zero-DCE [21] method. However, we try to make our model meet the requirements of real-time applications. In reference [20], low-light images can be converted into normal-light images through a combination of linear and gamma transformations. So, we use gamma correction to enhance low-light images.

The LE-curve based on gamma correction is defined as Equation (7). Ref. [20] shows the synthetic under-exposed image includes gamma transformation and linear transformation. So we add the variable b as the linear transformation.

$$LE(I(x); t, b)^{(i)} = I^{(i)}(x)^t + b \quad i \in \{R, G, B\} \tag{8}$$

To ensure better enhancement performance, LE-cures are applied to the RGB three channels separately. So $t = (t_R, t_G, t_B)$ and $b = (b_R, b_G, b_B)$ are valid.

Even though the gamma correction can enhance the contrast of a low-light image quickly, there is a specific issue that needs clarification. Since the variable t is the exponential part of the gamma function if multiple iterations are performed the derivation will increase rapidly during backpropagation. This makes it is difficult to converge, resulting in training failure. Therefore, the iterative number can only be 1 when using gamma correction enhancement which was verified during subsequent training. Although gamma correction can only be iterated once, it still achieves pleasing enhancement effects.

3.2. LLE-NET

To adapt the algorithm to input images of different resolutions and reduce the computational burden, the input image is downsampled to $3 \times 128 \times 128$. To keep less change in the low-light regions, each input pixel value should be within the normalized range of [0, 1]. Divide the pixel values represented as integers by 255 to normalize each pixel value to the range of [0, 1]. When enhancing the input image, perform channel-wise operations on the R, G, B channels. Therefore, for channel $i \in \{R, G, B\}$, $t = (t_R, t_G, t_B)$ and $b = (b_R, b_G, b_B)$ should be predicted.

Figure 2 illustrates the detailed structure of LLE-NET when the LE-curve is a cubic curve. The resized images are applied as the input of LLE-NET, which contains three convolutional layers with a simplified channel attention layer [43]. After downsampling, the image is passed through a 3×3 convolution for dimensionality expansion, followed by average pooling for a 1/2 downsampling operation. The GeLu activation function [44] is utilized in the attention layer to improve gradient preservation. Moreover, a sigmoid operation is applied to ensure that the values of each feature map are within the [0, 1] range. Similar operations continue until the feature map dimension is reduced to (64, 16, 16). Further reduction in dimensionality is achieved through the two-dimensional adaptive average pooling operation(AdaptiveAvgPool2D) to obtain a dimension of (64, 1, 1). After the adaptive average pooling layer, the subsequent layers consist of a flattened layer followed by a linear layer. The predicted result is to generate a $6n$-dimensional vector, where n is iteratively numbers. Parameters $\{t_n, b_n\}_{j=1}^{j=n}$ are used to construct n iteration-specific cubic curves for iterative enhancement. Each iteration applies three LE curves for the three channels in RGB color space. The blue dashed box combined with the green dashed box in the figure constitutes the complete network architecture of LLE-NET with four iterations. The network outputs 24-dimensional data, including t and b for RGB 3 channels used in each iteration. There are six parameters used per iteration with four iterations; the network's output data are, therefore, 24-dimensional.

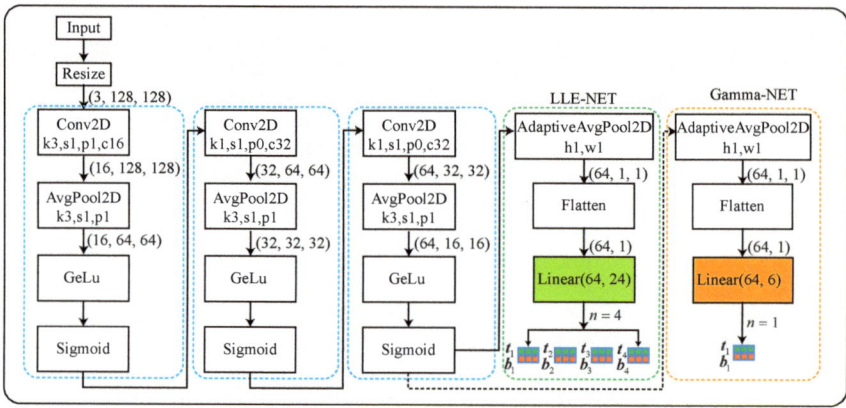

Figure 2. Architecture of LLE-NET and Gamma-NET.

After obtaining t_n and b_n through LLE-NET, plugging them into Equation (7) yields enhancement curves for each iteration. Referring to the algorithm flow in Figure 1, enhance each input image with the LE curve to obtain the image after this iteration's enhancement until the entire iteration is completed.

3.3. Gamma-NET

We use the same network as LLE-NET when the LE-curve is gamma correction, and set n is equal to 1. If the LE-curve is gamma correction, the enhancement network is remarked as Gamma-NET, as shown in Figure 2. The blue dashed box and the orange dashed box in Figure 2 form the complete structure of the Gamma-NET network. Since the number of iterations is $n = 1$, the output dimension of the linear layer is 6. In fact, when n is equal to 1, we can regard Gamma-NET as adaptively estimating gamma correction parameters through a deep-learning network. From the perspective of network architecture, Gamma-NET and LLE-NET only differ in the output of the linear layer. In fact, when the number of iterations for LLE-NET reduces to 1, the network structures of the two are identical with the only difference being in the enhancement curves.

After obtaining the enhancement curve parameters through Gamma-NET, plugging these parameters into Equation (8) yields specific low-light enhancement curves. By enhancing the original input images with these enhancement curves, the final enhanced images can be obtained.

3.4. Non-Reference Loss Function

We define the spatial consistency loss, exposure control loss and color constancy loss to be the same as those in Zero-DCE [21]. The spatial consistency loss L_{spa} maintains the distinction between adjacent regions in both the input and enhanced images, ensuring spatial coherence.

$$L_{spa} = \frac{1}{K} \sum_{i=1}^{K} \sum_{j \in \Omega(i)} (|Y_i - Y_j| - |I_i - I_j|)^2 \tag{9}$$

In Equation (9), K denotes the count of local areas, and $\Omega(i)$ represents the four adjacent neighborhoods (top, bottom, left, right) around a specific local area i. Y and I correspond to the average intensity values of the local area in the enhanced and original images, respectively. The dimension of each local region is defined as 4×4 [21]. Figure 3 visually explains the concept of spatial consistency loss.

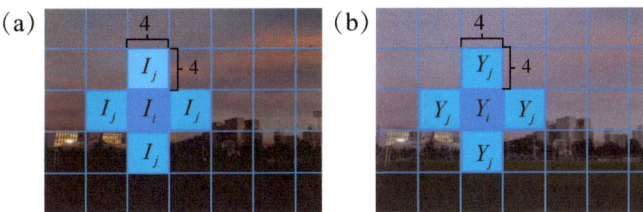

Figure 3. An illustration of the spatial consistency loss. (**a**) Definition of local areas in the input image. (**b**) Definition of loal areas in the enhanced image.

The exposure control loss L_{exp} seeks to maintain the brightness level of the enhanced images, and it is defined as

$$L_{exp} = \frac{1}{M} \sum_{i=1}^{M} |Y_k - E|. \tag{10}$$

In Equation (10), E is defined as the grayscale value in the RGB color space [45], M denotes the count of distinct local areas each sized 16×16, Y is the mean intensity value of a local region in the enhanced image [21]. Based on experimental evaluations, E is determined to be 0.6.

The color constancy loss L_{col} aims to rectify any possible color shifts in the enhanced image and establish interconnections between RGB channels [21].

$$L_{col} = \sum_{\forall (p,q) \in \varepsilon} (J^p - J^q)^2, \quad \varepsilon = \{(R,G),(R,B),(G,B)\} \tag{11}$$

In Equation (11), J^p and J^q denote the mean intensity values of the p and q channels, respectively, in the enhanced image [21].

Due to the adoption of curve enhancement instead of pixel-wise enhancement in Zero-DCE [21], the monotonicity of surrounding pixels is maintained according to the properties of curve derivatives. Therefore, we discard the illumination smoothness loss from Zero-DCE [21] and introduce the local contrast loss L_{con}. Actually, according to the result of the ablation study, the illumination smoothness loss does not affect the enhancement results.

To make the dark-light regions in the enhanced image clearer, we introduce the local contrast loss L_{con}. Figure 4 demonstrates the method used to calculate the local contrast loss. The definition of the local contrast loss is Equation (12)

$$L_{con} = \frac{1}{M} \sum_{i=1}^{M} \frac{I_{max} - I_{min}}{I_{max} + I_{min} + 10^{-8}}. \tag{12}$$

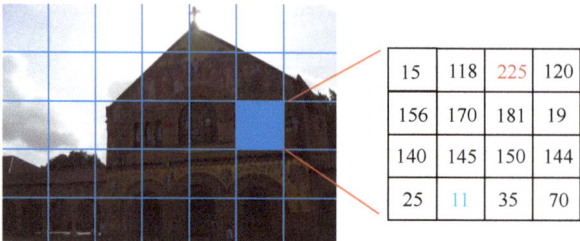

Figure 4. An illustration of the local contrast loss. The pixel values of the single-channel in the subregion, as shown in the enlarged portion in the figure, are represented by blue for the maximum and red for the minimum values of the local region pixels.

In (12), M denotes the quantity of local regions, each with a size of 4×4. I_{max} and I_{min} correspond to the maximum pixel and minimum pixel values in the enhanced image.

The total loss function is defined as Equation (13), where $\lambda_{spa}, \lambda_{exp}, \lambda_{col}$, and λ_{con} are the weights for $L_{spa}, L_{exp}, L_{col}$ and L_{con}.

$$L_{total} = \lambda_{spa} L_{spa} + \lambda_{exp} L_{exp} + \lambda_{col} L_{col} + \lambda_{con} L_{con} \qquad (13)$$

The non-reference loss function for Gamma-Net is the same as LLE-NET, but the loss weights are different from the loss weights of LLE-NET.

4. Experiments

We evaluate LLE-NET and Gamma-Net through experiments conducted on a system comprising an Intel(R) Core(TM) i7-10700k CPU @3.80GHz, 32 GB RAM, and a single NVIDIA GeForce RTX 3060 GPU (with 12 GB memory) running on the PyTorch 1.12 platform. We compare our approach against several state-of-the-art methods, conducting comprehensive qualitative and quantitative assessments to affirm its effectiveness.

4.1. Implementation Details

LLE-NET and Gamma-Net utilize unpaired data for training. Part 1 of SICE [2] comprises 360 multi-exposure images, while the LOL dataset [35] contains 485 training images and 15 test images. The complete training dataset combines the training images from Part 1 of SICE and LOL. To expedite model training, we can randomly choose 400 images from the combined dataset for the training task. Experimental results indicate that a smaller training set yields similar training outcomes compared to the complete training dataset. If there is no strict requirement on training time, it is recommended to use the complete dataset. However, if training time is restricted it is advisable to use random sampling from the complete training dataset as the training dataset. In theory, random sampling should yield enhancement effects similar to those of the complete training dataset. However, practical testing has found that it is best to have over 20% of normal or over-exposed images in the randomly sampled training dataset.

Before training, we first resize training images and testing images to dimensions of $128 \times 128 \times 3$. The initial filter weights for each layer are initialized using a standard Gaussian distribution with zero mean and a standard deviation of 0.02. We utilize the ADAM optimizer with default parameters, keeping a constant learning rate of 10^{-4}. LLE-NET iteratively enhances four times for input image. The weights $\lambda_{spa}, \lambda_{col}, \lambda_{exp}$ and λ_{con} are set to 40, 15, 5, and 8 for LLE-NET, respectively. The weights $\lambda_{spa}, \lambda_{col}, \lambda_{exp}$ and λ_{con} are set to 35, 15, 5, and 8 for Gamma-Net, respectively. The iteration number for LLE-Net is set to 4. The iteration number for Gamma-Net is set to 1, so Gamma-Net is as same as gamma correction. LLE-NET and Gamma-Net adopt the same training dataset. The training dataset in this paper consists of randomly sampled data from the complete training dataset. We selected training weight files with better visual evaluation results as the training outcomes.

4.2. Experimental Evaluation

We contrast our approaches with several state-of-the-art methods: LIME [14], RetinexNet [35], MBLLEN [33], EnlightenGAN [40], RUAS [29], Zero-DCE [21], SCI medium [37]. The images for comparison are generated using publicly available source code with recommended parameters.

Table 1 compares the trainable parameters and GFLOPs. The GPLOPs are measured when processing $1200 \times 900 \times 3$ image and the inference time tested in LIME [14] dataset is the running time of different methods. Since RetinexNet has the highest GFLOPs but the slowest computational speed, the runtime of this algorithm is no longer provided. The inference time of Gamma-Net is close to Zero-DCE++ [21]. Compared to other algorithms in Table 1, LLE-NET and Gamma-NET have lower GFLOPs values, giving them a better advantage in terms of runtime. Table 1 presents the runtime of various methods from loading the model to completing the LIME [14] dataset enhancement. LLE-NET exhibits remarkable inference speed, achieving 400 fps on a single GPU for images sized $640 \times 480 \times 3$ while maintaining pleasing enhancement quality. The enhancement model based on gamma correction attains an impressive inference speed of 800 fps for images sized $640 \times 480 \times 3$ on a single GPU. The inference time of Gamma-Net based on the GPU platform can reach 0.01s when it processes 1080×1920 images.

Table 1. Computation efficiency of different methods. The trainable parameters for an input image of size $1200 \times 900 \times 3$, GFLOPs, inference time based on GPU platform in LIME [14] dataset. The best results are highlighted in bold.

Method	Parameters (K) ↓	GFLOPs ↓	Time (s) ↓
RetinexNet [35]	555	587	-
MBLLEN [33]	450	301	21.9512
EnlightenGAN [40]	8000	273	16.1921
RUAS [29]	**3.4**	3.5	5.5745
Zero-DCE [21]	79	85	3.3182
SCI medium [37]	5.877	188	4.0959
LLE-NET (ours)	76	**0.7515**	2.9972
Gamma-Net (ours)	75	0.7517	**2.8852**

We visually compare different methods on the LIME dataset [14] is shown in Figures 5 and 6.

It can be seen from Figures 5 and 6 that LIME [14] cannot recover the building clearly, and the enhanced image of RetinexNet [35] has a painting-like texture. SCI medium [37] and RUAS [29] exhibit uneven exposures, especially where bright regions in the enhanced image are over-enhanced. Deep learning enhancement algorithms based on the Retinex theory, such as RetinexNet, RUAS, and SCI medium, exhibit overexposure phenomena.

The enhanced images of EnlightenGAN [40] and Zero-DCE [21] appear slight color deviation. The images enhanced by MBLLEN exhibit higher clarity and lesser color distortion compared to LLE-NET. The enhanced image using LLE-NET or Gamma-NET is more similar to the enhanced image using MBLLEN [33]. However, LLE-NET has fewer GFLOPs and faster processing speed compared to MBLLEN. In cases where the enhancement effects are similar, LLE-NET is more suitable for applications with high demands on processing speed. Particularly, LLE-NET retains the advantages of high similarity and low color distortion similar to MBLLEN. Therefore, even if the enhancement effect is slightly inferior to MBLLEN, LLE-NET is still considered more suitable for real-time application scenarios. Compared to Zero-DCE and EnlightenGAN, LLE-NET and Gamma-NET have fewer color distortions. LLE-NET and Gamma-Net tend to under-enhance the low-light images. However, they preserve the bright regions of the input image as faithfully as possible. From the visual effect evaluation, LLE-NET and Gamma-NET are more similar to the original input image.

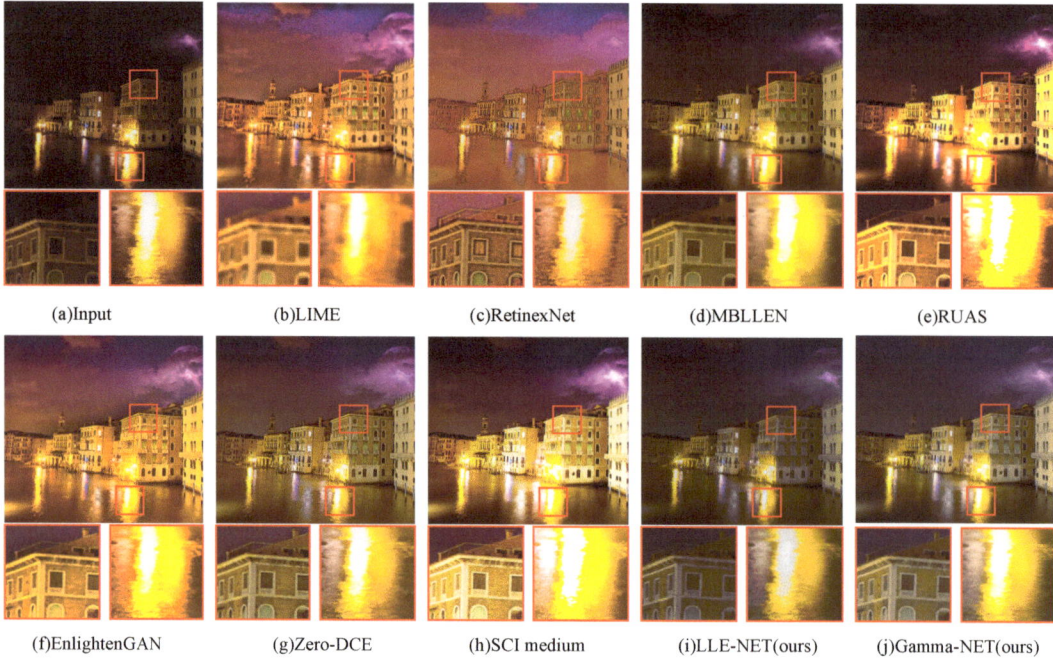

Figure 5. First visual comparison of different methods on LIME [14].

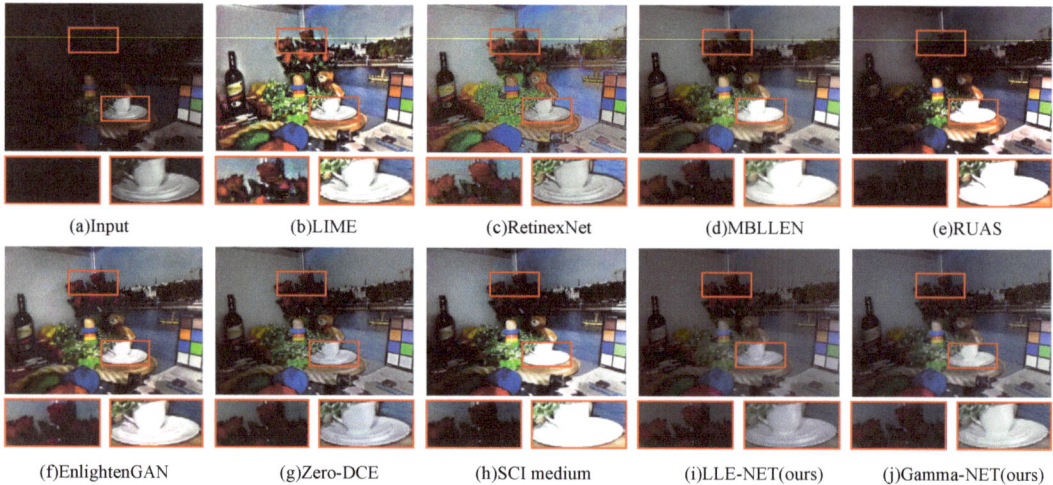

Figure 6. Second visual comparison of different methods on LIME [14].

Qualitative and quantitative evaluations are performed on the standard image set used by previous works including DICM [46] (64 images), LIME [14] (10 images), MEF [47] (17 images), NPE [48] (84 images), VV [49] (24 images). The reference qualitative comparisons are shown in Table 2 which gives the detailed results of five datasets in terms of Peaking Signal-to-Noise Ratio (PSNR,dB), Structural similarity (SSIM), Mean Absolute Error (MAE), and Learned Perceptual Image Patch Similarity (LPIPS) [50]. The detailed results in five datasets are presented in Table 2. The MBLLEN algorithm excels in SSIM and LIPIS metrics, whereas the LLE-NET algorithm outperforms in terms of PSNR and MAE metrics. It can be concluded that images enhanced using LLE-NET have better performance in terms of similarity and smaller color distortion, and are especially suitable for applications such as SLAM. The evaluation metric results are consistent with the visual assessment. We can conclude that the LLE-NET and Gamma-NET algorithms ensure enhancement while maximizing similarity to low-light images. Gamma-NET and Zero-DCE have similar evaluation indicators. It can be seen that using Gamma-NET can achieve similar effects to Zero-DCE. The inference speed of Gamma-NET increases obviously compared to Zero-DCE. Because there is no established ground truth for the enhanced images, using reference qualitative methods cannot fully evaluate the quality of enhanced images. Therefore, non-reference qualitative methods are introduced.

Table 2. Mean quantitative comparison between our method and state-of-the-art methods on DICM [46], LIME [14], MEF [47], NPE [48], VV [49]. Bold indicates the optimal outcomes.

Dataset	Method	PSNR ↑	SSIM ↑	MAE ↓	LPIPS ↓
DICM	MBLLEN	18.2286	**0.7271**	1520.6005	**0.1981**
	RUAS	10.7435	0.6088	6945.4501	0.3509
	EnlightenGAN	13.2887	0.6082	3434.5043	0.2353
	Zero-DCE	14.5836	0.6391	2500.3813	0.2292
	SCI-medium	9.4584	0.5115	8606.4664	0.4096
	LLE-NET	**18.7514**	0.7180	**946.5415**	0.2251
	Gamma-Net	14.1608	0.6352	2684.1659	0.2535
LIME	MBLLEN	14.3632	0.5512	3060.0568	0.2800
	RUAS	12.7033	0.5522	4184.1014	**0.2390**
	EnlightenGAN	10.4526	0.3762	6373.8652	0.3260
	Zero-DCE	12.7292	0.4673	3716.9237	0.3205
	SCI-medium	10.1090	0.3750	7311.8408	0.3533
	LLE-NET	**16.6399**	**0.5587**	**1462.218**	0.3071
	Gamma-Net	13.4485	0.5057	3055.1416	0.2880
MEF	MBLLEN	16.1754	**0.5963**	1855.8897	**0.2510**
	RUAS	12.0177	0.5755	4624.5877	0.2633
	EnlightenGAN	12.6525	0.4397	3934.1041	0.2906
	Zero-DCE	13.6976	0.4444	3034.4384	0.2999
	SCI-medium	10.2258	0.3960	6835.2636	0.3595
	LLE-NET	**17.5471**	0.5581	**1225.4604**	0.2759
	Gamma-Net	14.0117	0.4812	2702.0425	0.2818
NPE	MBLLEN	19.5104	**0.7448**	1052.0196	**0.1556**
	RUAS	10.3375	0.6025	6571.6485	0.3412
	EnlightenGAN	12.6337	0.6552	3783.2525	0.1888
	Zero-DCE	13.8611	0.6519	2817.4149	0.1813
	SCI-medium	9.0282	0.5091	8514.8493	0.3855
	LLE-NET	17.7302	0.7360	1128.3872	0.1813
	Gamma-Net	14.1781	0.545	2575.9487	0.3921
VV	MBLLEN	17.7058	**0.7113**	1177.6664	0.3196
	RUAS	11.2388	0.6107	5559.8106	0.4134
	EnlightenGAN	11.5388	0.4948	4728.1429	0.5199
	Zero-DCE	13.8369	0.5316	2820.4735	0.4026
	SCI-medium	9.8914	0.4629	7278.1504	0.5279
	LLE-NET	**18.1330**	0.6238	**1042.4784**	0.3763
	Gamma-Net	13.6904	0.6814	2819.8596	**0.1903**
Average	MBLLEN	17.19668	**0.67404**	1733.2466	**0.24086**
	RUAS	11.40816	0.58994	5577.1196	0.32156
	EnlightenGAN	12.11326	0.51482	4450.7738	0.31212
	Zero-DCE	13.74168	0.54686	2977.9263	0.2867
	SCI-medium	9.98208	0.42828	7373.39696	0.40196
	LLE-NET	**17.76032**	0.63892	**1161.0171**	0.27314
	Gamma-Net	13.8979	0.5697	2767.43166	0.28114

Non-reference qualitative comparisons of the Perceptual index (PI) [51] and Natural Image Quality Evaluator (NIQE) [52] on five datasets are listed in Table 3. As we can see, Zero-DCE [21] obtains the best score in terms of PI and NIQE. LLE-NET and Gamma-Net achieve good scores compared to other methods. Since non-reference qualitative comparison is closer to the judgment standard of the human eye, taking into account the content of Figures 5 and 6, Zero-DCE exhibits superior performance in contrast and saturation of the enhanced image. However, there is noticeable color distortion present as well. Color distortion is detrimental to tasks such as vision SLAM. Since algorithms cannot excel in all metrics, we need to choose low-light image enhancement algorithms according to different requirements of tasks.

Table 3. Perceptual Index (PI) ↓/Naturalness Image Quality Evaluator (NIQE) ↓ on different datasets. Bold means the best results.

Method	Average	DICM	LIME	MEF	NPE	VV
MBLLEN	3.84/4.43	3.75/4.20	3.63/4.50	3.91/4.73	3.43/4.54	4.48/4.18
RUAS	3.54/4.59	3.83/4.78	3.09/4.23	2.77/3.69	3.87/5.68	4.14/4.60
EnlightenGAN	3.34/3.90	3.11/3.48	2.83/3.66	2.45/3.22	2.96/4.11	5.35/5.01
Zero-DCE	**2.94/3.60**	3.08/3.60	3.00/3.95	2.43/3.28	2.86/3.93	3.33/3.22
SCI-medium	3.03/3.65	3.51/3.79	2.99/4.18	2.56/3.44	2.56/3.44	3.55/3.42
LLE-NET	3.15/3.80	3.19/3.75	3.00/3.95	2.88/3.52	3.09/4.39	3.61/3.39
Gamma-Net	3.11/3.73	3.17/3.69	3.19/3.99	2.76/3.38	3.52/3.32	2.96/4.25

To assess and contrast the performance and efficiency of different methods, Figure 7 shows the relationship between PI and GFLOPs. The enhanced performance of Gamma-Net is similar to Zero-DCE [21]. LLE-NET and Gamma-Net, using global lookup tables for high-resolution images, can accelerate inferring speed. Combining the runtime data in Table 1, it can be observed that LLE-NET runs at a higher frame rate than Zero-DCE, while Gamma-NET surpasses both LLE-NET and Zero-DCE. In fact, considering the frame rate processing indicator, Gamma-NET is essentially twice as fast as LLE-NET and Zero-DCE.

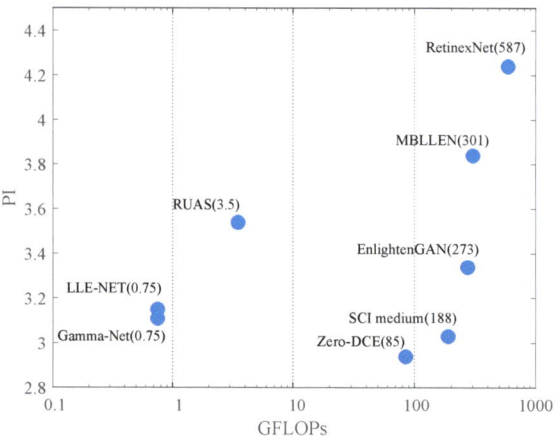

Figure 7. Comparison of performance and efficiency. Average PI↓ is calculated on five real-world datasets. GFLOPs↓ is measured on a 1200 × 900 × 3 image.

Limitations. The LLE-NET and Gamma-NET algorithms do not perform exceptionally well in non-reference metric evaluation. In fact, visually, images enhanced using these two methods tend to have an overall dark brightness. The enhanced image's texture details are not clear compared to MBLLEN, and they are noticeably affected by noise. The contrast and color saturation of the enhanced images are lacking compared to the Zero-

DCE and EnlightenGAN methods. Since a pixel-wise mapping similar to the Zero-DCE algorithm was not employed, the enhanced images exhibit the drawbacks of traditional image enhancement algorithms, such as low contrast and relatively low color saturation. Due to the absence of a noise filtering module, noise in the input image directly affects the effectiveness of the enhanced image. It may be beneficial to introduce a noise removal module while enhancing images to further improve the quality of the enhanced images.

Although our methods can not achieve the best score in every index, our approach demonstrates strong competitiveness in overall performance, particularly given its similarity to input images and its inference speed.

4.3. Ablation Study

In order to evaluate the impact of each loss component, the results of LLE-NET trained using different combinations of loss weights are shown in Figure 8. Figure 8b shows the enhancement image by the weights combination of $(40, 15, 5, 8)$. During the ablation study process, we found that setting the weight of L_{spa} to zero is not feasible. Therefore, we decided to decrease the weight of L_{spa} to 30. From Figure 8b,c, L_{spa} reduce noise and preserve the overall contrast of the enhanced image. From Figure 8b,d, L_{col} prevents the color deviation of the enhanced image. From Figure 8b,e, L_{exp} improves the overall exposure of enhanced images. From Figure 8b,f, L_{con} improves the local contrast of the enhanced images. Besides, the value of L_{con} influences the value of L_{spa}. Figure 8 illustrates the significant contribution of each loss in achieving the final enhancement result. Table 4 presents the metrics of non-reference qualitative comparisons. These metrics show the significance of the divergence loss function.

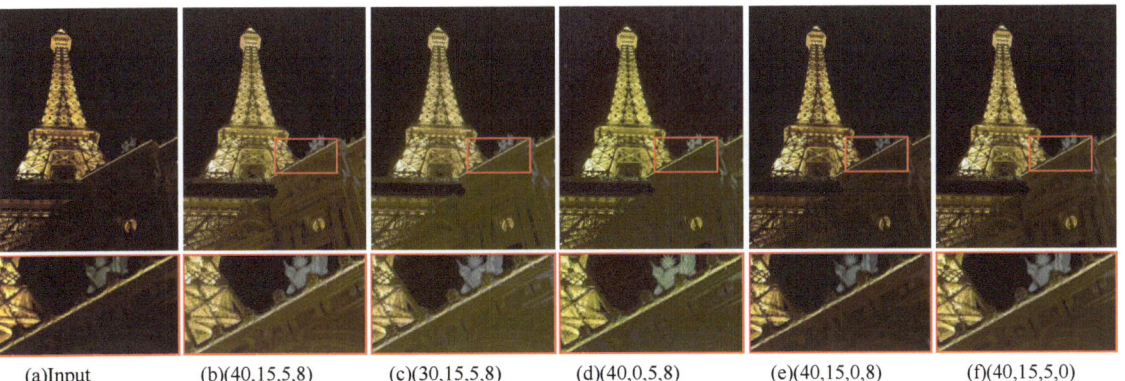

Figure 8. Different combinations of loss weights $(\lambda_{spa}, \lambda_{col}, \lambda_{exp}, \lambda_{con})$. (**a**) Input image. (**b**) Loss weights are $(40, 15, 5, 8)$. (**c**) Loss weights are $(30, 15, 5, 8)$. (**d**) Loss weights are $(40, 0, 5, 8)$. (**e**) Loss weights are $(40, 15, 0, 8)$. (**f**) Loss weights are $(40, 15, 5, 0)$.

Table 4. Perceptual Index (PI) ↓/Naturalness Image Quality Evaluator (NIQE) ↓ on different combinations. Bold means the best results.

	(40, 15, 5, 8)	(30, 15, 5, 8)	(40, 0, 5, 8)	(40, 15, 0, 8)	(40, 15, 5, 0)
PI↓	**2.9957**	3.21121	3.1610	3.0962	3.0469
NIQE↓	**3.948**	4.2345	4.2512	3.9505	3.9963

4.4. Effect of Parameter Setting

The parameter E is included in the loss function L_{exp}, as shown in Equation (10). During training, it was observed that this parameter affects the enhancement results. By comparing the parameter values set to 0.4, 0.5, 0.6, 0.7, it was observed that a generally superior effect is attained when E is configured to 0.6. Figure 9 presents qualitative comparisons for different values of E in LLE-NET. It can be observed that as the value of E increases, there is a corresponding rise in image brightness. However, when $E = 0.7$, noticeable noise artifacts appear in the enlarged images.

(a)Input   (b)E=0.4   (c)E=0.5   (d)E=0.6   (e)E=0.7

Figure 9. A visual comparison among the results using different well-exposedness level, E. (**a**) Input image. (**b**) Enhanced image when $E = 0.4$. (**c**) Enhanced image when $E = 0.5$. (**d**) Enhanced image when $E = 0.6$. (**e**) Enhanced image when $E = 0.7$.

The impact of training epochs on this research was investigated, revealing that higher epochs do not necessarily yield better results. It was observed that setting the epoch value too high leads to increased image noise and loss of details, while lower epochs result in less noticeable enhancements in image brightness. Thus, it is advisable not to opt for higher epoch values during training. The experiments found that typically, setting the epoch value to below 50 is sufficient, with around 20 epochs often meeting the requirements. Figure 10 illustrates the training results for different epochs in Gamma-NET. It can be seen that at epoch 3, enhancement in dark regions is achieved, with further improvement at epoch 8. However, by epoch 11, noise becomes noticeable in the darker regions of the image. It was noted that setting the epoch value too high results in noise becoming a significant part of the enhanced image, thus it is recommended to use slightly lower epoch values in practical network applications.

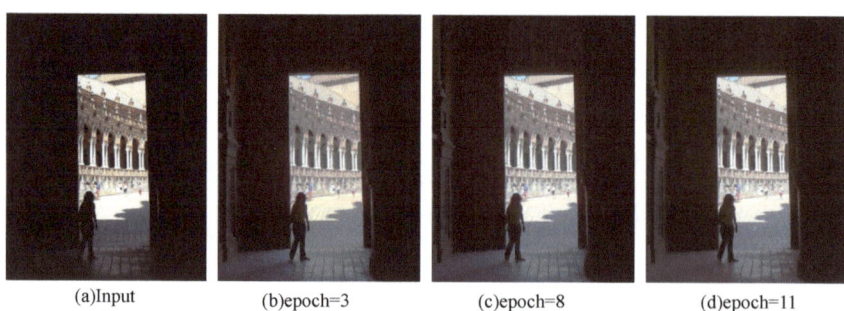

(a)Input   (b)epoch=3   (c)epoch=8   (d)epoch=11

Figure 10. A visual comparison among the results using different epoch. (**a**) Input image. (**b**) Enhanced image when $epoch = 3$. (**c**) Enhanced image when $epoch = 8$. (**d**) Enhanced image when $epoch = 11$.

4.5. Effect of Training Data

The training dataset for the LLE-NET network and Gamma-NET influences the enhancement results. Figure 11 illustrates the impact of various datasets on enhancement outcomes. Two datasets were used in this research: the LOL dataset [35] and the first part of the SCIE dataset [2]. Experimental results revealed a significant influence of the training set on data augmentation results. Figure 11b shows the results after training with the LOL dataset, indicating lower overall image brightness and poor enhancement in dark areas. The first part of the SCIE dataset includes a total of 3021 images which are divided into 360 groups with and without reference assessment, each group containing images with varying brightness levels. A composite training set was assembled by merging images from both the LOL and the initial section of the SCIE dataset, culminating in a sum of

3506 images, as shown in Figure 11c. It can be observed that training with a combination of low and high-light images can effectively improve enhancement results. During training, it was found that one complete training cycle takes about 30 min. To speed up training, a random selection of 400 images was used for training, as shown in Figure 11d. It was found that this approach yielded training results comparable to using the complete training set. Therefore, in scenarios where training time is a constraint, constructing a dataset with a combination of low and high-light images and training with a smaller random subset of images can still achieve good enhancement results. The dataset is composed of randomly selected images and must include approximately 20% of images that are either normal or over-exposed. Considering algorithm applicability and contrast enhancement of the enhanced images, this study recommends using a combined dataset of low and high-light images for training and suggests training with a random sample of 200–500 images. For example, training with 200 images takes approximately 4 min.

(a)Input   (b)LOL dataset   (c) The first part in SCIE and LOL   (d)Randly selected dataset

Figure 11. A visual comparison among the results using different training datasets. (**a**) Input image. (**b**) Enhanced image when the training dataset is the LOL dataset. (**c**) Enhanced image when the training dataset is the first part in SCIE and LOL dataset. (**d**) Enhanced image when the training dataset is randly selected from the first part in SCIE and LOL dataset.

5. Conclusions

In this research, the framework of LLE-NET and Gamma-NET is proposed without paired training datasets, and an appropriate loss function is defined. By comparing with existing algorithms, we concluded that using LLE-NET can achieve better image enhancement effects. Firstly, the LLE-NET and Gamma-NET algorithms achieve comparable results to MBLLEN with smaller models, meeting the requirements for real-time applications. Secondly, compared to the Zero-DCE and EnlightenGAN algorithms, LLE-NET and Gamma-NET algorithms exhibit fewer color distortions and better image similarity. They achieve optimal results in PSNR and MAE evaluation metrics. Therefore, the algorithms overall meet the requirements of our design, providing higher processing speeds and image similarity while meeting enhancement requirements. In terms of algorithm processing speed evaluation, when the input image size is 640×480, the processing speed of LLE-NET can reach 400 fps, and Gamma-NET can reach 800 fps.

Despite the algorithms performing well in some aspects, limitations still exist. The lack of paired training datasets makes it challenging to perform denoising simultaneously with image enhancement using Zero-shot methods. Therefore, researching network structures that simultaneously remove noise and enhance low-light images holds greater application value.

Author Contributions: Conceptualization, X.C.; methodology, X.C.; software, X.C.; validation, X.C.; writing—review and editing, X.C.; project administration, J.Y.; funding acquisition, J.Y. All authors have read and agreed to the published version of the manuscript.

Funding: This research received no external funding.

Data Availability Statement: The source code will be made publicly available at https://drive.google.com/drive/folders/1KLM1i06PZKDtFgkIdPgq7_fShYb2oSV6?usp=sharing, accessed on 14 April 2024.

Conflicts of Interest: The authors declare no conflicts of interest.

References

1. Moran, S.; Marza, P.; McDonagh, S.; Parisot, S.; Slabaugh, G. Deeplpf: Deep local parametric filters for image enhancement. In Proceedings of the IEEE/CVF Conference on Computer Vision and Pattern Recognition, Seattle, WA, USA, 13–19 June 2020; pp. 12826–12835.
2. Cai, J.; Gu, S.; Zhang, L. Learning a deep single image contrast enhancer from multi-exposure images. *IEEE Trans. Image Process.* **2018**, *27*, 2049–2062. [CrossRef] [PubMed]
3. Yang, S.; Zhou, D.; Cao, J.; Guo, Y. LightingNet: An integrated learning method for low-light image enhancement. *IEEE Trans. Comput. Imaging* **2023**, *9*, 29–42. [CrossRef]
4. Wu, W.; Weng, J.; Zhang, P.; Wang, X.; Yang, W.; Jiang, J. Uretinex-net: Retinex-based deep unfolding network for low-light image enhancement. In Proceedings of the IEEE/CVF Conference on Computer Vision and Pattern Recognition, New Orleans, LA, USA, 18–24 June 2022; pp. 5901–5910.
5. Li, C.; Qu, X.; Gnanasambandam, A.; Elgendy, O.A.; Ma, J.; Chan, S.H. Photon-limited object detection using non-local feature matching and knowledge distillation. In Proceedings of the IEEE/CVF International Conference on Computer Vision, Montreal, BC, Canada, 11–17 October 2021; pp. 3976–3987.
6. Wang, W.; Wang, X.; Yang, W.; Liu, J. Unsupervised face detection in the dark. *IEEE Trans. Pattern Anal. Mach. Intell.* **2022**, *45*, 1250–1266. [CrossRef] [PubMed]
7. Gao, H.; Guo, J.; Wang, G.; Zhang, Q. Cross-domain correlation distillation for unsupervised domain adaptation in nighttime semantic segmentation. In Proceedings of the IEEE/CVF Conference on Computer Vision and Pattern Recognition, New Orleans, LA, USA, 18–24 June 2022; pp. 9913–9923.
8. Ye, J.; Fu, C.; Zheng, G.; Paudel, D.P.; Chen, G. Unsupervised domain adaptation for nighttime aerial tracking. In Proceedings of the IEEE/CVF Conference on Computer Vision and Pattern Recognition, New Orleans, LA, USA, 18–24 June 2022; pp. 8896–8905.
9. Xin, Z.; Wang, Z.; Yu, Z.; Zheng, B. ULL-SLAM: Underwater low-light enhancement for the front-end of visual SLAM. *Front. Mar. Sci.* **2023**, *10*, 1133881. [CrossRef]
10. Su, Y.; Wang, J.; Wang, X.; Hu, L.; Yao, Y.; Shou, W.; Li, D. Zero-reference deep learning for low-light image enhancement of underground utilities 3D reconstruction. *Autom. Constr.* **2023**, *152*, 104930. [CrossRef]
11. Song, S.; Chen, W.; Liu, Q.; Hu, H.; Huang, T.; Zhu, Q. A novel deep learning network for accurate lane detection in low-light environments. *Proc. Inst. Mech. Eng. Part D J. Automob. Eng.* **2022**, *236*, 424–438. [CrossRef]
12. Tang, H.; Zhu, H.; Fei, L.; Wang, T.; Cao, Y.; Xie, C. Low-Illumination image enhancement based on deep learning techniques: A brief review. *Photonics* **2023**, *10*, 198. [CrossRef]
13. Peng, B.; Zhang, X.; Lei, J.; Zhang, Z.; Ling, N.; Huang, Q. LVE-S2D: Low-light video enhancement from static to dynamic. *IEEE Trans. Circuits Syst. Video Technol.* **2022**, *32*, 8342–8352. [CrossRef]
14. Guo, X.; Li, Y.; Ling, H. LIME: Low-Light Image Enhancement via Illumination Map Estimation. *IEEE Trans. Image Process.* **2017**, *26*, 982–993. [CrossRef]
15. Jobson, D.J.; Rahman, Z.u.; Woodell, G.A. A multiscale retinex for bridging the gap between color images and the human observation of scenes. *IEEE Trans. Image Process.* **1997**, *6*, 965–976. [CrossRef]
16. Arici, T.; Dikbas, S.; Altunbasak, Y. A histogram modification framework and its application for image contrast enhancement. *IEEE Trans. Image Process.* **2009**, *18*, 1921–1935. [CrossRef] [PubMed]
17. Kim, W. Low-light image enhancement: A comparative review and prospects. *IEEE Access* **2022**, *10*, 84535–84557. [CrossRef]
18. Li, C.; Guo, C.; Han, L.; Jiang, J.; Cheng, M.M.; Gu, J.; Loy, C.C. Low-light image and video enhancement using deep learning: A survey. *IEEE Trans. Pattern Anal. Mach. Intell.* **2021**, *44*, 9396–9416. [CrossRef] [PubMed]
19. Zhang, Y.; Teng, B.; Yang, D.; Chen, Z.; Ma, H.; Li, G.; Ding, W. Learning a Single Convolutional Layer Model for Low Light Image Enhancement. *IEEE Trans. Circuits Syst. Video Technol.* **2023**. [CrossRef]
20. Lv, F.; Li, Y.; Lu, F. Attention guided low-light image enhancement with a large scale low-light simulation dataset. *Int. J. Comput. Vis.* **2021**, *129*, 2175–2193. [CrossRef]
21. Li, C.; Guo, C.; Loy, C.C. Learning to enhance low-light image via zero-reference deep curve estimation. *IEEE Trans. Pattern Anal. Mach. Intell.* **2021**, *44*, 4225–4238. [CrossRef] [PubMed]
22. Wu, C.; Dong, J.; Tang, J. LUT-GCE: Lookup Table Global Curve Estimation for Fast Low-light Image Enhancement. *arXiv* **2023**, arXiv:2306.07083.
23. Dhal, K.G.; Das, A.; Ray, S.; Gálvez, J.; Das, S. Histogram equalization variants as optimization problems: A review. *Arch. Comput. Methods Eng.* **2021**, *28*, 1471–1496. [CrossRef]
24. Ibrahim, H.; Kong, N.S.P. Brightness preserving dynamic histogram equalization for image contrast enhancement. *IEEE Trans. Consum. Electron.* **2007**, *53*, 1752–1758. [CrossRef]
25. Chen, S.D.; Ramli, A.R. Preserving brightness in histogram equalization based contrast enhancement techniques. *Digit. Signal Process.* **2004**, *14*, 413–428. [CrossRef]
26. Dhal, K.G.; Sen, M.; Das, S. Cuckoo search-based modified bi-histogram equalisation method to enhance the cancerous tissues in mammography images. *Int. J. Med. Eng. Inform.* **2018**, *10*, 164–187.
27. Muniraj, M.; Dhandapani, V. Underwater image enhancement by modified color correction and adaptive Look-Up-Table with edge-preserving filter. *Signal Process. Image Commun.* **2023**, *113*, 116939. [CrossRef]

28. Shi, Z.; Feng, Y.; Zhao, M.; Zhang, E.; He, L. Normalised gamma transformation-based contrast-limited adaptive histogram equalisation with colour correction for sand–dust image enhancement. *IET Image Process.* **2020**, *14*, 747–756. [CrossRef]
29. Liu, R.; Ma, L.; Zhang, J.; Fan, X.; Luo, Z. Retinex-inspired unrolling with cooperative prior architecture search for low-light image enhancement. In Proceedings of the IEEE/CVF Conference on Computer Vision and Pattern Recognition, Nashville, TN, USA, 20–25 June 2021; pp. 10561–10570.
30. Bao, S.; Ma, S.; Yang, C. Multi-scale retinex-based contrast enhancement method for preserving the naturalness of color image. *Opt. Rev.* **2020**, *27*, 475–485. [CrossRef]
31. Zhang, W.; Dong, L.; Pan, X.; Zhou, J.; Qin, L.; Xu, W. Single Image Defogging Based on Multi-Channel Convolutional MSRCR. *IEEE Access* **2019**, *7*, 72492–72504. [CrossRef]
32. Tian, F.; Wang, M.; Liu, X. Low-Light mine image enhancement algorithm based on improved Retinex. *Appl. Sci.* **2024**, *14*, 2213. [CrossRef]
33. Lv, F.; Lu, F.; Wu, J.; Lim, C. MBLLEN: Low-Light Image/Video Enhancement Using CNNs. In *BMVC*; Northumbria University: Newcastle upon Tyne, UK, 2018; Volume 220, p. 4.
34. Chen, C.; Chen, Q.; Xu, J.; Koltun, V. Learning to see in the dark. In Proceedings of the IEEE Conference on Computer Vision and Pattern Recognition, Salt Lake City, UT, USA, 18–23 June 2018; pp. 3291–3300.
35. Chen, W.; Wang, W.; Yang, W.; Liu, J. Deep retinex decomposition for low-light enhancement. In *British Machine Vision Conference*; British Machine Vision Association: Glasgow, UK, 2018.
36. Zhang, Y.; Guo, X.; Ma, J.; Liu, W.; Zhang, J. Beyond brightening low-light images. *Int. J. Comput. Vis.* **2021**, *129*, 1013–1037. [CrossRef]
37. Ma, L.; Ma, T.; Liu, R.; Fan, X.; Luo, Z. Toward fast, flexible, and robust low-light image enhancement. In Proceedings of the IEEE/CVF Conference on Computer Vision and Pattern Recognition, New Orleans, LA, USA, 18–24 June 2022; pp. 5637–5646.
38. Hui, Y.; Wang, J.; Shi, Y.; Li, B. Low-light Image Enhancement Algorithm Based on Exposure Prediction and Hybrid Feature Weighted Fusion Strategy. *Proc. J. Phys. Conf. Ser.* **2022**, *2281*, 012017. [CrossRef]
39. Zhu, J.Y.; Park, T.; Isola, P.; Efros, A.A. Unpaired image-to-image translation using cycle-consistent adversarial networks. In Proceedings of the IEEE International Conference on Computer Vision, Venice, Italy, 22–29 October 2017; pp. 2223–2232.
40. Jiang, Y.; Gong, X.; Liu, D.; Cheng, Y.; Fang, C.; Shen, X.; Yang, J.; Zhou, P.; Wang, Z. Enlightengan: Deep light enhancement without paired supervision. *IEEE Trans. Image Process.* **2021**, *30*, 2340–2349. [CrossRef] [PubMed]
41. Hui, Y.; Jue, W.; Li, B.; Shi, Y. Low light image enhancement algorithm based on improved multi-objective grey wolf optimization with detail feature enhancement. *J. King Saud Univ.-Comput. Inf. Sci.* **2023**, *35*, 101666. [CrossRef]
42. Zhu, A.; Zhang, L.; Shen, Y.; Ma, Y.; Zhao, S.; Zhou, Y. Zero-shot restoration of underexposed images via robust retinex decomposition. In Proceedings of the 2020 IEEE International Conference on Multimedia and Expo (ICME), London, UK, 6–10 July 2020; pp. 1–6.
43. Chen, L.; Chu, X.; Zhang, X.; Sun, J. Simple baselines for image restoration. In *European Conference on Computer Vision*; Springer: Cham, Switzerland, 2022; pp. 17–33.
44. Hendrycks, D.; Gimpel, K. Gaussian error linear units (gelus). *arXiv* **2016**, arXiv:1606.08415.
45. Mertens, T.; Kautz, J.; Van Reeth, F. Exposure fusion: A simple and practical alternative to high dynamic range photography. In *Computer Graphics Forum*; Wiley Online Library: Oxford, UK, 2009; Volume 28, pp. 161–171.
46. Lee, C.; Lee, C.; Kim, C.S. Contrast enhancement based on layered difference representation of 2D histograms. *IEEE Trans. Image Process.* **2013**, *22*, 5372–5384. [CrossRef] [PubMed]
47. Ma, K.; Zeng, K.; Wang, Z. Perceptual quality assessment for multi-exposure image fusion. *IEEE Trans. Image Process.* **2015**, *24*, 3345–3356. [CrossRef] [PubMed]
48. Wang, S.; Zheng, J.; Hu, H.M.; Li, B. Naturalness Preserved Enhancement Algorithm for Non-Uniform Illumination Images. *IEEE Trans. Image Process.* **2013**, *22*, 3538–3548. [CrossRef]
49. Vonikakis, V. Busting Image Enhancement and Tonemapping Algorithms. Available online: https://sites.google.com/site/vonikakis/datasets (accessed on 1 January 2021).
50. Zhang, R.; Isola, P.; Efros, A.A.; Shechtman, E.; Wang, O. The unreasonable effectiveness of deep features as a perceptual metric. In Proceedings of the 2018 IEEE/CVF Conference on Computer Vision and Pattern Recognition, Salt Lake City, UT, USA, 18–23 June 2018; pp. 586–595.
51. Blau, Y.; Michaeli, T. The perception-distortion tradeoff. In Proceedings of the 2018 IEEE/CVF Conference on Computer Vision and Pattern Recognition, Salt Lake City, UT, USA, 18–23 June 2018; pp. 6228–6237.
52. Mittal, A.; Soundararajan, R.; Bovik, A.C. Making a "Completely Blind" Image Quality Analyzer. *IEEE Signal Process. Lett.* **2013**, *20*, 209–212. [CrossRef]

Disclaimer/Publisher's Note: The statements, opinions and data contained in all publications are solely those of the individual author(s) and contributor(s) and not of MDPI and/or the editor(s). MDPI and/or the editor(s) disclaim responsibility for any injury to people or property resulting from any ideas, methods, instructions or products referred to in the content.

Article

Greedy Kernel Methods for Approximating Breakthrough Curves for Reactive Flow from 3D Porous Geometry Data

Robin Herkert [1,*], Patrick Buchfink [2], Tizian Wenzel [3], Bernard Haasdonk [1], Pavel Toktaliev [4] and Oleg Iliev [4]

1. Institute for Applied Analysis and Numerical Simulation, University of Stuttgart, 70569 Stuttgart, Germany; haasdonk@mathematik.uni-stuttgart.de
2. Department of Applied Mathematics, University of Twente, 7522 NH Enschede, The Netherlands; p.buchfink@utwente.nl
3. Department of Mathematics, Universität Hamburg, 20146 Hamburg, Germany; tizian.wenzel@uni-hamburg.de
4. Fraunhofer ITWM, Technical University Kaiserslautern, 67663 Kaiserslautern, Germany; pavel.toktaliev@itwm.fraunhofer.de (P.T.); oleg.iliev@itwm.fraunhofer.de (O.I.)
* Correspondence: robin.herkert@mathematik.uni-stuttgart.de

Abstract: We address the challenging application of 3D pore scale reactive flow under varying geometry parameters. The task is to predict time-dependent integral quantities, i.e., breakthrough curves, from the given geometries. As the 3D reactive flow simulation is highly complex and computationally expensive, we are interested in data-based surrogates that can give a rapid prediction of the target quantities of interest. This setting is an example of an application with scarce data, i.e., only having a few available data samples, while the input and output dimensions are high. In this scarce data setting, standard machine learning methods are likely to fail. Therefore, we resort to greedy kernel approximation schemes that have shown to be efficient meshless approximation techniques for multivariate functions. We demonstrate that such methods can efficiently be used in the high-dimensional input/output case under scarce data. Especially, we show that the vectorial kernel orthogonal greedy approximation (VKOGA) procedure with a data-adapted two-layer kernel yields excellent predictors for learning from 3D geometry voxel data via both morphological descriptors or principal component analysis.

Keywords: machine learning; kernel methods; two-layered kernels; porous media; breakthrough curves

MSC: 68T05; 65D15; 46E22; 76S05

1. Introduction

The reactive flow in porous media plays an important role for many industrial, environmental and biomedical applications. Since the reactions occur at the pore scale, 3D pore scale simulations are very important. At the same time, pore scale measurements are difficult or impossible, and, usually, some averaged quantities are measured. One such quantity of interest that can be measured is the breakthrough curve, i.e., the time-dependent integral of the species over the outlet. These breakthrough curves can be computed from a reaction–advection–diffusion equation on a porous medium, which is numerically solved. However, this usually leads to very high computational costs, which might be prohibitively high in a multiquery application, e.g., optimization of the geometry of the porous medium. In that case, a surrogate model for the full order simulation model (FOM) is required. A promising way of obtaining an adequate surrogate model is the use of machine learning (ML) techniques. ML techniques are nowadays widely spread and employed for a variety of tasks, including the estimation of damage for buried pipelines [1] or automatic vision-based sewer inspection [2]. ML algorithms are developed and tested for porous media flows with different complexity. The literature in this area is very rich, and we cite some exemplary papers simply to point to the place of our research. Numerous papers discuss predicting permeability from microscale geometry. For example, see [3–5] and the references therein. At the next level of complexity, e.g., in [6], the capability of using deep learning techniques has been shown in the case where the velocity field is predicted from the morphology of a porous medium. On the same topic, improvement is achieved by incorporating coarse velocities in the learning process, see [7]. In the last decade, the application of ML techniques for the simulation of passive and reactive transport has rapidly grown. One of the directions in this case is using ML to predict reaction rates when those are very expensive in the case of complex reactions. This can be implemented without taking into account the geometry, see e.g., [8–10], or predicting the rate from structure features, see, e.g., [4,11,12], to name just a few. Recently, the potential of using machine learning models as surrogates for predicting breakthrough curves for varying physical parameters, i.e., Damköhler and Peclet numbers, on a fixed porous medium geometry [13] has been reported.

In the current paper, we address the task of predicting the breakthrough curves for varying geometries of the porous medium with fixed Damköhler and Peclet numbers. Our work is in the same direction as that of [4,11], but there are essential differences. In [11], ML addresses the impact of the structural features on the effective reaction rate to overcome the limitation of the well-mixing assumption. Pore scale reactive flow in an inert skeleton is considered there. In [4], pore scale colloid transport is considered as a part of a filtration problem. Steady-state problems are solved. In our case, our pore scale geometry is in fact a two scale media, as the active washcoat particles are nanoporous. We consider the diffusion of the species within the washcoat, where the reaction occurs. Furthermore, while the other papers discuss different neural network algorithms, we consider a kernel-based method, namely, VKOGA. To the best of our knowledge, such studies have not yet been discussed in the literature.

Because of the computationally demanding simulation of the FOM, we are limited to a scarce data regime as we can only afford to compute a few samples. Furthermore, the input dimension (the number of elements of the discretization of the porous medium) and the output dimension (the number of time steps used during the FOM simulation) are very high. This yields a challenging task for machine learning techniques [14]. For this purpose, greedy kernel approximation schemes [15,16] have been shown to be efficient. These meshless approximation techniques can be combined with deep learning techniques to yield two-layered kernels [17,18], which have also already been successfully applied for certified and adaptive surrogate modeling for heat conduction [18], as well as surrogate modeling of chemical kinetics [8].

Our work is organized as follows: In Section 2, we introduce the underlying equations of the 3D porous medium reaction–advection–diffusion model. In Section 3, we give an overview on greedy kernel methods and two-layered kernels. The numerical experiments are provided in Section 4, and we conclude our work in Section 5.

2. Problem Formulation

2.1. Geometry

In the current paper, we consider artificially generated voxel-based geometries on the unit cube $\Omega = [0,1]^3$ as geometries for porous filter fragments. These consist of the solid skeleton, Ω_s, free pores, Ω_f, and effective porous space (washcoat or unresolved porosity region) Ω_w. Accordingly, we assume that the porous geometry sample can be represented as a union of non-overlapping domains $\Omega = \Omega_s \cup \Omega_f \cup \Omega_w$. Each of the domains Ω_w, Ω_f is represented as a union of non-overlapping volume voxels:

$$V_{i,j,k} = [(i-1)h; ih] \times [(j-1)h; jh] \times [(k-1)h; kh], i,j,k = 1, \ldots, N_h, \ h = 1/N_h,$$

where N_h is the number of voxels in each dimension. This leads to a uniform grid with $N_V = 150^3$ elements (voxels). The assignment of the voxels to the three subdomains is stored within two boolean arrays (a third one is not necessary as it can be calculated from the other two). That means each porous sample is represented by a vector $\mathbf{z} \in \{0,1\}^{2N_V}$.

Depending on the application and the production process, the structure of the porous space in real filters could be strongly irregular and highly anisotropic. Nevertheless, for certain types of filters, the micro structure of porous media could be represented as a combination of regular shaped nanoporous granules and solid binder material [19]. We use this representation to reconstruct the porous domain Ω_f and the washcoat domain Ω_w and later, using existing experimental data on porosity, to generate a series of artificial porous geometries that could be used as models for real filter fragments. The size of each sample in voxels, $N_h = 150$, is chosen according to a representative volume element (RVE) study on the one hand and the amount of computational work to generate enough data for training on the other hand. In order to generate each porous sample, we use an analytical spheres piling algorithm for the washcoat region, then voxelize analytical spheres and distribute voxelized solid material (binder) uniformly and randomly, covering the washcoat skeleton surface. The main varying parameter during the generation of the samples was the washcoat volume fraction ϵ_w; thus, in order to generate each sample, the target value of ϵ_w was set, but depending on geometry realization, the resulting value of ϵ_w for a generated sample could differ by more than 5%. A typical porous sample generated with this two-step procedure with porosity $\epsilon = 0.553$ is depicted in Figure 1.

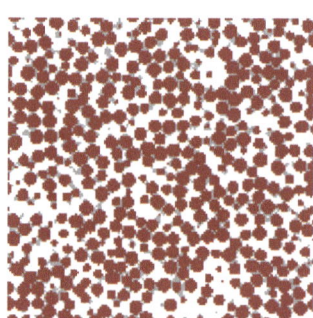

Figure 1. Isometric (**left**) and middle plane (**right**) view of a typical porous sample; colors: brown—washcoat (Ω_w), grey—solid (binder, Ω_s), white (transparent)—free pores (Ω_f), green—inlet boundary section, opposite of the (non-visible)—outlet section. GeoDict visualization [20].

In addition to the typical porous geometry characterization parameters, such as porosity ϵ, phase volume fraction (for washcoat) ϵ_w, and phase specific surface area (for free pores) A_S, we also compute the integral Minkowski parameters as morphological features. A complete list of parameters with their definitions for each porous sample can be found in the supplementary Section A. In total, 59 artificial porous samples were generated for further processing. The geometry generation time per sample varied greatly depending on the porosity, from the minimum of 6 wall-clock seconds (wcs) to the maximum of 222 wcs, with the average of 111 wcs for a system with 40 cores Intel Xeon CPU E5-2600 v2, 2.8 GHz. On the contrary, the time for evaluation of geometric parameters was almost the same for all samples and did not exceed 2 wcs.

Both the generation and parameter evaluation phases for each geometry were performed with the GeoDict software (Release 2022) [20] and Python scripts.

2.2. Governing Equations for FOM

Different approaches can be used to describe the flow and transport of chemical species through the porous medium at the pore-scale. Many of them are based on solving convection–diffusion–reaction (CDR) equations for the species transport and (Navier–)

Stokes equations for the bulk flow. Thus, we consider, as the FOM solution in the current paper, the solution of the CDR equation for a species of interest and additionally assume, based on typical filtration application conditions, that (i) flow Reynolds numbers are sufficiently small $Re \ll 1$ and Stokes equations are valid for any sub-region of the pore space Ω_f, and (ii) the concentration of the species of interest, c, is much smaller than the bulk mixture concentration. Although these are rather strict assumptions, they work well for catalytic filtration applications and are in fact the standard in this field. This justifies a one-way coupling approach when the solution of the flow equations can be decoupled from the species transport equation. We also restrict ourselves to scalar CDR equations with a linear source term. This type of source term can be used to describe a first order sorption–desorption process in porous media (Henry isotherm). According to the aforementioned assumptions, the CDR equation for species concentration, $c \geq 0$, can be written in dimensionless form as

$$\partial_t c - \Delta c + \text{Pe}_L \, \nabla \cdot (\mathbf{v} c) + \text{Da}_L \, c = 0, \quad x \in \left(\Omega_f \cup \Omega_w\right), \, t > 0, \quad (1)$$

where Da_L, Pe_L are the parameters: $\text{Da}_L = \frac{k_R L}{D}$ is the piece-wise-constant Damköhler number, $\text{Pe}_L = \frac{u_{in} L}{D}$ is the Peclet number, $L, D > 0$ are the characteristic length and diffusion coefficient, respectively; u_{in} is the inlet velocity, $k_R(x) \geq 0$ is the reaction rate constant and reaction occurs only in the washcoat region:

$$k_R(x) = \begin{cases} 0, & \mathbf{x} \in \Omega_f, \\ k_r > 0, & \mathbf{x} \in \Omega_w. \end{cases}$$

In Equation (1), the characteristic diffusion time was used as a time scale. Moreover, we fix the parameter values, $(\text{Pe}_L, \text{Da}_L) = (5, 0.1)$, and thus, consider only a convection-dominated regime for each geometry. For the numerical solution, Equation (1) was complemented with zero initial conditions, Dirichlet conditions for the inlet boundary section and zero Neumann conditions for the outlet boundary section and all other boundaries, see Figure 1. Based on the solution of Equation (1), a quantity of interest, the breakthrough curve, can be evaluated as an integral concentration over the outlet section of the geometry, Γ_{outlet}:

$$a(t) = \int_{\Gamma_{\text{outlet}}} c(x, t) \, d\sigma. \quad (2)$$

For the velocity $\mathbf{v}$ within Equation (1), the stationary Stokes equations in Ω_f were considered:

$$\begin{aligned} \mu \Delta \mathbf{v} &= \nabla p, \\ \nabla \cdot \mathbf{v} &= 0, \end{aligned} \quad (3)$$

where $p : \Omega_f \to \mathbb{R}$ is the pressure and $\mu \in \mathbb{R}_+$ is the dynamic viscosity of the gas mixture. Velocity inlet–pressure outlet boundary conditions were used for system Equation (3).

Thus, at the first step of the overall solution procedure, the velocity field $\mathbf{v}$ was determined as a solution of system Equation (3). In the second step, due to (ii), using the predetermined velocity field, the concentration field c and integral Equation (2) were computed. Both steps were performed with the PoreChem software (Release 1.0 beta) [21].

3. Kernel Methods

Kernel methods [22] comprise versatile tools for scattered data approximation, revolving around the notion of a symmetric kernel $k : \Omega_d \times \Omega_d \to \mathbb{R}$. An important type of kernel is given by strictly positive definite kernels, i.e., kernels such that the so-called kernel matrix $k(X_N, X_N) = (k(\mathbf{x}_i, \mathbf{x}_j))_{i,j=1}^N$ is positive definite for any choice of pairwise distinct points $X_N = \{\mathbf{x}_i\}_{i=1}^N \subset \Omega_d$, $N \in \mathbb{N}$. In the context of machine learning, the set X_N

is often referred to as the training set X_{train}, i.e., $X_N = X_{\text{train}}$. In the following, we focus on the popular class of radial basis function kernels on $\Omega_d \subseteq \mathbb{R}^d$, which can be expressed as $k(\mathbf{x}, \mathbf{x}') = \phi(\|\mathbf{x} - \mathbf{x}'\|)$ using a radial basis function $\phi : \mathbb{R} \to \mathbb{R}$. Popular instances of such kernels are given by the following:

$$k(\mathbf{x}, \mathbf{x}') = e^{-\epsilon^2 \|\mathbf{x}-\mathbf{x}'\|^2} \qquad \text{Gaussian kernel,}$$

$$k(\mathbf{x}, \mathbf{x}') = (1 + \epsilon \|\mathbf{x} - \mathbf{x}'\|) e^{-\epsilon \|\mathbf{x}-\mathbf{x}'\|} \qquad \text{Matérn 1,}$$

$$k(\mathbf{x}, \mathbf{x}') = (3 + 3\epsilon \|\mathbf{x} - \mathbf{x}'\| + \epsilon^2 \|\mathbf{x} - \mathbf{x}'\|^2) e^{-\epsilon \|\mathbf{x}-\mathbf{x}'\|} \qquad \text{Matérn 2,}$$

which are also later on used in Section 4. As we do not know about the regularity of the target function, we apply kernels that are infinitely smooth (Gaussian kernels) or finitely smooth (Matérn kernels) in order to cover various possible regularities of the target function. The parameter ϵ is the so-called shape parameter, which allows us to tune the width of these kernels.

Given not only the input data $\{\mathbf{x}_i\}_{i=1}^N$ but also the corresponding (possibly vector-valued) target values $\{\mathbf{f}_i\}_{i=1}^N \subset \mathbb{R}^b$, $b \geq 1$, a well known representer theorem states that the optimal least squares kernel approximant is given by

$$s_N(\mathbf{x}) = \sum_{i=1}^N \alpha_i k(\mathbf{x}, \mathbf{x}_i), \tag{4}$$

with coefficients $\{\alpha_j\}_{j=1}^N \subset \mathbb{R}^b$. These coefficients can be computed directly by solving the regularized linear equation system $(k(X_N, X_N) + \lambda I)\alpha = y$, where $\alpha \in \mathbb{R}^{N \times b}$ and $y \in \mathbb{R}^{N \times b}$ refer to a collection of the coefficients and target values in arrays. The regularization parameter $\lambda \geq 0$ allows us to steer the robustness to outliers/noise versus the approximation accuracy in the training points. The value $\lambda = 0$ corresponds to kernel interpolation. For this case $\lambda = 0$, the assumption on the strict positive definiteness of the kernel still ensures the solvability of the system.

Greedy kernel approximation: In order to obtain a sparse kernel model, one strives to have a smaller expansion size $n \ll N$ within Equation (4). For this, greedy algorithms can be leveraged, which select a suitable subset of centers X_n from X_N. For this, they start with $X_0 = \{\}$ and iteratively add points from X_N to X_n as $X_{n+1} := X_n \cup \{\mathbf{x}_{n+1}\}$, according to some selection criterion. While there are several selection criteria in use in the literature, we focus on the f-greedy selection criterion, which reads

$$\mathbf{x}_{n+1} := \operatorname{argmax}_{\mathbf{x}_i \in X_N \setminus X_n} |\mathbf{f}_i - s_n(\mathbf{x}_i)|.$$

This residual-based selection criterion incorporates the data point of the largest error, i.e., directly aims at minimizing the maximal absolute error of the kernel model. An efficient implementation of such greedy kernel algorithms is provided by the VKOGA package [15], and a comprehensive analysis of the convergence of such greedy kernel algorithms was provided in [16]. Because of the greedy strategy, VKOGA is often a superior method compared to other kernel-based strategies. Other methods for obtaining sparse, kernel-based models are sparse Gaussian processes [23,24], support vector regression (SVR) [25] or the reduced support vector set approach [25]. The computational efficiency of VKOGA kernel models is shown, for example, in [26], where a comparison of VKOGA with support vector machines was performed, which revealed that VKOGA results in sparser models and, hence, less computational time for training. Similarly, less computational time for prediction was observed in [13], where Gaussian processes and VKOGA were compared. In [27], a comparison of VKOGA and SVR over other ML techniques was performed in a turbulent flow prediction scenario. The study revealed that those kernel methods gave the best performance regarding the quality of the approximated discrete-time dynamics.

Two-layered kernels: In order to incorporate feature learning into kernel models, we make use of two-layered kernels [17,18]: These make use of a base kernel k, as given above, and combine it with a matrix $\mathbf{A} \in \mathbb{R}^{d \times d}$, such that the two-layered kernel is given by

$$k_{\mathbf{A}}(\mathbf{x}, \mathbf{x}') = k(\mathbf{A}\mathbf{x}, \mathbf{A}\mathbf{x}') = \phi(\|\mathbf{A}(\mathbf{x} - \mathbf{x}')\|). \quad (5)$$

With this, the two-layered kernel can be optimized to the given data $(\{\mathbf{x}_i\}_{i=1}^N, \{\mathbf{f}_i\}_{i=1}^N)$ by optimizing the first layer matrix $\mathbf{A} \in \mathbb{R}^{d \times d}$. Thus, this two-layered structure may considerably improve the performance of the kernel model, especially for medium- to high-dimensional input data, where an equal importance of all features is highly unlikely. The strength of two-layered kernel models and their superior performance over shallow kernel models has been observed, for example, when applied to heat conduction [18] or when used as a surrogate model for chemical kinetics [8]. We investigate whether this behavior can also be observed for our current problem. For the optimization of the matrix $\mathbf{A}$, we employ the fast-gradient-descent-based mini-batch optimization proposed in [17] and extended it to vector valued target values $b > 1$ in [18]. The overall idea is to leverage an efficiently computable leave-one-out cross validation (LOOCV) error loss, which, thus, makes the kernel generalize well to the unseen data. In particular, this cross validation error loss makes use of both input and target values, i.e., it is a supervised optimization.

The matrix $\mathbf{A}$ makes the two-layered kernel $k_{\mathbf{A}}$ even more interpretable: The large singular values with corresponding right singular vectors within the singular value decomposition of the matrix $\mathbf{A}$ correspond to the more important features within the data set, while the smaller singular values with the corresponding right singular vectors correspond to the less important features within the data set.

In the following Section 4, we make use of the notion "single layered kernel" to refer to the standard kernel k, while we make use of the notion "two-layered kernel" to refer to (optimized) kernels $k_{\mathbf{A}}$.

4. Numerical Experiments

In this section, we present the numerical experiments. The goal is to approximate breakthrough curves Equation (2) from voxel data, which characterizes the geometry of the porous medium. As explained in Section 2, the voxel data are described by a vector $\mathbf{z} \in \{0,1\}^{2N_V}$. In our numerical experiment, we choose $N_V = 150^3$. We discretize a breakthrough curve $a(t)$ on an equidistant temporal grid t_i, $i = 1, \ldots, n_t$, as the vector $\mathbf{a} := (a(t_i))_{i=1}^{n_t} \in \mathbb{R}^{n_t}$ with $n_t = 500$ time steps.

We compare two different kernel-based models for learning the breakthrough curves (see Figure 2), in which either morphological features (MF) prescribed by expert knowledge (see Section A) are extracted or principal component analysis (PCA) features are learned from the data using a PCA. The kernel function k is chosen to be either a shallow one-layered or a two-layered kernel. We refer to these models in the scope of our paper as MF-1L-kernel and MF-2L-kernel or PCA-1L-kernel and PCA-2L-kernel, depending on the depth of the kernel (one-layered/two-layered) and whether we extract morphological features or PCA features.

Both types of models (MF) and (PCA) are based on a feature map $\Phi : \mathbb{R}^{2N_V} \to \mathbb{R}^{n_f}$ with n_f features and a kernel function $k : \mathbb{R}^d \times \mathbb{R}^d \to \mathbb{R}$ with $d = n_f$, such that the resulting kernel models using the single-layer or the two-layered kernels are given as

$$s_n(\mathbf{z}) = \sum_{i=1}^n \alpha_i k(\Phi(\mathbf{z}), \Phi(\mathbf{z}_i)), \quad \text{respectively,} \quad s_n(\mathbf{z}) = \sum_{i=1}^n \alpha_i k(\mathbf{A}\Phi(\mathbf{z}), \mathbf{A}\Phi(\mathbf{z}_i)), \quad (6)$$

with coefficients $\alpha_i \in \mathbb{R}^b$, $b = n_t$ and centers $\mathbf{z}_i \in \{0,1\}^{2N_V}$ for $i = 1, \ldots, n$. The expansion size n is fixed to $n = 10$. Choosing smaller values for n would worsen the results presented in the next subsections considerably, while increasing n would only influence the approximation quality on the test set slightly.

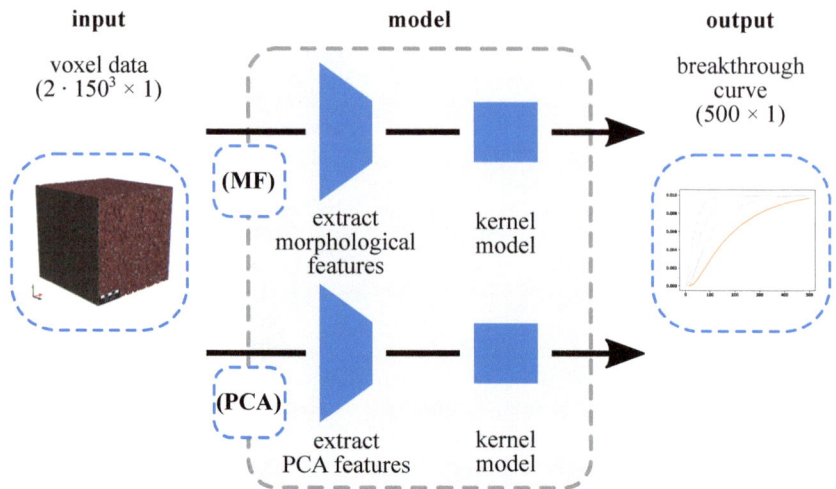

Figure 2. Two feature extraction-strategy-based models to approximate breakthrough curves from voxel data: Model with morphological features (MF), and model with PCA features (PCA).

All of these models involve hyper-parameters, which are listed in Table 1. Suitable values for the hyper-parameters are determined via an LOOCV on the training data set. Note that in the cases where two-layered kernels are applied, no LOOCV for the shape parameter is performed, and instead, the matrix **A** is optimized using the procedure described in the previous section. The kernel function and the regularization parameter are determined via LOOCV in both cases.

Table 1. Hyper-parameters of the kernel function k, shape parameter ϵ and regularization parameter λ used during LOOCV of the MF-based models and PCA-based models.

Hyper-Parameter	Values
kernel fun.	Matérn 1, Matérn 2, Gaussian kernel
Shape parameters	1, 1/2, 1/4, 1/8, 1/16, 1/32
Regularization parameters	$0, 10^{-2}, 10^{-3}, 10^{-4}, 10^{-5}, 10^{-6}$

In the following, we discuss the generation of the training and test data (Section 4.1), the training and results of the (MF) models based on morphological features (Section 4.2) and of the (PCA) models based on PCA features (Section 4.3).

4.1. Training and Test Data

In total, we consider $n_s = 59$ samples $X := \{\mathbf{z}_i\}_{i=1}^{n_s}$ of voxel data $\mathbf{z}_i$ and the corresponding time-discretized breakthrough curves $\mathbf{a}_i$ (see Figure 3). The breakthrough curves $\mathbf{a}_i$ are obtained by solving Equations (1) and (3) based on the geometry described by the corresponding voxel data $\mathbf{z}_i$. The average computational cost of solving Equations (1) and (3) for one sample is 7514 wcs with a standard deviation of 286 wcs on a workstation with two Intel Xeon Gold 6240R (48 cores in total).

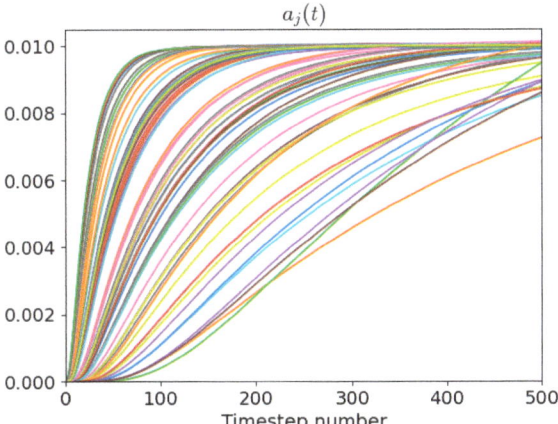

Figure 3. All breakthrough curves $a_i(t)$ computed from the voxel data $\mathbf{z}_i$ for $i \in \{1, \ldots, 59\}$. Different colours correspond to breaktrough curves computed from different geometries.

We use an approximate 80–20% training–test split, which results in $n_{s,\text{train}} = N = 47$ training samples $X_{\text{train}} = X_N$ and $n_{s,\text{test}} = 12$ test samples X_{test} with $X = X_{\text{train}} \cup X_{\text{test}}$ and $X_{\text{train}} \cap X_{\text{test}} = \emptyset$. To demonstrate robustness with respect to the choice of the training–test split, we consider three different random splits, where we use the same three random splits to measure the performance of each model. As an error measure, we use a relative error on the test set

$$e_{\text{rel}} = \frac{1}{|X_{\text{test}}|}\sqrt{\sum_{\mathbf{z}_i \in X_{\text{test}}} \frac{\|\mathbf{a}_i - s_N(\mathbf{z}_i)\|^2}{\|\mathbf{a}_i\|^2}}. \qquad (7)$$

4.2. Kernel Models on Morphological Features

Because of the high dimensionality of the input space, it is necessary to apply some reduction technique before training the machine learning model. In this section, we extract $n_f = 6$ morphological geometry features that describe the porous medium. These are the porosity, the washcoat volume fraction, the volume of free pores, the surface area for the free pores, the integral of mean curvature of the free pores and the integral of total curvature of the free pores. For further information on how they are computed, see supplementary Section A. Thus, the machine learning model can be represented by setting $\Phi = \Phi_{\text{MF}}$ in Equation (6) $\Phi_{\text{MF}} : \mathbb{R}^{2N_V} \to \mathbb{R}^{n_f}$ the mapping that computes the morphological features from a given geometry.

For the first experiment, we use shallow kernels and present the approximated breakthrough curves in Figure 4. We observe that except for the red outlier curve in the bottom diagram, all curves are well approximated. This corresponds to the relative test error presented in Table 2, where we see that for the first two data splits, a relative error of approximately 0.01% can be achieved; whereas, for the third split, we only achieve an error of approximately 0.42%. We further observe from Table 2 that for the first two data splits, exactly the same hyper-parameters (kernel function, shape parameter and regularization parameter) are chosen. However, they are chosen differently for the third data set, which may be due to the red outlier curve being part of the test set for the third data split.

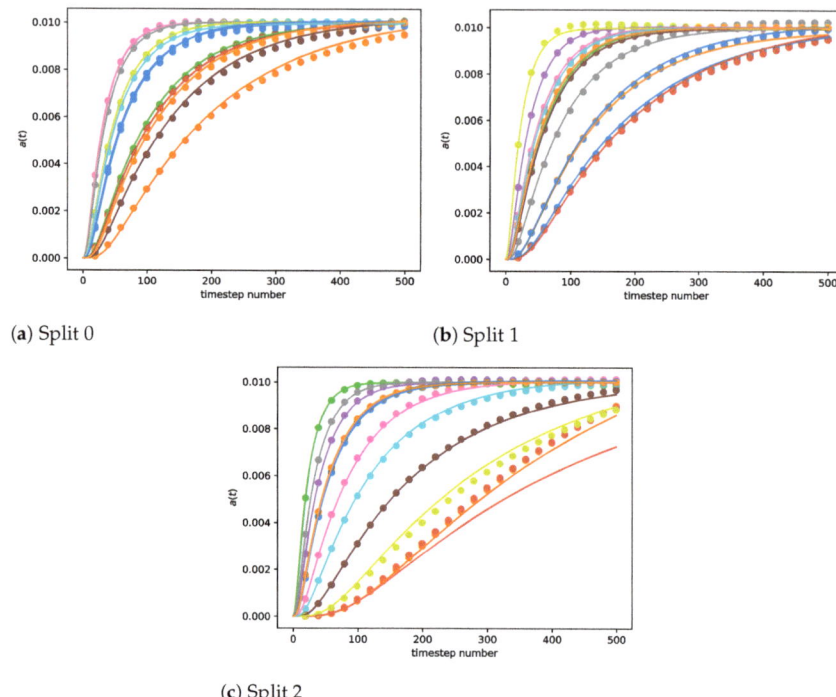

(a) Split 0

(b) Split 1

(c) Split 2

Figure 4. MF-1L-kernel: Predicted breakthrough curves on the test set X_{test} for three different training–test splits. Solid: Breakthrough curves, dotted: predictions. The different colors correspond to the different breakthrough curves.

Table 2. MF-1L-kernel: Relative error (7) and the selected hyper-parameters from Table 1 for three different training–test splits (0–2).

Split	Rel. Err.	Kernel Fun.	Shape Parameter	Reg. Par.
0	$1.49 \cdot 10^{-3}$	Matérn 1	1.00	$1.00 \cdot 10^{-2}$
1	$1.60 \cdot 10^{-4}$	Matérn 1	1.00	$1.00 \cdot 10^{-2}$
2	$4.23 \cdot 10^{-3}$	Matérn 1	$2.50 \cdot 10^{-1}$	$1.00 \cdot 10^{-4}$
average	$1.51 \cdot 10^{-3}$			

For the next experiment, we included two-layer optimization of the kernel model and present the approximated breakthrough curves in Figure 5. We observe that a similar approximation quality can be achieved using two-layered kernels. All breakthrough curves except for the red outlier curve in the bottom diagram are well approximated. The relative test error (see Table 3) is slightly improved for the third data split. However, for the first and second split, it becomes slightly worse. We observe that similar to the experiment with shallow kernel models, for each data split, the Matérn 1 kernel is selected and that for the third split, a smaller regularization parameter is selected than for the first and second one. To compare the shape transformations by the first layer, we present the first layer matrix **A** in Table 3. For an easier comparison, the matrix **A** is visualized using the color-map at the bottom of the table. We observe that the matrices look very similar for each data split.

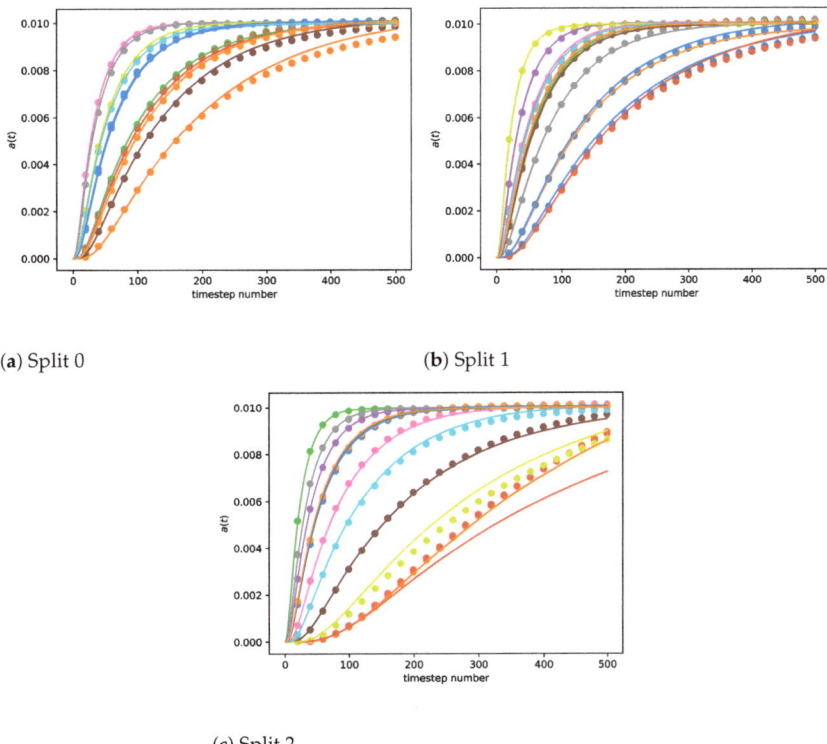

(a) Split 0 (b) Split 1

(c) Split 2

Figure 5. MF-2L-kernel: Predicted breakthrough curves on the test set X_{test} for three different training–test splits. Solid: Breakthrough curves, dotted: predictions. The different colors correspond to the different breakthrough curves.

Table 3. MF-2L-kernel: Relative error (7) and the selected hyper-parameters from Table 1 for three different training–test splits (0–2).

Split	Rel. Err.	Kernel Fun.	A	Reg. Par.
0	$1.54 \cdot 10^{-4}$	Matérn 2		$1.00 \cdot 10^{-3}$
1	$2.37 \cdot 10^{-4}$	Matérn 2		$1.00 \cdot 10^{-3}$
2	$3.99 \cdot 10^{-3}$	Matérn 1		$1.00 \cdot 10^{-4}$
average	$1.46 \cdot 10^{-3}$			

4.3. Kernel Models on PCA Features

Next, we use the PCA to define a feature map Φ. In order to be comparable to the previous experiment, we choose the number of features as $n_f = 6$. Following the idea of the PCA [28], we choose the PCA feature map $\Phi_{PCA}(z) = U_{n_f}^T z$ based on the first n_f left-singular vectors $U_{n_f} \in \mathbb{R}^{2N_V \times n_f}$ of the matrix $Z := (z)_{z \in X_{train}} \in \mathbb{R}^{2N_V \times n_{s,train}}$ via the SVD

$$Z = U\Sigma V^T \qquad \text{with} \qquad U_{n_f} := U(:, : n_f) \qquad (8)$$

and set $\Phi = \Phi_{PCA}$ in Equation (6) (technical note: The voxel data are saved as a boolean array $z \in \{0,1\}^{2N_V}$. To compute the SVD, we convert these data to a floating point number, which is why $Z \in \mathbb{R}^{2N_V \times n_{s,train}}$).

In Figure 6, we present the prediction of the breakthrough curves for the PCA-1L-kernel model on the test set X_{test} for the three different randomized training–test splits. We observe that many of the breakthrough curves are well approximated and a mean relative error of approximately 0.5–1.3% (see Table 4) can be achieved. However, some breakthrough curves are badly approximated, especially the two blue curves for the first data split. We observe that three different kernels, three different shape parameters and three different regularization parameters are chosen for each data split. We further observe from Section 4.3 that $n_f = 6$ is also a suitable choice in the sense that a small test error is achieved for that setting compared to higher and smaller values of n_f.

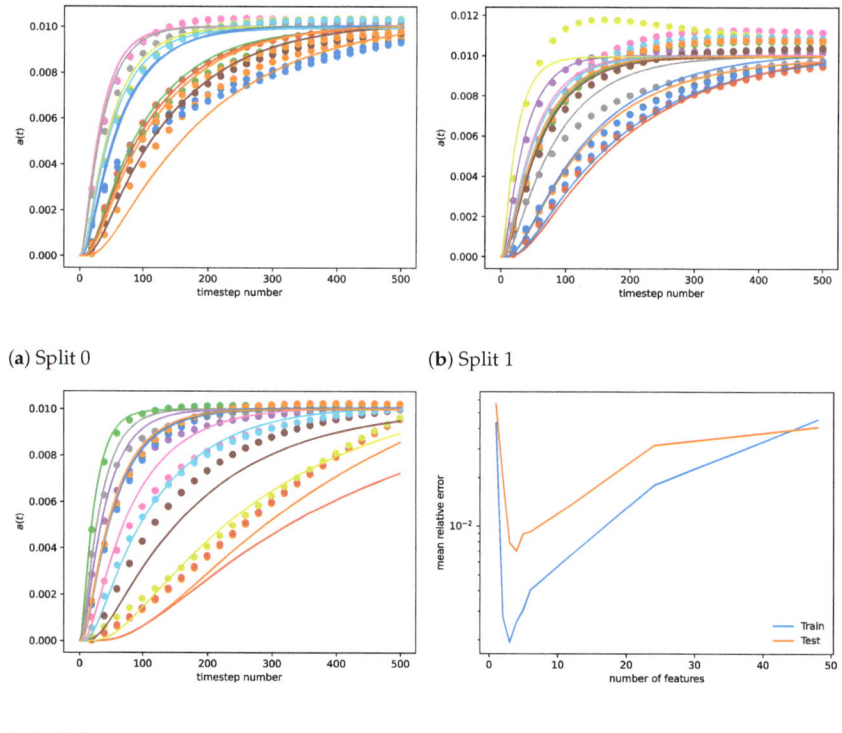

Figure 6. PCA-1L-kernel: (**a–c**): Predicted breakthrough curves on the test set X_{test} for $n_f = 6$ and three different training–test splits. Solid: Breakthrough curves, dotted: predictions. The different colors correspond to the different breakthrough curves. (**d**): Relative test and train error (Equation (7)) over n_f.

Table 4. PCA-1L-kernel: Relative error (7) and the selected hyper-parameters from Table 1 for three different training–test splits (0–2).

Split	Rel. Err.	Kernel Fun.	Shape Parameter	Reg. Par.
0	$9.62 \cdot 10^{-3}$	Matérn 1	$6.25 \cdot 10^{-2}$	$1.00 \cdot 10^{-3}$
1	$4.77 \cdot 10^{-3}$	Gaussian kernel	$6.25 \cdot 10^{-2}$	$1.00 \cdot 10^{-4}$
2	$1.34 \cdot 10^{-2}$	Matérn 2	$2.5 \cdot 10^{-1}$	$1.00 \cdot 10^{-2}$
average	$9.26 \cdot 10^{-3}$			

For the next experiment, we consider the PCA-2L-kernel model. The results for the analogous experiments to the previous paragraph are presented in Figure 7. We chose again $n_f = 6$ to be consistent with the previous experiments. However, as we observe in Section 4.3, for $n_f = 3$, slightly better results could have been achieved.

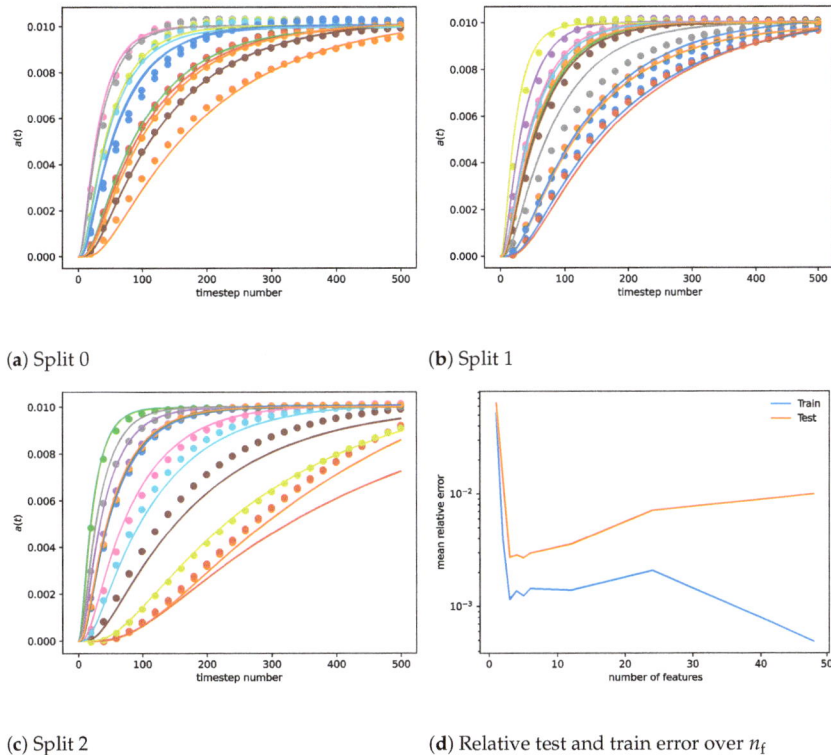

(**a**) Split 0   (**b**) Split 1

(**c**) Split 2   (**d**) Relative test and train error over n_f

Figure 7. (**a–c**): Top and left: Predicted breakthrough curves on the test set X_{test} for $n_f = 6$ and three different training–test splits. Solid: Breakthrough curves, dotted: predictions. The different colors correspond to the different breakthrough curves. (**d**): Relative test and train error (Equation (7)) over n_f.

We observe that the results from the shallow kernel models are considerably improved by using two-layered kernels. The relative errors from Table 5 can be reduced to 0.08–0.7%, and we do not observe badly approximated curves for the first data split anymore. Compared to the the MF-2L-kernel experiments from the previous section, we also observe that the approximation qualities are quite similar. This means that the PCA features transformed by the first layer of the two-layered kernel are able to describe the geometry almost as well as the morphological features. This shows the strength of two-layered kernels, as the PCA feature extraction is purely data-based, and no expert knowledge had to be used.

Table 5. PCA-2L-kernel: Relative error (7) and the selected hyper-parameters from Table 1 for three different training–test splits (0–2).

Split	Rel. Err.	Kernel Fun.	A	Reg. Par.
0	$7.94 \cdot 10^{-4}$	Matérn 1		$1.00 \cdot 10^{-3}$
1	$1.10 \cdot 10^{-3}$	Matérn 2		$1.00 \cdot 10^{-2}$
2	$7.05 \cdot 10^{-3}$	Matérn 1		$1.00 \cdot 10^{-4}$
average	$2.98 \cdot 10^{-3}$			

We further observe from Table 5 that, again, similar hyper-parameters are selected for each data split. For example, the same kernel (Matérn 1) was selected for the first and third data split. Moreover, we see similarities in the first layer matrices **A** of the kernels. For all three matrices, the entries in the left upper 3×3 block are considerably larger than the other entries, which means that the first three modes are the important ones. Compared to Table 3, there are larger differences between the first layers. This can be explained by the fact that in contrast to the MF-feature map, the data-based PCA-feature map is different for all three data splits. This is due to the linear mappings defined by the PCA modes being different in each split.

Lastly, we compare the mean errors averaged over the three different training–test splits in Table 6. We observe that the models based on morphological feature extraction work very well in combination with both one-layered and two-layered kernels. In contrast, combining one-layered kernels with PCA feature extraction yields an average error that is almost one order of magnitude larger. This error is considerably improved by applying two-layered kernels, and almost the same accuracy as with the morphological feature extraction is achieved.

Table 6. Mean relative test errors, averaged over the three training–test splits.

	1L	2L
MF	$1.51 \cdot 10^{-3}$	$1.46 \cdot 10^{-3}$
PCA	$9.26 \cdot 10^{-3}$	$2.98 \cdot 10^{-3}$

4.4. Runtime Discussion

In this subsection, we compare the runtimes of the different methods in Table 7. We compare the time needed for the computation of the feature map added to the feature extraction time on the test set (first column), the time needed for LOOCV, the training time of the final model and the evaluation time on the test set. Note that the full order model solves and the morphological feature extraction are performed on a different machine (workstation with two Intel Xeon Gold 6240R (48 cores in total)) than the PCA feature extraction and kernel model training (performed on a computer with 64 GB RAM and a 13th Gen Intel i7-13700K processor) due to licensing limitations. We observe that the LOOCV for the two-layered models is way more expensive than for the shallow models, which is due to the optimization of the first layer. However, it is still considerably lower (approximately 30 times for the MF-2L-kernel and 7 times for the PCA-2L-kernel) than the generation of a single training sample (7514 wcs). Furthermore, the LOOCV time and final model training of the MF-kernel models is less expensive than the training on the morphological features. However, the computation of the PCA feature map is less expensive than the computation of the morphological features. Moreover, the evaluation time of the PCA-kernel models is larger than the evaluation of the MF kernel models. Since the computation of the morphological features i.e., the evaluation of Φ_{MF} takes approximately 2 wcs per sample, the MF approaches have a larger overall evaluation time (summing evaluation time of MF extraction and MF-1L-kernel/MF-2L-kernel). Compared to the FOM, this results in a speed-up of almost 6 orders of magnitude for the PCA kernel models and 3 orders of magnitude for the MF kernel models. Nevertheless, in both cases, the evaluation times are considerably lower than the computation of the training samples.

Table 7. Runtime comparison of the machine learning methods in wcs averaged over the three training–test splits.

Model	Feat. Map	LOOCV Time	Final Model Train Time	Eval. Time
FOM	-	-	-	$9.02 \cdot 10^4$
MF extraction	$9.40 \cdot 10^1$	-	-	$2.40 \cdot 10^1$
MF-1L-kernel	-	$5.90 \cdot 10^0$	$9.95 \cdot 10^{-4}$	$2.91 \cdot 10^{-4}$
MF-2L-kernel	-	$2.01 \cdot 10^2$	$2.12 \cdot 10^{-1}$	$2.67 \cdot 10^{-4}$
PCA feat. map comp.	$1.28 \cdot 10^1$	-	-	-
PCA-1L-kernel	-	$2.29 \cdot 10^1$	$1.36 \cdot 10^{-3}$	$1.83 \cdot 10^{-1}$
PCA-2L-kernel	-	$9.18 \cdot 10^3$	$8.63 \cdot 10^{-1}$	$2.13 \cdot 10^{-1}$

5. Conclusions and Outlook

In this work, we demonstrated how breakthrough curves can be predicted from the geometry of a 3D porous medium. We presented two approaches on how to treat the high dimension of the input data: For the first approach, we computed morphological features of the geometries and learned a mapping from these morphological features to the breakthrough curves. For the second approach, we computed PCA features of the geometry data set and learned a mapping from these PCA features to the breakthrough curve.

We observed that the MF approach worked well in combination with one-layered kernels and that both approaches worked well in combination with two-layered kernels. This is compelling, as the morphological features used in the study are well-known informative and predictive quantities for porous media, and in contrast, the PCA feature extraction approach is purely data-based. Thus, the results indicate the strength of using two-layered kernels, as they automatically adapt to the relevant features. We further observed that the scarce-data situation did not prevent these approaches from easily predicting the high-dimensional outputs.

The future work will focus on how ideas from convolutional neural networks can be combined with the framework of deep multi-layered kernels. Moreover, we will investigate whether data augmentation (rotating/reflecting geometry samples without changing the breakthrough curves) can further improve the PCA-feature approach while avoiding the computation of expensive FOM solutions.

Author Contributions: Conceptualization, R.H., P.B., T.W., B.H., P.T. and O.I.; methodology, R.H., P.B., T.W. and B.H.; software, R.H., P.B., T.W. and P.T.; writing—original draft preparation, R.H., P.B., T.W. and P.T.; writing—review and editing, R.H., P.B., T.W., B.H., P.T. and O.I.; visualization, R.H., P.B., T.W. and P.T.; supervision, B.H. and O.I.; funding acquisition, B.H. and O.I. All authors have read and agreed to the published version of the manuscript.

Funding: Funded by BMBF under the contracts 05M20VSA and 05M20AMD (ML-MORE). The authors acknowledge the funding of the project by the Deutsche Forschungsgemeinschaft (DFG, German Research Foundation) under Germany's Excellence Strategy - EXC 2075 - 390740016.

Data Availability Statement: The code to reproduce this study got published on 6 June 2024 and is openly available at https://doi.org/10.18419/darus-4227, accessed on 1 May 2024.

Conflicts of Interest: The authors declare no conflicts of interest.

Appendix A

In the following, morphological features, i.e., geometry parameters are listed that were computed based on the voxel representation of the porous samples. We assume that we already have a voxel representation of the domain Ω and its subsets $\Omega_f, \Omega_w, \Omega_s$, where $\Omega_f, \Omega_w, \Omega_s$ are the free pores, washcoat and solid domains, respectively.

1. Porosity ϵ:
$$\epsilon := \frac{|\Omega_f|}{|\Omega|}.$$

2. Washcoat volume fraction ϵ_w:
$$\epsilon_w := \frac{|\Omega_p|}{|\Omega|}.$$

3. Volume of the free pores V:
$$V := |\Omega_f|.$$

4. Surface area for the free pores phase S:
$$S := |\partial \Omega_f|.$$

5. Integral of mean curvature for free pores phase, c_f. For smooth surfaces, this quantity is usually defined by the integral
$$c_f := \frac{1}{2} \int_{\partial \Omega_f} \left(\frac{1}{k_1} + \frac{1}{k_2} \right) ds,$$
here, ds is a surface element of $\partial \Omega_f$, and k_1 and k_2 are the two principal curvatures from the respective surface element. Since the boundaries of the voxelized geometry are piece-wise flat, the software package computes an approximation of this quantity for our phase boundaries.

6. Integral of total curvature for free pores phase, ct_f. For smooth surfaces, this quantity is usually defined by the integral
$$ct_f := \int_{\partial \Omega_f} \left(\frac{1}{k_1 k_2} \right) ds,$$

here, ds is a surface element of $\partial \Omega_f$, and k_1 and k_2 are the two principal curvatures from the respective surface element. The software package computes an approximation of this quantity for our piece-wise flat phase boundaries.

References

1. Zhao, N.; Li, D.Q.; Gu, S.X.; Du, W. Analytical fragility relation for buried cast iron pipelines with lead-caulked joints based on machine learning algorithms. *Earthq. Spectra* **2024**, *40*, 566–583. [CrossRef]
2. Hu, C.; Dong, B.; Shao, H.; Zhang, J.; Wang, Y. Toward purifying defect feature for multilabel sewer defect classification. *IEEE Trans. Instrum. Meas.* **2023**, *72*, 1–11. [CrossRef]
3. Wu, J.; Yin, X.; Xiao, H. Seeing permeability from images: Fast prediction with convolutional neural networks. *Sci. Bull.* **2018**, *63*, 1215–1222. [CrossRef] [PubMed]
4. Marcato, A.; Boccardo, G.; Marchisio, D. From computational fluid dynamics to structure interpretation via neural networks: An application to flow and transport in porous media. *Ind. Eng. Chem. Res.* **2022**, *61*, 8530–8541. [CrossRef]
5. Gärttner, S.; Alpak, F.O.; Meier, A.; Ray, N.; Frank, F. Estimating permeability of 3D micro-CT images by physics-informed CNNs based on DNS. *Comput. Geosci.* **2023**, *27*, 245–262. [CrossRef]
6. Santos, J.E.; Xu, D.; Jo, H.; Landry, C.J.; Prodanović, M.; Pyrcz, M.J. PoreFlow-Net: A 3D convolutional neural network to predict fluid flow through porous media. *Adv. Water Resour.* **2020**, *138*, 103539. [CrossRef]
7. Zhou, X.H.; McClure, J.E.; Chen, C.; Xiao, H. Neural network–based pore flow field prediction in porous media using super resolution. *Phys. Rev. Fluids* **2022**, *7*, 074302. [CrossRef]
8. Döppel, F.; Wenzel, T.; Herkert, R.; Haasdonk, B.; Votsmeier, M. Goal-Oriented Two-Layered Kernel Models as Automated Surrogates for Surface Kinetics in Reactor Simulations. *Chem. Ing. Tech.* **2023**, *96*, 759–768. [CrossRef]
9. Laloy, E.; Jacques, D. Speeding up reactive transport simulations in cement systems by surrogate geochemical modeling: Deep neural networks and k-nearest neighbors. *Transp. Porous Media* **2022**, *143*, 433–462. [CrossRef]
10. Silva, V.; Regnier, G.; Salinas, P.; Heaney, C.; Jackson, M.; Pain, C. Rapid Modelling of Reactive Transport in Porous Media using Machine Learning. In Proceedings of the ECMOR 2022, Hague, The Netherlands, 5–7 September 2022; European Association of Geoscientists & Engineers: Hague, The Netherlands, 2022; Volume 1, pp. 1–9. [CrossRef]
11. Liu, M.; Kwon, B.; Kang, P.K. Machine learning to predict effective reaction rates in 3D porous media from pore structural features. *Sci. Rep.* **2022**, *12*, 5486. [CrossRef] [PubMed]
12. Marcato, A. Deep Neural Networks as Scale-Bridging Tools for Flow and Transport Modelling in Porous Media. Ph.D Thesis, Politecnico di Torino, Torino, Italy, 2023.
13. Fokina, D. Machine Learning Algorithms for Solution of Convection-Diffusion-Reaction Equation at Pore-Scale. Ph.D Thesis, Fachbereich Mathematik, RPTU Kaiserslautern, Germany, 2023.
14. Grigo, C.; Koutsourelakis, P.S. A physics-aware, probabilistic machine learning framework for coarse-graining high-dimensional systems in the Small Data regime. *J. Comput. Phys.* **2019**, *397*, 108842. [CrossRef]
15. Santin, G.; Haasdonk, B. Kernel Methods for Surrogate Modeling. In *Model Order Reduction*; De Gruyter: Berlin, Germany, 2021; Volume 2. [CrossRef]
16. Wenzel, T.; Santin, G.; Haasdonk, B. Analysis of target data-dependent greedy kernel algorithms: Convergence rates for f-, $f \cdot P$- and f/P-greedy. *Constr. Approx.* **2023**, *57*, 45–74. [CrossRef]
17. Wenzel, T.; Marchetti, F.; Perracchione, E. Data-Driven Kernel Designs for Optimized Greedy Schemes: A Machine Learning Perspective. *SIAM J. Sci. Comput.* **2024**, *46*, C101–C126. [CrossRef]
18. Wenzel, T.; Haasdonk, B.; Kleikamp, H.; Ohlberger, M.; Schindler, F. Application of Deep Kernel Models for Certified and Adaptive RB-ML-ROM Surrogate Modeling. In *Proceedings of the Large-Scale Scientific Computations*; Lirkov, I., Margenov, S., Eds.; Springer: Cham, Switzerland, 2024; pp. 117–125. [CrossRef]
19. Kato, S.; Yamaguchi, S.; Uyama, T.; Yamada, H.; Tagawa, T.; Nagai, Y.; Tanabe, T. Characterization of secondary pores in washcoat layers and their effect on effective gas transport properties. *Chem. Eng. J.* **2017**, *324*, 370–379. [CrossRef]
20. Math2Market. GeoDict simulation Software Release 2022; Math2Market GmbH: Kaiserslautern, Germany, 2022. Available online: https://www.geodict.com/Solutions/aboutGD.php (accessed on 9 December 2022).
21. Iliev, O.; Toktaliev, P. On pore scale numerical simulation of complex homogeneous reactions with application to filtration processes. In Proceedings of the FILTECH 2022, Cologne, Germany, 8–10 March 2022; ISBN 978-3-941655-19-5.
22. Wendland, H. *Scattered Data Approximation*; Cambridge Monographs on Applied and Computational Mathematics; Cambridge University Press: Cambridge, UK, 2005; Volume 17. [CrossRef]
23. Leibfried, F.; Dutordoir, V.; John, S.; Durrande, N. A tutorial on sparse Gaussian processes and variational inference. *arXiv* **2020**, arXiv:2012.13962.
24. Snelson, E.; Ghahramani, Z. Sparse Gaussian processes using pseudo-inputs. *Adv. Neural Inf. Process. Syst.* **2005**, *18*, 1257–1264. [CrossRef]
25. Schölkopf, B.; Smola, A.J. *Learning with Kernels: Support Vector Machines, Regularization, Optimization, and Beyond*; MIT Press: Cambridge, MA, USA, 2002. [CrossRef]
26. Wirtz, D.; Karajan, N.; Haasdonk, B. Surrogate modeling of multiscale models using kernel methods. *Int. J. Numer. Methods Eng.* **2015**, *101*, 1–28. [CrossRef]

27. Carlberg, K.T.; Jameson, A.; Kochenderfer, M.J.; Morton, J.; Peng, L.; Witherden, F.D. Recovering missing CFD data for high-order discretizations using deep neural networks and dynamics learning. *J. Comput. Phys.* **2019**, *395*, 105–124. [CrossRef]
28. Joliffe, I.T. *Principal Component Analysis*; Springer: Berlin/Heidelberg, Germany; New York, NY, USA, 2002. [CrossRef]

Disclaimer/Publisher's Note: The statements, opinions and data contained in all publications are solely those of the individual author(s) and contributor(s) and not of MDPI and/or the editor(s). MDPI and/or the editor(s) disclaim responsibility for any injury to people or property resulting from any ideas, methods, instructions or products referred to in the content.

Article

A Novel Underwater Wireless Optical Communication Optical Receiver Decision Unit Strategy Based on a Convolutional Neural Network

Intesar F. El Ramley [1,*], Nada M. Bedaiwi [1], Yas Al-Hadeethi [1,2], Abeer Z. Barasheed [1], Saleha Al-Zhrani [1] and Mingguang Chen [3]

- [1] Physics Department, Faculty of Science, King Abdulaziz University, Jeddah 21589, Saudi Arabia; nbedaiwi0005@stu.kau.edu.sa (N.M.B.); yalhadeethi@kau.edu.sa (Y.A.-H.); abarasheed@kau.edu.sa (A.Z.B.)
- [2] Lithography in Devices Fabrication and Development Research Group, Deanship of Scientific Research, King Abdulaziz University, Jeddah 21589, Saudi Arabia
- [3] Department of Chemical and Environmental Engineering, University of California, Riverside, CA 92521, USA; mchen041@ucr.edu
- * Correspondence: intesar@ramley.com

Abstract: Underwater wireless optical communication (UWOC) systems face challenges due to the significant temporal dispersion caused by the combined effects of scattering, absorption, refractive index variations, optical turbulence, and bio-optical properties. This collective impairment leads to signal distortion and degrades the optical receiver's bit error rate (BER). Optimising the receiver filter and equaliser design is crucial to enhance receiver performance. However, having an optimal design may not be sufficient to ensure that the receiver decision unit can estimate BER quickly and accurately. This study introduces a novel BER estimation strategy based on a Convolutional Neural Network (CNN) to improve the accuracy and speed of BER estimation performed by the decision unit's computational processor compared to traditional methods. Our new CNN algorithm utilises the eye diagram (ED) image processing technique. Despite the incomplete definition of the UWOC channel impulse response (CIR), the CNN model is trained to address the nonlinearity of seawater channels under varying noise conditions and increase the reliability of a given UWOC system. The results demonstrate that our CNN-based BER estimation strategy accurately predicts the corresponding signal-to-noise ratio (SNR) and enables reliable BER estimation.

Keywords: convolutional neural network (CNN); signal-to-noise ratio (SNR); bit error rate (BER); eye diagram (ED); computational methods; engineering problems; numerical simulations

MSC: 94-10

1. Introduction

Underwater wireless optical communication (UWOC) systems are showing promise as low-cost, high-capacity, energy-efficient ways to transmit data at high speeds of up to multi-gigabits per second (Gbps) over distances of 10 to 20 m [1,2]. Unlike traditional acoustic communication, UWOC offers higher bandwidth and lower latency, making it suitable for applications such as underwater exploration, environmental monitoring, and military operations [3]. However, the performance of UWOC systems is significantly influenced by various impairments, including scattering, absorption, and turbulence, which collectively deteriorate the signal quality and increase the bit error rate (BER) [4]. However, the challenges facing UWOC systems are becoming increasingly complex, necessitating effective solution options. One of these options is to optimise the optical receiver design circuitry [5] to render an optimum performance level for the overall receiver unit.

In an optical receiver, a decision unit (DU) with an accurate BER estimation is crucial to support the performance optimisation steps of the digital receiver systems in UWOC.

However, traditional BER estimation strategies, such as Monte Carlo simulations (MCSs) and analytical methods, are computationally intensive [6] and may not adapt well to the dynamics of the underwater environment. Pilot symbols and training sequences provide more real-time estimation but at the cost of reduced data throughput [7]. Error Vector Magnitude (EVM) and noise variance estimation offer alternative approaches but are often limited by their assumptions about the channel conditions [6,7], which makes the estimation strategy highly dependent on the full knowledge of the channel impulse response (CIR) temporal profile. Monte Carlo simulations are flexible and can handle complex systems but are computationally expensive. Analytical methods are efficient, but their success depends on the model accuracy level, which the appropriate decision unit should avoid. Empirical methods provide real-world accuracy but are impractical for initial design, i.e., it is design time not run time implementation knowledge. Hence, the choice of BER estimation method depends on the specific numerical needs and constraints of the communication system being analysed.

Recent advancements in machine learning (ML) technology solution options (see Figure 1), particularly CNNs in optical performance monitoring, have introduced a new technology to help design an efficient computational processor (for the DU) that deploys a CNN-oriented strategy. CNNs can learn complex patterns embedded in eye diagrams (composed of various pixels) that are generated in real-time (see Figure 2). These patterns are learned from the bit stream received at the input of the DU, making them suitable for dynamically adapting to the varying conditions in UWOC systems. CNNs recognise patterns in visual data, making them suitable for processing eye diagram images—a critical visualisation tool used in digital communication systems to evaluate signal integrity and quality. Eye diagrams encapsulate key performance metrics, including timing jitter and noise levels, providing a comprehensive snapshot of the signal's health. By utilising the capabilities of CNNs, it is possible to develop a more robust and efficient decision unit strategy that improves BER estimation accuracy and overall system performance. This CNN-based DU strategy does not depend on the transmission modulation format, channel stochastic impairments, and the need to set a fixed threshold during the design phase to estimate the BER. The CNN training data pool is continuously enhanced without reducing the data throughput. Additionally, it is worth mentioning that the DU implementation should not require knowledge of the CIR during the design or run time. This CNN solution approach to building a high-performance DU is the core of this study.

Using CNN technology is not new in optical communications. CNN networks have been previously used in optical performance monitoring (OPM) to measure the parameters of optical systems such as chromatic dispersion (CD), modulation format identification (MFI), and signal-to-noise ratio (SNR) [8–12]. Considering these measures to develop an affordable OPM system with great diagnostic capabilities is crucial. Further investigation and analysis are necessary to address the obstacles and issues that this field faces, including the natural factors in underwater environments and the accompanying phenomena, whether they are inherent optical properties (IOPs) such as absorption, scattering, and scintillation or apparent optical properties (AOPs), such as reflectance. Section 2 summarises the relevant published studies on ANNs, specifically focusing on CNNs. The purpose is to facilitate navigation and focus on implementing our proposed new CNN approach and the architecture and design elements.

This study first applies the CNN model directly on eye diagram images to predict SNR values through regression; subsequently, the BER is extracted from the SNR for UWOC receiver systems. The CNN model can provide accurate predictions at a reasonable cost, regardless of water type, pulse shape, and noise sources. It achieves a Mean Absolute Error (MAE) and Root Mean Squared Error (RMSE) in the range of 0.29–0.52 and 0.39–0.73, respectively, rendering it a fast and accurate way to assess the received signal inside the receiver of the UWOC system. Consequently, it becomes a core component in the decision unit, as depicted in Figure 3. The training of the CNN model is based on handling the nonlinearity of water channels under various noise environments, which helps identify and manage the UWOC systems' reliability even though the impulse response of the water channel is not yet fully characterised. Although the eye diagram images in this study have been generated from simulations, the model has proved that the concept can be conveniently expanded to assess real-time generated eye diagrams.

Our proposed tool is vital for researchers and communication engineers interested in UWOC because of the difficulty of measuring SNR in real-world scenarios. Thus, when a new pulse is received, an image of the corresponding eye diagram is generated at run-time. Then, the ML model can learn and deduce the SNR value with high accuracy. This reliable approach deals with the nonlinearity of channels in underwater environments, such as multiple scattering, turbulence, scintillation, propagation time jitter, and multipath effect, which causes intersymbol interference (ISI) and receiver thermal noise. Furthermore, the decision unit will be an ML base unit using the NN to pick the best-matched image to make a decision. Because training high-performance ML applications and big processing units take a long time, the Microsoft Azure Virtual Machine (VM) was used in this study. This study also used various other resources, including Python 3.9.13, TensorFlow and Keras 2.12.0, cloud computing, SQLite Database Management System (SQLite DBMS), and eye diagram images. The essential features for signal processing in a UWOC system are seawater type, channel model, pulse shape, pulse width, and the zero-position symbol. Based on these features, the proposed algorithm generates eye diagram images.

This study employed a CNN approach to perform regression analysis on eye diagram images to determine SNR values and, subsequently, the corresponding BER. The CNN contained a flattened feature map as the input, a hidden layer with a ReLU activation function, and an output layer with a linear activation function. The CNN took eye diagram images as inputs and processed them through subsequent layers to obtain feature maps. The first layer is called the convolutional layer. This study conducted 13 trials, each utilising different CNN models with filters ranging from 16 to 64.

Additionally, the feature map from the convolutional layer underwent max pooling. Five iterations of the convolutional and max pooling layers were performed. The last feature map was flattened to obtain the input values entering the Fully Connected layer (FC). Additionally, dropout (a regularisation technique) was used in the FC layer of the NN to tackle the overfitting problem. The dropout rate used was 0.45. The Adam optimiser and a learning rate of 10^{-5} were employed in all trials. Finally, the output layer of the CNN yielded predictions in the form of SNR values. In this study, our newly designed CNN instrument is equivalent to a computational processor for the optical receiver electronic circuitry decision unit. The training and validation loss exhibit minimal disparity, and the congruity in the performance metric suggests that the proposed model is more precise and comprehensive.

Additionally, if the neural network's size (the number of parameters) increases, the model's performance also increases. This study demonstrates that CNNs can make decisions using cost-effective functions with limited trainable parameters (ranging from 516,881 to 2,267,201). These decisions apply to various types of waters, even in the presence of ISI noise and fluctuations in the water environment. This study is organised as follows: Section 2 briefly reviews related studies. Section 3 reviews the basics of UWOC systems. Section 4 discusses the foundations of CNN modelling with basic theory. Section 5 presents the CNN algorithm design and implementation. Section 6 provides a comprehensive overview of the results of the SNR and BER predictions, the performance metrics, and the statistical summary of the obtained results. Sections 8 and 9 of the document discuss the conclusion and future studies, respectively.

2. Related Studies—A Brief Review

Artificial intelligence (AI) has caused significant reorganisation in many different industrial and scientific sectors as machines learn how to solve specific problems [13]. Computer algorithms acquire knowledge of the fundamental connections within a provided dataset and autonomously detect patterns to make decisions or forecasts [14]. Machine learning (ML) algorithms enable machines to implement intellectual activities by applying complex mathematical and statistical models [15]. Specifically, supervised and unsupervised ML methods have played an essential and effective role in optical communication, especially in detecting impairments and performance monitoring in UWOC systems. ML methods are important interdisciplinary tools that utilise eye diagram images as feature sources in several fields, including computer vision [16], equalisation [17], signal detection, and modulation format identification [18]. Some examples of techniques used in this study include Support Vector Machine (SVM) [19], k-means clustering to mitigate nonlinearity effects [20,21], Principal Component Analysis (PCA) for modulation format identification (MFI), optical signal-to-noise ratio (OSNR) monitoring [22], and Kalman filtering for OPM [23]. Reference [24] indicated that CNNs could achieve the highest accuracy compared to five other ML algorithms: Decision Tree (DT), K-Nearest Neighbour (KNN), Back Propagation (BP), Artificial Neural Networks (ANNs), and SVM. Figure 1 depicts the various applications of ML algorithms used in optical communication. This study provides a comprehensive review of ML solution applications in UWOC technology.

Neural networks, such as ANNs, CNNs, and recurrent neural networks (RNNs) are highly suitable machine learning tools. They are capable of learning the complex relationships between samples or extracted features from symbols and channel parameters such as optical signal-to-noise ratio (OSNR), polarisation mode dispersion (PMD), polarisation-dependent loss (PDL), baud rate, and chromatic dispersion (CD) [10,25–33]. The OSNR is a signal parameter that significantly impacts the effectiveness of optical links. The OSNR can be used to predict the bit error rate (BER), which directly gauges receiver performance [34]. Reference [35] proposed and demonstrated a system for compensating for fibre nonlinearity impairment using a simple recurrent neural network (SRNN) with low complexity. This method reduces computational complexity and training costs while maintaining good compensation performance.

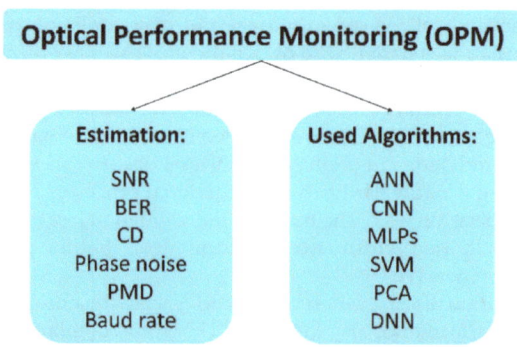

Figure 1. ML algorithms in optical performance monitoring.

Several methods based on automatic feature extraction can be used to obtain the features input into the neural network (NN). These methods use constellation diagrams, asynchronously amplitude histograms (AAHs), Asynchronous Delay Tap Plots (ADTPs), Asynchronous Single Channel Sampling (ASCS), In-phase Quadrature Histograms (IQHs) for SNR, and other parameter estimations. Here, we review the various works that display a range of OPM works utilising machine learning techniques to forecast signal-to-noise ratio (SNR) values through various approaches. In [36], a new machine learning OPM method is proposed that uses support vector regressors (SVRs) and modified In-phase Quadrature Histogram (IQH) features to estimate several optical parameters, including signal-to-noise ratio (SNR) and chromatic dispersion (CD). A deep learning algorithm in ref. [37] has been successfully applied in wireless communications, but it often results in challenging nonlinear problems. An ANN algorithm in [26] was developed to calculate the signal-to-noise ratio (SNR) using On-Off Keying (OOK) and Differential Phase Shift Keying

(DPSK) data. The training errors for OOK and DPSK were 0.03 and 0.04, respectively. The ANN is trained by sending a series of well-known symbols before being used as an equaliser. The parameters are modified to reduce discrepancies between the desired and ANN outputs [38]. Improving the ANN on the receiver can bring several benefits, such as reducing training time and complexity, maintaining high performance, achieving high data rates and bandwidth transmission capabilities, improving efficiency, and enhancing multipath delay robustness. Various studies have highlighted these advantages, including references [8,12,31,39–43]. A 10 Gbps NRZ modulation scheme measures the SNR using statistical parameters such as means and standard deviations obtained from the ADTP. The RMSE of the ADTP is 0.73. In [31,44–49], a DNN was employed to classify SNR from AAH and 16-QAM PDM-64QAM with an accuracy that can reach 100%. OSNR monitoring from 10 to 30 dB was achieved using 10 Gb/s NRZ-OOK and NRZ-DPSK from ASCS. Constellation diagrams were used in [50,51] to estimate SNR with errors less than 0.7 dB by designing CNNs with QPSK, PSK, and QAM modulation formats. The fundamental CNN algorithm for SNR estimation is presented in [52], and methods for preprocessing received signals and selecting optimal parameters are provided. The technique efficiently and accurately identifies the modulation format and estimates SNR and BER using 3D constellation density matrices in Stokes space.

Eye diagrams have been utilised in the literature to track OSNR, PMD, CD, nonlinearity, and crosstalk via NNs [53–55]. Observing an eye pattern involves various optical communication noises simultaneously (e.g., thermal noise, time jitter, and ISI); consequently, SNR decreases, and the signal declines when the noise levels rise. SNR is used to investigate the quality of the received signal in communication systems. Reference [56] presents a long short-term memory (LSTM)--based deep learning to simultaneously estimate SNR and nonlinear noise power. The test error is less than 1.0 dB, and the modulation types include QPSK, 16QAM, and 64QAM. The SNR monitoring method suggested in ref. [57] uses an LSTM neural network, a classifier, and a low-bandwidth coherent receiver to convert continuous monitoring into a classification problem. It is cost-effective and suitable with multi-purpose OPM systems because it achieves excellent classification accuracy and robustness with minimal processing complexity.

The eye diagram used to locate optical signal impairments by overlapping the symbols depicts the amplitude distribution over one or more-bit periods. SNR and BER indicate how well a system performs by assessing the signal quality based on various properties: eye height, eye width, jitter, cross percentage, and levels 0 and 1 (Figure 2).

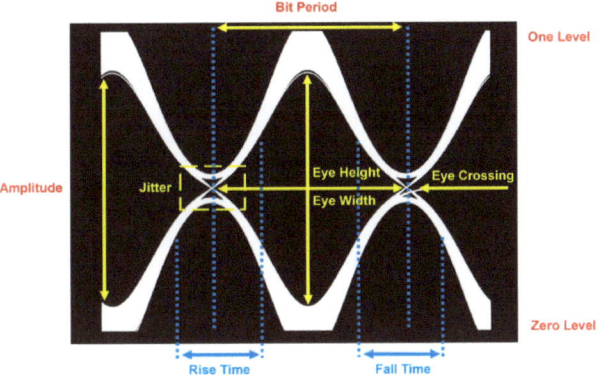

Figure 2. Eye diagram essential features.

SVM for classification and NN for regression were studied in ref. [25–27,38] using 64-QAM, 40 Gb/s RZ-OOK, 10 Gb/s NRZ-OOK, and DPSK. The input features from the eye diagram are mean, variance, Q-factor, closure, jitter, and crossing amplitude. The ANN reports a correlation coefficient of 0.97 and 0.96 for OOK and DPSK systems, respectively [58].

NN regression was developed to extract variance from eye diagram images, and SNR with a range from 4 to 30 dB was measured with a mean estimation error range of 0.2 to 1.2 dB for 250 km [25]. Another study used an ANN to extract 24 features from eye diagram images. The RSME values ranged from 1.5 to 2 for SNRs between 10 and 30 dB using NRZ, RZ, and QPSK for a data rate of 40 Gb/s [59]. Table A1 (in Appendix A) represents the studies from 2009 to 2024 that used ML to extract features from eye diagram images to obtain signal-to-noise ratios; the table also shows the implementations of the NN algorithms and model performance and compares these studies with ours. References [24,60,61] demonstrated the CNN-based algorithms on eye diagram images and discussed the CNN structure and implementations in detail. These studies have generated eye diagrams by run-time simulation or experimental setup and used classification techniques to obtain the SNR (see Table A2 in Appendix A). What is crucial to note is that while our study has created and implemented a new CNN structure for UWOC, previous efforts have primarily focused on optical fibre. Our approach to estimating SNR directly from eye diagrams, which involves 13 regression CNN models, is at the heart of the novelty of our study.

3. UWOC System Model

In the following sections, we will introduce our study as an innovative method for rapidly estimating bit error rate (BER) in technology. However, before doing so, we will provide concise explanations of two topics to help the audience understand the underlying challenges this study aims to address. These topics are (1) the digital signal evaluation cycle, in which the digital signal transforms from an optical digital signal on the transmitter (Tx) side to an electronic digital signal as an output of the optical receiver (Rx), and (2) the conventional BER estimation regimes, which include some familiar approaches: modified Monte Carlo (MC)-based estimation methods, the MC prediction method, and the Log-Likelihood Ratio-based BER model. The UWOC system generally consists of three fundamental components, as depicted in Figure 3: the transmitter unit, the water propagation channel, and the receiver section.

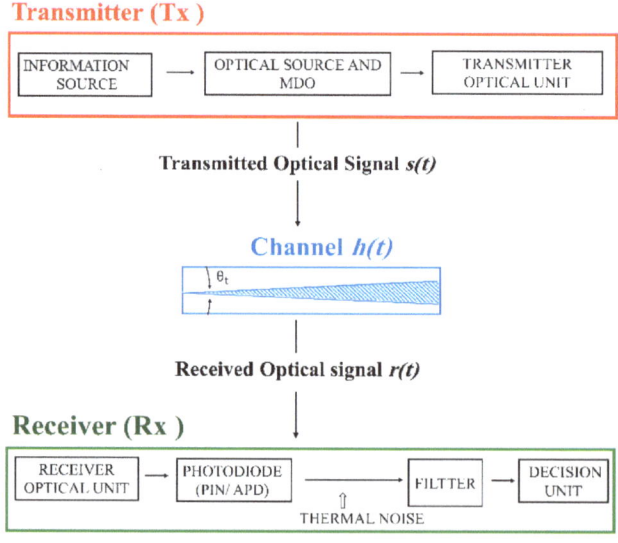

Figure 3. The layout of a typical UWOC system [62].

The photons propagate across the water in the underwater communication channel independently from each other through any medium, facing different sequenced sets of optical events: transmission, absorption, and scattering (elastic and inelastic). The impact on the transmitted optical signal includes attenuation, temporal and spatial beam spreading, deflection of its geometrical path, and amplitude and phase distortions [63]. Degradation, such as absorption and scattering, significantly impacts the UWOC's performance [59]. Turbulence is another degrading factor that causes beam spreading, beam wander, beam scintillation, and link misalignment. Oceanic water types can be classified as follows [64]: clean ocean water, pure sea water, turbid harbour water, and coastal ocean water. Furthermore, in turbid harbour water, several photons may arrive at the receiver with delays, intersymbol interference (ISI), and fading signal, reducing communication viability [65].

3.1. The Transmitter Unit

The transmitter unit utilises a beam-shaping optical unit to interface with the water propagation channel. The transmitter unit's modulator provides the needed modulation shaping characteristics to generate the information bit stream. Moreover, in UWOC systems, the driver circuit is another crucial part of the transmitter unit [66]. The main job of this device is to convert the electrical signal from the modulator into an optical signal that can be transmitted through the water channel. The driver circuit typically consists of a laser or LED driver that provides the necessary current to the light source, which emits the optical signal $s(t)$. The selection of the light source and driver circuit is determined by the particular system requirements, such as the desired data rate, transmission distance, power consumption [67], and optical characteristics of the water channel [68]. In the UWOC system, the LED setup is more affordable and straightforward, but the connection range is very constrained because of the incoherent optical beam and light spread in all directions [4]. Laser diodes are often used as the light source in UWOC systems due to their long ranges, high intensity of output power, improved collimation characteristics, narrow beam divergence [69], high efficiency, small size [70], high data rates, and low latencies [4]. The high-quality output of the coherent laser beam is quickly degraded by turbulence and underwater scattering. The laser-based UWOC system may reach a link distance of 100 m in clear water and 30 to 50 m in turbid water, while the LED-based UWOC may cover a linkspan of no more than 50 m [69].

3.2. UWOC Propagation Channel

In UWOC systems, water is the communication channel via which the optical signal $s(t)$ propagates. One of the challenges of the UWOC is that there is no definite mathematical expression for the impulse response function ($h_c(t)$). Hence, $h_c(t)$ must be reliably modelled to assess the scope of impacts on the propagated $s(t)$ due to water channel impairments like absorption, single/multiple scattering, scintillation, and turbulence. These degradations degrade $s(t)$ temporal and spatial quality, reducing the received OSNR [71] at the surface of the photodetector. There are many studies (e.g., [70–72]) that focus on solving the radiative transfer equation (RTE) analytically and numerically, which account for different sets of inherent optical properties (IOPs) that mainly include absorption and scattering. The analytical solutions of the RTE are based on a wide range of assumptions or rather simplifications. These solutions are considered benchmark limits for the numerical ones. The simplest and most well-known benchmark is the Beer-Lambert law (BLL) [71–73]. The main aim of numerical solutions is to conclude an extrapolated mathematical close form using a double gamma curve-fitting to conclude a temporal profile for $h_c(t)$, which accounts for impairments' impact limits for different water types and given link configurations. Once the $h_c(t)$ format is defined, we will be able to conclude the convolution $s(t)$ with $h_c(t)$, the product of which is the optical received signal ($r_{opt}(t)$).

In this study, we utilised the following $h_c(t)$ format versions: (1) double gamma functions (DGFs), (2) weighted double gamma functions (WDGFs), (3) a combination of exponential and arbitrary power functions (CEAPFs), and (4) Beta Prime (BP). The impairment scope of each $h_c(t)$ model is shown in Table 1. The CEAPF and BP formats might look different from the foundation DGF but can be reduced back to the DGF.

Table 1. List of models' channel impulse response functions.

Model Name	The Equation of the Model	Ref.
DGF	The closed-form expression of the double gamma functions (DGFs) is given as follows: $h(t) = c_1 \Delta t e^{-c_2 \Delta t} + c_3 \Delta t e^{-c_4 \Delta t}$, $t \geq t_0$, $\Delta t = (t - t_0)$ $t_0 = \frac{L}{v}$	[74]
WDGF	The weighted double gamma functions (WDGFs) model is given as follows: $h(t) = c_1 \Delta t^\alpha e^{-c_2 \Delta t} + c_3 \Delta t^\beta e^{-c_4 \Delta t}$, $t \geq t_0$, $\Delta t = (t - t_0)$	[75]
CEAPE	A combination of exponential and arbitrary power functions (CEAPEs) is given as follows: $h(t) = \frac{c_1 \cdot \Delta t^\alpha}{(\Delta t + c_2)^\beta} \cdot e^{-a.v(\Delta t + t_0)}$ $c_1 > 0, c_2 > 0, \alpha > -1$ and $\beta > 0$	[76]
BP	Beta Prime (BP) distribution is given as follows: $h_{BP}(t) = \frac{\Gamma(\beta_1+\beta_2)}{\Gamma(\beta_1)\Gamma(\beta_2)} \cdot \frac{t^{\beta_1-1}}{(1+t)^{\beta_1+\beta_2}}, t > 0$	[77]

$C_1, C_2, C_3, C_4, \alpha, \beta, \beta_1$, and β_2 are double gamma curve-fitting parameters. v is the light velocity for the seawater medium under consideration. L is the linkspan distance between the Tx and Rx.

3.3. The Receiver Unit

An optical detection system or a receiver is one of the main components of UWOC. The optical signal will go through an optical filter and focusing lens on the receiver side. The photon detector will then capture it. Since a photodiode can only transform light intensity variations from an LD or laser into corresponding current changes [78,79], a trans-impedance amplifier is cascaded in the following stage to convert current into voltage. The transformed voltage signals will then go through a low-pass filter responsible for shaping the voltage pulse to reduce the thermal and ambient noise levels without causing significant inter-symbol interference (ISI) [80,81].

Further signal processing programmes are bypassed through a signal quality analyser for demodulation and decoding [82]. An equalisation is a tool used to reshape the incoming pulse, extract the timing information (sampling), and decide the symbol value. A PC or BER tester will finally collect and analyse the recovered original data to evaluate several important performance parameters, such as BER. In optical receivers, many types of photodetectors can be used; for more details, see ref [62]. The most functional OWC systems use a PIN or an avalanche photodiode (APD) as a receiver [83]. The UWOC receiver system must meet specific requirements to address the effects of noise and attenuation. The receiver's most significant parameters are a large FOV, high gain, fast response time, low cost, small size, high reliability, high sensitivity and responsivity at the operating wavelength, and high SNR [83]. The APD can provide higher sensitivity and gain faster response times. It could also be used in longer UWOC links (tens of metres) and wider bandwidths but at a much higher cost and complex circuits. The noise performance of these two devices is the most significant difference. The main source of noise in PIN photodiodes is thermal noise, while in APD, it is shot noise [79,82,84–86].

However, the PIN photodiode appears to be a more favourable technology for shorter wavelengths than the APD for the UWOC system [4]. To process and understand the received data, the decision unit in an optical receiver converts the signal into discrete binary values. It compares the sampled voltage to a reference level or threshold (D_{th}). With the use of the received optical signal, this procedure estimates the underlying BER based on which a decision will be made if the bit is "0" or "1" for binary $s(t)$ [87–89].

3.4. Digital Signal Evaluation Cycle from Optical to Electronic—A Mathematical Viewpoint

The digital signals evaluation cycle is based on the illustration in Figure 4. The main components of a typical optical receiver system (Rx), as explained in Section 3.2, include a photodetector, preamplifier/amplifier, filter/equaliser, and decision unit (DU). The received optical signal $r_{opt}(t)$ can be described as follows:

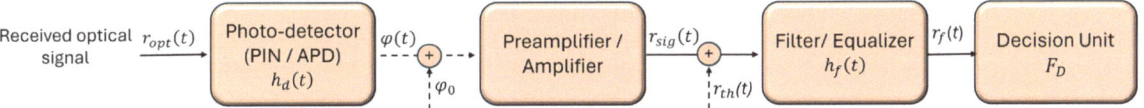

Figure 4. Typical direct detection optical receiver model.

In a typical optical digital communication system, the transmitted optical signal $s(t)$ can be represented as follows [5]:

$$s(t) = \sum_{k=-\infty}^{\infty} a_k h_p(t - kT) \tag{1}$$

where T is the signalling period, for a binary (OOK) signal format, if τ is the timespan of each bit within a symbol, then T = τ, so 1/T is the bit rate. a_k is the energy received in the kth symbol; for binary system $a_k \in \{0, 1\}$, the $h_p(t)$ is the transmitted optical pulse. Typically, the $s(t)$ experiences temporal and spatial distortions while propagating through a medium channel (air, fibre optic, or water), depending on the profile of the propagation channel impulse response $h_c(t)$. The received optical signal $r_{opt}(t)$ is the footprint of the convolutional impact of $h_c(t)$ on the $s(t)$. Hence, $r_{opt}(t)$ can be expressed as follows:

$$r_{opt}(t) = s(t) \otimes h_c(t) \tag{2a}$$

$$r_{opt}(t) = a_0 h_p(t) \otimes h_c(t) + \sum_{\substack{k=-\infty \\ k \neq 0}}^{\infty} a_k h_p(t - kT) \otimes h_c(t) \tag{2b}$$

where $\otimes$ denotes the convolution operation. The $r_{opt}(t)$ is the received optical signal. In this study, we consider a binary direct detection Rx, as depicted in Figure 4. Without losing generality, we will assume that the Rx includes a PIN photodetector with an internal gain (g) equal to one. The photodetector converts the input photons of $r_{opt}(t)$ into electronic signal $r_{sig}(t) =$, which can be expressed as follows:

$$r_{sig}(t) = \sum_{j=1}^{N(t)} h_d(t - t_j) \tag{3a}$$

where $\{t_j\}$ denotes the photoelectron emission times. Therefore, the filter electronic signal output $r_f(t)$ is

$$r_f(t) = \sum_{j=1}^{N(t)} h_d(t - t_j) \otimes h_f(t) + r_{th}(t) \tag{3b}$$

If we assume that $h_d(t) = \delta(t)$, then Equation (3b) takes the following form:

$$= \sum_{j=1}^{N(t)} h_f(t) + r_{th}(t) \tag{3c}$$

We should note that the assumption of $h_d(t) = \delta(t)$ is valid for modern fast-response PIN detectors. The first term is the signal component $r_{sig}(t)$, and the second term $r_{th}(t)$ is the AGTN. In Equation (3), $\{t_j\}$ is the set of photoelectrons' arrival times governed by Poisson statistics. $N(t)$ represents the stochastic counting process, which is an inhomogeneous process with a time-varying rate intensity of $\{a_k\}$ in Equation (1).

It is expected that the DU in Figure 4 will be able to estimate $r_f(t)$ as an accurate replica of $s(t)$. The accuracy and speed of decision-making, which is comparable to the function $s(t)$, heavily relies on the computational processing strategy of the DU. This strategy minimises the BER to meet the receiver's performance goals.

4. BER Computational Strategies for Decision Unit—Background Tutorial

In this section, before presenting our novel technique for CNN-based bit error rate (BER) estimation technology, we need to briefly present tutorial descriptions for the conventional BER estimation regimes, which include some familiar approaches: the Monte Carlo (MC) prediction method, the Log-Likelihood Ratio-based BER model, and the modified MC-based estimation approaches.

4.1. BER Estimation Schemes—A Brief Review

Many techniques may be used to conclude bit error rate estimation. This subsection provides a synopsis of the conventional MC simulation to reveal that the execution time for low BER is very long. This subsection presents three techniques: quasi-analytical estimation, importance sampling theory, and tail extrapolation probabilities.

Such solutions demand assumptions regarding the actual system behaviour, and the effectiveness is greatly dependent on the presumed parameters, which likely have to be altered for various systems of communication. Predominantly, finding the ideal model or suitable parameters is not easy. Next, a number of new BER estimators based on the LLR distribution were introduced; nevertheless, they have a few shortcomings, such as being dependent on the SNR uncertainty estimation and the specific channel features. However, all the aforementioned approaches demand awareness of the transmitted bit stream, while the estimator certainly does not know transmitted data in practical situations. In contrast, our new CNN imaging computational processor requires no prior information.

4.2. Monte Carlo (MC) Method Simulation

The MCS approach is predominantly used for BER estimation in communication systems [90,91]. This estimation approach is implemented by passing N data symbols through a model, which reflects the influencing features of the underlying digital communication system by counting the error numbers that take place at the receiver. The simulation run includes noise sources, pseudo-random data, and device models, which process the digital communication signal. In conclusion, the MC simulation processes a number of symbols, and eventually, the BER is estimated.

Let us assume that we have a standard baseband signal model representation, as shown in Equation (2), and the decision unit is using the Bernoulli decision function $I(a_k)$ expressed as follows:

$$I(a_k) = \begin{cases} 1 \text{ if } \hat{a}_k \neq a_k \\ 0 \text{ otherwise} \end{cases} \quad (4)$$

where $a_k \in \{0, 1\}$ as defined in Section 3.4, and the ^ sign refers to the assembled average of the variable. Accordingly, the BER can be indicated in terms of the probability of error p_e as follows:

$$p_e = P(\hat{a}_k \neq a_k) = P[\, I(a_k) = 1] = E[I(a_k)], \quad (5)$$

where E[.] is the expectation operator, $P(\hat{a}_k \neq a_k)$ is the probability that the instant value of a_k does not equal its average $\hat{a}_k$. If we take into consideration the entire stream of symbols in Equation (2b), then the BER is estimated by utilising the ensemble average of p_e:

$$\hat{p}_e = \frac{1}{K} \sum_{k=1}^{K} I(a_k) \quad (6)$$

where K is the maximum number of symbols (the bit stream size) in Equation (2b). Equation (7) helps to determine the estimation error, and its variance will be given as follows:

$$\varepsilon = p_e - \hat{p}_e = \frac{1}{K}\sum_{k=1}^{K}(p_e - I(a_k)) \tag{7}$$

This means that the variance of ε can be expressed as:

$$\sigma_\varepsilon^2 = \frac{p_e(1-p_e)}{K} \tag{8a}$$

Hence, we can write the normalised estimation error as follows:

$$\sigma_n = \frac{\sigma_\varepsilon}{p_e} = \sqrt{\frac{(1-p_e)}{K.p_e}} \tag{8b}$$

For a small BER, Equation (8b) can be simplified to

$$\sigma_n \cong \sqrt{\frac{1}{K.p_e}} \tag{8c}$$

Here, σ_n is an indicator for the target accuracy we must aim at. Consequently, we can determine the required K for a target performance as given below:

$$K \cong \frac{1}{\sigma_n^2 p_e} \tag{8d}$$

Equation (8d) indicates that a small BER value requires a large, simulated signal bit stream. For example, to configure a system with a BER of 10^{-6}, we require no less than 10^8 bits in the signal stream. This numerical limitation ensures that the MC simulation trial size will satisfy the central limit theorem. This operational limitation means the decision unit will take a long time to estimate a trusted value of BER. Accordingly, MC simulation is impractical for a baud rate larger than 100 MBit. It is worth mentioning that in our discussion, we assumed that the bit errors were independent.

4.3. Importance Sampling Scheme

As earlier concluded, a small BER demands a large K. From a DU point of view, this is considered a fatal limitation of MC implementation, specifically for spread spectrum (SS) systems [92] (such as CDMA systems) in which every transmitted bit must be modulated via the SS code with an abundance of bits.

A modified MC method called the importance sampling (IS) method can be utilised to decrease BER simulation complexity for SS systems [93]. Further, ref. [94] introduces a method for estimating the bit error rate (BER) based on IS applied to trapping sets. Considering the IS approach, the noise source statistics in the system are biased so that bit errors occur with greater p_e, thus minimising the needed execution time. For instance, for a BER equal to 10^{-5}, practically, we artificially degrade the performance of the channel, pushing the BER to 10^{-2}.

To explain the IS approach, let $g(\cdot)$ be the original noise probability density function (PDF) and let $g^*(\cdot)$ be the rising noise PDF utilising an external noise source. Hence, the weighting coefficient can be expressed as follows:

$$w(x) = \frac{g(x)}{g^*(x)} \tag{9a}$$

For a simple threshold-dependent decision element, the expression that describes an error takes place as soon as there is a significant excursion of the threshold D_{th} as follows:

$$a_k = 0 \; for \begin{cases} error\ count = 1\ if\ x_k \geq D_{th} \\ error\ count = 0\ otherwise \end{cases} \quad (9b)$$

Then, p_e is given as follows:

$$p_e = \int_{-\infty}^{\infty} I(x)\, g(x) dx \quad (9c)$$

$I(x)$ is an indicator function, which equals 1 when an error takes place; otherwise, it equals 0. Hence, we can express that with regard to the natural estimator of the expectation (i.e., sample mean) as follows:

$$\hat{p}_e = \frac{1}{K} \sum_{k=1}^{K} I(x_k) \quad (9d)$$

Hence, concerning the PDF of the noise (i.e., $r_{th}(t)$ in Equation (4)) and using Equations (9c) and (9d), we obtain

$$p_e = \int_{-\infty}^{\infty} I(x)\, \frac{g(x)}{g^*(x)} g^*(x) dx = \int_{-\infty}^{\infty} I^*(x)\, g^*(x) dx = E[I^*(x)] \quad (9e)$$

Equation (9e) is not just a mathematical expression; it represents the noise processes statistics that influence, and the prediction is achieved with regard to $g^*(\cdot)$. As in the preceding subsection, we may attain the estimator using the sample mean;

$$\hat{p}_e = \frac{1}{K} \sum_{k=1}^{K} I^*(a_k) = \frac{1}{K} \sum_{k=1}^{K} w(a_k) I(a_k) \quad (9f)$$

Regarding Equation (9d), in Equation (9f), the weight parameter $w(x)$ needs to be evaluated at a_k. This means reducing the σ_e, which can be accomplished by establishing external noise of biassed density.

IS-based BER estimation performance relies crucially on the biassing scheme $w(x)$. An accurate estimate of the BER can be attained with a brief simulation run time if a good biassing scheme is configured for a specified receiver circuitry system. Contrarily, the BER estimate might even converge at a slower rate than the conventional MC simulation. This implies the IS technique must not be regarded as a generic approach for estimating every receiving system's bit error rate (BER).

4.4. Tail Extrapolation Scheme

We should keep in mind that the BER estimation obstacle, in essence, is a numerical integration problem if we regard the eye diagram (ED) in Figure 5, measured for an experimental system with SNR = 20 dB. It is possible to determine the worst case of the received bit sequence.

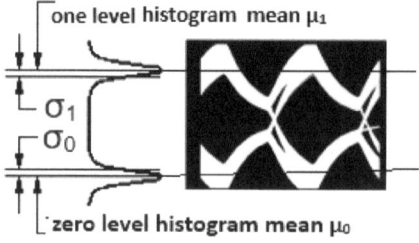

Figure 5. Probability density function (PDF) tails obtained from an eye diagram (ED).

When we regard the PDF of the eye section in lines A and B, the lower bound on the PDF (green line) is the worst-case bit sequence, and the small red area contains all of the bit errors. The BER of the given system can be thought of as the area under the tail of the probability density function.

Generally, we could not depict the sort of distribution to which the slopes of the bathtub curve in ED belong. However, we may presume that the PDF file is affiliated with a specific class and then accomplish curve-fitting on the obtained data. That technique for estimating the bit error rate (BER) is known as the tail extrapolation (TE) method [95].

When we set multiple thresholds for the lower bound, the number of times the decision metric surpasses every D_{th} is recorded, and a standard MC simulation can be executed. A wide category of PDFs is then detected. The tail region is typically identified by certain members of the Generalised Exponential Class (GEC) and is identified as follows:

$$f_{v,\sigma,\mu}(x) = \frac{v}{2\sqrt{2}\,\Gamma(\frac{1}{v})} e^{-[\frac{x-\mu}{\sqrt{2}\,\sigma}]^v} \tag{10a}$$

where $\Gamma(\cdot)$ is the gamma function, μ is the mean of the distribution, and σ is related to the variance V_v through

$$V_v = \frac{2\sigma^2\,\Gamma(\frac{3}{v})}{\Gamma(\frac{1}{v})} \tag{10b}$$

where the parameters (v, σ, μ) are then adjusted to find the PDF that best fits the data sample; therefore, the BER could be estimated via the integral evaluation of the PDF for D_{th}. Nevertheless, which class of PDF and which D_{th} should be selected is not frequently clear. Generally, it is hard to evaluate the estimated BER accuracy [95].

4.5. The Method of Quasi-analytical Estimation

The abovementioned methods analyse the received signal components (data and noise) at the receiver's output. At this point, we consider solving the BER estimation problem utilizing the succeeding two stages:

1. One handles the transmitted signal $r_f(t)$ in Equation (4);
2. The other handles the noise component $r_{th}(t)$.

First, we presume that the noise is denoted as the Equivalent Noise Source (ENS) and, second, that the ENS probability density function is known and determinable.

Therefore, we can assume that an ENS with an appropriate distribution can closely evaluate the receiver's performance. This approach is known as quasi-analytical (QA) estimation [96]. We can calculate the BER with ENS statistics using the noiseless waveform. More precisely, we can allow the simulation to calculate the influence of signal changes in the non-existence of $r_{th}(t)$ and superimpose the $r_{th}(t)$ on the noiseless signal component.

The noise statistics assumption results in a significant drop in computation run time. Nevertheless, this may create a risk of complete miscalculation. The appropriateness of the QA estimation will rely on how well the assumption matches actuality [97]. Hence, predicting ENS statistics before they occur for a linear system may be challenging.

4.6. Estimating BER Based on the Log-Likelihood Ratio

A receiver can implement soft-output decoding to reduce the signal stream's BER (e.g., a posteriori probability (APP) decoder). The APP decoder may output probabilities or Log-Likelihood Ratio (LLR) values. Let $(a_k) 1 \leq k \leq K \in \{+1, -1\}$ be the bit stream and let X_k; $k = 1, 2, \ldots, K$ represent the received values. Hence, the definition of LLR can be expressed just as follows:

$$LLR_k = LLR(a_k|X_k = x_k) = \log \frac{P(a_k = +1|X_k = x_k)}{P(a_k = -1|X_k = x_k)} \tag{11a}$$

Hence, when using Baye's theorem, we obtain the following:

$$LLR_k = \log\frac{P(a_k = +1)}{P(a_k = -1)} + \log\frac{P(a_k = +1|X_k = x_k)}{P(a_k = -1|X_k = x_k)} \quad (11b)$$

In Equation (11b), the first term on the RHS represents a priori information, and the second represents channel information. The hard decision expression is implemented by computing the LLR sign as follows:

$$a_k = \begin{cases} +1 \; if \; LLR_k(a_k|\,x_k) > 0 \\ -1 \; otherwise \end{cases} \quad (11c)$$

In [98], some basic properties of LLR values are extracted, and new BER estimators are proposed based on the statistical moments of the LLR distribution. If we are examining the succeeding criterion:

$$P(X = +1 \,|\, Y = y) + P(X = -1 \,|\, Y = y) = 1$$

Solving Equation (11b) utilising the criterion mentioned above permits us to derive a posteriori probabilities $P(a_k = +1 \,|\, x_k)$ and $P(a_k = -1 \,|\, x_k)$; then, we can write the following:

$$P(a_k = +1\,|\,x_k) = e^{(LLRk)}/1 + e^{(LLRk)} \; \text{and} \; P(a_k = -1\,|\,x_k) = 1/1 + e^{(LLRk)} \quad (11d)$$

If LLR_k = A, then we could infer the probability that the hard decision of bit k^{th} is wrong and

$$p_k = 1/1 + e^{-A} \quad (11e)$$

Now, the BER estimate can be expressed as follows:

$$\hat{p_{e,1}} = \frac{1}{K}\sum_{k=1}^{K} p_k \quad (12a)$$

$$\hat{p_{e,2}} = \int_y g_A(y)\frac{1}{1+e^y}dy \quad (12b)$$

The constraints of the LLR method are as follows:
1. The first estimate of BER given by Equation (12a) may not be as efficient as the second BER estimate given by Equation (12b) since $g_A(y)$ is usually Gaussian and smooth.
2. The second estimator is extra complicated to execute because an estimate of $g_A(y)$ ought to be computed (for instance, utilising a histogram) prior to the integral.
3. Both methods are sensitive to channel noise variance as the LLR distribution vigorously relies upon the accuracy of the SNR estimate. We should note that the earlier estimators implicitly presume that the SNR is well-known to the decoder.

5. CNN Model Solution Framework Foundations

5.1. Receiver Performance Indicators

This study highlights the receiver's performance by modelling a decision unit strategy. The UWOC receiver unit performance is influenced by the water channel signal impairments and various noise sources on the receiver side, such as electronic thermal, optical background, dark current, and shot noise—reference [4] reviewed such noise sources. Generally, the leading performance indicators for a digital receiver are SNR and BER. The SNR is represented by the following:

$$SNR = \frac{P_S}{P_N} \quad (13)$$

where P_S and P_N represent the signal power and noise power, respectively.

The BER is defined as the probability of incorrect identification of a bit by the decision circuit of the underlying receiver [81]. It is one of the most important metrics for assessing signal quality and estimating communication system performance. If the number of error bits received is N_e and the total bits is N_t, then the BER is as follows:

$$BER = \frac{N_e}{N_t} \qquad (14)$$

The relation between SNR and BER is embedded in the following formula:

$$BER = \frac{1}{2} \cdot erfc\left(\frac{\sqrt{2 \cdot SNR}}{2}\right) \qquad (15)$$

5.2. Test Data

In this study, eye diagrams and their SNRs are used as the source of feeding the CNN with the required testing data. A Python code was written and ran on a Microsoft Azure VM to generate 576 received pulses, including some random noise; then, the eye diagram pattern images were drawn, and their related SNRs based on the received pulses were calculated. For eye pattern generation, we used four-channel models, including the following:

- DGFs with distances of 5.47 m and 45.45 m for harbour and coastal waters, respectively, and (20°, 180°) field of view (FOV).
- WDGFs and CEAPFs with distances of 10.93 m and 45.45 m for harbour and coastal waters, respectively, and 20° FOV.
- BP with 5 m and 10 m distances for harbour and coastal waters, respectively, and 180° FOV.

We also utilised two transmitted pulse shapes, Gaussian and Rectangular, to implement a binary OOK modulation in our simulation. The range of pulse widths (FWHM) was 0.1 to 0.95. It is worth mentioning that pulse widths beyond 0.6 are unrealistic, but we added these scenarios as a "burn test" for our solution. The ranges of the FOV values across channel models were not similar because we had to use the published double gamma fitting parameters (shown in the last row of Table 1) and their corresponding FOV value ranges.

After that, the names of the images and SNR values were stored in an SQL database, while the images were stored in one folder. Consequently, the data were ready to have CNNs applied to them. These test data have some properties, and they are as follows:

The background of the eye diagram images is black, while the diagram itself is white (greyscale) to speed up and simplify the CNN calculations. All the eye diagram images' sizes (height × width) are 2366 × 3125; this size was taken from the shapes of the images' arrays (it is already an output from the code). The SNR has a normal distribution (which means there is no bias in our data before applying ML), as shown in Figure 6. The minimum SNR value is 0.5723, the maximum SNR value is 8.1478, the mean is 3.0004, and the standard deviation is 1.5061.

The data preprocessing steps before applying the CNN:

1. Loading the images' names and SNRs from the database.
2. Converting the data into a 'pandas' data frame.
3. Shuffling the data frame.
4. Using TensorFlow library on Python, we conducted the following:
    - Loaded the eye diagram images based on their names and normalised them using max normalisation (dividing each pixel by 255).
    - Split the dataset into training (70%) and validation (30%).
    - Converted the colour mode from RGB into grayscale.
    - Used the images' original size instead of resizing them to keep the resolution high.

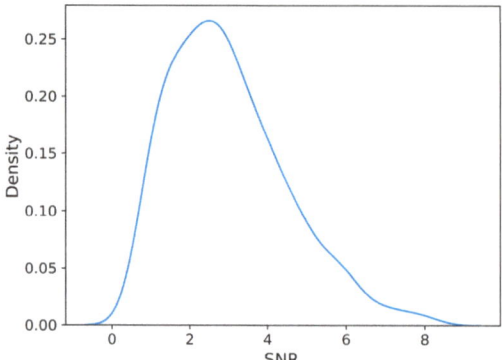

Figure 6. Density vs. SNR.

5.3. Machine Learning—Neural Networks (NNs)

Neural networks (NNs) are computing algorithms that include processing units known as neurons that are organised into layers. These layers are connected via weights; each cell has a different weighted function. Many researchers have investigated neural networks since the 1960s [99–101]. NNs were developed based on how biological nerves transmit information and analyse data, and they are mainly used to increase computing performance [102]. NNs can be used for supervised learning in both classification and regression, and they can also be used in unsupervised learning.

A general NN structure consists of at least the input of data and the output layer, which allows NNs to make predictions on new input middle-level layers known as hidden layers, which process the outputs of previous layers [26]. The neurons have various coefficients, such as bias (θ_0) and weights (θ_i), which are modified during the training process to obtain the optimum values that make the loss as low as possible. The correlations between input-output datasets that constitute the attributes of the device or system under study are discovered using NNs. The model outputs are compared to the true desired outputs, and the error is calculated [103]. For the training phase, the sample is represented as (x, y), where the input and output are x and y, respectively. Each node makes calculations on the (x) values that are entered into the neural network, and then the value of $(z^{(L)})$ is obtained. After that, the expected values of $(a^{(L)})$ are found via applying the activation function $f(x)$ on $(z^{(L)})$; the process is repeated as represented by the following equations [102]:

$$z^{(L)} = \theta_0 + \sum_{i=1}^{n} \theta_i x_i \tag{16a}$$

where $z^{(L)}$ is the predicted output of each layer, which is the input for the next layer.

$$a^{(L)} = f\left(z^{(L)}\right) \tag{16b}$$

The form of the hypothesis function or activation function (the final output in the last layer) is represented as follows:

$$y_{pred} = a^{(l)} \tag{17}$$

where i is the cell number, L is the layer number, l is the last layer number, and f is the activation function. Note that Equation (15) is similar to linear regression in which a predictor x variable and a dependent y variable are included in the model, and they are linearly related to one another. In this case, the output variable y was predicted based on the input variable x. The linear regression model is represented by the equation shown below:

$$y = mx + c \tag{18}$$

Equation (18) is the foundation equation for NNs, where θ_i or m is the slope or rate of predicted y based on the best-fit line and θ_0 or c is y-intercept. Figure 7 represents the functions of neurons in NNs.

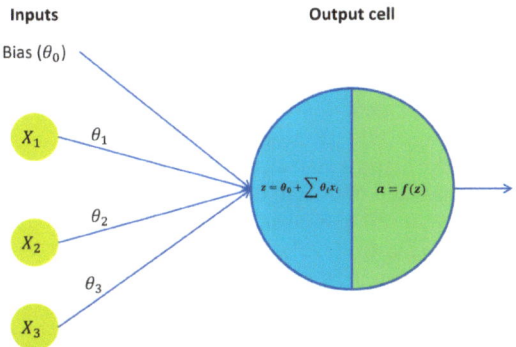

Figure 7. Components and the functions of an artificial neuron.

The most significant and often utilised component of neural networks is data propagation in both the forward and the reversed (or back) directions. This propagation is crucial for performing quick and efficient weight adjustments. The term "forward propagation", which describes moving information from the input to the output direction, has been the subject of the whole discussion up to this point. However, the neural network did not achieve practical significance until 1986, when the Back Propagation mechanism (BP) was employed [104,105]. Back Propagation is a technique used to train neural networks to adjust the weights and increase the model's generalisation to make it more reliable. The error rate of forward propagation is fed back through the NN layers. It analyses, compares, and evaluates the outcomes before going back oppositely from the outputs to the inputs and adjusting the weights' values. This process is performed endlessly until the weights are optimal. A reverse calculation of the weight values is carried out by finding the difference between the predicted and real values, followed by partial derivation, and Back Propagation is used to adjust the assumed weight values. After the output of each layer $a^{(L)}$ is calculated, the result is passed through a function; the goal is to minimise the cost function J, and the result is then passed through the loss function, as described in Section 6. After reaching the expected value $a^{(l)}$ (whether regression or classification), we find the delta error rate $\delta^{(l)}$ by subtracting the predicted from actual values $y^{(t)}$ as follows:

$$\delta^{(l)} = a^{(l)} - y^{(t)} \qquad (19)$$

where $y^{(t)}$ is not numbers but matrices with one column (vector) because several cells are in each layer. The general equation for Back Propagation is as follows:

$$\delta^{(L)} = \left(\theta^{(L)}\right)^T \delta^{(L+1)} \cdot f'\left(z^{(L)}\right) \qquad (20)$$

where f' is the first derivative of the activation function, T is the transpose matrix of $\theta^{(L)}$, and · is a dot product, not a matrix product. A conventional neural network (CNN) is a kind of deep feed-forward neural network that is one of the most effective learning algorithms used in many applications, with significantly higher accuracy [106]. A CNN is the best algorithm for analysing image data [106] and for solving problems in several visual recognition tasks, such as identifying traffic signs, biological image segmentation, image classification [107], speech recognition, natural language processing, and video processing [108]. The power of a CNN is its ability to extract features from samples with different requests at a fast speed [88] and handle high-dimensional inputs. A CNN offers two significant benefits over other ML algorithms [107]: (a) automated feature extraction from images utilising feature extraction without the requirement for feature engineering or data restoration, and (b) the algorithm complexity is significantly reduced by a network topology with local connections and weight sharing. The way the attention mechanism works allows it to extract the most important information from an image and store its contextual relationship to other image elements [106]. The main layers of a CNN are the convolutional layer, pooling layer, and neural network layer. First, the convolutional layer applies several filters to input images to extract features (produce feature maps) and decrease their size [93]. The convolutional layer's final output is obtained by merging these feature maps [109]. Decreasing the number of network parameters and computations requires that the feature map size be reduced again in the pooling layer by selecting the essential features and obtaining the maximum values. The advantages of max pooling are that it decreases training time and controls overfitting [109]. After repeating these layers several times, the output will enter into a neural network as flattened input values [110]. These values go through FCs that reach the final output of the CNN. The activation function could be used in a CNN on convolutional, hidden, and output layers.

6. CNN Model Architecture, Design, and Implementation

6.1. Model Solution Architecture and Design

Microsoft Azure VM was used to develop a Python code that draws eye diagram images and calculates SNR values via a multiprocessing technique. These images were saved in a folder on the VM, whereas their names and SNRs were stored as reference data in an SQL database. This study used SQLite DBMS to store information on 576 rows of eye patterns and related SNRs. The meta dataset used to generate eye diagrams consists of water type, channel model, pulse shape, pulse width, and the signal state (0 or 1), which is the value of position zero on eye diagrams. Another code was developed using the OOP paradigm to retrieve data from the database and train 13 CNN models via a training set to make decisions for testing images using the validation set. Then, the error between actual and predicted SNRs was calculated. The errors include the MAE and the RMSE for training and testing data. The BER values were extracted based on the original and predicted SNRs and the performance of the CNN models was measured. A schematic representation of the methodology for this study is shown in Figure 8. Consequently, the ML works as a decision unit in the optical receiver, which is the primary goal of this study.

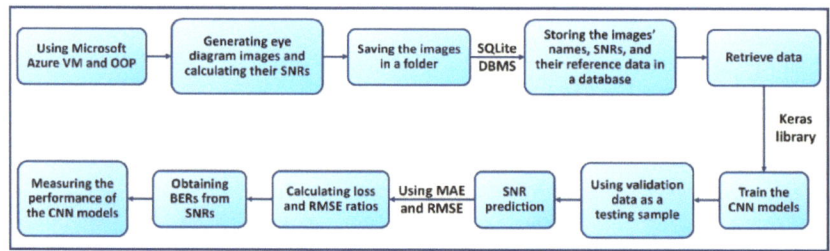

Figure 8. A schematic representation of predicting SNRs with various numbers of filters.

6.2. Model Dataset

Eye diagram images were generated using a multiprocessing technique on Azure VM with the following components: Windows 11 Pro operating system, x64-based processor, Intel Xeon Platinum 8171M CPU @ 2.60GHz 2.10 GHz, 32 GB RAM, 127 GB Premium SSD LRS Storage, and eight virtual CPUs. The following attributes are required to generate the eye diagrams and conclude the SNR: water type, the channel model, optical pulse shape, and pulse width. Table 2 shows the details of these attributes. The corresponding SNR values were stored in an SQL database. Some examples of the created eye patterns are shown in Figure 9.

Table 2. The required attributes for generating eye diagram images and calculating SNR.

Metadata	Values
Water types	Harbour and coastal waters
Channel models	DGF, WDGF, CEAPF, and BP
Pulse shapes	Gaussian and Rectangular
Pulse widths	0.1, 0.15, 0.2, 0.25, 0.3, 0.35, 0.4, 0.45, 0.5, 0.55, 0.6, 0.65, 0.7, 0.75, 0.8, 0.85, 0.9, 0.95
Centre positions on the eye diagrams	0/1

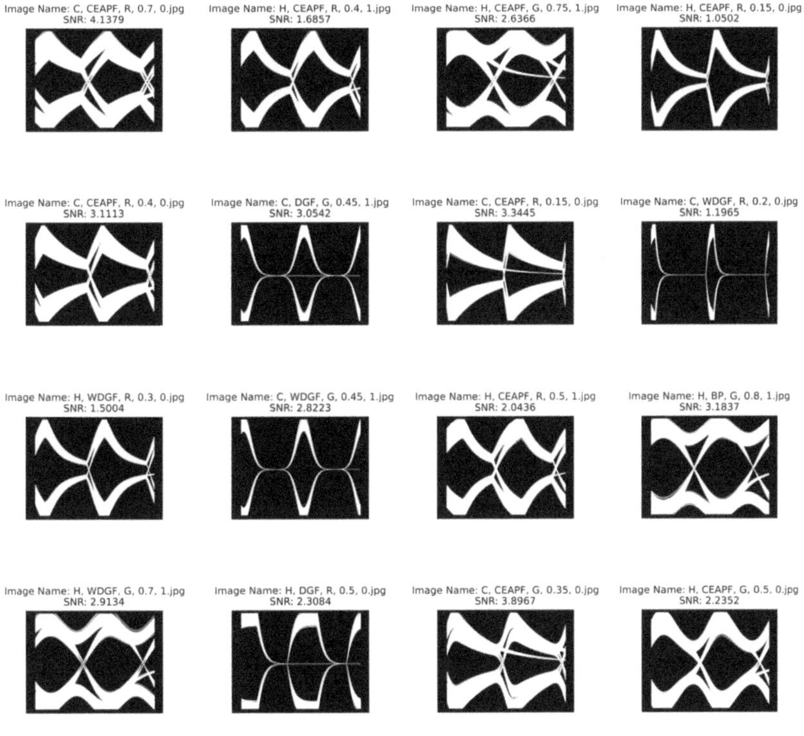

Figure 9. Examples of eye diagram images.

6.3. CNN Algorithm

CNNs are widely used in optical communications and networking. Regarding UWOC, ref [111] proposed a constellation diagram recognition and evaluation method using deep learning (DL). ML is applied in networking systems to address tasks in the physical layers. These tasks include monitoring systems, assessing signal degradation effects, optimising launch power, controlling gain in optical amplifiers, and adapting modulation formats. It is also used in nonlinearity mitigation [15]. The optical receiver can serve as an OPM in addition to its primary function of receiving data. A signal waveform is graphically represented in an eye diagram to locate optical signal impairments. The amplitude distribution over one or more-bit periods is depicted by overlapping the symbols. Eye diagrams are employed to evaluate the strength of high-speed digital signals [53]. A data waveform is typically applied to the sampling oscilloscope's input to create them. Then, all conceivable one-zero combinations are overlapped on the instrument's display to cover three intervals [54]. Pulses are spread out beyond the period of a single symbol because of the ISI, which results from temporal variations between light beams arriving at the receiver from multiple pathways. At data rates greater than 10 Mbps, ISI seriously impairs the system's performance. A clustering algorithm is used to identify anomaly attacks without being aware of the attacks beforehand. In ref. [112], a groundbreaking application of ML in optical network security has been reported. The findings showed that ANNs have a significant potential for detecting out-of-band jamming signals of various intensities with an average accuracy of 93%. Using TensorFlow and Keras 2.12.0, were used.

The CNN algorithm is used on eye diagram images to predict the values of SNR in different cases based on UWOC. To organise the inputs in a particular way or convert the relationship to a function that might predict an output, a CNN learns associations between the properties of the input data it receives. In this study, eye diagrams represent signals, and the result for SNR prediction and its magnitude is the type of impairment. This study's total number of samples is 576 eye diagram images, split into 404 and 172 for training and testing data, respectively.

The structure and implementation of the CNN in this study are as follows:

1. The dimensions of the input eye diagram images are 2366 × 3125 pixels, with a resolution of 600 dpi.
2. The network includes convolutional layers with a filter size of 10 and a stride of 1. The filters range from 16 to 64, increasing by four at each step. There is no activation function applied.
3. There are three non-overlapping max-pooling layers with a size and stride 3.
4. Flattened values refer to the input values that will be fed into the NN.
5. This study refers to the hidden layer as FC and uses the ReLU activation function to reduce the CNN calculations by setting negative values to zero.
6. The ultimate output of the CNN is the prediction of the signal-to-noise ratio (SNR) using a linear activation function, which is appropriate for regression tasks.

The Functional API model was used with the Adam optimiser, and the learning rate is equal to 1×10^{-5}. Figure 10 shows the model structure; each circle represents convolutional and max pooling layers. The architecture contains five convolutional and max pooling layers. Each output of these layers comes with an input of the next layer; notice that the connection path between the flattened, hidden, and output layer is the weights (small random numbers at the beginning), and the weights affect the layer's output as seen in Equations (15) and (16). Figure 11 shows the CNN structure and its implementations.

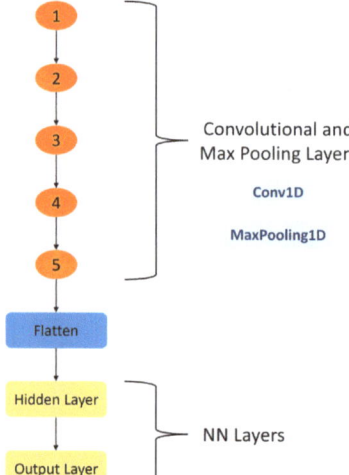

Figure 10. The CNN architecture.

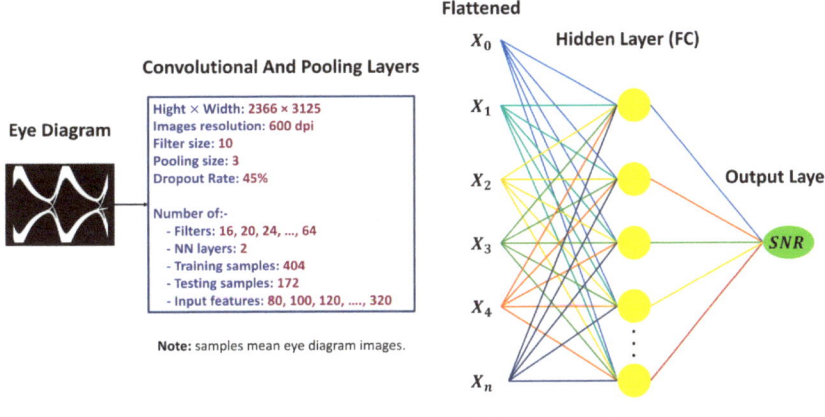

Figure 11. The CNN architecture and implementation.

6.4. SNR Prediction

This study constructed the CNN layers using the Keras library with the Functional API model. The loss error for the training sample, or the difference between the predicted and actual values, was also calculated. The cost function, or the cost error function, is the cumulative total of all errors for the training set. The cost function, which measures the model's accuracy, essentially refers to how far the predicted value is from the real data. The cost function's minimum value is determined throughout the CNN model learning phase. The task is to identify the model weights resulting in the cost function having a minimum value. Gradient descent optimisation (GD), a fundamental approach for CNN model optimisation, is employed to achieve this [113–115]. The equation of GD is as follows:

$$\theta_j := \theta_j - \alpha \frac{\partial}{\partial \theta_j} J(\theta_0, \theta_i) \qquad (21)$$

By substituting the partial derivative of $J(\theta_0, \theta_i)$ we obtain the following:

$$\theta_j := \theta_j - \alpha \frac{1}{m} \sum_{i=1}^{m} \left(h_\theta \left(x^{(i)} \right) - y^{(i)} \right) . x_j^{(i)} \qquad (22)$$

where j = 0, 1, 2, ..., n and m is the number of samples.

This study used MAE as a loss function, while the RMSE was used as a metric function to measure the model's performance. MAE is the mean of absolute differences between predictions and real results where all individual deviations are even more critical, and the RMSE is measured as the average of the square root of the sum of squared differences between predictions and actual output. The mathematical formulas of them are as follows:

$$\text{MAE}\left(y_{true}, y_{pred}\right) = \frac{1}{n_{images}} \sum_{i=1}^{n_{images}} \left| y_{true} - y_{pred} \right| \qquad (23)$$

$$\text{RMSE}\left(y_{true}, y_{pred}\right) = \sqrt{\frac{1}{n_{images}} \sum_{i=1}^{n_{images}} \left(y_{true} - y_{pred}\right)^2} \qquad (24)$$

where n_{images} is the variable that represents the number of eye diagram images in the testing sample.

This CNN programme retrieves the SNR (True) from the database and computes the predicted SNR value by processing the run-time-generated eye diagram images. The MAE is calculated by comparing SNR (True) and SNR (Predict). Moreover, the BER values are extracted from SNR, as shown in Figure 12.

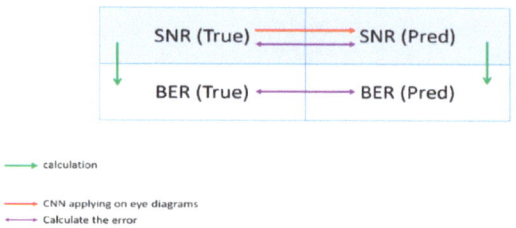

Figure 12. Scheme of calculating the MAE of True and Predicted data.

7. Results and Discussion

The proposed CNN models have successfully predicted SNR with high performance. Figures 13–15 depict the learning curves, which show the training and validation results for both loss and RMSE and their ratio in relation to the validation values. We discarded the scatter plot because it created point-overlapping distortion. The graphs in this study, referred to as "standard hyperparameters," display the dropout rate, learning rate, and number of epochs. The quantity of filters utilised in this study was modified, as indicated in Tables 3 and 4. The training and validation curves show a gradual decrease in loss and RMSE as the number of epochs increases, eventually converging to a similar value. The loss and RMSE in training and validation curves gradually decrease with epochs, and they become close to each other. When the number of filters (16, 20, 24, and 28) in the CNN architecture increases, the training and validation loss and RMSE decrease, as seen in Figure 13. The crucial metrics are the loss and RMSE ratios, approximately equal to 1. This indicates that the models are highly accurate and efficient in predicting the actual SNR values. Figures 14 and 15 demonstrate a decrease in both the loss and RMSE. However, a slight divergence was observed between the training and validation curves, indicating a minimal gap between the loss and RMSE values for the training and validation datasets.

Table 5 provides a comprehensive summary of the models' performance via train/validation loss and train/validation RMSE at the last epoch, as well as the number of trainable parameters and the loss and RMSE ratios. The equation for each one is as follows:

$$\text{Loss Ratio} = \frac{\text{Loss}}{\text{Validation Loss}} \qquad (25)$$

$$\text{RMSE Ratio} = \frac{\text{RMSE}}{\text{Validation RMSE}} \qquad (26)$$

The nearer to 1 the ratio is, the more fitting the model is so that the model can make a correct decision, and the more likely the predicted SNR will approach the actual value.

The statistical analysis includes the results' minimum, maximum, and mean information. For example, the training time ranges between 8.33 and 10.99, whereas the range of predicting time ranges from 0.1732 to 0.2098. We observed no significant fluctuation in time, although the number of filters changed. The maximum difference between 1 and loss or RMSE ratios are 0.3381 and 0.4153, respectively, using 48 and 56 filters in CNN implementation. In contrast, the minimum difference between 1 and loss or RMSE ratios are 0.0297 and 0.0183, respectively, when using 20 filters. In addition, the average of the $|1 - Loss\ Ratio|$ is 0.2107, and for $|1 - RMSE\ Ratio|$ it is 0.2551, which is very close to zero, as shown in Table 3.

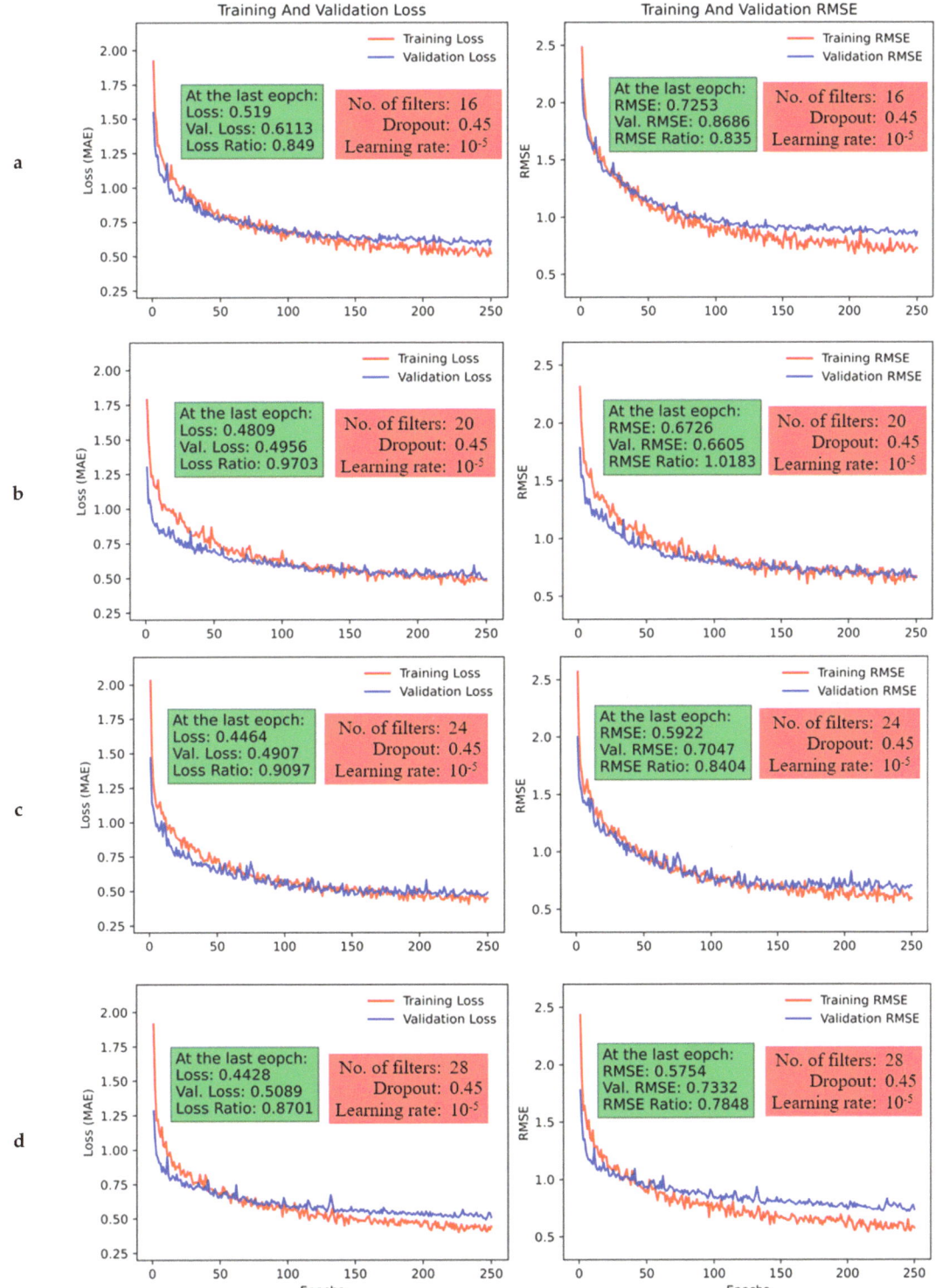

Figure 13. Learning curves of CNN regression models using (**a**) 16, (**b**) 20, (**c**) 24, and (**d**) 28 filters, measured via loss and RMSE.

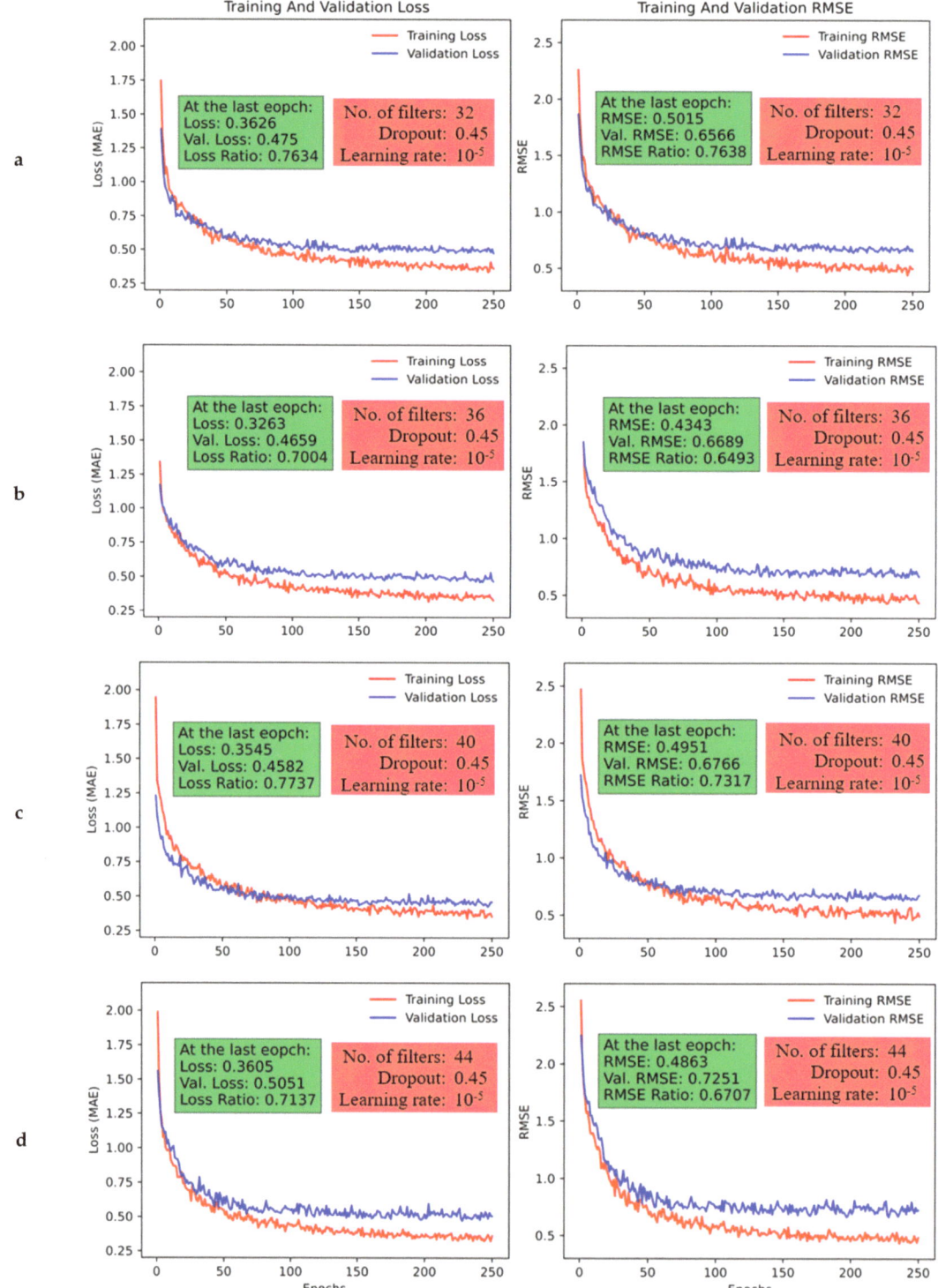

Figure 14. Learning curves of CNN regression models using (**a**) 32, (**b**) 36, (**c**) 40, and (**d**) 44 filters, measured via loss and RMSE.

Table 3. Statistical analysis of results information.

	Min	Max	Mean
Training Time (h)	8.33	10.99	9.6915
Predicting Time (s)	0.1732	0.2098	0.1855
Loss	0.2911	0.5190	0.3739
Validation Loss	0.3605	0.6113	0.4730
RMSE	0.3869	0.7253	0.5070
Validation RMSE	0.5178	0.8686	0.6779
Loss Ratio	0.0297	0.3381	0.2107
RMSE Ratio	0.0183	0.4153	0.2551
Number of Filters	16	64	40
Number of Parameters	516,881	2,267,201	1,369,161

Table 4 displays the constant hyperparameters and their corresponding values used in this study, including the colour mode of the eye diagram images, the optimisation of the model, and other hyperparameters as shown in this table. The primary implementation motivation for the set of hyperparameters in Table 4 is to ensure that the CNN engine achieves its optimum model accuracy fitting and safely operates within a region away from the over-fitting and under-fitting boundaries. Moreover, this stable fitting region is broad enough for optimum processing time.

The Pearson correlation coefficients between the number of parameters and other results' information are displayed in Table 6. Loss, validation loss, RMSE, and validation RMSE have strong correlations, indicating that the cost function decreases while the CNN size increases. Therefore, the performance of the CNN model is enhanced by increasing its size.

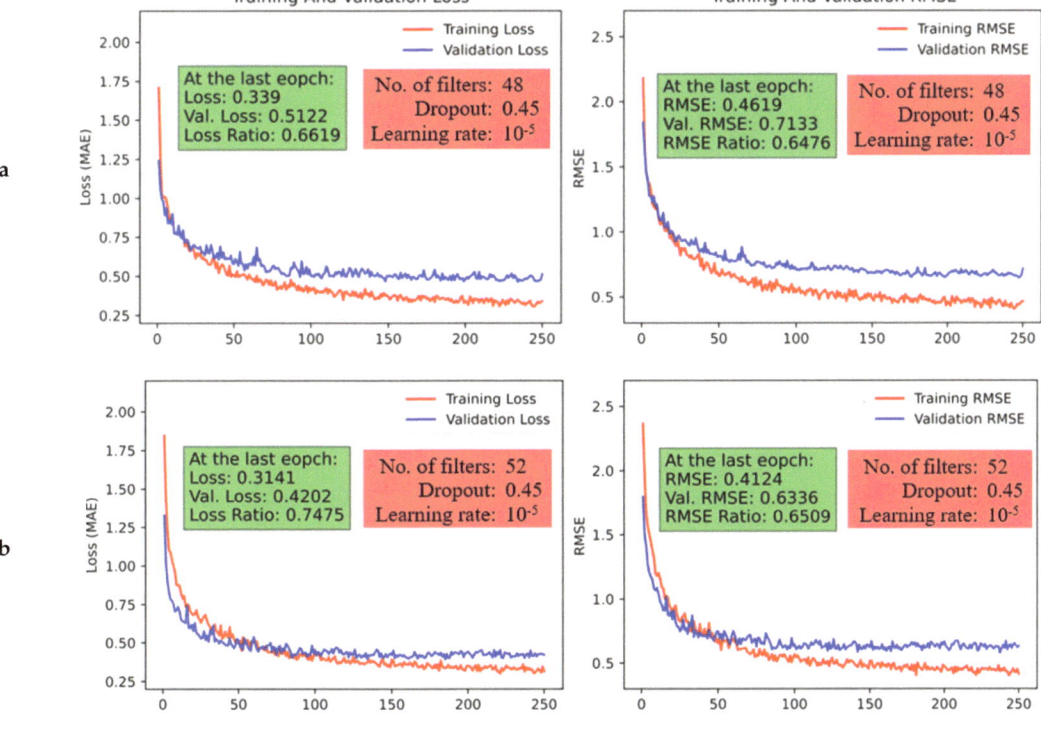

Figure 15. *Cont.*

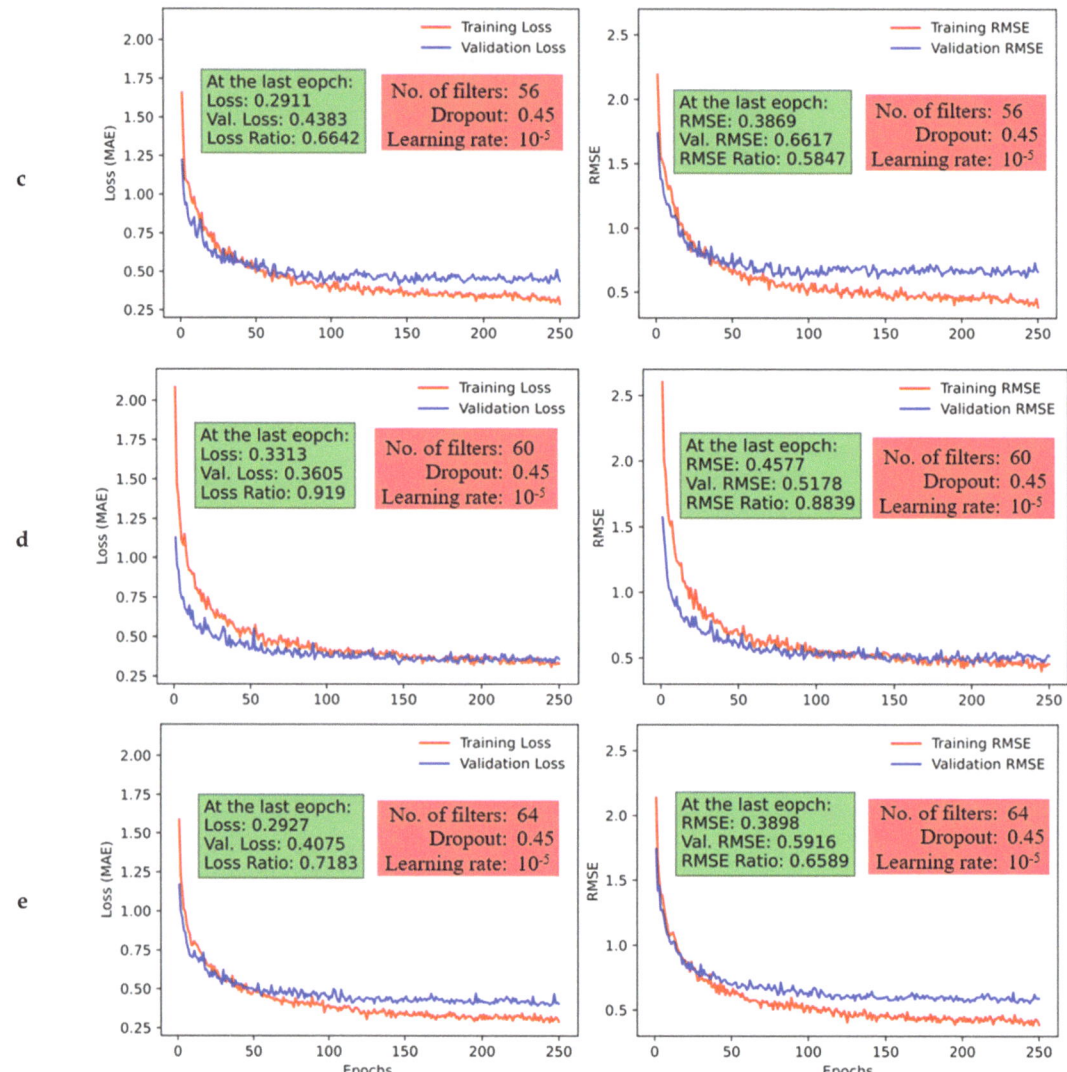

Figure 15. Learning curves of CNN regression models using (**a**) 48, (**b**) 52, (**c**) 56, (**d**) 60 and (**e**) 64 filters, measured via loss and RMSE.

Table 7 represents the Pearson correlation coefficient between the number of filters and other results' information, like training and predicting times, loss, and RMSE, and the validation for both interpretations of these correlations. On the other hand, the graphs below, Figures 16–19 show the relationship between the number of filters used in the CNN models and their information. Figure 16 shows the weak correlation between the number of filters and training and predicting times, which indicates that the curve is almost constant. While it is expected that increasing the number of filters in a CNN would result in increased computations and, therefore, more time to complete them, using a highly capable VM mitigates the impact of increased computations on time, making it negligible.

Table 4. Standard hyperparameters for CNN model platform structure.

Standard Hyperparameters	Values
Colour mode	Grayscale
Eye diagram image size (height × width)	2366 × 3125
Model	Functional API
Optimizer	Adam
Loss function	MAE
Metric	RMSE
Batch size	15
No. of convolutional layers	5
No. of max pooling layers	5
Filters size	10
Filters stride	1
Pooling size	3
Pooling stride	3
No. of hidden layers	1
Activation function in the hidden layer	ReLU
Activation function in the output layer	linear
Learning rate	10^{-5}
Epochs	250
Dropout rate	0.45

Table 5. Performance summary of the dataset's model regarding training and validation for loss and RMSE.

Training Time (h)	Predicting Time (s)	Loss	Validation Loss	RMSE	Validation RMSE	Loss Ratio	RMSE Ratio	No. of Filters	No. of Parameters
9.82	0.18551209	0.519	0.6113	0.7253	0.8686	0.8490	0.8350	16	516,881
10.12	0.18702742	0.481	0.4956	0.673	0.6605	0.9703	1.0183	20	651,301
8.84	0.18525898	0.446	0.4907	0.592	0.7047	0.9097	0.8404	24	787,801
9.86	0.18294497	0.443	0.5089	0.575	0.7332	0.8701	0.7848	28	926,381
8.96	0.18577732	0.363	0.475	0.502	0.6566	0.7634	0.7638	32	1,067,041
10.19	0.18203078	0.326	0.4659	0.434	0.6689	0.7004	0.6493	36	1,209,781
9.97	0.18092463	0.355	0.4582	0.495	0.6766	0.7737	0.7317	40	1,354,601
10.62	0.18176481	0.361	0.5051	0.486	0.7251	0.7137	0.6707	44	1,501,501
10.09	0.19424853	0.339	0.5122	0.462	0.7133	0.6619	0.6476	48	1,650,481
10.99	0.18315452	0.314	0.4202	0.412	0.6336	0.7475	0.6509	52	1,801,541
9.08	0.18004519	0.291	0.4383	0.387	0.6617	0.6642	0.5847	56	1,954,681
9.12	0.17316376	0.331	0.3605	0.458	0.5178	0.9190	0.8839	60	2,109,901
8.33	0.20982659	0.293	0.4075	0.39	0.5916	0.7183	0.6589	64	2,267,201

Table 6. Pearson correlation coefficients between a number of parameters and results' information and their interpretation.

	No. of Parameters	Interpretation
Loss	−0.8977	Strong linear inverse correlation
Val. loss	−0.7891	Strong linear inverse correlation
RMSE	−0.8863	Strong linear inverse correlation
Val. RMSE	−0.7029	Strong linear inverse correlation
No. of filters	0.9997	Very strong linear direct correlation

Their correlation coefficients range from medium to very strong concerning loss, validation loss, RMSE, and validation RMSE. When the number of filters increases, the capacity of the model (trainable parameters) also increases, which allows it to fit the training data better and improve its effectiveness (see Figure 17). In contrast, the loss and RMSE ratios are close to 1, as seen in Figure 18, which means the model makes good decisions.

Table 7. Pearson correlation coefficients between a number of filters and results' information and their interpretation.

	No. of Filters	Interpretation
Training Time	−0.1923	Very weak linear inverse correlation
Predicting Time	0.1793	Very weak linear direct correlation
Loss	−0.9053	Very strong linear inverse correlation
Validation Loss	−0.7897	Strong linear inverse correlation
RMSE	−0.8429	Strong linear inverse correlation
Validation RMSE	−0.6416	Moderate linear inverse correlation

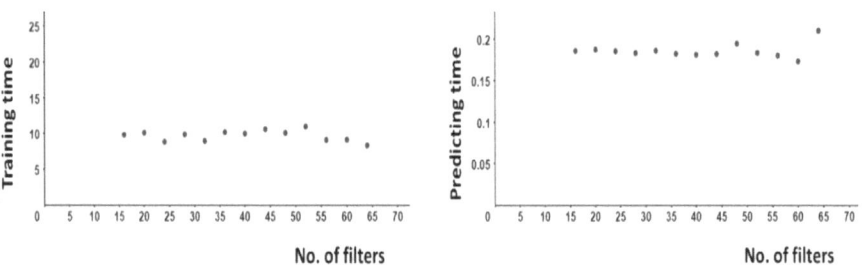

Figure 16. Number of filters vs. training and predicting time for all CNN models.

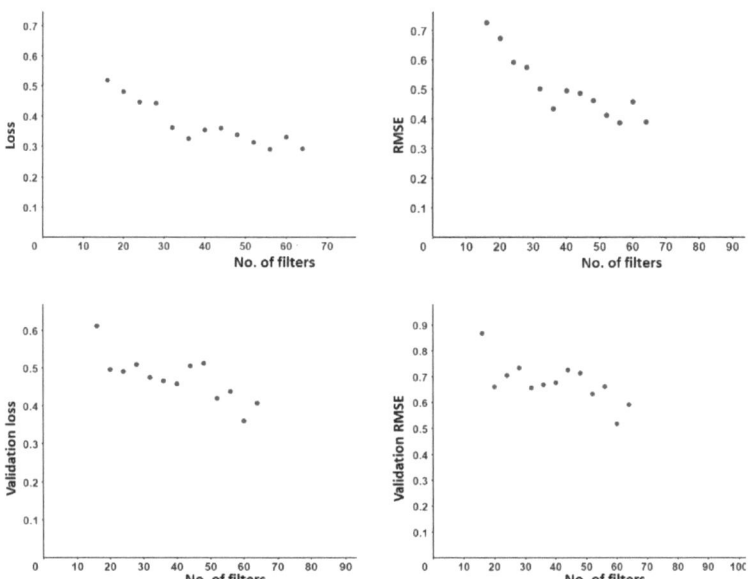

Figure 17. Number of filters vs. training and validation for both loss and RMSE for all CNN models.

On the other hand, the positive upward curve displays a very strong linear direct correlation between the number of filters and the number of parameters; it forms a perfectly straight line (see Figure 19). The reason is that the total number of values inside all filters increases when the filters are increased. These are considered parameters, so the number of trainable parameters increases.

To assess the performance of the CNN models that work on the optical receiver, which can handle the ISI noise in UWOC, the relationship between the actual and predicted values of SNR and BER is drawn in Figure 20. This result illustrates the models' outcomes using a 0.45 dropout rate and a learning rate of 10^{-5} with 28 filters, as shown in the figure below.

CNN models can predict correct results for harbour and coastal waters using Gaussian and Rectangular optical pulse shapes, with different pulse width ranges from 0.1 to 0.95, using DGF, WDGF, CEAPF, and BP channel models. The trend in the curves is similar to the identity function, represented by the red line ($y=x$), which means the actual values are close to the predicted ones in both SNR on the left and BER on the right. This shows that the CNN model can decide correctly in various situations involving various types of water, ISI noise, and water environment variations.

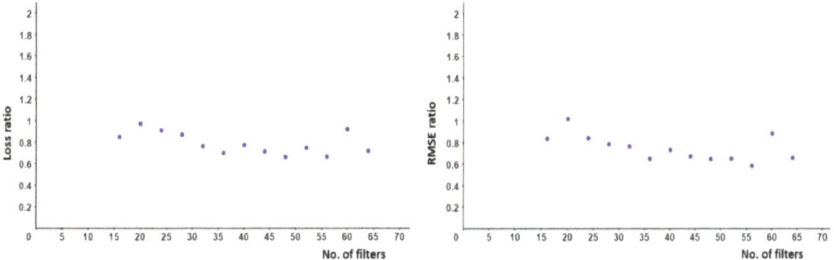

Figure 18. Number of filters vs. loss and RMSE ratios for all CNN models.

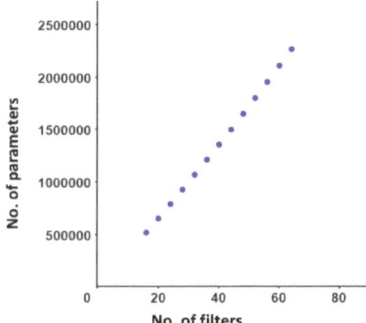

Figure 19. Number of filters vs. number of trainable parameters for all CNN models.

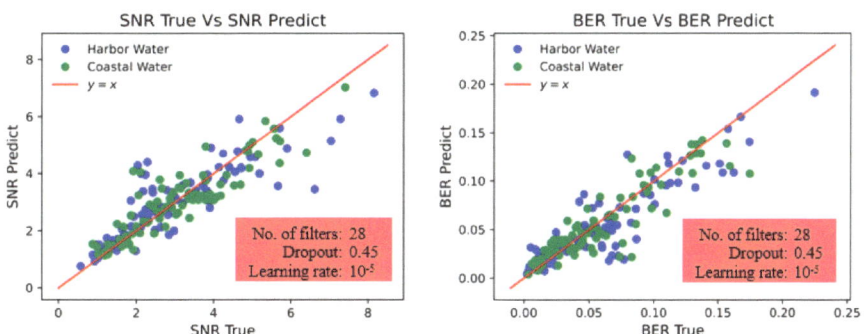

Figure 20. Performance of the CNN models, the true versus the predicted SNR (**left**) and BER (**right**) values. Various channel models are employed to simulate the behaviour of water in harbours (represented by the colour blue) and coastal areas (represented by the colour green) for different pulse widths.

The relation between SNR and BER, which represents the performance of the optical receiver, is drawn, as represented in Figure 21, using a 0.45 dropout rate and a 10^{-5} learning rate with 28 filters. From the graphs, we can conclude that the suggested CNN models perform well in making accurate decisions for various instances involving various types of waters, ISI noise, and underwater environment variations.

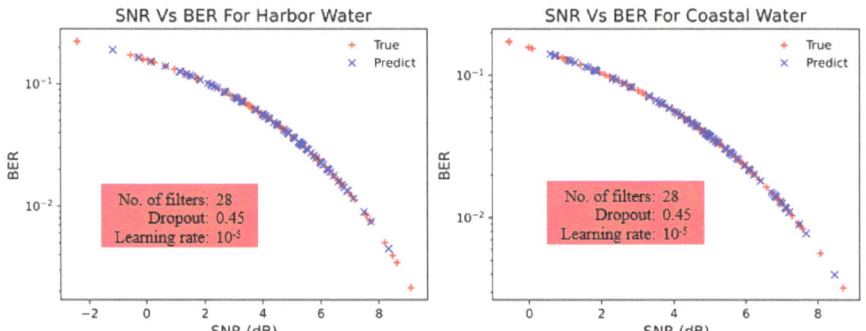

Figure 21. SNR vs. BER for harbour water (**left**) and coastal water (**right**). The true (red) and predicted (blue) values are for different pulse widths using different channel models.

Regarding the high BER values, it means small SNRs are included in our models. This is due to this study's significant noise and channel fluctuations. Although the SNRs are caused by received pulses that pass through noisy channels, the models can predict SNRs accurately.

8. Conclusions

This study successfully demonstrated the implementation of a novel CNN-based decision unit strategy in an optical receiver of UWOC systems. The proposed CNN models are found to predict SNR effectively with high performance, with the train and validation losses and RMSE demonstrating convergence towards smaller values. The results show an inverse strong correlation between the number of parameters in the model and the cost function, suggesting that increasing the CNN model's size enhances its performance. Even in diverse water types with fluctuating noise levels and environment variability, employing a CNN model as a decision unit in an optical receiver enables efficient decision-making with a low-cost function.

Our innovative CNN tool's architecture and supporting mathematical formulations made it agnostic to the UWOC model and transmission modulation format. Hence, if any or all channel models in Table 1 are proven not to partially or fully satisfy the linear time-invariant system (LTIS) condition requirements, replacing any or all of these models with ones that comply will not impact the CNN tool computational software algorithm. Still, it might require altering the hyperparameters of the CNN model platform structure shown in Table 4 to ensure optimum model accuracy fitting, but from a hardware perspective, we do not expect any necessary change to the hosting math processor of the DU. It is worth mentioning that LTIS requirements are translated in terms of channel path loss, mean delay, Root Mean-Square delay spread, and the constancy of the frequency bandwidth with the model temporal profile broadening with linkspans.

9. Future Studies

In future studies, we plan to elevate the effectiveness of our ML model for the UWOC system through a two-pronged strategy: dataset expansion and CNN refinement. The first cornerstone of our approach is the extension of our dataset. We aim to generate more eye diagram images, diversifying and enriching the data available for the ML model. This broader dataset will fortify the model's learning capabilities and enhance its predictive precision. Simultaneously, we propose a strategic refinement of our CNN's hyperparameters. We contemplate introducing two or three hidden layers into the network's architecture, which could amplify the model's ability to detect intricate features and, in turn, boost its accuracy.

We are also considering altering activation functions in both the convolutional and hidden layers (e.g., Tanh, Leaky ReLU, ELU, and SELU), aiming to introduce varying degrees of nonlinearity that could potentially enhance the model's learning and generalisation from the data.

Additionally, we will explore the employment of non-overlapping filters in our convolutional operations. This adjustment could help retain original input data information, minimising information loss during the convolution process and potentially leading to more robust predictions. Aside from these strategies, we also plan to incorporate the capabilities of large language models, like GPT-4. We envision utilising these models for tasks such as automated hyperparameter tuning and predictive modelling based on text mining of recent research trends. Furthermore, they could aid in automatic feature extraction from eye diagram images and augment our dataset by generating synthetic images based on textual descriptions of various UWOC scenarios. These models can also help interpret the CNN model's results and enhance our understanding of the network's decisions. Lastly, we could facilitate knowledge transfer by identifying parallels between UWOC and other fields and refining our CNN techniques and approaches. Through this holistic strategy, integrating both traditional methods and advanced AI techniques, we aim to significantly elevate the accuracy and efficiency of our CNN model in UWOC.

Author Contributions: Conceptualisation, I.F.E.R. and Y.A.-H.; Methodology, N.M.B. and S.A.-Z.; Software, I.F.E.R., N.M.B. and S.A.-Z.; Validation, I.F.E.R., N.M.B. and A.Z.B.; Formal analysis, I.F.E.R. and Y.A.-H.; Investigation, I.F.E.R., S.A.-Z., Y.A.-H. and A.Z.B.; Writing—original draft, I.F.E.R.; Writing—review and editing, N.M.B., S.A.-Z., Y.A.-H., A.Z.B. and M.C.; visualisation, I.F.E.R. All authors have read and agreed to the published version of the manuscript.

Funding: The Deanship of Scientific Research (DSR) at King Abdulaziz University (KAU), Jeddah, Saudi Arabia, under grant no. (GPIP-1512-130-2024).

Data Availability Statement: The digital image SQL database can be provided upon request through the corresponding author's email.

Acknowledgments: This study was funded by the Deanship of Scientific Research (DSR) at King Abdulaziz University, Jeddah, Saudi Arabia, under grant no. (GPIP-1512-130-2024). The authors, therefore, acknowledge DSR's technical and financial support with thanks.

Conflicts of Interest: The authors declare no conflicts of interest.

Appendix A

Table A1. Recent studies use the ML approach to obtain SNR using eye diagrams.

Ref.	Year	Type of Modulation	Data Rate	Optical Fibre/UWOC	Distance	ML Tec.	Sim./Exp.	Train: Test	Input	Hidden Layers	Hidden Neurons	SNR Range (dB)	BER	Performance
[25]	2017	PDM-64QAM	32 Gbaud	Fibre	250 km	NN, regression	Exp. To generate an eye diagram	1664:832	variance from the eye diagram	1	3	4–30	------	mean estimation error range from 0.2–1.2 dB
[58]	2009	NRZ-OOK RZ-DPSK	10 Gb/s 40 Gb/s	Fibre	------	ANN	Sim.	------	Q-factor, closure, jitter, crossing-amplitude from eye diagram	1	12	16–32	------	correlation coefficient = 0.91 (@10G) correlation coefficient = 0.96 (@40G)
[26]	2009	RZ-OOK RZ-DPSK	40 Gb/s	Fibre	------	ANN	Sim.	135:32	Q-factor, closure, jitter, Crosspoint, mean, standard deviation from eye diagram	1	12	16–32	------	RMSE = 0.57, 0.77
[116]	2021	NRZ-OOK	10 Gb/s	Fibre	100 km	ANN	Sim	145: 41	factor, noise power, eye amplitude, eye height, eye closure, eye-opening factor, extinction ratio at min BER, and RMS jitter	1	5	15–30	------	MSE = 1.12
[8]	2009	NRZ-DPSK	40 Gb/s	Fibre	50 km	NO	------	500–1500 for training	six features	------	------	25, 35	------	------
[68]	------	NRZ-OOK	1.25 Gbps	UWOC	1.5–6 m	NO	Exp	------	------	------	------	------	1×10^{-7}	------
[59]	2012	NRZ, RZ and QPSK	40 Gb/s	Fibre	------	ANN	Sim	------	24 features from the Eye diagram	1	10	10–30	------	RMSE = 1.5 : 2
Our study	2024	NRZ-OOK	2 Gb/s	UWOC	12 m	CNN	Sim	404:172	Eye diagram	1	80–320	(−2.42–9.11)	0.0022–0.2247	MAE = 0.291 RMSE = 0.387

Table A2. CNN algorithm structure and implementations that utilise eye diagram images for SNR prediction.

Ref.	[24,60]	[61]	Our Work
ML technique	CNN	CNN	CNN
Input data	Eye diagrams	Eye-opening, height, width, closure.	Eye diagrams
Images format	jpg	No	jpg
Approach	Classification	classification	Regression
No. of convolutional and pooling layers	2	3	5
No. of filters	C1 = 6 C2 = 12	C1 = 60 C2 = 80 C3 = 180	Unified for all convolutional layers, and it ranges from 16 to 64
Filter size	5	3	10
Pooling size	2	2	3
activation functions	Sigmoid in the whole CNN	ReLU for each convolutional layer and soft-max	ReLU for hidden layer Linear for output layer
No. of hidden layers	0	2	1
No. of elements of the fully connected feature map	192	FC1=360 FC2=120	Range from 80 to 320 According to no. of filters
Dropout	No	yes	45%
Backpropagation	Yes	Yes	Yes
No. of output nodes	20	No	1
Output	4 modulation formats 16 SNR	modulation formats, OSNR, ROF, and IQ skew	SNR
No. of epochs	35	No	250
Modulation format	RZ-OOK, NRZ-OOK, RZ-DPSK, and 4PAM	QAM and QPSK	NRZ-OOK
Data rate	25Gbaud	32 Gbaud	2 Gb/s
Collecting eye diagrams way	Simulating signals and displaying eye diagrams using the oscilloscope	Experimental	Simulating everything using Python
Colour mode	Coloured converted into grayscale	Coloured	Black and white in RGB convert to grayscale
Original image size	900×1200	224×224	2366×3125
Resized image	28×28	No	No
Resolution	Low	Low	High (600 dpi)
No. of models	1	2	13
Prediction time	0.46 s	No	Range from 0.17 to 0.20 s
SNR range	(10–25) dB	(15 to 40) dB	(−2.42–9.11) dB
BER range	No	No	0.0022–0.2247
Total no. of images	6400	1170	576
Performance	100% accuracy	99.57% accuracy	MAE = 0.29–0.52 RMSE = 0.39–0.73
Learning curves existence	No	No	Yes
UWOC/ Fibre	Fibre	Fibre	UWOC
Year	2017	2019	2024

References

1. Aldin, M.B.; Alkareem, R.A.; Ali, M.A. Transmission of 10 Gb/s For Underwater Optical Wireless Communication System. *J. Opt.* **2024**, 1–12. [CrossRef]
2. Tian, R.; Wang, T.; Shen, X.; Zhu, R.; Jiang, L.; Lu, Y.; Lu, H.; Song, Y.; Zhang, P. 108 m Underwater Wireless Optical Communication Using a 490 nm Blue VECSEL and an AOM. *Sensors* **2024**, *24*, 2609. [CrossRef] [PubMed]
3. Qu, Z.; Lai, M. A Review on Electromagnetic, Acoustic, and New Emerging Technologies for Submarine Communication. *IEEE Access* **2024**, *12*, 12110–12125. [CrossRef]
4. Álvarez-Roa, C.; Álvarez-Roa, M.; Raddo, T.R.; Jurado-Navas, A.; Castillo-Vázquez, M. Cooperative Terrestrial–Underwater FSO System: Design and Performance Analysis. *Photonics* **2024**, *11*, 58. [CrossRef]

5. Ramley, I.F.E.; AlZhrani, S.M.; Bedaiwi, N.M.; Al-Hadeethi, Y.; Barasheed, A.Z. Simple Moment Generating Function Optimisation Technique to Design Optimum Electronic Filter for Underwater Wireless Optical Communication Receiver. *Mathematics* **2024**, *12*, 861. [CrossRef]
6. Proakis, J.G.; Salehi, M. *Digital Communications*; McGraw-Hill: New York, NY, USA, 2008.
7. Sklar, B. *Digital Communications: Fundamentals and Applications*; Pearson: London, UK, 2021.
8. Anderson, T.B.; Kowalczyk, A.; Clarke, K.; Dods, S.D.; Hewitt, D.; Li, J.C. Multi impairment monitoring for optical networks. *J. Light. Technol.* **2009**, *27*, 3729–3736. [CrossRef]
9. Khan, F.N.; Zhou, Y.; Lau, A.T.; Lu, C. Modulation format identification in heterogeneous fiber-optic networks using artificial neural networks. *Opt. Express* **2012**, *20*, 12422–12431. [CrossRef]
10. Khan, F.N.; Shen, T.S.R.; Zhou, Y.; Lau, A.T.; Lu, C. Optical performance monitoring using artificial neural networks trained with empirical moments of asynchronously sampled signal amplitudes. *IEEE Photonics Technol. Lett.* **2012**, *24*, 982–984. [CrossRef]
11. Shen, T.S.R.; Sui, Q.; Lau, A.T. OSNR monitoring for PM-QPSK systems with large inline chromatic dispersion using artificial neural network technique. *IEEE Photonics Technol. Lett.* **2012**, *24*, 1564–1567. [CrossRef]
12. Tan, M.C.; Khan, F.N.; Al-Arashi, W.H.; Zhou, Y.; Lau, A.T. Simultaneous optical performance monitoring and modulation format/bit-rate identification using principal component analysis. *J. Opt. Commun. Netw.* **2014**, *6*, 441–448. [CrossRef]
13. Marsland, S. *Machine Learning: An Algorithmic Perspective*; Chapman and Hall/CRC: Boca Raton, FL, USA, 2011.
14. Khan, F.N.; Fan, Q.; Lu, C.; Lau, A.T. An optical communication's perspective on machine learning and its applications. *J. Light. Technol.* **2019**, *37*, 493–516. [CrossRef]
15. Musumeci, F.; Rottondi, C.; Nag, A.; Macaluso, I.; Zibar, D.; Ruffini, M.; Tornatore, M. An overview on application of machine learning techniques in optical networks. *IEEE Commun. Surv. Tutor.* **2018**, *21*, 1383–1408. [CrossRef]
16. Li, P.; Yi, L.; Xue, L.; Hu, W. 56 Gbps IM/DD PON based on 10G-class optical devices with 29 dB loss budget enabled by machine learning. In Proceedings of the 2018 Optical Fiber Communications Conference and Exposition (OFC), San Diego, CA, USA, 11–15 March 2018; pp. 1–3.
17. Liao, T.; Xue, L.; Hu, W.; Yi, L. Unsupervised learning for neural network-based blind equalization. *IEEE Photonics Technol. Lett.* **2020**, *32*, 569–572. [CrossRef]
18. Zha, X.; Peng, H.; Qin, X.; Li, G.; Yang, S. A deep learning framework for signal detection and modulation classification. *Sensors* **2019**, *19*, 4042. [CrossRef] [PubMed]
19. Wang, D.; Zhang, M.; Li, Z.; Cui, Y.; Liu, J.; Yang, Y.; Wang, H. Nonlinear decision boundary created by a machine learning-based classifier to mitigate nonlinear phase noise. In Proceedings of the 2015 European Conference on Optical Communication (ECOC), Valencia, Spain, 27 September–1 October 2015; pp. 1–3. [CrossRef]
20. Zhang, J.; Chen, W.; Gao, M.; Shen, G. K-means-clustering-based fiber nonlinearity equalization techniques for 64-QAM coherent optical communication system. *Opt. Express* **2017**, *25*, 27570–27580. [CrossRef]
21. Zhang, L.; Pang, X.; Ozolins, O.; Udalcovs, A.; Popov, S.; Xiao, S.; Hu, W.; Chen, J. Spectrally efficient digitized radio-over-fiber system with k-means clustering-based multidimensional quantization. *Opt. Lett.* **2018**, *43*, 1546–1549. [CrossRef]
22. Khan, F.N.; Yu, Y.; Tan, M.C.; Al-Arashi, W.H.; Yu, C.; Lau, A.P.T.; Lu, C. Experimental demonstration of joint OSNR monitoring and modulation format identification using asynchronous single channel sampling. *Opt. Express* **2015**, *23*, 30337–30346. [CrossRef]
23. Zibar, D.; Gonzalez, N.G.; de Oliveira, J.C.R.F.; Monroy, I.T.; de Carvalho, L.H.H.; Piels, M.; Doberstein, A.; Diniz, J.; Nebendahl, B.; Franciscangelis, C.; et al. Application of machine learning techniques for amplitude and phase noise characterization. *J. Light. Technol.* **2015**, *33*, 1333–1343. [CrossRef]
24. Wang, D.; Zhang, M.; Li, Z.; Li, J.; Fu, M.; Cui, Y.; Chen, X. Modulation format recognition and OSNR estimation using CNN-based deep learning. *IEEE Photonics Technol. Lett.* **2017**, *29*, 1667–1670. [CrossRef]
25. Thrane, J.; Wass, J.; Piels, M.; Diniz, J.C.M.; Jones, R.; Zibar, D. Machine learning techniques for optical performance monitoring from directly detected PDM-QAM signals. *J. Light. Technol.* **2016**, *35*, 868–875. [CrossRef]
26. Wu, X.; Jargon, J.A.; Skoog, R.A.; Paraschis, L.; Willner, A.E. Applications of Artificial Neural Networks in Optical Performance Monitoring. *J. Light. Technol.* **2009**, *27*, 3580–3589.
27. Jargon, J.A.; Wu, X.; Choi, H.Y.; Chung, Y.C.; Willner, A.E. Optical performance monitoring of QPSK data channels by use of neural networks trained with parameters derived from asynchronous constellation diagrams. *Opt. Express* **2010**, *18*, 4931–4938. [CrossRef] [PubMed]
28. Shen, T.S.R.; Meng, K.; Lau, A.T.; Dong, Z.Y. Optical performance monitoring using artificial neural network trained with asynchronous amplitude histograms. *IEEE Photonics Technol. Lett.* **2010**, *22*, 1665–1667. [CrossRef]
29. Zibar, D.; Thrane, J.; Wass, J.; Jones, R.; Piels, M.; Schaeffer, C. Machine learning techniques applied to system characterization and equalization. In Proceedings of the 2016 Optical Fiber Communications Conference and Exhibition (OFC), Anaheim, CA, USA, 20–24 March 2016; pp. 1–3.
30. Reza, A.G.; Rhee, J.-K.K. Blind nonlinear equalizer using artificial neural networks for PAM-4 signal transmissions with DMLs. *Opt. Fiber Technol.* **2021**, *64*, 102582. [CrossRef]
31. Chan, C.C.K. *Optical Performance Monitoring: Advanced Techniques for Next-Generation Photonic Networks*; Academic Press: Cambridge, MA, USA, 2010.
32. Hauske, F.N.; Kuschnerov, M.; Spinnler, B.; Lankl, B. Optical performance monitoring in digital coherent receivers. *J. Light. Technol.* **2009**, *27*, 3623–3631. [CrossRef]

33. Geyer, J.C.; Fludger, C.R.S.; Duthel, T.; Schulien, C.; Schmauss, B. Performance monitoring using coherent receivers. In Proceedings of the 2009 Conference on Optical Fiber Communication, San Diego, CA, USA, 22–26 March 2009. [CrossRef]
34. Szafraniec, B.; Marshall, T.S.; Nebendahl, B. Performance monitoring and measurement techniques for coherent optical systems. *J. Light. Technol.* **2012**, *31*, 648–663. [CrossRef]
35. Zhao, Y.; Chen, X.; Yang, T.; Wang, L.; Wang, D.; Zhang, Z.; Shi, S. Low-complexity fiber nonlinearity impairments compensation enabled by simple recurrent neural network with time memory. *IEEE Access* **2020**, *8*, 160995–161004. [CrossRef]
36. Saif, W.S.; Ragheb, A.M.; Nebendahl, B.; Alshawi, T.; Marey, M.; Alshebeili, S.A. Machine learning-based optical performance monitoring for super-channel optical networks. *Photonics* **2022**, *9*, 299. [CrossRef]
37. Honkala, M.; Korpi, D.; Huttunen, J.M.J. DeepRx: Fully convolutional deep learning receiver. *IEEE Trans. Wirel. Commun.* **2021**, *20*, 3925–3940. [CrossRef]
38. Skoog, R.A.; Banwell, T.C.; Gannett, J.W.; Habiby, S.F.; Pang, M.; Rauch, M.E.; Toliver, P. Automatic identification of impairments using support vector machine pattern classification on eye diagrams. *IEEE Photonics Technol. Lett.* **2006**, *18*, 2398–2400. [CrossRef]
39. Ziauddin, F. Localization Through Optical Wireless Communication in Underwater by Using Machine Learning Algorithms. *J. Glob. Res. Comput. Sci.* **2024**, *15*, 1.
40. Fan, X.; Xie, Y.; Ren, F.; Zhang, Y.; Huang, X.; Chen, W.; Zhangsun, T.; Wang, J. Joint optical performance monitoring and modulation format/bit-rate identification by CNN-based multi-task learning. *IEEE Photonics J.* **2018**, *10*, 1–12. [CrossRef]
41. Jargon, J.A.; Wu, X.; Willner, A.E. Optical performance monitoring by use of artificial neural networks trained with parameters derived from delay-tap asynchronous sampling. In Proceedings of the 2009 Conference on Optical Fiber Communication, San Diego, CA, USA, 22–26 March 2009; pp. 1–3. [CrossRef]
42. Wu, X.; Jargon, J.A.; Paraschis, L.; Willner, A.E. ANN-based optical performance monitoring of QPSK signals using parameters derived from balanced-detected asynchronous diagrams. *IEEE Photonics Technol. Lett.* **2010**, *23*, 248–250. [CrossRef]
43. Dods, S.D.; Anderson, T.B. Optical performance monitoring technique using delay tap asynchronous waveform sampling. In Proceedings of the Optical Fiber Communication Conference, Anaheim, CA, USA, 5–10 March 2006; p. OThP5.
44. Chen, H.; Poon, A.W.; Cao, X.-R. Transparent monitoring of rise time using asynchronous amplitude histograms in optical transmission systems. *J. Light. Technol.* **2004**, *22*, 1661. [CrossRef]
45. Dong, Z.; Khan, F.N.; Sui, Q.; Zhong, K.; Lu, C.; Lau, A.T. Optical performance monitoring: A review of current and future technologies. *J. Light. Technol.* **2016**, *34*, 525–543. [CrossRef]
46. Cheng, Y.; Zhang, W.; Fu, S.; Tang, M.; Liu, D. Transfer learning simplified multi-task deep neural network for PDM-64QAM optical performance monitoring. *Opt. Express* **2020**, *28*, 7607–7617. [CrossRef]
47. Wan, Z.; Yu, Z.; Shu, L.; Zhao, Y.; Zhang, H.; Xu, K. Intelligent optical performance monitor using multi-task learning based artificial neural network. *Opt. Express* **2019**, *27*, 11281–11291. [CrossRef]
48. Khan, F.N.; Zhong, K.; Zhou, X.; Al-Arashi, W.H.; Yu, C.; Lu, C.; Lau, A.P.T. Joint OSNR monitoring and modulation format identification in digital coherent receivers using deep neural networks. *Opt. Express* **2017**, *25*, 17767–17776. [CrossRef]
49. Xia, L.; Zhang, J.; Hu, S.; Zhu, M.; Song, Y.; Qiu, K. Transfer learning assisted deep neural network for OSNR estimation. *Opt. Express* **2019**, *27*, 19398–19406. [CrossRef]
50. Kashi, A.S.; Zhuge, Q.; Cartledge, J.; Borowiec, A.; Charlton, D.; Laperle, C.; O'Sullivan, M. Artificial neural networks for fiber nonlinear noise estimation. In Proceedings of the 2017 Asia Communications and Photonics Conference, Guangzhou, China, 10–13 November 2017; pp. 1–3.
51. Wang, D.; Zhang, M.; Li, J.; Li, Z.; Li, J.; Song, C.; Chen, X. Intelligent constellation diagram analyzer using convolutional neural network-based deep learning. *Opt. Express* **2017**, *25*, 17150–17166. [CrossRef]
52. Cho, H.J. Deep Learning Based Optical Performance Monitoring for Digital Coherent Optical Receivers. Ph.D Thesis, Georgia Institute of Technology, College of Engineering, Atlanta, GA, USA, 2021. Available online: http://hdl.handle.net/1853/66065 (accessed on 17 July 2024).
53. Derickson, D. Fiber optic test and measurement. In *Fiber Optic Test and Measurement/Edited by Dennis Derickson*; Prentice Hall: Upper Saddle River, NJ, USA, 1998.
54. Jargon, J.A.; Wang, C.M.J.; Hale, D. A robust algorithm for eye-diagram analysis. *J. Light. Technol.* **2008**, *26*, 3592–3600. [CrossRef]
55. Rajbhandari, S.; Faith, J.; Ghassemlooy, Z.; Angelova, M. Comparative study of classifiers to mitigate intersymbol interference in diffuse indoor optical wireless communication links. *Optik* **2013**, *124*, 4192–4196. [CrossRef]
56. Wang, Z.; Yang, A.; Guo, P.; He, P. OSNR and nonlinear noise power estimation for optical fiber communication systems using LSTM based deep learning technique. *Opt. Express* **2018**, *26*, 21346–21357. [CrossRef] [PubMed]
57. Ye, H.; Jiang, H.; Liang, G.; Zhan, Q.; Huang, S.; Wang, D.; Di, H.; Li, Z. OSNR monitoring based on a low-bandwidth coherent receiver and LSTM classifier. *Opt. Express* **2021**, *29*, 1566–1577. [CrossRef]
58. Jargon, J.A.; Wu, X.; Willner, A.E. Optical performance monitoring using artificial neural networks trained with eye-diagram parameters. *IEEE Photonics Technol. Lett.* **2008**, *21*, 54–56. [CrossRef]
59. Ribeiro, V.; Costa, L.; Lima, M.; Teixeira, A.L.J. Optical performance monitoring using the novel parametric asynchronous eye diagram. *Opt. Express* **2012**, *20*, 9851–9861. [CrossRef]
60. Wang, D.; Zhang, M.; Li, Z.; Li, J.; Song, C.; Li, J.; Wang, M. Convolutional neural network-based deep learning for intelligent OSNR estimation on eye diagrams. In Proceedings of the 2017 European Conference on Optical Communication (ECOC), Gothenburg, Sweden, 17–21 September 2017; pp. 1–3. [CrossRef]

61. Zhang, Y.; Pan, Z.; Yue, Y.; Ren, Y.; Wang, Z.; Liu, B.; Zhang, H.; Li, S.-A.; Fang, Y.; Huang, H.; et al. Eye diagram measurement-based joint modulation format, OSNR, ROF, and skew monitoring of coherent channel using deep learning. *J. Light. Technol.* **2019**, *37*, 5907–5913. [CrossRef]
62. Al-Zhrani, S.; Bedaiwi, N.M.; El-Ramli, I.F.; Barasheed, A.Z.; Abduldaiem, A.; Al-Hadeethi, Y.; Umar, A. Underwater Optical Communications: A Brief Overview and Recent Developments. *Eng. Sci.* **2021**, *16*, 146–186. [CrossRef]
63. Oubei, H.M.; Shen, C.; Kammoun, A.; Zedini, E.; Park, K.-H.; Sun, X.; Liu, G.; Kang, C.H.; Ng, T.K.; Alouini, M.-S.; et al. Light based underwater wireless communications. *Jpn. J. Appl. Phys.* **2018**, *57*, 08PA06. [CrossRef]
64. Petzold, T.J. *Volume Scattering Functions for Selected Ocean Waters*; Scripps Institution of Oceanography La Jolla Ca Visibility Lab: La Jolla, CA, USA, 1972.
65. Singh, M.; Singh, M.L.; Singh, G.; Kaur, H.; Kaur, S. Modeling and performance evaluation of underwater wireless optical communication system in the presence of different sized air bubbles. *Opt. Quantum Electron.* **2020**, *52*, 1–15. [CrossRef]
66. Zhang, H.; Gao, Y.; Tong, Z.; Yang, X.; Zhang, Y.; Zhang, C.; Xu, J. Omnidirectional optical communication system designed for underwater swarm robotics. *Opt. Express* **2023**, *31*, 18630–18644. [CrossRef] [PubMed]
67. Yu, C.; Chen, X.; Zhang, Z.; Song, G.; Lin, J.; Xu, J. Experimental verification of diffused laser beam-based optical wireless communication through air and water channels. *Opt. Commun.* **2021**, *495*, 127079. [CrossRef]
68. Li, D.-C.; Chen, C.-C.; Liaw, S.-K.; Afifah, S.; Sung, J.-Y.; Yeh, C.-H. Performance Evaluation of Underwater Wireless Optical Communication System by Varying the Environmental Parameters. *Photonics* **2021**, *8*, 74. [CrossRef]
69. Loo, J.; Mauri, J.L.; Ortiz, J.H. *Mobile Ad Hoc Networks: Current Status and Future Trends*; CRC Press: Boca Raton, FL, USA, 2016.
70. Sun, X.; Kang, C.H.; Kong, M.; Alkhazragi, O.; Guo, Y.; Ouhssain, M.; Weng, Y.; Jones, B.H.; Ng, T.K.; Ooi, B.S. A Review on Practical Considerations and Solutions in Underwater Wireless Optical Communication. *J. Light. Technol.* **2020**, *38*, 421–431. [CrossRef]
71. Geldard, C.T.; Thompson, J.; Popoola, W.O. An Overview of Underwater Optical Wireless Channel Modelling Techniques: (Invited Paper). In Proceedings of the 2019 International Symposium on Electronics and Smart Devices (ISESD), Badung, Indonesia, 8–9 October 2019; pp. 1–4. [CrossRef]
72. Johnson, L.; Green, R.; Leeson, M. A survey of channel models for underwater optical wireless communication. In Proceedings of the 2013 2nd International Workshop on Optical Wireless Communications (IWOW), Newcastle Upon Tyne, UK, 21 October 2013; pp. 1–5. [CrossRef]
73. Al-Kinani, A.; Wang, C.; Zhou, L.; Zhang, W. Optical Wireless Communication Channel Measurements and Models. *IEEE Commun. Surv. Tutor.* **2018**, *20*, 1939–1962. [CrossRef]
74. Tang, S.; Dong, Y.; Zhang, X. Impulse response modeling for underwater wireless optical communication links. *IEEE Trans. Commun.* **2013**, *62*, 226–234. [CrossRef]
75. Dong, Y.; Zhang, H.; Zhang, X. On impulse response modeling for underwater wireless optical MIMO links. In Proceedings of the 2014 IEEE/CIC International Conference on Communications in China (ICCC), Shanghai, China, 13–15 October 2014; pp. 151–155. [CrossRef]
76. Li, Y.; Leeson, M.S.; Li, X. Impulse response modeling for underwater wireless optical channels. *Appl. Opt.* **2018**, *57*, 4815–4823. [CrossRef]
77. Boluda-Ruiz, R.; Rico-Pinazo, P.; Castillo-Vázquez, B.; García-Zambrana, A.; Qaraqe, K. Impulse response modeling of underwater optical scattering channels for wireless communication. *IEEE Photonics J.* **2020**, *12*, 1–14. [CrossRef]
78. Kodama, T.; Sanusi, M.A.B.A.; Kobori, F.; Kimura, T.; Inoue, Y.; Jinno, M. Comprehensive Analysis of Time-Domain Hybrid PAM for Data-Rate and Distance Adaptive UWOC System. *IEEE Access* **2021**, *9*, 57064–57074. [CrossRef]
79. Kaushal, H.; Kaddoum, G. Underwater optical wireless communication. *IEEE Access* **2016**, *4*, 1518–1547. [CrossRef]
80. Khalighi, M.A.; Uysal, M. Survey on free space optical communication: A communication theory perspective. *IEEE Commun. Surv. Tutor.* **2014**, *16*, 2231–2258. [CrossRef]
81. Agrawal, G.P. *Fiber-Optic Communication Systems*; John Wiley & Sons: Hoboken, NJ, USA, 2012.
82. Zhu, S.; Chen, X.; Liu, X.; Zhang, G.; Tian, P. Recent progress in and perspectives of underwater wireless optical communication. *Prog. Quantum Electron.* **2020**, *73*, 100274. [CrossRef]
83. Ghassemlooy, Z.; Popoola, W.; Rajbhandari, S. *Optical Wireless Communications: System and Channel Modelling with Matlab®*; CRC Press: Boca Raton, FL, USA, 2019.
84. Kharraz, O.; Forsyth, D. Performance comparisons between PIN and APD photodetectors for use in optical communication systems. *Optik* **2013**, *124*, 1493–1498. [CrossRef]
85. Zhao, Z.; Liu, J.; Liu, Y.; Zhu, N. High-speed photodetectors in optical communication system. *J. Semicond.* **2017**, *38*, 121001. [CrossRef]
86. Farr, N.; Chave, A.; Freitag, L.; Preisig, J.; White, S.; Yoerger, D.; Sonnichsen, F. Optical Modem Technology for Seafloor Observatories. In Proceedings of the OCEANS 2006, Boston, MA, USA, 18–21 September 2006; pp. 1–6. [CrossRef]
87. Lee, H.-K.; Moon, J.-H.; Mun, S.-G.; Choi, K.-M.; Lee, C.-H. Decision threshold control method for the optical receiver of a WDM-PON. *J. Opt. Commun. Netw.* **2010**, *2*, 381–388. [CrossRef]
88. Palermo, S. CMOS Transceiver Circuits for Optical Interconnects. In *Encyclopedia of Modern Optics*, 2nd ed.; Guenther, B.D., Steel, D.G., Eds.; Elsevier: Oxford, UK, 2018; pp. 254–263.

89. Shieh, W.; Djordjevic, I. Optical Communication Fundamentals. In *OFDM for Optical Communications*; Shieh, W., Djordjevic, I., Eds.; Academic Press: Oxford, UK, 2010; pp. 53–118.
90. Kryukov, Y.; Pokamestov, D.; Brovkin, A.; Shinkevich, A.; Shalin, G. MCS MAP FOR LINK-LEVEL SIMULATION OF TWO-USER PD-NOMA SYSTEM. *Proc. Eng.* **2024**, *6*, 151–160. [CrossRef]
91. Tsipi, L.; Karavolos, M.; Papaioannou, G.; Volakaki, M.; Vouyioukas, D. Machine learning-based methods for MCS prediction in 5G networks. *Telecommun. Syst.* **2024**, *86*, 705–728. [CrossRef]
92. Qiu, Y.; Gan, Z.; Pan, Y. Research on application of software simulation to spread spectrum communication systems. *J. Syst. Simul.* **1999**, *11*, 461–464.
93. Wikipedia. Importance Sampling—Wikipedia, the Free Encyclopedia. Available online: https://en.wikipedia.org/wiki/Importance_sampling (accessed on 28 May 2024).
94. Cavus, E.; Haymes, C.L.; Daneshrad, B. Low BER performance estimation of LDPC codes via application of importance sampling to trapping sets. *IEEE Trans. Commun.* **2009**, *57*, 1886–1888. [CrossRef]
95. Jeruchim, M.C.; Balaban, P.; Shanmugan, K.S. *Simulation of Communication Systems: Modeling, Methodology and Techniques*; Springer Science & Business Media: Berlin/Heidelberg, Germany, 2006.
96. Jeruchim, M. Techniques for estimating the bit error rate in the simulation of digital communication systems. *IEEE J. Sel. Areas Commun.* **1984**, *2*, 153–170. [CrossRef]
97. Shin, S.K.; Park, S.K.; Kim, J.M.; Ko, S.C. New quasi-analytic ber estimation technique on the nonlinear satellite communication channels. *IEE Proc.-Commun.* **1999**, *146*, 68–72. [CrossRef]
98. Land, I.; Hoeher, P.; Sorger, U. Log-likelihood values and Monte Carlo simulation-some fundamental results. In Proceedings of the International Symposium on Turbo Codes and Related Topics, Brest, France, 4–7 September 2000; pp. 43–46.
99. Kabrisky, M. *A Proposed Model for Visual Information Processing in the Human Brain*; University of Illinois at Urbana-Champaign: Champaign, IL, USA, 1964.
100. Giebel, H. *Feature Extraction and Recognition of Handwritten Characters by Homogeneous Layers*; Springer: Berlin/Heidelberg, Germany, 1971; pp. 162–169. [CrossRef]
101. Fukushima, K. Cognitron: A self-organizing multilayered neural network. *Biol. Cybern.* **1975**, *20*, 121–136. [CrossRef] [PubMed]
102. Cui, N. *Applying Gradient Descent in Convolutional Neural Networks*, 1st ed.; IOP Publishing: Bristol, UK, 2018; Volume 1004. [CrossRef]
103. Boutaba, R.; Salahuddin, M.A.; Limam, N.; Ayoubi, S.; Shahriar, N.; Estrada-Solano, F.; Caicedo, O.M. A comprehensive survey on machine learning for networking: Evolution, applications and research opportunities. *J. Internet Serv. Appl.* **2018**, *9*, 1–99. [CrossRef]
104. Rumelhart, D.E.; Hinton, G.E.; Williams, R.J. *Learning Internal Representations by Error Propagation*; California Univ San Diego La Jolla Inst for Cognitive Science: La Jolla, CA, USA, 1985.
105. LeCun, Y.; Boser, B.; Denker, J.S.; Henderson, D.; Howard, R.E.; Hubbard, W.; Jackel, L.D. Backpropagation applied to handwritten zip code recognition. *Neural Comput.* **1989**, *1*, 541–551. [CrossRef]
106. Khan, A.; Sohail, A.; Zahoora, U.; Qureshi, A.S. A survey of the recent architectures of deep convolutional neural networks. *Artif. Intell. Rev.* **2020**, *53*, 5455–5516. [CrossRef]
107. Krizhevsky, A.; Sutskever, I.; Hinton, G.E. Imagenet classification with deep convolutional neural networks. *Commun. ACM* **2017**, *60*, 84–90. [CrossRef]
108. Koushik, J. Understanding convolutional neural networks. *arXiv* **2016**, arXiv:1605.09081. [CrossRef]
109. Al Bataineh, A.; Kaur, D.; Al-khassaweneh, M.; Al-sharoa, E. Automated CNN Architectural Design: A Simple and Efficient Methodology for Computer Vision Tasks. *Mathematics* **2023**, *11*, 1141. [CrossRef]
110. Bataineh, A.A. A comparative analysis of nonlinear machine learning algorithms for breast cancer detection. *Int. J. Mach. Learn. Comput.* **2019**, *9*, 248–254. [CrossRef]
111. Zhou, Z.; Guan, W.; Wen, S. Recognition and evaluation of constellation diagram using deep learning based on underwater wireless optical communication. *arXiv* **2020**, arXiv:2007.05890. [CrossRef]
112. Natalino, C.; Schiano, M.; Di Giglio, A.; Wosinska, L.; Furdek, M. Field demonstration of machine-learning-aided detection and identification of jamming attacks in optical networks. In Proceedings of the 2018 European Conference on Optical Communication (ECOC), Rome, Italy, 23–27 September 2018; pp. 1–3. [CrossRef]
113. dorronsoro, J.R.; González, A.; Cruz, C.S. Natural Gradient Learning in NLDA Networks. In *Connectionist Models of Neurons, Learning Processes, and Artificial Intelligence*; Mira, J., Prieto, A., Eds.; Springer: Berlin/Heidelberg, Germany, 2001; pp. 427–434. [CrossRef]
114. Ruder, S. An overview of gradient descent optimization algorithms. *arXiv* **2016**, arXiv:1609.04747. [CrossRef]
115. Amari, S.-I. Natural gradient works efficiently in learning. *Neural Comput.* **1998**, *10*, 251–276. [CrossRef]
116. Rai, P.; Kaushik, R. Artificial intelligence based optical performance monitoring. *J. Opt. Commun.* **2024**, *44*, s1733–s1737. [CrossRef]

Disclaimer/Publisher's Note: The statements, opinions and data contained in all publications are solely those of the individual author(s) and contributor(s) and not of MDPI and/or the editor(s). MDPI and/or the editor(s) disclaim responsibility for any injury to people or property resulting from any ideas, methods, instructions or products referred to in the content.

MDPI AG
Grosspeteranlage 5
4052 Basel
Switzerland
Tel.: +41 61 683 77 34

Mathematics Editorial Office
E-mail: mathematics@mdpi.com
www.mdpi.com/journal/mathematics

Disclaimer/Publisher's Note: The statements, opinions and data contained in all publications are solely those of the individual author(s) and contributor(s) and not of MDPI and/or the editor(s). MDPI and/or the editor(s) disclaim responsibility for any injury to people or property resulting from any ideas, methods, instructions or products referred to in the content.

www.ingramcontent.com/pod-product-compliance
Lightning Source LLC
LaVergne TN
LVHW072323090526
838202LV00019B/2339